THE
CAMBRIDGE HISTORY
OF THE BIBLE

VOLUME 2

THE WEST FROM
THE FATHERS TO THE
REFORMATION

THE
CAMBRIDGE HISTORY OF
THE BIBLE

VOLUME 2

THE WEST FROM
THE FATHERS TO THE
REFORMATION

EDITED BY

G. W. H. LAMPE

*Ely Professor of Divinity
in the University of Cambridge*

CAMBRIDGE
AT THE UNIVERSITY PRESS
1969

Published by the Syndics of the Cambridge University Press
Bentley House, 200 Euston Road, London N.W. 1
American Branch: 32 East 57th Street, New York, N.Y. 10022

Library of Congress Catalogue Card Number: 63–24435

Standard Book Number: 521 04255 0

Printed in Great Britain
at the University Printing House, Cambridge
(Brooke Crutchley, University Printer)

CONTENTS

Preface   *page* vii

I THE OLD TESTAMENT: MANUSCRIPTS, TEXT
   AND VERSIONS   I
   by the Rev. Professor Bleddyn J. Roberts, D.D., *Professor of
   Hebrew and Biblical Studies, University College of North Wales,
   Bangor*

II THE HISTORY OF THE TEXT AND CANON OF THE
    NEW TESTAMENT TO JEROME   27
    by the late C. S. C. Williams

III EARLY CHRISTIAN BOOK-PRODUCTION: PAPYRI
     AND MANUSCRIPTS   54
     by T. C. Skeat, *Keeper of Manuscripts, British Museum*

IV JEROME   80
    by the late Fr E. F. Sutcliffe, S.J., *Old Testament Professor at
    Heythrop College*

V THE MEDIEVAL HISTORY OF THE LATIN VULGATE   102
   by Raphael Loewe, *Lecturer in Hebrew, University College, London*

VI THE EXPOSITION AND EXEGESIS OF SCRIPTURE   155
    1 TO GREGORY THE GREAT   155
    by the Rev. G. W. H. Lampe, *Ely Professor of Divinity, University
    of Cambridge*

    2 FROM GREGORY THE GREAT TO ST BERNARD   183
    by Dom Jean Leclercq, O.S.B., D.TH., *Professor at the Pontifical
    Institute S. Anselm, Rome*

    3 THE BIBLE IN THE MEDIEVAL SCHOOLS   197
    by Beryl Smalley, F.B.A., *Vice-Principal, St Hilda's College, Oxford*

    4 THE BIBLE IN LITURGICAL USE   220
    by the Rev. S. J. P. van Dijk, O.F.M.

    5 THE STUDY OF THE BIBLE IN MEDIEVAL JUDAISM   252
    by Erwin I. J. Rosenthal, LITT.D., *Reader in Oriental Studies,
    University of Cambridge*

v

VII THE 'PEOPLE'S BIBLE': ARTISTS AND
COMMENTATORS   *page* 280
  by the Very Rev. R. L. P. Milburn, *Dean of Worcester*

VIII BIBLE ILLUSTRATION IN MEDIEVAL MANUSCRIPTS   309
  by Professor Francis Wormald, *formerly Director of the Institute
  of Historical Research, London University*

IX THE VERNACULAR SCRIPTURES   338
  1 THE GOTHIC BIBLE   338
    by M. J. Hunter

  2 ENGLISH VERSIONS OF THE SCRIPTURES BEFORE WYCLIF 362
    by Geoffrey Shepherd, *Professor of English Medieval Language
    and Literature, University of Birmingham*

  3 THE WYCLIFFITE VERSIONS   387
    by Henry Hargreaves, *Lecturer in English, University of Aberdeen*

  4 VERNACULAR SCRIPTURES IN GERMANY AND THE LOW
    COUNTRIES BEFORE 1500   415
    by W. B. Lockwood, D.LITT., *Professor of Germanic and Indo-
    European Philology, University of Reading*

  5 VERNACULAR SCRIPTURES IN FRANCE   436
    by C. A. Robson, *Fellow of Merton College and Lecturer in French
    Philology and Old French Literature, University of Oxford*

  6 VERNACULAR SCRIPTURES IN ITALY   452
    by Kenelm Foster, O.P., *Lecturer in Italian, University of Cambridge*

  7 VERNACULAR SCRIPTURES IN SPAIN   465
    by Margherita Morreale, *Professor of Spanish Language and
    Literature, University of Bari*

X ERASMUS IN RELATION TO THE MEDIEVAL
BIBLICAL TRADITION   492
  by Fr Louis Bouyer, D.D., *of the French Oratory, formerly Professor
  in the Faculty of Theology of the Institut Catholique de Paris*

Bibliography   509

Notes on the Plates   536

Plates   *between pages* 540–1

Indexes   541

PREFACE

The present volume, a companion to *The Cambridge History of the Bible: The West from the Reformation to the Present Day*, edited by Professor S. L. Greenslade, is principally concerned with the history of the Bible in medieval western Europe.

The era of the Reformation clearly represents a dividing line in the story of the Bible in western Europe, as in the history of western Christianity itself. A proper starting-point for this volume is not so easy to determine. The Scriptures themselves grew out of the living traditions of Israel and of the Christian Church. They embody the historical memory of a community, its pattern of life and worship, its traditional preaching, and catechetical and ethical teaching. A history of the Bible, however, presupposes the existence of a Canon of Scripture. It must deal with a distinct collection of literature already accepted as authoritative and normative for the thought and practice of the community in which its component parts had come into being. This volume, therefore, begins at a time when the books of the Bible were already in existence. It can take no account of the process, itself the most important part of the history of the Bible, by which the living tradition of Israel came to find expression in the individual books of the Law, the Prophets and the Writings, and by which the Christian gospel found its literary form in the fourfold Gospel and came to be reflected in the other books which later became the New Testament. These and similar matters, which fall outside the scope of this volume, will receive detailed treatment in a further volume, the first in chronological order, *The Cambridge History of the Bible: from the Beginnings to Jerome*. The first three chapters of this volume give a kind retrospective survey of matters more fully dealt with in the other volume, on the ground that readers primarily concerned with the medieval period would find such a summary useful: the volume is in that sense self-contained. Indeed, the process by which these particular books came to be recognized as uniquely authoritative, as the fountain-head of the Church's continuing tradition and as the standard to which that tradition must constantly be referred, cannot be ignored in a work which treats of the subsequent history of these books as a single 'Holy Bible'. The first two chapters accordingly provide a backward glance to the history, first of the text of the Old Testament in Hebrew and in other versions, and of the final stages in the formation of its Canon, and secondly of the recognition of the canonicity of the New Testament and of the development of its textual tradition.

Other chapters describe the process by which the Scriptures have been handed down: the methods of book-production in the early centuries, the nature of the papyri and the other manuscripts which comprise the oldest witnesses to the scriptural text; and also the methods and materials used by the copyists and illuminators of the middle ages.

The central part of the volume discusses the exposition and exegesis of the Bible. Five aspects of this have been selected. The first is the patristic exegesis which, building on the reinterpretation of the Old Testament which had already been carried out in the primitive Church, interprets the Scriptures of both Testaments as a book about Christ and the Church and finds in them an armoury for apologetic, and a guide both in doctrinal controversy and in the edification of believers. The second and third show the way in which the Bible became, less in the form of a book as such than of an influence which permeated the Church's devotional life, the basis of medieval European culture, especially in the monasteries and the schools. The fourth aspect is specifically liturgical: the embodiment of scriptural material in the actual forms of public worship. The fifth is different: the opposing tradition of Jewish exegesis in which the Hebrew Scriptures were expounded outside the framework of the Catholic Church's life and thought but which at the same time exerted influences on Christian thinking which affected subsequent history.

The permeation of European culture by the Scriptures is illustrated by the presentation of biblical themes in medieval art and by the history of the translation of the Scriptures into the vernacular speech of western European countries. Particular attention has been paid in this book to the early history of the English Bible, but consideration has also been given to the vernacular Bible on the Continent, especially in Spain where the history of the vernacular Scriptures has been relatively little studied and where the contact between Christians and Jews produced particularly interesting results.

Preface

A select bibliography for each chapter has been appended. So far as possible, footnotes to the chapters have been kept to the minimum, but the detailed history of the Latin Vulgate text, which is necessarily highly complex, has required the addition of a special system of references which will be found in the bibliography.

The volume has been some ten years in preparation. It is only just to the contributors to point out that some articles were written in 1957–9. In bringing the volume to completion and seeing it through the press, the editor has been assisted by the officers of the Cambridge University Press.

CHAPTER I

THE OLD TESTAMENT: MANUSCRIPTS, TEXT AND VERSIONS

The Old Testament textualist is today more concerned with the story of the textual transmission up to the middle ages than ever before. It is from its manuscripts that he derives both the text itself and the variants for his *apparatus criticus*, and his interpretation of the medieval transmission controls, to a large extent, his choice of readings. Consequently, the relevance of the present survey of the medieval transmission lies not so much in providing information about textual activities but in an appraisal of their use in the contemporary textual situation. The topic as a whole falls into two fairly exclusive sections, namely the Hebrew (Massoretic) text, and the Versions.

THE HEBREW (MASSORETIC) TEXT

The traditional view of the Hebrew transmission was that the textual minutiae of the Law as the most significant part of the Scriptures were fixed for all time under the influence of Rabbi Aqiba (*c.* A.D. 55–137), and the standardization of the remainder followed soon afterwards, to produce the official Massoretic text. From that time onward all manuscripts were scrupulously transcribed according to the archetype, and scrutinized by official scribes, so that a correct transmission was assured. Rabbinic evidence, it was said, supported this reconstruction.

On four occasions in rabbinic writings we are told, with a few variations, that three scrolls of the Law, with minor textual divergences, were deposited in the Temple court, and in each case of divergence it was ruled that the majority reading was authoritative. The fact that the legend is set in the Temple area shows that discussion about text standardization goes back at least to the time before A.D. 70, the date of the sack of Jerusalem. Again, it is stated that Rabbi Aqiba studied each instance of the use of the grammatical particles and based his exegesis on

I

their usage, and this, it is argued, must surely represent a definitive phase in the standardization. The fact that the comment is derived from the Babylonian Talmud (*Shebu'oth* 26 *a*), a standard rabbinic work redacted in the sixth century, shows that the rabbinic tradition was soundly based.

During the past hundred years, however, and especially because of the work of Paul Kahle in the present century, the tradition has been challenged, and counter-challenged. At present, experts who can rightly claim outstanding authority are not only contradictory but often mutually exclusive in their testimony. The present survey cannot pretend to offer a verdict on either side, but rather, by means of introducing an independent perspective, seeks to tell the story as a whole with a reasonable sense of proportion.

The discovery of the Dead Sea scrolls provides a suitable starting-point, because they provide actual specimen texts from the time before Aqiba's 'standardized' text-form. But the fact that there are two distinct groups of 'Dead Sea' biblical texts is highly important. On the one hand we have the texts from Qumran, which are sectarian and probably from the pre-Christian and early Christian era, and, on the other, we have the texts from Murabba'at and Masada, which represent the orthodox rabbinic transmission from the second century A.D.

The latter are less well known to the average reader, but for the present survey they demand pride of place. It is beyond dispute that they form part of the literary remains of the Jewish army in the bar Cochba revolt in A.D. 132–5, the last vain attempt to oppose Roman domination. Not all the texts are available for general scrutiny, but it is reported that they contain fragments from the three sections of rabbinic scriptures, the Law, the Prophets and the Writings, and are identical with the text which became recognized as standard. Rabbi Aqiba, whose name figures so prominently in the so-called standardization, was directly involved in the revolt, and consequently it is reasonable to assume that the standardized text was available before his time. The relevance of the conclusion, however, will be discussed when the question of standardization must once again be raised.

The Qumran biblical manuscripts do not represent the orthodox transmission, and consequently it is only by implication that they relate to the Massoretic text. They belong to a dissident sect, whose independence of orthodoxy was fundamental and is to be observed in such important issues as the religious calendar, the priestly hierarchy, apocalyptic teaching and the interpretation of Scripture—all matters on which orthodox Judaism of those times held rigid views. It lies to hand to suggest that in its transmission of Scripture the sect of the scrolls was no less non-conformist, and consequently it is at least precarious to use the Qumran scrolls indiscriminately to demonstrate the early history of rabbinic textual transmission.

In actual fact, the Qumran biblical scrolls, mainly from caves one, four and eleven, range from near-identity with the Massoretic text to a text-form which closely approximates to the parent text of the oldest of the Versions, the Greek Septuagint, with instances, too, of variations between the two. That is, there is a considerable variety of text-forms, with far-reaching divergences; it does not appear that the sect subscribed to any one traditional or established text-form of the Hebrew Old Testament.

But among the variety the one text-form which is predominant has strong affinities and probable identity with the rabbinic text. One of the Isaiah manuscripts from cave one is particularly relevant, namely *1QIsb*. It belongs to the first century A.D. and, though it is badly worn and consequently has lost a substantial amount of text, it is generally regarded as practically identical in both text and orthography with the current text. Indeed, so similar are they and so insignificant are the divergences that the scroll has hardly been given the notice it deserves from scholars. But from the text-historian's point of view it is just these features that make it one of the most significant of the Qumran scrolls. Its comparatively late date places it in a period when any tendency by the sect to accept an orthodox text-form can be discounted. By the same token, it is very unlikely that orthodox Judaism at that time would have chosen as archetype for its own text-form a text out of those transmitted by the Qumran sect. The obvious conclusion is that its existence among the scrolls points to its existence also in orthodox circles long before the time of Aqiba, and it could be as early as the beginnings of the Qumran sect itself.

Another Isaiah text from cave one indirectly supports this view, namely *1QIsa*. Compared with the accepted text, the divergent readings in this scroll are numerous and more far-reaching than in *1QIsb*. In the main, however, they fall into clearly defined categories of grammar, orthography and normal textual corruption, scribal errors and the replacement of difficult readings by simple ones; only rarely do they

3

point to recensional divergences in the sense presupposed, for instance, by some of the Samuel texts from cave four. That is, *1QIsa* again postulates the existence, at a time earlier than its own date, of a text which agrees essentially with the Massoretic text. Thus the cumulative evidence of Qumran, albeit by implication, points to the existence in the period before Christ of a text which approximates as nearly as is possible to the Massoretic text.

Finally, it may be noted that other fragments of biblical texts from caves one and four, and the lengthy scroll of Psalms from cave eleven, agree to such an extent with the Massoretic text that what was said above about *1QIsb* may well apply to the whole of the Old Testament.

We cannot discover how orthodox Judaism functioned in the period before Christ, but it is unlikely that the authorities countenanced such a wide freedom of textual transmission as that which obtained in Qumran. Josephus, in *Contra Apionem* i. 8, from the second century A.D., says that one mark of the sacred writings of the Jews is their textual inviolability, and it is consistent with what we know of Judaism, with its particularism and its strict hierarchical control, that it transmitted one text-form, whereas the sects were accustomed to the transmission of popular variant versions.

Historical data from rabbinic writings suggest how the rabbis proceeded with the task of transmitting the text. After the fall of Jerusalem in A.D. 70 the Pharisees, relieved of preoccupation with the Temple-bound Sadducees, turned their wrath on the apocalyptic sectarians such as the Zealots, the Essenes and the Christians, persecuted them and expelled them from the Synagogue. Constructively, they established under Johanan ben Zakkai of the first generation of Tannaite teachers (*c.* A.D. 10–80) a centre of study and piety at Jamnia (Jabne-el of biblical times) on the coastal plain, and this became the prototype of similar academies throughout Palestine. It is often assumed that final questions connected with the canonicity of some of the books of Scripture were settled at the Synod of Jamnia, but it is still an open question whether the interpretation is correct. It is still more difficult to decide whether or not steps were taken to establish the definitive text of the Old Testament. What Jamnia does show is that henceforth orthodox Judaism was to be rigidly controlled by the rabbis, who, in turn, were themselves bound to the Massorah, i.e. the tradition. There was freedom within the Massorah to debate and to decide, as is abundantly shown by references within the complex of rabbinic writings down to the middle ages, and controversy waxed strong, but it was always ordered and controlled and never again was orthodoxy to be torn asunder by schism or secession.

The existence of the Massorah can be traced back as far as any rabbinic activity; its usage in the Mishna, the earliest codification of rabbinic teaching, produced in the second century A.D., shows that it had always functioned in the disputations. 'The Massorah is a fence to the Law', said Rabbi Aqiba, who, though he belonged to the third generation of teachers, was primarily concerned with the maintaining of the Massorah, the tradition which he had received. The academy to which he belonged was at Bne Baraq (to the east of Joppa), although he had also attended those of Lydda and Jamnia. Obviously Massoretic studies in this period were pursued at a number of centres and under the guidance of a variety of families of rabbis in Palestine, and their *dicta* were treasured and transmitted, to a large extent orally, until the final redaction of the Mishna in the second century, and later in the Talmuds of Palestine and Babylonia, and in other rabbinic works down to the middle ages. And it is in this sense that biblical scholars always refer to the Hebrew Old Testament as the Massoretic text.

Rabbinic studies flourished also in Babylonia, for from the second century and later there is evidence of centres at Nehardea and at Sura. The former was destroyed in 259 and was replaced by the academy at Pum Bedita. Verdicts of the rabbis in these centres, too, were included in the collections referred to. It is from these sources that data are recoverable for the historical reconstruction of the textual transmission, and it is significant that they contain no hint of any divergent recension of the text, but rather assume that every care and attention was devoted to the transmission of the accepted, 'correct' form. The Babylonian Talmud, *Kethuboth* 106a, from the sixth century included among the officers who had been paid by the Temple authorities the 'book readers', men who corrected biblical manuscripts, and it is apparent that the office persisted into later Talmudic times.

This account, however, is oversimplified, as we have been forcibly reminded in a recent survey (1966) by H. M. Orlinsky of the Hebrew Union College, New York. Most of the material he uses as evidence was previously known, but his conclusions are new and quite sensational. He summarily denies that the Massoretic text as such ever actually existed, or can ever be constructed; divergences within the transmitted texts, as witnessed by rabbinic discussions and also by collations in subsequent biblical editions, demonstrate traditional and legitimate divergences. For Orlinsky, then, all that can be claimed for any given edition is that it represents *a* Massoretic text, and not *the* Massoretic text. This is hardly the right occasion to enter into the controversy: what may be stressed, however, is that the key-word is still Massoretic—whether it be *a* or *the* Massoretic text.

In a general sense, then, it is correct to think of the transmission as the work of the scribes, including, possibly from the time of Ezra, an expertise in matters of interpretation. At the same time, the title *sopher*, 'scribe', is both traditionally and etymologically attached to the official copyists. A ninth-century rabbinic work, *Massekheth Sopherim*, contains the traditions of scribal instructions and data; and numerous Talmudic references connect with the word *sopher* the work of counting. Thus, the scribes reckoned every letter of the Torah, established that the middle consonant in the Torah was in Lev. xi. 42, the middle word in Lev. x. 16, the middle verse Lev. xiii. 33. The middle of the Psalter was Ps. 78: 38.

These and other products of scribal activity came to be inserted in the margins of manuscripts, at the top and bottom of columns, and at the end of individual books. Much later they were assembled in separate collections, of which a few have survived. Particular interest attaches to three or four which, in part at least, are still extant. They include the above-mentioned *Massekheth Sopherim*, *Diqduqe Ha-te'amim* attributed to Aaron ben Asher in the tenth century, and *Ochla we-Ochla* which was edited from manuscripts and published by Frensdorff in 1864; but the most convenient for current usage, despite some serious basic misconceptions, is the collection made by C. D. Ginsburg, and published in four volumes, *The Massorah*, 1880–1905. Appropriately, the scribal notes contained in these collections are collectively called *Massorah* or *Massoreth*—'the body of tradition'—and the persons responsible for its transmission *ba'ale ha-massoreth*, 'the masters of the tradition'. The notes include such items as irregularly shaped letters and unusual features of grammar, and draw attention to textual interference by the scribes in matters of exegesis, especially where the traditional, consonantal text was still retained. But it must be stressed that they are not uniform, nor do they always agree with the texts they accompany.

An outline of such Massoretic annotations obviously needs to be illustrated from actual texts, but the following will serve to indicate the kind of material included in them: *Tiqqune Sopherim*—scribal emendations—which often avoid anthropomorphism in the original text; *'Itture Sopherim*—scribal omissions; *Qre* and *Kethib*—divergences between what was recited and the written consonantal text (although most of these first became obvious only after the introduction of vocalization). There are also scribal marks which denote that the text was corrupt or wrong, and such passages were designated (in the Babylonian Massorah) *Demish*. Lists of such marks—actually dots, *puncta extraordinaria*—have been transmitted and their existence is postulated even as early as the Mishna.

Other scribal peculiarities, such as the suspended consonants *nun* in Judges xviii. 30, and *ayin* in Ps. 80: 14, and a number of enlarged and diminished consonants, have only incidental significance and denote the initial or the middle consonant of a book. Some interest may attach to the presence in some manuscripts of an enlarged initial consonant for Isa. xl. 1.

The survival of the two main traditions of Massoretic activity in Babylon and Palestine is seen in the two divergent Massoroth, those of *Madinhae* (eastern) and *Ma'arbae* (western) respectively. Failure to recognize the distinction between them resulted in the erroneous view, prevalent until the work of Paul Kahle in the present century, that the Massorah of the text was uniform because it reflected a basic uniformity in the text transmission. Nowhere is the divergence more obvious or more relevant than in the systems of vocalization which were superimposed on the consonantal text and which were developed both in Palestine and Babylon between the late fifth century and the ninth century A.D. In Babylon sporadic use of vocalic consonants and dots was made to assist and to formalize the correct recitation of the hitherto unvocalized, consonantal text in synagogue worship. In the eighth century, probably under the influence of the Qaraites, a non-rabbinic Jewish sect, refinements were introduced into the vocalization which ultimately produced the complicated scheme of supralineal pointing which still survives in the so-called Babylonian vocalization. During the same period, and under the same impetus, a parallel process was applied to the texts transmitted in Palestine. A primitive Palestinian supralineal vocalization was in due course replaced by the Tiberian pointing which is the one normally used today for the Hebrew Bible. The supremacy of the Tiberian system over the Babylonian is to be explained mainly by the disappearance of Babylon from Jewish history as a result of the Islamic conquest of Mesopotamia, though it is to be noted in passing that Babylonian influence, inspired by the Qaraite movement and perpetuated by outstanding personalities such as Saadya Gaon and the academies at Pum Bedita and Sura, played an important part in the subsequent history of European Judaism.

The earlier, primitive phases of the vocalization in both transmissions are almost wholly unknown, except for incidental and until recently incomprehensible references in late rabbinic works, but actual examples were discovered in fragments of biblical texts from the Cairo Genizah, an ante-chamber in the synagogue in which discarded manuscripts were deposited. The account of their significance forms an important part of Kahle's Schweich Lectures (published as *The Cairo Geniza*, 1947, and its second edition, 1959). Subsequent scrutiny of important fragments of these texts has been published in the Annual of the Hebrew University, *Textus*.

The Genizah fragments—over 200,000 in all—were removed from the Cairo synagogue, where they had been assembled in the ninth and tenth centuries A.D., and deposited in the main in libraries in Leningrad, and in England, notably at the Cambridge University Library, the Bodleian at Oxford, the British Museum and the John Rylands Library, Manchester (which acquired what previously formed the Gaster Collection), and in the U.S.A. They range from about the sixth century to the tenth and relate to all aspects of synagogue worship and pedagogy, and include biblical texts (many of them vocalized), Mishna, Talmuds, Targums, liturgies, hymns and prayers, and even private papers. Recent discoveries among the Genizah fragments contain texts with both Babylonian and Tiberian vocalizations, and form a valuable addition to other fragments by which it is now possible, albeit tentatively, to reconstruct the framework for the whole history of vocalization. They also include fragments where the words are only partly written and vocalized, the so-called 'abbreviated system'; and whereas specimens of Palestinian and Tiberian pointings had been available since early in this century, a recent fragment with Babylonian abbreviated texts has thrown further light on this interesting phase. Moreover both this and another fragment from the Rylands collection contain both

Babylonian and Tiberian vocalizations. From the standpoint of textual transmission, it might be argued that the main body of the fragments generally supports the traditional view that the text had long been fixed. But the exception of one very significant feature, namely the transmission of the divine name, indicates that such a generalization is misleading. It is remarkable how frequently the manuscripts show divergences not only in the change from Yahweh to Adonai and conversely, but also of interchange between Elohim and Yahweh. That there were ancient divergent transmissions of the divine name is shown by the Elohistic and Yahwistic redactions in collections of Psalms, but it is remarkable that a similar divergence was allowed to persist long after the text was apparently established in other respects, and this underlines the need to scrutinize other, less obvious, inconsistencies.

The adoption of one scheme of vocalization from the rather chaotic multiplicity of Simple and Complex Babylonian, and the Palestinian and Tiberian, and various modified forms within each group—for they were not in any way homogeneous—was not the end of a phase in the struggle for supremacy, for controversy still persisted. There were disputes between two contemporary families of Tiberian Massoretes, ben Asher and ben Naphtali. The former flourished in the ninth and tenth centuries, presumably also the latter, though so apparently complete was the ultimate supremacy of ben Asher that most of the traces of the history of the ben Naphtali tradition have been expunged, and the main evidence of its existence lies in Massoretic lists of variations between the two transmissions. In their present form, the lists indicate that the conflict dealt mainly with minutiae of vocalization and especially accentuation, but underlying these apparently innocuous variants are issues of more far-reaching significance. What might appear to be the concern of the Massoretes simply for the 'correct' rendering of Scriptures in synagogue worship was actually their desire to retain divergent traditions. For the general purposes of the Old Testament textualist, however, its main importance lies in its providing the means of identifying biblical manuscripts from the middle ages. The oldest and best list of differences between ben Asher and ben Naphtali is that by Mishael ben Uzziel, *Kitab al Khilaf*, probably composed in the tenth century but now reconstructed from later works and Genizah fragments. This work is now completely edited by L. Lipschütz; the first part, *ben Ascher–ben Naftali*, appeared in 1937, and the remainder was

9

published as an appendix to *Textus*, vol. II, in 1962, with an introduction in vol. IV, 1964.

With the introduction of the name ben Asher we move into the period when lengthy and complete manuscripts of the text are available, for there are codices extant which carry ben Asher colophons. They are the oldest copies of the Old Testament Scriptures apart from the Dead Sea scrolls and the Genizah fragments, and consequently need to be listed separately; they also form the basis of most modern editions of the text, or at least provide important sources for the *apparatus criticus*. They are:

1. The British Museum manuscript *Or 4445*, which consists of the Pentateuch, written probably in the early tenth century, on the authority and during the lifetime of Aaron, the chief though not the first of the ben Asher family.

2. The so-called Babylonian codex of the Prophets, actually dated A.D. 916. At one time it was known as the St Petersburg Codex, but it is now catalogued in the Leningrad Library, *MS Heb. B. 3*. It was edited and published under the title *The Petersburg Codex of the Prophets* by H. L. Strack, 1876.

3. The Cairo codex of the Prophets, preserved in the Qaraite synagogue in Cairo from 895, is the oldest dated Hebrew manuscript extant, and was produced by Moshe ben Asher, the father of Aaron.

4. The Aleppo codex comes from the first half of the tenth century, and once contained the whole Old Testament; consequently it is the most significant of all the ben Asher manuscripts. Furthermore it is argued that this text was acclaimed by Maimonides in the twelfth century as the model codex. At least from the fifteenth century it was preserved in the Sephardic synagogue in Aleppo, and so carefully was it guarded that it was almost impossible to consult. Even so, one page was photographed, and in 1887 formed the frontispiece of a book on Hebrew accents (Wickes, *A treatise on the accentuation of the twenty-one so-called prose books of the Old Testament*). The codex was reported destroyed in the upheavals in the Lebanon in the 1940s, but in 1960 the President of the State of Israel proclaimed that it had been recovered, and it has now become the basis of a new edition of the Massoretic text edited by M. H. Goshen-Gottstein in the Hebrew University, and in 1965 a *Sample edition of the Book of Isaiah* appeared.

5. Finally, the *Leningrad Codex, B 19a*, written in 1008 and vouched

for by the copyist in a colophon as based on the text of Aaron ben Asher. Since 1937 it has been used as the basis of the only current critical edition of the Massoretic text, namely Kittel's *Biblia Hebraica*, third and subsequent editions.

It has been assumed that the ben Asher text marks the end of the formal history of the Massoretic text, but not all manuscripts from the middle ages belong to this tradition. Three Erfurt codices from the eleventh to the fourteenth centuries, and the *Reuchlin Codex*, the oldest biblical manuscript in Germany, contain elements which are recognizably ben Naphtali. In the past, they have not been rated as significant for the history of the classical text, but, as scholars become better informed about Massoretic activities in general, it is more than likely that renewed attention will be paid to these divergent transmissions. One is again conscious of Orlinsky's assertion, already referred to, that there never was really a text which could be designated as *the* Massoretic text.

The establishment of the ben Asher text, however, produced an interesting side-effect on the transmission of the accompanying Massoretic notes. The Massorah became conventional because it had no longer any real purpose to serve; and gradually its minutely written script became rendered in geometric and artistic designs as embellishments around the margins of the manuscript, sometimes in grotesque shapes of dragons and occasionally in intricate and fanciful lines, to give an outlet to the artistic urges of the scribe.

An exquisite example of the ornamental Massorah is to be found in a fifteenth-century Spanish manuscript in Aberdeen University, and in a discussion of it (*The Aberdeen Codex of the Hebrew Bible*, 1958) Dr Cecil Roth gives the history of this feature of Hebrew scribal activity, with three excellent photographs from the manuscript itself. The codex also contains eight folios of ben Asher and ben Naphtali variants, which were included in the manuscript. Dr Roth urges that they are to be regarded simply as a convenient vehicle for introducing scribal art and letter illumination into the initial pages (in this instance eight) of the scroll. Another instance of ornamental Massorah is *B.M. Or. 2626–8*, again of Spanish provenance, late fifteenth century.

In the late fifteenth and early sixteenth centuries printed Hebrew bibles begin to appear, and outstanding among them are rabbinic bibles, because they contain along with the Massoretic text important Targumic renderings to which reference will be made later, and the polyglot texts, because they include many of the Versions. For the history of the Massoretic text, however, special interest attaches to the *Second rabbinic bible* of 1524/5 edited by Jacob ben Chayim. The edition is a critical one, based on the collation of a considerable number of manuscripts, and supplied with a Massorah created by the editor himself. It became the main basis of practically every subsequent edition of the text until Kittel's *Biblia Hebraica*[3]. But it had two serious faults. First, the manuscripts available to ben Chayim were, by his own plaintive admission, recent and of unknown provenance. Secondly, he seems not to have been able to deal with the vicissitudes which had beset the transmission even during the four or five centuries since the emergence of the ben Asher text. The Erfurt Codices provide an instance of what had happened, and there is hardly a manuscript—and there are a goodly number from this period—which had retained a pure ben Asher text. The very fact that ben Chayim composed his own Massorah shows that he was not ignorant of the divergent elements which were present in his manuscript sources, but was unable to accommodate them.

Subsequent printed bibles perpetuated the hybrid text of ben Chayim and occasionally introduced additional, equally mixed, text-forms, but they served well. They include the Hebrew text of the *Complutensian Polyglot* (1514–17), and the editions of Michaelis (1720), Kennicott (1776–80), and J. B. de Rossi (1784–98). Lists of variants from nearly 700 and 1,500 manuscripts and printed bibles accompanied the last two respectively, and during the heyday of biblical criticism the editions of Baer-Delitzsch and C. D. Ginsburg were published with their Massoroth, and Kittel's first two editions were supplied with an *apparatus criticus* to include manuscript evidence, Version variants and conjectural emendations to the text.

There appears to be no doubt that *Biblia Hebraica*[3] with its return to an authentic ben Asher text from the early eleventh century marks an important step in the scientific study of the textual transmission. It renders possible, too, an appreciation of the relevant Massorah, rather than assuming a Massoretic composition which has no textual value at all. The edition is a lasting tribute to Paul Kahle and his assessment of the Cairo Genizah fragments and of subsequent manuscripts. But the extent to which this departure really involves a drastic modification of earlier theories is still a controversy, and the edition might well be displaced as a definitive text either by the Hebrew University Bible, or by

Orlinsky's conclusion that it can be no better than *a* Massoretic text, one among many.

To some degree the reaction is illuminated by the latest Hebrew Old Testament to be published in Britain, namely N. H. Snaith's edition for the British and Foreign Bible Society (*Sepher Torah u-Nebi'im u-Kethubim*), which will replace the Letteris and Ginsburg editions. A detailed introduction to the edition is still awaited, but Snaith has briefly outlined the background ('New Edition of the Hebrew Bible', *Vetus Testamentum*, VII, 1957, pp. 207/8), and again in *Textus*, vol. II, 1962. The text is based on the original readings of some fifteenth-century Spanish manuscripts (*British Museum, Or. 2626–8*, the Yemenite *B.M. Or. 2375*), and the *Shem Tob MS* from the Sassoon library, and the editor claims that the resultant text is practically identical with the Kahle (*Biblia Hebraica³*) edition of the ben Asher standard text.

That Principal Snaith decided that only the ben Asher type of text can henceforth really satisfy the Hebraist is a tribute to the epoch-making work of Kahle and the publication of *Biblia Hebraica³*, but if his claim that the ben Asher text is not limited to strictly ben Asher manuscripts is substantiated, further scrutiny of Spanish manuscripts might well be worth-while. In any case it is a challenge to the view, popularly accepted, that, soon after the ben Asher text appeared, scribal interference with it was universal and brought all later manuscripts into disrepute. Thus, recent textual studies emphasize that for the Hebrew Old Testament actual medieval manuscripts are basic. At present, and unless some discovery is made of more fundamental significance than the Dead Sea scrolls, critical editions must be based on medieval codices, whether they be regarded as *the* Massoretic or merely *a* Massoretic text.

THE VERSIONS

The relevance of the middle ages for the Versions of the Old Testament is quite different from that for the Hebrew text, for it is in this period that we see much of their origin and early history. In a sense this is true even of the oldest of the Versions, and the most important, namely the Greek rendering commonly known as the Septuagint; it is obviously true of the Latin renderings—both the early Old Latin and the later Vulgate—as well as the Aramaic renderings of the Targums and the others. Nevertheless, the prehistory of the Versions must be included, for without it we fail to see the whole significance of many prominent features in the medieval transmission. At the same time, it is necessary to note that much of this prehistory actually results from recent discussion as well as discovery; consequently the present survey must often be concerned with items undreamed of by the medievalists themselves.

The actual Versions consist, of course, of the Septuagint and its daughter versions on the one hand, and renderings more closely related to the Massoretic text such as the Targums, the Samaritan recension and the Arabic version on the other. The Syriac Peshitta, as we shall see, has its own category.

The Septuagint

Throughout the history of the Christian Church the most important of the Versions has been the Septuagint. It assumed priority as early as the first century: apparently it was used by Paul when he wrote to the churches, and on the whole it was the rendering used for the Gospels in their present form. On the other hand, orthodox Judaism either refused to recognize it from an early period or quickly expunged it from among its Scriptures, for there are but few and indirect indications of its existence in any of the rabbinic works. Consequently, the history of its transmission must be regarded as largely independent of the Massoretic text except that, from time to time, significant attempts were made by Christian Fathers to achieve its alignment with the more fixed and, in a sense, more authentic Hebrew text.

Recently discovered manuscripts from the pre-Christian and early Christian periods provide pointers for the early history. They include the *John Rylands Papyrus 458* from the second century B.C., and *Papyrus Fouad 266* in Cairo from the late second or early first century B.C., both of which contain fragments of Deuteronomy. Qumran cave four has produced a papyrus fragment of Leviticus, and two leather fragments of Leviticus and of Numbers. The last mentioned still await publication. Their major importance is that on the whole they confirm the implications of the Letter of Aristeas, and the testimony of Philo and Josephus that by the second century B.C. the Greek rendering of the Torah was not only complete and uniform but was also well distributed throughout the Hellenistic Diaspora and in Palestine itself. The only caveat that should be entered is that the scholars who have collated the Rylands papyrus are not wholly agreed on its affinities (e.g. Kahle argues that it is related to one of the recensions, namely the Lucianic).

From Qumran caves one, four, five and six come biblical texts in

Hebrew which, according to reports, are related to the parent text of the Septuagint historical books. Particular interest attaches to Samuel fragments from cave four, because the text-form shows more obvious affinities with the Septuagint than do the others. Of course, it has long been agreed that the parent text of the Septuagint Samuel contained recensional divergences from the Massoretic text, but the extent of the recension has been debated. Those who minimized it argued that many of the textual differences merely reflect Hellenistic tendencies, others explained them as deriving from actual Hebrew variants. The present discovery obviously supports the second alternative, and it may be assumed that since the rendering of Samuel is demonstrably a fairly literal translation of its Hebrew parent text the presence of interpretation elsewhere, at least in the historical books, should be admitted only where no other explanation is possible.

But the problem of Greek–Hebrew relationships is not thereby disposed of, for though the presence of interpretation in the Septuagint generally is undoubted, its nature and its extent are debated. It is probable that during the third century B.C. a rendering of the Torah in *koiné* Greek was produced by a duly commissioned body of Jerusalem (orthodox) Jews for apologetic purposes and for liturgical use in the synagogues of the Hellenistic Diaspora. This agrees with the historical core of the Letter of Aristeas. In the rendering interpretative elements bear typically Jewish characteristics, in which such items as antianthropomorphisms and antianthropopathisms loom large, as they also do in the Aramaic Targums. Likewise the Septuagint rendering of the historical books may well be a true rendering of a Hebrew parent text, albeit in a different recension from the Massoretic. It used to be claimed for it that some legendary features in the Massoretic Samuel–Kings had been rationalized and the persons of the kings idealized, all under the influence of Greek interpretation. But discrepancies of this kind are not necessarily Hellenistic, or confined to the Greek–Hebrew texts; one need only think of the similar discrepancies between Samuel–Kings and Chronicles in the Hebrew bible. The question is further complicated by traces of multiple translators as well as divergent parent texts. At the same time we cannot deny Hellenistic influence; for instance, it is difficult to explain away such obvious interpretative elements as the polemic against Hellenistic heathenism in the Greek Isaiah—a text whose parent Hebrew is almost identical with the Massoretic. There are other hints of what has been appropriately called 'Galuth-psychology', that is, the introduction of Hellenistic philosophical overtones. Thus, Proverbs and Job can be regarded as a fruitful source of Hellenistic hermeneutics, and even the comparatively literal rendering of Ecclesiastes betrays occasional Hellenisms. The theory has inevitably evoked opposition, which is mainly based on the view that the only satisfactory key to the Version is Jewish (orthodox) hermeneutics. If, however, the history of the Old Testament text and interpretation in the pre-Christian era must be regarded from one basic standpoint, with one uniform parent text and one uniform exegesis, more questions seem to be raised than answered. The debate continues, vigorously conducted with scholars such as G. Gerleman and J. W. Wevers on opposite sides, and promises to be one of the most fruitful examinations of the Septuagint of recent times.

A parallel controversy is centred on the nature of the Greek text and the early textual transmission of the Version. On the one hand Kahle has a considerable following for his view that during the pre-Christian era there were numerous Greek renderings of the Old Testament and that what the Letter of Aristeas describes is the standardization rather than the rendering of the Torah text in Greek. The other books were subsequently standardized by the Christian Church and the name Septuagint, having lost favour among the Jews, was given to it for convenience. In other words, despite the evidence of Philo and Josephus and the statement in the Prologue to Ecclesiasticus, it is assumed that there was no authorized Septuagint text before the second century A.D. On the other hand, the traditional view is still strongly defended by many scholars and has the implicit approval of the editors of modern critical texts of the Septuagint. Obviously this does not deny the existence of variant Greek texts in the pre-Christian era, for in the New Testament itself although the quotations are predominantly Septuagintal use is made of other renderings—some of them identifiable, such as the pre-Theodotionic readings in the Book of The Revelation and elsewhere. It would appear, however, that Kahle and his school are overstating the case when they make it depend on the assumption that the existence of other Greek versions necessarily precludes the existence of the Septuagint as a recognized version in the time immediately before the New Testament.

The Chester Beatty and related papyri from the early Christian era, whose discovery was a sensation in the 1930s, seem now to be assuming their proper place in the textual history of the Version; and, especially in their contribution to post-Pentateuchal books, their importance is even greater than the Dead Sea scrolls or the pre-Christian Septuagint fragments. For Ezekiel, *Pap 967/8* provides a substantial amount of text from the second century A.D. which, it has been argued, either helps to establish the case for an early alignment of the Septuagint with the Hebrew text, or for the view that already doublets occur in the text which betoken a conflation of two divergent traditions, one of which had a strong affinity with the Massoretic text. For Daniel, the same papyrus manuscript gives a text which is true Septuagint and not Theodotionic, which is the source of all other extant manuscripts of this book, with one late exception. Yet another collection of early Greek manuscripts, housed in Berlin until their destruction in the last war, but fortunately discussed by O. Stegmuller in 1939, can be briefly mentioned. They are on papyrus and parchment from the early third to the seventh centuries A.D. and contain texts which range from straightforward Septuagint to a fifth- or sixth-century lectionary which clearly stands outside the normal Septuagint transmission and which represents either a far-reaching recension or a completely new Greek translation.

The rival Greek translations from the second century A.D.—Aquila, Symmachus and Theodotion—have again become the centre of attention because of yet another of the Dead Sea scrolls. It is a leather fragment from an unidentified cave, probably in the Murabba'at area, and contains fragments of the Minor Prophets in Greek. There are two conflicting views about their significance. Father Barthélemy, writing in *Revue Biblique*, 1953, asserts that the text, from the late first century A.D., consists of a revision of the old Septuagint from the pre-Christian era, similar in pattern to the rather later renderings of Aquila, Symmachus and Theodotion, and is also the text used by Justin Martyr in the second century in his *Dialogue with Trypho* in which he refutes Jewish charges of Christian interference with the Septuagint. That is, Barthélemy continues, the text of the Greek Minor Prophets shows that there was current among both Jews and Christians in the second century A.D. a common Greek bible acceptable to both parties, and which was itself a revision of the earlier Septuagint. The opposite view is taken by Kahle, and published in *Theologische Literaturzeitung*, 1954, and his *Cairo Geniza* (2nd edition), 1959. Accepting a verdict by

C. H. Roberts that the fragment belongs to the period 50 B.C. to A.D. 50, and asserting that agreement with the three translations of Aquila, Symmachus and Theodotion is only sporadic, he concludes that the manuscript is yet another of the *Vulgärtexte* which were abundant in Judaism before the Bible texts, both Hebrew and Greek, were standardized. The similarity with the text of Justin Martyr, Kahle continues, is to be explained by his having made use of Lucian's recension which, in turn, can be shown to have existed in pre-Christian times, as witness Kahle's interpretation of the above-mentioned *Rylands Papyrus* of the Pentateuch. According to this hypothesis, texts used by the Fathers postulate a variety of text-forms current during the early stages of the history of the Greek bible. The present manuscript of the Minor Prophets belongs to the same group, and, together with Aquila, Symmachus, Theodotion and Lucian, reflects attempts made at that time to establish agreement between the Greek and Hebrew texts.

It is difficult to see how a compromise solution satisfactory to both sides can be offered. The Chester Beatty and other papyri show textual divergences, as indeed do all the manuscripts of the Septuagint; throughout its history free transmission was always one of its characteristic features, and, despite attempts to fix a standard form, there appears to have been no recension for which the claim was made that it was an authoritative text. In other words, if there was at any time a recognized Septuagint text-form it was at the beginning, and the divergences were introduced during the transmission over the centuries.

It is against this background that we look at Origen's *Hexapla*. At some time between 230 and 240 Origen, the first scholar in our sense in the history of the Church, produced what was to become yet another recension of the Septuagint on the basis of the Hebrew text. That the latter was supremely important to him is suggested by the order of columns in the *Hexapla*—first the Hebrew text and the same in transcription, columns three and four Aquila and Symmachus, and only in column five does his reconstructed Septuagint appear, with the use of Aristarchean signs to mark additions and omissions in relation to the Hebrew. Why Theodotion's version is placed in column six, after the Septuagint, is not clear, nor why parts of the poetical books were placed in additional columns, though from a note by Eusebius that they were found in a jar in a cave near the Dead Sea we might venture a guess that these were early precursors of the Dead Sea scrolls, and that the relevance of the Greek Minor Prophets from the caves is thereby still further increased.

Of the colossal *Hexapla*, and of its abbreviated *Tetrapla*, there are no extant remains, but mention should be made of the *Milan Palimpsest* from the tenth century, discovered in 1894 by Cardinal Mercati, which contains some Psalms in all columns except the Hebrew. Unfortunately, the manuscript is still unpublished, but the transcription column has been examined from the point of view of Hebrew orthography and grammar. Field's collection of Hexaplaric material in 1895 (reissued in 1965) is now being superseded by a section in the *apparatus criticus* of the latest critical edition of the Septuagint text, the *Göttingen Septuagint*.

The controversy about the early history of the Version is bound to affect modern views about the recensions of its text. It is at first sight difficult to dismiss a tradition, which goes back to Jerome in the late fourth century, that there were three recensions current at his time: the Hesychian in Alexandria, the Lucianic in Constantinople and Antioch, and the Hexaplaric in Palestine; but reference has already been made to Kahle's view that at least the Lucianic was based on a pre-Christian divergent text. There is, moreover, abundant evidence from before and after Jerome's time that the transmission of the text itself was by no means controlled by local or recensional principles. The sources for the evidence, of course, are the Great Codices and the uncials and minuscules from the fourth century onwards. They are all admittedly 'mixed' texts. For instance, whereas it is generally agreed that *Codex Marchalianus* (*Q*) belongs, with others, to a fairly well-defined family of texts with Hesychian characteristics, and that Hexaplaric readings are to be recovered largely from another group of manuscripts, it is nevertheless from the margins of *Q* that many of the best Hexaplaric readings are actually obtained. Again, the well-known *Codex Vaticanus* (*B*) is regarded as the best of the so-called non-recensional texts, but the presence of Hexaplaric infiltration in this text is admitted. So little is known about the early history of the recensions and their purpose that any assessment of their relevance for the general transmission is inconclusive, and also carries with it a possible danger in that it might suggest a completely wrong standpoint for their use in textual reconstruction.

Nowhere is this more obvious than in current attempts to produce critical editions of the Septuagint. There have been two major projects, each with its independent approach to the task. The one is the Cambridge edition, *The Old Testament in Greek*, begun in 1906 under the editorship of Brooke and McLean, later joined by St John Thackeray and subsequently taken over by T. W. Manson, and abandoned at his death. It largely adopts the principles applied by H. B. Swete for the three-volume *The Old Testament in Greek* (1887–91 with several later editions), and uses as basic the text of *Vaticanus*, whose lacunae are supplied from the text of *Codices Alexandrinus* and *Sinaiticus*. The *apparatus criticus* provides variants from uncials, selected minuscules, daughter translations, Philo and Josephus and some early Christian writings. Obviously there is no pretence that the result represents a standard critical text; by using the British Museum *Codex Alexandrinus*, which is largely a Hesychian witness, to augment *Vaticanus*, the editors implied that their text was to be little more than a conventional rendering which, together with the *apparatus criticus*, could be used by each individual student to reconstruct or to explain the Version as he wished. It is significant that Professor Manson more than once explained that in his view to reconstruct an 'original' Septuagint is not only hypothetical but also impossible on *a priori* grounds. The edition covers Genesis (1906) to Tobit (1940), and the regrettable and untimely death of the editor in 1958 caused its cessation. A re-issue of Swete, however, with a revised *apparatus criticus*, might go far towards redeeming the situation.

In some ways Rahlfs's *Septuaginta* (1935) follows the same principle, for the text is based on the three Great Codices, *Vaticanus*, *Sinaiticus* and *Alexandrinus*, with a much shorter *apparatus criticus* of variant readings than the Cambridge edition.

The other edition is the *Göttingen Septuagint*, which, since 1922 and more ambitiously since 1931, has appeared with regularity and colossal industry. The origins of the edition are to be found in the principles formulated by de Lagarde late in the nineteenth century. Essentially it means that in the first instance all available sources for Septuagint readings, which include manuscripts of all kinds, daughter translations and quotations from the Fathers, should be classified according to the recensions—Hexaplaric, Lucianic and Hesychian—to provide 'Text-Families' on lines similar to those of the New Testament. The next step was to reconstruct the pre-recension text, which should, in theory, correspond to the original text. The work obtained its main inspiration and impetus through Rahlfs and later Ziegler, who, however, has established the case for the addition of one further recension, called *The Catena Group* and based originally on early commentaries of the Fathers from which readings were included in later manuscripts. But it has been pointed out that the texts in this group contain readings which overlap with the older recensions—a conclusion which reduces the validity of their witness to the existence of a self-contained 'family' or recension.

A still more ambitious edition along the lines of de Lagarde and the *Göttingen Septuagint* is the *Text of Joshua in Greek* produced by Max L. Margolis and published in four fascicles in 1931–8.

The comparative merits of the two principles of editing as exemplified in the Cambridge and Göttingen texts are difficult to assess. The former, it may be complained, is inconclusive and does little more than provide material for further analysis and speculation; but it has the advantage of being realistic. Its text is produced from actual historical text-forms, particularly *Codex Vaticanus*, which, since the appearance of the Sixtine edition in 1587, has provided the basis for the major Septuagint studies of Holmes and Parsons, Swete, and, to a large extent, the *Concordance* of Hatch and Redpath. Indeed it is the only manuscript from among the Great Codices which can safely be used; for *Alexandrinus* is, as we have seen, representative of the Hesychian recension, and comparatively large portions of the Old Testament have been lost from *Sinaiticus*, which, in any case, is so closely related to *Vaticanus* as to make its choice arbitrary. Moreover, it is only such an edition as the Cambridge that can possibly accommodate the view that there never actually existed an *Ur-Septuagint* in the sense postulated by the Göttingen edition.

On the other hand the Göttingen text has the merit of being the logical product of a recognized historical method and analysis, and has to a considerable extent justified itself by demonstrating the existence of some well-defined text-families. Furthermore, the practical benefits of the classification are clearly indicated in the *apparatus criticus*, and the fact that a very large number of readings are adduced from a great variety of sources adds to the immediate practical uses of the edition. Obviously the main criticism, and a fundamental one which is almost universally recognized, is that the resultant text is hypothetical, eclectic and unreal, and one which probably never existed except in the mind of the editor; a corollary is that even the system by which the text is achieved is not without possible criticism along the same lines.

Nevertheless, the practical benefits of the edition far outweigh its academic shortcomings, and its use is not limited to the scholars who subscribe to its postulates.

Other Versions

The other Versions may briefly be divided into two groups according to their Jewish and Christian origins. Jewish renderings come under the general title of Targums and consist mainly of translations and expansions into Aramaic. How ancient these renderings may have been is difficult to say, but the Babylonian Talmud, *Megillah* 3 a, attributes their origin to Ezra, and Kahle has argued that unofficial Aramaic translations were current from the fourth century B.C., when, under the Persian regime, Aramaic became an official language in Asia Minor.

Hypotheses about the history and transmission of the Targums reflect the same two basically different standpoints as in the case of the Septuagint. Kahle's interpretation assumes that the standardized translation was a later emergence from a number of unofficial, free and popular renderings. The other view which, in the absence of contemporary outstanding Targum exponents, must be called traditional, assumes that free renderings are developments from an earlier fixed translation.

Extant Targumic texts are generally to be found in printed editions of the rabbinic printed bibles and the polyglots from the fifteenth and sixteenth centuries, but many later and critical editions have been produced in the nineteenth and twentieth centuries. Substantial manuscript additions have become available from the Cairo Genizah, and augmented in 1956 by the identification of a complete Targum manuscript of the Pentateuch, the *Neofiti Codex I* of the Vatican which belongs to the fifteenth century, but whose significance is far greater than its date would suggest.

Targums are divided into two groups: those which, by their adherence to the Massoretic text and the prestige they claim in the tradition, were official translations, and others, free and paraphrastic, which were unofficial. Of the former the Pentateuch Targum of Onqelos is usually explained as having been officially redacted in the second century A.D. as a literal rendering of the newly produced Massoretic text, and parallel to Aquila's Greek translation—indeed, the two names have frequently been identified. An important edition was produced by A. Berliner in 1884, but substantial additions of manuscripts from the middle ages in the Genizah fragments have changed some of the readings as well as modifying the general picture of the transmission. The standard Targum to the Prophets is called by the name of Jonathan ben Uzziel, but again the version is sometimes identified with Theodotion, and a possible pointer in favour of this view is that the Mishna itself is confused in its references both to the identity of Jonathan and of the Targum. As a rendering it is not so faithful to the Massoretic text as is Onqelos, and it bears obvious traces of having been redacted from earlier renderings; the fact that it quotes Onqelos, especially in passages relating to the Torah, bears out both the fact that it had mixed origins and also had official status as a translation. As with Onqelos, the most common sources of the Targum Jonathan are the rabbinic and polyglot bibles. But mention should be made of Lagarde's *Prophetae Chaldaice* (1872) and of critically edited texts of Joshua and Judges by Prätorius (1899–1900) and Isaiah by Stenning (1949, reprinted 1953) and a concordance to the whole Targum Jonathan by Kosowski (1940). More important is the recent publication, in four volumes, of A. Sperber, *The Bible in Aramaic*, 1959–62. Volume I has Targum Onqelos, vol. II, the Former Prophets (Targum Jonathan), vol. III, the Latter Prophets (Targum Jonathan). Volume IV is to contain treatments of textual problems raised by the edition.

Unofficial Targums are numerous and vary considerably both intrinsically and in interest for the textualist. Indeed, even Targums to the Pentateuch from this class need careful scrutiny because freedom of paraphrase has permitted, for example, not only the final compilation of the Mishna to be presupposed (second century A.D.) but also one of the wives of Mohammed and a daughter to be mentioned as wives of Ishmael in Gen. xxi. 21! Nor is this an isolated historical pointer to the middle ages.

The most interesting of the Targums are those of the Pentateuch, and, because of the recently discovered Neofiti I, pride of place goes to what was previously called the Fragment-Targum, or Jerusalem II. There is now a complete copy of 450 folios of this Targum excellently preserved, and it also provides evidence for a degree of 'infiltration' of the Onqelos text into the text of the unofficial Targums. Portions of the text of this Targum were printed in the first rabbinic bible, 1516–17 and later reprinted: other texts were published in 1899 by Ginsberger (*Das Fragmententhargum*): still other material was discovered in the

Genizah manuscripts and discussed by Kahle (*Cairo Genizah*[2], 1959), and undoubtedly Neofiti I, under the direction of its editor, Diez Macho, will necessitate a fresh examination of the whole Targum.

Another Pentateuch Targum, wrongly called Jonathan, hence Pseudo-Jonathan, is based on Targum Onqelos with numerous elaborations of rabbinic provenance. The question of their relationships and period is still unsettled, but additions to the text from the Cairo Genizah manuscripts help to clarify the picture.

Targums to the Writings obviously come into the list of unofficial Targums for, because of the omission of these books from the synagogue lectionaries, there was no need of an official Targum. The texts vary from literal renderings as in the Targum to Esther (which may be official, as witness the important role played by this book in the history of the synagogue) to very free paraphrases, as in some Psalms.

The text of the Samaritan Pentateuch has recently become a subject of concern. It is well known that the Abisha scroll at Nablus was always regarded as a standard text, and because of its antiquity it ranked as a major source of textual variants. And especially under the influence of Paul Kahle it has become one of the most important witnesses to the early, pre-Massoretic text of the Pentateuch. But the Abisha scroll has now been twice photographed, and in 1959 its text was edited and published by Pérez Castro, accompanied by photographs and a lengthy introduction. The scroll, far from being a pre-Christian text, is merely a collection of medieval texts, written by Abisha ben Pinhas in 1085. Consequently the actual text of the Samaritan Pentateuch cannot claim antiquity except by implication. The fact that in some cases Samaritan readings are paralleled by some Qumran texts does not mean that the former text-form receives complete vindication. The full implications of Castro's publication have not yet been assessed, but it appears unlikely that in future an appeal to the Samaritan text will carry the same authority as previously. In this context, too, mention should be made of the Arabic rendering of the Pentateuch by Saadya Gaon in the tenth century, which became part of the Samaritan transmission.

The second group of early Versions relates to the history of the Septuagint, and as part of the Christian transmission of Scripture they reflect the vicissitudes of the Church in the same way as its dogma and politics. For western Christendom the main interest lies in the Latin Versions. As early as the late second century A.D. there appear to have been free renderings of the Septuagint to produce daughter translations in Latin, and fragments from Europe and North Africa were later assembled and became known as Old Latin texts (or *Itala*). The standard list of these texts, made by Sabatier in 1743-9, has received continuous though sporadic additions; the most recent and ambitious collection made by the abbots of Beuron, 1949-54, goes to the end of Genesis.

The Vulgate marks a departure from the Septuagint, at least theoretically, for its original text cannot any longer be constructed. It is well known that Jerome, commissioned by Pope Damasus in 383 to produce a Latin bible, first of all revised Old Latin texts on the basis of the Hexaplaric Septuagint, and extant remains include the Psalter and, possibly, parts of Job and Song of Songs. After 390, however, Jerome produced the Vulgate based on the Hebrew text, and explained his principle and methods in the *Prologus Galeatus*, which accompanied the first section of his translation, Samuel–Kings. Opposition to the rendering was violent from the outset, and it was not until the eighth century that the Vulgate was popularly received. Meanwhile the rendering had been interspersed with readings from the Old Latin, and the uncertain nature of its transmission is well illustrated by two editions of the Vulgate which appeared in the late sixteenth century. After the Council of Trent a revision—the Sixtine—was produced under the auspices of Pope Sixtus V in 1590, but four years later, under Clement VIII, it was replaced by the Clementine, which is still recognized as the official version, except that since 1945 the Pontifical Biblical Institute's new translation of the Psalms from the Hebrew has been included in the breviary. In 1907 the Benedictines began a critical edition of the Vulgate, and books have appeared regularly since 1926. The work, *Biblia Sacra iuxta latinam Vulgatam*, is based on the modern principle of the establishment of manuscript families, but it is generally admitted that, despite some very important clarifications in the history of the Version, the resultant text cannot confidently be claimed to represent the original Vulgate. (See also chapters IV and V.)

Finally, the Syriac Peshitta. This is yet another version transmitted by the Church, though possibly having Jewish provenance and consequently a somewhat greater relevance for the Hebrew Old Testament. Its origins are unknown, but there are traces in quotations by Syriac Fathers of a pre-Peshitta rendering, possibly for propaganda among proselyte Syrians such as the royal family in Adiabene, eastwards of the

Tigris, who became converts around the beginning of the Christian era. But there was also a pre-Peshitta New Testament, whose existence strengthens the opposite view, that the Syriac Version always was Christian; and the fact that the Peshitta—like the Vulgate—represents a Hebrew parent text and contains sporadic traces of rabbinic exegesis does not necessarily preclude a Christian origin. Some of the numerous Christian Peshitta manuscripts, such as the Codex *Ambrosianus* (sixth to seventh century A.D.), stress that the Psalms were translated from Hebrew.

At the same time, the characteristically free transmission of the Bible text characterizes the Peshitta as much as any other Version, and it is demonstrable that the influence of the Septuagint is frequently present; consequently the textual evidence of the Version, especially where it departs from the Massoretic text and confirms the Septuagint, loses force.

As a whole, two distinct standpoints may be seen emerging from a mid-twentieth-century survey of the Old Testament Text and Versions. On the one hand the authenticity of the Massoretic text stands higher than at any time in the history of modern textual criticism, a standpoint which is based on a better assessment of the history of the Jewish transmission. Coupled with it is an increased knowledge of Hebrew lexicography and of the cognate languages which shows that difficulties in the *textus receptus* do not always justify textual emendation. On the other hand, interest in the Versions has become increasingly centred on their own intrinsic relevance and their intricate history. Appeal to the Versions for purposes of textual emendation, though obviously still valid, is made with the greatest caution; but the scrutiny of the Versions, especially of the Septuagint and Targums, for exegesis and interpretation has produced important results, and is likely to prove interesting and profitable.

CHAPTER II

THE HISTORY OF THE TEXT AND CANON OF THE NEW TESTAMENT TO JEROME

THE TEXT

The aim and object of the textual critic is to deduce from all the available material what the original author wrote. None of the original manuscripts of the New Testament exists, and, until the age of printing began in the fifteenth century, all manuscripts were copied by hand. Mistakes arose inevitably in the process. The reader is challenged to copy out a page of the New Testament fairly rapidly without an error: mistakes were easier to make in the early days of the Church, when words were not separated in writing, and when punctuation and Greek breathings and accents were absent from the capital (uncial) letters employed. Alterations to the text during the process of transmission could be either accidental or intentional. By accident, words or lines were omitted by a scribe whose eye passed over one word or phrase to another similar to it (haplography) or they were written by him twice (dittography). The former error constantly occurred at the end of a sentence or a phrase, when the scribe's eye had left the original to concentrate on the copy, so that, of two phrases ending in a similar or identical way, one is omitted (homoioteleuton). Sometimes a scribe working in a scriptorium, and hearing the original text being read out, would be guilty of errors of ear rather than of eye; αι, ει, η are constantly confused; even ἡμεῖς is written for ὑμεῖς, 'we' for 'you', cf. Col. i. 7. For the critic such errors have often a value, because, unless they are pure accidents that might happen to a number of scribes independently, they point to textual relationship: the more errors that one manuscript has in common with another, the greater is the probability of their affinity.

Less often the scribes 'corrected' their texts intentionally. They harmonized one Gospel with another, one account of Paul's conversion in Acts with either of the other two, one account of the Lord's supper with another or with familiar liturgical usage, the epistle of Jude with that of II Peter or references to the Old Testament with the text (usually the Septuagint, sometimes the Hebrew) familiar to themselves. Occasionally they took offence at language which had been used innocently at first but which seemed in a later age to be heretical or at least derogatory to the Lord or his followers. Sometimes they incorporated gossipy details about New Testament figures into the text, sharing the interests of the authors of the Apocryphal Gospels; the 'western' scribe(s) of Acts especially may be accused of this fault. Sometimes they added suitable names, e.g. Jesus, Paul, to an opening paragraph or other words to make the situation clearer, perhaps for lectionary purposes; or they made 'suitable' endings to a paragraph or to a book, cf. Mark xvi. 9–20. But the total number of 'intentional' variants in proportion to the whole New Testament is very small. These variants also are valuable to the critic. Not only do they throw light on the minds of the scribes but also they help to trace relationship between manuscripts which have, for instance, the same insertion in the same place; for example, the *Pericope Adulterae*, John vii. 53–viii. 11, is placed after Luke xxi. 38 in manuscripts belonging to fam.[13] but at the end of John in manuscripts belonging to fam.[1] (see below, p. 31).

Of the total number of New Testament manuscripts that must have been written, those that are extant are probably only a fraction. And yet the number of those surviving is vast. In comparison with the manuscripts of any ancient pagan text, for example of Virgil, those for the New Testament are overwhelming and the oldest are far nearer in time to the authors than are the manuscripts of any pagan work. We have for the New Testament more than 66 papyri and 230 uncial manuscripts, 2,500 minuscules (written in running or cursive writing) and about 1,600 lectionaries for use in church services: in addition there are the Versions, the oldest being the most valuable, for example, the Syriac, Old Latin, Coptic, Armenian and Georgian, not to mention the Arabic and Ethiopic. In addition there are the quotations in the Fathers, sometimes of great value, especially if they are in extended form rather than short citations from memory and if the patristic scribes have refrained from making the quotation conform to the text of the New Testament current in their own day. These citations help often to localize the text; e.g. the Latin *k*, *Codex Bobbiensis*, gives us an African text almost identical with that of Cyprian, *c.* A.D. 250.

The papyri and some of the other most valuable manuscripts of an early date were preserved in the dry sands of Egypt; elsewhere the climate and soil were too damp for them to survive, with a few exceptions.

In some of the older textbooks and commentaries it was the custom to cite the textual evidence by enumerating as many manuscripts as possible for or against a variant. Even some modern critics, like Tischendorf and Vogels, have been opposed to any strict grouping of manuscripts, though usually they have laid great stress themselves on certain evidence; the former valued ℵ, *Codex Sinaiticus*, his own discovery, very highly, and the latter, the evidence of the Versions. Since the days of Westcott and Hort, however, it has become increasingly recognized that the critics' task is to go behind the comparatively late Byzantine, ecclesiastical or (as Hort called it misleadingly) 'Syrian' text to discover the readings of the Alexandrian and western texts, which the Byzantine scribes were wont to conflate. The term 'western' is largely a misnomer, as evidence for this text is found in Egypt early in the second century and in many of the early eastern Fathers; but frequently the Latin versions support such readings as well as the Graeco-Latin texts, lending colour thereby to this appellation. It remains true that a 'Byzantine' manuscript may sometimes preserve a good reading, found now to be supported by an early and recently discovered papyrus. Usually in an *apparatus criticus* only the more important representatives of the textual families are given and the evidence of the late text, vouched for by the mass of late minuscules, is given by a siglum such as ω or ς. It must be noted, however, that sometimes a minuscule, though written later than some of the uncial manuscripts, may witness to a good text; for example, 33 (ninth–tenth century) has a good 'Alexandrian' text, and 1739 (tenth century) seems to give the text of Paul known to Origen in the third century. It is a truism that manuscripts must be weighed and not counted.

Building on the work of Westcott and Hort, of Ferrar and of Lake, B. H. Streeter (*The Four Gospels*, 1924) put forward his theory of local texts, into which the most important manuscripts then known could be grouped. The influential centres of Christian life in the Mediterranean world of the first few centuries A.D. were Alexandria, Antioch, Caesarea, Italy and Gaul, Carthage and Byzantium.

Streeter's primary authority for the Alexandrian family was B, *Codex Vaticanus* (fourth century), and the secondary authorities were ℵ, *Codex Sinaiticus*, cited as S by Merk and Bover (also fourth century), L, *Codex Regius* (eighth century), and the Coptic Versions, both Bohairic and Sahidic (see below for Versions). His patristic authorities under this heading were Origen, before 231 when he moved from Alexandria to Caesarea, and Cyril of Alexandria, *c.* 430.

For the primary text of Antioch he chose the older Syriac manuscript, Syr^s or Sinaitic Syriac, and as secondary support the other manuscript of this old Syriac text, Syr^c or Curetonian Syriac.

For the text of Caesarea he put first Θ, the Koridethi manuscript (ninth century), the text of which had not been discovered till 1906 nor published till 1913. His secondary authorities were fam.[1] and fam.[13], 28, 565, 700 and the text of Mark v. 31 ff. in W, the Washington or Freer manuscript (fourth or fifth century) discovered in 1906.

As the primary authority for Italy and Gaul, Streeter put D, *Codex Bezae*, the famous fifth-century Graeco-Latin codex, with two Old Latin manuscripts as secondary support: *b*, the fifth-century *Codex Veronensis*, and *a*, the fourth-century *Codex Vercellensis*. The patristic authorities under this heading were (1) Tatian, *c.* 170, who took back to the East from Rome his Diatessaron, a harmony of the four Gospels (probably in Syriac, soon to be translated into Greek, rather than vice versa). To many modern scholars it seems closely connected with a postulated Latin harmony current in the West which underlay harmonies made later in Dutch, Italian, French and Early English just as in the East the Syriac Diatessaron may have been the basis of Armenian, Persian and Arabic harmonies. Streeter was concerned with Tatian's basic text, which was presumably that of Rome *c.* 165 but altered at times to suit his own heretical tendencies. The other authority was (2) Irenaeus, *c.* 185, who had moved from Asia to Gaul.

The primary evidence for Carthage or North Africa was that of *k*, the Old Latin *Codex Bobbiensis* (fourth or fifth century). The Washington manuscript, W, in its text of Mark i. 1–v. 30 supports this text as a secondary authority and so does *e*, the fifth-century *Codex Palatinus*. Here patristic support was given by Cyprian, *c.* 250, whose text is often identical with that of *k*.

The Byzantine text was considered comparatively worthless. In the Gospels it is represented by the manuscripts S V Ω; E F G H.

Streeter added manuscript evidence of a 'tertiary' and supplementary character. A beginner, however, may be content to memorize the primary, secondary and patristic evidence under each locality, noting that this grouping applies only to the Gospel manuscripts. For the rest of the New Testament, manuscripts are grouped chiefly as Alexandrian, western and Byzantine.

Since Streeter's work appeared, his grouping of the material has been modified, even by those prepared to accept a form of grouping at all. The third-century papyrus codex, 𝔓[45] (Chester Beatty), has been discovered and confirms to some extent the conclusions reached by Streeter, Lake, Blake and others. At the same time it has become clearer that the half-dozen text-types were the results of a process of growth and revision; the manuscripts attesting a text-type are windows, as it were, looking on to that development at different stages. Further, Streeter's view that Origen used an Alexandrian text till 230, and a Caesarean text after his removal to Caesarea in 231, has been proved erroneous. He used a Caesarean text at Alexandria before using first an Alexandrian and then a Caesarean text at Caesarea. This is not so absurd as it sounds; as T. Ayuso has shown, there was a pre-Caesarean group of manuscripts in Egypt before there was a later Caesarean group in Palestine; the former is attested by 𝔓[45], W, fam.[1], 28, and fam.[13] and the latter by Θ, 565, 700, Origen, Eusebius and the Armenian and Georgian Versions.

Again, it is usually considered now to be a forlorn hope to attempt to reconstruct the exact text-type, e.g. of Alexandria or of Caesarea, though it may be possible to reconstruct the text of a smaller group, like that of the minuscules making up fam.[13], which consists now of 13, 69, 124, 174 (outside Mark), 230, 346, 543, 788, 826, 828, 983 and 1689, or of fam.[1], which consists now of 1, 22, 118, 131, 209, 872 (for Mark), 1278, 1582, and 2193. While textual families and clans and their archetype may be determined with some exactness, text-types are a wider category, and the full evidence for their definition lies among the myriad manuscripts no longer extant. Nonetheless, Streeter's theory of local texts is a good working hypothesis, provided that its limitations are noted.

Similarly, for the Pauline epistles, following the work of Zuntz one may postulate a 'proto-Alexandrian' group represented by 𝔓[46] (Chester Beatty), B, 1739, Coptic, Clement of Alexandria and Origen, and one may weigh a variant attested by the best of these against a western reading found in the manuscripts D (Claromontanus), F and G. For these epistles there seems to be no certain evidence that a 'Caesarean' group ever existed as a kind of half-way house between the Alexandrian and western text-types.

Though Streeter was not concerned in *The Four Gospels* with the rest of the New Testament, it has been increasingly clear since 1924 that the textual evidence outside the Gospels falls into three main groups, Alexandrian, western and Byzantine. For Acts, the Alexandrian evidence includes $\mathfrak{P}^{45}$ (Chester Beatty) B א A C Ψ 33, and the western group includes D (Codex Bezae) $\mathfrak{P}^{29}$ $\mathfrak{P}^{38}$ and $\mathfrak{P}^{48}$, *h* (the African Latin manuscript Floriacensis) and the Harklean Syriac marginal readings (see below). The papyri show that western variants were known in Egypt as early as the third century, if not before. The Latin Versions also, of course, lend support to this group, as do the citations from Cyprian and Augustine.

Similarly, for the Catholic epistles the Alexandrian group is represented by B א A C Ψ 33 and 104 with $\mathfrak{P}^{20}$ and $\mathfrak{P}^{23}$. On the western side there is no manuscript of the calibre of D (Bezae) of the Gospels or D (Claromontanus) of Paul. The minuscules that witness best to this type are 917 1829 1874 1836 1898 181 88 and 915; but the Latin Version older than Jerome's lends valuable support to these minuscules, especially *ff* (*Corbeiensis*), a tenth-century manuscript of James, *s* (*Fragmenta Vindobonensia*) of the fifth to sixth centuries, containing fragments of James and I Peter, and *h* (*Floriacensis*) of the fifth century containing fragments of I and II Peter and I John; the citations by Tertullian (*fl.* A.D. 200) and Cyprian (*fl.* A.D. 250) are important.

The evidence for the Apocalypse falls into three main groups which cannot be localized precisely in each instance:

(*a*) A C א $\mathfrak{P}^{47}$ (Chester Beatty) and $\mathfrak{P}^{18}$ and the Leningrad codex 025 are among the least revised manuscripts; Hippolytus also may be classed with C. These manuscripts, however, do not seem to have been derived from a common ancestor.

(*b*) 046, sometimes called Q or (misleadingly) B_2, a tenth-century manuscript, with some forty minuscules represents a more revised text with many Semitisms removed.

(*c*) Codex 1 and other minuscules approximate to the Textus Receptus based on the mass of late minuscules.

During the last few years much research has been carried out on the Byzantine or ecclesiastical text. No longer can it be considered entirely worthless or consisting of late and conflated readings; following von Soden's work scholars are investigating the textual stream of minuscules written between the fifth and tenth centuries; the citations of Leontius, John of Damascus and Photius show how varied are the currents in that stream. The origin and unity of this Byzantine river are still under discussion.

Considerable light, it is hoped, will be thrown on the history of the Byzantine text and even of some of the local texts by the increasing study of the lectionaries, of which there are over 1,600; most of these collections of lessons for the Church's year are taken from the Gospels (*Evangeliaria*), though about one-fifth are from the Acts and Epistles (*Praxapostoli*); the earliest lectionary manuscripts are not older than the ninth century and most are much later but, as American scholars are proving, they are valuable as witnesses especially to the Caesarean and Byzantine text-types of the Gospels.

The Syrian Versions

Tatian the 'Assyrian' as he called himself may have come from Adiabene before reaching Rome soon after the middle of the second century. Besides his *Oration to the Greeks*, he composed a careful mosaic of the four Gospels, the Diatessaron or Evangelion da-Mehallete (gospel of the mixed), to form one continuous life of Christ. After his expulsion as a heretic with Encratite leanings, he took his Diatessaron, which he may have composed in Rome or Antioch, back to his native land. An old Latin harmony may have been produced on the basis of this work, which was to influence various versions in the West in ways hitherto almost unsuspected; but the main influence of the Diatessaron seems to have been exercised in the East. Whether Tatian wrote originally in Syriac or in Greek, a Greek form of the Diatessaron must soon have been made; from it was derived a small fragment of the Greek Diatessaron, discovered at Dura Europus in 1933, dated before 256. Unfortunately the original Syriac (or Greek?) text of the Diatessaron is lost and it has to be reconstructed from Arabic, Armenian, Persian, Latin, Dutch and other evidence, and from quotations in the Syriac writings, for example the *Demonstrations* of Aphraates or the *Liber Graduum*.

33

Ephraem wrote a commentary on the Diatessaron, extant only in Armenian, of which Moesinger published a Latin translation in 1876; Leloir's recent edition and translation are indispensable for the study of this work. In 1888 Ciasca edited the text of an Arabic version of the Diatessaron; Marmadji published the text of another Arabic manuscript in 1935. Though the Syriac basis of the Arabic version is clear, it is unfortunate that that basis was harmonized with the Syriac Vulgate or Peshitta (see below). The Persian evidence to which attention was drawn by Messina (*Diatessaron Persiano*, 1951) consists of a sixteenth-century manuscript, based apparently on one three hundred years older; it preserves many Tatianic readings but not, unfortunately, the original order of the sections of the Diatessaron. In the West, the Latin evidence consists largely of the *Codex Fuldensis*, which Victor of Capua ordered to be made in 546. Again it is unfortunate that the later Latin Vulgate text has swamped the older Latin version of the Diatessaron, scribes tending to assimilate the text to that current in their own day. The Dutch evidence is provided by manuscripts published by Meyer in 1835, by Bergsma in 1895–8, and by Plooij with C. A. Phillips and Barnouw in 1929–36. The Dutch version(s) of a Latin Diatessaron may rest on more than one Latin translation; the Latin Vulgate does not seem to have affected this Latin basis as much as it affected the *Codex Fuldensis*. The Italian evidence is found in two dialect versions, Venetian and Tuscan, of the thirteenth to fourteenth centuries, published by Vaccari, Vattasso and Todesco in 1937. It seems that Tatian made some slight use of apocryphal works as well as of the four Gospels, namely, the Gospel according to the Hebrews and the Protevangelium of James.

The evidence for the Diatessaron being what it is, the reconstruction of its text is exceedingly delicate and questions still debated about it are: (*a*) was it written originally in Syriac or in Greek? (*b*) did it or a Latin harmony have much influence on writers and scribes in the West? (*c*) did it cease to have influence in the East when the Syriac version of the separate gospels came to predominate? and (*d*) were scribes of Greek manuscripts strongly influenced by the Diatessaron to harmonize one gospel text with another, as von Soden thought? In brief, (*a*) the Greek fragment found at Doura does not settle the question finally but proves only that the Diatessaron in Greek was current within eighty years of its composition. Internal evidence, however, may suggest a Greek original; if Tat^arab represents the text of Tatian in Mark ix. 15, Tatian's note of joy (shared with D and several Old Latin manuscripts) suggests a transposition of Greek letters, προσχαίροντες for προστρέχοντες. (*b*) Despite F. C. Burkitt's view, it seems that the Diatessaron had considerable influence in the West as well as the East, traces of it being found in medieval German, French and early English lives of Christ. (*c*) Though in the fifth century Rabbula of Edessa and Theodoret of Cyrrhus destroyed 400 and 200 copies of the Diatessaron respectively, it was not altogether wiped out, particularly in remote areas, but continued in use alongside the fourfold Gospel. (*d*) The scribes of Greek manuscripts were often liable to harmonize one Gospel with another in passages which Tatian did not use; but it may well be that their knowledge of the Diatessaron aggravated this tendency, particularly of some of the western scribes, as of D. It would be as absurd to deny this influence altogether as it is to attribute every harmonization to Tatian's influence.

There is some slight evidence in Aphraates' *Demonstrations*, in the commentaries of Ephraem Syrus (extant only in Armenian) and in the *Liber Graduum* that Tatian put out a version of Acts and possibly of Paul's epistles; cf. Eusebius, *h.e.* 4. 29. 6, 'It is said that he dared to alter some of the apostle's expressions'.

The Old Syriac (O.S.) or Syr^vet

Distinct from the text-types associated with B and with D stands the Old Syriac, represented by the Sinaitic Syriac manuscript, Syr^s, written *c.* 400, and the Curetonian Syriac manuscript, Syr^c, written *c.* 450. The Version itself may be much older than the fifth century, possibly dating back to *c.* 200 or earlier.

It is uncertain whether this Version preceded Tatian's Diatessaron or whether it was later and, to some extent, influenced by it; nor is it known if this Version arose in Edessa or Osrhoene or, as Torrey thinks, at Antioch. It has become clearer recently that it was not entirely replaced later by the Peshitta or Syriac Vulgate but that it was widespread and that traces of it survived in patristic writers as late as the twelfth century, as Vööbus suggests (*Early versions of the N.T.*).

Mrs Lewis's discovery of Syr^s in St Catherine's monastery on Mt Sinai in 1892 enlarged a knowledge of this Version hitherto based on Cureton's edition in 1858 of Syr^c, a manuscript from the Nitrian desert. The great majority of scholars accept the view that of the two manuscripts Syr[s] is the older, showing fewer signs of having been assimilated to Greek manuscripts. The Version seems to be based on a Greek text of the four separate Gospels (Evangelion da-Mepharreshe) no longer extant. Either this hypothetical Greek text or its Syriac translation errs on the side of brevity; this is more likely than the hypothesis that the short text of Syr[vet] is nearer to the original than any other text-type, even that of B. For there are over 200 omissions from Matthew's text alone in this Version. It is unsafe to treat the Syriac omissions as if they were all on a par with what Westcott and Hort called 'non-western interpolations' into (i.e. western omissions from) the Greek texts of the Gospels, especially of Luke, or as if they had a good claim to represent the original text.

The Peshitta Version

Manuscripts of the Peshitta or Vulgate Syriac abound to the number of about 320; some go back to a comparatively early date. There are two fifth-century manuscripts of Matthew and Mark in the British Museum and about fifty manuscripts of the Gospels belonging to the sixth. Codices of Paul, Acts and the Catholic epistles include some of the same period.

According to F. C. Burkitt, Rabbula, bishop of Edessa, 411–35, did for the Peshitta what Jerome did for the Latin Vulgate, and the view is now widespread that Rabbula was responsible for this Version. Recently A. Vööbus has thrown serious doubt on this hypothesis, which has never had the support of Syriac writers. An earlier date than Rabbula's for this Version is suggested by its exclusion from the New Testament Canon of II Peter, II and III John, Jude and Revelation; but these were accepted as canonical in this area before the end of the fourth century. Vööbus has also pointed to a manuscript of the Pseudo-Clementine Recognitions, dated 411, which gives more quotations from the Peshitta than from the Syr[vet].

This Version, the work apparently of several hands, seems to be based on Old Syriac manuscripts revised in the light of the Greek textual tradition which crystallized later into the Byzantine text. Omissions in the Old Syriac text are repaired and sentences are refined in other ways to conform with Greek manuscripts. Like the Latin Vulgate in the West, the Peshitta made its way into favour gradually in the East. The older view of scholars that this Version was a second-century one is now universally discarded.

J. H. Ropes (*The beginnings of Christianity*, III) shows that in Acts the Peshitta preserves many Old Syriac readings in a text not unlike that of the old uncial Greek manuscripts.

The Philoxenian and Harklean Versions

It has been debated often whether the Version produced by Polycarp for Bishop Philoxenus in 508 was re-edited in 616 by Thomas, sometimes said to be bishop of Harkel (the latter doing no more than adding marginal notes in the light of a few Greek manuscripts), or whether Thomas made a complete revision of the Philoxenian Version, noting in addition important variants from the text. On the latter view, Polycarp's Version is lost except for the manuscripts of the lesser Catholic epistles and Revelation, the textual value of which has been variously assessed. In the light of Philoxenus' commentary on John this latter view is the more probable (cf. Vööbus, *op. cit.* pp. 110 ff.). On any view, all are agreed that the marginal readings of the Harklean in Acts lend most valuable support to the western text-type of this book.

The Palestinian Syriac Version

The Palestinian Syriac (or Christian–Palestinian–Aramaic) Version is represented by three eleventh- or twelfth-century manuscripts of lectionary fragments of the Gospels, Acts and Pauline epistles. The lectionary was based on or adapted to a Greek one. The date of this Version is variously given between the fourth and sixth centuries. The text, especially of the Synoptic Gospels, has affinity with the Palestinian tradition, particularly with the Caesarean text, though it preserves some ancient Syriac readings.

The Old Latin Version(s)

The origin of the Old Latin translation of the New Testament is unknown; it is usually sought in North Africa or in Syrian Antioch, rather than in Rome, where the church used Greek during the first two centuries A.D. Pope Victor, *c.* 190, used Latin for his treatises, according to Jerome, and Novatian, *c.* 200–60, did the same; Milan rather than Rome was the first see to adopt Latin for its liturgy. However, as Souter says, 'Society from top to bottom was bilingual in Italy, and Greek and Latin were referred to usually by the simple phrase "both languages".' Though Greek was the official language for the church at Rome for so long, elsewhere in Italy the need for translations into Latin may have been more pressing. The presence of Latin-speaking Christians at Pompeii before the city was destroyed in A.D. 79 may be suggested by the palindrome-anagram written as a square, Rotas-Opera-Tenet-Arepo-Sator, which possibly means 'A Pater noster O' written as a cross with 'n' as the centre. More recent scholars like G. Bardy and C. Mohrmann support the view that Latin translations were made first at Rome; at least a case for Italy being their place of origin can be made. Some of the translators, it is true, knew Semitic languages and the western scribe(s) of Acts had a dangerously small knowledge of Hebrew. This, however, does not prove that the Latin translations originated in Antioch, for converted Jews with a knowledge of Hebrew or Aramaic probably helped with the translations far from Palestine, producing a superficial resemblance to the Old Syriac Version.

The close agreement of the New Testament text used by Cyprian with that of *k*, *Bobbiensis*, has been urged as a plea for the North African origin of the Old Latin texts. Probably, however, translations into Latin were made in several places and by many hands. 'In the early days of the faith', wrote Augustine, 'everyone who happened to get possession of a Greek manuscript and who thought that he had any facility in both languages, however slight it might be, ventured to translate it' (*De Doct. Christ.* 2. 11. 16).

It is possible, as Lietzmann suggested, that the earliest Latin version of Paul's epistles was made by Marcionites at Rome hoping to convert the uneducated. To judge from von Soden's study of the text of Paul in Marcion and Tertullian, Marcion's text was not based on an African translation but a European; and the Marcionite and Catholic translations were independent one of another.

Lists of the manuscripts of the Old Latin Version may be found elsewhere, for example, Souter's Greek Testament (2nd ed., 1947, pp. xviii ff.) and Streeter, *The Four Gospels* (1926, p. 606).

There are two, or possibly three, main types of Old Latin texts: (i) the European, *a b c d ff*² and *q* (Gospels), *d gig.* (Acts), *d g* (Paul), *ff m* (Catholic epistles), *g* (Rev.); (ii) the African *k e* (Gospels), *r* (Paul), *h* (the rest of the New Testament); and possibly (iii) the Italian, if Augustine's text of the *De Doct. Christ.* originally had 'Itala' and if he was not referring to the later Latin Vulgate when he used the term.

It is impossible to decide whether the European and African text-types stem from the same roots; some evidence suggests that the same translations lie at the base of each: for example, Mark ix. 15 cited above; but we must note that this was a Tatianic variant and those who allow for the influence of the Diatessaron on western manuscripts would attribute this transposition of letters or error here to Tatian. At the same time, there are wide divergences between the two types that far outweigh any resemblances.

According to Jülicher in his study of the Old Latin text of Acts, based on *gig.* and Cyprian's citations, a revision of the Old Latin on the basis of a Greek manuscript was made *c.* 350. Solecisms and barbarisms were removed; the youthful Augustine with his fastidious taste for classical Latin was offended before his conversion at the crudity of such Old Latin texts as he knew; in later years he grew to love the Old Latin Version, which he quoted as impartially as he quoted the Vulgate, just as in our day one may quote the Authorized Version or Revised Version (or Revised Standard Version) indifferently. In time the Latin Vulgate tide swept the Old Latin Version(s) into remote nooks and corners of the empire in the West, where it lasted for 500 years after Jerome's revision, the Vulgate, was made.

The Coptic Versions

Christianity probably reached Egypt before the end of the first century, though Eusebius does not relate the history of the church there before the time of Bishop Demetrius (188–231); but the discovery of the Greek New Testament papyri in Egypt dated to the second or third century (especially $\mathfrak{P}^{52}$, $\mathfrak{P}^{45-47}$ and $\mathfrak{P}^{66}$), and of the Gnostic library at Nag Hammadi as well as the work of Gnostic writers such as Valentinus and Heracleon, all point to the introduction of Christianity into Alexandria at least before the second century began.

The Sahidic Version (*Cop^{sa}*): Between 1911 and 1924 G. Horner published the then known fragments of the New Testament in the southern dialect, making of them a patchwork which covered most of the New Testament. Since then other manuscripts in this and similar dialects have been found, such as the early-seventh-century Chester Beatty Coptic papyri of John and the beginning of Matthew, and the fourth- or fifth-century fragments of John ii. 12–xx. 20 in sub-Achmimic (published by Sir H. Thompson in 1924). A papyrus codex of Acts,

4-2

written *c.* 310 with Deuteronomy and Jonah oddly included; the Chester Beatty Coptic text of Acts; the other Beatty Coptic text of the Pauline epistles; two ninth-century manuscripts containing Paul and Hebrews which were discovered at Harmouli; another Harmouli manuscript of the same date with the text of the Catholic epistles, are all among the recent discoveries.

The need for a Coptic translation from Greek was felt sooner in southern Egypt than in the north; the life of Antony, which records his conversion after hearing a lesson in church from Matt. xix. 21, suggests that he heard it read in Coptic *c.* 270. The monks of Pachomius, *c.* 320, must also have needed the Scriptures in translation.

In the Gospels Cop^{sa} sides not only with the B-type of text but also with the 'pre-Caesarean', having some of the western readings which this group contains; the more aberrant variants of D are absent; the same tendency to side with D but not to include its wilder additions is found in Acts. For the rest of the New Testament Cop^{sa} agrees more with the B-type of text.

The Bohairic Version (Cop^{bo}): The manuscripts of this Version are numerous but comparatively late. G. Horner published a text based on the then known fragments between 1898 and 1905. Since then, a ninth-century catena of the Gospels has come to light and there are fragments of tenth-century Gospel codices; codices of Acts and Paul are of even later date.

A fragment of a parchment codex of the Pauline epistles from Deir al-Bala'izah, near Assiut, of the fourth or fifth century, lends colour to the view that the Bohairic Version may have influenced some of the readings in the sub-Achmimic Gospel of John already mentioned; yet many scholars are reluctant to date Cop^{bo} as early as the middle of the third century and some still urge a seventh- or eighth-century date for the Version.

Textually, Cop^{bo} agrees closely with the B-type of text, especially with 'secondary' Alexandrian manuscripts.

The precise relationship between Cop^{sa} and Cop^{bo} is still undetermined.

For the remains of the New Testament in other Egyptian dialects, Achmimic and Fayyumic, cf. B. M. Metzger, *The evidence for the Versions*, in M. M. Parvis and A. Wikgren's *New Testament manuscript studies*, 1950.

Other Versions

Among the more important of the other Versions, which include the Ethiopic, Arabic, Gothic, Nubian, Sogdian, Old Slavic and Persian, are the Armenian and Georgian.

Manuscripts of the Gospels and printed editions of the Armenian Version are based on a text or texts going back to a translation from the Greek but containing echoes of Syriac phrases; the affinity of the text (for the Gospels) is with the Caesarean clan, cf. E. C. Colwell (*The Journal of Religion*, XVII (1937), 48–61) and the present writer (*J.T.S.* XLIII (1942), 161–7). At the same time a study of the Gospel citations in Armenian Fathers, such as that carried out by S. Lyonnet in 1950, shows that Agathangelos, Koriun, Eznik, Pseudo-Gregory, John Mandakuni and others used earlier translations from the Syriac rather than the Greek. Though no manuscript of this early Version survives, it may be cited as Arm[1] as opposed to that based on Greek manuscripts (Arm[2]). Research also on the oldest ritual manuscript, the *Rituale Armenorum*, confirms this view. It is not yet clear how far the basic Syriac texts of Arm[1] depended on a Diatessaron or on a text like that of Syr[vet]; while Lyonnet favours the theory of an Armenian Diatessaron, Vööbus rejects it. While, therefore, Lazar of Pharpi's view must be set aside that the first Armenian version of the New Testament was made from the Greek and the other Armenian tradition of Koriun and Moses of Chorene must be accepted, that it was made from Syriac sources, yet the study of the extant Greek-based manuscripts is by no means valueless if it throws light on the spread of manuscripts of Caesarean character through Cappadocia into Armenia.

The study of the Old Georgian Version is proceeding apace; as this Version was based very largely on the Old Armenian, it will be of great value in throwing additional light on the Armenian evidence. It may be noted that a Caesarean element has been found in the best and earliest Gospel manuscript, Adysh, written in 897, and in the other Georgian textual strata represented by the Tbet' manuscript (995) and the Opiza manuscript (913). The Gospels have been edited by R. P. Blake in the *Patrologia Orientalis* with a Latin translation; Mark, *P.O.* XX, 3 (1929); Matthew, XXIV, 1 (1933); John, XXVI, 4 (1950); cf. M. Brière's edition of Luke, XXVII, 3 (1955).

For the other Versions, reference may be made to M. M. Parvis and

A. Wikgren, *New Testament manuscript studies* (1950), pp. 45 ff. (by B. M. Metzger) and to A. Vööbus, *Early versions of the New Testament* (1954), pp. 133 ff. and 243 ff.

THE CANON

The Old Testament formed the Scriptures of the earliest Christians; gradually some Christian writings were placed on a par with it, not by any decree of a council nor by the fiat of a pope or bishop but by the common agreement of the faithful; the spiritual intuition of the Church came slowly to decide which of its writings should be regarded as 'canonical' (the word 'canon' from meaning a rod or bar, a rule or model, was applied to a rule of doctrine or practice and to a list of accepted and recognized books). The early history of the growth of the Canon of the New Testament is lost in obscurity. Three steps may be assumed to have been taken before the process was complete. (*a*) A Christian writing was found helpful and inspiring. (*b*) It became a recognized and authoritative source of Church teaching, accepted locally as such. (*c*) It was considered apostolic, either because it was connected with the apostles themselves or with 'apostolic men' presumed to have been in their circle, or because it was accepted in sees which traced their connection with the apostles. A work which had a strong claim (even if unfounded, according to many modern scholars) to have been written by one of the twelve apostles, for example, the Gospels of Matthew and John, would be likely to win recognition as an authoritative book sooner than others. The problem is complicated by lack of evidence. It has been suggested, for example, that Valentinus the Gnostic was himself the author of the recently discovered 'Gospel of Truth'. Even if this were so, it could not be inferred that every New Testament citation in this work proves the book to which it belongs to have been for him in class (*c*) above, rather than in (*a*) or (*b*). 'Valentinus' may allude to Rev. ii. 17, iii. 12, v. 3–8 and xiv. 1, without proving more than that Revelation was known in his circle and found helpful. To be helpful and inspiring a work threw light on the life, character and teaching of Christ or of his early followers and it harmonized with all that was known of God as seen in Christ and in them; the spiritual intuition of the Church rightly rejected the apocryphal Gospels from the accepted list of books, because they failed on both counts. But a work which won acceptance under (*a*), (*b*) and (*c*) in one locality might not do so for many years, if at all, throughout the whole Church. The *Shepherd* of Hermas was accepted by Clement of Alexandria and Origen and included in the Clermont list; fragments of it in Coptic and scraps in Middle Persian among the Manichean texts at Turfan attest its popularity. It was included in *Codex Sinaiticus*, and Athanasius said that it was helpful to converts but not canonical (cf. *De Inc.* 3, *ad Afros*, 5), and Eusebius placed it among the disputed books. In the West, the Muratorian canonist excluded it, as did Tertullian but not Irenaeus; the Pseudo-Cyprianic *Adversus Aleatores* quotes it as divine Scripture. Similarly the *Epistle of Barnabas* was accepted by Clement of Alexandria and Origen and included in *Codex Sinaiticus*; the Clermont list places it after the Catholic epistles; Jerome ascribed it to Barnabas but denied that it was part of Scripture. Again, the *Revelation of Peter* seems to have been accepted by the Muratorian canonist and by Clement of Alexandria, though not by Hippolytus; Eusebius placed it among the disputed books. The Clermont list includes it, but prefaces its name with a line, which may mean that it stands in a different category from the books already mentioned in the list. According to Sozomen in Palestine in the middle of the fifth century it was used as a lectionary each Good Friday. These works are instances of the literature which nearly became 'canonical' but which the good sense of the Church rejected in the end.

The Pauline epistles, the earliest Christian writings, were largely occasional letters, written to meet the needs of particular readers. It is not known how collections of them came to be made. Two theories have been advanced. (*a*) Paul's letters were copied and circulated to neighbouring churches, cf. Col. iv. 16. As time went on small collections grew into larger ones until eventually the thirteen or fourteen (i.e. without or with Hebrews) became recognized as forming the Pauline canon. A local church might have copies of Romans, I Corinthians and Ephesians before A.D. 70, all the rest except the Pastorals and Hebrews by A.D. 100 and the Pastorals by A.D. 120 or 130. With such a theory of gradual growth the name of Harnack is often associated. (*b*) E. J. Goodspeed, J. Knox and C. L. Mitton have urged strongly that the Pauline epistles were, as a collection, unknown for a generation after Paul's death until *c*. A.D. 90 when a Pauline canon was put out, headed by Ephesians, the work of a Pauline disciple, as an introductory epistle. This collection was probably made in or near Ephesus and possibly by Onesimus, Philemon's slave, who probably became bishop of Ephesus later. It may be that the 'publication' of Acts (which shows no knowledge of the extant Pauline epistles), *c.* A.D. 80, revived interest in the figure of Paul and led to the formation of a Pauline canon. If Ephesians is dated after *c.* A.D. 90, it may be significant that it and other works of that or of a later date show acquaintance with Paul's epistles, the author of Ephesians knows the other nine letters (Hebrews and the Pastorals being excluded) and his work is known to the authors of Revelation, Hebrews, *I Clement*, I Peter, the Fourth Gospel, to Ignatius, Polycarp, to the author of James, to Marcion, the Pastoral writer and to the author of II Peter. These eleven writers know not only Ephesians but also most of the other nine Pauline letters, though we cannot be certain that 'Revelation' used II Corinthians or II Thessalonians, that 'Heb.' used II Thessalonians or Philemon, that *I Clement* used Colossians, I and II Thessalonians or Philemon, that I Peter used II Corinthians, Philippians, Colossians or Philemon, that Polycarp used Colossians or Philemon or that James used II Corinthians, Colossians, II Thessalonians or Philemon. The argument from silence is precarious and the findings of the Oxford Committee, *The New Testament in the Apostolic Fathers*, 1905, on the positive evidence were somewhat too cautious. It should be added that on the evidence of that Committee the three Pastoral letters were just possibly known to Barnabas and possibly to Ignatius; I and II Timothy probably to Polycarp; I Timothy just possibly and Titus possibly to *I Clement*. Here again the Committee was probably overcautious; W. L. Knox has argued convincingly that Ignatius knew II Timothy, which in turn shows knowledge of Acts. It seems striking that whereas the author of Acts, no doubt Luke, did not have a collection of Paul's letters, the eleven early writers between *c.* A.D. 90 and 125 did so.

Polycarp, whose date, according to P. N. Harrison, is A.D. 135 for the bulk of his epistle and who, according to others, may be dated ten or fifteen years earlier, knew without any doubt I Peter, which he quoted fully as if it were an authoritative document at least in his local church, i.e. belonging at least to class (*b*) above. Like Clement of Rome, it is possible that he knew Acts but it is not at all certain that he knew Hebrews, as Clement of Rome did (without attributing it to Paul). Polycarp's knowledge of the Pauline letters is mentioned above.

Marcion's influence on the Canon has been variously estimated.

(i) According to Harnack, whose edition of the text of Marcion (1924) is the standard one, Marcion's influence was profound. His mutilated gospel of Luke and bowdlerized edition of ten Pauline epistles was the first New Testament Canon, which had a creative effect on the canon accepted later by the Great or Catholic Church. But this, like much that Harnack wrote about Marcion, gives the schismatic too much credit. From the early days of the Church, the conception of canonicity was not unknown, at least in connection with the Old Testament. The sayings of the Lord had had for Paul a final authority, carefully distinguished from his own advice, cf. I Cor. vii. 10, 12, 25, 40; I Thess. iv. 14; Ignatius, *Philad.* 8. 2. It may be that Marcion accelerated the tendency of Christians to place Paul's epistles on a par with the written Gospels and the Old Testament, but the tendency was already there, cf. Ignatius, *Philad.* 5. 1 'taking refuge in the Gospel as the flesh of Jesus and in the Apostles as the presbytery of the Church'. (It is uncertain whether 'Gospel' here means a written one.) Cf. Polycarp 12. 1, 'As it is said in these Scriptures, Be ye angry and sin not, and, Let not the sun set on your wrath'. II Pet. iii. 15–16 puts a collection of Pauline letters alongside 'the other scriptures', i.e. probably the Gospels and Old Testament; this work is probably to be dated *c.* A.D. 125–35. II Peter may have given 'the other scriptures' class (*b*) status, and Paul's letters, such as he had, class (*a*) only. The other theory (ii) is preferable to Harnack's, namely, that Marcion selected from the Christian writings that were known in Pontus, Asia and Rome to be both helpful and authoritative and by excision and emendation he adapted some of them to suit his own anti-Semitic and biblical-Gnostic views.

The Latin Marcionite Prologues to Paul's epistles, found in many Latin Vulgate manuscripts, but in no Old Latin manuscript, were recognized as Marcionite by de Bruyne. Their order in the Marcionite *Apostolicon* was as follows:

Galatians are Greeks. These accepted the word of truth first from the apostle but after his departure were tempted by false apostles to turn to the Law and to circumcision. The apostle recalls these men to the faith of truth [cf. II Thess. ii. 13], writing to them from Ephesus.

Corinthians are Achaeans. These also likewise heard the word of truth from the apostle and were perverted variously by false apostles, some by the wordy eloquence of philosophy, others led on by the sect of the Jewish Law. The apostle recalls these men to the true and evangelical wisdom, writing to them from Ephesus [by Timothy].

Romans are in the region of Italy. These were reached beforehand by false apostles and under the name of our Lord Jesus Christ had been led on to the Law and the Prophets. The apostle recalls these men to the true and evangelical faith, writing to them from Athens.

Thessalonians are Macedonians in Christ Jesus, who having accepted the word of truth, persevered in the faith even under persecution from their own citizens; and moreover they did not accept what was said by false apostles. The apostle congratulates these men, writing to them from Athens.

Laodiceans are of Asia. These, having accepted the word of truth, persevered in the faith. The apostle congratulates these men, writing to them from Athens.

Colossians; these also, like the Laodiceans, are of Asia. They too had been reached beforehand by false apostles, and the apostle himself does not come to them; but he corrects them also by a letter; for they had heard his word from Archippus, who also accepted a ministry to them. So the apostle, already in bonds, writes to them from Ephesus.

Philippians are Macedonians. These having accepted the word of truth persevered in the faith and they did not receive false apostles. The apostle congratulates these men, writing to them from prison at Rome by Epaphroditus.

To *Philemon* he composes a private letter by Onesimus his slave. But he writes to him from Rome out of prison.

The Marcionite 'Laodiceans' is Ephesians. Marcion thus rejected the Old Testament and issued his version of Luke and ten Pauline epistles; the Great Church was impelled to include among its recognized books not less than Marcion had done, but more. Yet though Marcion's canon was closed, the list of authoritative books in a centre of church life *c.* 150 was not closed yet; the Montanist heresy, not the Marcionite, impelled the Church towards closing its canon. Just as Old Testament prophecy 'ceased with Ezra' and the Canon was closed in effect with him, so the Christian Church began to close its Canon in the face of the fantastic prophetic claims of Montanism.

Justin became a Christian probably in Asia and towards the middle of the second century went to Rome. He used the four Gospels, referring to them as the 'memoirs of the apostles', relying chiefly on Matthew and least of all on John, which, as Streeter suggested, he may have been seeking to introduce to the West. For there was a remarkable reluctance in many quarters to accept the Fourth Gospel, owing perhaps to a preference for Mark's chronology or to a doubt about the apostolic origin of this Gospel or to a failure to realize that the Fourth Evangelist was using terms that suggested Gnosticism as weapons with which to combat it; no doubt he gave these 'memoirs' class (*b*) status and since in the liturgy at Rome they were read together with lections from the Old Testament, they were beginning there to acquire class (*c*) status also. He would probably have classed Paul's letters in class (*a*), i.e. as helpful and inspiring, but though he knew Romans, I Corinthians, Galatians, Ephesians and Colossians, he hesitated, no doubt, to quote them (he does not even quote Paul by name in any extant work) for fear of appearing tarred with the Marcionite brush. He knew 'Hebrews', but in common with those in the West he would have given it only class (*a*) status and not connected it with Paul. On the other hand he would have given Revelation class (*b*) status at least, for he speaks of it as 'a Revelation made to a man named John, one of the apostles of Christ'; he accepted its claim to inspiration. The work of his pupil Tatian has been mentioned above. His careful mosaic of the Four Gospels with only an occasional reference to an apocryphal New Testament work shows that he felt free to alter the text to suit his purposes and yet that he attached greater value to these four than to any other Gospels; for Tatian they had at least class (*b*) status. Eusebius, who did not know Tatian's work at first hand, says that he dared to alter some of the apostle's expressions with a view to correcting the style in which they were composed. If so, he gave the same status to Paul's letters as Justin had.

The Anti-Marcionite Prologues are sometimes dated *c.* A.D. 160. They are found in twelve Latin manuscripts of Mark, thirty-three of Luke, and ten of John, Luke's being found also in Greek, the original language of all three; Matthew's is missing. Dom de Bruyne's arguments for their homogeneity and anti-Marcionite tendency convinced Harnack, Lietzmann and F. L. Cross. One must contrast his arguments in the *Revue bénédictine*, XL (1928), 193 ff. with those of E. Gutwenger, *Theological Studies*, VII (1946), 393 ff.; B. W. Bacon, *Journal of Biblical Literature*, XXXII (1913), 194 ff. and XLIX (1930), 43 ff.; and R. G. Heard, *Journal of Theological Studies*, n.s. VI (1955), 1 ff. It may be that, after all, the prologues did not originally form one unit. Even if the Marcan prologue echoes second-century western traditions, the Lucan seems dependent on Irenaeus and belongs to the third century, though it may well incorporate some accurate biographical details about Luke; the Johannine prologue may be as late as the fifth or sixth century, the text of it being very corrupt. They run:

...Mark related, who was called curt-fingered, because his fingers were rather short in relation to the size of the rest of his body. He was Peter's interpreter. After the departure [death?] of Peter himself, this same man wrote the gospel in the regions of Italy.

Luke is a Syrian of Antioch, a physician by trade, who was a disciple of apostles and later followed Paul until his martyrdom. He served the Lord without distraction, unmarried, childless, and he fell asleep at the age of eighty-four in Boeotia, full of the Holy Spirit. When the gospels were already in existence (that according to Matthew written in Judaea, that according to Mark in Italy), this man was impelled by the Holy Spirit and wrote this whole gospel in the regions of Achaia. He makes plain by the preface this very point, that before him other gospels had been written, and that it was necessary to set forth for the believers from among the Gentiles the accurate narrative of the dispensation, that they should not be distracted by the Jewish fables nor miss the truth through deception by heretical and vain fantasies. We received therefore as most necessary immediately at the beginning the birth of John, who is the beginning of the gospel, in that he was a forerunner of the Lord and a partaker both in the preparation of the gospel and in the plan of baptism and the fellowship of the Spirit. A prophet among the twelve calls to mind this dispensation. And afterwards the same Luke wrote the Acts of the Apostles; and later John the Apostle from among the Twelve wrote the Apocalypse on the island of Patmos, and, after this, the gospel.

The gospel of John was shown forth and given to the churches by John while still in the body, as Papias of Hierapolis, a cherished disciple of John, has recorded in his *exoterica* [*exegeseis?*], that is, in his last five books. For he wrote the gospel while John dictated it aright. But Marcion the heretic, when he had been rejected by him owing to his contrary opinions, was expelled by John. He had in fact brought writings or letters to him from the brethren who were in Pontus.

For the years A.D. 180–230 the position about the Canon becomes clearer; to take the centres of church life in turn:

Alexandria: Clement (*fl.* A.D. 200) accepted the four Gospels and took Acts to be written by Luke; he knew, but did not give scriptural value to, the Gospel according to the Hebrews and the Gospel according to the Egyptians. He accepted Hebrews among the Pauline letters, which included the Pastorals; we are reminded that 𝔓46, the third-century

Chester Beatty papyrus, (alone) places Hebrews immediately after Romans, i.e. prominently among the letters sent to churches. He accepted also I Peter, I and II John and Jude; also *I Clement* (Codex A includes *I* and *II Clement* at the end) and *Barnabas* (which is included in *Codex Sinaiticus*); also the Revelation of John and that of Peter; the *Preaching of Peter* and the *Shepherd* of Hermas; and he quotes the *Didache* once as Scripture.

Origen, his successor as head of the Catechetical School (*fl.* 230), distinguished between the accepted books and the disputed books of the New Testament; among the former he put the four Gospels, the fourteen Pauline letters (i.e. including Hebrews, though, as he said, 'who wrote it, God knows'), Acts, I Peter, I John and Revelation. Among the disputed books he placed James, which he is the first of the Fathers to mention by name, II and III John, Jude, II Peter, *Barnabas* and also the *Shepherd* of Hermas, about which he strikes a rather apologetic note (Eus. *h.e.* 3. 3. 6). Though he was of a more critical turn of mind than Clement, he may be said to have had a full canon, for the 'disputed' books belonged to it no less than the accepted; cf. *Codex Sinaiticus* (ℵ).

Syria: The Diatessaron and perhaps the Acts were accepted and some of the Pauline epistles; even later the church here was most conservative; about 350, according to the *Teaching of Addai*, the Law, Prophets and Gospel were read before the people, the letters of Paul and Acts 'and along with them shall you read nothing else besides'; the Gospel was the Diatessaron. No doubt the situation before 230 was the same.

Western: (i) *European.* The Muratorian Canon, published by L. A. Muratori in 1740, exists in an eighth-century copy in Latin done by an ignorant scribe, but it is based on a Greek original *c.* 180–200 which was probably translated into Latin after the fourth century; whether it was the work of Victor or of Hippolytus or someone else, it seems to give a list of books accepted in Italy before A.D. 200. The opening is lost but Luke is called the third book of the Gospel; after Luke, John is dealt with at length, as though it needed a defence (Hippolytus wrote such a defence, which implies local attacks on it); then come 'the Acts of all the Apostles', the thirteen Pauline epistles (including the Pastorals, but excluding Hebrews); 'Laodiceans' and 'Alexandrians' are mentioned but rejected. Jude is included (with the word '*sane*', 'indeed', which may imply some local doubts), I and II John, Wisdom, the

Revelation of John and the Revelation of Peter 'which some reject' for lectionary purposes.

Hebrews is not mentioned, for though it was well known in the West, for example to Clement of Rome, it was not considered Pauline or scriptural until the time of Hilary of Poitiers. The omission of I Peter is surprising, especially as Hippolytus accepted it along with I and II John and the Revelation of John; Zahn emended the text of the *Muratorianum*, line 72, to read 'One epistle of Peter which alone we accept', supposing that thirteen letters have dropped out from the Greek 'original', and P. Katz emended lines 68 f. to run 'of the afore-mentioned John two [epistles] in addition to the Catholics are held' (*J.T.S.* 1957, pp. 273 f.); Victor of Rome knew two letters of John certainly. It is possible that III John was bound up with and considered part of II John but this is unlikely in view of the fact, to which Harnack drew attention, that the Latin translator of III John is not the same as that of I and II John; presumably there was a time in the West when only I and II John were in use; probably the Muratorian canonist did not include III John.

Irenaeus (*fl.* A.D. 180) had moved as a young man from Asia to Gaul; he is the first to write explicitly of a 'New' Testament (*Adv. haer.* 4. 9. 1) which was now being placed alongside 'the old covenant' to which Paul had referred (II Cor. iii. 14). Irenaeus could counter the Gnostic claim to possess secret traditions with the open tradition of the bishops of Rome and Ephesus, for both sees could claim to have had apostolic foundation. He could maintain that it was impossible for the Gospels to be more or fewer than the four, though his arguments from the four regions of the world, the four winds or the four faces of the Cherubim are unconvincing (*Adv. haer.* 3. 1. 1). It is unnecessary henceforth to note the acceptance of the four Gospels. For Irenaeus, the Pauline epistles had also status (*a*) and (*b*) and were on their way to acquiring status (*c*); he ranks them with the Old Testament though he does not preface any of his 200 and more citations from them with the words 'Scripture says'. He cites them all except Philemon. In *Adv. haer.* 4. 16. 2 he seems to cite Jas. ii. 23; if so, he cites all the Catholic epistles except II Peter and III John. He was familiar with Hebrews but took the western view that it was not Pauline. He quoted Revelation often, taking it to be by John 'the disciple of the Lord', in his view the beloved disciple. He accepted Acts too on the guarantee of the Pauline letters, whereas Tertullian accepted the latter on the guarantee of the former.

Hippolytus (*fl.* 200), whether or not the author of the Muratorian Canon, in his extant works shows familiarity with the whole of our canon except Philemon, II and III John and Jude, though he cited Jas. i. 1 as though it came from Jude. His defence of Revelation has been noted already.

(ii) *African*. In A.D. 180, when Christians on trial at Scili were asked what they had in their church chest, Speratus replied: 'The books and the letters of Paul, a righteous man.' 'The books' probably meant the Prophets and the Gospels.

Tertullian, *fl.* 200, as a lawyer took a legal view of the New Testament 'instrumentum'; he accepted the thirteen letters of Paul as an 'apostolicum instrumentum', but he attributed Hebrews to Barnabas. His 'instrumentum Johannis' included the Fourth Gospel, I John and Revelation, which he attributed to John the Apostle. Both the Old and the New Testaments were to him divine Scripture, so that he could speak of the 'instrumentum utriusque testamenti'. His penchant for tracing apostolic descent can be seen in his saying that the church in Rome 'associates the Law and the Prophets with the evangelical and apostolic books' (*praescr.* 36). He seems also to have valued the *Shepherd* of Hermas, but later in life he rejected it because of its 'laxity' towards post-baptismal sin.

By *c.* 200 the broad outline of the Canon had become clear.

During the third and fourth centuries the tendency was to stress the criterion of apostolicity; an exception was Dionysius of Alexandria (*fl.* 250), who accepted Revelation in his 'canon' but rejected it as being not by John, the author of John and I John, in a most scholarly dissertation based on considerations of style and thought (Eus. *h.e.* 7. 25. 17–27).

Eusebius of Caesarea (*fl.* 325) gave his own views (*h.e.* 3. 25), distinguishing between the accepted books (the Gospels, Acts, Pauline letters including Hebrews, I John and I Peter), the disputed books (James, Jude, II Peter, II and III John), and the rejected books (the *Acts of Paul*, the *Shepherd* of Hermas, the *Revelation of Peter*, *Barnabas*, the *Didache*, the *Gospel of the Hebrews* and 'the Revelation of John, if it seem proper, which some as I said reject, but which some class with the accepted books'). His 'canon' was made up of the accepted and disputed books. In addition he knew several apocryphal works, such as the Gospels of Peter and of Thomas.

The Coptic Version included all the books in our modern canon, the Sahidic Version including also the *Shepherd* and *I Clement* and (with the Achmimic) the *Acts of Paul*. In his famous Festal letter of 367 Athanasius gave a list of books which coincides with those in our canon, but putting the fourteen Pauline letters before Revelation. His acceptance of Revelation was followed by Basil of Caesarea and Gregory of Nyssa; but Gregory of Nazianzen and Chrysostom rejected it. Athanasius favoured the reading of the *Didache* and the *Shepherd* for edification; but by 367 he had given up the *Shepherd*. His list may be compared with that known as the Clermont list, from the sixth-century *Codex Claromontanus*, which probably gives the accepted usage of Egypt *c.* 320. In error, no doubt, a scribe has omitted Philippians, I and II Thessalonians and probably Hebrews. The seven Catholic epistles are marked with a line, probably denoting a paragraph and difference of authorship from Paul's; a similar mark prefaces *Barnabas*, Revelation and Acts and three similar marks stand before the *Shepherd*, the *Acts of Paul* and the *Revelation of Peter*. This again may be compared with the list of *Codex Sinaiticus* (‭א‬) *c.* 350, which has the books of our canon, Acts being placed between the fourteen Pauline epistles and the Catholic epistles, and which also has *Barnabas* and the *Shepherd*.

The *Shepherd* was never to be found among Syriac-speaking Christians, who remained on the whole conservative; Aphraates's *Demonstrations*, *c.* 350, show knowledge of the Diatessaron as well as of the Separated Gospels, fourteen Pauline letters, probably the apocryphal III Corinthians also, and of Acts; Ephraem Syrus, who wrote a commentary on III Corinthians, had the same 'canon'. The Sinaitic Syriac list of the same date included the Separated Gospels, Acts and fourteen Pauline letters; 'this is all'. Theodore of Mopsuestia's 'canon' (*fl.* 420) was the same. The Syriac Peshitta list, however, *c.* 410, included James, I Peter and I John, the twenty-two books corresponding to the number of letters in the Hebrew and Syriac alphabets. Chrysostom (*fl.* 380) and Theodoret (*fl.* 440) had the same canon. In the Philoxenian Syriac the Catholic epistles and Revelation were added, but Syr[pal] did not include Revelation till its revision in the eleventh century. The position in the East may be seen from the synod of Laodicea (*c.* 363), which forbade the reading of uncanonical books and which, in its later fourth-century canon 60, gives a list coinciding with our canon (except for Revelation); or it may be seen from the list of Amphilochius of Iconium (*fl.* 380); he included Hebrews 'which some mistakenly reject'; 'of the Catholic letters some say seven, others only three, one of James, one of Peter and one of John'; 'the Revelation of John some accept but the majority call it uncanonical'.

For the views of Christians in the West during this period, the Cheltenham list, discovered by Mommsen, may be quoted; it is believed to show what the 'canon' was in North Africa *c.* 360. It includes the Gospels, thirteen letters of Paul (i.e. not Hebrews), Acts, Revelation, Letters of John three, and Letters of Peter two; after the last two items a conservative scribe familiar with the 'canon' of Cyprian a century earlier has written 'one only'. It omits Hebrews and Jude. A generation later than the Cheltenham canonist, the synod of Carthage in 397 included Hebrews after the thirteen Pauline letters and allowed martyrologies to be read in church on martyrs' feasts. By the time of the Council of Carthage, Hebrews was included among the Pauline epistles; for Ambrose, Rufinus, Jerome, and Augustine in his early days followed the lead of Hilary in the West in accepting Hebrews, though Pelagius rejected it and Ambrosiaster, and Augustine after 409, reckoned it anonymous. Jerome consciously followed eastern rather than western custom in accepting it. It was Jerome's Vulgate and Augustine's support for Jerome (e.g. in the *De Doct. Christ.* 2. 12) which helped to establish our canon. The so-called 'Gelasian decree', which is really of the sixth century, follows the Vulgate.

CHAPTER III

EARLY CHRISTIAN BOOK-PRODUCTION: PAPYRI AND MANUSCRIPTS

PREHISTORY OF THE CHRISTIAN BOOK:
PAPYRUS AND PARCHMENT

The discoveries of the present century have completely revolutionized our ideas of the early Christian book and its ancestry. Handbooks written thirty years ago, or even less, are now largely obsolete, and it is only today that it is becoming possible to envisage the basic problems which have still to be solved. This advance in knowledge has been all the more dramatic because no early Christian writer has anything to tell us about the way in which Christian, or indeed any, books were written and circulated. Nor are pagan writers of the contemporary Graeco-Roman world much more informative: in common with the general paucity of technological literature, no treatise on ancient book-production has come down to us, and we have had to glean what knowledge we could from casual references and allusions, often incomplete or ambiguous.

Now, however, the picture is altered to the extent that finds of papyri, predominantly in Egypt, have provided us with hundreds of specimens of works of literature produced during the period in which Christian literature was born: and, still more recently, the astonishing discoveries in the deserts of Palestine have revealed numerous examples of the types of books and writing materials with which the earliest members of the Church would have been familiar and which they would have used themselves in daily life.

Three distinct types of writing material, papyrus, parchment, and wooden tablets, contributed, though in very different ways, to the formation of the Christian book, and all were in common use in Palestine and most of the Near East during the first century A.D. The first which we shall consider is papyrus. This legendary material, once used so widely throughout the whole of the ancient world that Pliny describes it as co-existent with civilization, has, after its virtual eclipse during the middle ages, once more become familiar through the tens of thousands of examples which have come to light in Egypt, mainly during the last hundred years. With the aid of these specimens, and numerous modern experiments, we can now form a much better picture of the method of its manufacture than we could from the *locus classicus* in Pliny's *Natural History*, in which he attempts to describe the process in language which is neither as clear nor as precise as could be wished.

The papyrus plant, *Cyperus Papyrus* L., is a species of reed which once grew in the greatest profusion in Egypt, particularly in the marshes of the Nile Delta, and also in other parts of the Near East, including Palestine, where it is still to be found in the neighbourhood of Lake Huleh. Today, ironically, it has completely died out in Egypt, and can only be seen there either in the Cairo Botanical Gardens or, immortalized in stone, in the papyrus columns beloved of the Egyptian architect. The plant grows with its roots submerged in water, from which the jointless stem, triangular in section, rises to a height of 10–15 feet, ending in a tuft of flowers. For the manufacture of papyrus the plant was cut down and the stem was divided into sections, the length of which determined the height of the papyrus roll which was to be made. From these sections the outer rind was stripped off, and the soft pith, while still fresh, cut lengthwise into thin strips. These strips were laid side by side, slightly overlapping, on a hard surface, and a second layer was laid over them, the strips running at right angles to those in the first layer. The two layers were then consolidated by hammering and pressing, and then dried. The sheet thus formed was then trimmed, and the surface smoothed with pumice and burnished with rounded polishers of shell or ivory. Finally, a number of sheets were pasted together with flour paste to make long lengths which were then rolled up for storage or transport.

Newly made papyrus was white in colour, or nearly so, although it yellowed with age, like paper. Dio Chrysostom (A.D. 30–117) records how booksellers artificially 'aged' papyrus books by plunging them in wheat, to yellow them and give them an appearance of antiquity. Specimens now to be seen in museums vary in colour from a very pale yellow or beige to a deep brown or purplish-black, the last-named being characteristic of papyri which have been affected by damp and partially carbonized. On the whole, the thinnest and finest papyri are the earliest, one New Kingdom specimen measured by Professor Černý being only 0·1 mm in thickness; by contrast, some papyri of the Byzantine period are almost as thick and stiff as card.

The individual sheets of papyrus varied greatly, both in height and width, the broadest sheets being considered the hall-mark of the finest quality. According to Kenyon, an average size of sheet during the Graeco-Roman period would be 25 cm high and 19 cm broad, the former figure representing the height of the roll as finally made up. The joins of the sheets were so skilfully made as to be almost invisible, and certainly scribes paid little attention to them, carrying the writing across the junctions without any apparent difficulty.

Papyrus was always rolled up in such a way that the horizontal fibres were on the inside and thus not subjected to strain, while the vertical fibres, which naturally had more 'give', were on the outside. The side with the fibres running horizontally was the one intended to receive the writing, and as such was more carefully smoothed and finished. It is customary to describe this side as the 'recto' and the side with vertical fibres as the 'verso' in order to distinguish them. It is an axiom of papyrology that scribes always used the recto of the papyrus first, and the verso was only written on, if at all, after the recto had been used. It is very rare for the same work to be continued from the recto to the verso; much more frequently the verso of a discarded roll was employed, as a cheaper form of writing material than new papyrus, for the reception of a different work altogether, and lengthy tax-registers or accounts, which would be discarded after a fairly limited period, formed a prolific source of this second-class writing material. The famous roll of Aristotle's *Constitution of Athens*, for example, is written on the back of a roll containing agricultural accounts.

Details of the development of Greek writing must be sought in the manuals of palaeography, but some idea of the general appearance of a typical Greek book at the beginning of the Christian era may conveniently be given here, if only because it differed so greatly from the book of today. The text consisted of a succession of columns of writing, the lines of writing within the columns being parallel to the length of the roll. To those familiar with the exquisite regularity of the finest medieval manuscripts most papyri present a relatively unsophisticated appearance. The Graeco-Roman scribe wrote entirely by eye, without the aid of any ruled lines either to guide the writing or to mark the borders of the columns, which in fact often slope markedly from left to right. Nor was much trouble taken to 'justify' the lines (to bring them to a regular margin on the right), though a filling-mark (>) was sometimes used for this purpose. Although it is sometimes stated that scribes used the horizontal fibres of the papyrus as guides to keeping their lines of writing straight, this is not borne out by the papyri, which often show the scribe writing at a slight angle to the fibres. The truth is that the fibres of the papyrus tend to mask defects in straightness and regularity, whereas a smooth and fibreless material like vellum highlights such imperfections.

In the columns of writing the text ran on continuously, without any division of words and few, if any, accents or breathings and little or no punctuation. Any kind of aids to the reader such as capital letters, italics, divisions of text, cross-headings, title-pages, lists of contents, indexes, footnotes, illustrations, bibliographies, etc., were entirely unknown. In addition to these (to us) shortcomings, the physical difficulty of reading from a roll has often been emphasized. The reader needed both hands for the purpose, the right to hold the roll, the left to hold the initially unrolled portion, and to roll it up as the reading proceeded. Cumbersome though this sounds, long practice probably made it an automatic process; certainly, as we shall see, ancient readers in general were in no hurry to adopt what seems to us the infinitely more convenient codex type of book. Finally, when the reader came to the end of the roll, he had to re-roll it in the reverse direction in order to make it ready for the next reader; as ancient authors never make mention of this essential 'chore' one suspects that it was left to servants or slaves.

Few subjects are more obscure than the methods of ancient book-production. We do indeed hear of booksellers, and it is clear that production on a commercial scale existed; for example, Cicero's friend Atticus was an active publisher and kept a large staff of slaves to produce copies of books. And apart from individual publishers, the great libraries such as that at Alexandria also functioned as centres of book-production. But of practical procedure we know nothing for certain. It has been confidently asserted, and just as energetically denied, that an 'edition' was produced by means of one person dictating the 'copy' to a roomful of slaves writing simultaneously; but clearly dictation would give no advantage in the case of single orders. Possibly both dictation and visual copying were employed according to the needs and circumstances of the case. How the scribe carried out his task is again a matter for conjecture: there is virtually no evidence for the use of chairs, tables or desks, and it would appear that the scribe sat on a stool or even on the ground and rested the section of the roll on which he was writing on his knee, holding the remainder of the roll with his free hand.

The date of the invention of papyrus is unknown, but its use in Egypt can be traced back to the fourth millennium B.C., and it retained its predominant position in that country until long after the Arab conquest in 640–5. Although the decline and eventual extinction of the papyrus industry in Egypt is generally ascribed to the rivalry of paper, which finally replaced it in the tenth or eleventh century A.D., it is in fact difficult to establish whether the dying out of the papyrus plant was the result, or the cause, of the disappearance of the material. During the whole of this immense period of time almost no change can be detected in the method of manufacture, except a very gradual decline in quality.

From Egypt papyrus was exported, from a very early date and certainly centuries before the Christian era, to many parts of the ancient world, and the only reason why so few papyri have been found outside Egypt is that apart from a few exceptions, such as the Dead Sea caves, it is in Egypt alone (and then only in certain parts of the country) that the soil and the climatic conditions are dry enough to enable it to survive. A few papyri written in neighbouring countries have been discovered in Egypt and give us valuable information about writing habits in their countries of origin, but for the most part inferences have to be drawn from, for example, linguistic evidence, representations on monuments, impressions on clay sealings, and the like. In Assyria papyrus was certainly in use as early as the eighth century B.C., since the word used by the Assyrians to denote papyrus has been found in texts of that date. This papyrus was no doubt imported from Egypt, although some centuries later (perhaps under the Seleucids) the papyrus plant was introduced into Mesopotamia and papyrus was presumably manufactured there. Papyrus must have been equally well known in Syria and Palestine, and in fact the Murabba'at cave has produced a Hebrew papyrus, written in Phoenician script, which has been ascribed on palaeographical grounds to the seventh century B.C.—the oldest Semitic papyrus in existence. In later centuries the conquests of Alexander and the subsequent incorporation of Palestine in the empire of the Ptolemies, who ruled it from 304 to 200 B.C., must have greatly fostered the use of papyrus imported from Egypt, and indeed a number of Greek papyri written in Palestine in the middle of the third century B.C. have come to light in Egypt.

Before we leave the subject of papyrus, two major misconceptions, often reflected in older handbooks (and in some of more recent date), must be cleared away. The first is the supposition that papyrus was relatively expensive, and that its everyday use was restricted accordingly. In fact, the prices which have come down to us suggest that a roll of papyrus was by no means an expensive commodity; and in any case the lavish manner in which papyrus was often used, with wide margins and large unwritten areas, shows that the cost of the material was never a limiting factor. Furthermore, although, as has been pointed out, inscribed rolls or sheets of papyrus could easily be re-used either by washing off the original writing or by writing on the verso, this expedient was employed in only a minority of cases, and many discarded rolls which could have been used in this way were thrown away on the rubbish-heaps of Oxyrhynchus and elsewhere. The truth is that the consumption of papyrus in the ancient world was on a scale which almost passes belief. The celebrated Egyptian story of the travels of Wen-Amon (*c.* 1090 B.C.) represents him as carrying 500 blank rolls of papyrus 'of the finest quality' to Phoenicia to barter for wood. From a papyrus account of 258/7 B.C. we learn that one section of the accounting staff of Apollonius, the Finance Minister of Ptolemy II, received and used 434 rolls of papyrus in 33 days; this, moreover, was merely part of the travelling staff which accompanied Apollonius on his tours of the provinces, and not the permanent Treasury staff at Alexandria, the requirements of which must have been infinitely greater.

Another misconception which it is equally necessary to dissipate is the idea that papyrus is a particularly fragile material, of very limited durability. It is true that papyri which have survived to the present day, after centuries of desiccation, although they may be handled with reasonable care, can be crushed to powder between the fingers. But all the evidence indicates that in its original state papyrus was at least as durable as the best hand-made paper, if not more so. This proposition could be supported by numerous examples, of which only a few can be quoted here. Pliny, for instance, speaks of having seen autograph letters of the Gracchi, which must have been some 200 years old, while

Galen mentions having handled rolls 300 years old without suggesting that they were in any way fragile or that they were indeed anything out of the common. The famous 'find' of manuscripts of Aristotle at Scepsis, where they had been hidden in a cellar to save them from the attentions of the Attalid kings of Pergamum, was followed by their transport to Athens, where they were seized by Sulla and carried off as spoils of war to Rome, subsequently forming the basis of the edition of Aristotle's works by the philosopher Andronicus of Rhodes in the middle of the first century B.C.: thus, despite their vicissitudes, the manuscripts, which must have been on papyrus, remained usable for over 250 years. Finally must be mentioned the specimens, rare it is true, of papyri which have survived in Western Europe, the most ancient of which are documents from Ravenna written in the fifth century A.D.; although these papyri have been continuously above ground since the time of their creation, they have survived to modern times without any of the benefits of present-day conservation techniques. But the most striking example of all of the durability of papyrus is of a different kind: this is the fact that the Qumran leather scroll of Samuel (4QSam^a), when beginning to deteriorate, was strengthened on the back with a strip of papyrus, which has helped to preserve it. Yet we are continually informed that parchment and vellum are greatly superior to papyrus in durability!

The myth of the fragility of papyrus can thus be discarded once and for all, and, as we shall see, other grounds must be sought for its gradual replacement by parchment and vellum as the principal, and eventually the sole, material for book-production.

At this point a few words may be said about pens and inks. The pen used by the ancient Egyptians was a slender rush, *Juncus maritimus*, the end of which was cut at an angle and then chewed in the mouth, producing something like a very fine brush. With this simple implement the Egyptians produced miracles of craftsmanship both in their hieroglyphic writing and their vignette illustrations. The Greeks, on the other hand, invariably used, at least as early as the third century B.C., a reed with a much thicker stem, *Phragmites aegyptiaca*, the end of which was cut to a point, forming a nib, which was then slit as in modern pens. The Romans used the same reed-pen, which has remained in use in the East down to the present time. Metal pens with split nibs have also been found on Roman sites, perhaps as substitutes in areas where suitable reeds were not available.

The most ancient form of ink is undoubtedly that employed by the ancient Egyptians from time immemorial, made from carbon, obtained as lamp-black or soot, mixed with thin gum to hold it in suspension and provide adhesion. The Egyptians used this in the form of solid cakes which were ground up and mixed with water just like the present-day Indian or Chinese ink. Owing to its totally inert composition this ink is not subject to fading and, as the oldest Egyptian papyri prove, is virtually everlasting. A later invention is the metallic-based ink, usually made from an infusion of oak-galls mixed with green vitriol (iron sulphate). This ink undergoes chemical changes which can, in course of time, liberate minute quantities of sulphuric acid which may eat right through the writing material. It has sometimes been suggested that metallic inks were introduced specifically for writing on parchment, the greasy surface of which gives poor adhesion for carbon inks, but this explanation is not borne out by the evidence. Traces of metallic ink have, for instance, been found on the Lachish ostraca of the sixth century B.C., whereas the ink of the Dead Sea scrolls is mainly, if not entirely, carbon. The Talmud prescribed the use of carbon ink for writing the books of the Torah, and this practice has been followed for writing the Torah down to the present day, although metallic ink came into general use among Jews of the middle ages. Practically all Greek papyri use carbon ink, but from the fourth century A.D., and perhaps earlier, Greek parchment manuscripts used metallic ink: notable examples of the use of metallic ink are the *Codex Sinaiticus* and the *Codex Alexandrinus*; the latter has sustained serious damage as a result of the ink eating through the parchment. The general canon enunciated by Driver (*Semitic Writing*, 1954, p. 89) that carbon ink was used for parchment and metallic ink for papyrus, however true it may be for Semitic manuscripts, is almost exactly the reverse of the practice of the Greek scribes.

The second basic type of writing material to be considered is the group formed by leather, parchment and vellum. These must be taken together, since they merely represent different methods of utilizing the skins of the smaller quadrupeds, mainly sheep, goats and calves, for writing material. The terms parchment and vellum are virtually in-distinguishable, since though by derivation vellum means a preparation from skins of calves, it is now customarily used as a generic term, irrespective of the source of the material. Parchment (Latin *pergamena*) owes its name to the kings of Pergamum in Asia Minor, one of whom, the bibliophile Eumenes II (197–158 B.C.), is credited with having invented it during a temporary shortage of papyrus. Pliny quotes this story on the authority of Cicero's contemporary Varro, but our confidence is somewhat shaken when he follows it up with another quotation from Varro, to the effect that papyrus was invented after the founding of Alexandria by Alexander the Great! However this may be, parchment is a convenient term since it is not linked with any particular animal, and it will accordingly be used in the succeeding paragraphs.

The difficulty of differentiating between leather prepared for writing and parchment is illustrated by describing the normal process of manufacture, which has changed little over the centuries. After flaying, the epidermis, with the hair or wool, is removed from the outer side of the pelt, and the flesh from the inner, after soaking in a bath of lime. This is followed, in the case of leather, by tanning; but for parchment the skin, after liming, is washed, placed in a stretching frame, and allowed to dry. It is then shaved on both sides with a heavy iron knife to the required thickness, smoothed and whitened with pumice and chalk, and finally trimmed. The fineness of the resulting product depends upon the extent to which the reduction by shaving is pursued. The skin or dermis consists of three layers, the outermost being known from its granular appearance as the grain layer, the next one below, containing the roots of the hair follicles, as the papillary layer, and the innermost layer, next to the flesh, as the reticular layer or corium. In the finest quality parchment the two outer layers are completely removed, leaving only the reticular layer. Today, skins are split into layers by machinery, but in antiquity the reduction had to be effected by laborious scraping. Possibly it was this final reduction to the reticular layer which constituted the innovation of Eumenes.

Parchment has two sides, known as the 'hair side' and the 'flesh side'. The hair side, which was originally towards the outside of the skin, is clearly distinguishable in the coarser types of parchment by its yellow colour, rougher surface, and clearly visible remains of the hair roots. By contrast the flesh side, the original inner side, is whiter and smoother. In the case of documents, therefore, where only one side of the parchment has to be used, it is usual to write on the flesh side because of its better appearance, much as the writer on papyrus used the recto. Despite the superiority of the flesh side, it is usually the hair side, with its rougher and more absorbent surface, which holds the ink better than the smooth and shiny flesh side, from which ink tends to flake off. Often, when the leaves of an ancient manuscript are turned over, revealing alternate openings of flesh side and hair side, there is a surprising difference of legibility in favour of the hair side.

Despite the predominance of papyrus, leather rolls for written records were occasionally used in ancient Egypt, the earliest example known being of the sixth Dynasty, though most date from the New Kingdom. In the Persian empire leather was certainly in use in the fifth century B.C., since the Greek historian Ctesias speaks of the 'royal skins' on which the acts of the Achaemenid kings were chronicled. Actual examples of Persian parchments have survived through the discovery in Egypt, in the early 1930s, of a leather bag containing some twenty letters, of which thirteen were complete or nearly so. All were written on parchment, in Aramaic, and were addressed to an official of the Persian administration in Egypt; though undated, they can be assigned to the later years of the fifth century B.C. A number of the letters emanated from 'Aršam, the Persian satrap of Egypt, and what gives them an especial interest is that 'Aršam was not in Egypt at the time, the letters being written in Babylon or Susa. We know from the Aramaic papyri which have been found in Egypt that 'Aršam used papyrus whilst in that country, and we may perhaps infer that the Persians when in their homeland had a definite preference for parchment, since they could, of course, have perfectly well imported papyrus from Egypt had they wished to do so. This preference for parchment continued into the Parthian period, from which have survived three documents found at Avromān in Persian Kurdistan: these comprise one bilingual, in Greek and Middle Iranian, dated 88 B.C., one wholly in Greek, dated 22–21 B.C., and one wholly in Iranian, dated 12–11 B.C. Similarly at Doura on the Euphrates parchment is the normal material for documents in both Greek and Aramaic until the Romans captured the town in about A.D. 165; thereafter papyrus becomes the commonest material, and is used exclusively by the Roman military authorities until the town was captured and destroyed by the Persians in 256.

The foregoing documents are of non-literary character, and are written on separate pieces of parchment, often roughly prepared. They show no trace of ruled lines or margins, nor of any special preparation of the material for writing, and thus give us little or no idea of the probable appearance of contemporary literary works.

In any case, these discoveries have now been completely eclipsed by the astonishing finds in the Dead Sea caves and elsewhere in the Judaean desert. These sites have now produced fragments, some extensive but for the most part very small, of nearly 800 manuscripts, said to range in date (with a few exceptions) from the end of the third century B.C. to the second century A.D. All, where ascertainable, are in the form of rolls, and the great majority are on skin or parchment, though a small proportion, which fluctuates considerably from cave to cave, are on papyrus. The main body of texts are in Hebrew or Aramaic, in various scripts, but there are a few in Greek, both on parchment and papyrus. It is only quite recently that specimens of the scrolls have been subjected to technological examination, with interesting results. The methods of manufacturing the skins and preparing them for writing have been found to correspond, in remarkable degree, with the directions incorporated in medieval rabbinic literature. The skins were not steeped in lime, indeed lime was not used at all; instead, the skins were cured with salt and then treated with flour and other vegetable substances to remove the hair, clean the substance, and loosen the fibre structure. Three kinds of skin were distinguished, the first being whole-hide leather, while the other two were formed by splitting the skin into an inner and outer layer. After the processes of salting and flouring already described, all three types of skin are stated to be 'tanned', but in fact this 'tanning' amounts to no more than brushing over the surface, on both sides, with a gall-wood dressing which coloured it a dark yellow-brown. The object of this dressing was said to be to improve the surface for writing and to make erasures and alterations difficult, thus protecting the integrity of the text.

The rabbinic rules also prescribed which religious writings were to be written on each of the three different kinds of parchment, and also which side of the skin was to be used for writing in each case. Thus, the whole-hide skin was reserved for the Torah which must be written on the hair side. Of the split skins, the outer skin was be inscribed on the flesh side, and the inner skin, which was presumably, as we have seen, the finest material, was to be inscribed on the hair side. Horizontal lines to guide the writing, which hung from the lines, and vertical lines to mark off the margins, were ruled with a dry point, a practice which scribes of the third century A.D. regarded as an essential feature of a manuscript, and of which they traced the origin back to Adam, which at any rate shows that it was no recent innovation. This ruling is in sharp contrast to the practice of scribes on papyrus, who, as already stated, needed no such aids. To form rolls, the separate skins were sewn together; whereas medieval rabbinic regulations prescribe the use of sinews for this purpose, the sewing in the Dead Sea scrolls appears to be of vegetable origin. Although these joins were made very neatly, they are inevitably much more prominent than those in papyrus rolls, and scribes consequently avoided writing across them.

The stage is now set for considering the beginnings of the Christian book. If we consider the everyday world in which the earliest Christians lived, we might have expected that they would adopt as the vehicle for their literature either the parchment scroll of contemporary Judaism, or the papyrus roll universal throughout the Gentile world, or both. But in fact they did neither of these things: in this, as in other matters, the men who 'turned the world upside down' had different ideas.

THE ORIGIN OF THE CODEX

Today the codex form of book, that is, the book with separate leaves secured down one side, and with writing on both sides of the leaf, is virtually universal, and was so throughout the middle ages. The story of its ultimate origins is a long one, and the stages by which it gained this ascendancy are complex. There can be no possible doubt that the form of the codex derives from the multi-leaved writing tablets used by both the Greeks and the Romans. The classic form of Graeco-Roman writing tablets consisted of two or more (the largest number known is ten) thin rectangular wooden boards, held together down one side by means of strings passing through holes pierced near the inner edge. The inner surfaces of the boards were slightly hollowed out, and the cavities filled with a thin layer of black wax. On this wax, writing was traced with a metal stylus. This device formed an ideal vehicle for rough notes and memoranda, as alterations or deletions could be effected with the greatest ease by reversing the stylus and using its flattened end to smooth the wax and enable the correction to be written; or the whole surface could be smoothed, thus obliterating the writing, and enabling the tablet to be used again and again.

Although most of our knowledge comes from Greece and Rome, waxed tablets were certainly used in other parts of the Near East, as is shown not merely by representations of them in Neo-Hittite reliefs, but by the actual example of the magnificent ivory tablets, still bearing traces of their original green wax, recently found at Nimrud and dating from the eighth century B.C. Their distribution was thus extensive; but the Romans seem to have had a special predilection for them, employing them for permanent records such as wills and registrations of birth. And before the middle of the first century B.C. the Romans took what proved to be a momentous step: for the bank of wooden leaves, which they called a *codex* (from *caudex*, a log of wood), they substituted a bundle of sheets of parchment, sewn or tied together, which served much the same purpose and possessed decided advantages in lightness, portability and general convenience. The principle of indefinite reusability was preserved, since although the writing now had to be in ink, the carbon ink then in use could easily be washed or scraped off as required. These rough parchment notebooks, which the Romans called *membranae*, must have spread rapidly to the Near East, since it is virtually certain that it is notebooks of this type to which Paul refers in II Tim. iv. 13, when he asks Timothy to bring with him, not only the cloak left behind at Troas, but 'the books, especially the *membranae*', his use of the Latin term confirming the theory that the parchment notebook was of Roman invention. (It is worth noting that the New English Bible at this passage has been sufficiently influenced by the results of the latest research to translate it 'the books, above all my notebooks'.)

From the rough parchment codex used for ephemera it may seem only a short step to the employment of a codex, whether of parchment or papyrus, for the permanent reception of literary works. But this step was slow in coming, and for centuries yet the public remained mesmerized by the papyrus roll to which it had for so long been accustomed. The first indications of the next step are to be found in certain poems of Martial written between A.D. 84 and 86. The poems in question are a series of distichs meant to accompany gifts exchanged by well-to-do Romans at the Saturnalia. The gifts include writing tablets, of ivory or costly woods, or, in one case, of parchment, this last providing us with another example of the parchment notebook. But the innovation consists in five couplets intended to accompany copies of famous books

(Homer, *Iliad* and *Odyssey*; Virgil; Cicero; Livy; and Ovid, *Metamorphoses*), all of which are described as being written on parchment, and, in at least three cases and probably in all, in the form of codices.

Nearly all the distichs emphasize the compendiousness of the parchment codex (in tacit but obvious contrast to the papyrus roll), and the Cicero is specifically recommended for taking to read on a journey. Both these sentiments are echoed in another poem of Martial, advertising a revised edition of his own poems, in which he urges those who wish to possess his poems, and in particular to read them on a journey, to buy a copy of the new edition written in parchment codices, which takes up so little space that it can be held in one hand instead of needing a whole bookcase; and he concludes by giving the name and address of the bookseller from whom they can be obtained. Here then we have, for the first time on record, an instance of not merely a single copy, but an entire edition of a literary work being published in parchment codices.

Despite the efforts of Martial and his publisher, the venture does not seem to have been a success, and it is a long time before we hear again of parchment codices on any large scale. But the invention was not wholly forgotten, for we have a minute fragment of a page of a parchment codex containing a Latin historical work, which has been dated both on palaeographical and philological grounds to *c*. A.D. 100. We have also two single leaves from Greek parchment codices, one containing the *De falsa legatione* of Demosthenes, the other the lost *Cretans* of Euripides, which have been variously dated on the evidence of the script to the second century, to *c*. A.D. 100, or even to the late first century A.D.

The fact that, despite its obvious advantages, the parchment codex failed to secure a foothold indicates that the reading public of the Graeco-Roman world was conservative in its outlook (it is noticeable that Martial never commends his innovation as a *novelty*), and that, whatever possible advantages the parchment codex might have, they were simply not interested in the new form. But some other people were.

CHRISTIANITY AND THE CODEX

One possible reason why the parchment codex failed to catch on is that in the public mind parchment was associated with rough, untidy drafts or notes, whereas papyrus was traditionally the 'right' material for books. However this may be, a very short time after Martial's experiment someone conceived the idea of making a codex, not of parchment, but of papyrus. Where and by whom the idea was first tried out we do not know; but we do now know that the new form is directly connected with the earliest days of Christianity, and that the inventor may actually have been a Christian.

Realization of this fact has been slow in coming. Possibly the earliest hint of it is to be found in the article 'Writing' which Kenyon contributed to Hastings's *Dictionary of the Bible* as far back as 1902, and which includes the observation: 'There are signs, however, that it [the codex form] was early taken into use among the Christians for their private copies of the Scriptures. The evidence at present available is too scanty to justify dogmatism, but it is certainly the case that several of the earliest examples of the codex form contain Christian writings, and that the majority of the third century containing Christian writings are in the codex form.' A few years later and, it would seem, independently, C. R. Gregory in his *Canon and Text of the New Testament* (1907), pp. 322–3, put forward as 'a mere theory, a hypothesis', the suggestion that the change from the roll to the codex form, which he assigned to about the year A.D. 300, was motivated by the Christians: 'The theory touches the person or persons who made the change, who invented leaf-books. I am ready to believe that leaf-books are due to a Christian; that a Christian was the first one who felt the need of a change, and who effected the change.' And he goes on to suggest that the reason for the change was the need of the Christians to be able to refer quickly to different passages of Scripture when engaged in theological debates.

In assigning the change from roll to codex to about the year 300 Gregory added, 'a new papyrus may to-morrow show that the change came earlier'. This prophecy was fulfilled by later discoveries, above all by the finding, in about 1930, of the Chester Beatty biblical papyri. This group of eleven early Christian manuscripts, all on papyrus and all in codex form, and ranging in date from the early second century to the fourth, justified their editor, Kenyon, in observing: 'Not only do they confirm the belief that the Christian community was addicted to the codex rather than to the roll, but they carry back the use of the codex to an earlier date than there has hitherto been any good ground to assign to it.' Finally the whole question was investigated in depth in the magisterial monograph by C. H. Roberts, 'The Codex', in 1954.

While it is true that the statistics quoted by Roberts need to be re-calculated to take account of discoveries since 1952, these have not materially altered the general picture.

As Roberts shows, the most effective way of approaching the problem is to classify all extant fragments as coming either from rolls or codices, and to tabulate the results chronologically. Taking first pagan literature, Roberts gives the percentage of codices to rolls among fragments which have been dated second century as 2·31 per cent; among those dated second–third century, 2·9 per cent; among those dated third century, 16·8 per cent; among those dated third–fourth century, 48·14 per cent; and among those dated fourth century, 73·95 per cent. Thus, in the case of pagan literature, the codex barely existed before A.D. 200, and did not achieve a sizeable proportion until after A.D. 250.

When, however, we turn to Christian literature, the position is entirely different. If we take as a whole all the Christian biblical fragments which have been found in Egypt and which were written up to the end of the fourth century or not long thereafter, we find that, on the figures given by Roberts, these total 111, sixty-two coming from the Old Testament and forty-nine from the New. Of these 111, ninety-nine are from codices and only twelve are from rolls. If, however, we examine the evidence more closely, we find the proportion of codices to be even higher than would at first sight appear. First, five of the twelve rolls are on the backs of rolls already written on the recto, that is, the scribe had no option but to adopt the form of the earlier writing, and their witness is therefore irrelevant. Secondly, of the remaining seven rolls, three are probably Jewish, and another three possibly so. Thus, out of over a hundred Christian texts, only one—a roll of the Psalms—is an unequivocal example of the roll form.

When we shift the emphasis to the earliest surviving examples of Christian papyri, the contrast with pagan literature is, if anything, even more sharply drawn. There are now at least eleven Christian biblical papyri which can be assigned to the second century, and at least another three or four which can be placed on the borderline between the second and third centuries. Of these fourteen or fifteen specimens, every one is a codex. The proportion of codices to rolls is thus 100 per cent, whereas for pagan literature during the same period the proportion is only 2·5 per cent. Despite the fact that the overall number of Christian texts is so much smaller than the pagan, the discrepancy remains overwhelming, and has been so consistently reinforced by further discoveries that it cannot possibly be the result of chance; and we must now seek the cause.

In the past, all sorts of reasons have been put forward to explain the Christian preference for the codex. Thus, it has been claimed that papyrus codices were cheaper than rolls because both sides of the material were used, and that most of the earlier Christians came from the poorer classes, to whom the economy would be a strong motive. Against this it should be pointed out that while it is true that none of the early Christian codices have the appearance of *éditions de luxe*, they equally reveal no attempt to make the most of the available space; and in any case, the supposed dearness of papyrus has already been shown to be mythical. Another argument is that codices were more convenient for peripatetic missionaries to carry about with them. As Roberts points out, this is an application to the Christians of the argument put forward (unsuccessfully) by Martial in urging the parchment codex upon his readers. In fact, a papyrus roll, when tightly rolled, as it customarily was, to a small diameter could contain a surprising amount of material: thus, a papyrus 6 m in length could easily be rolled up into a cylinder no more than 5 or 6 cm in diameter, which could be comfortably held between the thumb and forefinger. If anything, a roll could probably be more conveniently carried in a fold of the garment than a codex with its projecting and vulnerable edges. Lastly there is the argument put forward, as we have seen, by C. R. Gregory, to the effect that the codex form was more convenient for quick reference in theological controversy. This is a pure hypothesis, and it is at least doubtful whether it could be justified on practical grounds. Without any system of chapter or verse divisions, finding one's way about the text would be no easier in a codex than in a roll, indeed a roll, in which the eye could survey perhaps four or more columns of writing at a glance, might well be the superior. Nor were Christians the only controversialists of the ancient world.

Roberts accordingly rejected all these would-be explanations, and sought, rightly, for a deeper and more compelling reason behind the Christian addiction to the codex. The solution he proposed was ingenious, and has found a wide measure of support.

In the first place, it must be remembered that the surviving examples of Christian codices are common provincial productions, and can in no circumstances be regarded as probable trend-setters. The origin of the Christian codex must therefore be sought in a period considerably earlier than the earliest surviving examples: as Roberts has pointed out, 'so universal is the use of the codex by Christians in the second century that the beginnings of this process must be taken back well into the first century'. This conclusion has lately been reinforced by the publication of a fragment from a papyrus codex of Genesis in Yale University Library (P. Yale 1) which the editor assigns to the late first century, 'perhaps between A.D. 80 and 100', thus making it the earliest Christian papyrus in existence. If this judgement is accepted, the origin of the Christian codex must be placed not later than A.D. 70. This condition is fulfilled by the solution propounded by Roberts, to which we now turn.

Roberts begins by arguing that Mark, when he came to write down his Gospel in Rome in or shortly after A.D. 70, would have employed the rough parchment notebook which, as we have seen, was in common use in Rome for notes and literary drafts. Roberts further suggests that the traditional association of Mark with the church of Alexandria reflects a real link between the Alexandrian church and the West, and that Mark's Gospel was the first authoritative Christian writing to reach Egypt. He further assumes that it was Mark's original autograph manuscript, in the parchment notebook, which so reached Egypt, and argues that it would have been regarded with such veneration by the Alexandrian Christians that copies taken from it would have been made in the same codex form, but utilizing the universal writing material of Egypt, papyrus. The papyrus codex, once established and backed by the authority of Alexandria in bibliographical matters, would have rapidly spread to other Christian writings both inside and outside Egypt.

As will be seen, this explanation involves acceptance of, not one, but a whole chain of hypotheses, all unproved and, in all probability, unprovable; and apart from this, there are several points about which doubts can be expressed. For instance, many other literary works must have started life as drafts in parchment notebooks and been subsequently transferred onto papyrus rolls, and it is not clear why the Alexandrian Christians should have felt the need to adopt any different procedure in multiplying copies of Mark's Gospel. Even if we accept Roberts's theory of the extraordinary reverence attaching to Mark's original manuscript in the parchment notebook, we have still to explain why, if format was of such vital importance as to compel adoption of the codex form, it did not equally compel adoption of parchment as the writing material. For the moment, at any rate, Roberts's theory cannot be regarded as more than a working hypothesis.

Whatever the explanation of its origin may be, the fact remains that the papyrus codex *was* invented, and that within a very short space of time it won acceptance as the only possible format for the Christian Scriptures. Such radical innovations are usually the work of individuals rather than committees—or churches—and we may perhaps imagine the invention as originating with some leading figure in the early Church, who, whatever the ultimate source of his inspiration, succeeded both in devising a distinctive format for Christian manuscripts of the Scriptures, differentiated equally from the parchment roll of Judaism and the papyrus roll of the pagan world, and in imposing its use throughout the Church. Here the reader may reasonably ask whether there is any other evidence pointing to the existence of such a dominating genius at work in the field of the earliest Christian literature. The answer is, surprisingly, yes.

Hand in hand with the papyrus codex goes a palaeographical peculiarity which, right from the earliest period, enables one to distinguish, almost at a glance, manuscripts of Christian literature from all others—the so-called *nomina sacra*. This term denotes certain stereotyped abbreviations, or rather compendia, for a limited number of words of divine significance or association, such as the Greek equivalents of 'God', 'Lord', 'Father', 'Jesus', 'Christ', 'Son', 'Man' (included through the influence of the term 'Son of Man'), 'Cross', 'Spirit', and a few others. These compendia are marked off from the surrounding text by a horizontal line above the letters, and one of them, I̅H̅S̅ or I̅H̅C̅ for 'Jesus', has survived to the present day. These compendia are found in virtually all Christian manuscripts, although some are so fragmentary that they provide no opportunity for the use of *nomina sacra*.

Why the early Christians should have taken this surprising step remains a mystery. Possibly it was a deliberate attempt to differentiate the Christian Scriptures from other literary forms, to mark them out as sacred books by investing them with a species of *cachet*. However this may be, the significant fact is that the introduction of the *nomina sacra* seems to parallel very closely the adoption of the papyrus codex; and it is remarkable that those developments should have taken place at almost the same time as the great outburst of critical activity among Jewish scholars which led to the standardization of the text of the Hebrew bible. It is no less remarkable that they seem to indicate a degree of organization, of conscious planning, and uniformity of practice among the Christian communities which we have hitherto had little reason to suspect, and which throws a new light on the early history of the Church.

Before we leave the papyrus codex, some technical points may be adverted to. The most primitive type of codex was that formed by piling the sheets of papyrus one on top of the other and doubling them over in the middle, thus making a single huge quire. The resultant bundle was held together by means of threads passing through holes stabbed right through the codex, not in the fold but some way inwards from it. If no precautions were taken, this produced a very awkwardly shaped volume, since the leaves near the centre of the book projected beyond those at the beginning and end, with consequent exposure to wear and damage; this defect could be overcome by cutting the sheets narrower and narrower as the centre of the book was approached, and examples of this are found, but it must have been a cumbersome process. Another defect of the single-quire codex was that the scribe had to calculate pretty exactly the number of leaves he required, since under- or overestimating would result in blank pages at beginning or end, with consequent waste of material. It is not therefore surprising that the alternative was tried of forming the codex of a number of quires, as in the modern book. In some cases, as in the Chester Beatty codex of Gospels and Acts, quires of only two leaves—a single sheet folded in half—were used, but larger quires, of six, eight, ten or twelve leaves, also occur at different times. These various arrangements overlapped for long periods, and no steady development can be traced. Eventually the single-quire codex faded out, and the multi-quire form, usually with quires of eight leaves, achieved universal acceptance; but by this time the papyrus codex itself had been superseded by the parchment codex.

In most papyrus codices the sheets were cut from papyrus already made up into rolls, with the result that the joins in the material are visible in the pages. An exception is the group of Coptic Manichean codices, which despite their present lamentable state were originally *éditions de luxe*, made up of individual sheets of papyrus of fine quality and specially prepared for writing on both sides. The question of sides, the so-called 'recto' and 'verso' of the papyrus, is important because it may be possible, from the order in which the sides follow each other, to infer the original contents of an entire codex from a few small fragments. In making up a single-quire codex, the natural method is to pile up the sheets one on top of the other with the 'recto' uppermost in each case. When a codex so made up is opened, one of the two leaves exposed to view will show the fibres running horizontally, the other vertically. This incongruity was clearly felt, since the practice arose of arranging the sheets with 'recto' facing upwards and downwards alternately, so that the opened book would show either horizontal fibres or vertical fibres on both of the facing pages. Similar variations are possible in the case of multi-quire codices.

Finally, just as the papyrus roll could be protected by being enclosed in a parchment sheath or *capsa*, so the papyrus codex needed protection from external wear and tear. No early papyrus codex in Greek has preserved any trace of a binding; but the great find of Coptic Gnostic papyrus codices made at Nag Hammadi in Upper Egypt in 1947 has provided us with no fewer than eleven leather bindings, all more or less intact, which enable us to form some idea of the external appearance of the earliest Christian books. These bindings, which are presumably of the same period as the manuscripts they contain, and thus range in date from the end of the third century to the beginning of the fifth, are in fact more like satchels or envelopes than bindings as we know them today. Many have triangular or rectangular flaps which cover the fore-edge of the manuscript, and to which long leather laces were attached, intended to be wound two or three times round the closed book. Within these covers the papyrus codices were attached with leather thongs.

SUPREMACY OF THE PARCHMENT CODEX

The change to the parchment codex now to be described is a complex one, since it affected Christian and non-Christian literature alike, and in the case of the latter involved not only the change of form from roll to codex but also the change of material from papyrus to parchment, whereas in the case of Christian literature the change was a straightforward one from the papyrus codex to the parchment codex. Moreover, all these changes were gradual processes and overlapped for considerable periods, with the result that, for instance, in non-Christian literature of the fourth century A.D. we find the papyrus roll, the papyrus codex, and the parchment codex all competing for popularity.

The complete dominance achieved by the papyrus codex in the field of early Christian literature, and its long survival, prove that it was a perfectly adequate form of book, and in the course of the second century it was apparently beginning to influence certain forms of non-Christian literature: there are eleven fragments of non-Christian papyrus codices which are assigned to the second century, though they are still enormously outnumbered by the fragments of papyrus rolls. During the third century there is a marked change in the situation. About one-sixth of the non-Christian texts are now in codex form, and of these some half-dozen are parchment codices. From the same century comes the earliest example of a New Testament parchment codex. But the real watershed is the year 300. The celebrated Edict of Diocletian (301), imposing a freeze on prices and wages, specified maximum rates of pay for scribes writing in parchment codices; this shows, better than any assemblage of fragments, how common the parchment codex was becoming. Then, in 332, we have the letter of Constantine the Great to Eusebius, bishop of Caesarea, ordering him to supply fifty vellum bibles for use in the new churches which he was building in Constantinople. These volumes were specifically ordered to be 'written on prepared vellum, easy to read and conveniently portable, by professional scribes with an exact understanding of their craft', and the letter makes it clear that no expense was to be spared. It is plain that by this date the parchment codex had come to be regarded as the supreme form of the Christian book, and superior to the papyrus codex, at least for such official and ceremonial purposes.

The triumph of the parchment codex is signalized not only by the literary evidence quoted above, but by the actual survival of two magnificent Greek bibles written at precisely this period—the *Codex Sinaiticus* and the *Codex Vaticanus*. It has even been suggested that these two great bibles are survivors from the consignment ordered by Constantine, and though this cannot be proved, and is in fact on the whole improbable, it is certainly true that they represent accurately the type of book which Constantine had in mind. And although they are the only two parchment codices of the Bible to have come down to us from this period in a reasonably complete state, they are not isolated specimens. Indeed, in the latest list of manuscripts of the Greek New

Testament there are at least sixteen fragments of other parchment codices written in the fourth century. From the fourth century also comes the most ancient manuscript of the Old Latin version of the New Testament, the *Codex Vercellensis*, in parchment codex form, while in the field of pagan literature we have monumental parchment codices such as the *Codex Palatinus* of Virgil or the famous palimpsest of the *De Republica* of Cicero, a manuscript which resembles the *Codex Sinaiticus* in its combination of external magnificence and astonishing scribal lapses.

Nevertheless it must not be inferred that the supremacy of the parchment codex involved the disappearance of the papyrus codex. On the contrary, it displayed a remarkable vitality. In Egypt it remained in common use down to the sixth or seventh century, and even later. In the case of Greek classical literature it even seems to have staged a revival in the fifth century, the proportion of papyrus codices to vellum codices being almost twice as great then as in the fourth century. In the West, remnants of eight Latin papyrus codices, written in France or Italy, have survived all the hazards of the middle ages down to the present day. These codices, all containing Christian or legal texts, show that here also the papyrus codex long resisted the competition of parchment. It is true that Roberts quotes a letter written to Ruricius, bishop of Limoges, in the first half of the fifth century, in which the remark occurs 'a papyrus book is less capable [i.e. than a parchment one] of resisting damage, since, as you know, it deteriorates through age'. But this may be countered by the fact that when Cassiodorus, writing to the monks of Vivarium in Southern Italy about 550, says he is leaving them a manuscript of the Pauline epistles for them to work on and purify the text on the lines laid down by him, he specifically mentions that the manuscript was a papyrus codex.

As in the case of the change from roll to codex, all sorts of reasons have been put forward to explain the change from papyrus to parchment. For instance, it has been stated that parchment was cheaper than papyrus. But we have no information about the relative prices of parchment and papyrus at any period. Again, it has been suggested that papyrus was basically unsuitable for a codex, because it was difficult to fold, or cracked when folded. This is simply untrue, as is shown by the examples of papyrus codices which have survived more or less intact; by experiments with modern papyrus; and by the existence of a large number of private letters and other documents which for transmission have been folded up into extremely small shapes, and unfolded by the recipients without damage. This is, in fact, part of the more general claim that parchment was tougher, longer-lasting, and more resistant to damage than papyrus—a claim largely based upon the supposed fragility of papyrus, which has already been shown to be illusory. Some writers have even suggested that parchment was preferred to papyrus because it offered scope for manuscript illumination; yet Egyptian scribes for thousands of years had produced papyri illustrated with coloured drawings, and coloured illustrations do occur, though rarely, in Greek papyri.

Another possible explanation is the following. The sole source of papyrus, then as always, was Egypt, whereas parchment could be produced anywhere. The continued use of papyrus, in competition with parchment, thus depended upon uninterrupted commerce with Egypt. If the fall of the Western Empire caused increasing dislocations of such trade, parchment would naturally obtain the preference. This explanation does not, however, explain the replacement of papyrus by parchment within Egypt itself.

It will be seen, therefore, that it is very difficult to find practical reasons for the supersession of the papyrus codex by the parchment codex. One is almost driven to conclude that it is a mistake to search for a purely practical explanation, and that the need for a change of writing material may reflect some deeper, psychological cause, associated with the great changes which came over the ancient world in the fourth century. Possibly papyrus was seen, to an increasing extent, as a symbol of the old order which was passing away; if so, its survival into the sixth and seventh centuries for manuscripts, and much longer than that for documents, must be ascribed to sheer conservatism. Here, for the time being, the question must be left without any clear solution.

It now remains to give some account of the technical make-up and external appearance of the parchment codex, and for this purpose it may be convenient to take a single example of a manuscript which has been the subject of intensive study and analysis—the *Codex Sinaiticus*. This manuscript, now one of the greatest treasures of the British Museum, consists of parchment from both sheepskin and goatskin. The parchment is finely prepared and thin in relation to the size of the book. Originally the double sheets must have measured about 40 × 70 cm, so that when doubled over they formed pages 40 × 35 cm. The makers of parchment codices had learnt from the papyrus codex the disadvantages of the single-quire codex, so that all parchment codices, so far as is known, are in multi-quire format. The *Codex Sinaiticus* consists, with a few exceptions, of quires of eight leaves, a figure which remained the most popular make-up throughout the middle ages. In the quire, the sheets of parchment were arranged so that (*a*) flesh side faced flesh side and hair side hair side throughout the quire, and (*b*) flesh side was on the outsides of the quire. This arrangement became stereotyped in later Greek (though not Latin) manuscripts. The pile of sheets was then folded over to form the quire, and two vertical rows of small holes were pricked right through the eight leaves, near the fore-edge, to act as guides for the ruling lines. These lines were ruled with a hard point, always on the flesh side, so that they appear as raised lines on the hair side. The lines to guide the writing were ruled right across the double leaf, and then vertical lines were added to mark the margins of the columns of writing. Each page contained four narrow columns of writing, except in the poetical books of the Old Testament, which were ruled for two broad columns to the page. At a normal opening, therefore, eight narrow columns are presented to the reader's view, and it has often been claimed that this arrangement is derived from the succession of columns in a papyrus roll. The suggestion is, however, groundless, since in the first place the *Codex Sinaiticus* is exceptional in having as many as four columns to the page, most codices, whether papyrus or parchment, having only one or two, and secondly, narrow columns of the proportions found in the *Codex Sinaiticus* are by no means characteristic of papyrus rolls. After ruling, the writing area on each page was rubbed down with an abrasive to enable the ink to take a secure hold.

The quires were numbered to keep them in the correct order when the book was bound, but at this point our knowledge comes to an end, since neither the *Sinaiticus* nor any of the other great parchment codices have preserved any traces of their bindings. When Constantine wrote to Eusebius of Caesarea, as mentioned above, ordering bibles for the churches in Constantinople, Eusebius tells us that the manucripts were supplied in 'expensively worked containers' though it is uncertain whether this means bindings of the satchel- or envelope-type found on the Gnostic codices from Nag Hammadi, which could easily be given a more luxurious appearance by decorating the leather, or some kind of decorated book-boxes.

The *Codex Sinaiticus* is a fitting point at which to end this survey, since it represents in fully developed form the type of book which was to dominate Christianity for the next thousand years. Changes of scale indeed took place, from the huge bibles of the Romanesque period to the astonishing small bibles of the thirteenth century, with parchment pared thin as India paper and almost literally microscopic script; but the basic method of construction remained unaltered. Nor did manuscript illumination, with its panoply of decorated initials, borders and miniatures, affect the make-up of the books so embellished. Towards the end of the period, it is true, paper had begun to supplant parchment; but this change was far from complete when the final revolution took place—the invention of printing—and the manuscript book, which had moulded the minds of men for upwards of five thousand years, vanished for ever from the scene of everyday life.

CHAPTER IV

JEROME

An outline of Jerome's life will help to indicate his place in history and also some of the influences to which he was subjected and which have left their mark on his biblical work. Much effort has been devoted to establishing his chronology, but as the evidence consists largely in the rather vague remarks contained in his writings the dates assigned are in part only approximate, and even today there is no complete agreement among scholars. The dates accepted here are those of F. Cavallera, except that the date of Jerome's death should perhaps be 420 and not 419, the date given by that biographer. The date of his birth is at the latest 347, and may have been a year or two earlier.

Jerome was born at Stridon on the borders of Pannonia and Dalmatia, not far from Aquileia at the head of the Adriatic. This place is mentioned nowhere except in the last section of Jerome's *De Viris Illustribus*; it was destroyed in an invasion of the Goths, and its very site is today a matter of speculation. His parents were Christian, but apparently not particularly zealous in their attachment to their religion. They were in easy circumstances, and after his early education in his native place they were able to send their son to Rome at the age of about twelve for further studies. Here he was fortunate enough to have the celebrated grammarian Donatus as his teacher. Under his tuition Jerome gave himself ardently to the study of the great classical writers. His natural eagerness to learn was stimulated in this literary pursuit by the charm of the music of words. He was delighted by the rhythms of the poets and the harmonious cadences of the great prose writers. This devotion to the pagan classics persisted until the famous dream at Antioch in 374–5, in which he heard himself condemned before the celestial tribunal: 'Ciceronianus es, non Christianus.'[1]

From that time he devoted himself to Christian learning with the same ardour that he had previously shown towards the classics, and more than fifteen years later he was able to say that in the intervening time he had never had in his hands Tully, Maro, or any pagan author.

[1] *Ep.* 22. 30.

Yet so tenacious was his memory that classical passages often came spontaneously to his lips as he dictated.

The course in 'Grammar' was followed by that in 'Rhetoric'. It is not known who were his instructors during these years. Victorinus is mentioned by Jerome, but he never speaks of him as his master, as he does of Donatus. Quintilian provided the principles; the students composed and declaimed their own pieces; and the orators in the law-courts were living models for young aspirants. There the learner heard the foremost advocates, ignoring the merits of the case, 'in feigned wrath insulting and tearing one another to pieces'.[1] Does this experience perhaps explain the violent language later used by Jerome in the course of his controversies? The final stage of these studies, concluded at about the age of twenty, was the course in philosophy. We hear of his study of the works of Cicero and Seneca, of his introduction to logic under a learned teacher through the *Isagoge* of Porphyry, of his study of Aristotle and the commentaries on his logic by Alexander of Aphrodisias.

During his stay at Rome this devotee of the classics had been at considerable pains to collect a 'library' which he took with him when he later travelled to the East.[2] It would be a mistake, however, to suppose that all his youthful energy was absorbed in the pursuit of learning. One of his letters reveals that when he was living an ascetic life in the desert of Chalcis, with only scorpions and wild beasts for company, he 'was often present at dances with girls'. Nor, he frankly confesses, did he pass these years of his youth without grave sin;[3] and it was through fear of hell that he condemned himself 'to such a prison as the desert'.[4] But it was also at Rome that the Christian devotion of the people and of earnest companions awoke in him a sense of his duty to God. With these friends he used to visit the catacombs, and it was in Rome that he received his long-deferred baptism.

These years at Rome inaugurated a career of study that was to last until his dying day. From Rome he travelled to Trèves, where the emperor at that time held his court. Perhaps the intention of his family was that he might gain a position in the imperial service; but of this there is no record. It seems certain, however, that the flourishing monastic life, which owed its inception to the visit of Athanasius during

[1] *PL.* 26, 340 B.   [2] *Ep.* 22. 30.
[3] *Ep.* 7. 4.   [4] *Ep.* 22. 7.

the course of his first exile, either planted or fostered in Jerome's mind the idea of embracing it himself. In the meantime his knowledge of Christianity must have been considerably enlarged by the arduous task, undertaken at the request of Rufinus, of copying Hilary's commentary on the Psalms and his treatise *De Synodis*. Later he requested his friend Florentinus to make him copies of these same two works.[1] From Trèves he travelled to his home at Stridon and visited friends who were living a monastic life at nearby Aquileia. Some sudden disturbance (*subitus turbo*) caused his departure, without a definite aim, on a long and exhausting journey through Thrace, Pontus, Bithynia, Galatia, Cappadocia and Cilicia, to arrive, a very sick man, at Antioch, where he received hospitality and care from his friend Evagrius. This was in 374.

In the following year, when he had recovered his strength sufficiently, he retired to the desert of Chalcis, where he gave himself up to the rigour of an ascetic life and to the study of the Bible and patristic literature. With the help of copyists he continued to enlarge his library, and was by now well supplied with biblical manuscripts. He tells Florentinus that he will have copied and send him whatever he desires.[2] Curiously enough, the desert offered him the opportunity, which he eagerly grasped, of beginning the study of Hebrew. This he did under the instruction of a converted Jew. The labour and difficulty of the task, undertaken at the age of about 30, are feelingly described by him.[3] Finally, discord having broken out among the monks concerning theological questions and the schism at Antioch, Jerome abandoned the desert and returned to that city.

In Antioch Apollinarius, bishop of the neighbouring city of Laodicea, used at that time to deliver lectures on the Bible. Jerome, who was 'possessed by a wonderful eagerness to learn', seized the opportunity and attended the course frequently and with much profit to his knowledge of the Scriptures. He never embraced the heretical opinions of his teacher.[4] As these lectures were given in Greek, the pupil from Stridon had evidently made remarkable progress in that language. He thus became acquainted with the principles of the exegetical school of Antioch. In this city, too, Jerome was ordained by Bishop Paulinus, but on condition that he should retain the freedom of a monk and not

[1] *Ep.* 5. 2.   [2] *Ep.* 5. 2.
[3] *Ep.* 125. 12.   [4] *Ep.* 84. 2.

be obliged to minister in a particular church. It was probably at this time, also, that he went to Beroea, where he received permission to copy the Aramaic gospel of pseudo-Matthew, which he later translated into Greek.[1]

From Antioch Jerome now made his way to Constantinople, perhaps repelled from the one city by the discord provoked by the schism and attracted to the other by the reputation of Gregory Nazianzen, its bishop from 378. Helped by this 'most eloquent man', he continued there his study of Scripture; he calls the bishop 'my teacher',[2] and says that he rejoices to have had his instruction. Perhaps owing to his influence, Jerome now translated fourteen homilies of Origen on Jeremiah, fourteen on Ezekiel, and seven on Isaiah. At this time, too, he wrote his commentary on the vision of Isaiah.[3] In this, after one paragraph devoted to the explanation of such matters as who Uzziah was and the length of his reign, he passes on to the spiritual sense of the text, which was the real purpose of the 'history'. Jerome took no part in the Council of 381, but the assembling of the bishops at Constantinople gave him the opportunity to gain the friendship of Gregory of Nyssa and Amphilochius of Iconium. A testimony to Jerome's wide interests is the translation, made at this time, of the *Chronicle* of Eusebius. He inserted some details of Roman history which had not been of interest to the Greek author, and added a continuation from 325 to the death of Valens in 378.

In 382 Paulinus of Antioch and Epiphanius, bishop of Salamis in Cyprus, set out from Constantinople to attend the council at Rome which was to open towards the close of that year. Jerome had now lost the chief attraction which had kept him in Constantinople, for Gregory Nazianzen had resigned the see and retired to Cappadocia. He was therefore glad to accompany the two bishops to Rome. His familiarity with the city and his mastery of both Latin and Greek made him an ideal guide and interpreter; and he was anxious to help the cause of his friend Paulinus. Pope Damasus soon recognized Jerome's wide knowledge and literary ability, and utilized his services as a secretary.[4] He also entered into correspondence with him, seeking the solution to various scriptural difficulties. More important by far, the pope entrusted to his secretary the revision of the Gospels in Latin. The existing

[1] *PL.* 23, 613 B; 26, 78 A.   [2] *Ep.* 52. 8.
[3] *Epp.* 18 A, 18 B.   [4] *Ep.* 123. 9.

codices presented such variations in the text that readers were at a loss to know which they could trust. As the reviser expressed the situation in his preface dedicated to the pope, there were almost as many versions as codices.[1]

This lamentable state of affairs was due in part to the carelessness of copyists, partly to unintelligent emendation, partly to errors of translation. A frequent source of error was the insertion in one Gospel of elements of another, under the mistaken idea that fuller details found elsewhere must have been accidentally omitted. Jerome's emendation was carried out with the aid of Greek manuscripts which were, in Jerome's own words, 'ancient'. To spare susceptibilities (custom and tradition are strong forces) only those passages were corrected which deviated from the sense of the original; the rest was allowed to stand as it was.

From this the reader will appreciate the importance of this version of the Gospels. It represents in Latin the text of Greek codices which were already ancient (*veteres*) in the late fourth century and therefore much closer in time to the archetypes than any complete Greek manuscripts now extant. No preface to the revision of the rest of the New Testament is known to exist, but in various places Jerome states that he revised the New Testament to bring it into agreement with the authoritative Greek text.[2] There is no sound reason for limiting the reference of all these statements to only a part of the New Testament; and there are good reasons for accepting them at their face value. The manuscripts of the Gospels and epistles all give the Vulgate version, and this unity of tradition indicates a unity of origin. This is supported by the uniformity of the recension, in which the same principles are followed, and also by the fact that it is all characterized by Jerome's style.[3]

Other biblical work carried out at this time was the correction of the Latin Psalter by the aid of the Septuagint, of which it was a translation. This was not a thorough revision, though the text was in large measure corrected.[4] It is commonly held that this revision is that known today as the Roman Psalter, which is still in use in the Basilica of St Peter. This identification has been challenged by Dom de Bruyne; his arguments have not been found convincing, though they are not destitute of all probability. At any rate, in the expert opinion of Vaccari,

---

[1] *PL.* 29, 526 C.   [2] E.g. *ep.* 71. 5.
[3] See A. Vaccari in *Biblica*, I (1920), 535–41.   [4] *PL.* 29, 1117 B.

the existing Roman Psalter is of the type used by Jerome for his revision.[1]

Close attention was demanded by the collation of Aquila's Greek version with the original Hebrew. The purpose of this was to discover whether anti-Christian bias had led the second-century Jew into some infidelities in his translation. The outcome, so Jerome informed Marcella in a letter, was favourable to the translator and led to the discovery of various passages which supported the Christian faith.[2] Later he praises Aquila as 'diligent and careful' in his work. A less arduous undertaking was the translation of two of Origen's homilies on the Song of Songs. Jerome was still under the spell of the Alexandrian's allegorical inter-pretations, and in his short preface he extols him as the master exegete (*PL.* 23, 1117A). All this biblical labour was accompanied by zealous efforts to promote the ascetic life and by indignant protests against the worldliness and self-seeking that tarnished the lives of some among the Roman clerics and monks. The inevitable happened. Feelings were alienated and attacks were provoked. How had Jerome dared to make alterations in the Gospels against ancient authority and against the opinion of the whole world?[3] It must be admitted that the language of his reply was not calculated to conciliate. His critics are 'little two-footed asses'. His ascetical teaching was held responsible for the early death of the high-born Blesilla. 'How long will it be before the hateful brood of monks is driven from the city?'[4]

Apart from this desire of his enemies, however, Jerome's own inclinations had awakened a longing to be away from city life. Even the social duties of visits with their idle conversations were little to his taste. Apart from the monk's abhorrence of all signs of worldliness in Christians, the scholar with his 'incredible passion for learning'[5] deplored the hindrances to his pursuits and longed for the quiet and leisure of the country. When the protecting hand of Damasus was withdrawn by death late in 384, Jerome's position became increasingly difficult. Calumnies were spread against him. So in 385 he took ship from Ostia to settle at Bethlehem.

Others felt the same call and travelled with him. These were his young brother Paulinianus, a priest Vincentius, and some monks who settled with him in his new home. The journey was broken at Cyprus,

[1] See A. Vaccari, *Scritti di erudizione e di filologia*, I (Rome, 1952), 211–21.
[2] *Ep.* 32. 1.   [3] *Ep.* 27. 1.   [4] *Ep.* 39. 8.   [5] *PL.* 25, 839 A.

where Jerome was received by the 'venerable bishop Epiphanius'. Thence to Antioch and its bishop Paulinus. Here, probably, the party was joined by Paula and her daughter Eustochium. In the intense cold of winter they started south together. The places visited by the pilgrims in Palestine are described in *Epistle* 108. 8–13. After Palestine, Egypt, with a visit to the innumerable monks of Nitria and to Alexandria. Thence back to Bethlehem, where it took three years to build the two monastic houses, one for Paula and her community and one for Jerome and his monks. In addition, Paula built a hospice for pilgrims 'because Mary and Joseph had not found a lodging'.[1]

It was during this Egyptian tour that Jerome became acquainted with Didymus, the blind biblical scholar. Deprived of eyesight at the age of five, he had never learnt the characters of the alphabet; yet Jerome, whose standard of learning was unusually high, calls him 'the most erudite man of his time'. He consulted him about various biblical difficulties and was a frequent attendant at his lectures.[2] He gratefully acknowledges the help he received; but he is careful to point out that he did not adopt the errors of the 'seer' (as the blind old man was called, after the style of the ancient prophets of Israel). These errors he had imbibed through his implicit confidence in Origen. At his visitor's request Didymus dictated three books on Hosea and five on Zechariah and dedicated them to him.[3] Thus Jerome attended lectures by a foremost exponent of the Alexandrian school, as he had attended earlier those of Apollinarius of the more literalist school of Antioch, and those of the Cappadocian Gregory Nazianzen.

Once he had settled at Bethlehem, Jerome's travels abroad were over. Within Palestine he must have spent some considerable time at Caesarea working in the famous library founded by Pamphilus and Eusebius, where the original copy of Origen's *Hexapla* was preserved. With this authentic copy, he tells us, he collated all the books of the Old Testament.[4] There, too, he found and read Eusebius' six volumes in defence of Origen. He tells us also that in company with the most learned of the Jews he went round the country and visited the sites of ancient cities.[5] This can scarcely refer to the first pilgrimage with Paula. That was for the purpose of devotion rather than study, and would not have been sufficiently exhaustive.

[1] *Ep.* 108. 11.   [2] *PL.* 25, 820 A.   [3] *PL.* 25, 820 A, 1418 A.
[4] *PL.* 26, 595 B.   [5] *PL.* 29, 401 A.

Rome had forced on the scholar many distractions from study; life at little Bethlehem brought new calls on his time. There was the care of the monastery under his charge; the instructions and exhortations delivered to his monks; a vast correspondence with various countries and notably with Augustine in Africa; visits and the care of pilgrims who, incidentally, were his 'postmen' and made intercourse by means of letters possible; the needs of many fugitives at the time of the sack of Rome by Alaric in 410; the composition of controversial works against Rufinus, Jovinian, Vigilantius, Pelagius (that against Helvidius had been written at Rome); the armed attack on his monastery in 416 by Pelagian monks who set fire to the building; his own constant ill-health. Mention must be made of some at least of his non-biblical works. He wrote lives of Malchus and Hilarion. These, like that of Paul the hermit, written at Antioch, were designed to attract recruits to the monastic life. The translation of the rule of Pachomius would serve the same purpose, but was undertaken not on Jerome's initiative but at the request of Latin monks in Egypt, ignorant of Coptic and Greek. The preface says that he summoned a secretary and dictated 'in our language' a version of an existing Greek translation.[1] The work, *De Viris Illustribus*, derived in part from Eusebius, is a valuable list of Christian writers and their works. Its purpose was to demonstrate to the pagan world the erudition and ability of so many adherents of the new religion. He also translated a volume on the Holy Spirit by his friend Didymus.

Jerome was sensitive and emotional, warm and faithful in affection, quick and vehement in his anger against all that he conceived to be contrary to revealed truth. His friendship with Rufinus suffered a severe breakdown, but in his mind it was the other party who made its continuance impossible. The violence of his language on occasions was due to the strength of his feelings and his ardent temperament. He thought it right to reprove Paula for extreme grief at the death of Blesilla;[2] but he himself was deeply affected by the death of his friends. F. Cavallera, the author of the standard biography, cannot be accused of any bias against the saint, but his description of him is not wholly laudatory. Jerome, he writes, was sensitive, easily impressionable, suspicious, irascible, exaggerating insults he received and not sparing of blows in return, prompt to irony and sarcasm, but also with feelings of tenderness and ardent in affection. He was passionately devoted to

[1] *PL.* 23, 63 A.   [2] *Ep.* 39. 6.

his faith and unwearying in his labours to make the truths of religion better known: the impelling motive of all his biblical study and writing.

Finally, he was an artist in words with a delicate sensitivity for the beauty of language. He refers frequently to the style of his compositions. He knew that it should be adapted to the subject, and his writings exhibit two styles, the one studied and even rhetorical (as in his first *Epistle*, on the woman struck seven times by the sword of the executioner), the other simple and straightforward as in his commentaries. In such works, as he remarks in a letter to Damasus, the meaning is more important than the language, though, even so, he excuses his inability to polish what he had written, as the weakness of his eyes made it necessary for him to dictate.[1]

It must be observed here that his works were intended to be of use to his contemporaries, and therefore use words in the sense familiar in his time. Error sometimes arises when this fact is overlooked. Thus *plerique* means 'many'; *satis*, 'exceedingly', as in 'Exulta satis, filia Sion' ('Rejoice exceedingly...'); *instrumentum* is the term often used of the Old and New Testaments.

Among the first labours undertaken by Jerome after his settlement in Palestine was the revision of the existing Latin version of the books of the Hebrew Canon. Its original had been the Septuagint, and Jerome was now able to make his revision with the aid of Origen's *Hexapla*. The greatest importance attaches to his second revision of the Psalms, which came to be known as the Gallican Psalter, either because this version first became popular in Gaul or, more probably, because it became widely known through manuscripts copied in that country. The need for it is stated in the preface to be because the Roman revision had already been disfigured by the fault of copyists and presented 'more of the old error than of the new emendation'. The text was provided with the critical signs used by Origen, showing what was present in the Greek but not in the Hebrew, and what had been added from the Hebrew in the version of Theodotion. The same practice was followed in the other books of the Bible that he revised. So powerful was the tenacity of custom in the very widely used Psalter that this version was never replaced by Jerome's later translation from the Hebrew, and thus it came to have a permanent place in the Latin bible. The revision did not follow the Greek slavishly, but occasionally corrected it by the Hebrew.

---

[1] *Ep.* 21. 42.

Other books published were Job, Chronicles, Proverbs, Ecclesiastes and the Song of Songs. Of these only the text of Job is extant, together with two prefaces, one to Chronicles and one to the 'Books of Solomon'. A request from Augustine for copies could not be met because 'through someone's deceit' a large part of the work had been lost.[1]

It is to be regretted that Jerome did not compose a formal treatise on the interpretation of Scripture. He has left us only scattered remarks on the subject, though these are numerous. In three places he lays it down that the Scriptures should be understood in three ways, justifying this principle by reference to the Septuagint version of Prov. xxii. 20 as a command to write the Scriptures in our hearts in a threefold manner. The triple interpretation is explained differently in the three passages, except that in each the literal sense is placed first. In two of them a connection is made with the threefold concept of man as body, soul and spirit, thus showing a dependence on Origen.

In the latest of these passages to be written, in the commentary on Ezekiel,[2] written between 410 and 414, the first sense is the literal, and ethical precepts from I Cor. x. 8–10 are given as examples. The second, or tropological, is illustrated by I Cor. ix. 9, where the ox is taken as a metaphor for the Christian preacher (though many would take the argument as being *a minore ad maius*). Of the third, 'the sublime and sacred way of understanding', the instance is Paul's interpretation of marriage as a mystery embodied in Christ and the Church. In spite of this repeated insistence on threefold exegesis, Schade could find only four examples of it in Jerome's works.[3] One is admittedly dubious, two are questionable and none fits the theoretical schemes. An instance, however, is to be found in *ep*. 21. 28, on the Prodigal Son. The son himself provides the literal sense of the parable; allegorically he is a figure of publicans and sinners; and according to the mystical sense the parable prophesies the future calling of the Gentiles.

In general the exegesis proposed is confined to two senses, the literal and the spiritual; and the scriptural basis of this division is the teaching of Paul that the letter kills but the spirit gives life (II Cor. iii. 6). The literal is also called the historical, this being the form in which it so frequently occurs. The spiritual sense also receives other names. It is called *anagoge* and *tropologia* but without any precise difference in

[1] *Ep*. 134. 2. [2] *PL*. 25, 147 CD.
[3] L. Schade, *Die Inspirationslehre des hl. Hieronymus* (Freiburg i.B., 1910), p. 109.

application. The former (literally 'elevation') is employed in the middle ages of texts which lead the soul up to the contemplation of celestial beatitude. By Jerome it is used of the ascent from a bare and strictly literal sense to an allegorical application (e.g. *PL.* 25. 164C). Similarly tropology, with the meaning of 'figure of speech' or 'trope', may be no more than a metaphor, as in *ep.* 129. 6, where the land flowing with milk and honey is explained as signifying 'abundance of all things'. But elsewhere, also by tropology, the same phrase is taken to refer to 'the church of Christ in which we as suckling children are reared by faith to be capable of taking solid food'.[1]

Jerome says that 'each of these senses requires the other'. This is in connection with the two doors of the Temple (Ezek. xli. 23) 'which are the means of showing forth the mysteries of both Instruments', that is, Testaments.[2] But he insists that the spiritual sense must be founded on the literal.[3] They both 'run on the same lines'; that is, the spiritual must develop naturally out of the literal.[4] Still, he allows that, though the literal sense gives the exegete no liberty, 'tropology is free and is limited only by these laws, that it must be a pious meaning keeping close to the language of the context and must not violently conjoin really disparate matters'.[5] The justification for this search for higher meanings seems to be that all Scripture is intended for our religious instruction, for which some passages do not appear to be well adapted; and that, as Scripture gives us 'divine utterances', they must reflect the wisdom of Almighty God and be full of deep and hidden mysteries. But Jerome's attitude to these 'pious' developments certainly underwent a change in the course of his career. The first commentary he wrote was composed at Antioch about 375 on the prophet Obadiah. Of this he was later ashamed, and he wished it to be destroyed; and in fact we should have known nothing of it, had not its author asked pardon for it in the preface to his later work on the same book.[6] His 'mind was on fire with mystical knowledge', and he explained the book allegorically, taking no account of the literal sense. This was before the commencement of his Hebrew studies in the desert. He had started his career under the influence of the prevailing mentality and with a profound admiration for Origen, but this gradually changed. In the preface to Malachi,[7]

---

[1] *Com. in Jer.* 11. 5. [2] *PL.* 25, 404B. [3] *Ep.* 129. 6.
[4] *PL.* 25, 387A. [5] *PL.* 25, 1281D–1282A.
[6] *PL.* 25, 1097A. [7] *PL.* 25, 1543A.

written in 406, he writes that Origen was the author of three volumes on the prophet 'but he simply did not touch the literal sense, and, after his manner, was wholly engaged in allegorical interpretation'. And in Jerome's work on Jeremiah, his last and unfinished commentary, the spiritual interpretations are comparatively rare, and he several times speaks of Origen as 'doting' in his allegorical interpretations.

Concerning the 'typical' meaning of Scripture Jerome has left no doubt as to his mind, though of this subject too there is no express treatment. 'Everything', he says, 'that concerned Israel proceeded in image and shadow and type.'[1] Types are acted predictions. 'Let us follow the rule that all the prophets did much that was typical of our Lord...and whatever at the actual time happened concerning Jeremiah was a prophecy of the future concerning the Lord.'[2] These general expressions, however, were not meant to be pressed. 'A type indicates a part', and 'those who were partial types of our Lord are not to be thought to have done as types of him all that they are reported to have done.'

The difficulty experienced by the novice in Hebrew studies in the desert of Chalcis may well be imagined when we remember that the Hebrew texts at his disposal were all in manuscript and contained only the consonants; the vowel signs were invented after his time. There were, moreover, no dictionaries, no concordances, no grammars. Only those who already knew how words were pronounced could give expression to the characters. The pronunciation of words when once heard had to be stored in the memory. No wonder he speaks of the labour and difficulty: 'How often I despaired and how often I gave up and in my eagerness to learn started again.'[3] Clearly his initial lessons could not suffice. Before attempting work on Chronicles he obtained the help of a Doctor of the Law from Tiberias and with him went carefully through the whole book.[4] For Job, the most difficult book of the Old Testament, he secured at considerable expense as tutor a renowned Jew from Lydda.[5] What Jerome says of the help he received from this learned man has sometimes been misunderstood: 'whether I made progress under his tuition I do not know; this only I know, that I could not have translated what I had not previously understood.' This is only a modest way of saying that it must be left to others to

---

[1] *Ep.* 129. 8. [2] *Com. in Jer.* 11. 21–3. [3] *Ep.* 125. 12.
[4] *PL.* 29, 401 B. [5] *PL.* 28, 1081 A.

judge of the success achieved. One instructor is mentioned by name. This was Baranina, who for handsome payment, both at Jerusalem and at Bethlehem, made his visits by night like another Nicodemus.[1] The mastery Jerome achieved in the knowledge of the Hebrew vocabulary may be judged by a sentence written in 400.[2] Speaking of 'Rissah' he says that he can remember no occurrence of the word except in Num. xxxiii. 21—no help from a concordance, we must remember—and in a non-canonical book called 'Little Genesis', otherwise known as 'Jubilees'. And his memory had not betrayed him. In his turn Jerome had himself become a teacher, and to such good effect that Paula, Eustochium, and Blesilla used to sing the Psalms in Hebrew. As for the science of etymology, it was unknown in those days, and it is not surprising that Jerome in this matter was not more advanced than others of his age.

In his earlier period, before he became immersed in his study of the Hebrew Scriptures, Jerome acknowledged the canonicity of the books known as deuterocanonical. This name was first used in the sixteenth century by Sixtus Senensis and has since passed into common use in the Latin Church as a convenient label to cover Tobit, Judith, Wisdom, Ecclesiasticus, the two Books of Maccabees, Baruch, and the Greek parts of Esther and Daniel. It was not intended to denote an inferior degree of authority, but only as a recognition of the fact that the canonicity of these writings had not always met with universal consent in the Church. And the most notable dissident was the recluse of Bethlehem. He nowhere refers to his change of view or to the reason for it. But it is plausible to suggest that the implicit faith he came to give to the Hebrew text—'the Hebrew truth' (*Hebraica veritas*), as he commonly calls it— led to the opinion that where the true text was to be found, there also the true Canon was to be sought, which he thereupon adopted from the contemporary opinion of the Jewish rabbis. The change is to be dated from about 390, as most of his literary work can be dated with exact or approximate accuracy. As an example of his earlier attitude may be cited the commentary on the Epistle to the Galatians, where Mattathias is mentioned as spoken of in 'the treasury of the Scriptures';[3] his name occurs only in I Maccabees. Later, in the prologue to his version from the Hebrew of the Books of Samuel and Kings, he gives a list of the Hebrew books and then goes on to say that whatever is not in that

[1] *Ep.* 84. 3.   [2] *Ep.* 78. 20.   [3] *PL.* 26, 384 c.

catalogue is to be reckoned among apocryphal writings. He mentions by name Wisdom, the Book of Jesus the son of Sirach (Ecclesiasticus), Judith, Tobit, and Maccabees.[1] Elsewhere he speaks similarly of Baruch.[2] Various other passages could also be quoted.

This attitude was never abandoned. The reference to Baruch, just given, is found in the commentary on Jeremiah, the last to be undertaken. Yet these later years produced a number of expressions that speak in an opposite sense. The reader gains the impression that the lessons on the Canon which Jerome had learnt in his youth still exercised their influence, which caused them, perhaps almost unnoticed by the author, to find expression in the writings of his advanced years. Thus Judith is said to give her name to a 'sacred volume' (*ep.* 65. 1, which dates from 397). Ecclesiasticus is called 'holy Scripture' in the commentary on Isaiah, 408–10.[3] Wisdom is styled 'Scripture' in the last commentary, that on Jeremiah.[4] And these are only a small selection of the texts that could be mentioned.

In the case of the New Testament Jerome recognized as canonical all the writings so recognized today. He was too well-informed not to know that doubts existed both about the canonicity of the Epistle to the Hebrews and about its authorship. But he accepted it himself as having the testimony of tradition, following, he says, 'the authority of ancient writers'. He condemns Marcion and Basilides for rejecting it,[5] and speaks of it as 'Scripture'.[6] Many attributed the epistle to Barnabas or Clement, but, he writes, 'it is of no consequence whose it is' (*ep.* 129.3); that is, as the context shows, as regards the question of canonicity. He himself seems to favour Pauline origin understood in the sense that Paul's Hebrew script was rendered by another into eloquent Greek.[7]

The commentaries on the New Testament are few in number. Of the Gospels, only that of Matthew is treated, and of the epistles of Paul those to the Galatians, the Ephesians, Titus and Philemon. These commentaries were composed at the pressing request of friends, sometimes at least against the exegete's inclination. He tells Paula and Eustochium in the preface to Ephesians that they had forced him to undertake the work in spite of his unwillingness and reluctance.[8] This attitude may appear surprising, but it is readily intelligible in the

[1] *PL.* 28, 556 A.   [2] *PL.* 24, 680 A.
[3] *PL.* 24, 67 A.   [4] *PL.* 24, 798 D.   [5] *PL.* 26, 555 A.
[6] *PL.* 26, 578 C.   [7] *PL.* 23, 617 B–619 A.   [8] *PL.* 26, 440 A.

circumstances. Others could do useful work on the New Testament, but for the elucidation of the Old Jerome possessed unique qualifications and he must have felt that all his available time and energy would be most profitably devoted to that work. In fact with his many distracting duties he did not live to accomplish all he had hoped for. The commentary on Jeremiah was left incomplete and that projected on the Song of Songs was never written.[1] His especial interest and delight was in the prophetical literature, and we have his commentaries on the other three major, and the twelve minor, prophets. There is besides only the commentary on Ecclesiastes and short notes on most of the Psalms. The homilies on the Psalms are addresses given to his monks at Bethlehem and, suitably to their purpose, are devoid of erudition. They were intended to help his audience in the devout recitation or singing of the Psalter. They seem to have been written down as orally delivered. Their unstudied character may be judged by a remark in the course of the commentary on Psalm 88 (89): 'What I forgot to say at the beginning I will say now.'

The function of an exegete, Jerome writes, is 'to discuss what is obscure, to touch on the obvious, to dwell at length on what is doubtful'.[2] Elsewhere he says that the commentator should 'briefly and plainly elucidate what is obscure' and should so write that his own explanation of another's words does not itself need explanation.[3] But in the matter of brevity he is far from attaining his own ideal. But eloquence has no place in a commentary; on the contrary, it should be written in 'simple speech'.[4] In composing his work he acknowledges his use of earlier writers, as his purpose is not to give personal views of his own but the treasures of traditional wisdom. Much, however, is inevitably the fruit of his own study. He desired in particular to give the West the benefit of the learning and piety of the Greek writers who were not familiar to those of Latin speech. On difficult matters various opinions are recorded and at times the reader is left to his own judgement to decide which explanation is the best (e.g. *PL.* 24, 681 A).

In the works on the Old Testament erudition is naturally more in evidence. A Latin translation is given of the Hebrew original and also of the Septuagint Greek, which in Latin dress had so long been the text used in the West. There are frequent references to the versions of the

[1] *PL.* 26, 22 A. [2] *PL.* 26, 400 C. [3] *PL.* 25, 1118 B.
[4] *PL.* 26, 401 B.

later Greek translators, Aquila, Symmachus and Theodotion, and in many places he sets forth the views of learned Jews. Indeed, he says more than once that part of his purpose was to give to Latin ears the erudition of 'the masters of the synagogue'.[1]

This brief sketch would be sadly incomplete without a mention of the impelling motive that guided all this literary activity. Jerome had a natural ardour for study and learning, but he subordinated this to a higher supernatural zeal and devotion to the written Word of God. In his prefaces he manifests his reliance on the power of prayer to help him to write on the Scriptures in the same spirit as that in which they were written. That was his impelling motive; to make them better known and better understood.

In the present context, the name Septuagint may cover also its Latin derivative just as it did in the language of the times we are concerned with. It was the version Jerome learnt in his boyhood.[2] Even after his translation of the Psalms from the Hebrew it was in this version that he sang them with his community of monks; and, of course, it was the words they sang that he endeavoured to explain for their edification.[3] This illustrates both his wisdom in allowing for the force of custom and providing for the spiritual good of others, and also his respect for the words and phrases that had been used in the Church since the days of the apostles. And yet his attitude to the Version had necessarily undergone a change. In his youth it was universally held in the highest esteem as the vehicle of the word of God, an esteem heightened by the common belief that it had been inspired by the Holy Ghost. This belief was founded on the story that the seventy elders, separated in seventy cells, found at the conclusion of their task that all had produced identically the same translation. As his studies advanced Jerome learnt that this picturesque detail was an addition to the original account of Aristeas and of no authority.[4] Moreover, in the course of his revision of the Old Latin with an eye on the original Hebrew his attention was drawn more and more to the imperfections of the Greek texts. There was no codex that could be said to represent faithfully the authentic text of the Septuagint. Alexandria and Egypt used the recension of Hesychius, Constantinople and Antioch that of Lucian, and in the territory between these two the text held in honour was that of Origen's *Hexapla*.[5] Then

---

[1] *PL.* 25, 1455 D. [2] *PL.* 23, 448 A.
[3] *PL.* 28, 1326 B. [4] *PL.* 28, 150 A. [5] *PL.* 28, 1325 A.

besides this variety of recensions the text had not been kept pure but had become disfigured by the carelessness of copyists.[1] He thus became gradually convinced that no revision of the Old Latin could be entirely satisfactory and that greater benefit would accrue to the Church of God by an entirely new version direct from 'the Hebrew truth'. Some had been critical and even scandalized at his revision, which in their ignorance or prejudice they accused of falsifying the sacred text. Augustine, more enlightened, approved of the revision. But even he disapproved of the new venture of a translation from a language known in the Church (apart from some convert Jews) only to the translator.[2] He therefore tried to dissuade Jerome from continuing with the task and urged him to return to the work of revision.

Skill in translating is fostered by practice, and Jerome was no novice at the art when he commenced the arduous task of translating the Old Testament from the original Hebrew. His previous work of the kind had been from the Greek of Origen and Didymus but it had enabled him to form definite principles. These he set down in the letter 57 to Pammachius which he speaks of as a treatise 'On the best style of translating'. The desired ideal is fidelity to the sense without undue adherence to the words as such, for a translation must be true to the character of the language into which it is made, and this cannot be achieved by slavish reproduction of words. It is true that the principle of 'sense by sense and not word by word' is said not to apply to holy Scripture, 'where even the *ordo verborum* is a mystery'.[3] This does not mean the order of the words, but, by a usage attested elsewhere in Jerome's writings, something like 'the precise character of the words'. In the preface to Job the translation is said to follow at times the words, at times the sense, at times both at once,[4] though this statement is not altogether clear in meaning. Certainly Jerome often neglects the words when they represent mere repetition which would be alien to Latin taste. He even at times inserts words of his own for the sake of clarity, as in Gen. xxxi. 47, 'each according to the propriety of his own language'. And in the following verse he explains the name Galaad 'that is, the Witness Heap'. In places a neat Latin phrase has an ethos quite absent from the simplicity of the Hebrew, as 'if in silent thought thou answer' for 'if thou shouldst say in thy heart' (Deut. xviii. 21).

---

[1] *PL.* 28, 1323 B.   [2] *PL.* 22, 566.   [3] *Ep.* 57. 5.
[4] *PL.* 28, 1081 A.

Another characteristic that not only distinguishes Jerome's Latin style from that of the Hebrew but produces a very different literary impression is the unwillingness of the translator to repeat the use of the same word. For instance, in Gen. xv. 9 the Hebrew uses the same word three times to specify that the age of the heifer, the she-goat and the ram is three years, whereas the Latin has *triennis, trima, trium annorum*. Or again, in II Sam. vii. 13–16 the one Hebrew word meaning 'for ever' is rendered *in sempiternum, in aeternum, iugiter*. A marked feature of Jerome's style is the separation of nouns from their dependent genitives. Thus in Gen. xxiv. 32 where the Hebrew reads 'He gave straw and fodder for the camels and water to wash his feet and the feet of the men with him' the translation in all manuscripts but one has *dedit paleas et foenum et aquam ad lavandum pedes camelorum et virorum qui venerant cum eo*. This trick of style is responsible for the idea expressed by several writers that Jerome strangely thought it the practice to wash the feet of camels. This idiom does not tend to clarity. In the sentence 'The apostle commands women's heads to be veiled in churches on account of the angels' the order of the words in Latin is *velari capita in ecclesiis feminarum*.[1]

It might be thought that the Latin style of the version would make it difficult to recognize the wording of the underlying Hebrew. Actually, especially in the historical books, this is not so, once the characteristics of the translation are taken into account. And it is widely acknowledged that Jerome's Hebrew manuscripts were in close agreement with the recension in use today. Mistakes found in the one are found in the other. So the rather meaningless 'tribes' appears in II Sam. vii. 7, whereas the true reading 'judges' is preserved in the parallel passage in I Chron. xvii. 6. In the Pentateuch some remarks of Jerome show that his text agreed with extant manuscripts even in the matter of vowel letters (*matres lectionis*). He comments that in Gen. xxiii. 16 the name Ephron is first written with *wau*, and then a second time without it.[2] This is also the case in our own printed editions. He remarks, too, that in Exodus the word 'cherubim' is consistently written without *wau*, though in other books it occurs frequently with it.[3] So, again, we still find it. Differences of meaning do not necessarily demonstrate differences in the Hebrew texts. They may merely reflect different ways of vocalizing the same consonants. Thus, in Ps. 2: 9,

[1] *PL*. 26, 130B. [2] *PL*. 23, 973A. [3] *Ep*. 29. 6.

where the Massoretic vocalization gives 'Thou shalt crush them with a rod of iron', Jerome's version from the Hebrew has *pasces eos*, the verb being read as in Ps. 22 (23): 1, 'the Lord is my shepherd': a meaning that harmonizes badly with the 'rod of iron'. Again, the present Hebrew reading of Ps. 71 (72): 12 means 'he will rescue the poor man at his entreaty', wheareas Jerome, with the same consonants, renders it 'he will rescue the poor man from the mighty'.

All manuscripts when copied, and in particular when frequently copied, gradually deviate in some degree from the exact wording of the archetype, and the Latin translation under consideration has inevitably been no exception to the rule. For accurate textual work recourse must be had to critical editions if available, and the decisive factor must be sought in the evidence and not in the judgement of the editor. Here it is worth remarking that in some cases at least in the writings of Jerome it would never be possible to determine with certainty which of the variant readings was the one intended. Even if there were a codex extant which was known to have been copied at Bethlehem under the author's direction, we could not be sure that all its readings were correct. With his multifarious occupations he could not, as he himself says, check all the copies made;[1] and when he did himself revise, he would inevitably in places improve his own text. Thus two readings would be in circulation, both stemming from the author but without, it might well be, any sure criterion to distinguish the earlier from the later reading. At times—and this is important—other evidence besides that of the text itself must be taken into consideration.

A clear instance of this necessity is the well-known reading *ipsa* in Gen. iii. 15. Of this it may be asserted with confidence that it is not Jerome's own text, and that he wrote, or rather dictated, *ipse*. This is the reading of Ottobonianus (of the seventh or eighth century), one of the three principal textual witnesses. And in *Quaestiones Hebraicae in Genesim*, a work composed before the translation of the Pentateuch, we find the Old Latin quoted as 'ipse servabit', followed by the comment that the Hebrew, with 'ipse conteret', is superior. That the latter is the genuine reading adopted by Jerome in his version of Genesis is shown by a citation in Leo the Great, using 'conteret'. This is evidence that Leo depended on Jerome's text. As the subject of 'conteret' Leo has 'semen mulieris', and this ('The seed of the woman') shows that he

[1] *Ep.* 71. 5.

could not have found *ipsa* in the text.[1] It is of interest to note that
F. Drewniak[2] has shown that *ipsa* did not arise out of the application
of the text to the Blessed Virgin, and was not the origin of that
application.

Jerome had the oral assistance of Jewish teachers, and this is reflected
in the occasional agreement of his version with the Targum. He also
had the existing Greek versions, not only of the Septuagint but also of
Aquila, Symmachus and Theodotion. Aquila's may have been intended
as a 'running vocabulary'. It was of the most slavish character, rendering the Hebrew word for word without regard for the exigencies of the
Greek language. Aquila's work was thus of assistance in fixing the
meanings of words, and his influence can still be traced in the Latin
Version. It should also be mentioned that occasionally Jerome gives a
revised translation in his later commentaries as on Hosea xi. 8.[3] Thus
if it is claimed, and rightly claimed, that Jerome was the most successful
of the ancient translators, it is also true that he owed his success in part
to the advantage of having previous workers in the same field. Since
his time great progress has been made in the exact understanding of
Hebrew. The discovery and decipherment of ancient Semitic literatures,
as the Babylonian and Ugaritic, have thrown much light on the Bible,
and passages still obscure to Jerome can now be more accurately
comprehended and translated.

The name 'Vulgate' has been avoided in the foregoing pages, as
at the time of Jerome's activity the expression 'editio vulgata' meant
the Old Latin Version then commonly used in the West or, according to the context, the Septuagint from which it had been derived.
The name, of course, could not be transferred to the new translation
from the Hebrew till that had taken the place in general use previously
enjoyed by the Old Latin. The subsequent history of the Version
belongs, however, to another chapter. Here it suffices to say that it
did not receive the title of 'Vulgate' till the sixteenth century, though
long before that it had acquired the right to it. The 'textus vulgatus'
spoken of in the thirteenth century was the particular recension drawn
up in the University of Paris and received with wide favour.

The Vulgate, as we now know it, contains Jerome's translation of

---

[1] *PL.* 54, 194A.
[2] *Die mariologische Deutung von Gen. 3: 15 in der Väterzeit* (1934).
[3] *PL.* 25, 919BC.

the Hebrew books of the Old Testament Canon, with the exception of the Psalms; of the Hebrew and Aramaic of Esdras and Daniel, as also of the Greek parts of the latter and Esther; and his translation from Aramaic of Tobit and Judith. The Psalms are those of the Gallican Psalter. And the remaining books, Wisdom, Ecclesiasticus, the two Books of Maccabees and Baruch, are in the Old Latin Version. These were neither translated nor revised by Jerome. The New Testament is in the form revised by him.

Besides much biblical exegesis in his letters, there are three books that must be introduced to the reader. The first is the *Liber de Nominibus Hebraicis*. Inspired by earlier work by Philo and Origen, Jerome collected all the proper names of both Testaments and assigned to each its traditional meaning. Some of these traditional etymological explanations he sets down with a protest as doing violence to the names ('violentum'). But a good knowledge of Hebrew does not necessarily imply an understanding of the science of etymology, which had not then been born. The main interest of the book is consequently for the history of exegesis, as these interpretations long remained in favour.

The second, *Liber de Situ et Nominibus Locorum Hebraicorum*, is a gazetteer of the towns, mountains, rivers, and other geographical names occurring in the Bible. As the preface informs the reader, it is a translation of a work by Eusebius of Caesarea, for whom Jerome had a high esteem. He made some few changes and additions. This work is not disfigured by etymologies.

The third is the *Liber Hebraicorum Quaestionum in Genesim*. All three were in hand at the same time and date from about 389–92. This one, on selected passages of Genesis, was of a character till then completely unknown. It was meant to be the first of a series, but the continuation seems to have been abandoned. The purpose was to correct erroneous opinions about the Hebrew books, and mistakes in the Latin and Greek codices. As the popular etymologies in the Hebrew bible lose their point in translations, these also are explained, as, for example, the name of Cain in Gen. iv. 1. The probable explanation of its discontinuance is that this plan was overtaken by the decision to produce a translation of the whole Hebrew bible.

The lifelong labours of Jerome all bear witness to his ardent devotion to Holy Scripture. For him 'knowledge of the Scriptures' means 'the riches of Christ' and 'ignorance of the Scriptures is ignorance of Christ'.[1] Hence his exhortations to his correspondents: 'I beg you, dear brother, live with them, meditate on them, make them the sole object of your knowledge and inquiries.'[2] And to a priest: 'Frequently read the divine Scriptures; rather, never let the sacred text out of your hands. Learn what you have to teach. . . The speech of a priest should be seasoned with the words of Scripture.'[3] 'Make knowledge of the Scriptures your love and you will not love the vices of the flesh' (*ep.* 125. 11). And in the explanation of the Scriptures, he reminds his readers, we always stand in need of the Spirit of God.[4]

[1] *PL.* 23, 936A and 24, 17B. [2] *Ep.* 53. 10.
[3] *Ep.* 52. 7 f. [4] *PL.* 25, 1159B.

CHAPTER V

THE MEDIEVAL HISTORY OF THE LATIN VULGATE*

In a letter written to Jerome in 403, Augustine mentioned that in Eoa (Tripoli) a bishop had caused a disturbance, and had nearly lost his flock, through reading a lesson from Jonah in Jerome's new Latin version. Jerome replied that the trouble was doubtless due to his improved rendering of the Hebrew *qiqqayon* (*gourd*), for which he had replaced the earlier *cucurbita* by *hedera*, itself admittedly not a perfect rendering.[1] The incident is a fair example of perhaps the most formidable kind of opposition against which any revised or new translation of the Scriptures may have to struggle: if the student is to appreciate adequately the forces at play, it is essential for him to gain some insight into the minds of the laity as well as the scholars and theologians ranged for or against innovation. As for the case in point, we may remind ourselves of the widespread recognition in Jonah and his experiences of a type of Christ,[2] and there are plentiful examples from the second century onwards of Jonah's frequent representation in early Christian iconography. These reflect the strength of the popular notion of the plant that shaded Jonah as a *gourd*, a notion too sturdy to give way before Jerome's proposed *ivy*—a point with which Rufinus, in castigating Jerome, makes sarcastic play. With one doubtful exception, the surviving monuments will have none of the ivy, *tout simple*; they show either the plain gourd, or compromise with a hybrid invention exhibiting features of both gourd and ivy.[3]

* For abbreviations, etc., see the bibliography below, p. 511 ff. For *sigla* indicating manuscripts of the Vulgate see the introductory portions of *Biblia Sacra* and *Novum Testamentum* there cited.

[1] *Ep. Hieronymi* 104, 112; *C.S.E.L.* 55 (ed. I. Hilberg), pp. 241, ll. 3, 392, *P.L.* 22, 833, §5, 930; *In Jon.* 4, 6; *P.L.* 25, 1148B.

[2] See, e.g., Hilary, *In Ps.* 69 (68), §5, *P.L.* 9, 473 A; Jerome, *Ep.* 53, §8; *C.S.E.L.* 54, p. 458, l. 10, *P.L.* 22, 546 below.

[3] Rufinus, *Apologia* II, §35, *P.L.* 21, 614A. H. Leclercq, art. 'Jonas' in *Dictionnaire d'Archéologie chrétienne et de Liturgie*, VII, col. 2574 below, 2593 f., quoting *in extenso* from

Fig. 1

HISTORY OF THE VULGATE TEXT
TO THE RENAISSANCE

(see *caveat*, below, p. 112)

Symbols as used in the Oxford edition of the New Testament and the Rome (Benedictine) edition of the Old Testament (in brackets following N.T. symbol where applicable). Main families shown in large Greek majuscules. For Π, see Quentin, pp. 353 f.; Ψ, Γ, pp. 361 f., 384; Berger (3), pp. 137 f.; Lowe, III, no. 383; Ω, below, p. 145; Λ, Δ, Fischer (3), pp. 8–9. Bracketed numbers as follows:

(1) Benevento, MS B.M. Add. 5463. See Berger (3), p. 91.
(2) See below, p. 134 n. 3.
(3) Below, p. 135 n. 7.
(4) Below, p. 141 n. 1; see Fischer (1), p. 10 on MSS St Gall 6, 7, etc.
(5) See below, p. 134 n. 2.
(6) Below, pp. 143–4.
(7) MS B.M. Royal I A xviii. See Glunz (2), p. xvi.
(8) E.g. MS Copenhagen, Royal Library Gl. Kgl. s. 10; see Glunz (2), p. xvi.
(9) Below, p. 146 n. 3.
(10) Below, p. 150 n. 2.
(11) Below, p. 145 nn. 2, 3.
(12) See C. Lindberg, MS Bodley 959, 1959, p. 19 (Acta Universitatis Stockholmiensis, VI).

The diagram here presented is modified from that of Glunz (1), facing p. 177; cf. Quentin, p. 352, and Glunz's own remarks (2), p. 2. Recent students have been critical of Glunz's findings, which ought to be viewed with circumspection unless checked from the MSS and from the conclusions of Berger, De Bruyne, Quentin, etc. Ayuso in his various studies greatly exaggerates the influence of the Spanish Latin bible beyond the Iberian peninsula. Fischer (4), p. [15] f., emphasizes the role of Italy as the centre of textual diffusion, the best texts coming from Italy and southern Gaul. Spanish texts are Italian-based, and exercised a limited external influence, in France only. Insular influence cannot be established for the early stages of Vulgate history; for most books of the Old Testament there are no Irish MSS and for the New Testament few apart from the Gospels. No early MS written outside Ireland and imported there has survived.

I am grateful to Messrs Tauchnitz of Leipzig, publishers of the late Dr Glunz's *Britannien und Bibeltext*, for permission to use his diagram; but should make it clear that the introduction of substantial changes by me gives the diagram here printed an independence of the original.

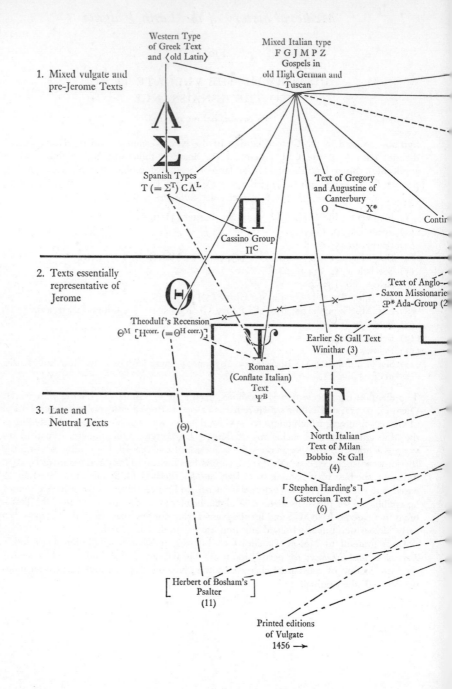

1. Mixed vulgate and pre-Jerome Texts

Western Type
of Greek Text
and ⟨old Latin⟩

Mixed Italian type
F G J M P Z
Gospels in
old High German and
Tuscan

Λ
Σ

Spanish Types
T (= Σ^T) C Λ^L

Text of Gregory
and Augustine of
Canterbury
O   X*

Contir

Π

Cassino Group
Π^C

2. Texts essentially representative of Jerome

Θ

Text of Anglo-
Saxon Missionarie
℘* Ada-Group (2

Theodulf's Recension
Θ^M ⌈H^corr. (=Θ^H corr.)⌉

Ψ

Earlier St Gall Text
Winithar (3)

Roman
(Conflate Italian)
Text
Ψ^B

Γ

3. Late and Neutral Texts

(Θ).

North Italian
Text of Milan
Bobbio St Gall
(4)

⌈ Stephen Harding's ⌉
⌊ Cistercian Text ⌋
(6)

⌈ Herbert of Bosham's ⌉
Psalter
(11)

Printed editions
of Vulgate
1456 ⟶

Fig. 1

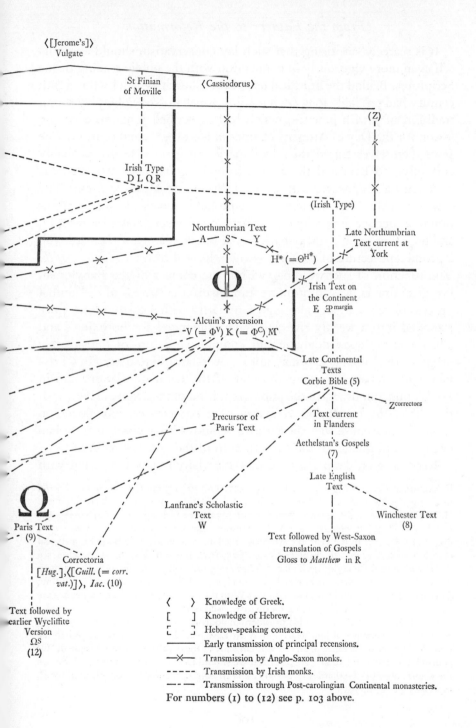

⟨[Jerome's]⟩
Vulgate

St Finian
of Moville

⟨Cassiodorus⟩

(Z)

Irish Type
D L Q R

(Irish Type)

Northumbrian Text
A— S— Y

Late Northumbrian
Text current at
York

H* (=Θ^H*)

Φ

Irish Text on
the Continent
E ⅌^margin

'Alcuin's recension
V (= Φ^V) K (= Φ^C) M'

Late Continental
Texts
Corbie Bible (5)

Z^correctors

Precursor of
Paris Text

Text current
in Flanders

Aethelstan's Gospels
(7)

Late English
Text

Ω

Lanfranc's Scholastic
Text
W

Winchester Text
(8)

Paris Text
(9)

Text followed by West-Saxon
translation of Gospels
Gloss to *Matthew* in R

Correctoria
[*Hug.*],⟨[*Guill.* (= *corr.*
vat.)]⟩, *Iac.* (10)

Text followed by
earlier Wycliffite
Version
Ω^s
(12)

⟨   ⟩   Knowledge of Greek.

[   ]   Knowledge of Hebrew.

⌐   ⌐   Hebrew-speaking contacts.

———   Early transmission of principal recensions.

—×—   Transmission by Anglo-Saxon monks.

- - - -   Transmission by Irish monks.

— — —   Transmission through Post-carolingian Continental monasteries.

For numbers (1) to (12) see p. 103 above.

It is scarcely surprising that such lay conservatism should assert itself even more vigorously in connection with the public reading of the Scriptures. Behind the liturgical use of the Church, which by the eighth century had probably long been reading Jonah in November, lay a long tradition of Jewish practice, which had prescribed Jonah as a proper lesson for the Day of Atonement since at least the second century. The Jews themselves traced their lectionary—in general terms, probably correctly—to Ezra and the return from Babylon, and attributed the pentateuchal lectionary, with poetic intuition, to Moses himself.[1] The Jewish weekly sabbath readings were probably themselves a generalization of a practice originally customary on a few special occasions only, and they thus point the way back to the Babylonian New Year festival, a prominent feature of which was the rehearsal of the *Creation Myth*. The function of such reading, within the context of the Babylonian liturgical drama, was to promote and ensure the success of the annual process of renewal: and although familiarity with a custom long since extended into a weekly rite will have obliterated for both Jews and Christians the quasi-dramatic and compulsive nature of the possible origin of the lectionary, it may not be over-fanciful to descry in Christian conservatism regarding the text of the Latin translation, and in Jewish punctiliousness in the public rendition of the original Hebrew of the Bible, the inarticulate *residuum* of a concern lest any deviation should compromise the efficacy of a religious act whose purpose had once been to guarantee the perpetuation of the order of nature.[2]

Resistance on the part of the Christian laity to any tampering with

E. Michon in *Revue Biblique*, n.s. XII (1915), 527. The *Atlas of the Early Christian World*, by F. van der Meer and C. Mohrmann (English translation, 1958, by M. F. Hedlund and H. H. Rowley), contains several specimens of Jonah; see plates 90, 107–8, 167, 579–80.

[1] For the Church, see Ordo xiii A, M. Andrieu, *Les Ordines Romani du haut moyen âge*, II (1948), 485. In the year 385 Ambrose read and expounded the book on a special occasion, including the 4th chapter; *Ep.* 20, §25, *P.L.* 16, 1001. For the Synagogue, see the *Baraitha* in the Babylonian Talmud *Megillah* 31 a; Nehemiah viii. 1–8, Babylonian Talmud *Babha Qamma* 82 a; Mishnah *Megillah*, iii, end; Jerusalem Talmud *Megillah* iv, § 1 (f. 75 a); cf. *Sifrey* on Deut. xvi. 1 § 127. (With the exception of the last, these texts are all available in English, French, or German translations.)

[2] S. H. Hooke, at the end of his presidential address to the Folk-Lore Society, 1937, reports the experience of Jane Harrison at an Easter celebration in Greece. When she remarked on the exuberance of an old woman's joy at the occasion, the latter replied, 'Of course I am happy; if Christ were not risen we should have no harvest this year'. See on the whole subject B. Gerhardsson, *Memory and Manuscript*, 2nd ed. (Copenhagen, 1964), especially pp. 67 f., 165 f.

the biblical text in the setting of the *cultus* was reinforced by a pervasive linguistic factor operative throughout the churches of the West. During the first four Christian centuries the Latin-speaking Christian community had forged its Latinity into an instrument adjusted to all aspects of its activity as an *Ideengemeinschaft*, domestic no less than ceremonial and public; and it was the interaction of this Christian Latin tradition with the norms identifiable in the writings of the greatest non-Christian authors that was to produce the successive renascences within western Christendom that culminated in the fifteenth-century Renaissance. The lexical innovations of Jerome's revised translation were to contribute to this christianized Latin, but the essential foundations had been laid before Jerome's time and remained, on the whole, impervious to neologistic interference. The extent to which the emergent Romance languages (both in the form spoken by Christians and in the Judaeo-Romance dialects) reflect the vocabulary of the Old Latin bible is evidence of its continued popularity as against what is now called the Vulgate; and the naturalization of the older biblical vocabulary in its various new linguistic settings reinforced such reluctance as already existed towards the adoption of the new version.[1]

As regards ecclesiastical leadership, although we may suppose that the theological climate in which scriptural innovation was received would be conditioned by sensitivity towards any attempt to saddle heretical notions on to the wording of Holy Writ, such hesitancy may be here discounted on account of Jerome's own staunch orthodoxy and attitude towards Arianism. A more potent cause for dissatisfaction with change was the fact that, as regards the Old Testament, the Septuagint (and along with it, its largely dependent early Latin versions) had come to be accepted as the bible of the Church, with a supposed miracle accompanying its production to guarantee its quality of verbal inspiration. It was for this reason that Augustine,[2] who

[1] On the whole subject see C. Mohrmann's numerous studies, especially (1). For the influence of the Old Latin bible on the Romance languages see J. Schrijnen, 'Le Latin chrétien devenue langue commune', in *Collectanea Schrijnen* (Nijmegen–Utrecht, 1939), pp. 335 f. (=*Revue des Études Latines*, XII, 1934, 96 f.); D. S. Blondheim, *Les Parlers Judéo-Romans et la Vetus Latina* (Paris, 1925); H. F. Muller, *A Chronology of Vulgar Latin*, Beiheft 78 of *Zeitschrift für Romanische Philologie* (Halle, 1929), esp. pp. 169 f.

[2] For Augustine's view of the inspiration of the Septuagint, see *Civ. Dei* XVIII, 43, *C.S.E.L.* 40, ii, p. 337, *P.L.* 41, 604; further references in Index to Augustine, *P.L.* 46, 602, *s.v. Septuaginta*. Augustine's scriptural quotations are assembled by Bonnardière, but not with textual questions primarily in view. For Augustine's own alleged revision,

may have revised at least parts of both Testaments in order to improve the fidelity of the Latin to the Greek, its clarity, and its latinity (in that order of priority), criticized Jerome for basing himself on the Hebrew instead of what had long been known as the *editio vulgata*—a name that Jerome's own version was not to usurp for a number of centuries, perhaps not until after the thirteenth (see also p. 99), whilst the prestige enjoyed by the old version was to be inherited by the new one no more quickly. It was not until the Council of Trent that the seal was set on the process, and Jerome's version declared a repository of orthodox Christian biblical doctrine, irrespective of any merits that it might possess as a translation *vis-à-vis* the original texts and the Renaissance Latin versions that were, by the sixteenth century, challenging its accuracy.[1]

In any case, it is necessary to remind ourselves that we ought not to speak too glibly of 'Jerome's' translation. It is certain that some books (e.g. Job and the Minor Prophets) owe their revision for the 'Vulgate' to Jerome personally; others were taken over by him unchanged from the Old Latin (p. 100). Thus the Vulgate form of at least the Catholic and Pauline epistles—perhaps of all the New Testament other than the Gospels—derives from an unknown editor, working at Rome, not later than the last decade of the fourth century. (See Frede (2), pp. 34* f.) The earliest manuscript of the Vulgate Gospels, from the first half of the fifth century, possibly contemporary with Jerome himself, is St Gall 1395 (Turner; *C.L.A.* 984; Fischer (4), p. [15]). A further important point is the fact that pandects (one-volume bibles of the kind produced by Cassiodorus or like the surviving *Codex Amiatinus*, see below, pp. 116 f.) were very rare exceptions. The Bible normally circu-

De Bruyne (2), especially pp. 521 f., 567 f., 576, 602, 605, 606; the subsequent influence of this revision in Spain, e.g. on the Mozarabic Psalter, is considered, but De Bruyne overestimated Augustine's textual activity: see Frede (2), p. 35*, above. For Augustine's criticism of Jerome's reversion to the Hebrew bible, *Ep.* 71, ii, §4; *C.S.E.L.* 34 (ed. A. Goldbacher), p. 252; *P.L.* 33, 242. His appreciation of Jerome's Vulgate, called by him *Itala*, *de Doctrina Christiana*, II, 22 (chap. xv), *P.L.* 34, 46; see Burkitt, pp. 57 f., 64.

1 Cassiodorus' *Institutiones* (*post* 511) illustrate the incipient communication to Jerome's (hexaplaric) text of the mystical prestige of the Greek: I, xv, §5, ed. Mynors, p. 44, *P.L.* 70, 1127 C (*corrumpi nequeunt quae inspirante Domino dicta noscuntur*); also §9, p. 46, ll. 19 f., *P.L.* 1128 *infra*, §11, p. 47, *P.L.* 1129 B; Fischer (2), p. 62. In 1267 Roger Bacon could write *exemplari vulgato, quod est Parisiense* (*Opus Tertium*, ed. Brewer, p. 92), but he also uses the term *Vulgata* (if obliquely) of pre-Jerome versions: *Opus Minus*, pp. 341 f. See also E. F. Sutcliffe, 'The Name "Vulgate"', *Biblica*, Rome, XXIX (1948), 345 f.

lated in smaller codices containing a single book or more often a group (Gospels, Octateuch, etc.); and when one-volume bibles were produced, sub-units of heterogeneous provenance would be used as prototypes. (The early-ninth-century St Germain Bible (G) is exceptional in reflecting, comparatively faithfully, a north Italian one-volume bible of the seventh century. The fact that Bede and others single out for mention the one-volume bible brought with other books by Benedict Biscop and Ceolfrid from Rome to Jarrow, indicates how rare a pandect of the Bible was considered to be (Fischer, pp. 37, 42 f., (2), 66, 77).) Since the pandects themselves were generally intended for reference purposes at an important centre, they would again be copied piecemeal by those interested in individual biblical books of importance to their own concerns.

Thus in the centuries following Jerome's death, the spread of both the new version and the Old Latin remained ungoverned by self-conscious consistency or the canons of responsible textual criticism. The primary task of the missionaries who first carried abroad knowledge of the Bible in Latin was the inculcation of a practical ethic allied to a Christian faith, and the type of text upon which they based their preaching was a matter of accident. Heterogeneous interpolations would be included to meet the requirements of the immediate situation, and the text thus modified would become perpetuated as it was diffused in the course of missionary activity. That this procedure was as respectable in the study as in the field is shown by Gregory the Great. In his *Moralia in Job*, complete late in the sixth century, he stated explicitly that he would use Jerome's text as his basis, but would not hesitate to adopt the Old Latin wherever it lent itself better to his own emphasis on moral and ascetic interpretation. Thus, in order to stress the ever-contemporary relevance of the Incarnation, he prefers at Luke ii. 11 the Old Latin *natus est nobis hodie salvator* against Jerome's *vobis* (Vulgate manuscripts X* Y G D^c W have preserved *nobis*). Similarly in Luke xv. 7, when elaborating the spiritual discipline necessary to achieve penitence, Gregory follows the older *peccatore poenitentiam agente* against Jerome's *habente* (Z I X* 𝔉 𝔓 E R *agente*).[1] One is reminded of the rabbinic device of revocalizing a word in the Hebrew text ('read it not as *HaLiKhoth* but as *HaLaKhoth*') in order to justify some essay into

[1] See Glunz (2), pp. 5 f., 11 f., 17; *P.L.* 75, 516; 76, 1104, 1248. For dogmatic sources of corruption in the Vulgate see Berger (3), p. viii.

allegorical or moral exegesis—except that rabbinic exegesis was meant for a Jewish public that was at least superficially familiar with its own Bible, and a body of tradition regarding the 'literal' meaning was already in existence.[1]

By the time of Jerome's death in 420 the controversy that his revision had stimulated was beginning to wane. By the year 404 Augustine had been quoting the Gospels in Jerome's version whilst adhering to the older one for Acts,[2] and by *c.* 406 Pelagius was using the Vulgate text of Paul. By the seventh century the new version was on the way to winning domination, and during the four centuries that followed Jerome's death a situation emerged controlled by three factors. The first is the importance of Italy and its adjunct, southern Gaul, for the dissemination of the Latin bible and of good texts of it. Secondly, there was the pull of liturgical tradition, at least as far as the more familiar biblical texts were concerned; and thirdly some tendency towards local homogeneity. As ecclesiastical centres in certain areas grew in importance, waves of missionary activity might carry a text-form, stamped with the marks of the earliest preaching of Christianity in the province concerned, beyond the natural or politically probable frontiers of its currency. The classic example of this process is the introduction of a south Italian text-type into Northumbria by Ceolfrid and Benedict Biscop (see below, p. 117). From Wearmouth and Jarrow, where Irish texts were also current, texts carried by missionaries to Gaul, Switzerland, and Germany both transmitted to the Continent in the ninth century Alcuin's Northumbrian-based bible, and also reinforced the Irish tinge that was independently being injected into texts of other parentage produced in Europe (see below, pp. 130 f.). But the Northumbrian instance is exceptional, and ought not to be generalized to a degree that would obscure the central significance of Italy as a disseminator of texts.[3]

As regards the pull of liturgical conservatism, distinction must be drawn between the various parts of the Bible, according to the extent to which they were familiar at a popular level (that is, in the New Testament, between the Gospels and the remainder). The Old Testa-

---

[1] See, for this device, *Encyclopaedia Judaica*, II, 74 f. (N. H. Torczyner).
[2] See Augustine, *Acta contra Felicem*, *C.S.E.L.* 25 (ed. J. Zycha), pp. 801 f., *P.L.* 42, 519; Burkitt, pp. 57 f.
[3] On all this see Frede (1), pp. 11 f.; Fischer (4), pp. [15 f.], [53 f.], (2), p. 77.

ment, with the exception of the Psalter, had never been a people's book in western Christendom before Jerome,[1] except among a few Christians of immediate Jewish antecedents. The history of the Psalter is instructive. Jerome's final revision *iuxta hebraicam veritatem* (above, pp. 84 and 88) never won popularity at all; his second, the so-called Gallican Psalter, early achieved a wide currency in Gaul, particularly through the influence of Gregory of Tours at the end of the sixth century. Its present wide acceptance may possibly be connected with the diffusion of the New Hymnary that ousted the old Benedictine Hymnary not long after the reign of Charlemagne; but the earlier ascendancy of the 'Roman' Psalter that is attached to Jerome's name, but which is in fact an earlier Latin version, was maintained throughout Italy until the pontificate of Pius V (1566–72).[2] This Roman psalter-text had itself begotten several others, connected with Italy, Gaul, Spain, and England, one of them (the so-called Verona Psalter) corresponding with the quotations of Augustine from the Psalms and being a partially retouched Italian text. (The oldest Latin psalter current in North Africa, as used by Tertullian and Cyprian, has disappeared, but it underlies the Cassino Psalter (MS Cas. 557) edited by A. Amelli in *Collectanea Biblica Latina*, I, Rome, 1912.)[3] This process is not peculiar to the Psalter. It ought therefore to be clear that isolated manuscripts are to be expected which, although produced in an ecclesiastical environment that had evolved a substantially stabilized text of its own, nevertheless show (in part or *in toto*) an alien text, recognizable as such from the inclusion of some significant particular. One obvious touchstone is the form of Hebrew names, the sometimes surprising Greek shapes of which were retained in the Old Latin bible but brought into line with the Hebrew original by Jerome (e.g. *Ambacum* for *Habacuc*). The presence of identifiable particularities will point to movements of some interest— the migration of historically well-known figures within the Western Church, or the temporary resort of more shadowy ones to sit at their feet.

As a result of advances in palaeographical knowledge, and greatly

---

[1] Berger (3), p. 3.

[2] Walafrid Strabo, *de rebus ecclesiasticis*, §25; *P.L.* 114, 957 A.

[3] Weber, p. viii, referring to A. Vaccari, *Filologia Biblica e Patristica* (*Scritti di erudizione e di filologia*, I, Rome, 1952), chap. x, pp. 207–55, especially p. 208. For the Cassino Psalter, see B. Capelle, *Revue Bénédictine*, Maredsous, XXXII (1920), 113–31.

improved modern techniques of facsimile reproduction and other mechanical aids—together with a greater appreciation of the necessity for team-work in the scientific reconstruction of the history of the Latin bible—many of the findings of the pioneers of Vulgate scholarship in the late nineteenth and early twentieth century are now being subjected to a fresh examination that sometimes clearly leads to quite new conclusions. This is largely due to the scholarship of the two great Benedictine institutions, in Rome and in Beuron, Germany, concerned with the critical publication of the Vulgate and with the recovery of the Old Latin bible text. Earlier schemes must be regarded as of tentative and questionable value. While, therefore, it may be provisionally claimed that Jerome's Vulgate reached the ninth century along a twofold or threefold line of transmission based on broad geographical generalizations, this must not be allowed to obscure the supremacy of Italy as a centre of diffusion. Her dominating role is indicated decisively by a statistical analysis of the provenance and distribution of all known surviving manuscripts of the Latin bible earlier than 800.[1] And because of the constant tendency towards textual admixture (see above, p. 110), the attempt to construct diagrammatic genealogies ought to be acknowledged as artificial and of doubtful historicity. (See Fig. 1, pp. 104–5.)

With this reservation, it may be said that whereas on the whole Italy adopted Jerome's bible, North Africa long clung to the Old Latin, whose progressively Europeanized vocabulary had culminated in the text of the Vulgate itself. One example is the Johannine epistles, which in the fifth and sixth centuries were circulating in the West in a form (frequently used by Augustine) of advanced Europeanization, distinctive features being, for example, the use of *saeculum* for κόσμος (I. ii. 2, Vulgate *mundi*) and *palam fieri* for φανεροῦσθαι (I. i. 2, Vulgate *manifestata est*). Because of its popular diffusion, this text sometimes contaminated the true Vulgate, especially in Spanish manuscripts.[2] Of the Insular texts, those from Ireland show a conflation of Jerome with the Old Latin (below, pp. 131 f.); England, apart from the popularity of the *Psalterium Romanum*, shows remarkably little of the Old Latin bible. Spanish texts take Jerome as their base but are characterized by the inclusion of many doublets, glosses, and legendary accretions. The

---

[1] Fischer (4), pp. [53 f.].

[2] H. von Soden, *Das Lateinische Neu Testament in Afrika zur Zeit Cyprians* (Leipzig, 1909), p. 354; Thiele, pp. 10, 38, 42.

tendency towards conflation was particularly great in the case of the New Testament, since here the differences between Jerome and the Old Latin are much slighter than in the Old Testament. In Gaul, the Old Latin New Testament tended to survive alongside Jerome's Old Testament, the usage of Avitus of Vienne (*d.* 515) being here instructive. Southern Gaul was, however, in constant touch with the basic text as evolving in Italy, though Gaul's role as the alleged early meeting-ground *par excellence* for Insular and Spanish text-types has been unduly stressed; but from the tenth century the reaction of the two set in.[1] Germany, where the influence of the Carolingian renaissance was greatest, constituted the true point of confluence of biblical texts, mainly from Italy, but also from France, Ireland, England, and Spain.

These broad classifications may be elaborated slightly into the following sevenfold analysis of texts current down to the ninth century (i.e. prior to the recensions of Alcuin and Theodulf). Some of the more important manuscript testimony is here shown in each case, together with the *sigla* by which it is indicated in the critical editions and scholarly literature.[2]

(i) EARLY ITALIAN TEXTS: *Codex Fuldensis* (New Testament F), Milan (M) and Harley (Z) Gospels.

(ii) EARLY SPANISH TEXTS: Ashburnham Pentateuch (G), *Codex Cavensis* (C), Toledo Codex (T in New Testament, Σ^T in Old Testament).

(iii) ANGLO-SAXON TEXTS:
   (*a*) Pure Italian Text (of Gospels) in Northumbria: *Codex Amiatinus* (A), in part, Lindisfarne Gospels (Y).
   (*b*) Mixed Italian Text at Canterbury: 'St Augustine's' Gospels (O).

(iv) IRISH TEXTS:
   (*a*) Produced in Ireland: Book of Armagh (D in New Testament), Rushworth Gospels (R).
   (*b*) Written on the Continent: Echternach Gospels, margin ($\mathrm{E}^{marg.}$).

(v) LANGUEDOC TEXTS: *Codex Colbertinus* (c) (with Gospels in Old Latin).

---

[1] See on all this Berger (3), p. 2, and Fischer (4), p. [54], correcting Berger.
[2] After White, following Berger (3); Kenyon, p. 246, following Wordsworth and White, arranges slightly differently.

(vi) OTHER GALLIC PRE-ALCUIN AND PRE-THEODULF TEXTS: (Limoges, Fleury, Chartres, Tours, etc.) Corbie Psalter (M).

(vii) SWISS TEXTS (ESPECIALLY ST GALL): Codices partly written by Winithar of St Gall (S).

It is necessary to emphasize that the categories here postulated are far from watertight. For example, an elaborate collation of eight separate chapters of the Octateuch has listed ninety-one readings which may be taken as significant for type-classification because they are unaffected by any tendentious factors. Concerning eighteen of these, a group of eight major Spanish codices (C Σ^T(T) X Λ^L B Σ^M Σ^O and manuscript 2 of the Madrid Academy of History) are in agreement (e.g. *famulis*, not *famulabus* in Exod. ii. 5): but they are also in accord with members of other groups. It is the variants reflecting the revisions of Alcuin and Theodulf that serve to set manuscripts clearly apart from the remainder. Again, a group of Cassino manuscripts ranging in date from the tenth to the fifteenth centuries show distinct affinities with the Spanish family and are derived, *via* an intermediary, from the *Codex Cavensis* (C).[1] In general, however, it should be borne in mind that the affiliation of manuscripts of the Latin bible has hitherto been determined too much by factors external to the text itself, for example format, decoration, and above all headings and introductory matter.[2] The authorship of the numerous prefaces composed for the various books may sometimes be established, and sundry fixed points in history and in geography thereby achieved. From the *minutiae* of textual variation associated with the inclusion or omission of certain prefaces it was regarded as possible, with a greater or less degree of certainty, to reconstruct the pedigrees. In recent decades, however, greater attention has been paid to the text itself and to its concordance with what the writings of the Latin Church

[1] Quentin, pp. 235 f., 298 f., 353 f., 360. For the Spanish connections of 'Italian' manuscripts deriving ultimately from Rome (rather than Milan, as Berger had thought), see pp. 361 f., 384. This recension may be identified by its canonical order and certain interpolations, e.g. at Judges ii. 6—*tabernacula sua et in* [*possesionem*]. For C, see below, pp. 121 f.

[2] For the prefaces, see Berger, 'Les Préfaces jointes aux livres de la Bible', *Mémoires Présentés à l'Académie des Inscriptions et Belles-Lettres*, Paris, XI, 2 (1904); F. Stegmuller, *Repertorium Biblicum Medii Aevi. I. Initia Biblica, Apocrypha, Prologi* (Madrid, 1950); Sparks, p. 116 n. Fischer (4), pp. [3], [31], emphasizes the risks inherent in deducing textual history from evidence of this kind.

Fathers show of the methods by which it was handled. (This is well illustrated in De Bruyne (1), pp. 373 f.; (2), pp. 521 f.)

The permanent significance of Italy in the recensional history of Jerome's version finds a link, geographically, in the first identifiable individuals to concern themselves with it. In 547 Victor, bishop of Capua, edited a New Testament text preserved by the *Codex Fuldensis*, a manuscript at one time in the hands of Boniface.[1] Victor addressed himself to correcting orthography, scribal errors, and syllable division (according to Greek, not Latin grammatical theory); and in the Pauline epistles he introduced some new readings from a north Italian text. His edition included a gospel harmony, descending (through the Old Latin) from Tatian's, a Vulgate text being substituted which was substantially similar to that which furnished the sixth-century prototype for (the Gospels of) the *Codex Amiatinus* and other Northumbrian manuscripts, and which is related to manuscript St Gall 70; but the text is, throughout, of Italian origin. Outside the Gospels, the influence of Victor's text is not to be traced; its gospel harmony was, however, widely diffused in the middle ages, and it furnished the prototype for the earliest translations into Old High German and Tuscan.[2]

Better known in this connection is the name of Flavius Cassiodorus Senator (*c.* 485–580) of Scyllacium (Squillace), who enjoyed a public career under Theodoric and retired, after Belisarius' entry into Ravenna, to the monastery of Vivarium which he had founded on his own estate (identified with the ruins of San Martino, south of Squillace). He here enjoined upon the brethren a particular concern for letters both sacred and secular. The library of Vivarium was dispersed after Cassiodorus' death, but some of the manuscripts reached the Lateran Library in Rome, and their diffused influence was not negligible.[3]

The editorial undertaking of Cassiodorus has been largely misunderstood and overestimated, as has the alleged surviving testimony to the

---

[1] On Victor see G. Bardy in *Dictionnaire de Théologie Catholique*, 15, 1, cols. 2874 f. (1950). On his text see Fischer (4), pp. [16 f., 23]; *C.L.A.* 1196.

[2] Fischer (4), pp. [16 f., 18, 19, 21, 23–5].

[3] For Cassiodorus see M. Cappuyns in *Dictionnaire d'histoire et de géographie ecclésiastiques*, x (Paris, 1949), col. 1349 (new ed., 1961). References to extant manuscripts, allegedly from Cassiodorus' library, are given by Fischer (2), p. 63 n. 26. For the site of Scyllacium see B. Courcelle, *Mélanges d'Archéologie et d'Histoire*, 55 (Paris, 1938), p. 259.

text-form as he finally approved it. (The whole issue is discussed by Fischer (2), who dismisses as unfounded Cappuyns' claim that A is a direct and faithful copy of Cassiodorus' Vulgate.) There is no evidence that he attempted a revision of the text, as opposed to the improvement of its external form (spelling, latinity, etc.; see below, p. 119); and it is of crucial significance here that the text-form which he comments on in his exegetical writings is the Old Latin.[1] He himself records[2] having three different copies of the Bible prepared: a nine-volume text (i.e. an Old Latin text, serving as Cassiodorus' own working copy); the famous illustrated one-volume *Codex grandior littera clariore conscriptus*, containing for the Old Testament the earlier, hexaplaric revision by Jerome based on the Septuagint,[3] for the Gospels probably the Vulgate text, and for the remainder of the New Testament the Old Latin; and also a second, smaller one-volume bible (*pandectem... minutiore manu*) containing the Vulgate throughout. Misunderstanding has been bred by the temptation, natural enough, to postulate for Cassiodorus' own *Codex grandior* many or all of the details of the surviving eighth-century *Codex Amiatinus* (A)—a manuscript with which it is certainly connected, but in regard to external features only. Of the actual text-form of Cassiodorus' three bibles, whether Old Latin, hexaplaric, or Vulgate, nothing is known, and an alleged influence on the subsequent transmission of the Latin bible has not been substantiated in regard to any of them.[4]

The *Codex grandior* of Cassiodorus was certainly at one time in

[1] See Fischer (2), p. 59, against De Bruyne's assertion that Maccabees is Cassiodorus' recension (*Les anciennes traductions latines des Macchabées, Anecdota Maredsolana*, 4, Maredsous, 1932), and pp. 61–2.

[2] The relevant sources, with the crucial wording in each case, are: (*a*) *Codex grandior. Instit.* 1, 14, 2–3, ed. Mynors, p. 40, ll. 6 f., *P.L.* 70, 1125 C: *...in codice grandiore littera conscripto...in quo septuaginta interpretum translatio veteris testamenti...continetur; cui subiuncti sunt novi testamenti libri...Hic textus...patris Hieronymi diligenti cura emendatus*, etc.; (*b*) the *Lesser Pandect. Instit.* 1, 12, 3–4, ed. Mynors, p. 37, ll. 20 f., *P.L.* 70, 1124 B: *...pandectem...minutiore manu...aestimavimus conscribendum... Hieronymum omnem translationem suam...colis et commatibus ordinasse*; (*c*) *the working copy* is repeatedly referred to by Cassiodorus as *novem codices*, and illustrated as such in A (f. 5ʳ); e.g. *Instit.*, preface, ed. Mynors, p. 8, l. 6, *P.L.* 70, 1109 B. See further Mynors's index, p. 174. Cf. also 1, 5, 2, ed. Mynors, p. 23, *P.L.* 70, 1116 C; Fischer (2), pp. 58 f., 65.

[3] Cassiodorus' language, as quoted in note 2 (*a*) above, disposes of the supposition that Jerome abandoned his hexaplaric revision of the Old Testament in favour of his revision from the Hebrew.

[4] See Fischer (2), pp. 68 f., 74, and (4), pp. [25–6].

England, having been brought to Northumbria by Ceolfrid, who was responsible for the production in Jarrow, before 716, of the *Codex Amiatinus*[1] now in Florence, as well as two other single-volume bibles no longer completely extant.[2] Bede, Ceolfrid's contemporary, in referring to a picture of the Tabernacle stated by Cassiodorus to have been included by him in the *Codex Grandior* (*in pandectis majoris capite*), says that he himself had seen it;[3] and the *Codex Amiatinus* contains just such an illustration, on what are now its folios 2ᵛ–3ʳ. Palaeographical evidence, however, indicates that the *prolegomena* to the *Codex Amiatinus* are to be referred to the same period and scriptorium as the text itself, and that they cannot be identified with Cassiodorus' original.[4] The sequence of contents follows, almost exactly, one of the three canonical orders cited by Cassiodorus himself, but instead of the hexaplaric text of the *Codex Grandior* a Vulgate-type text has been substituted throughout.[5] What, however, renders the textual identification between the *Codex Grandior* and the *Codex Amiatinus* out of the question is the heterogeneous quality of the latter. The prototype of its Gospels was a sixth-century Roman text adapted to the local requirements of Naples, a circumstance underlined by the presence in another celebrated Northumbrian manuscript, the *Lindisfarne Gospels* (Y), of a gospel text very close to that of the *Codex Amiatinus* and also a Naples calendar.[6] Little information is available for the provenance of the originals copied for the remainder of the text of the *Codex Amiatinus*. The prototype for Samuel was from northern Italy or Gaul, and the three solomonic books presuppose an Italian prototype. The text of Wisdom and Ecclesiasticus is a poor one, and its shortcomings may reveal its provenance when the critical text of the Vulgate for these books is published. The Tobit agrees with the text-form in Bede's commentary, and was perhaps emended by Bede himself on the basis of texts deriving from Italy through St Gall. The Psalter was based on a corrupt Irish text, emended conjecturally so as to furnish a *Psalterium iuxta hebraeos*. The Pauline

---

[1] *C.L.A.* III, 299; Fischer (2), pp. 65 f.

[2] Fragments survive; MSS British Museum Add. 37,777, and 45,025 (*C.L.A.* 177).

[3] *Historia Abbatum*, II, § 16, ed. C. Plummer (Oxford, 1956), I, p. 379, *P.L.* 94, 725 A, also 91, 454 C; cf. Cassiodorus *in Ps. 15* (*14*), *P.L.* 70, 109 A, B.

[4] Fischer (2), p. 68 n. 37.

[5] Bede, *Hist. Abbatum*, II, §15 (see note 3), [*Ceolfridus*]... *tres pandectes novae translationis, ad unum vetustae translationis quem de Roma adtulerat, ipse super adiungeret.*

[6] Quentin, p. 449; Fischer (2), p. 71.

epistles follow a good text, probably Roman; Acts allies with the Spanish C and Σ^T in pointing to the Roman text contained in a manuscript of the Vallicelli Library in Rome (B. 25), and has been emended, partly in agreement with the text of Bede's commentary. The Catholic epistles contain a substantial Irish element.[1] Such a hotchpotch is precisely what one would expect—Cassiodorus' own pandects were doubtless no less heterogeneous in their own way. The *Codex Amiatinus* is a Vulgate manuscript, though not a unity—still less a faithful copy of Cassiodorus' Vulgate text contained in the lesser pandect not known ever to have been brought to England, and it has no connection with the Old Latin nine-volume bible of Cassiodorus illustrated (together with his other two bibles) in the well-known portrait on f. 5^r of the *Codex Amiatinus*. (On the historical importance of these illustrations, particularly that of the Tabernacle, see now C. Roth, 'Jewish Antecedents of Christian Art', *Journal of the Warburg and Courtauld Institutes*, London, XVI, 1–2, 1953, p. 37.) The *Codex Amiatinus* is certainly connected with Cassiodorus' *Codex Grandior*, but in regard to external features only. And of the contents of the *Codex Amiatinus*, it was the Gospel text alone that was to enjoy any significant circulation.[2]

Though the *Codex Amiatinus* can do no more than give us an impression of the format of the *chef d'œuvre* of Cassiodorus' scriptorium, we do know something of the way in which he set to work to create it. From his *Institutions* we gather that fundamental to his whole endeavour was the principle that all appropriate resources and techniques familiar in connection with the liberal arts must be applied to the study of the Scriptures. For this purpose he assembled a staff of translators and grammarians to collate the whole Bible, and provided them with a library of the works of the Fathers.[3] A Greek text was also available for comparison, but it is to be assumed that no one at Vivarium would have been competent to refer to the Hebrew. Chapter-division was provided

[1] Fischer (2), pp. 74–7; (4), p. [26]. On the Irish affinities of A, see *prolegomena* to *Biblia Sacra, Genesis*, p. xxiv; Quentin, p. 448; Chapman, *Revue Bénédictine*, XXXVIII (1926), pp. 139 f.; XXXIX (1927), pp. 12 f.; T. J. Brown in the *Lindisfarne Gospels*; E. A. Lowe, *English Uncial* (1960).

[2] Fischer (4), p. [27].

[3] *Instit.* 1, 27, ed. Mynors, p. 68, *P.L.* 70, 1140 D; Jones, pp. 28 f. For Cassiodorus' exegetical methods, see Smalley (2), pp. 30 f. See also *Instit.* 1, 8, ed. Mynors, pp. 32 f., *P.L.* 70, 1119. Jones, p. 33, refers to the collecting of manuscripts from Africa and elsewhere; but the object of such search seems to have been biblical commentaries, and not specifically codices of the Bible.

for the emergent Latin text, as were chapter headings, together with the division of each verse (in so far as the Vulgate, not the hexaplaric, Latin was concerned)[1] into *cola et commata*. The latter device had been applied by Jerome himself, and had been extended before Cassiodorus to the whole Bible; but his insistence upon it seems to have won him the reputation for carrying it right through the text.[2]

His own description[3] of the editorial processes whose observance he required is worth summarizing, since it constituted the programme for all attempts at improvement (rather than amplification) of the text until the end of the medieval period. In effect, it was only the surface which was being touched. There is nothing to suggest any intuition on Cassiodorus' part of the relative value of manuscripts as representing various textual traditions whose affiliations and antecedents ought to be investigated and evaluated. Nevertheless, the conservatism of his approach to his task is remarkable. The work can be entrusted to few only, and these must be learned. Hasty emendation of presumed scribal errors must be eschewed. The authority of two or three ancient and emended *codices* is sufficient to override the accepted canons of Latin usage where solecisms occur, and the rules of Latin prosody have no relevance to the Bible. Grammatical peculiarities supported by good manuscript testimony must be preserved, since a text known to be inspired cannot be susceptible to corruption (*corrumpi. . .nequeunt quae inspirante Domino dicta noscuntur*). Apart from these considerations, accuracy in Latin accidence is to be carefully observed in accordance with the context, especially regarding the use of the ablative or accusative cases after prepositions that can govern either. Division of sentences into *cola* and *commata* is to be carried throughout the text, the interchange of *b* and *v* being avoided, and the euphonically modified form of prepositions is to be preferred where they are prefixed as compounds to verbs. Any irrational orthographical variants are to be corrected from Jerome's codices (*quos. . .in editione LXX interpretum*

[1] For Jerome's use of *cola* and *commata*, see note 2 (*b*) on p. 116, and Fischer (2), pp. 59, 67, who emphasizes its restriction to Vulgate (and not hexaplaric or Old Latin) texts.

[2] The claim that Cassiodorus first extended it to the whole Bible is not now tenable (*op. cit.* p. 68). He seems, however, to have added it in Psalms: *Instit.* 1, 15, 12, ed. Mynors, p. 49, *P.L.* 70, 1130A; cf. also 1, 1, 2, ed. Mynors, p. 4, l. 16, *P.L.* 70, 1107B, and 15, 9, Mynors, p. 46, l. 22, *P.L.* 70, 1128D.

[3] *Instit.* 1, 15, ed. Mynors, pp. 41 f., 42, 44, 47 f., *P.L.* 70, 1126 f., 1126C, 1127D and C, 1129B.

emendavit, vel quos ipse ex Hebraeo transtulit—a form of words that might conceivably mean Jerome's own holographs or fair copies). (Fischer (2), p. 60, dismisses the suggestion as pure supposition; but the language here cited would surely bear the interpretation.) Hebrew Scripture, 'or its professors' (*vel eius doctores*), may be consulted as a possible source of an appropriate emendation (*decora correctio*), but the context seems to limit this to orthography, particularly of biblical names; and all such editorial treatment is to be conservatively applied. Biblical methods of expression, metaphor, and idiom must be preserved, even if outlandish by Latin standards, as must also the 'Hebraic' forms of proper names—save for the grammatical inflexion of such of them as lend themselves to it—since in the interpretation of the names divine mysteries are enshrined.[1]

In approaching Vulgate history on the basis of surviving manuscripts and of what can be inferred from them of their forbears, it will be convenient to begin with Spain.[2] Like the Irish text, and for similar reasons, the Spanish Latin bible long maintained a somewhat sequestered existence. The Spanish Church, pinned between the Moors and the Pyrenees and for centuries not greatly susceptible to extraneous influences, developed its own text-form and impressed upon it a characteristic orthography of its own. The occasional migration of an early Spanish text to Gaul or Italy ought not to be exaggerated into a picture that would suggest a central importance for the Spanish text-type (so, for example, the parent of the *Codex Ottobonianus* (O), written in the seventh or eighth century at an Insular centre in northern Italy). Conversely, prolonged Spanish 'protectionism' was to hinder the acceptance of even the Alcuinian text-form: it was only with the thirteenth century that the convenience of the little Paris bibles (see below, p. 146) virtually smuggled the Paris text across the Spanish frontier.

The history of the Spanish Vulgate begins with Jerome himself, who in the year 398 supervised the work of scribes sent by Lucinus Baeticus

---

[1] Mynors, pp. 47–8, *P.L.* 70, 1129 C; Jones, p. 104 n. 2.

[2] Berger (3), pp. 8 f.; De Bruyne (1), pp. 373 f.; Upson Clark, pp. 100 f.; Ayuso (2), especially p. 122. Although Ayuso (whose writings are bibliographically useful) is quoted extensively in this section, his conclusions require scrutiny where they differ from De Bruyne. See now Fischer (3).

from Spain specially to copy his texts.[1] Jerome had not, by then, completed his final revision, the text of which must have been sent subsequently to Lucinus' widow Theodora and his continuators: but no extant Spanish texts derive from Lucinus' without contamination.[2] Between Lucinus, therefore, and what can be inferred from the study of existing manuscripts lies a cypher text which is ancestor of all the Spanish types. The emergence of the earliest of these leads us to the enigmatic figure of Peregrinus—a shadowy personage who, if he existed at all, seems to have flourished in northern Spain around the middle of the fifth century. It may be that what he edited was not the complete Bible at all, as generally alleged.[3] At any rate his orthodox corrections of the heretical *Canons* of Priscillian (*d.* 385) are often found in Spanish manuscripts alongside a distinctive text of the Pauline epistles. To Peregrinus have also been credited certain prefaces to biblical books intended not for Jerome's final translation of the Old Testament from the Hebrew, but for the earlier one based on the hexaplaric Greek. The prefaces in question are to the hexaplaric Latin of Job, which survives, and of Chronicles, which does not; but the latter preface was taken over by Theodulf, and thus preserved in his own biblical recension (it is, indeed, a characteristic feature of Spanish manuscripts to introduce books exhibiting a basically Vulgate text with prefatory material taken over from the Old Latin bible).

These prologues, when taken in conjunction with a distinct series of biblical books, may point to the preparation of a biblical recension, conceivably by Peregrinus; at least it must ante-date Isidore (625), and since it presupposes knowledge of the whole Vulgate including the pseudo-Hieronymean preface to Acts, it is unlikely to be much earlier than 450.[4] The text of this recension is reflected in certain portions of the ninth-century *Codex Cavensis* (C), which, though written after 850,

---

[1] *Ep.* 71, §5, *C.S.E.L.* 55, pp. 5 f., *P.L.* 22, 671; *Ep.* 75, §4, *C.S.E.L.* 55, p. 33, *P.L.* 22, 688.

[2] Fischer (4), p. [8], n. 46, p. [33]. For Samuel all Spanish texts without exception have been subjected to Italian influence.

[3] Fischer (4), p. [13], questions the very existence of Peregrinus as an individual and contends that Peregrinus' text, and probably also the associated hexaplaric prefatory matter, derived from Italy, perhaps Rome, and was possibly diffused to Spain under Gregory the Great (Fischer (3), pp. 40 f., 45). On Peregrinus see also De Bruyne (1), pp. 384–5; and Ayuso (3), pp. 151 f.; (1), pp. 378–9, 520 f.; (2), p. 122 (c).

[4] Ayuso (1), pp. 381–5, and p. 351 no. 13; (3), p. 143.

probably in Asturias, rests in general on an Italian text. C contains mainly a good Vulgate, and is dependent (formally) on the Tours bibles, its ornamentation betraying Carolingian influence. For the New Testament, C represents the prototype of Σ^T, which has however corrupted it with Old Latin readings (Fischer (4), pp. [12], [28], [35]). It is wrong to refer the *complete* text of C uncritically to Peregrinus (p. [36]). It is a mistake to claim to recognize as Peregrinus' text that contained in the so-called 'Isidore' Bible, dated 960, now at León (*Codex Gothicus*, Λ^L),[1] a text of very mixed composition. The canonical order in C has likewise been referred to the same editor: with one slight discrepancy it is the order actually followed by Isidore, doubtless as being the one in common use at his time, although differing from that which Isidore had himself proposed.[2] Further items that have been (if questionably) associated with Peregrinus are a colophon found after Esther in the Roda Bible[3] referring to the work of collating editions, and the production of a single-volume text; and also a prologue to Baruch found in C and other manuscripts.

The character of the text as allegedly left by Peregrinus is supposed to be observable in the text of Proverbs found in the *Codex Cavensis* and other manuscripts, which contain likewise a note on Proverbs as well as the prologue to the Pauline epistles which is attributed, with greater confidence, to Peregrinus. The outstanding feature is the extensive interpolation, matter not found in the Massoretic text having been introduced into the Vulgate from older Latin versions. Typical of this Spanish Vulgate are the two additional verses at the end of Joshua that are found in the Septuagint and, in Latin, in e.g. Λ^L. Of the interpolations in Proverbs the source is, in some places, demonstrably the hexaplaric Greek: in one case it cannot have been, unless Peregrinus' own hexaplaric text was itself corrupt, so that the immediate source

[1] The claim is Ayuso's (1), p. 354 n. 21. See now Fischer (3), pp. 9 f. The archetype of Λ^L was essentially Spanish for Baruch only. It dates from the ninth century and has suffered substantial Spanish overlay in the form of supplement and marginal glossation; Fischer (4), p. [30]. The Psalter is the type of Theodulf's; Sainte-Marie, pp. xxxiii f. Ayuso (1), p. 369, claims that the marginalia of the Calahorra Bible reflect an archetype of possibly fifth century, conceivably Peregrinus' text: *La Biblia de Calahorra*, *E.B.* 1 (1942), 241 f., and *Sefarad*, Madrid, II (1942), 465, and III (1943), 461.

[2] Isidore, *Etym.* VI, ii, *P.L.* 82, 229, and 230B f.; De Bruyne (1), p. 399; Ayuso (3), p. 168.

[3] MS Paris, B.N. *lat.* 6; also *lat.* 11553: De Bruyne (1), pp. 393 f., 400, 401.

may be some pre-Hieronymic Latin Proverbs.[1] The following are typical examples:

iii. 28 C Σ^T Roda Bible + *non enim scis quid superventura pariat* (v.l. *pariet*) *dies*.

xiii. 4 *piger*] C + *in desideriis est*.

xvi. 7 C (partly) Σ^T Roda Bible^marg. Vat. 5729 + *qui excipit disciplinam in bonis erit, qui autem custodit vias suas custodit animam suam, diligens autem vitam parcet ori suo*.

Of forty-four such interpolations in Proverbs, thirty-five are unattested outside Spanish manuscripts and the dependent Theodulfian texts, and some are peculiar to the *Codex Cavensis*. Alcuin later excluded them all (save at Prov. xiv. 21) from his own revision: but the post-Carolingians, progressively more anxious to assemble a text that should fully reflect the patristic exegesis with which it was becoming almost fused (see below, p. 140), gradually reintroduced such matter (mainly through Theodulf's bible) into what became in the thirteenth century the 'Paris' bible. Thence many of the examples under consideration passed ultimately into the printed Clementine text.[2]

Spanish codices also show inconsistency of affiliation as between the various groups of biblical books found between the same covers;[3] and in view of the amount of qualification that has been called for in the previous section, it is somewhat naïve to describe as 'Peregrinus' Bible' the texts that were circulating in the Peninsula at the time of Isidore, bishop of Seville from *c.* 599 to 636, and distinguished as a champion of orthodoxy no less than as an encyclopaedic compiler, through whom the salvage of the mind of antiquity was passed to western medieval Christendom.[4] Isidore himself owed his education to Leander, his brother and predecessor, who had founded the school of Seville to whose further establishment Isidore himself contributed

[1] Hexaplaric, Prov. x. 4; xv. 5; xxix. 27, De Bruyne (1), p. 392; non-hexaplaric, ix. 18, De Bruyne, *ibid.* and p. 388.

[2] For interpolations outside Proverbs, see Ayuso (3), pp. 108 f., 110, 146. Cf. Denifle, pp. 269 f., 584.

[3] For Spain particularly, see Fischer (4), p. [32].

[4] For Isidore see, most recently, Fontaine; also Menéndez Pidal, pp. 397 f. For full bibliographical material see Ayuso (1, p. 504); E. Dekkers and Ae. Gaar, 'Clavis Patrum Latinorum', *Sacris Erudiri*, iii (Bruges–Hague, 1961), Ed. 2, 267 f.

substantially. Isidore's manifold writings show no independent knowledge of Greek, although the presence of Byzantines in Spain would
have afforded him the opportunity to learn it. It is conceivable that
under the shadow of the controversy of the Three Chapters he saw in
Greek the language of heresy, and deliberately held himself aloof from
it.[1] If that is so, analogous considerations might account for his
ignorance of Hebrew (save for what he had taken over from Jerome,
etc.), since Isidore himself wrote controversially against the Jews, with
whom he could easily have established contact in Visigothic Spain had
he wished to do so. He does, however, betray some knowledge (possibly
at first hand) of Jewish customs.[2]

Isidore's editorial approach to the Bible was perhaps prompted by
the discrepancy between the contemporary Spanish text[3] and text-types
current outside the Peninsula. It is customary to symbolize the group
of manuscripts containing the text attributed to him as Σ, but it cannot
be regarded as certain that Isidore's own bible edition has in fact survived.[4] Of the Σ-family the major representative is Σ^T (T in the New
Testament), which originally came from Seville; since in the rubrics to
its prologues it never refers to Isidore as *beatus*, it would seem to reflect
an early archetype.[5] The recension is characterized by a general reversion to the pure Vulgate text and therefore to the *hebraica veritas*, as
against the heavily interpolated earlier text-type of 'Peregrinus'.
Certain distinctive features and inclusions serve to identify manuscripts
in which an Σ-type text is found: in particular, a general preface beginning *Vetus testamentum ideo dicitur* (a disquisition included also in
Isidore's *Etymologies*),[6] in which a canonical order broadly correspond-

---

[1] So (tentatively) Fontaine, pp. 849 f., 851; cf. Menéndez Pidal, p. 404.

[2] Isidore's *de fide Catholica contra Judaeos*, *P.L.* 83, 449 f.; A. Lukyn Williams,
Adversus Judaeos (Cambridge, 1935), pp. 216 f. For his possible knowledge of Jewish
customs, see *P.L.* 83, 523, 744–5, and S. Katz, *Jews in the Visigothic and Frankish
Kingdoms in Spain and Gaul* (Cambridge, Mass., 1937), pp. 64 f.

[3] For Peregrinus' alleged influence on Isidore, see Ayuso, 'Los elementos extrabíblicos de los Profetas', *E.B.* VI (1947), 393–4.

[4] Fischer (3), p. 7; (4), pp. [28, 36], also [37].

[5] See *Novum Testamentum*, I, p. xiii, no. 23; *Biblia Sacra, Genesis*, p. xvii; Quentin,
pp. 316 f. Full bibliography in Ayuso (1), p. 352, no. 15, see also *E.B.* II (1943), 150 f.;
IV (1945), 278 f.; VI (1947), 395. Fischer (3), p. 7, adheres to the tenth-century dating,
against Ayuso's attempts to see in it a copy of Isidore's own codex.

[6] *Biblia Sacra, Genesis*, pp. 38 f.=*Etym.* VI, 1, *P.L.* 82, 229. Cf. p. 122 n. 2 above.
See Ayuso, *E.B.* II (1943), 176 f. and VI (1947), 393 f.; also (3), pp. 161 f. and De
Bruyne (1), pp. 373 f.

ing to the Jewish one is detailed. It is that canon, and not those of Cassiodorus or Peregrinus, which is followed in manuscripts of this group. Amongst other pointers are the omission, as lacking full canonical authority, of Baruch and the epistle of Jeremy, the presence of certain prologues to the Twelve Minor Prophets, to be credited partly (it is said) to Peregrinus and in part to Isidore himself, and a summary to each biblical book that discusses its contents with an introductory formula beginning *De*....[1]

This more faithful Vulgate recension of Isidore did not succeed in ousting the earlier Spanish bible, and in the course of the seventh century a conflated, 'Peregrinus–Isidore' type of text evolved, embracing additional matter; and this, as an archetype, is supposed to underlie several existing Spanish codices.[2] While the Visigothic culture of Spain was at its zenith a few specimens of the Spanish bible-text filtered abroad, to Italy and St Gall and also (perhaps by direct transmission) to Ireland; but some recent investigators have overestimated the diffusion of Spanish influence allegedly due to them. It was not until the Carolingian period that further development was to take place.[3] The Frankish empire achieved no more than a march beyond the Pyrenees, the effect of which was to isolate Catalonia from the remainder of Spain throughout its subsequent history, and which fostered a permanent stream of immigration from Aquitaine into the north-west of the Peninsula. But although Spain was to prove generally unreceptive to the most lasting achievement of Carolingian biblical endeavour, the so-called Alcuin bible, she nevertheless made an important contribution to the biblical scholarship encouraged by Charlemagne's court, in the infiltration of Spanish-type texts and in the person of Theodulf.

[1] For the Prologues see Ayuso, *E.B.* VI (1947), 394. There are clear affinities with Isidore's *de ortu et obitu patrum*, *P.L.* 83, 129 f. For the summary, see Ayuso, 'Los elementos extrabíblicos del Octateuco', *E.B.* IV (1945), 35 f., 40.

[2] Ayuso, *E.B.* II (1943), 169 f.; (3), pp. 154 f., where he lists (no. 604) seven codices, all in Spanish collections, assigned by him to this group.

[3] Ayuso (2), pp. 118 f. For the possibility of early Spanish contacts with Ireland not through Gaul, see J. N. Hillgarth, 'The East, Visigothic Spain and the Irish', *Studia Patristica*, IV (= *Texte und Untersuchungen*, Berlin, 79) (1961), pp. 444 f. See also below, p. 131 n. 1. For Italy and Switzerland see Berger (3), pp. 137 f., 140 f. (For the so-called 'Legionensis'-group, dating between *c.* 940 (the Oña Bible) and 1190, see Fischer (3), p. 8; (4), p. [33].)

Theodulf was born (*c.* 760) of Gothic stock in northern Spain, where he was also educated; and when he fled from the Moors into France, he took his library with him. Having first been appointed abbot of Fleury and St Aignan, he was made bishop of Orleans by Charlemagne at some time between 781 and 794. After Charlemagne's death he was accused of conspiring against Louis the Pious and was deposed and imprisoned (818); but he had been released before his death, which occurred in 821. On Theodulf see, apart from works mentioned in the bibliography, M. Manitius, *Geschichte der lateinischen Literatur des Mittelalters*, I, Munich, 1911, 537 f.; Ch. Cuissard, *Théodulfe Évêque d'Orléans*, Orleans, 1892, pp. 88, 174 f.; *C.L.A.* V, no. 576, VI, no. 768; F. J. E. Raby, *Christian Latin Poetry*[2], Oxford, 1953, pp. 171 f.; [W. Wattenbach], W. Levinson, and H. Löwe, *Deutchlands Geschichtsquellen im Mittelalter*, II, *Die Karolinger*, Weimar, 1953, pp. 195 f.; Fischer (4), pp. [50] f. His education is reflected in a reading list that he compiled in verse; it contains no Greek author save Chrysostom, whom he must have read in Latin translation.[1] There is no evidence that he ever studied Hebrew. He was much influenced by the Spanish Christian poets, particularly Prudentius, and was of course familiar with the works of Isidore. In addition to promoting the cultivation of learning in the cathedral schools and the cloister, Theodulf also introduced parish schools and the exposition of the Bible at a popular level (*ad docendum plebes*): *Qui Scripturas scit, praedicet Scripturas.*[2] In the conclusion to his own verse proem to the Bible, he enunciates the importance of its regular study:[3]

> crebra sit in sancta tibimet meditatio lege,
>   instato monitis nocte dieque suis...
> Nec solum ut doctus, sed et ut sis iustus amato...
>   Lectio crebra tenet, mens quod acuta capit...
> Quod bene mente capis humili sermone profare,
>   ne fastu amittas quod studiosus habes.

Codices of the Bible belonging to the Theodulfian family are designated by the symbol Θ: in external features, such as orthography,

---

[1] *M.G.H., Poetae*, I, 543, *P.L.* 105, 331 C; see J. T. Muckle, 'Greek Works Translated Directly into Latin before 1350, I (before 1000)', *Mediaeval Studies*, IV (New York, 1942), 37; A. Siegmund, *Die Überlieferung der griechischen christlichen Literatur in der lateinischen Kirche bis zum zwölften Jahrhundert* (Munich, 1949), pp. 91 f.

[2] *Capitula ad Presbyteros*, XXVIII, *P.L.* 105, 200 A; cf. XX, *ibid.* 196 D.

[3] *Carmina*, II, ll. 219 f., *M.G.H., Poetae*, I, 538, *P.L.* 105, 304 C, *Biblia Sacra, Genesis*, p. 59.

they are painstakingly and accurately written in a minute but legible hand, the format of the codices being perhaps inspired by Spanish pandect bibles similar to C.[1] The group includes the celebrated Paris manuscript[2] (Θ^M, Θ in the New Testament) with marginal corrections supposed to have been carried out under the supervision of Theodulf himself. But the most primitive testimony to his text is now held to be not Θ^M, but rather the closely related variants added to the ninth-century Bible of St Hubert, in the British Museum (Θ^H, H in the New Testament).[3] Yet evidence for Theodulf even purer than that in Θ^H is sometimes afforded (at least as far as concerns the Psalter *iuxta hebraeos*) by Λ^L.[4]

Theodulf's text (which he was at pains to improve continuously) is essentially eclectic, produced in the first instance as a work of scholarly reference;[5] and although the strong Spanish cultural background is made manifest by ornamental features, particularly by the horseshoe-shaped arches that surmount the canonical tables in Θ^H,[6] his text-type is fundamentally an Italian one and not (with the exception of three books) Spanish. (Theodulf's prototype(s) approximated to a tenth-century Milan text; his interpolations for Samuel reflect an Italian text probably of the fifth century. Spanish antecedents for Theodulf's text can be authenticated in the case of Baruch only, and, in the earlier Theodulf bibles, Wisdom and Ecclesiasticus.)[7] Of earlier codices it is to O,[8] a seventh–eighth-century incomplete Octateuch or Heptateuch of Spanish descent written in northern Italy, that Θ^H attaches itself

[1] Fischer (1), p. 8; (4), p. [50].

[2] B.N. *lat.* 9380. L. Delisle, 'Les Bibles de Théodulphe', *Bibliothèque de l'École des Chartes*, XL (Paris, 1879), 1 f.; *Novum Testamentum*, I, p. xii, no. 11; Quentin, p. 250; *Biblia Sacra, Genesis*, p. xxxiii; *C.L.A.* V, no. 576.

[3] MS Add. 24,142. *Novum Testamentum*, I, p. xii, no. 10; Quentin, pp. 251, 256f.; *Biblia Sacra, Genesis*, p. xxxii; Ayuso, 'Los elementos extrabíblicos de los Paralipómenos, Esdras, Tobías, Judit y Ester', *E.B.* V (1946), 39. Earlier scholars accepted the supremacy of Θ^M for the whole Bible: Berger (3), pp. 149 f.; Quentin, pp. 249, 257. Glunz (1), pp. 15, 107, emphasizes that the original hand of Θ^H is very close to the Northumbrian text. Cf. *Novum Testamentum*, I, 709.

[4] See above, p. 122 n. 1. Power (2), pp. 255–6 n. 3, on Ps. 8: 9, 32: 4 (*aestas*); cf. Sainte-Marie, *in locc.* and p. xxxiii n. 21.

[5] Fischer (4), pp. [50] f.

[6] Quentin, pp. 257 f., 259 f., with illustration; Ayuso, *E.B.* VI (1947), 399 f.; (2), p. 120, 4; (3), p. 155.   [7] Fischer (4), pp. [6] f., n. 50, [51].

[8] MS Vatican *Lat.* 66; cf. above, p. 120. Quentin, p. 432; *Biblia Sacra, Genesis*, pp. xxxi, xlii. *C.L.A.* I, no. 66 ('written apparently in North Italy').

most closely. (Various features suggest that it was written in an Insular centre in Italy. Ayuso ((2), pp. 115 f., (3), p. 155) argues not only for its Spanish dependence, but even for its Spanish scribal origin; he also questions the usual assumption that O, when complete, was an Octateuch, suggesting rather a Hexateuch.) Where Θ^H parts company with O, the influences to which it is most subject are those of an Alcuinian text—which it cites frequently in the margin—very close to Φ^V (MS Rome, Vallicelli B. 6) (see below, p. 138), and those of Spanish texts dependent on Isidore as represented by descendants of Σ^T.[1] The divisions of Isidore's canon are likewise followed, and prefatory material drawn from him and Peregrinus is found in some members of the Θ group, which mostly ignore chapter-division within the text, in spite of displaying at the beginning chapter-lists that agree substantially with those of A.[2] As regards their extra-biblical contents, Θ-manuscripts tend to include the pseudo-Augustinian *Speculum de Scriptura Sacra*.[3]

If Theodulf concerned himself with textual questions by citing marginal variants differentiated by sigla ($\bar{a}$ = Alcuin, etc.), he had no interest in, or understanding of, versional ones: and in his verse preface to the Bible he has nothing to say about either. After listing the Canon, with intaglio-like descriptions of the contents of each book (ll. 1–136), he turns to homiletics and *parenesis* (cf. extracts, p. 126). In spite of his employment of critical sigla, the marginal variants soon corrupted his text, which he himself was deliberately improving as he went along; and it thus becomes of very uneven quality.[4] Theodulf's edition, though scholarly (it prefers, for instance, Jerome's Psalter *iuxta hebraeos* to the popularly current Gallican Psalter), was, it seems, not executed according to any sufficiently determined principles; and indeed his own linguistic equipment would have been inadequate for scientific biblical scholarship. But in spite of this, his text is not devoid of all contact with the original. It has been shown that the Psalter *iuxta hebraeos* in Θ bears marks of correction made not *via* any hexaplaric text, but direct from

---

[1] See above, p. 124 n. 5. Berger (3), pp. 165 f., 170; Quentin, pp. 263 f.

[2] Found in Θ^M and Θ^A (i.e. *Codex Aniciensis*, an Octateuch, in the Chapter Library at Puy). Quentin, pp. 261, 263, 264; De Bruyne (1), pp. 379 f. (on the preface *Si aut fiscellam* to the hexaplaric Job). *C.L.A.* VI, no. 768. Regarding affinities between Θ and the Northumbrian text of A, traceable to the dependence of each on south Italian archetypes, see *C.L.A.* VI, p. xx.

[3] Quentin, pp. 263 f.   [4] Berger (3), p. 145; Kenyon, p. 260.

the Hebrew, apparently by a number of independent hands; and it is probable that careful examination would show the same situation in other parts of the Old Testament.[1] Since these psalter-readings, being attested by Θ^{H}, ascend to the ninth century, such recourse to the Hebrew is (in time at least) near enough to Theodulf himself conceivably to owe something to his inspiration or to his pupils.

Theodulf's bible suffered from the competition of the contemporary, more precisely planned and successfully disseminated Alcuinian version. As a result, manuscripts containing it are not numerous and its influence was not great[2]—although many of the interpolations that it had inherited were to be taken up into the (basically Alcuinian) scholastic Bible (see below, p. 140), and some of its hebraizing renderings were to find a future in the productions of a few later students of the twelfth and thirteenth centuries (see below, pp. 145, 152).

The legend of the Spanish parentage of Theodulf's bible text dies hard; but if the notion must be abandoned, Theodulf's own origins may permit us to attach him as an appendix to the Spanish part of our story. In spite, therefore, of the existence of a yet further late Spanish text, hybrid in quality, formed in Catalonia (probably at Ripoll—represented by the Ripoll and Roda Bibles, MSS Vatican *Lat.* 5729 and Paris B.N. *lat.* 6 respectively) in the tenth or eleventh century and still essentially based on Isidore,[3] the history of the Vulgate in medieval Spain may here be brought to a close.

It is appropriate at this point to consider the contribution of Insular Christianity to the transmission of the Vulgate; and in so doing one should distinguish between the parts played by the Anglo-Saxon and Irish churches respectively. (See the chart, pp. 104–5.) England herself had received the Latin bible through two streams. The Gospels that Augustine of Canterbury (*d. c.* 604) brought from Rome represented

[1] Power (2), especially pp. 238, 257–8. Regarding Exodus, see Power (1); Fischer (4), p. [51], speaks of assistance obtained from a Jewish convert to Christianity, but this is apparently an inference from the signs of Hebrew expertise: there is no unequivocal evidence for such collaboration.

[2] Berger (3), p. 145; Quentin, pp. 250 f. For a description of the external features of Theodulf bibles see Fischer (1), p. 8; (4), pp. [50] ff. where he traces its influence in northern France after 822, in St Gall about the same time, and in Spain in the tenth century.

[3] Ayuso, *E.B.* II (1943), 166–70; (1), p. 366, nos. 73 and 74; (3), p. 156.

a mixed Italian text which combined Old Latin readings with Jerome's: it is the text typified by O (see below, p. 136 n. 4) and by the original hand in X. As for the text brought to Northumbria by Ceolfrid from Italy, the Gospels were in the Vulgate form; but in so far as the *Codex Amiatinus* (exclusive of its Gospels) typifies the type of text circulating in northern England, that text was, for the remainder of the Bible, of very heterogeneous provenance. Both these two streams flowed south-ward again to contribute to the mixed texts current in Europe. The more significant stream was the Northumbrian, inasmuch as it formed (when joined by an Irish tributary) the bible carried by Boniface (*d.* 755) and the Anglo-Saxon missionaries to Germany and Switzer-land; it is represented by the original hand in ℙ.[1] Moreover, being current at York, it formed the backbone of Alcuin's revision of the Vulgate (see below, p. 136), and it thus came to be substantially pre-served in the Vulgate as subsequently transmitted.

Whereas the Anglo-Saxon gospellers were missionaries by design, the Irish monks proved to be missionaries in spite of themselves.[2] Finding themselves impatient of monastic discipline at home, and yet impelled by ascetic ideals, they frequently wandered abroad in search of their personal salvation—as, for example, did Columbanus—only to find that their sincerity, personality, and learning won for them the admiring emulation of those with whom they came into contact. Irish houses had succeeded in maintaining some classical learning: a know-ledge of Greek was, in northern and western Europe, effectively an Irish monopoly, and the Irish bible carries signs of correction made immediately from the Greek text.[3] Irish learning was prized, and the Irish sufficiently sought after as teachers for aspiring pupils even to go to Ireland themselves to seek them out.[4] Indeed, in the seventh century no continental monastery of any importance was without some Irish link. New houses were founded by the Irish monks, who were to be found as far afield as Spain. Within the British Isles, where Irish

[1] *Novum Testamentum*, I, p. xi, no. 7; *C.L.A.* v, no. 578, cf. also II, no. 125 (MS Corpus Christi College, Cambridge, 197). T. J. Brown has now shown that ℙ may well have been produced in the Lindisfarne scriptorium (see *Lindisfarne Gospels*).

[2] For the Irish bible see Kenney, chap. 7, pp. 623 f.; Glunz (1), pp. 67 f.; (2), pp. 106 f.; Cordoliani, pp. 5 f.

[3] Kenney, index, p. 797; Glunz (1), pp. 68 f., 76, 84.

[4] Bede, *Hist. Eccl.* III, 3, ed. C. Plummer (Oxford, 1896), I, p. 132, *P.L.* 95, 120 C; III, 27, p. 192, *P.L.* 95, 165 B.

missionary activity was a matter of deliberate policy, Iona was established in 563 as a lighthouse whose beam was trained on Scotland, Northumbria, and Wales, and from there, in 635, the centre at Lindisfarne was founded. Alcuin was to pay tribute to Irish missionary zeal: Irishmen were to be found at the court of Charlemagne (*d.* 814); and John the 'Scot' (i.e. Erigena) was a prominent member of the court of Charles the Bald (843–77).[1]

Irish monasticism, for all its leaning towards scholarship, was always conscious that the ultimate use of the Bible lay in its being a guide, of universal import, for life and for law.[2] In order to show its immediate relevance to given situations, and to the ascetic ideal that they sought to preach, the Irish permitted themselves some textual liberty: modifications, at first perpetrated homiletically, were already finding their way into the Old Latin text before the Vulgate reached Ireland. It is these spontaneous alterations and simplifications that give the Irish bible its characteristic flavour.[3] Thus, at Mark xi. 26 (*si vos non dimiseritis, nec pater vester... dimittet vobis*), Q adds (as object to *dimiseritis*) *hominibus*. In John i. 47 (*ecce vere israhelita in quo dolus non est*) for *vere* D E 𝔓^marg. R gat. read *vir*.

The early history of the text in Ireland cannot yet be adequately reconstructed and it has not, hitherto, been sufficiently differentiated from that of the Anglo-Saxon text-form of Northumbria.[4] Irish evidence is plentiful for the Gospels only, and for the Old Testament (other than the Psalter) is identified as such in but a single manuscript (St Gall 10 (tenth–eleventh century)). The Old Latin tradition, prior to St Patrick (*d. c.* 463), is exemplified by *Codex Ussher I* (MS Trinity College, Dublin, A. 4. 15). The introduction of Jerome's bible by Finian of Moville, probably from Italy, in the sixth century, gave rise to a dual progeny—a mixed text developed alongside the more purely preserved Hieronymic tradition that was not to achieve supremacy in Ireland before the tenth century. Irish bibles did, indeed, contribute

[1] Alcuin, *M.G.H.*, *Epist.* p. 437, l. 15, *P.L.* 100, 501 A; Smalley (2), pp. 38 f. On the missionary zeal of Irish monks see also Glunz (1), pp. 68–77; cf. also Hillgarth (cited above, p. 125 n. 3).

[2] For Irish biblicism in Canon law, see especially P. Fournier, 'Le Liber ex Lege Moysi et les tendances bibliques du Droit Canonique irlandais', *Revue Celtique*, xxx, 3 (1909), 221 f., especially pp. 228 ff.; summarized by Kenney, p. 250.

[3] *Novum Testamentum*, I, 715 f.; Glunz (1), pp. 80, 81, 86.

[4] Berger (3), pp. 29 f.; Glunz (1), p. 133 n. 45; Cordoliani, pp. 5, 31.

influentially to the Northumbrian text-form going out to Europe from Jarrow and Monkwearmouth, but the text known as *Celtic* is more properly to be described as definitively Irish.[1] Its main testimony is found in the Gospel manuscripts D, E, L, Q and R—the major representative being the *Book of Armagh* (D)[2] which, apart from a corrupt orthography, is close to the *Codex Amiatinus* (see above, pp. 117 f., 130). Similarly the seventh-century *Book of Durrow* (MS Trinity College, Dublin, A. 4. 5),[3] which preserves a very pure Hieronymic text, stands near to both the *Codex Amiatinus* and the *Lindisfarne Gospels*. The eagerness with which the Irish were welcomed as teachers on the Continent in the decadent Merovingian period gave to the Irish bible a wider circulation than that enjoyed by texts deriving from alien sources in Italy and in England, while in Germany Irish manuscripts closely rivalled the imported Italian and French texts; but it should be borne in mind that this conclusion is based on the distribution of those manuscripts which happen to have survived, and that in each case (except that of France) locally produced codices outnumber the foreigners.[4] Irish bibles, which have left traces on the Spanish text and, in Italy herself, at Bobbio, were accepted authoritatively as mastercopies and as norms for correctors. So substantial was the Irish strain injected into the continental Vulgate (particularly during the eighth and ninth centuries, perhaps under the impact of Danish raids on Ireland) that Irish features have survived down to the printed Clementine text of 1592.[5] In post-Carolingian times the influence of Irish philological competence was operative, especially through the schools of Laon and Auxerre, as a counterweight to the tendency of incipient scholasticism to introduce variants in order to point explicitly within the text itself towards the authoritative exegesis of the Fathers. In this way certain Old Latin readings were restored to the post-Alcuinian text.

External features of the Irish bible that serve to identify Irish

[1] *Novum Testamentum*, I, 707 f., 713; Cordoliani, p. 12, instances the Matthew text in the Clairemont Gospels (MS Vatican *Lat.* 7223, fifth–sixth century, *C.L.A.* I, no. 53), which has numerous coincidences with MS Ussher I (see preceding page); see also Cordoliani, pp. 13, 28.

[2] See Frede (1), pp. 57 f.

[3] *C.L.A.* II, no. 273. See now the facsimile edition (see bibliography, *s.v. Durrow*).

[4] Fischer (4), pp. [53] f. Of the surviving codices in Germany earlier than 800, the native and total imported manuscripts are almost exactly equivalent (61:60).

[5] Glunz (1), pp. 78, 85, 87 f.

manuscripts are (palaeographical considerations apart) the absence of prefatory material and chapter titles, etc., and in the Psalter the division into three groups of fifty psalms each. The lines of the transmission of the Irish text to Europe, which may be traced through E and the margin of 𝔓, at first run independently of the purer Vulgate stream that flows from Northumbria to the Continent; but the two converge in the eighth-century Anglo-Saxon missionary bible. The *Codex Fuldensis* left by the English Boniface at Fulda contains some glosses in Erse, and this and the ninth-century Gospels of St Gatian from Tours (gat.: MS Paris, B.N. *nouv. acq. lat.* 1587), probably both written and corrected in Ireland, must presumably have been at Alcuin's disposal.[1] The palaeographical features of the Irish bible rapidly receded, naturally enough, in face of the emergent dominance of the Carolingian hand; and reference in the ninth-century St Gall library *Catalogue*[2] to Irish-style manuscripts (*libri scottice scripti*) indicates clearly that these were, calligraphically, distinct from the majority.

If Alcuin's bible is generally regarded as being more intimately associated with the Carolingian empire than Theodulf's bible, this does not mean that Alcuin's edition enjoyed (as has frequently been supposed) any official sponsorship in the sense of having been issued *cum privilegio Maiestatis*. It is important that the biblical interests and endeavours of Charlemagne and Alcuin should not be confused by identification. Charlemagne (sole ruler 771–814) was concerned with the promotion of education[3] for what were, effectively, clerical reasons —the good governance of his realm through the instrumentality of an efficient body of clergy under his close control. But if he was alive to the contribution that an improved biblical text could make towards the orderliness that he so cherished, he also stood personally committed to Christianity as he understood it, and his conversation and correspondence reflect a genuine interest in theological matters. This partially

[1] See also Cordoliani, pp. 17, 23.

[2] MS St Gall, 728, f. 4. This catalogue has been edited several times; F. Weidmann, *Geschichte der Bibliothek von St Gallen* (St Gall, 1841), p. 364; G. Scherrer, *Verzeichnis der Handschriften der Stiftsbibliothek von St Gallen* (Halle, 1875), p. 233. With Kenyon, p. 260, compare Glunz (1), p. 76.

[3] For this see especially *M.G.H., Capit. Reg. Franc.*, p. 46, § 16; *Admonitio Generalis*, dated 789, *ibid.* pp. 52 f., 59, § 72; *Epistola de litteris colendis*, to be dated 786–801, *ibid.* p. 78; J. de Ghellinck, *Littérature latine au moyen âge*, I (Paris, 1939), 85; Ganshof, pp. 7 f.; Glunz (2), pp. 73–4.

accounts for the occurrence during his reign of several attempts, independent of Alcuin's, at reforming the biblical text. Apart from Theodulf's enterprise there is manuscript evidence of other undertakings,[1] in particular that of Maurdramnus, abbot of Corbie (772–81), whose bible[2] (M in the Old Testament) foreshadows Alcuin's, though it is of stronger Spanish affiliation; it constitutes the earliest datable Carolingian minuscule manuscript. There is also the so-called 'Ada' group, produced in the court school between 781 and 814, the text of which, like Alcuin's, reflects an Anglo-Saxon prototype.[3] It is no doubt to such endeavours as these, rather than to Alcuin's, that Charlemagne was alluding in his claim to have corrected the text of both Old and New Testaments 'long since' (*iam pridem*), seeing that the Encyclical in which he made the claim must have been composed before 29 May 801, whereas Alcuin's revision had been completed only in the previous summer.[4]

Alcuin was born near York, *c.* 730–5: he went to Aachen to take charge of Charlemagne's palace school *c.* 782, and was from 796 until his death in 804 abbot of St Martin's at Tours.[5] In York he had received from Egbert and Aelbert, and from the resources of a fine library, as good a schooling as could be had in Europe. (For the contents of the library, cf. Alcuin, *Vers. de Sanctis*, 11, 1535 f. Stephens considers that the only work in the library in Greek was Priscian. Alcuin's reference to *Hebraicus quod populus bibit imbre superno* means, of course, the biblical heritage in translation.) Alcuin acquired a very slender knowledge of Greek—enough to enable him to find Greek *soubriquets* and renderings for his pupils' names, but not enough to save him from absurd etymology and inaccurate inflexion; Greek references in his

---

[1] MS Paris, B.N. *lat.* 11553; Metz Municipal Library, MS 7 (destroyed 1944). Cf. also Winithar's verses, to be dated probably before 780, *M.G.H.*, *Poetae*, pp. 89 f.; Fischer (1), p. 6 n. 11, and p. 17.

[2] MS Amiens Municipal Library, 6, 7, 9, 11, 12; cf. also MS Paris, B.N. *lat.* 13174, ff. 136, 138; *C.L.A.* vi, no. 707; Fischer (1), p. 6 n. 9; (4), p. [46].

[3] MSS Trier, Stadtsbibliothek 22, Paris, B.N. *nouv. acqu. lat.* 1203 (Godescalc Gospels), Vienna, Nationalbibliothek *lat.* 1861 (Psalter); Quentin, p. 268; *C.L.A.* vi, p. xxvii; Fischer (1), p. 9; (4), p. [47].

[4] *Capit. Reg. Franc.* (see p. 133 n. 3), p. 80, § 28: *iam pridem universos veteris ac novi instrumenti libros, librariorum imperitia depravatos, Deo nos in omnibus adiuvante, examussim correximus.* Fischer (1), p. 18.

[5] For Alcuin's biography see Gaskoin; Kleinclausz; Duckett; [Wattenbach], Levison, Löwe, pp. 225–36, with very full bibliography.

own writings are derivative.[1] Assertions that Alcuin knew Hebrew may be disregarded: where he does allude to it, he borrows from Jerome, and the nearest that he ever got to Jewish scholarship was to hear Peter of Pisa—later a member of Charlemagne's court—dispute at Pavia with a Jew named Lullus.[2] Devotion to biblical scholarship was, in Alcuin, intimately linked with practical ethical endeavour and orthodox *apologia*;[3] the real, i.e. mystical, significance of Holy Writ was to be found in the Fathers, and in them only, but as an essential substructure the literal, historical sense must first be appreciated.[4] When he came to revise the text it was this last consideration that directed the endeavour that was called forth, as it had been from the early missionaries, by an outside situation that demanded a pragmatic application of Christian ethics—namely, Charlemagne's need for an authoritative and grammatical text, and the promotion of religion and culture in the Frankish empire.[5]

Charlemagne had directed that all copying of the Gospels and Psalms (though conceivably no more than the liturgically essential portions of the Bible were in his mind, Ganshof, p. 9) must be carried out by responsible hands (*perfectae aetatis homines scribant cum omni diligentia*);[6] and such surviving, pre-Alcuinian bibles as those written by the contemporary Winithar of St Gall[7] emphasize, in their carelessness and corrupt state, the justification for his injunction. In a letter written at Eastertide, 800, to Gisela and Rothrude, Charlemagne's sister and daughter, Alcuin says that he is busy with the king's charge

---

[1] M. L. W. Laistner, *Thought and letters in western Europe*, p. 192; Stephens, pp. 34 f. But some of his biblical corrections derive immediately from the Greek, not *via* the Old Latin. See Glunz (1), p. 132.

[2] *Ep.* 172, *M.G.H., Epist.* p. 285, *P.L.* 100, 314c (*Ep.* ci).

[3] Cf. *De virtut. et vitiis*, 5, *de lectionis studio: beatissimus est, qui divinas scripturas legens, verba vertit in opera, P.L.* 101, 616–17; *Vita S. Vedasti* (composed *c.* 800), preface, §3, *P.L.* 101, 666 A, B, *defensores qui . . . doctrina veritatis castra Dei viriliter defendere valeant.*

[4] *In Gen., cap. 49, Interpr.* 231, *P.L.* 100, 558–9; *prius historiae fundamenta ponenda . . . allegorice culmen priori structurae superponatur.* For Alcuin's view of the manifold senses of Scripture, see *in Cant.* iv, 11 (*Favus distillans*), *P.L.* 100, 652 below; *Confessio Fidei*, iii, §36, *P.L.* 101 A; *Ep.* 232 (229) *ad Gyslam, P.L.* 100, 510 D, *M.G.H., Epist.* p. 41, l. 45, *in* [*sacris scripturis*] *quid credere, quid sperare, quid amare, quid fugere debeamus, ostenditur.*

[5] Glunz (2), pp. 24 f.

[6] *Cap. Reg. Franc., M.G.H.* I, p. 60, §72. Cf. Cassiodorus (above, p. 119) *a paucis . . . doctisque faciendum*, ed. Mynors, p. 42, *P.L.* 70, 1126c.

[7] MSS St Gall, 2, 11, 40, 44, 70, 907, 1398 *b*. Berger (3), pp. 117 f., 129; Fischer (1), pp. 10, 17; (4), pp. [22], [53]. See above, p. 134 n. 1.

(*praeceptum*) to emend the text of both Testaments.[1] These words have generally been construed to imply a specific injunction to Alcuin, to which the 'Bible of Alcuin' is due; but it has also been asserted that no more is meant than that Alcuin was working, like others, within the framework of Charlemagne's general directive.[2] Having turned natur-ally to the Northumbrian schools, then the best in western Europe, for the source material for his task (or at any rate for his basic gospel text), he probably began work after the arrival in Tours of books from York in 797.[3] It was complete in time for him to present it, through the agency of his pupil Fridugis, to Charlemagne, at his coronation as emperor in Rome at Christmas, 800. (*M.G.H.*, *Epist.* pp. 418–20, *P.L.* 100, 368 D, 374 B; Ganshof, p. 14 n. 3.)

In Alcuin's time, two types of gospel text were current in North-umbria. A south Italian text, brought to Canterbury by Augustine, is typified by three seventh-century manuscripts (O, X, Z);[4] and of these O and X, which contain a Roman form of text, come from the abbey of St Augustine, Canterbury. It was the text found in Z—a mixed Italian text with Old Latin quotations, and with some attempt at smoothing grammar and style—that was adopted as Alcuin's school text. The availability in Northumbria, even before Alcuin's time, of a form of the Gospels associated with southern England is paralleled by the fact that in the eighth century there could be produced at Canter-bury a manuscript[5] exhibiting the same kind of text as O and X, but written in a script modelled on the Northumbrian style. But alongside the text infiltrating from the south there were also current in the north of England the Vulgate Gospels and the remainder of the Bible in the text brought to Monkwearmouth and Jarrow by Ceolfrid in the seventh century and reflected in A and Y (see above, pp. 117, 130).[6] This latter type was well known at York; and the O X Z type, carried from York

[1] *M.G.H.*, *Epist.* pp. 322 f., *P.L.* 100, 923 C.

[2] Berger (3), p. 187, etc. (see Ganshof, pp. 9 f., 12 n. 1); Fischer (1), p. 19; (4), p. [46].

[3] Alcuin, *Epist.* 121, *M.G.H.*, *Epist.* p. 177, *P.L.* 100, 208 C. More evidence is required to substantiate the Northumbrian source, at any rate for books other than the Gospels (Fischer (1), p. 19, cf. Glunz (1), p. 133; (2), pp. 29 f.).

[4] O=MS Bodleian Library, Auct. D. 2. 14; X=MS Corpus Christi College, Cam-bridge, 286; Z=MS British Museum, Harley 1775. Glunz (2), pp. xx, 29 f.

[5] MS British Museum, Royal, I. E. vi.

[6] MS Durham A. II. 17 (mid-eighth century) is claimed by Turner (pp. 198 f.) to be the original of Y.

to Tours, was being copied there in Alcuin's time. (Fischer (4), p. [50], emphasizes that the putative prototypes used by Alcuin have not survived.) In his revision of the Bible—or at any rate of the Gospels—Alcuin leaned heavily on both, and the result of his efforts may be observed clearly in two late ninth-century manuscripts in the British Museum.[1] No new recension was envisaged: and there is no evidence of any grasp of the problems of textual criticism. Alcuin's severely practical aim was to afford, through correct latinity, an intelligent avenue of approach to Holy Writ.[2] Editorial activity was limited to the purgation of errors in punctuation, grammar, and orthography. On these subjects Alcuin had written treatises, that on orthography being principally based on Bede and Cassiodorus (whose own approach to textual improvement of the Bible clearly influenced Alcuin).[3] But whereas Cassiodorus had been conscious of his responsibilities towards Jerome's own solecisms of latinity (see above, p. 119), in Alcuin's revision some of these were 'corrected' away.[4] As examples of readings introduced by him, Mark vi. 32 *in navem* for *in navi*; Luke xix. 37, *discipulorum* for *discentium*; John vii. 8 *nondum [impletum]* for *non*, etc., can be cited. Characteristic orthographical features are the assimilation of prepositions prefixed to stems (cf. Cassiodorus, p. 119), and the form of certain proper names, e.g. *Moyses*, not *Moses*.[5] Of greater significance for the future, however, was the replacement of the Psalter *iuxta hebraeos*—Jerome's own final version—by the Gallican Psalter based on the hexaplaric Greek, in Alcuin's biblical pandects.[6]

Textually, the Alcuinian bibles show remarkable constancy, and as regards external features these single-volume Scriptures remained unchanged for half a century. They consist of 420–50 folios according to the amount of illumination, dedicatory matter, etc., that they include; they measure ± 50 cm × 35–9 cm; and they are disposed in double columns of 50–52 lines each. Extra-biblical features are the verse prologues of Alcuin, found in some manuscripts, and colophons at the end

[1] MSS Harley, 2823, and Add. 11,849, the latter probably written at Tours. Glunz (2), pp. 30, 49–50.

[2] Glunz (1), p. 128.

[3] *Grammatica, P.L.* 101, 849; *de Orthographia, ibid.* 901 (ed. A. Marsili, Pisa, 1952). See [Wattenbach], etc., p. 230. Cf. above, p. 135 n. 6, and pp. 119f.

[4] Fischer (1), pp. 18–19.

[5] Glunz (1), pp. 127 f. n. 39, 132; (2), pp. 49, 50.

[6] Fischer (1), p. 19. Cf. above, p. 111, and Burkitt in *Journal of Theological Studies,* xxx (1929), 396.

of each Gospel recording the stichometry.[1] During the abbacy of Alcuin himself the products of the Tours scriptorium were still calligraphically poor, irregular, and indeed inferior orthographically to e.g. Maurdramnus' bible[2] (see above, p. 134). Under his successor Fridugis (807–34) technical ability advanced to a point beyond which improvement in the script itself was not possible. A conventional use of differently coloured inks, and various styles—capitals of two kinds, uncial, half-uncial, large and small minuscule—in regular positions established a pattern that indicated the structure of the text itself. The golden age under Adalhard (834–43) and Vivian (843–51) gave the Carolingian empire its finest specimens of book-production in such splendidly illuminated manuscripts as the Grandval Bible (Φ^c, K in the New Testament), the Lothair Gospels, and the bible presented by Vivian to Charles the Bald in 846.[3] Tours was sacked by the Normans in 853, but by *c.* 880 the abbey was again producing books of the calibre of the Vallicelli Bible (Φ^V, V in the New Testament).[4]

Manuscripts belonging to the Alcuinian family are designated by the symbol Φ[5] (Alcuin having borne the soubriquet *Flaccus*);[6] and the *Vallicelli Codex* (Φ^V, V in the New Testament) is said to afford the best evidence for Alcuin's text,[7] even though older Alcuin bibles are extant. The earliest of them all, at St Gall,[8] is too rough a copy to be identifiable with that presented to Charlemagne in 800: calligraphically it is not a unity, orthographically it is irregular, and altogether it is to be regarded as an experimental model only. But the presentation volume, if it was indeed prepared at Tours, cannot have been substantially different. (Fischer (1) concludes that the gift was intended as testimony to Alcuin's training of the monks at St Martin's rather than as an

---

[1] Fischer (1), pp. 6 f., 14 f. For the verse prologues, see *Biblia Sacra, Genesis*, pp. 44 f.; *M.G.H., Poetae*, pp. 287 f.; *P.L.* 101, 731 B f. For stichometry, see Berger (3), p. 363; *Novum Testamentum*, I, 736; Glunz (2), p. 50.

[2] Fischer (4), p. [49].

[3] Φ^c, MS British Museum Add. 10,546; Lothair Gospels, MS Paris, B.N. *lat.* 266; Vivian's presentation bible, MS Paris, B.N. *lat.* 1.

[4] MS Rome, Vallicelli Library, B. 6. See below, n. 7.

[5] *Biblia Sacra, Genesis*, pp. xxvii f.; in *Novum Testamentum* (see I, p. xiv) Φ had not yet been adopted as a symbol. Φ^V appears there as V.

[6] E.g. *Ep.* 145, *M.G.H., Epist.* p. 232, l. 32, p. 234, l. 16, *P.L.* 100, 268 A, D.

[7] Berger (3), pp. 197 f. But Quentin indicates the priority of T (MS Tours, 10—an Octateuch) and Φ^R (MS Paris, B.N. *lat.* 3—a complete bible). Cf. Berger (3), pp. 204 f., 242. For the Gospels, MS Tours, 22 ($\overline{\text{M}}$) is also of major significance.

[8] MS 75. See *C.L.A.* VII, no. 904; Fischer (1), p. 10.

example of his own scholarly achievements (pp. 6 f., 12, 19; Rand, pp. 337–42 f., 374).) It was the sudden rise of Tours to a position of supremacy among the Carolingian scriptoria that diffused, through these sumptuously ornamented bibles, the text as revised by Alcuin—in a format perhaps intended to suggest the value of his own scholarly reputation. (The Bamberg Bible—Staatliche Bibliothek MS Bibl. 1— produced some thirty years after Alcuin's death, contains his portrait.)[1] Indeed, it is true to say that the textual influence of Alcuin's bible was less widespread than the influence of its external features;[2] and it is to these, and not to any official sponsorship, that is due the prominence which Alcuin's text came to enjoy throughout the empire. A modern analogy is to be sought not in the position of King James's 'Authorized Version' of the English bible, but rather in the success with which dictionaries bearing the imprint of a well-known Press will drive rival publications from the market. It was Alcuin's personal achievement to have injected vitality into an already existent tendency towards textual purification, and the Vulgate was henceforth to be, effectively, Alcuin's Latin text.[3] Although the conservatism of monastic scriptoria is demonstrated by the continued production of pre-Alcuin and mixed Alcuin texts,[4] the sedulous introduction of Alcuinian corrections[5] indicates that the strictly Alcuinian text was, by the late ninth century, coming to be regarded as a norm. Texts that had been current in England in the eighth century were still being copied there, together with Irish texts, up to three centuries later; but the monastic reforms of King Alfred (871–901), based as they were on scholars brought over from the Continent, promoted the infiltration of Alcuin's texts, especially into the convents.[6]

Alcuin's bible constitutes a landmark, inasmuch as the Vulgate text was not henceforth to be determined by the pragmatic selection of whichever particular text, out of several possibilities all traditionally associated with 'Jerome', appeared most apposite to the immediate situation as viewed from the standpoint of Augustinian ethics. With

---

[1] Berger (3), p. 206; Rand, p. 358; Fischer (1), pp. 12 ff., 19.
[2] Fischer (4), p. [52].   [3] Fischer (1), p. 19.
[4] E.g. Leofric's Gospels, MS Bodleian, Auct. D. 2. 16; similarly MS British Museum, Cotton, Tib. A. 2 (*c.* 900). Glunz (2), pp. 54 f.
[5] E.g. MS British Museum, Harley 2797, written at St Geneviève, Paris. Glunz (2), pp. 51 f.   [6] Glunz (2), pp. 59 f., 61, 65 f., 68, 70.

the Carolingian age there begins a veneration for the Fathers that invests their views on the meaning of Scripture with dogmatic authority.[1] No less integral to incipient scholasticism was logical realism, that is, the notion that every substance has, corresponding to itself, a noun. Since the substantial significance of Holy Writ is embodied in its patristic exegesis, it was felt to be desirable that the text should itself show some unmistakable pointer towards that significance—in just the same way that the language of the Aramaic Targum (translation) of 'Onqelos had earlier been formulated so as to embody much of the official Jewish interpretation of the Pentateuch.[2] Such an attitude reduces all questions of textual nicety to quite secondary importance, and opens the door to tendentious alteration. As an example, we may cite Luke xii. 35, *Sint lumbi vestri praecincti et lucernae ardentes*, where the addition of *in manibus vestris* is found first in E, a manuscript written not earlier than the mid-ninth century. The surplus reflects the identification, by Gregory, of *lamps* with *good works*, which had been taken over by Bede.[3] The history of the Vulgate thus becomes the history of its exegesis.

And yet textual conservatism remained the order of the day for two centuries. Post-Carolingian monastic reforms were dominated by asceticism, by liturgical considerations, and by the cultivation of humility—with which a critical handling of the scriptural text was held to be incompatible. Libraries were rarely maintained. Further advance had to await the combination, in the twelfth century, of the fruits of an address to inconsistencies found within the Fathers themselves as ebulliently exposed by Abelard, and the competence of a few scholars in Hebrew and, perhaps, to a lesser extent, in Greek.[4]

Nevertheless, reports and occasionally evidence have come down to us of attempts made in the interval to improve the text of the Vulgate,[5] although it is not until the thirteenth century that we encounter, in the 'Paris' bible, an enterprise whose influence was widely and effectively diffused (see below, pp. 145 f.). Manuscript St Gall, 75, the earliest extant Alcuin bible, was heavily corrected by Hartmut (abbot 872–83) and his

---

[1] Glunz (2), pp. 32, 82 f.; Smalley (2), pp. 35, 37 f.
[2] See Kahle, *The Cairo Genizah*[2] (Oxford, 1959), pp. 194 f.
[3] Cf. *P.L.* 76, 1124 A and 92, 195 C. See further Glunz (2), pp. 82 f., 90 f., 101, 116.
[4] See Glunz (2), pp. 32–49; Smalley (2), pp. 39 f., 44.
[5] Smalley, *ibid.*

assistants: it thus brought its influence to bear on the text current in St Gall in the ninth century—i.e. the earlier, very corrupt text of Winithar (see above, p. 135), which was henceforth to be crossed both with Alcuin (thanks to a Spanish tributary channelled through Rome and Milan)[1] and with Theodulfian corrections. Assertions that have made biblical correctors of Dunstan, archbishop of Canterbury 959–88,[2] of Olpert, abbot of Gembloux early in the eleventh century, and of Franco Scholasticus of Liège, his junior by a generation, seem to go beyond the evidence.[3] Peter Damian (1007–72) states[4] that he had the whole Bible corrected: *emendare curavimus—licet cursim, et per hoc non exacte*. Nothing can be said about the alleged elimination of scribal errors from the text to which Theotger, abbot of St George's in the Black Forest, and Herino of Hirschau (Hirsauge) are supposed to have addressed themselves *c.* 1090.[5]

Slightly greater substance may be allowed to the claim made by Milo Crispinus for Lanfranc of Bec[6] (*c.* 1005–89), that together with his pupils he engaged in correcting the text of the Bible and of the Fathers (*secundum orthodoxam fidem studuit corrigere*) and that his work was widely accepted within the Church. As a master of dialectic and a defender of orthodox theology against the rationalism of Berengar of Tours in the matter of transubstantiation, Lanfranc (abbot of Caen and archbishop of Canterbury) showed himself a champion of tradition and of the doctrine of the universal church. His reform of English monasticism and ecclesiastical administration, and particularly his introduction of the False Decretals (which brought England into line with the Canon law of the general church), are in character; and a

[1] Berger (3), pp. 120–29, 137 f., 140; Quentin, pp. 361 f., 380 f., 384.

[2] *Vita, amatore B,* §37, ed. W. Stubbs, *Memorials of St Dunstan*, Rolls Series, London, LXIII (1874), 49 (*ut...mendosos libros...corrigeret*); Glunz (2), p. 159, note.

[3] Sigebert of Gembloux, *de Scriptoribus Ecclesiasticis*, §164; *P.L.* 160, 585 B (Franco); *Gesta Abbat. Gemblacensium, P.L.* 160, 625 B (Olpert). C. Vercellone, *Variae Lectiones Vulgatae Latinae Bibliorum Editionis*, I (Rome, 1860), p. xvii note. Glunz, *ibid.*

[4] *De Ordine Eremitarum, P.L.* 145, 334 C. Cf. Berger (3), p. 141.

[5] J. Mabillon, *Annales Ordinis S. Benedicti*, V (Paris, 1713), p. 277; Martin (1), p. 57. E. Nestlé, 'Die Hirschauer Vulgata-Revision', *Theologische Studien aus Württemberg*, X (1889), 305–11.

[6] *Vita, P.L.* 150, 55 C. Cf. also the contemporary tribute to him of Clement III, quoted by F. Liebermann in the *English Historical Review*, XVI (1901), 331. For Lanfranc see A. J. Macdonald, *Lanfranc* (2nd ed., 1944); Z. N. Brooke, *The English Church and the Papacy, etc.* (1931), pp. 57–83, 117–31; R. W. Southern in *Studies...presented to F. M. Powicke* (1948), pp. 27 f.; Smalley (2), pp. 46 f.

'correction' of the biblical text so as to make it conform to orthodoxy would fall into place beside these achievements. Such 'correction' amounts to the prosecution of the early scholastic treatment of the Bible outlined above (see p. 140), through which modifications were introduced so as to point explicitly towards the exegesis of the Fathers.[1] Lanfranc was thus bringing the English bible into line with that of eleventh-century Europe. In one Gospel manuscript[2] interlinear glosses are found which, like Lanfranc's own commentary to the Pauline epistles[3] and the *Gloss* to the whole Bible that was, by 1137, already in process of becoming recognized at Paris as the standard commentary of the Western Church (below, pp. 145 f., 190, 205),[4] depend closely on Remigius of Auxerre's digest of patristic commentaries. A fair sample of Lanfranc's improved readings is at Luke v. 25, *tulit lectum in quo iacebat*, where *lectum* is a new insertion intended to point to the exegesis, adapted from Ambrose by Bede,[5] which equates the *bed* with the human body. Substantial manuscript testimony to Lanfranc's text is available from the late eleventh century onwards.[6] It may be exemplified by William of Hales' Bible (in the New Testament W),[7] dated 1254, which is a copy of a Salisbury manuscript more than a century older.[8]

Significant, too, as a pointer towards the future, are occasional allusions to the comparative application to the Vulgate text of a linguistic competence that went beyond the study of the norms of Latin grammar. In the ninth century Greek studies had perhaps been directed at patristic rather than at biblical scholarship; but John the Scot had compared the Latin text of the Gospel of St John with more than one Greek text,[9] and relics of a similar approach to the Psalter, possibly

[1] Glunz (2), p. 163.

[2] MS British Museum, Royal, I. B. xi; Glunz (2), pp. xvii, 159 f.

[3] *P.L.* 150, 101 f.

[4] Smalley (2), pp. 46 f., 63 f., 71.

[5] Ambrose, ed. C. Schenkl, *C.S.E.L.* 32, part IV, p. 184, l. 16, *P.L.* 15, 1639 B. Bede, *P.L.* 92, 388 D.

[6] MS Wadham College, Oxford, ii (A. 10. 22), of 1070 or shortly after. Glunz (2), pp. xvii, 166 f.

[7] MS British Museum, Royal, I. B. xii. Glunz (2), pp. xvii, 184.

[8] MS Salisbury Cathedral, 148. Glunz (2), *ibid.*

[9] *Comm. in Iohann., P.L.* 122, 302 C, etc. See E. Nestlé, 'Scotus Erigena on Greek Manuscripts of the Fourth Gospel', *Journal of Theological Studies*, XIII (Oxford, 1912), 596. M. Cappuyns, *Jean Scot Érigène: sa vie, son œuvre, sa pensée* (Louvain and Paris, 1933), p. 225. See also Smalley (2), pp. 43 f.

connected with Sedulius Scotus, are also extant.[1] There is no evidence that Hebrew studies were cultivated in the early scholastic period, with the possible exception of disciple(s?) inspired by Theodulf (see above, p. 129). In the eleventh century, however, the cultivation of Hebrew began to eclipse that of Greek, though Odo, bishop of Cambrai, had, while abbot of St Martin's, Tournai (i.e. not later than 1105), had a quadruple psalter prepared that exhibited the transliterated Greek alongside the three Latin versions.[2] Contact with Jewish scholars is attested for Sigebert of Gembloux in Metz, *c.* 1070, for Abelard,[3] and (somewhat later) from the Jewish side also.[4] This renewed interest in Hebrew scholarship was to bear fruit in the twelfth and thirteenth centuries, but the results fall mainly within the field of exegesis, and they qualify for mention here only in so far as textual repercussions can be demonstrated.[5] On this score the corrected bible,[6] dated 1109, of Stephen Harding, third abbot of Cîteaux,[7] deserves inclusion by virtue of its apparent intention; for in an inserted note Harding records the origin of his text and hints at its purpose. Having transcribed the fullest of a number of texts that he had assembled, he erased such passages of the Old Testament as were not to be found in the Hebrew, availing himself of the assistance of a converted Jew with whom he conversed in French. Since Harding requests readers not to restore the erased passages, and forbids improper use of the book *auctoritate Dei et nostrae*

[1] Kenney, p. 568 note 375; A. Allgeier, 'Exegetische Beiträge zur Geschichte des Griechischen vor dem Humanismus', *Biblica*, XXIV (Rome, 1943), 261 f., 264 (MSS 24–6).

[2] It may be confidently identified with MS Paris, B.N. *nouv. acqu.* 2195; see L. Delisle, *Mélanges de Paléographie et de Bibliographie* (Paris, 1880), pp. 150 f.; *Palaeographical Society*, ed. E. A. Bond and E. M. Thompson, II (London, 1873–83), Pl. 156; V. Leroquais, *Les Psautiers manuscrits latins des Bibliothèques de France*, II (Mâcon, 1940–1), no. 373, p. 142, with full bibliography.

[3] Sigebert: *Gesta abbat. Gemblacensium*, continued by Godeschalc, *P.L.* 160, 641 B. Smalley (2), pp. 79, 80 note. Abelard: *Problemata Eloissae*, §36, *P.L.* 178, 718 A. On Abelard's fictitious *Dialogue* with a Jew, see H. Liebeschütz in *The Journal of Jewish Studies*, XII (1961), 1 f., 12.

[4] See e.g. Z. Kahn, 'Le Livre de Joseph le Zélateur', *Revue des Études Juives*, I (Paris, 1880), 238, 239, 242; J. Katz, *Exclusiveness and Tolerance* (*Scripta Judaica* 3) (Oxford, 1961), pp. 106 f.

[5] On the whole subject see Berger (4); Smalley (1); (2), pp. 82, 102 f.; Loewe (2).

[6] MSS Dijon, 12–15 (formerly 9 *bis*). See [P. Quarre], *Saint Bernard et l'Art des Cisterciens* (Dijon, 1953), p. 30.

[7] F. 150ᵛ of vol. 2. The ascription of this correction to Alberic, Harding's predecessor (*Gallia Christiana*, IV, 984), rests on a confusion; see Martin (1), p. 17; Denifle, pp. 267 f., 462; Berger (4), pp. 9 f.; Loewe (2), p. 233.

congregationis, he seems to have intended it as a model for Cistercian use.[1] His text reflects a precursor of the heavily interpolated Paris bible[2] (see below, pp. 145f.), but Theodulf's influence is to be detected, particularly in the canonical order followed[3] (see above, p. 128). Another Cistercian who cultivated a similar approach was Nicholas Manjacoria of Rome; himself a Hebraist, he also used Jewish assistance, and showed in his writings (to be dated towards the middle of the century) an incipient critical sense that led him to reject the Hebrew as testimony to the Vulgate except where his Latin manuscripts were reciprocally at variance.[4] In his *Libellus de corruptione et correptione Psalmorum*, written shortly after 1145, he too alludes to a specifically Cistercian psalter-text, and criticizes the assumption (as had Harding, by implication) that the fullest text is necessarily the most accurate.[5] He had previously carried out a revision of the Bible, removing superfluities from its text,[6] and although his version has not hitherto been identified in any manuscript its character may be reconstructed from his surviving *prolegomena*—entitled, in a fifteenth-century manuscript,[7] *Suffrageneus Bibliothecae*. The terms of reference were to remove additions to the original Vulgate, to restore modified or corrupt readings (*transformata reformare*), and to replace the genuine text where this had been arbitrarily deleted.[8] The treatise categorizes numerous passages from all parts of the Old Testament (but none from the New) that have suffered damage from each of the specified causes; and the material designated as surplus shows that Nicholas, like Harding, started from

[1] Cf. Mabillon's note in his edition of St Bernard, *P.L.* 182, 1119, §2; also below, note 4 and p. 145 n. 1. Berger (2), p. 8.

[2] Denifle, pp. 269, 475, as against Martin (1), pp. 65 f., who takes it to be Θ.

[3] Martin (1), p. 19; Berger (4), p. 11.

[4] On Manjacoria see Denifle, pp. 270 f.; Berger (4), pp. 12 f.; Wilmart, pp. 136 f. (to p. 136 n. 2, add reference to MS Venice, St Mark's, *olim* 133, *Catalogue* by J. Valentinelli, II (1869), 134). Denifle, p. 272; Berger (4), p. 13 (*in his tantummodo hebraicos codices michi censui consulendos, in quibus nostri aperte sibi invicem dissonarent*). MS Montpellier Medical School, 294 (late twelfth century); Wilmart, pp. 138 f., 141 f., 142. F. 144ʳ: *psalterium...ad exemplar nostrum idest Cisterciensis ordinis emendare*).

[5] F. 158ʳ. Wilmart, pp. 141 f.; Smalley (2), p. 80. The incident concerned took place between 1140 and 1145 (Wilmart, p. 142).

[6] F. 145ᵛ. Wilmart, pp. 139, 142 (*bibliothecam studiose conscriberem multisque superfluitatibus expiarem*).

[7] Venice, St Mark's, 178 (*olim lat.* 289), ff. 141–81; *Catalogue* (see above, note 4), IV (1871), 126. J. P. P. Martin, *Introduction à la Critique...du Pentateuch*, I (Paris, 1887), pp. cii f. [8] Denifle, p. 272, §3; Berger (3), p. 13.

what was later to become the 'Paris' text.[1] Again like Harding, he followed the canonical order of Isidore and Theodulf (see above, pp. 124, 128), save for the inversion of Job and Psalms. By the end of the twelfth century this Paris text was establishing itself as a supposedly uniform and recognized recension, traces of which can be detected in the Psalter-text of Herbert of Bosham,[2] although the latter (writing soon after 1190) took an Alcuinian text as the basis of his edition, and was substantially influenced by Theodulf, by direct reference to the Hebrew, and by Jewish exegesis.[3]

The development of the so-called Paris text[4] of the Bible was a contributory cause of the emergence of the University of Paris from the episcopal school, and its establishment as commanding a certain recognition was the result of the same process. In itself, the text (which is symbolized in the critical apparatus of *Biblia Sacra by* Ω) forms the culmination of the tendency that we have noticed since early post-Carolingian times, by which the text became progressively more adapted so as to point specifically towards the exegetical treatment of the Fathers. The *Sentences* of Peter Lombard, finished in 1152, comprise a systematic theology based essentially on patristic exegesis as digested in the *Gloss*[5] to the Bible, the expansion of which on the Psalms and Pauline epistles into the *Magna Glosatura*[6] was due to Lombard himself and his pupil and posthumous editor, Herbert of Bosham. It is possible to illustrate the organic interdependence of the text, in its twelfth-century form, and the *Gloss*, and to point to the dependence of the *Sentences* on both.[7] Thus in Matt. xviii. 10, *quia angeli eorum in caelis semper vident faciem patris mei*, some scholastic texts, the

---

[1] Denifle observes that the matter marked by Nicholas as superfluous and to be deleted at I Sam. v. 6 and v. 9 is likewise omitted in Harding's text.

[2] MS St Paul's Cathedral, London, Case B. 13; see B. Smalley, 'A Commentary on the *Hebraica* by Herbert of Bosham', *Recherches de Théologie Ancienne et Médiévale*, XVIII (Louvain, 1951), 29 f.; Loewe (1). For date, see Loewe, p. 63 n. 2.

[3] The basic text is of the type of Sainte-Marie's O (=MS Bodleian, Auct. E. inf. 2, Berger (3), p. 399, Sainte-Marie, p. x), but it is affected by Ω^M and Θ^K. See Sainte-Marie, p. xiv. The Symbol O used on pp. 120, 127n. 8, and 136 refers to two other MSS.

[4] The basic study is Denifle's. See also Martin (2), 1888, pp. 444 f., 1890, pp. 301 f.; Glunz (2), pp. 221 f.

[5] On its development see Smalley (2), pp. 46 f., and pp. 197 ff. of the present volume; above, p. 142 n. 4. It is printed, *P.L.* 113–14.

[6] *P.L.* 191–2.

[7] Glunz (2), pp. 255 f.; Smalley (2), p. 64.

Gloss, and the *Sentences*[1] omit *in caelis*, following the exegesis of Jerome which here recognizes the doctrine of guardian angels: the sphere of activity of these must be not in heaven, but on earth. The *Sentences* had immediately become a standard theological textbook; lecturing on the *Magna Glosatura* was instituted after Peter Lombard's death in 1160, and attracted to him a posthumous reputation for heterodoxy. When his views were, by implication, condemned at the Synod of Sens in 1164, those who favoured his scholastic method—and with it, inevitably, the form of the Vulgate text that was integral both to his exegetical digests and his own systematic theology—were forced into a standpoint of opposition in which the University of Paris was germinally present. The primacy won by the Paris school of theology served both to consolidate and to disseminate the form of text there current, particularly in view of the appearance at this time of bible manuscripts in small, one-volume format on thin parchment which could easily be carried among a wandering scholar's personal effects.[2]

At some time in the first third of the thirteenth century a single codex may have been selected as a master-copy for future use and designated the *exemplar Parisiense*; but if any such archetype ever existed, it is no longer identifiable. Its character may, however, be reconstructed from comparison of the Paris codex Ω^J with two others.[3] In view of its integration with the *Gloss* and the latter's underlying patristic sources which frequently start from non-Vulgate readings, it is not surprising that the 'Paris' text was a heavily interpolated and corrupt representation of the Vulgate, contaminated by material from the margin and from corrected erasures. A marginal form of text-critical apparatus was also provided.

The Paris text, then—for all its encrustation, still basically the text

[1] *In caelis* is omitted, e.g., in MSS Trinity College, Cambridge, B. 5. 3 and B. 5. 5; Glunz (2), pp. xviii, 256. Cf. *Gloss*, *P.L.* 114, 146C; Jerome, *in Matth.*, *P.L.* 26, 130B; Peter Lombard's *Sentences*, II, *dist.* XI, 1, ed. the St Bonaventure Franciscans, Quarracchi, Florence, I (1916), 334, *P.L.* 192, 673.

[2] Glunz (2), pp. 222, 224, 265, 267, 269. Some specimens of these small-format bibles are reproduced in *The New Palaeographical Society*, ed. E. M. Thompson, etc., 1st Series (London, 1911–12), no. 217, the English examples being, however, earlier than the French one (MS British Museum, Add. 31,830, c. 1252–75. Comprising 480 folios, it measures 5¾ in. by 4 in.).

[3] Ω^J = Paris, B.N. 16719–22; cf. B.N. 15554, ff. 1–146, and *ibid*. ff. 147–253. Denifle, pp. 285 f., 291, 568, 571. Glunz (2), pp. 261, 282, denies that a single, definitive master-copy ever existed at Paris. Cf. Martin (2), 1889, p. 446.

of Alcuin—was a natural growth that arose to meet the needs of the masters and scholars of the Paris schools. It was in no sense a specially edited or officially sponsored text—though the Paris doctors may have touched it up in places in the interests of consistency—but the fruit of private enterprise on the part of the Paris stationers, over whom the University exercised limited control through the grant of privilege.[1] The text was frequently issued from the bookshops accompanied by the *Gloss*;[2] yet the extent to which text and *Gloss* were harmonized, both in such copies and also in the unglossed bibles, varied according to the judgement of whoever controlled the scriptorium. The result was that, owing to irresponsible copying, manifold variation on a large scale soon became widespread.[3] The complexion of this mass-produced 'text' is reflected in the strictures passed on it by Roger Bacon[4] in the second half of the thirteenth century and by the attempts which, already before his time, were being made to remedy its shortcomings (see below, pp. 148 f.). In one respect only did the Paris text achieve a uniformity that was to be perpetuated, and that was its canonical order and its revised chapter-division; and it is the latter which became its distinguishing external characteristic.[5] In view of the international provenance of the student body at Paris, and the existence of numerous systems of chapter-division from late antiquity and the early medieval period that sometimes enjoyed localized currency and were therefore found in bibles that scholars brought with them from their native lands, there was felt in the Paris schools the absolute need for a standardized canonical order and system of capitulation. The new arrangement is ascribed to Stephen Langton, and it is substantially the one in use today.[6] Langton was

---

[1] See Denifle, pp. 282, 568, 571. Roger Bacon, *Opus Minus*, Brewer, p. 330, refers to *multi theologi infiniti et stationarii Parisiis*; Smalley (2), p. 334 n. 4. Glunz (2), pp. 268–70. H. Rashdall (ed. F. M. Powicke and A. B. Emden), *The Universities of Europe*[2] (1936), I, 421 f.

[2] Smalley (2), pp. 334 f.

[3] Denifle, p. 278; Glunz (2), pp. 270, 272.

[4] The relevant passages are: *Opus Minus*, Brewer, pp. 330, 333; *Opus Tertium*, p. 92. They have been frequently reproduced. (Briefly, Smalley (2), p. 334.)

[5] Berger (1), pp. 53 f.; (3), pp. 10 f.; Denifle, pp. 290 f.; Martin (3), 1889, p. 447, 1890, p. 302.

[6] Berger (2), p. 11, substantiates the attribution by reference to MS Lyons, 340 (note at the beginning of Proverbs). Denifle, p. 281; Smalley (2), p. 222; Martin (3), 1889, pp. 447 ff., 1890, p. 304. Martin draws attention particularly to MS Paris B.N. 14417, ff. 125–6. Smalley (2), p. 222. On earlier chapter-divisions see the *prolegomena* to *Biblia Sacra, Genesis*. The differences are tabulated by Martin, p. 466. The subdivision into

teaching in Paris until June 1206, when he was made a cardinal; between that year and 1231, the date of the earliest known dated Paris bible,[1] written at Canterbury, Langton's chapter system had gained currency at Paris, and had come to be disseminated widely alongside Peter Lombard's *Sentences* and other textbooks in use in the Paris schools. Bacon, writing about 1267, misconstrued the situation when he contrasted the corrupt, 'modern' text of Paris—which he assumed to have been deliberately established some forty years previously—with the text found in earlier manuscripts: for many of the interpolations and corruptions in the 'Paris' text antedate that text by centuries.[2] But by Bacon's time the origin of the Paris text was already obscure; and in any case, the main target of his attack was rather the attempts that had been made to remedy its shortcomings—attempts which, he complained, left confusion worse confounded.[3]

Bacon's criticisms had been adumbrated over a century before by Hugh of St Victor (*d.* 1141);[4] and we have already noticed the attempts of Stephen Harding and Nicholas Manjacoria in the first half of the twelfth century to improve matters. Textual criticism had, moreover, figured in a casual and unsystematic way in the biblical lectures of Stephen Langton[5] at the end of the century, but it was not until the second quarter of the thirteenth century that correction of the Bible was taken seriously in hand.[6] The initiative came from the two new mendicant orders, priority lying with the Dominicans, although it was the Franciscan *Correctoria*[7] which, profiting from the experience of their

verses was subsequent, and the current system is not older than the sixteenth century; Martin (3), p. 458, and 1890, p. 304.

[1] MS Paris, Mazarine Library, 29; Berger (2), p. 11 n. 3; Denifle, pp. 282, 290. It should be noted that up to the end of II Samuel this manuscript follows the older capitulation.   [2] Denifle, pp. 277–83, 573; Glunz (2), p. 282.

[3] *Opus Tertium*, Brewer, p. 94: *unde eorum correctio est pessima corruptio et destructio textus Dei*, etc.; *Opus Minus*, p. 347.

[4] *De Scripturis*, 9, *P.L.* 175, 18A: *ita tandem omnia confusa sint ut pene nunc cui tribuendum sit, ignoretur.* Denifle, p. 276.

[5] Martin (3), 1889, p. 456; Smalley (2), pp. 220, 335.

[6] The fundamental study is by Denifle. See also Berger (1), pp. 46 f.; (2), pp. 10 f.; (4), pp. 26 f.; Glunz (2), pp. 284 f.; Smalley (2), pp. 335 f.; E. Mangenot, art. 'Correctoires', in *Dictionnaire de la Bible*, II (1899), col. 1022, is still of importance.

[7] *Correctorium* is the conventional term for these *apparatus*, which should properly be termed *correctiones*; see Hody, p. 418; Glunz (2), p. 285 n. 2. *Correctorium* (*-us*) is strictly the title assigned to tracts on the prosody, etc., of difficult words in the Bible,

predecessors, were to exercise the greater influence; and few of the later *Correctoria* are entirely independent.[1] Chronological data are afforded by the enactment of the Dominican Chapter General in 1236 that bibles of the Order[2] be standardized according to the corrections prepared in the Province of France—an enterprise that is presumably to be identified with the *Correction* of Theobald and possibly also with the *correctio parisiensis secunda*.[3] According to Roger Bacon,[4] the Dominicans produced this supposedly second *Correction c.* 1248, but conceivably there was one enterprise only, elaborated over a number of years. In any case, in 1256 the Dominicans rejected and proscribed what they termed the 'Corrections of Sens',[5] no doubt intending to replace them with an improvement upon the earlier ones, newly prepared by the prior of their Paris house, Hugh of St Cher. Of the Franciscans' *Corrections*, that attributed to William le Breton (F)[6]—in due course to be utilized by Stephanus for his fourth edition of the Bible, 1538–40, the edition cited in the apparatus to *Biblia Sacra* as e—depends on the two 'Paris' *Corrections*.[7] This compilation was surpassed in point of scholarship by that of William of Mara [MS Vatican 3466 (D)], a friend of Bacon (whose principles of textual criticism it closely follows), and also by a further *Correction* [MS Vatican 4240 (E)], found in a group of manuscripts, which has much in common with the *Correction* of William of Mara.[8]

after the style of Alexander Neckam's *Corrogationes Promethei*, for which see P. Meyer, *Notices et Extraits de la Bibl. Nationale*, XXXV, 2 (Paris, 1897), 641; R. Loewe in *Mediaeval and Renaissance Studies*, IV (London, 1958), 18.

[1] Denifle, p. 544; Mangenot (see p. 148 n. 6), col. 1025.

[2] Berger (2), p. 11, pointed to MS Paris, B.N. *lat.* 17 as being the bible from which the Dominicans started: essentially the Paris text, it agrees with citations from the 'Sens Bible' in the Sorbonne *Correctorium*, i.e. *F* (see this page), MS B.N. 15554, ff. 147 f. By 'Sens Bible' is, of course, to be understood the 'Sens corrections'; Denifle, p. 284.

[3] See Martène and Durand, *Thesaurus novus anecdotorum*, IV (Paris, 1717), col. 1676, B, §34; Berger (1), p. 57; (4), p. 30; Mangenot (see p. 148 n. 6), col. 1023.

[4] *Opus Maius*, ed. S. Jebb (1733), p. 49; Berger (4), p. 27.

[5] *Thesaurus novus* (see note 3), col. 1715, E, §23. Cf. note 2.

[6] MS Paris, B.N. 15554, ff. 147 f., cf. note 2. Berger (1), pp. 58 f., 62; Mangenot, col. 1024.

[7] The fluidity of terminology used in the *Correctoria* complicates the task of establishing interdependence; cf. Denifle, p. 285. For Stephanus in this connection, see J. Wordsworth, *Old-Latin Biblical Texts: No. I, The Gospel according to St Matthew* (Oxford, 1883), Appendix I, pp. 49, 50. Cf. Berger (1), p. 58.

[8] Berger (1), pp. 63–4, identifies *D* and *E*; Denifle distinguishes them, p. 265. See also Berger (4), pp. 32 f., and Denifle, pp. 298, 545, but cf. p. 311.

Manuscripts of these *Correctoria* have been categorized into thirteen groups, listed serially *A–N*. Of these, groups *A*, *D*, and *E* refer to the Greek bible independently of the Old Latin, and are provided (in some manuscripts) with prologues setting forth the principles of criticism that they follow.[1] That of group *A*, specifically attributed to Hugh of St Cher and cited in the apparatus to *Biblia Sacra* as *Hug.*,[2] used red underlinings and supralinear points as critical symbols, and claimed to take as its authorities the commentaries of Jerome, pre-Carolingian codices, and Hebrew manuscripts. The door was thus opened to matter irrelevant for the recovery of Jerome's text, the dominating consideration being to assimilate the Latin to the original. Sounder principles animated the author of the *Correctorium Vaticanum*, i.e. *D*, who is to be identified with Bacon's *homo sapientissimus*[3] and, through him, with William of Mara: it is consequently cited by *Biblia Sacra* as *Guill.* (*cor. vat.* in the New Testament). This corrector's self-discipline prevented his very considerable Hebrew competence, and his knowledge of Greek, from interfering with his reconstruction of the Latin Vulgate. He explicitly rejects, as wrong-headed procedure, the branding of the Latin as spurious wherever it cannot literally reproduce Hebrew or Greek idiom; and he appreciates that contemporary Hebrew manuscripts are not *ipso facto* preferable to older Latin ones. The author of *E* (MS Vatican *Lat.* 4240), Gerard of Huy,[4] though standing close to *D*, knew less Hebrew than he, but surpassed him both in Greek and in judgement; and his approach reminds one of that of Nicholas Manjacoria (above, p. 144). Comparison with the Hebrew and Greek, he writes, must be circumspect, and the slavish following of the originals must be eschewed; reference ought not to be made to them save in the case of the discrepancy of the oldest Latin codices, unless it is a case of remedying such palpable inner-Latin corruptions as *saeculi* for *sacculi* at Proverbs xvi. 11. Patristic quotations, which often follow the non-Hieronymic version, should be discounted as evidence. Matter omitted

---

[1] Denifle, pp. 264 f., 596 f.

[2] MS Vatican Ottob. 293; Denifle, pp. 264, 293. MS Paris, B.N. 16719 (Denifle's *B*) is also cited, in the apparatus to *Biblia Sacra*, as *Iac.*

[3] Denifle, pp. 265, 295, 298, 545, 553. Berger (4), pp. 32 f., 35, 45. Brewer, pp. 89, 92 below, 94.

[4] So Denifle, p. 477. Berger (1), p. 64, asserted that this could not be so in spite of the reference to Gerard in MS Vatican *Lat.* 4240, since the occasional vernacular words included are in French, not in Flemish. See also Berger (4), pp. 46 f.

in the various manuscripts under review is underlined, the authority concerned being indicated by a superscribed initial—*h*[*ebraeus*], *o* (= Septuagint), *t* (= Greek), *a*[*ntiqui*], *m*[*oderni*], *aug*[*ustinus*], *ier*[*onymus*], *gr*[*egorius*], *B*[*eda*], *R*[*abanus*], *gl*[*osa*]. The author concludes with a conventional invitation of constructive criticism and the improvement of his work.[1]

For all its soundness, this approach achieved less than might have been hoped. Above all, since the *Correctoria* largely circulated as *apparatus* unaccompanied by any diacritically marked text, side by side with their multiplication their corruption increased progressively.[2] Both *E* and *D* regard Alcuin's bible as basic; but the correctors had an inadequate number of significant codices for comparison and none, it seems, anterior to the ninth–tenth century (this is, at least, demonstrably so in the case of Proverbs).[3] References to 'Charle[magne]'s bible' seem in fact to indicate the first bible of Charles the Bald.[4] In a few places only may *E* and *D* have had at their disposal readings that they themselves appreciated as pre-Carolingian, and references to the bible of Gregory the Great[5] do not appear to signify the text of scriptural quotations in Gregory's own works. In general, the correctors misconstrued (and rejected) pre-Alcuinian readings as 'modern', inasmuch as it was in the Paris text that they found them, ensconced there by the *Gloss* and its patristic antecedents. It is noticeable that *E* makes less use of Bede than do *B*, *C*, *D*, or *F*, and senses that in default of a critically sound text of Bede his quotations ought not to be relied on; yet had pre-Alcuinian manuscripts been available to him, he would have realized that they gave him warranty to make a freer use of Bede.

In spite, therefore, of the bias in Bacon's language that it has become usual to discount, his complaint[6] that the *Correctoria* (or at any rate, as he, a loyal Franciscan, put it, those of the Dominicans) had served merely to make matters worse, must broadly be accepted: and it was the Paris bible, as the natural issue of Alcuin's bible and the precipitate of patristic exegesis to which the scholastics had wedded it, that was in due course to confront the Renaissance editors of the early prints,

[1] All this is treated more fully in Denifle, pp. 306 ff.
[2] Bacon, *Opus Minus*, ed. Brewer, p. 333. Berger (1), pp. 51 f., 65 f.; (2), pp. 9 f., 13 f.
[3] Denifle, pp. 587 f., 590.
[4] Cf. above, p. 138 n. 3; Denifle, p. 591.
[5] Bacon, *Opus Minus*, ed. Brewer, p. 335; Denifle, pp. 301, 591–2.
[6] See above, p. 147 n. 4; Smalley (2), p. 335.

and indeed to leave its mark on the Clementine edition of the Vulgate of 1592.

The Renaissance, and the fortunes of the Latin bible in the age of printing, lie outside the scope of the present chapter: but the story as it has been here presented has its own epilogue, still set on the stage of the thirteenth century and linked to the foregoing account of the *Correctoria* by a common Franciscan connection. An awakened interest in Greek, and even more so in Hebrew, animated a few adventurous minds within both mendicant orders—the Dominicans largely in virtue of their concern for evangelizing among the Jews, and the Franciscans perhaps because of a striving to recreate as far as possible in their own experience the spiritual background for the ministry of Jesus. The impact of this incipient Orientalism was to elicit from the Church, instigated by Raymond Lull at the Council of Vienne in 1312, a directive that Chairs for the teaching of Greek, Hebrew, Aramaic and Arabic should be established at Paris, Bologna, Salamanca, and Oxford.[1] Although as far as England was concerned this injunction was to remain virtually a dead letter[2] until the sixteenth century, some seventy years before its enactment the interest in biblical scholarship of Robert Grosseteste, bishop of Lincoln until his death in 1253, bore fruit in the shape of a new Latin translation of the Old Testament made direct from the Hebrew. This rendering, which was an attempt to wring the last drop of significance out of the Hebrew text, was prepared probably by some unknown English Franciscans with Jewish assistance.[3] It was written between the lines of Hebrew manuscripts, some of them being specially written for the purpose, and came to be known as the *Superscriptio Lincolniensis*. The Hebrew is rendered literally save where, by a paradox, rabbinical exegesis scarcely intended by the Jewish commentators to be taken *ad litteram* has nevertheless been adopted, on the principle that any Jewish exegesis must, *ex hypothesi*, be 'literal'.[4] The

[1] See C. J. Hefele, *Histoire des Conciles*, ed. H. Leclercq, VI (Paris, 1914), 689; Berger (4), p. 57.

[2] An ex-Jewish convert called John of Bristol was teaching Hebrew and Greek at Oxford in 1320–1. See C. Roth, 'Jews in Oxford after 1290', *Oxoniensia*, XV (1950), 63; H. Rashdall, *The Universities of Europe* (see above, p. 147 n. 1), III, 161 f.

[3] See Loewe (3), pp. 211 f., 226 f.

[4] Loewe, 'The Jewish Midrashim and Patristic and Scholastic Exegesis of the Bible', *Studia Patristica*, I (= *Texte und Untersuchungen*, Berlin, 63), 1957, pp. 501 f., 512 f.;

value of prefixed particles and suffixed pronouns, etc., is clearly brought out, resort being made where necessary to Latin neologism. Thus, at Psalm 45:3, for the Hebrew *yophy āphīthā* (Authorized Version *thou art fairer*), the Gallican Psalter has *speciosus forma* and the Psalter *iuxta hebraeos* has *decore pulchrior es*, both versions sensing, but being unable fully to express, the significance of the reduplication in this form of the Hebrew root ʏᴘʜ = *beautiful*. The nuance of that reduplication is here a quantification, which the *Superscriptio* catches (the Hebrew form being verbal) by coining *speciosissimasti*. The whole text of Psalms survives, in several manuscripts, and portions of several other books of the Old Testament also: and it may have been the translator's (or sponsor's) intention or ambition to extend the same treatment to the whole of the Hebrew bible. Although the experiment was to have no future, the manuscript evidence indicates progressive improvement and elaboration; and a passing remark of Henry of Cossey, an early-four-teenth-century Cambridge Franciscan, may imply that the possibility of its approval by the papal *Curia* had at least been mooted. It was not until the Renaissance versions of Pagninus, Arias Montanus, and Munster that anything similar was to see the light.[1]

It may be helpful to visualize the history of the Latin bible with the help of a sustained astronomical metaphor, Hebrew and Jewish mono-theism being pictured as the centre of a solar system. Around it moves a planet, the Hebrew bible, possessing its own moon, the Greek trans-lation. Under the impact of Jesus and Paul the central object erupted, to throw off Christianity as a second planet, charged with sufficient energy to generate its own atmosphere of patristic tradition, and possessed of sufficient gravitational pull to attract the Greek bible—the 'moon' of the Hebrew bible—into orbit round itself. Christianity also acquired a second satellite in the shape of the Latin bible, compounded as it were out of the interplanetary dust of the Latin-speaking world. The Latin bible—which, down to at least the age of Charlemagne, often amounted for practical purposes to the Gospels, with perhaps the Pauline epistles and the Psalms—has from time to time been exposed to the gravitational pull of other objects that form part of the cluster

also 'The "Plain" meaning of Scripture in Early Jewish Exegesis', in *Papers of the Institute of Jewish Studies, London* (Jerusalem, 1964), pp. 140 f.

[1] Loewe (3), pp. 213 f., n. 39; Berger (4), pp. 49 f.; Smalley (2), pp. 342 f.; Loewe (4).

that includes Judaism, Christianity, Greek philosophy and European humanism; and the outcome has been sundry attempts at improving its language by Roman classicism or by Hebraic realism in diction. Yet the patristic tradition that had nurtured the specialized vocabulary of early Latin Christianity has enveloped the Latin bible with an air that Christians could breathe: so that such waves of hebraization, or of classicism, that have affected the atmosphere of the Church have given it but a transient negative charge. Thus it has come about that the Vulgate has always been held fast to its own orbit, whereas some of its own vernacular and other satellites have been captured, especially in the countries of the Reformation, by the gravitational pull of the original Hebrew of the Old Testament, and the Greek of the New.

CHAPTER VI

THE EXPOSITION AND EXEGESIS
OF SCRIPTURE

1. TO GREGORY THE GREAT

The ways in which the Bible was interpreted by the Church of the first six centuries had already been partly determined by the Christian communities of the apostolic age itself. From the earliest stage to which the tradition of the Church can be traced, the Scriptures of the Old Testament had been interpreted as a book about Christ. The decisive act of God in human history had taken place; the Gospel events stood as the central and focal point of God's dealings with mankind. The promises to Israel, and the long chain of events in which, according to the Scriptures, these promises were worked out in divine judgements and in saving acts of mercy and deliverance, had reached their fulfilment in the life, death and Resurrection of Christ. This fulfilment could only be apprehended as such in the light of the ancient promises and the entire course of Israel's history, as this had been interpreted in the prophetic-historical tradition of the Old Testament. Conversely, the Scriptures could be rightly understood only when they were seen in the new perspective of the age of fulfilment which had now dawned. God had so acted in Christ that the focal point of history, which gave meaning to the whole process, no longer lay in the remote past, in the deliverance from Egypt, the Sinai Covenant and the entry into the Promised Land. A greater exodus had taken place, a new covenant had been established, and the promised age of the Spirit, the last days foretold by the prophets, had now begun. The eschatological hope had taken on a new significance, for the ground for it was now to be found in recent events through which the end itself had been brought proleptically into the present age. The end was not to be an entirely fresh act of God, but the consummation and completion of what had already been decisively accomplished in Christ.

The Lucan Resurrection-narratives ascribe the fundamental Christian reinterpretation of the Scriptures to the risen Christ himself. It was 'necessary' that the Messiah should suffer and enter into his glory; and this necessity was grounded in the Scriptures. 'Beginning from Moses and from all the prophets, he expounded to them in all the scriptures the things concerning himself.' 'All the things which had been written in the law of Moses and the prophets and the psalms concerning me had to be fulfilled.' 'Then he opened their mind to understand the scriptures; and he said to them, "Thus it has been written, that the Messiah should suffer and rise from the dead on the third day, and that repentance for forgiveness of sins should be preached to all the nations"' (Luke xxiv. 26–7, 44–7).

In this scene is summed up the revolution in scriptural exegesis which was effected in the primitive Church. It was in the light of Easter that the Scriptures took on a new meaning, and the belief that Christ's death and Resurrection happened 'according to the scriptures' was already embodied in the very early kerygmatic tradition received by Paul and transmitted by him to his converts. Whether this reinterpretation originated with Jesus himself, in the sense that he believed that they pointed to the nature and course of his own mission, cannot be determined with certainty. We face one of the most difficult problems of New Testament study when we inquire whether it is historically true that Jesus interpreted his own destiny in terms of scriptural prophecies, or whether the primitive Christian tradition read this interpretation back from its own post-Resurrection standpoint into the story of his mission. It is, however, at least highly probable that Jesus regarded his mission as the fulfilment of the work of the prophets who had declared God's judgement and mercy towards Israel; that he saw his inevitable rejection and death as the necessary climax of the divine purpose revealed in the Scriptures, and that he himself, and not only the primitive Church, identified his own person in some sense with the symbolical figure of the Son of Man in Daniel's vision. In particular, it is difficult not to believe that he applied to himself those passages in Scripture which, like the 'Servant Songs', speak of a righteous sufferer.

However this may be, his followers were united in the belief that God's promises had been uniquely and decisively fulfilled in him. Hence they sought to interpret his life of obscurity and rejection, and especially the scandal of a crucified Messiah, as well as the Lordship which they had come to recognize through the Resurrection, by reference to the Old Testament. The Church thus depended for its understanding of itself, and of the Gospel on which its life was founded, upon its interpretation of the Scriptures as a book about Christ. In that book it found the key to its understanding of the historical traditions about his deeds and words, so that the subject of the apostolic preaching was Jesus as seen in the light of Scripture, and it was Jesus as interpreted by Scripture who provided the theme of the Gospels.

Christ was the fulfilment of the scriptural promises. The manner of this fulfilment could be understood and communicated in terms of prophecies and types. In the case of the former, passages of Scripture were taken to refer directly to him; there was an immediate correlation between prophecy and fulfilment, so that the apostolic testimony to his life, death and Resurrection was an open assertion, after the event, of what the prophets of Israel had already declared in a more concealed and mysterious fashion before the time. Thus the Church's foundation was the dual witness of the apostles and prophets, and in the course of time their twofold testimony came to be embodied in the canonical Scriptures of the Old and New Testaments.

Typology similarly detected and set forth the fulfilment of the divine purpose in the Gospel events. In them the saving acts of God in ancient times were seen to be recapitulated: Jesus acted like a new Moses or a new Elijah; his death and Resurrection were a new and greater Exodus; his temptations re-enacted the Deuteronomic testing of Israel in the wilderness. At almost every point the evangelists, often by means of subtle hints and allusions, convey their belief that what God had accomplished in Christ was analogous to his great acts recorded in the Scriptures.

The remarkable fact is that this drastic reinterpretation of the Old Testament as the key to the understanding of the Gospel, and as a record whose true meaning was unintelligible except in relation to its Christian fulfilment, was carried through so rapidly that an established tradition of prophetical and typological exegesis had been built up by the time that the Pauline epistles were composed. Whether or not written collections of prophetic testimonies on the lines of Cyprian's *Testimonia* were in circulation in the apostolic churches, standard interpretations of Old Testament passages in relation both to Christ and the Church were already embodied, by the time of the earliest New

Testament writings, in the tradition of missionary preaching, catechetical teaching and liturgy.

The Church's interpretation of the Scriptures was revolutionary as regards its content; but its method was not wholly novel. The idea of promise and fulfilment was familiar to the prophets themselves, and an elementary typology was used by such prophets as Hosea and the Second Isaiah. For the former, God's acts in the Exodus period pointed to a future dispensation of judgement and mercy when the time of the wilderness sojourn would be re-enacted. The fulfilment of the type still lay, as is usual in the prophets, in the as yet unrealized future. For Deutero-Isaiah, however, the age of fulfilment was already at hand. The wonders of the Exodus, which themselves recapitulated the Creation, were about to be reproduced in a new act of deliverance from Babylon. There was to be a real correspondence between God's past acts and the coming restoration of Israel.

In the Dead Sea scrolls the relation between the Scriptures and the recent past and the future takes a different form. The biblical commentaries assume that recent events were foretold by the prophets, and the interpretation of their prophecies assumes, like Christian exegesis, that the present is related to the past, not simply by an inner logic in the historical process but by the overriding action of the consistent purpose of a transcendent God. Fulfilment corresponds to promise. But in the Qumran commentaries on Habakkuk and Nahum this belief does not find expression in typology. The Old Testament books are regarded as a storehouse of oracles relating not to their own time, but to the present or the recent past. The original context and meaning of a passage are disregarded; they do not establish a pattern of divine action which can now be seen to be recapitulated in the recent events. Rather, a prophetic interpretation has to be read into the text by means of allegory. In the commentaries an allegorical exegesis is introduced by such phrases as 'Interpreted, this saying concerns...'. Thus Isa. v. 10–14 is made to refer to 'the scoffers in Jerusalem', and Isa. liv. 11, 'interpreted...concerns the priests and the people who laid the foundations of the council of the community'. Habakkuk ii. 4, 'the righteous shall live by his faith', meant to Paul the righteousness of faith as opposed to legal works, which was present in Abraham and which, by a typological correspondence, has been manifested again in its completeness in the new covenant established through Christ. The

Commentary on Habakkuk, however, makes it allude to those who put their trust in the community's Teacher of Righteousness. The original meaning has no importance.

Like all allegory, these interpretations are arbitrary. They depend upon the belief that the Scriptures are an assortment of oracles whose meaning is revealed to those who have the insight to discern it and apply it to the contemporary scene. No objective criteria can be established to determine whether the insight of the commentator is correct; so that the presupposition of this kind of exegesis must be that the ingenuity of the allegorist comes by a kind of inspiration. Exegesis, in fact, is a form of prophetic activity. In some Christian writers, such as 'Barnabas' and Clement, this presupposition becomes rather more explicit; the interpreter can discern spiritual allegories because he possesses a special *gnosis* (knowledge). Again, however, there is no criterion for distinguishing true *gnosis* from false.

Allegory of this kind is quite distinct from the detection of parallels between God's acts in the past and what are believed to be his acts in the present or hoped for in the future. A simple typology of analogous situations is common in Judaism. It underlies the structure of many prayers in which the recollection of past mercies gives assurance for the future: 'God, who didst...grant us...' It is also present in much Jewish rhetoric, where the past history of the nation is recalled in order to commend a particular attitude towards present events or future hopes. Psalm 78 is an example of this, and in a Christian context it determines the form of Stephen's apologia in Acts vii, where the history of Israel is expounded in such a way as to convince the audience that Christ is the climax of a succession of prophets and saviours, whereas the present leaders of Judaism stand in a succession of blindness and apostasy. The view of Scripture implied here takes full account of the literal sense; indeed this is essential for the application of the text to the present situation. In the allegorical commentaries among the scrolls, however, no attention is paid to the literal meaning of the text. The Scriptures have been turned into oracles or parables. These need not necessarily have any reference to the providential ordering of history; the rabbis made extensive use of allegory in order to elicit moral and spiritual edification from the text of the Law, and several forms of allegorical exegesis were applied by them for this purpose to the Song of Songs.

It is true that rabbinic allegory tends to be less fully developed and elaborate (indeed, fanciful) than that of the Alexandrian Jewish tradition represented by Philo; but the difference lies in content rather than in method. Paul's application of the Deuteronomic prohibition against muzzling the ox to the Church's duty to maintain its ministers is a good example of the rabbinic use of allegory. Philo, on the other hand, is concerned, like some of the Hellenistic interpreters of Homer, to read a system of philosophy into the Scriptures and in so doing to eliminate apparent obscurities and morally offensive passages. His idea that Abraham's wanderings signify the progress of the soul towards contemplation, and that the wives of the patriarchs stand for moral virtues, has no parallel in Palestinian Judaism. Nevertheless, the Scriptures, especially the Law, were treated in both these branches of Judaism as a treasury of hidden teaching to which the allegorist possessed the key.

The New Testament writers follow Jewish precedent in finding in the Old Testament direct prophecy of events in the distant future, types which, as historical events, foreshadow Christ or the continuing life of the Church (and can thus, as in I Cor. x. 1–11, afford moral examples to it) and, rarely, allegories. The first two of these categories arise out of the conviction that the Gospel events are the climax of God's purposes in history; and the nature of Christian belief implied that prophecies which in Jewish exegesis were referred to a still unrealized future were now for the most part actually fulfilled in Christ. Indeed, the testimonies used by Matthew are introduced by the formula, 'that the saying of the prophet...might be fulfilled', suggesting that the Gospel events had been providentially designed to furnish the fulfilment of what had been predicted. In some cases the narratives were constructed or shaped in order to satisfy the requirements of the prophecies to which they were related. This procedure is particularly obvious in the Matthaean infancy narratives, which seem to have been largely built upon the proof texts of Isa. vii. 14, Mic. v. 1–3, Ps. 72: 10 ff., Hos. xi. 1, Jer. xxxi. 15, and the obscure testimonium, 'He shall be called a Nazaraean'.

Since the decisive event in the history of God's dealings with his people had taken place, the historical records in the Old Testament took on an abundance of fresh meaning. In countless passages foreshadowings of the Gospel could now be discerned. Hence typology is much more frequent and much richer than in Jewish literature. Usually it is straightforward. The original event is seen to be recapitulated in the fulfilment; there is a clear analogy between the two, so that the latter is illustrated and explained by the former, and vice versa. The kind of typology which requires an allegorical interpretation of the original text is less common, though it is present in the analogy between Melchisedek and Christ in the Epistle to the Hebrews. Melchisedek is not a straightforward type of Christ. There is no real parallel between the two as historical figures, and the analogy depends upon the discovery of an allegorical reference to Christ in the fact that Genesis provides Melchizedek with no genealogy, that he was a king and a priest, that his kingdom's name denotes 'peace' and his own name 'king of righteousness'. It is arguable that Matthew's 'out of Egypt have I called my son' also requires arbitrary allegorizing in order to be made applicable to Christ, but this is probably wrong; Matthew may not intend to discard the literal meaning of the text, but rather to show that the historical event of the Exodus was reproduced in the life of Christ as the embodiment of the true Israel. The famous 'allegory', as Paul calls it, of Sarah and Hagar is a striking example of allegorical typology: that is to say, historical analogy which requires the allegorizing of the Old Testament narrative.

Non-historical allegory of the kind employed by the rabbis is very rare in the primitive Church's handling of Scripture. Paul's application of Deut. xxv. 4, mentioned above, is perhaps the only instance. It is, however, significant that by the time of the writing of Mark, Christian interpreters were already allegorizing the parables of Jesus into moral discourses for homiletic purposes. The most notable instances are Mark's explanation of the parable of the sower and Matthew's of the parable of the wheat and the tares. This tendency, which was operating at an early stage of the tradition, as witness the different application made by Luke and Matthew of the parable of the lost sheep, foreshadows the allegorical exegesis of New Testament material by Origen and others in the following centuries. Nothing in the New Testament really corresponds to Philo's allegories, although the exegetical methods of the Epistle to the Hebrews sometimes resemble his, and it is possible that its author knew his work. Hebrews, however, though it uses allegory, does so in order to construct an historical typology. Its thought is dominated by the belief that the God who spoke in the past by the prophets has in these last days spoken to us by a Son. The content of its exegesis is therefore radically different from that of Philo, in whom historical interest has been replaced by concern for philosophical and ethical truth. The difference between Philo and any early Christian writer really lies in the fact that the object of the former was to reinterpret the Old Testament as a book about certain timeless truths, whereas the latter was writing what was in fact, although it did not come to be so called for another century or more, a 'New Testament': a record and interpretation of a new 'Exodus', a final revelation of God, and a new covenant, in the light of which the Old Testament received a new significance as actual history.

All these precedents were employed in the Christian interpretation of the Bible in the first six centuries after the apostolic age. Two particularly difficult questions confronted the Church during this period: the relation of the apostolic writings to traditions believed to have been handed down independently of these documents, and the manner in which the Old Testament should be interpreted. The former question concerns the history of the Canon; the latter concerns us now.

Like the New Testament writers, the Fathers approach the Old Testament in the conviction that the divine purposes in history are revealed in a pattern of promise and fulfilment, and that this means that the Old Testament can in principle be applied at every point to Christ and the Church. The fulfilment of prophecy furnished proof of the Christian claims about Jesus. It could be used in apologetic directed towards Jews who were familiar with the prophecies, and also towards pagans whom the Church approached with the Septuagint in one hand and the apostolic testimony in the other (later reinforced, by Lactantius and others, with the claim that the Sibylline oracles concurred with the prophets in foretelling Christ). It could also be used to assure Christians themselves of the truth of their faith. Typological exegesis could be employed at all levels, from the citation of simple *exempla* from Scripture for the encouragement or admonition of the Church in its life and conduct, to an elaborate sacramental typology by which, especially in the case of baptism, the history of Noah's deliverance (cf. I Pet. iii. 18–22), the Exodus, the water from the rock, the entry into the Promised Land, and other saving events in Israel's history were seen as having been recapitulated in Christ's death and Resurrection and as shared in by the believer through a sacramental *mimesis* (enactment).

In the early Church, however, the prophetic interpretation of history was combined with certain assumptions about the written word of the Old Testament which created many difficulties. It was assumed, as it had been in Jewish exegesis, that the Scriptures were a library of oracles. These oracles are embodied in various outward forms: law, history, prophecy, psalms, wisdom sayings; and this very diversity means that the oracles of God lie concealed under the external forms. To discover them, the exegete must penetrate beyond the literal sense; he must understand that he is confronted by symbols and riddles, and he must elicit the spiritual meaning by treating as secondary, or even discarding, the outward sense, the author's intention, and the context in which a passage occurs. The literal meaning is a husk containing and concealing the inner kernel of truth; and truth concerning faith, morals, worship, Church life and order generally, is in principle extractable from every part of Scripture: for the formation of the Canon of the Old and New Testaments gives value to every part of the Bible. At every point the Holy Spirit has inspired the original writers, and the same Spirit can reveal the meaning to those to whom he gives the insight to apprehend it.

This conception of Scripture presents a constant inducement to the exegete not to rest content with plain historical typology but to pass over into allegory. The principle of unity in the Bible is no longer a pattern of promise and fulfilment disclosed in the historical process itself. It is rather that a unified system of eternal spiritual truth is contained in every part of Scripture. The Scriptures no longer contain 'mysteries' in the New Testament sense of the word: revelations of the purposes of God which were formerly hidden from men's understanding. They *are* mysteries, in the sense of outward forms through which timeless spiritual truths are mediated to the initiate who can perceive them. The basis for this kind of allegorical exegesis is the Platonic notion of the relation of the sensible and temporal order to the intelligible and eternal, together with the Alexandrian tradition of the allegorizing of Homer and classical mythology, and the Philonic interpretation of the Scriptures in terms of ethics and philosophy. Not every Christian exegete favoured the allegorical method. Many who did employ it also made use of historical typology; but the two are easily combined and it is often hard to draw a clear line of distinction between them. Allegory was also a temptingly useful weapon both in apologetic against contemporary Jewish literalism (the rabbis came to discourage the use of allegory because of the advantages which Christian propaganda derived from it), and against Marcion's rejection of the Old Testament.

Another unfortunate presupposition was that because Christ is the central reference-point of the whole Bible, therefore every single part of it is in principle capable of a Christological interpretation. Further, the whole Bible has reference also to the Church, so that any passage which bears the slightest verbal or conceptual association with Christ or the Church may properly be applied to either. Tyconius and Augustine explicitly adopt the principle that passages relating to Christ also refer to his Body. This carries with it the further assumption that there is an unbroken continuity between the Old Testament and the New. Passages from the former can therefore be applied directly and indiscriminately to Christ and the Church. Hence Clement of Rome believed that the institution of bishops and deacons in the apostolic churches was by no means an altogether new thing; it 'had been written' long before in Isaiah lx. 17 (*I Clem.* 42. 5).

This attitude did much to invalidate the typological method of exegesis universally employed in the Church. Properly used, this method should confine itself to the discernment of true analogies between historical events, without overlooking the fact that there is much discontinuity in the history of God's dealings with his people, as well as continuity; that the fulfilment of his purposes in the New Testament is often paradoxical and that it takes place against, as well as in accordance with, the ancient expectations of Israel. Christ superseded and abolished much that was rooted in past history, while on Israel's side there was a long tradition of disobedience and rejection which had to be repudiated, as well as of faith and hope which could be fulfilled. After the breach between Church and Synagogue had become absolute, the element of discontinuity came to be less clearly appreciated than it was in the apostolic age; and the Church, confident that it was the true Israel, tended to assume that its history reached back in unbroken continuity to Abraham. Thus the pattern of divine action in the two Testaments came to be regarded as uniform and static, and too little recognition was given to the fact that the relation of promise to fulfilment involves contrast as well as harmony, particularly in regard to the Gospel events themselves. This failure to realize that fulfilment may involve transformation meant that the Old Testament types and prophecies were often referred to the New Testament at their original level of meaning. The primitive Church understood that they cannot always bear the deeper significance which the transference imposes on them, and that this was especially true of the Christological images of 'prophet' and 'Messiah'. Even in the apostolic age, however, this principle was not followed thoroughly, and in the following centuries the types of the Mosaic sacrifices and priesthood, to take one example, were often applied directly to the work of Christ and to Christian worship without a due recognition that they must be reinterpreted and given a new and more profound significance if they are to be useful in illuminating the nature and meaning of their anti-types.

This assumption of the uniformity of the scriptural revelation easily opened the door to that combination of historical typology with allegory which is characteristic of so much patristic exegesis. When it is combined with the further assumption that events in the past may have occurred simply because they were providentially intended to illustrate events in the distant future, history as such loses all value. This is even more true when it is thought that they were ordained merely to teach moral lessons. Even such exegetes as Origen, who make most concessions to this kind of allegorism, usually allow that the literal meaning is worth preserving; but the advantages of unhistorical allegorism as a means of evading the difficulty caused by absurd or offensive passages in the Old Testament made it hard to resist. When applied to the New Testament its dangers became more apparent. It was easy to treat the Gospel narratives like the Old Testament history: to make them serve as symbolical prefigurations of the work of Christ through the Spirit in the Church. Thus Origen not only allegorizes parables such as that of the Good Samaritan, making it a lesson about Christ, fallen man, the Church and the sacraments, but tends at times to defend the miracle stories against the attacks of such opponents as Celsus by treating them as symbolic prefigurations of the 'greater works' to be performed by Christ in the Church when he raises the spiritually dead and cures the spiritually blind. In this way the New Testament history, like that of the Old Testament, becomes parabolic. It is a symbolical description of the present existential situation of Christian believers. As applied to the Fourth Gospel it may be correct exegesis, and it is attractive in a Bultmannian age; but it is dangerous. Like the allegorical interpretation of the Old Testament, it knows no limits and can be controlled by no internal criteria. It could easily reduce the whole Gospel to myth and, as Heracleon's example shows, this could readily become Gnostic myth.

Individual Christian exegetes in the first six centuries exhibit great variety in their treatment of Scripture, and it is possible here only to pick out a few samples of their methods. It must be remembered, however, that certain lines of interpretation were laid down at a very early period and were followed in the main by all expositors of the Bible. These lines were chiefly related to the biblical foundations of liturgy. The selection and application of Old Testament types to the Christian sacraments became almost stereotyped, and catechetical teaching and preaching, as well as the liturgies themselves, tended to repeat a standard tradition of exegesis with relatively little variation as between local churches or individual expositors.

The pulpit, in the early centuries as always, offered the widest scope for individual ingenuity in exegesis; for where edification is the primary object, and where the congregation share the ancient love of rhetorical skill, the versatility of the allegorist knows no bounds. One might say that fanciful exegesis is allowable in the pulpit, for the preacher is doing no more than construct telling sermon illustrations; but since many of the Fathers wrote their serious expositions of entire books of the Bible in the form of homilies, and actually delivered them to an audience, the distinction between what is permissible in the study and in the pulpit was not clearly marked.

One of the earliest of the post-apostolic writings, Clement of Rome's letter to the Corinthians, is interesting in its use of the Old Testament. As a leader of the church at Rome, sending admonition and advice to a church afflicted by disorder and party-strife, Clement constantly refers to the Scriptures for examples, much in the style of a preacher. He uses texts to drive home his argument, and appeals to the Old Testament as authoritative, assuming that he and his readers agree that their situation and its problems are adumbrated in every part of the Septuagint. Clement's examples are moral: thus he brings forward lists of those who in the history of Israel exhibited certain vices which are prevalent in contemporary Corinth and certain virtues which that church ought to cultivate. Cain, Esau, Joseph's brethren, the antagonists of Moses, Aaron and Miriam, Dathan and Abiram, and Saul represent the disruptive forces of jealousy (4–6). A long list of the heroes of faith is adduced (9–12), similar in form to the great roll-call in Hebrews xi. In Hebrews, however, the list exhibited the quality of faithfulness towards God, and enduring trust and hope. Here the virtue commended is rather loyalty, contrasted with the schismatic temper of the Corinthians, and in several instances it is linked with hospitality, as against narrow and exclusive partisanship. This leads on to examples of humility (16–18). These are headed by the example of Christ himself, and this is attested by no less a passage than the fourth Servant Song in Isaiah liii. This vitally important Christological and soteriological prophecy thus becomes a paradigm of Christian behaviour. The moralism of the Apostolic Fathers, so often noticed by commentators, is thereby demonstrated, though it has to be remembered that Paul may have used the image of the Servant in a rather similar fashion in Philippians ii. The form of Clement's appeal to the Scriptures is not novel, but closely follows Jewish precedent. Allegorical typology is used: Rahab's scarlet thread, a recurring theme in patristic exegesis, is a sign of redemption through the blood of Christ (12. 7). Pure allegory, containing no historical analogy at all, is little used by Clement. An example of it, however, is to be found in his exegesis of Ps. 118: 19–20, in which the 'gates of righteousness' stand for brotherly love which may be equated with righteousness in Christ.

These various ways of applying Scripture to the present situation are typical of the early Christian writers. The interpretation of prophecy seems sometimes to be less a declaration of the fulfilment of God's purposes in Christ than an assimilation of Christian life and worship to Old Testament models. As early as the *Didache* (14. 3) Malachi's allusion to a 'pure sacrifice' is attached to the Christian Eucharist, the beginning of a process which profoundly affected the doctrines of the Eucharist and the Ministry, though in the *Didache* itself the Christian sacrifice seems to be identified with the entire act of corporate worship.

Such a use of prophecy seems arbitrary; but it was considered to be justifiable on the ground that the prophets were actually preachers of the Gospel before the event. Ignatius says that the prophets preached with reference to the Gospel; they set their hope on Christ and awaited him; they were saved in unity with Jesus Christ by faith in him; they have been numbered with us in the Gospel of our common hope (*Philad.* 5. 2). Patriarchs, prophets and apostles are one with the Church, for they proclaimed Christ (*ibid.* 9. 2). Hence, by the use of allegory prophecies can be applied to the Church's life even when their original sense seems unpromising. So the homily known as *II Clement* cites Isa. liv. 1, 'Rejoice, thou barren that bearest not . . .', as an allusion to the Church which was barren before children were given to it. 'Cry aloud, thou that travailest not' means, 'Let us not, like women in travail, grow weary of offering up our prayers to God in sincerity' (2. 1–2). By such means prophecy can be made to yield moral exhortation.

A much more elaborate form of allegorical exegesis, more akin to the Alexandrian tradition than the Palestinian, occurs in the same sermon (14), where 'God made man male and female' is an allegory of Christ and the Church, with the further idea that both Christ and the Church were pre-existent spiritual entities before their manifestation on earth. In pressing allegorical exegesis to these lengths, *II Clement* stands close to the probably Alexandrian *Epistle of Barnabas*. This document is packed full of allegorical typology of a most elaborate kind. The most famous instance of this is the revelation of Jesus and the Cross in the numerical symbolism of the 318 servants of Abraham (9). Scarcely less subtle is the interpretation of the ritual of the scapegoat as a detailed allegory of the Passion and glorification of Christ (7). More important, perhaps, is the insistence of 'Barnabas' that the provisions of the Law regarding unclean food were never intended to be taken literally. From the first they were meant to be understood spiritually: thus the taboo on pork was intended to teach us not to associate with swinish men. On this view the original text was a piece of ethical teaching disguised in the form of a law about food. The apparent meaning presents a kind of conundrum, to which the key is *gnosis*. This seems to mean little more than the ability to do this kind of exegesis. 'Barnabas' does not tell us explicitly what he believes to be its nature or its source, but, from the fact that both the interpreter and the scriptural author are said to possess it, it would seem that he thinks of it as a kind of inspiration, either to set the puzzle or to solve it. Whatever it may be, 'Barnabas' is undoubtedly very proud of it.

Justin, on the other hand, makes no such claim. He remains more firmly rooted in the tradition of Jewish and early Christian exegetical methods, but since his purpose in the *Dialogue with Trypho* is to commend the Christian interpretation of the Scriptures against that of Judaism his Christological typology is unusually extensive and detailed.

It does, of course, reproduce what were by now the accepted traditions of exegesis, such as an elaborate typological application of the story of Noah to baptism. Christians, like Noah, are saved by water, faith and the wood of the Cross (*Dial.* 138. 2). But he goes beyond the standard proof texts and types. Allegory is extensively used to support his typology and to multiply his store of proof texts. Gen. xlix. 10 ff., for instance, becomes an elaborate type of the entry into Jerusalem, the calling of Jew and Gentile, Christ's Passion, and the Christian's possession of the Spirit. An interesting variation in Justin's method appears in his handling of this passage. In *I Apol.* 32 it is treated by means of allegorical typology: the text foreshadows the entry into Jerusalem, the Passion, and the cleansing of believers by the blood of Christ. Incidentally, the narrative of the entry is modified to fit the text of Genesis (a process which may often have occurred at an early stage of the Gospel tradition): Christ, says Justin, found the ass's colt tied to a vine. In *Dial.* 52–4, on the other hand, the passage is treated as an almost pure allegory. It points to Christ's first and second coming; the ass and the colt stand for Jewish and Gentile believers; the robe and the garment denote the Spirit and the humanity of Christ; and so on.

One remarkable feature of Justin's exegesis is his assertion that the Logos speaks in Scripture in various 'persons'; sometimes as God, sometimes as Christ, sometimes as mankind in its relation to God. This is not an original idea. It is used very strikingly in the application of Psalm 102 to Christ by the writer to the Hebrews; but it becomes increasingly a major principle of patristic exegesis, and it was to be employed particularly, as by Augustine, in the exposition of the Psalms, where the 'person' can change in the course of a single verse of the text.

Justin's allegorical types are often extremely fanciful. It is worth noting, however, that although Trypho the Jew often objects to the content of Justin's interpretation of the Old Testament he does not radically challenge the validity of his methods. It is true, too, that even when Justin allegorizes most wildly his interpretations are usually related to historical events and not, like Philo's, to general philosophical and ethical truths. In this respect Justin resembles in his exegesis the Asiatic tradition represented by Melito of Sardis, whose *Homily on the Passion* expounds a detailed typology of the Passover and Exodus as applied to the death and Resurrection of Christ.

The relation which Melito envisages between Old Testament type and New Testament antitype is extremely close. They correspond to one another not merely because as events they are analogous, but because Christ was actually in some sense present in the events of the Exodus and the entry into the Promised Land (84). The pillar of cloud and fire was in fact the pre-existent Christ. In holding this belief Melito was in line with much patristic thought. The Old Testament types are significant because the fulfilment is already present in some degree in the foreshadowing; types and prophecies are sacraments (and the word *mysterion* is used both of them and of the Christian sacraments) of the Real Presence of Christ.

Elsewhere, Melito follows the established practice of grouping collections of texts as arguments for a particular topic: for instance, a number which prophesy the paschal mystery, including Isa. liii. 7 (61 ff.). He also, like Clement of Rome, lists biblical *exempla* of the Passion of Christ: the passover lamb, and the righteous sufferers of the Old Testament from Abel to the prophets (59). Both Justin and Melito differ markedly from Theophilus of Antioch, who resembles in his exegesis the style of Alexandria rather than of his Antiochene successors. There are passages in Theophilus' *Ad Autolycum* which recall Philonic allegory, particularly the well-known exposition of the Creation story in Book 2. Here sun and moon stand for God and man; the three days preceding the creation of the luminaries are images (*typoi*) of the trinity of God, Word and Wisdom; the fixed stars represent the righteous and the wandering planets those who forsake the law of God.

By this time the Church had been faced with the challenge of Marcion, a fundamental threat to the whole basis of the orthodox position, for it asserted that instead of being in unbroken continuity with the Old Testament the Gospel was absolutely discontinuous with it; the relation between them was one of direct opposition. The reaction against Marcion's revolutionary attitude was equally strong. It made orthodox expositors more than ever anxious to find all possible means, such as allegorical typology or pure unhistorical allegory, to wrest a Christian meaning out of even the most unpromising scriptural material, such as passages containing no obvious prophecies and those which appeared to be quite unedifying.

In Irenaeus the reaction took the form of a theological development of typology centred upon the biblical idea of Christ as the new, or second, Adam. Christ 'recapitulates' Adam and his story in two senses of the term: he sums up humanity in his incarnate person, and he re-enacts and reverses Adam's experience. Christ's work is not, as Marcion supposed, directed against the old order; its purpose is rather to renew and restore the old. In the light of this central belief the Gospel is seen as a recapitulation of the old dispensation, a fulfilment which reverses the Fall. Thus Christ corresponds to, and is identified with, Adam; Mary to Eve; the Cross to the tree of the Fall. Irenaeus' detailed application of his principle sometimes involves him in far-fetched analogies, but as a reply to Marcion and as a theological insight it is profoundly important. Moreover, Irenaeus is prepared to find a sort of development, rather than an absolute uniformity, in the Bible itself, and he speaks of God educating mankind in the Scriptures by revealing his truth in stages corresponding to man's capacity to receive it. It is regrettable that this concept, rather than the development of artificial allegory, was not adopted by the Church as its main line of defence against the Marcionite rejection of the Old Testament.

The ways in which allegorical exegesis were developed are well illustrated in Hippolytus. His extensive commentary on Daniel is mainly straightforward and literalistic, though he allegorizes the lions' den as Hades, and the lions as the devil's angels (3. 30. 2), and Daniel x is, not surprisingly, interpreted in a fully allegorical manner. In the story of Susannah, however, the literal sense is virtually ignored. Susannah represents the Church, the wicked elders its Jewish and Gentile persecutors, her bath becomes a detailed picture of Christian baptism in which the soap signifies the post-baptismal anointing (*Dan.* 1. 14). Hippolytus, too, is the Christian pioneer in the dangerous task of allegorizing the Song of Songs. It is given a mainly Christological reference, and a bewildering variety of Old and New Testament material is laid under contribution to support the very fanciful exegesis. In places, however, the content of the allegory is Philonic: that is to say, it is not related to Christ and the Gospel but to philosophical or other general concepts; thus the mention of two breasts in Song of Songs iv. 5 is interpreted either as the soul and the body or as two kinds of perception (alternative applications are common in this kind of allegory).

The Philonic method had already been imitated more wholeheartedly by Clement of Alexandria. This is made very clear in his treatment of the story of Sarah and Hagar (*str.* 1. 5. 30–1) which forms a striking contrast to Paul's handling of the same passage. Sarah is wisdom, Hagar is worldly *paideia*. Abraham progresses from an association with the latter to the former. Clement enthusiastically acknowledges his debt to Philo in his exposition of this passage. A very similar interpretation of Joseph being cast into the pit makes this, too, a picture of the soul's advance towards wisdom. Clement is one of the first Christian writers to bring the New Testament, as well, within the scope of allegorical exegesis. He does this, it is true, not in respect of the Gospel narratives but of the parable of the Good Samaritan, a happy hunting ground for preachers and commentators in pursuit of symbolism. Our neighbour is Christ who rescues us from the world-rulers of darkness who have almost done us to death with the wounds of lusts, anger, pleasures, etc.; Jesus is the doctor who cuts out the passions, pours the wine of David's vine into our wounded souls, applies the oil of the Father's compassion, and bids angels and principalities minister to us in return for the reward of deliverance from the vanity which pervades the world, and who must therefore be loved, as being our neighbour, equally with God (*q.d.s.* 28–9). Clement's example in allegorizing a parable of Jesus, itself a development of a process of interpretation which began during the formation of the Gospel tradition, was to be widely imitated.

Of a different kind is the biblical exegesis of the first great Latin writer, Tertullian. Broadly speaking, it is not until we come to Hilary and Ambrose that we find in the Latin authors the exuberant richness of Greek typological and allegorical exegesis. Tertullian disliked allegory, fearing that it might resolve the plain truth of Scripture into vague speculation, particularly in the exposition of the New Testament, whose clear teaching about such matters as the resurrection of the body and final judgement must be taken at its face value. So also, the parables must be interpreted by reference to their main purport rather than those details which seem to invite symbolical exegesis. Wherever possible the obscurities in the Old Testament must be resolved by being referred to Christ rather than by being allegorized moralistically; there is enough plainly intelligible material in the Bible to throw light upon its more enigmatic passages.

Cyprian also, following his 'magister' Tertullian, uses the Bible in an uncomplicated fashion, applying its literal sense, so far as he can, to the contemporary situation. His collection of prophetic *testimonia* may well represent the standard biblical equipment of the teacher or propagandist who requires an armoury of evidence for the truth of the Gospel. Such collections may perhaps have come into existence at a very early date, and they continued to be compiled. In the latter part of the fourth century we know from Epiphanius (*mens.* 1) that it was the practice of biblical students to annotate the Old Testament prophecies and classify them according to their literary genre. Epiphanius claims to distinguish ten such categories of prophecy, though his list contains only nine. It includes teachings, lamentations, prayers and narratives, together with other classes. An elaborate series of signs was marked into the text of prophetical passages to guide the reader. These inform him whether a prophecy comes under the heading of God's repudiation of his ancient people, the abrogation of the Law 'according to the flesh', the new covenant, the calling of the Gentiles, Christ himself, the promises to Israel, foreknowledge of the future, or obscurities in the Scriptures. Others indicate the relation of the Greek versions to one another and to the Hebrew. This code is too elaborate and artificial, but it shows how painstakingly Christian exegetes had worked through the prophecies and tried to bring some kind of order into their exposition, a strong motive being the constant need to defend the Christian reliance on those prophecies which Jewish exegetes interpreted in a quite different sense, making, for example, the key text Isa. vii. 14 refer to Hezekiah (as we learn from Justin's *Dialogue* and from Origen).

Clement and Origen stand in an exegetical tradition which, so far as method is concerned, appealed strongly to the Gnostics. Heracleon the Valentinian is the first commentator on the Fourth Gospel, perhaps the first author of a full-scale Christian commentary on any biblical book. His methods were evidently similar to those of Origen, to whom we owe our knowledge of his work. He uses allegory very freely: thus, the royal officer at Capernaum in John iv represents the demiurge; John iv. 36 alludes to the work of angelic powers; and Heracleon resembles Origen in a penchant for detecting important meanings in the grammatical details of the text.

Origen's methods, however, are more complex than this, and it is a matter of much dispute whether his exegesis follows any consistent principles. He works in conscious opposition to a literalism which might open the way to Judaistic interpretation or give a handle to the Marcionite attack on absurdities and inconsistencies in the text. At the same time he wants to beat the Gnostics at their own game and use Heracleon's methods to arrive at an orthodox result. Origen is a careful exegete, acquainted with Hebrew, and not, like his predecessors, slavishly attached to the Septuagint. Like Jerome alone among the Fathers, he applies an informed critical judgement to the text itself, and he also holds himself astonishingly free to reinterpret, sometimes in a most revolutionary way, the biblical framework of thought, especially in the realm of eschatology. Although Origen agreed with all orthodox Christians that all the canonical books are divinely inspired (following II Tim. iii. 16) and that they can therefore be used as a treasury of oracles, he recognizes that the human element in the Bible can be distinguished from the divine. The divine message is communicated through the earthly records, and these two aspects can be compared with the healing of the blind man by Jesus through the medium of clay (*fr.* 63 *in Jn.*). At times, too, he almost comes within sight of an idea of progressive revelation: not all the prophets were equally inspired (*Jn.* 6. 3, 16. 4). It is, however, significant that in his allegory of the divine word and the clay the latter has only a temporary function. Those who have recovered full vision can see Jesus without its aid. This typifies Origen's attitude to biblical history. For him it is not the constant medium of God's self-revelation. It is rather an outward and transient form which contains eternal spiritual truth. His attitude is thoroughly Platonist, and his kinship with Philo is thus very close.

This is the fundamentally important point where Origen reveals the gulf which divides his attitude from that of the biblical writers themselves. It is the basis for his prolific allegorism, for his application of it to the New Testament as well as the Old, and for his tendency to dissolve the literal sense of the text. Like so many of the Fathers, he is concerned to remove the offence caused to educated readers by the anthropomorphism and the apparent absurdity of certain parts of the Old Testament, and his anxiety to do this is sharpened by the cultured sarcasm of Celsus about the literal sense; but he extends the range of allegory far beyond this. In his view Scripture may have three senses, corresponding to the threefold division of man into body, soul and spirit (*princ.* 4. 2–3). These are the literal, the moral and the spiritual. How far he attached real importance to the literal is disputed; his attitude varied with the nature of the text under discussion. In most cases the literal meaning stands, and for simpler believers it may form the limit of their understanding. Much more important, however, is the hidden meaning, for which a higher degree of perception is required. He does not, for instance, deny the literal truth of the feeding of the multitude; indeed he does not want to reduce the miracles of Jesus to pure allegory (*Jn.* 20. 20); but he proceeds to allegorize the story in all its details (*Mt.* 11. 1). The literal meaning is often discussed first by Origen before he interprets the inner truth (cf. *Jn.* 13. 17), which is related to the former as the spirit is to the letter. Many passages, however, have no acceptable literal sense. Jesus was not literally taken to a high mountain by the devil, the Jewish food taboos make no sense (*princ.* 4. 3), the trees in Eden were not perceptible objects (*fr. in Gen.* 2. 9). In such cases the divinely intended meaning is the allegorical sense alone.

According to the systematic method of exegesis outlined in *De Principiis* 4, the allegorical sense is twofold: moral and spiritual. From time to time Origen does deal with a passage in all three ways. After giving the literal sense of the story of Lot, for instance, he offers a spiritual interpretation in which the story illustrates Israel's relation to the law, and then draws a moral lesson in which the characters in the narrative stand for virtues and vices (*hom. in Gen.* 5. 4). More often, however, the spiritual sense crowds out the moral, or the two are fused together. The possibility of more than one interpretation is often left open. Thus, the Song of Songs may be referred to Christ and the Church or else to the Word and the individual soul. Great importance is attached to more or less fanciful etymologies of names, in which respect Origen stands in an ancient tradition of Hellenistic philosophical allegory. Thus the successive camping-grounds of Israel in the desert are allegorized in Origen's *Homilies on Numbers* as signifying, through the meaning of the place-names, stages in the spiritual life. Origen is also fond of the symbolism of numbers.

It is hard to decide whether Origen rejects the historicity of some biblical narratives altogether. He probably does so in the case of the early chapters of Genesis; and he virtually rules out the historicity of the cleansing of the Temple and with it the vexed problem of reconciling the evangelists' chronology (*Jn.* 10. 23–5). Many other instances could be cited where Origen actually rejects the historical sense of a passage. Where it is not denied, it is often relegated to the background. The raising of Lazarus is a symbol of the awakening of the unenlightened from their spiritual sleep (*fr.* 79 *in Jn.*), and such episodes as the miracle at Cana are naturally taken in a parabolic sense.

This makes Origen a remarkably sympathetic and valuable commentator on the Fourth Gospel, whose author probably thought on similar lines to himself. His method is much less satisfactory when applied to writers who intended to record plain history. It tends to remove history from the sphere of revelation and to reduce the Gospel to a parable about certain moral and spiritual principles derived from philosophy. At one point Origen explicitly denies the principle on which historical typology rests, even though that traditional kind of exegesis is not absent from his writings: historical events, he maintains, are not to be taken as types of other historical events; they are types of spiritual realities (*Jn.* 10. 18). The correspondence is not between past promise and future fulfilment but between temporal shadow and eternal reality. Although Origen wrote his great commentary on John in order to provide a non-literalistic but orthodox counterblast to Heracleon's, he follows the latter's methods so closely as to leave himself with little room for manœuvre against Gnostic allegorizing; for in the last resort his exegesis very often depends upon his own imagination, and why should not another's imagination be as good as his? In practice, his safeguard against Gnosticism (which, as the *Gospel of Thomas* shows, could read its ideas out of the Bible by means of subtle modifications of the text as well as by full-scale allegorizing) lay in a principle which he did not directly derive from Scripture: his loyalty to the Church's rule of faith, which is a kind of distillation of what the Church traditionally held to be the main purport of the biblical revelation.

As a counterblast to narrow literalism, however, Origen's exegesis served his purpose well. The Arian controversy was to show the danger of literal exegesis as a criterion of doctrine. Not only was the *homoousion* (formulated in order to safeguard the implications of Scripture) attacked as unbiblical, but Arianism could rely on the support of a battery of proof texts. Prov. viii. 22, given the basic assumption that Wisdom is simply to be identified with the Son, was one of the most powerful of these, and Amos iv. 13 ('God creating *pneuma*', literally, 'wind', but translated 'Spirit') was almost as potent a weapon in the hands of those who assailed the deity of the Holy Spirit. Texts like these, interpreted on the assumption that the Septuagint text was verbally inspired and that the whole Bible tells of Christ, added much to the embarrassment caused to Athanasius by the passages in the Gospels which suggested the inferiority of the Son to the Father.

The methods of the Alexandrian exegetes exercised a great influence upon such western theologians as Hilary and Ambrose. Typical of their Origenistic allegorizing are Hilary's interpretations of the Psalms, including their enigmatic titles, and his exposition of Christ's walking through the cornfields, every detail of which has an inner meaning related to his mission to the world. Jerome, too, before he repudiated Origen, reproduced his exposition of the Song of Songs with great enthusiasm; he believed, also, that the titles of the Psalms indicated whether they were uttered in the 'person' of Christ, the Church, or the original prophet. Later, however, he disapproved of Origen's handling of Scripture and especially of his use of unsatisfactory Greek texts.

A different approach was followed by the Antiochenes. The spiritual sense (*theoria*) which Gregory of Nyssa, as an Origenist, equated with allegory (describing his allegorical *Life of Moses* as *theoria*) is sharply distinguished from allegory by the Antiochenes. Theodore of Mopsuestia is especially severe towards allegorists in his comment on Gal. iv. 24. They imagine inept fables, and give their folly the name of allegory, misusing the Pauline word as a ground for their abrogation of the sense of Scripture. The apostle treated historical facts as real, while using them as analogies. There could be no analogy if the historical facts did not stand as such. But the allegorizers do not allow Adam to be Adam, nor paradise to be paradise (a hit at Origen's treatment of Eden). If they were right, then there could be no reversal of Adam's fall by Christ. Pauline 'allegory' was different; it meant the comparison of real events in the past with others in the present.

Theodore classified the Psalms according to their 'argument'. Some refer to the life of David, some to post-Davidic history down to the Maccabees, beyond which time David's prophetic vision did not extend except for one or two Christological prophecies, such as Ps. 16: 10, which Theodore will allow. Yet it is permissible to use the Psalms in circumstances which resemble David's, and this Christ did when he adopted the cry of dereliction uttered by David at Absalom's revolt. Historical typology is, of course, acceptable, but the type must bear a real resemblance in its nature and in its effects to that which it signifies. The passover blood is an example of a true type (*Comm. in Jon.* proem.).

Chrysostom similarly holds that one must not try to control the sense of Scripture, nor to read one's own meaning into biblical allegories. When the Bible presents us with an allegory it also supplies the true interpretation (*Isa. interpr.* 5. 3). A very similar view is taken by Isidore of Pelusium: a great disservice is done, he thinks, by those who refer the whole Old Testament to Christ; this encourages heathens and heretics to reject those passages which *do* have reference to him (*epp.* 2. 195). Nor does Isidore believe that God utters prophecies that have no relevance for the time when they are spoken. Psalm 72 refers to Solomon as well as to Christ (Jerome thought it alluded only to Christ as the true Solomon, i.e. *pacificus*). Both the historical and the spiritual sense are to be respected and preserved (*epp.* 4. 203).

The Antiochenes, of course, do not rule out the spiritual sense. Diodore of Tarsus is said by Socrates (6. 3. 7) to have done so, but in his preface to the Psalms Diodore expressly denies this. The historical sense is the foundation for the spiritual, and if the latter subverts the former it is no longer true *theoria* but allegory. Paul's 'allegory' in Gal. iv. 24 did not violate this canon, but respected the historical meaning of the text. Severian of Gabala also remarks that it is one thing to preserve the historical sense and add to it the spiritual, and quite another to distort the historical sense into allegory (*creat.* 4. 2). Almost exactly the same judgement is made by Theodoret, who was, however, himself capable of fanciful allegorizing of Pentateuchal passages.

In the Latin West an attempt was made by Tyconius the Donatist to lay down certain rules in order to open up the recesses of Scripture and make its treasures of truth accessible. They are meant to be a guide to the traveller through the 'immense forest of prophecy'. Thus, one class of prophecies refers to Christ and to the Church as his Body. Sometimes the allusion is to Christ only, sometimes to the Church, sometimes to both in the same passage. Isa. liii. 4–6 refers to Christ, 10–11 to the Church; Isa. lxi. 10 to both; Matt. xxvi. 64 to Christ; II Thess. ii. 4 to both; Rom. i. 1–4, not, as one might expect, to Christ, but to those who are in Christ, i.e. the Church. The Body of Christ is composed of two parts, good and bad, corresponding to the right and the left side. Thus Song of Songs i. 5 alludes to Ishmael as Kedar and to Isaac as Solomon, signifying those whom God rejects and accepts. Another rule distinguishes between *genus*, prophecy embodying a general principle of God's dealings with man, and *species*, particular instances of this. A comparison of Jonah iii. 3 with Nahum iii. 3 shows that these particular prophecies about Nineveh also reveal general truths about man's relations with God. A further rule deals with times, seasons and numbers, and with the principle that the part may stand for the whole and vice versa. Hence there is no contradiction in the Evangelists' notes of time on Easter morning (dawn, while it was yet dark, and so on). The principle of *recapitulatio* tells us that a type and its fulfilment may be spoken of together, as in the case of the 'abomination of desolation' in Matt. xxiv. 15–16. Finally, just as prophecies about Christ may also have a reference to his Body, so those about the devil may refer to his Body, that is, the assembly of the wicked. Tyconius discerns one such allusion in Isa. xiv. 12.

Augustine adopts these principles, especially the first, of which he makes great use; but he thinks Tyconius optimistic if he believes that his rules will unlock every obscurity in Scripture, and he adds the warning that Tyconius, as a Donatist, must be treated with caution. These remarks occur in Augustine's *De Doctrina Christiana*, which contains some interesting observations about exegesis. He mentions that the Canon rests on the authority of the churches which possess apostolic sees and apostolic letters. Those books which are accepted by all churches are more authoritative than those received only in some places; those accepted by the majority, and by the more important, of the churches are preferable to those accepted by only a few and by the less important. He then treats of obscurities in Scripture. These, and the passages that are barren of prophetic interest, are divinely designed, and the Bible (as Tertullian asserted) can illuminate the obscurer passages by means of the vast quantity of plain teaching which it contains. Where a scripture might be open to misunderstanding, the ambiguity can be resolved by the aid of the Church's rule of faith. For instance, the punctuation of John i. 1–2, which could possibly be, '...et Deus erat; verbum hoc erat in principio apud Deum', must not be read in this way, for to do so would be contrary to the rule of faith concerning the equality of the persons of the Trinity.

Figurative passages must not be interpreted literally. This would be to understand them 'carnally'. To take signs for realities is 'miserabilis animae servitus'. But how is the literal to be distinguished from the figurative? First, whatever does not seem to conduce to good morals and true faith is figurative. Second, if anything wicked is ascribed to God or to the righteous it is to be taken figuratively. But note: customs change; what matters is the disposition of the people involved; thus, polygamy existed for a good purpose among the Old Testament saints. It must also be noted that all, or almost all, Old Testament history is to be taken both literally and figuratively. Some sins of the heroes of the Old Testament are recorded as warnings.

A figure need not always have one and the same meaning. It may vary with the context. Thus, 'shield' in Ps. 5: 13 denotes God's good pleasure, but in Eph. vi. 16 it signifies faith. Since, then, a figure may have several meanings, it does no harm to interpret it in a way which the author may not have actually intended, so long as this accords with the meaning given to it in other passages of Scripture. The Holy Spirit will have foreseen and approved of the interpretation.

Augustine grapples with problems of apparent inconsistencies and inaccuracies in the treatise *De consensu Evangelistarum*. The Gospel, he remarks, demonstrates the fulfilment of what had been foretold by the Law and the Prophets. It rests on the authority of the first preachers, the apostles, who saw Christ in the flesh, and recorded what they had seen and heard and also what they learned from Christ's parents and others about his birth, infancy and childhood. Matthew and John were eyewitnesses, Mark and Luke were authorized by apostles to write their Gospels. Others who have written about the acts of Christ and the apostles are not such as to command confidence; hence their works are excluded from the Canon. Further, they included material which is condemned by the catholic and apostolic rule of faith and by sound doctrine.

Though the Gospels are thus guaranteed by apostolic authority there are apparent discrepancies and inaccuracies in them. These problems, such as the difficulty of reconciling aspects of the infancy narratives and the details of the stories of Peter's denial, are attacked by Augustine on literary and historical grounds. At times he applies good textual criticism. Nevertheless, he also employs much less scientific arguments. He contends, for example, that all the prophets spoke with one voice; Matthew was not therefore wrong in ascribing Zechariah's prophecy to Jeremiah. Indeed, he was inspired to do so. For good measure, Augustine adds an allegorical interpretation of the passage in question.

A combination of quasi-rationalizing explanation with Origenistic allegory is seen in Augustine's interesting treatment of miracle stories. His handling of the feeding of the multitude is a good instance (*in*

Joannis evang. tract. 24). The purpose of miracles is to evoke by means of unusual divine actions (not necessarily greater actions than God normally performs) a recognition that the whole order of creation is miraculous. The government of the universe is a greater miracle than the feeding of five thousand with five loaves. God performs a more wonderful work when he creates a cornfield out of a few seeds; and it is only this same divine power which, in Christ, multiplied the loaves. The purpose was to enable men to discern the invisible God through his visible works, and so to desire to behold him invisibly.

The story is intended, too, to convey a message about Christ. A tale is not like a picture. It must not merely be looked at and admired; it is like the letters of a sentence which have to be read and understood. The real meaning is contained in every detail of the story. Christ on the mountain means that the Word is on high. His question to Philip is meant to teach by eliciting an admission of ignorance. The loaves which Jesus took are not the five, but loaves which he created. The five loaves are the Pentateuch; they are of barley, not wheat, because the grain of barley is hard to extract through its covering of chaff; and the meaning of the Old Testament is veiled in outward symbols. The boy is Israel, which carried the nourishment provided by the Old Testament but did not feed on it. The two fishes are the two anointed ones in the Old Testament, the priest and the king. Christ, who bears both these offices, is revealed in the barley grain, but hidden by the chaff. The Pentateuch, when broken by exposition, makes many books. But Israel was ignorant, the barley chaff still veiling their understanding. The five thousand are Israel under the Law (the same symbolism is intended by the five porticoes in John v. 2–9). They recline on the grass because their thoughts are carnal, and all flesh is grass. The fragments are the more secret teachings which the crowd could not receive. They were entrusted to those who were capable of teaching others also, namely the apostles. Hence there were twelve baskets. At the time, men could only see the miracle and marvel; we can read its meaning and believe.

A very similar piece of detailed exegesis is given by Augustine of the miracle at Cana (*in Joannis evang. tract.* 8–9). As a divine work it is parallel to the regular conversion of rainfall into wine; but because this happens every year it does not cause astonishment. The same Word who, incarnate, wrought the Gospel miracles effects the supreme miracles in his government of the universe. Why, then, be amazed at the changing of the water into wine? In becoming man the Word did not cease to be God. This is a work of the creative Word.

Its meaning is as follows: Christ has a bride whom he bought with his blood and to whom he gave the Spirit as a pledge. The Word is the bridegroom, the bride is human flesh, the womb of Mary is the bridegroom's chamber. Christ's answer to his mother shows that he is acting as God, who has no mother. When his hour is come, on the Cross, he will recognize his mother: the mother of his human weakness. The water is prophecy which has not yet been understood as revealing Christ. It was made into wine when Christ reinterpreted the Scriptures (Luke xxiv). Had Christ thrown away the water and replaced it by wine he would have signified that the Old Testament should be rejected; but he converted it into wine. The six waterpots are six ages: from Adam to Noah, Noah to Abraham, Abraham to David, David to the Exile, the Exile to the Baptist, the Baptist to the end of the world. Prophecy has continued through all the ages, but it is now fulfilled in Christ. Two or three measures: the Father and the Son; hence also the Spirit and the Trinity. The Law and the Prophets were originally for the Jews alone; hence, 'according to the purification of the Jews'. The first waterpot contains the mystery of Gen. ii. 24: Christ left his Father and his mother (the Synagogue). His bride is the Church, formed by the sacraments proceeding from the side of Christ. The second contains the ark, signifying the deliverance of the world by the wood of the Cross. The third contains Isaac, the type of the Passion, the seed in whom all nations will be blessed. The fourth contains Psalm 82: 8, the inheritance of Christ in all the nations. Prophecy belongs to all nations; hence *anatole* (east), *dysis* (west), *arctos* (north), *mesembria* (south), make an acrostic on 'Adam'. The fifth age or waterpot contains Daniel's stone cut without hands, which is Christ. The sixth contains the Baptist's prophecy of sons of Abraham being raised up out of stones (i.e. all nations). So the pots signify all nations. The two measures may be taken to mean circumcision and uncircumcision, and the three measures the three sons of Noah, that is, all mankind.

These specimens are fair examples of the kind of exegesis which Augustine produces in his homiletic commentaries. They are paralleled in their ingenuity by his sermons on the Psalms, which are rich in type and allegory and in which the preacher is rarely defeated even by a Latin text which is sometimes meaningless.

Augustine set a pattern for his successors which was followed, so far as method is concerned, during the remainder of this period. Of Gregory the Great it must be sufficient to remark[1] that his talent lay especially in the field of moral allegory. A good example of his exegesis is his comment on I Sam. xiii. 19–20 ('There was no smith to be found throughout all the land of Israel, for the Philistines said, "Lest the Hebrews make themselves swords or spears"'). The smiths are those who produce secular literature. Israel possesses only divine literature. The former cannot gain the victory without the aid of the latter; and the liberal arts ought to be studied by Israel, so that by their instruction we (Israel) may the better understand the divine *eloquia*. But the demons, represented by the Philistines, try to prevent us from acquiring secular knowledge by removing from the hearts of the faithful the desire to learn. Is this the first appearance of 'philistines' in the role of enemies of literary culture?

2. FROM GREGORY THE GREAT TO SAINT BERNARD

Two connected but distinct questions are to be considered here. The first is how Scripture was used: that is, what place it occupied in the various spheres of religious life. The answer is that it was read for self-instruction, and for public teaching; it was the manual for catechizing; as the source-book of corporate and private prayer it nourished both liturgical worship and individual piety; and from the treasure which it afforded material was drawn for preaching, art and iconography, and every branch of religious thought.

How was it interpreted? The starting-point was the text then current; the methods and intentions with which the text was handled were those of the time. Versions other than the Vulgate were scarcely known, still less the original text, but recourse was sometimes had to passages of the Old Latin versions transmitted by patristic writings and in a few manuscripts. The resources of philology were slight, being limited almost exclusively to traditional collections of *onomastica sacra*, consulted for the etymology of proper names. The important place occupied by allegory, however, in every branch of thought provided the exegesis of

[1] The exegetical methods of Gregory the Great, which are generally similar to those of his predecessors, are more fully discussed in the next section.

this period with its dominant orientation. These factors created both the strength and the weakness of all medieval interpretation of Scripture.

In all places and in each generation during this long period, one fact was especially responsible for creating the general atmosphere in which this exegesis developed and which made it fertile: the importance of monasticism in the contemporary life of the Church. Except, perhaps, in the ninth century, there were far fewer controversies than in the time of the Fathers, and the intellectual effervescence of the scholastic age was yet to come. The general tendency was more contemplative; the monks cultivated the spiritual life rather than speculation. It was only from the first half of the twelfth century that Scripture was widely employed in scholastic theology; its role in the schools is mentioned here only because it represents an element of transition to the following period, dealt with in the next section.

A chronological outline will provide an introduction to a description of the common and constant features of the interpretation of the Bible from Gregory the Great to St Bernard. This must be limited to the principal writers, seen in the context of their time, their environment, and the currents of thought which they represent.

The first and most important is Gregory himself (*d.* 604). All the others depend on him, and it was he who transmitted a large share of the heritage of the Fathers to the middle ages. For him, as for all of them, the Bible is the essential source of all religious learning. The greater part of his output consisted in commentaries on Job, Ezekiel, Kings and also on forty excerpts from the Gospels. Throughout his writings Gregory shows an enthusiastic admiration and esteem for Scripture. The Bible is really concerned with one subject: the revelation of God in Christ, which is the very condition of salvation. This light is given to men in every book of the Bible, both of the Old and the New Testaments. Between these two chapters in the religious history of mankind there are certainly differences, but also continuity and progress. Everything in the Bible is inspired; it constitutes, in the words of Ezekiel which Gregory explained in a passage of fundamental importance, a book 'written both within and without' (*intus et foris*) (Ezek. ii. 2).

Hence the inner meaning, the spiritual sense, should always be sought beneath the letter. Because this is hidden, effort is required: and this very obscurity is useful because it impels us to search. But in this process of seeking and finding, fanciful elements were introduced which are open to criticism: Gregory's exegesis includes explanations of numbers and of common or proper names which seem to us superficial, childish, or over-subtle. Nevertheless, Gregory warns us against an excess of allegory, and insists on the importance of the literal sense and on respect for history. In point of fact his method includes three necessary steps: we should first seek the historical sense, then build the typical sense on this foundation, and lastly deduce from the latter the moral sense. This is the plan which Gregory followed, not only in detailed verse-by-verse commentary but also as the basic scheme of the whole *Moralia in Job*. His treatment of the historical sense is less developed: this is fortunate, because here Gregory is less sound and less original owing to the limited philological resources of an age when knowledge of the original languages was almost unattainable in the West. Moreover, spiritual interpretation is in harmony with his deepest preferences. He is, above all, a moralist, concerned with Christian perfection; he repeatedly insists that the indispensable condition for understanding the Bible is to love it and to practise its teaching. 'We hear the words of God if we act upon them.' What he calls the 'eye of love' (*oculus amoris*) is what overcomes our incapacity to lay hold of the mysteries of God. Charity is both the end of Scripture and also the means which enables us to read it with profit and thus attain its object. 'Throughout Scripture God speaks to us for this purpose alone, to lead us to the love of himself and of our neighbour.'

One of the comparisons he developed most readily, and which sums up his whole notion of Scripture, is that which sees in it a mirror of the soul. In the inspired texts and in the people whose actions they describe, the Christian learns at one and the same time to know both God and also, by a kind of 'biblical hagiography', himself. In the strivings, faults and virtues of the saints of Scripture he sees the reflection of his own soul and its weaknesses, and also of its search for God. He thus learns from Scripture not only faith and charity but also humility and confidence.

By the bent of his character and his desire for interior perfection, Gregory gave a particular orientation to the exegesis of the subsequent centuries. To the new world which arose from the barbarian invasions he offered a teaching which was both acceptable and profound, expressed in easy and attractive language. He had drawn much from the great doctors of an earlier age: Ambrose, Jerome and

Augustine, and especially from Origen. From their teaching, however, he retained only what was of permanent relevance. This he disentangled from polemical elements whose purpose had been the refutation of errors that were now obsolete, so that the rich contribution of Christian antiquity could now be assimilated by the middle ages. It was to be received and lived out especially in the monastic milieu to which Gregory still belonged both by desire and by his special interest in St Benedict.

After Gregory there are only three important names in the seventh and eighth centuries. Isidore of Seville (*d.* 636) left no commentaries, properly so called, on entire books of the Bible, but he wrote 'Introductions' (*prooemia*) to several books of the Old and New Testaments, and biographical notices about individual characters in the Bible, and he was specially concerned with *quaestiones* posed by difficult passages. Even more important, he elaborated the *instrumenta studiorum* which were to remain in use during the whole of the middle ages; his *Etymologiae*, explanations of proper names, numbers, events and dates, which were extracted from earlier exegetes (especially Jerome), formed a kind of Christian encyclopaedia based on Holy Scripture. They became the handbook of Christian instruction for subsequent commentators.

The Venerable Bede (*d.* 735) also composed works on method. He gave special study to figures of speech (*De schematis et tropis*), after the example of Cassiodorus. He applied these principles in a long treatise on the tabernacle and the sacred vestments described in Scripture, in commentaries on several books of the Old and New Testaments, and in homilies on extracts from the Gospels. In all these works he displays his command of the scientific knowledge available at the time; and his restraint in the use of allegory, together with a kind of ingenuous simplicity, gives his commentaries a charm which is still attractive.

Lastly, Ambrose Autpert (*d.* 781), abbot of St Vincent in southern Italy, left a massive commentary in ten books on the Apocalypse. He borrowed many elements from his predecessors, but sometimes exhibited penetrating individual judgement concerning the mystery of history and the progress of the Church and the soul, with Mary's share in these.

Many lesser authors, who were often anonymous and whose works are still unpublished, also wrote about Scripture, especially in the British Isles where culture had found refuge. To these writers we owe glosses, treatises in the form of questions and answers, and connected commentaries. Ireland had a large share in these productions, which applied the technique of the 'grammar' of Latin antiquity to the inspired text. In Ireland, also, pocket Gospel books became widespread. These often had full-page illustrations; and as monks and pilgrims could carry them about easily from place to place they became widely known on the Continent and had a notable influence on iconography.

This period is also the golden age of *florilegia*: Isidore's *Sententiae*, for instance, are largely a collection of extracts from the Bible, elaborated in the manner of Gregory. But in the *Scintillae* of Defensor of Ligugé, as in many anonymous centos, the author's work consists merely in arranging the verses cited into chapters, which treat successively of the different articles of faith and the Christian virtues.

In the second half of the eighth century, at the beginning of the Carolingian era, there was a renewed output of exegetical works. They were not more original now than in the preceding period; often, as before, they simply repeated and transmitted to posterity the heritage of the Fathers and Gregory, but they were more numerous and more fully developed. Moreover the renewal of studies in cathedral and monastic schools stimulated the writing of *quaestiones*, whose purpose was to enlighten clergy and laity about the problems raised by obscure texts or the apparent contradictions between certain passages. Willibald of Stavelot, Smaragdus of St-Mihiel, Claud of Turin, Agobard of Lyons, Walafrid Strabo, Angelomus of Luxeuil, Sedulius Scottus, Florus of Lyons, Paschasius Radbert, abbot of Corbie, John Scotus Erigena, Chrétien Druthmar, Hincmar of Rheims and Remigius of Auxerre are the best-known of these commentators; others remained anonymous. All make use of the Fathers' explanations, but each, none the less, gives his work a personal element in harmony with his own bent and his favourite sources. The two most important writers of this period are Alcuin and Rabanus Maurus. The former not only wrote commentaries and exegetical *Interrogationes* on Genesis, but also undertook a revision of the Vulgate based on ancient manuscripts, which provided his contemporaries with a sounder version, and future critics with an important witness to its textual history (pp. 133 ff.). Rabanus Maurus left several elaborate commentaries which were often copied in later centuries, though some of them were merely abridgements of Origen.

In the tenth, and still more in the eleventh, centuries, as an accompaniment to the reform first of monasticism and then of the whole Church, new works appeared which were inspired by the Bible or were intended to make it better known. Odo of Cluny (*d.* 942) composed a long poem called the *Occupatio*, a verse paraphrase of sacred history. Bruno of Würzburg (*d.* 1045) explained those parts of Scripture which were sung at the Divine Office, especially the Psalms, canticles and the Lord's Prayer. Berno of Reichenau (*d.* 1048) set out to interpret the responsories in the Antiphoner in accordance with their biblical originals and to correct them if they had faulty readings. Lanfranc (*d.* 1089) assembled a series of citations from the works of Augustine and Ambrosiaster (the anonymous fourth-century writer who was identified with Ambrose) on the Pauline epistles. To St Bruno (*d.* 1101) are attributed commentaries on the Psalms and on Paul's epistles.

Several of these post-Carolingian authors claim that they have consulted the *Hebraica veritas*, or even that they have asked a Jew to help them with their interpretations and translations. Often this is only a literary fiction inherited from Jerome, whose own words often do duty for those of the supposed Jew; but at least this device shows that they were anxious not to despise the literal sense. These works, however artificial we may think them today, provided in those times of vital spiritual activity the most substantial nourishment available both for the pastoral activities of the Church and for the faith of the laity.

All these efforts devoted to the service of Scripture bore fruit, not so much in the sphere of doctrinal development as in that of the spiritual life. Three representative authors, all monks, should be mentioned. Peter Damian (*d.* 1072) incessantly appealed in the cause of the reform both of monasticism and of the whole Church to arguments drawn from the Bible, and especially from the Prophets. There he had found models which he commended to all for imitation. To describe the union of the soul with God he found his most suitable words and phrases in the Song of Songs, and the rich imagery of Scripture inspired his inexhaustible poetic genius. To doctrinal controversies he applied the 'principle of agreement' which enabled one passage of Scripture to be explained in the light of another, in the sense given to it by tradition.

Next, Othlo of St Emmeran (*d. c.* 1073) told of the interior struggles which were needed to overcome the temptations which the study of Scripture aroused in him concerning the apparent contradiction between the ideals which it offers us and the limitations of human efforts (*Liber de tentationibus suis*). When graces of illumination and strength had been granted him, he set himself the task of persuading the clergy in his *De cursu spirituali* that their faith should be nourished and their moral reformation stimulated above all through the Bible. Lastly, John of Fécamp (*d.* 1078), although he wrote neither commentaries nor treatises on scriptural problems, ceaselessly recalled his readers to the need to read Scripture and to relish it *in palato cordis*. His books of prayers, circulated under different names, especially Augustine's, enjoyed a very wide diffusion and influence.

The common characteristic in all this use of Scripture in the period from the seventh to the eleventh century was the constant link between the Bible and prayer, both public and private. During these great monastic centuries, contemplation found in the liturgy both its source and its expression, while private devotion was simply an extension of the mental attitude adopted in the Church's public prayer. The texts of the liturgy are chiefly made up of extracts from the Bible, collected and arranged in such a way as to make of them a poem of inexhaustible meaning and profundity. The liturgy develops men's inclination to read the Bible in order to discover yet more of the spiritual treasure which it contains, while the cycle of mysteries which is re-lived through the liturgy illuminates the most vital content of the sacred texts (and see section 4). The scriptural texts, especially those from the Psalms, pass into everyday life and prayer, and become the normal and spontaneous expression of the soul's contact with God. This is the reason why extra-biblical texts are written round so many manuscripts of the Psalms. It is not that the Psalms were commented on more than any other book of the Bible; recourse was had, rather, to the admirable commentaries of Augustine and Cassiodorus. But in order that they should penetrate further into daily life and prayer they were preceded and followed by titles or *capitula*, summaries or *argumenta*, with prayers or collects which asked that their meaning might be understood. Abridgements were made, such as the *Collectio psalterii* attributed to Bede, anonymous collections of the *Flores Psalmorum* and also the *Breviarium psalterii* composed for a lady by Bishop Prudentius of Troyes (*d.* 861) for recitation on journeys.

In the twelfth century there was a parallel development in the utilization and interpretation of Scripture to the two currents already distinguished: the Bible nourishes both learning and contemplation, both intellectual research and spiritual devotion. The first of these currents, which made Scripture the subject of academic study, became more and more important with the progress of scholasticism. From the early twelfth century, in the cathedral schools of large French towns, especially Laon, theological instruction was given in the form of *quaestiones* raised by commentaries on texts of the Bible. The masters' solutions became *sententiae*, almost always anonymous, and preserved by many manuscripts in different recensions (p. 198). Among these masters to whom clerics flocked in large numbers the greatest was Anselm of Laon, whose teaching played a decisive part in the elaboration of the *Glossa Ordinaria*, which was to become an important tool of the whole scholastic movement (pp. 145, 205). Peter Lombard and Peter Comestor, like Anselm of Laon, still only commented on Scripture according to the ideas of the Fathers, and they even used texts of Pelagius, which circulated under the name of Augustine. But Abelard, Gilbert de la Porrée, and even more their disciples, applied the methods of dialectic to the sacred text. At Paris the Victorines, who were in close touch with the schools of the city but also shared the claustral tradition of the Canons Regular, were able to bring into being an original blending of the new methods with the spiritual outlook of the monastic past. Hugh of St Victor initiated this, and his disciples continued his work. This use of the Bible by the scholastics, developing from the second half of the eleventh century onwards, is the subject of the next section.

It should be emphasized that the study of Scripture was remarkably fruitful in the monastic revival which began in the early twelfth century. In Italy Bruno of Asti, abbot of Monte Cassino and later of Segni, commented on Job, the Psalms, the Song of Songs, Joshua, Judith, Isaiah and the Apocalypse. In Anglo-Norman monasteries Gilbert Crispin, abbot of Westminster, Richard of Fourneaux, abbot of Préaux, Odo of Battle, abbot of Christ Church, Canterbury (to name only a few) composed commentaries which were read especially in England, where their manuscripts are still to be found. Laurence of Durham wrote the *Hypognosticon*, a long biblical poem similar to that of Odo of Cluny. In the empire, Honorius Augustodunus, probably of English origin though he lived in southern Germany (it is improbable that he was connected with Burgundy), commented on the Song of

Songs and Wisdom books. In the Rhineland, Rupert of Deutz arranged his treatise on sacred history around basic theological ideas which are indicated in such titles as *The Victory of the Word of God* or *The Works of the Holy Trinity*. He was also one of the first to give a Marian interpretation of the Song of Songs. Anxious to interpret everything in the light of Christ and the Church, saturated in patristic tradition and strongly influenced by Origen, he left a rich and noble output of biblical theology which was the most original of those produced by the Black Monks.

The new Orders founded just at this time also had some representatives in the field. Zachary of Besançon was outstanding among the Premonstratensians as the author of a harmony of the Four Gospels; as its model he chose the similar work of Ammonius of Alexandria after examining those of Tatian, Theophilus of Antioch and Augustine.

It was especially among the Cistercians that a vigorous biblical revival developed. Bernard of Clairvaux was its leader and set the tone, although he did not compose a single consecutive commentary on any book of the Bible. In his eighty-six *Sermons on the Song of Songs* the scriptural text is hardly more than the general theme and the element of continuity; it is sometimes merely a starting-point for a wide variety of developments. Nevertheless, all his writings, whether treatises, sermons, or letters, are full of the Bible. When he is not explicitly citing it he uses it constantly by borrowing its style and vocabulary, and even its thought. He had a profound and detailed knowledge of the many books of Scripture that he used, but especially of John's Gospel and the Pauline epistles. Consequently his theology is Johannine and, even more, Pauline.

In addition, he taught what should be the place of Holy Scripture in the life of the Christian, and especially the monk, adducing principles which are set out more than once in his compressed but poetic style. He insisted, too, on the unity of Scripture, in which there is told one and the same story of salvation which in turn finds its continuation in the lives of believers. Everything in the Bible has a meaning, and no detail of the text ought to be neglected. A number of texts have several possible meanings, not because the inspired writer foresaw or intended them, but because 'the Scriptures should be at the service of charity, and she can find within them as many lights as she desires'. Hence there is an element of freedom in this quest, a kind of inspiration by which God, as the master of Scripture, may be asked in prayer to assist its readers as he assisted its authors. Nevertheless, the detailed study of the actual text must not be neglected, and this can only be achieved in the Church, through living participation in the tradition and prayer of the *Catholica*, in the spiritual atmosphere of the celebration of the liturgy and the assiduous study of the Fathers. It is there that the love of God finds nourishment; the honey whose sweetness the soul tastes flows out of the letter. Enlightenment is thus received for the moral life, and joy in knowing the mysteries of God and their internal cohesion, and in discovering their depth, extent and sublimity. When their beauty and fecundity are realized a true experiential knowledge is attained, and the joy thus experienced kindles an ineffable rapture. In silence and contemplation the soul prays with groanings that cannot be uttered, and sings a melody audible to God alone; in thanksgiving it offers to the Father that divine sonship which it receives from the Word, the spouse of the soul, with the gift of the Spirit of the Father and the Son. The result of sacred reading is thus a song of love, *carmen spiritus*.

Thanks to the literary qualities and strongly individual character of his writings, St Bernard created a style of biblical theology which inspired disciples and admirers: Geoffrey of Auxerre, Isaac of Stella, Ailred of Rievaulx, Gilbert of Hoyland, Gilbert of Stamford among the Cistercians; Drogo, Arnald of Bonneval, Peter of Celle among the Black Monks (to name only a few); all of these continued his work, but not without adding elements of their own. The most original of all Bernard's friends was William of St-Thierry. Although he lacked the genius, penetration and facility of the abbot of Clairvaux, he sometimes showed greater knowledge and power of synthesis. Together, these monastic writers of the twelfth century assembled the elements of a true compendium of monastic theology whose inspiration, ideas and expression came from the Bible and the patristic commentaries on it, especially those of Origen.

The conclusion to be drawn from this chronological sketch is that, from the sixth century till the twelfth, renewal of interest in the Bible coincided with periods of ecclesiastical, and especially monastic, reform. Until the rise of scholasticism the tradition of exegesis was principally monastic. It extended the tradition of the Fathers and constituted, so to speak, a new patristic age. To the Church's given inheritance of doctrine it added the resources of a new sensitivity then gradually developing in the West. This blending of the most authentic elements of the past with a new ardour and freshness proved highly creative in the sphere of exegesis. To it we owe many varied and often beautiful works by means of which many generations of Christians lived their lives in the search for perfection. At the beginning and end of this development the two great names of Gregory and Bernard stand out to represent the labours of those anonymous monks who studied the Bible in order to live by it. Each, in his own way, represents a synthesis: a point of arrival for the thought which preceded him, and of departure for a renewal whose nature and direction he had prepared.

It is no longer necessary to prove that medieval laymen knew the Bible as well as clerics, and that everyone capable of doing so was encouraged to read it; the facts assembled by H. Rost[1] show this quite sufficiently. We need, however, to discern how this knowledge of the Bible provided education in the spiritual life and how completely it penetrated contemporary culture at every level.

The basis of the influence of Holy Scripture was the elementary fact that it was read; but the precise meaning of the term *lectio* needs to be established. It is applied to two different activities. In the schools, especially those where clerics were trained for pastoral duties, Scripture was read mainly to gain light on intellectual and moral problems. The text was examined, *quaestiones* were propounded, and these were answered by means of the *disputatio*. Knowledge is the principal object of the search: the problem is introduced by expressions such as *quaeritur* or *quaeri solet*, and the solution by the word *sciendum*. The text itself is all-important: it is the subject of the *lectio* and is called *sacra pagina*. On the other hand, in monasteries of the various rules, all of which were centres of an intense spiritual life, the monks pursued the traditional *lectio divina* of Scripture. Here it is not so much the text itself that is considered most important as the fact of reading it and gaining personal benefit from it. The aim is not so much to acquire ideas, since knowledge of the faith is presupposed, but rather to taste and savour the Word of God; thus the contemplative life of prayer and union with God might be strengthened. These two ways of reading Scripture were practised throughout the middle ages: the first developed primarily in twelfth-century scholasticism, the second remained in favour in the monasteries.

[1] *Die Bibel im Mittelalter* (Augsburg, 1939).

Both are marked by certain common characteristics which strictly belong primarily to the monastic *lectio divina* which was especially widespread in this period. The most important point to observe concerns the sources from which medieval men received their biblical education. These were of two kinds. The first was formed by the living environment in which the Bible was studied. This was the actual life of the Church as expressed in the liturgy. Thus Alcuin and Hervé of Bourg-Dieu (*d.* 1150) corrected the sacred text with a view to securing a more intelligent participation in divine worship. It was, moreover, especially from the text of the liturgy that they learnt to acquire a deeper understanding of the mysteries of which the Bible speaks. The Bible was, indeed, a 'book of life' for all: it spoke to each of the salvation of souls in Christ the giver of eternal life. It was for each to assimilate the teaching of the Bible and make it the rule of conduct, and, if he had pastoral duties, to impart to others the realities of which it speaks. Thus the Bible was the principal and often the only source for preachers, whether they were abbots and monks instructing other religious, or bishops and priests instructing the laity. The sermon was a liturgical act; scriptural commentary was an integral part of divine worship. Hence the liturgy provided an excellent initiation into the Bible and the Bible into the liturgy.

The second source of biblical education during the monastic centuries was patristic tradition. This, too, was completely in harmony with the spirit of the liturgy, which, indeed, borrows many of its texts from that tradition. The Fathers did little else but expound Scripture, even when they were not writing commentaries in the proper sense; hence they were often simply called *expositores*. Those of their writings which introduced the reader to the text itself and its immediate content, independently of the ancient doctrinal controversies which no longer interested the middle ages, were very widely copied, read and meditated on. Much was borrowed from Jerome, who was considered the master of historical exegesis, from Augustine's great commentaries on the Psalms and John, and from several other Latin Fathers; but among the Greeks only from those few, like Basil and John Chrysostom, whose works had been translated. The more, however, that the thought of the early middle ages is studied, the more the conclusion of modern scholars is confirmed that Origen was the most important source of all, especially through his commentaries translated into Latin by Jerome and Rufinus. Most of the allegories, symbols, images and even the actual phraseology come from Origen, either directly through the numerous transcripts of his own writings, or through intermediaries like Isidore, Rabanus Maurus and especially Gregory the Great. Gregory's teaching was derived from Origen, and contributed more than any other to forming the outlook of the middle ages. Contrary to received opinion, it therefore seems that the two great masters of medieval exegesis were not Jerome and Augustine but Origen and Gregory. It was especially in scholasticism that Augustine became dominant.

Within the atmosphere created by the liturgy and patristic tradition, two principal problems were presented to medieval exegetes, as those of every age. The first is the relation of the Old Testament to the New. Their solution, in brief, was that the interpretation of Scripture implies the discovery of the New Testament in the Old. This process had been carried out by the Apostles and the early Church. Christ announced the new revelation by unveiling the old, making clear that he himself had been foretold by it and that the New Covenant was already contained in it beneath the veils, those *involucra* which were waiting to be removed. All medieval exegesis, like that of the early Church, consisted in passing on from the literal to the spiritual sense of the Old Testament. This is why there was much more allegorizing of the Old Testament than of the New. The former required the perception of the mysteries, the *sacramenta*, under the veil of the letter. This broad view that the history of one and the same salvation developed through two different series of books had the advantage of keeping in sight the continuity which unites the two Testaments, called by St Bernard the *unitas Scripturarum*. Such an outlook explains the real greatness and fertility of medieval exegesis. Nevertheless, because that age, like antiquity as a whole, lacked any exact knowledge of chronology, historical context, literary forms, and the genius of the languages of the Bible, its writers applied this idea of development not only, rightly, to religious history on the grand scale, but also to particular facts. Completely artificial connections were made between texts which were quite unrelated except for a resemblance in external details or even in the actual words used in the Vulgate. In this way the great defect of medieval exegesis can be said to be an excess of literalism, or even more, an excess of historicism. At times it happened that, without the necessary modifications which the case required, examples, texts or ideas which were really valid only for deciding the relations between the leaders of Israel and the priests of the Old Covenant were applied directly to institutions like the hierarchy of the Church and the secular power.

The other major problem which faced the medieval exegete was that of the different senses of Scripture. It would be most interesting to trace the apparently very complex history of the lists of the senses of Scripture. They are formulated in various ways. Sometimes there are four senses: literal or historical; typical; moral or allegorical; and lastly anagogical. Sometimes there are only three. The first place is sometimes given to one, sometimes to another. Moreover, some authors divide and subdivide each sense. In point of fact, the senses should probably be reduced to three, in accordance with Gregory's division: history, typology, and the moral sense. In practice the letter was always treated first, then the spirit. The second sphere, spiritual exegesis, is that in which the interior life in all its forms finds its nourishment; in which, too, the hidden mystery is apprehended and applied to the life of the soul and all that concerns it: asceticism, mysticism, the Church, the sacraments and eschatology. In all these there is realized the sole object of the Scriptures, union with Christ. Every page of Origen's works had developed this fundamental idea, and if he was the favourite model of monastic commentators, this was because of his mastery of allegory, and consequently of the whole theory of the spiritual life. In the schools, however, and for purposes of theological controversy, more recourse was had to the literal sense as a source of solid arguments, and thus to the works of Jerome and Augustine which explained texts historically. In the cloister, where the principal aim was prayer and union with God, preference was given to the moral applications.

In both these milieux all the faculties of the soul, mind, memory, imagination and feeling were completely permeated by Scripture. There is no need to insist on the innumerable consequences of this in all spheres of medieval life. The Bible helped to form, not only medieval Latin, so deeply influenced by the Vulgate, but also the vernacular languages. It was glossed more often than any other text. It was often the basis of elementary education. The Psalter and other parts of Scripture were learned by heart. People learned to read by means of, and for the sake of, reading the Bible. Many of its phrases passed into vernacular languages and are still there under the form of similes and proverbs, common or proper names. Laws and social institutions found their principles and examples in Scripture. Literature was enriched by the influence of the whole Bible, not only in religious drama which began as a liturgical *mise-en-scène* of sacred history, but also in forms of literature as far removed from the Bible as parody. The art of book-production received a wealth of imagery in bibles that were versified and illuminated. Scenes from the Bible were represented everywhere: on doors, in frescoes, in sculptured capitals and tympana, in stained-glass windows and furnishings. Culture and the life of the Church were drawn into unity in and through the Bible. The Bible was the basic book of medieval culture, and medieval culture was essentially a biblical culture.

During these centuries when the highest intellectual activities consisted in reading, meditating and commenting on the Bible, scientific exegesis based on sound philology was lacking. Such explanations as were then given of biblical history have become obsolete. But though the progress of scientific knowledge replaced this provisional and imperfect philology by sounder methods, the religious spirit of the medieval commentators remains of permanent value. Their charity, their penetration of the mystery of Christ, and their experience of the realities of the spiritual life still make their works full of interest. Those humanists of sound and penetrating judgement who edited texts in the sixteenth and seventeenth centuries realized perfectly well that there was no need to rescue from oblivion the exegetes of the thirteenth century and later who had written historical commentaries on the Bible, but that it was important to publish those of the monastic centuries. The latter still deserve to be read because their authors knew how to extract what was most essential from the sacred texts: the means of leading souls to God. In this respect they represent an important stage in the history of the interpretation and use of the Bible.

3. THE BIBLE IN THE MEDIEVAL SCHOOLS

THE ACADEMIC BACKGROUND

The Latin Vulgate was a 'set text' in the theological faculties of schools and universities throughout the middle ages. Its central place as a teaching book goes far to explain both the achievements and the limitations of medieval exegesis.

Until the second half of the twelfth century the Bible was the only set book to be universally recognized. The term 'theology' had not come into use: *sacra pagina*, the sacred page of Scripture, denoted the whole subject to be studied. A master might expound some other text from the liturgy or the Fathers as an extraordinary measure; he might write a monograph or contribute to some current discussion; but his routine duty was to lecture on the sacred page. Clearly the Bible could not continue to hold this monopoly if science were to make any progress. The intellectual revival of the eleventh and twelfth centuries brought with it a desire to break up the old timetable. Place must be made for debate on those urgent problems which posed themselves in consequence of the Gregorian reform. The sacramental system of the Church had to be developed and her doctrines needed rethinking and clearer definition in the light of new knowledge of pagan philosophy. To treat such matters in the context of a lecture on Scripture, even on one of the Pauline epistles, so rich in theology, proved too cumbersome and haphazard. Recent work on the schools of the late eleventh and early twelfth centuries suggests that pupils took the initiative in sifting and sorting out the material of their master's lectures so as to arrive at a more systematic presentation. They made collections of his *Sentences* (opinions or weighty statements) on theological questions. A book of this kind encouraged reflection and systematization *à tête reposée*. Pupils promoted to be masters in their turn would take the further step of producing systematic textbooks. The Paris master, Peter Lombard, compiled *Sentences* in four books (probably finished in 1152) which covered the whole field of theology as it was then taught. This came to rank as a second set text. Lectures were given on the Lombard's *Sentences* as well as on the Bible. It became customary to discuss questions of doctrine in classes on the *Sentences*. The development of disputations as an essential part of the curriculum helped to differentiate the young discipline of theology from her elder sister, Bible study.

At first a lecturer on the *Sentences* was teaching the Bible at one remove. The Lombard's personal opinions, cautious and conservative as they were, had no binding authority in themselves. His shortish text includes nearly a thousand quotations from Scripture. Every book of the New Testament is represented there except for three Epistles (II Thessalonians, Titus and Philemon), and so is the vast majority of Old Testament books. Early commentators on the *Sentences* would adduce many more biblical texts in support of their arguments. It was not until the fourteenth century that commentators turned increasingly to philosophy and 'theology': they paid less attention to the Bible in practice, though still regarding it as their primary source in theory.

Meanwhile university men busied themselves in organizing and standardizing the teaching of Scripture itself. The unity of medieval culture is nowhere more visible than here. The same version of the Latin Vulgate with the same standard apparatus formed the subject of statutory lectures, prepared according to the same methods, throughout Catholic Europe. We may see in this a reflection of the fact that masters and students were all clerics, belonging to the same church. Whatever their place of origin, they could attend a foreign university because all spoke Latin. They could hope, moreover, that their qualifications might bring them promotion, if not in their own country, then at the papal curia or in some other branch of the Church universal. Yet we know that a bewildering diversity of local customs coexisted under any medieval government, ecclesiastical or secular. There were deeper reasons for the uniformity of biblical teaching. It derived first from the centralization of studies at Paris at a vital phase in their development, and secondly from the rise of the international mendicant Orders.

Paris, until about the middle of the twelfth century, was just one of a number of schools in northern France and the Rhinelands. A school would normally belong to a cathedral church. Its renown depended on the personality of the individual teacher. Students would travel round sampling the lectures at different schools, or would follow their master if he moved to another chair. Then more masters settled at Paris and teaching there became continuous; they gradually organized themselves into a university. Smaller schools began to look provincial and failed to attract pupils. Paris fashions in books and teaching methods were adopted elsewhere. The later middle ages saw a second, and this time a lasting, period of decentralization. Paris lost her monopoly, though not her eminence. The universities of Oxford and Cambridge grew up in England, and a larger number (in proportion to the area they served) in most other parts of Europe. The popes opened a faculty of theology for the instruction of the clergy at the Roman curia. It is by no means a foregone conclusion that all these centres would have kept faithful to Paris methods if the friars had not made Bible studies so peculiarly their own. The Dominican and Franciscan and later on the Austin and Carmelite friars set up houses of study with chairs attached to them wherever they found faculties of theology, beginning with Paris and Oxford. They also gave lectures on theology in some non-university cities and in universities such as Bologna which had not yet acquired a theological faculty. Thanks to their international organization, the mendicants could scatter or concentrate their men in key centres. A friar who qualified as a doctor of theology would normally teach for a year or two where he had taken his degree. Then his superiors would move him to another school or use him for pastoral or administrative work in his province. They might send an especially gifted doctor back to his chair for a second regency.

The jealousy and friction between secular and religious masters makes tangled history. Secular masters had had exclusive rights in theological teaching before the coming of the friars, except in monastic schools, which kept apart. The seculars resented competition from the new-comers. Yet however much they quarrelled about privilege, they resigned Bible studies to the friars by a kind of tacit surrender. What they really minded was rivalry in lectures on the *Sentences*, in disputation and in university preaching. The venerable old tradition that religious life in the cloister or hermitage should centre on *lectio divina* may explain this bloodless victory for the mendicants. Whatever the reason may be, the secular masters' contribution to Bible studies is negligible in comparison with the friars' until late in the fourteenth century: that means at least 150 years' pre-eminence. No local particularism in Bible studies could develop as long as teachers and books circulated freely over Christendom through the agency of international Orders.

A university course ran roughly as follows. Students had to qualify in the 'seven liberal arts' before they could read for a degree in theology. The arts course comprised the *trivium*, grammar, rhetoric and dialectic, and the *quadrivium*, music, astronomy, arithmetic and geometry; it was crowned by the study of philosophy. The content varied and widened as new books by Aristotle, or going under his name, with their Greek and Arabic commentaries, became available to the West, joining those Platonic and Neoplatonic texts which were known in translation. The richer content of the arts course affected Bible studies in that men of tough intellect preferred to spend longer as students and teachers of arts before passing to theology than had been the custom in the early twelfth century. The cry went up and was often repeated that promising scholars put off reading for theology until too late in life, even if they resisted the call of the 'lucrative sciences', medicine and law. This did not apply to the mendicants, since their students were forbidden to follow a university course in arts; they went straight to theology. But the friars provided a corresponding training in arts in their own *studia*. Hence all intending theologians, whether religious or secular, would have been prepared by an encyclopaedic education. They had learnt enough Latin grammar to read the required texts at least; they could dispute according to the rules of logic as taught in the schools; they had a knowledge of natural science and philosophy as understood at the time. Literary studies got submerged in the later twelfth century owing to the growing interest in logic and science. Even so, the most blinkered beginner would have picked up tags from the Latin classics and the most popular 'ancient fables' about the gods of Greece and Rome.

The course in theology was lengthened to eight years at Paris in the thirteenth century. The student attended compulsory lectures on Scripture. After taking his bachelor's degree he gave an elementary course of lectures himself, reading the Bible *cursorie*, without expressing his personal views on deeper matters. The *principium* or inaugural lecture was a solemn function. The *bachelarius biblicus* praised Scripture in general and introduced the text of his choice. On incepting as doctor he gave another *principium* at a more advanced level. The regent master in theology had a statutory duty to lecture on Scripture throughout the academic year. It was the custom to run two courses simultaneously, one course on a book of the Old, the other on a book of the New, Testament. The master dealt with any problem which might arise from his text and could air his opinions. His pace varied to suit himself. Some courses spread over two academic years. Some broke off unfinished because the master resigned his chair unexpectedly or miscalculated the time at his disposal.

Our knowledge of medieval exegesis in the scholastic period depends almost wholly on records of lectures, some by bachelors, many more by masters. We read them either in the master's own version, copied by a scribe or very occasionally in his autograph, or else in his pupils' notes, *reportationes*, taken down in class. The master's version may be properly prepared for publication, that is, ready to go to the stationer to be transcribed and circulated in a number of copies, or we may have only a copy of the rough notes which he took into class with him, intended for no eyes but his own; presumably he had no time to revise them before eager pupils pressed him to hand them over. *Reportationes* have sometimes come down in more than one version. Put two or three side by side and you have the same teaching expressed in different words, now more fully, now in a more condensed form according to the reporter's skill or habit, as the two or three pupils made their separate sheafs of notes. Another mark of the *reportatio* is that the lecturer is sometimes referred to in the third person: 'the master says...' A master had the duty of authorizing and revising one of the *reportationes* before it was published; but unofficial ones circulated, nevertheless. A brilliant study of Thomas Aquinas's secretaries has illustrated the difficulties which were experienced in getting clean texts of his lectures. He had skilled reporters, and yet the work was so exacting that he sometimes offered his own draft for copy to save undue strain. Like many great scholars he wrote in an almost illegible hand, the *littera inintelligibilis*. Some of his secretaries made a special study of transcribing it legibly, and there was a chain system for taking down his dictation. The Dominicans were so proud of him and so convinced of the value of his work as to give him every possible facility. Lesser men made shift as they could.

The origin and nature of these lecture commentaries make the study of medieval exegesis both technical and difficult. The reader has to struggle with copies deriving from defective, shoddy exemplars: scribes have made careless mistakes; they cannot be blamed for everything wrong in their text. The problems of anonymity and incorrect ascription beset him. The masters of *sacra pagina* from the eleventh to the end of the thirteenth centuries seem, with few exceptions, to have been a modest set of men who did not care to label their works with their names. Chance decided whether a lecture course should go down to posterity with the author's name correctly stated in the *incipit* or *explicit*. An outstanding teacher, especially if he brought glory to an Order, was likely to get due credit. On the other hand, a famous name drew apocrypha as a flypaper gathers flies—witness the long columns of 'pseudo-Albert', 'pseudo-Bonaventure', 'pseudo-Thomas' in the bibliographical notices on these doctors. Commentaries which were widely used, as we know from the number of surviving copies and of quotations in later writings, are still unattached to their author. One can only guess at their date and provenance. Fourteenth-century commentators had more *amour propre* than their predecessors. Perhaps they were conscious of living in a more competitive society and felt more anxious to assert themselves. They liked to send their finished commentaries to some high ecclesiastic, a pope, a cardinal, an archbishop or a provincial prior, with a dedicatory letter by way of a preface. It became fashionable to indicate one's name in a pun or allusion in one's prologue. Even so, fourteenth-century attributions are not all plain sailing.

The modern student can take courage, however, since he now has his indispensable reference book, the *Repertorium Biblicum Medii Aevi* by Professor F. Stegmüller. Here he will find a list of incipits of the books of the Vulgate with their prologues, a list of biblical commentators and writers on biblical subjects with incipits, and finally two volumes of *anonyma*. The *Repertorium* has made some sort of statistical analysis feasible at last. Which periods and which places in the middle ages saw a high output of commentaries and aids to study, and which a decline? Which parts of the Bible had most appeal for the scholars and teachers of a particular period? Naturally we are at the mercy of chance survival; it would be too simple to argue 'no record, therefore no lecture'. Courses reliably recorded as having been given are lost or still unidentified. The vast majority of courses can never have been published. We hear complaints of negligence but never of mass disobedience on the part of regent masters. Most of them must have made a show of complying with their statutory duties; and yet no record of their teaching has come down to us. One can only suppose that in such cases the lectures were too slight and unenterprising to be worth recording. Years which show a dearth of surviving commentaries need not signify a complete stop of teaching. What they do signify is loss of interest on the masters' part.

Here a word of warning is necessary to the student who embarks on the study of scholastic or pre-scholastic commentaries. He must not hope to find a precise terminology for the various types. He will meet *commentaria, commentariola, expositiones, glosae, glosulae, lectiones, lecturae* and *postillae*. *Lectiones* and *lecturae* (the latter term comes into common use only towards the end of the thirteenth century) denote lecture courses. 'Gloss' came to have the increasingly specialized meaning of a short comment inserted into the margin or between the lines of the text or of a collection of glosses of this kind. *Postilla*, a word of uncertain derivation, appears in the thirteenth century and normally means a commentary which originated in the classroom, but can be used more widely. 'Exposition' is a very general term. 'Commentary' is not very usual. It can refer to patristic; but it was customary to refer to the Father quoted *in originali*, meaning his original commentary (understood) as distinct from an excerpt. I have tried to avoid confusion by using the modern words 'lecture courses' and 'commentaries' to cover all exposition deriving from the schools.

AN HISTORICAL SURVEY

The cathedral schools of the tenth and early eleventh centuries produced little in comparison with those of the Carolingian period. This seems surprising in view of the Ottonian revival of learning; but the great scholars Ratherius of Verona and Gerbert, later Pope Sylvester II, who were also great eccentrics, took more interest in secular than in sacred studies. Untypical as they were, they reflect the bias of contemporary teaching. The revival of biblical studies, which prepared the way for the achievements of the scholastics, probably began with the teaching of Fulbert at Chartres, though none of his biblical work has come down to us. His pupils, Berengar of Tours and Lanfranc of Bec, were active exegetes. By the early twelfth century Scripture was being taught in a number of schools. The brothers Anselm and Ralph kept the most famous of these at Laon: it counted many of the outstanding masters and prelates of the day among its *alumni*.

Teaching in the pre-scholastic period took two forms. The master would gloss his text in the margin or between the lines. He aimed at assembling extracts from patristic or earlier medieval writers, who had in fact drawn largely from patristic, so as to make his text intelligible to beginners in the light of tradition. His successors would then be able to study the text together with its recognized, authoritative commentators. Books were scarce and time was limited. Classroom needs dictated short cuts. A monk in the cloister with all his religious life at his disposal might nibble or bite at the vast and difficult commentaries of the Four Latin Doctors and the Greek Fathers available in translation; the scholar with his degree to take was in a hurry. The need for glosses persisted all through the middle ages: a Middle English prologue to a glossed Apocalypse will show how readers depended on them. The writer of the prologue has just mentioned the Beasts:

> And full knowing of mickle truth
> That now is his, it is great ruth;
> What they mean in their kind
> Witness the gloss and ye shall find
> It as a key that will unlock
> The door that is full fast stuck.

The glossator could add remarks of his own in his prologue or on the text; his main task was to draw on his predecessors. Anselm and Ralph of Laon and a band of helpers planned and carried out a gloss on the whole Bible. Their apparatus had the same extraordinary fortune as the Lombard's *Sentences*. The Paris masters of the later twelfth century, led by Peter Lombard himself, accepted it as their standard guide. Scripture as expounded in schools and universities was a glossed text. These marginal and interlinear glosses were referred to as *Glossa* at first, later on as *Glossa Ordinaria* (pp. 142, 145, 190, 203, 214). The bibliographical myth which ascribed the marginal glosses to Walafrid Strabo and the interlinear to Anselm of Laon has done harm by obscuring the unity of the whole, and by putting a typical twelfth-century project back into the Carolingian period. Peter Lombard expanded the Laon text of the Gloss to form the *Magna glosatura* on the Psalter and Pauline epistles. His expansion was currently used for these two sections of Scripture. Gilbert de la Porrée, Anselm's pupil, had already prepared the way by his *Media glosatura*.

Secondly, masters of the late eleventh and early twelfth centuries made continuous commentaries. The material has come down to us partly in excerpts from lost lecture courses which have been reworked into collections of *Sentences* or other miscellanies. There was a strong preference for the Psalter and Pauline epistles as texts to be expounded, with the Hexaemeron coming third. It was a question of first things first. The Psalter claimed special attention on account of its place in the liturgical life of the clergy; the fondness for Paul and the Hexaemeron reflects interest in theology. The rest of the Bible suffered comparative neglect except that it received its gloss. When Peter Abelard, disgusted at the dullness of the old master at Laon, set himself up as a rival, he chose the prophecy of Ezekiel as being both 'dark' and *inusitata*; it gave the novice a chance to shine. The point of the story would have been lost on a later generation. There could be no higher tribute to the industry of succeeding masters.

The years from about 1120 to about 1200 saw the whole Bible brought into the classroom. It had all been glossed; now it could be lectured on. The impulse towards teaching the whole Bible seems to have begun at the abbey of St Victor of Paris, a house of canons regular. Hugh of St Victor thought deeply on the subject of Scripture as the story of man's salvation. He saw the two Testaments, followed by the later history of the Church, as forming the very stuff of theology and as the core of a Christian education. He discussed correct methods of exegesis and outlined an ideal syllabus, while setting an example by preparing commentaries. It seems that their scope was much wider than used to be thought and that he expounded three of the Gospels as well as many Old Testament books. Hugh's Victorine pupils carried his plans further; but the future did not lie with abbey schools; St Victor's ceased to be open to external pupils. The heirs of Victorine biblicism were secular masters. Peter Comestor or Manducator (he had eaten and digested the Scriptures) made a compendium of sacred history, the *Historia scholastica*, which ranked with the *Gloss* as a standard textbook. It sometimes served as a subject for elementary lectures. The Comestor also lectured on the four Gospels. Peter of Poitiers, a pupil of Peter Lombard, added a set of genealogical tables as a visual aid. Peter the Chanter and Stephen Langton (later archbishop of Canterbury) both lectured on the greater part of the Bible, including its apparatus of glosses.

Langton, the youngest and most productive of the Paris biblicists, left the schools in 1206. The next twenty years or so have less to offer. The masters who followed him reverted to the earlier practice of leaving an exposition of a single book, perhaps the Psalter, or a single group of books. No one had the gigantic appetite of the Eater. Men turned from Scripture to the thriving and enthralling subject of theology. The friars redressed the balance by dividing their energies between the two disciplines. Production soared. The sheer quantity of biblical commentaries and aids to study which came out between 1230 and 1270 would hardly be surpassed until the days of Erasmus and the Reformation and Counter-Reformation. The Dominican Hugh of St Cher and his friar helpers compiled a new apparatus to the whole

Bible, supplementing the *Gloss* with more excerpts from the Fathers, and drawing on commentators of the twelfth and early thirteenth centuries. A certain specialization of functions becomes apparent. We have commentaries from the great men of the period, Bonaventure, Thomas and Albert, representing part of their many-sided activity. We have more from obscure friars whose lecture courses on Scripture outweigh their recorded *Sentence*-commentaries or *quaestiones*. While no section of Scripture was neglected, the Wisdom literature appealed to teachers as never before. The Wisdom of Solomon fascinated men who admired pagan sages and whose reading of Aristotle had quickened their interest in ethics. Aids to study multiplied in the form of concordances to the Bible and the Fathers, biblical dictionaries and geographies of Palestine. A lecturer of the late thirteenth century could quote from a wider range of authors as indexing became more efficient. A higher standard of accuracy in quoting and reference was expected. The atmosphere of the classroom becomes less primitive. Oxford friars contributed both commentaries and new methods of tabulating. Robert Grosseteste makes a bridge between the two universities, since he worked in both Paris and Oxford. He was a passionate biblicist in the manner of Stephen Langton and did his utmost to promote biblical studies, first as lector to the Oxford Franciscans and then as bishop of Lincoln and chancellor of the university. He also bridges the gap between seculars and mendicants: a secular master himself, he taught at Greyfriars and warmly encouraged both mendicant Orders.

Slump followed boom. Output decreased sharply at Paris and Oxford alike in the last decades of the thirteenth century and the first decade of the fourteenth. It was the high peak of scholastic theology. Disputation on burning questions may have distracted men's minds from the more humdrum task of lecturing on Scripture. Then the friars made their second great effort as biblicists in the years about 1310 to the black death, 1348/9. We see them at work in Paris, Oxford, Cambridge, Toulouse, Avignon, Cologne, Florence, Bologna and Padua. Three books which enjoyed a spectacular success may be mentioned to illustrate their varied contributions. The Franciscan Peter Auriole made a *Compendium litteralis sensus totius Scripturae* giving a digest of each book of the Bible and grouping them according to a systematic order (legal, historical, poetical, prophetic, etc.). The Franciscan Nicholas of Lyra published his great *Postilla litteralis* on the whole Bible, setting out the fruits of his Hebrew scholarship. The Oxford Dominican Robert Holcot gave lectures on Wisdom which catered for contemporary taste by considering it as a biblical 'mirror for princes'. A type of commentary favoured in this period followed a conflated text of the Gospels or else the Gospels and Epistles as they were read in church through the liturgical year. The arrangement suited preachers who wanted material for Sunday and holy day sermons.

The mid-century was another comparatively barren period. The mendicants, hard hit by the plague, were occupied in attempts to reform themselves. The lull was broken when secular masters entered the field in force for the first time since the mendicants had arrived. John Wyclif incepted in theology at Oxford in 1372 or 1373 and died, still writing his *Opus evangelicum*, at the end of 1384. He began by postillating the whole Bible and went on to express strong views on the authority of Scripture. Wyclif was far too medieval to reject the Fathers or to imagine the sacred page wiped clean of its glosses, but he did reject the later traditions of the Church. He looked back to the early days when, as he thought, the Gospel had been rightly understood and followed. He brought up the problem of authority, which had been broached before, more brutally and directly. His attack on the religious Orders as not being grounded in Scripture, and his fiercely possessive attitude to its interpretation, represent a secular's revenge, all the sweeter for being long overdue, for the friars' monopoly. Most important of all, he made people think about Scripture as a whole, and about its place in theology, as a fundamental problem. At Paris too it was a secular master, John Gerson, who revived Bible studies, though he was orthodox and hostile to Wyclif and Hus. Gerson, regent in theology (1392) and chancellor (1395), pleaded for a return to the Scriptures from theological 'subtleties'. He set an example in his lectures on Mark. Two of his contemporaries, both seculars, Henry Totting of Oyta and Henry of Langenstein, left substantial biblical commentaries. They both taught at Paris before Gerson, but their existing lectures are connected with their regencies at Prague and Vienna after they had left Paris.

Totting and Langenstein introduce us to the last phase of medieval Bible study. The fifteenth century has never been surveyed from this point of view. It was a prolific period. The key men were Bohemians and Germans. The Hussite movement at Prague and its repercussions would make a good focus. The historian would have to take into account many other countries, however. The rise of universities in Italy, in the Spanish peninsula, in Scandinavia and to the east of the Rhineland signify new centres where lectures on Scripture were given. Religious masters enter the field again; the Austin friars are productive, the Carthusian monks even more so. Members of the older religious Orders of 'black' and 'white' monks had set up houses of study in the universities already in the thirteenth century, and may have made more mark on biblical studies in the later middle ages than they had earlier. Questions pose themselves which cannot yet be answered: did the return of the seculars and the pre-eminence of the Carthusians make for changes in the general trend of teaching? We know of this period mainly from humanist attacks on the scholastic approach to Scripture. The methods which came under fire were late-medieval. It would be desirable to start from the other end and see how these methods developed. How far did they differ from those of the thirteenth and early fourteenth centuries?

PROCEDURE AND CONTENT OF LECTURES

The Bible, if we abstract its sacred character, was only one of many texts which masters expounded in the schools. Their traditions went back to late antiquity, that is to a phase in the history of culture when creative writing had dried up and had been replaced by the study of venerated masterpieces belonging to a glorious past. A lecturer on the *Aeneid* would begin with an account of the authorship, place, date and purpose of the poem; he would then go through it line by line or word by word, explaining the grammar and the allusions to history, mythology and geography to be found there. Teaching on these subjects was given in the margin of lectures on the poets. The approach favoured pedantry, since the master took little interest in what we call 'literary appreciation'. Professor Marrou has pointed to the influence of contemporary school practice on Augustine's biblical exegesis. The collapse of profane scholarship in the fifth and sixth centuries joined ignorance to pedantry. Classical rhetors understood that the techniques of their subject had a history of development from primitive beginnings. This was lost sight of, and equal value given to texts of any period. Literary perspective vanished. The loss had a flattening effect on the study of any school text, the Bible included.

The ancient method of teaching, with its shrunken content, was learnt by every master of arts and ran no risk of being forgotten. The thirteenth-century influx of new philosophic and scientific texts led to a change in technique. Masters began to define the content of the book to be studied in terms of the four Aristotelian causes, efficient, material, formal and final. They focused on the meaning of their text by a process of division and subdivision. The teacher had to start from some kind of initial division by chapters. Twelfth- and thirteenth-century masters worked out the modern chapter-division of Scripture and of certain patristic texts. Thus students could follow the logical development of their author's argument with all its asides and consequences. The method was well chosen for application to Aristotelian books: the master could combine 'minute penetrating analysis with an astonishing breadth of accurate synthesis'. But Semitic literature lent itself less easily to feeding into a verbal mincing machine. The chapters themselves had been imposed more for convenience than because they corresponded to the author's leaps or pauses. Our hearts sink when a commentator of the early fourteenth century threatens to divide the Bible *usque ad indivisibilia*.

After his division of the whole book and then of the single chapter or group of chapters, the master makes use of his training in logic by enumerating the various meanings of the key words in each subdivision. Suppose that his word is *tempt* or *temptation*; he goes through the various ways in which men may be tempted. He quotes other passages from Scripture containing the word or referring to his theme. His predecessors' industry in making glossaries and concordances gives him ample opportunities. Moreover he starts with an apparatus of glosses, and custom allows him to expand on his master's lectures or on some other medieval expositor. Small wonder that the exposition tends to grow top-heavy.

Most scholars today would agree that a study of classical authors makes a good beginning; but it is clearly insufficient and misleading as the sole preparation for lecturing on oriental texts. The restraint of the authors they read in the arts course blocked the schoolmen's approach to biblical imagery. On the other hand, they tended to give their ideas very concrete expression. It comes as a surprise after the sophistication of scholastic debates, but anyone who has taught small children will feel at home with this side of medieval exegesis. A child will generally accept an authoritative statement that something happened; he shows an embarrassing curiosity as to how and why. The fish swallowed Jonah and cast him up alive after three days. This did not seem impossible: Augustine had seen at Carthage the skeleton of a fish which was large enough to hold a man. A student of Aristotle's *libri naturales* wanted to know further how Jonah resisted its *virtus digestiva* and how, given Aristotle's statement that fish do not breathe, he avoided suffocating. We shall slip into a class on the first Gospel and hear the master explaining the temptation in the wilderness. He shows us its significance as an opening to the ministry of Jesus; we see it too as a drama in the soul; but we also follow the story in all its outer detail. How did Jesus reach the pinnacle of the Temple? Did the devil carry him there and then assume human shape? Surely not. Jesus must have ascended at the prompting of the Holy Spirit. Perhaps the devil tempted him to pride, since people would see him flying miraculously through the air? Jesus foiled the devil's plan by making himself invisible. Where was the pinnacle of the Temple? Perhaps it means the gallery whence the priests would preach to the people gathered below. More probably it means the roof. The class imagines a Gothic spire; so the master sensibly explains that roofs in Palestine used to be flat. Then we follow Jesus up the very high mountain. Was it in the wilderness? More probably it was elsewhere, and was the highest in the world. Even so, all the kingdoms of the world could not have been visible. Jesus may have had the miraculous vision of the world spread out before him that we read of in legends of the saints. Alternatively the devil may have drawn on the ground or shown a map of the world. But in that case why should a mountain peak have been chosen? It seems more likely that the devil pointed in the direction of the various kingdoms, as someone standing high up might say to his companion: 'Look! That way lies Rome and that way France or Lombardy.' We reach more familiar ground when the master describes the exchange of *auctoritates* between our Lord and the tempter. Now we assist at a disputation where Christ answers a clever opponent. Some masters take part in it by supplying the right side with supporting texts from pagan sages. Cicero warns us against worldly ambition in his *De officiis*; when Christ resisted the temptation to turn stones into bread he was following the advice of Vegetius: the wise general never does what his enemy recommends, even if it seems good to him.

Teaching in the arts course bore a real, if superficial, resemblance to the teaching of Scripture. The Bible as a holy book demanded infinitely more from a lecturer than any other: 'God's Word is brief, but it ought not on that account to be expounded briefly.' Nor could it be. The master had before him a group of men who needed training for their responsibilities. His class consisted of future cardinals, prelates and cathedral *personae*, or leading officials of religious Orders, men who would run the Church and advise princes. Paris was the 'fourth wall of the *sacerdotium*' and the doctor a buttress of the whole building.

First he had to ground his pupils in Christian doctrine. After the teaching of theology proper had been made into a separate subject, the lecturer on Scripture still had to explain the points arising from his text and to warn his pupils against heretical interpretations. A lecture course on the Hexaemeron by Henry of Ghent makes the reader feel that he is walking through an exhibition of errors, both heathen and Christian, each error having its label and its appropriate rebuttal. Secondly the master taught his men the ideology of the medieval Church. He described, making lavish use of satire, society as it actually was, corrupt and acquisitive, and as it ought to be if each member did his duty. He laid special stress on the shortcomings of prelates, whose duties Gregory had defined for all time in his *Cura pastoralis*. It says much for the self-confidence of the medieval Church in her prime that students of theology were trained systematically to criticize their superiors.

The lecture course therefore fulfilled a dual purpose: it instructed the pupil in his duties and conduct. Since one of his main duties would be preaching, it provided him with matter for the sermons which he would give later on as a bachelor or master of theology and as a prelate. Exegesis had married homiletics. The marginal headings and the indexes of lecture commentaries show how they served as aids to preaching. The pulpit was the main instrument of propaganda, and the chair controlled the pulpit. The master would sometimes deliver sermons himself, but he had a far wider audience than his voice could ever reach. He prepared his students for preaching, and his lectures with their store of matter for sermons circulated outside the schools. That is why his personal allegiance was so important. His outlook would differ according to his status as a secular or as a member of a particular Order. Criticism of authority can run through endless shades of good and bad temper. The master might have his own personal message or his own brand of piety. He might be a keen papalist and high-church-man or he might be anti-establishment. One could be as 'anti-' as one liked, provided that one kept within the bounds of orthodox doctrine.

Just as theological *quaestiones* had swollen in content and tended to detach themselves from the lecture course, so homiletics came more and more to resemble skeleton sermons or addresses. They kept their place within the framework of the lecture but had less to do with the exposition of the text. Fourteenth-century commentaries will offer schemes for inaugural lectures, farewell addresses to a college or convent, funeral sermons and sermons for other days or occasions. 'Now, for our comfort and instruction', says John Hesdin, lecturing at Paris soon after the middle of the fourteenth century, 'we shall recommend this virtue...' He breaks off his exposition of the Epistle to Titus, at a text where Paul recommends a virtue, and describes and moralizes some personification of it. He presents his virtue as a statue or picture, sometimes in a sham antique setting. We should not accuse him of going off the point. He is adapting Paul's teaching to contemporary taste, which demands ingenuity and free rein for imagination. One type of lecture course resembles a collection of *exempla* or moral stories, strung together on the thread of the text, and the thread is slender.

The homiletic section often consisted of allegories and moralities. Some texts lent themselves to expansion in their literal sense; but the master would have been hard put to it without the scope offered by the spiritual senses. This brings us to the problem of the relationship between the literal and spiritual interpretation. These two modes have been described before; I shall only discuss the effects of school practice on their definition and use.

All schoolmen must have known the iconography of Gregory preparing his *Moralia in Job*. A dove perches on his shoulder with its beak to his ear, just as the evangelist writes at the dictation of the Holy Spirit in the form of a dove or of an angel. St Bernard had preached his sermons on the Song of Songs 'as the Holy Spirit spoke through his mouth'. The doctor of theology too believed that exegesis was a grace from heaven. His first lecture ended with a prayer for a blessing on himself and his class as he guided them through the holy book. But his was a different function from St Bernard's. Not for him the poetic diction and outpourings of the saint speaking to his elect at Clairvaux. The doctor had to get his pupils through the syllabus required for their degrees. He sat before them with the Bible on his desk. He undertook in his first lecture to expound according to the literal and spiritual senses, unless he chose to make a special exception for himself, which was unusual. He was obliged to tell them which of the senses he was treating at a given moment; they would want to know. What hardly mattered to monks imposed itself as essential in the schools. Worse still, his Bible was glossed. The glossators, unconcerned with his present problem, had not labelled their glosses as treating of this sense or that. He had to decide which gloss should be attached to which sense.

It was a heavy inheritance. The traditional doctrine said that Scripture had a literal or historical sense which was true and basic to the spiritual interpretation. No truth could be discovered by means of the latter which was not clearly revealed by the former. The difficulty was to apply this doctrine. Terminology had fluctuated. Did the terms *literal, historical, allegorical, moral* or *anagogical* refer to the method of exposition or to its content? The literal or historical exposition required a grammatical construing and explanation of the words and of the events they described. Where did it stop? *Allegoria* meant 'doctrine', that is the teaching of the text as distinct from its mere grammatical construction. Suppose that the sacred writer has expressed himself in parable or metaphor; is the teaching that he wishes to convey and which the lecturer must transmit to his class to be counted as part of the literal exposition or does it belong to the spiritual under the subheading *allegorical*? It would be absurd to say that the literal sense of a parable or metaphor is the same as its inner meaning. Yet if one puts them under two distinct headings, literal and allegorical, where should one put the master's allegorical interpretation, which he builds on his text for didactic or religious reasons according to the needs of the hour? It was not merely a question of classification. Vital problems entered in. Discussions with Jewish scholars brought up the interpretation of Old Testament prophecy. The Jews had been accused of interpreting Scripture 'according to the letter', instead of according to the life-giving spirit. Was their interpretation of Old Testament prophecy to be called 'the literal sense' of the prophecy, while the Christological interpretation went under the heading 'spiritual or allegorical'? This division seemed to clash with the received teaching that the literal sense was true and basic. It gave away too much to the Jews. Political controversies turned on the significance of certain texts. It was argued that the creation of the sun and the moon as the greater and lesser lights of the world and the two swords held by the apostles signified that secular government was inferior to or dependent upon ecclesiastical. If the interpretation of either passage in this sense were counted as 'spiritual', then, in order to conform to the rule that spiritual inter- pretation must be based on the literal, one would have to discover the same teaching clearly expressed elsewhere in Scripture according to 'the letter'. That would not be easy.

Masters of the twelfth and early thirteenth centuries made a patient, dogged effort to bring order into chaos. They worked their way to an agreed procedure. The literal-historical exposition of Scripture included *both* grammatical construction and lexicography *and* the explanation of whatever *allegoria* was contained in the parable, metaphor, prophecy or imagery of the text. The master had to commit himself to stating what he thought was included. He judged whether to put prophecies of the coming of Christ into the mouth of Balaam, of David or of Isaiah according to the literal sense of the prophecy. He gave due warning when he passed from the literal sense to the spiritual. The latter, as he made clear to his class, he based on a literal foundation. His spiritual exposition might keep to traditional typology or it might contain ingenious 'moralities' on the theme of bad prelates or lazy students. Moral or religious teaching, derived from the literal sense of a proverb or tale in the text, went under a subheading of the literal interpretation; it was called *moralitas secundum litteram*. Progress had been made, but the distinction between the senses was still only a school convention, a customary rule for teachers. It lacked a justification in theory. The old formulae decrying the literal sense as inferior to the spiritual and defin- ing the difference in such out-of-date terms as 'Littera gesta docet, quid credas allegoria etc.' lingered on to confuse the minds of masters and pupils. A statement seems to live forever when once it has got into the textbooks. Masters spoke as though the spiritual sense were something 'nobler' and 'higher' than the literal, although in practice they would include the teaching of the Sermon on the Mount with all its implica- tions for Christian life in their literal exposition. The sheer emotive force of words bedevilled attempts to use them correctly.

Thomas Aquinas reformulated current practice in terms of his own philosophy. This led him to lay more stress on the human agent of revelation and so made for a broader approach. The literal sense was defined as the sacred writer's full original meaning. It included the whole message which he meant to convey at the prompting of his inspiration for the benefit of his public whether present or future. Thomas's exposition of Job in the literal sense (he said that Gregory's *Moralia* sufficed for the spiritual) demonstrated how rich in meaning the literal sense could be if the book were treated as a discussion of the ways of Providence. The spiritual sense was defined as the meaning which God, the chief author of Scripture and of the events it describes, had put into sacred history. The sacred writers, who took part in it, could not understand a significance which had not yet been revealed. Their successors would discern it in the light of subsequent revelation. Thomas deduced from his premiss that no argument could be drawn from the spiritual interpretation, but only from the literal. The spiritual could be used for edification of the faithful, but not for proof.

The Thomist definition gained general acceptance, hesitating at first in some quarters, but later carrying conviction. It disposed of the difficulties arising from metaphor and prophecy and focused interest on the writer's original meaning. It restricted the use of moralities in political propaganda, where they had caused most muddle. The arguments in fourteenth-century polemics on relations between Church and State shift their ground. On the other hand, lecturers made free with Thomas's permission to use the spiritual senses for edification. What master would have cared to deprive his pupils of instruction in the technique of preaching? Allegories and moralities, no longer 'higher' or 'nobler', remained indispensable. They would last in exegesis just as long as the medieval sermon lasted.

BIBLICAL SCHOLARSHIP

Linguistic, textual and historical studies have waited to the end of this survey because biblical scholarship in the strict sense was a marginal subject. The most interesting developments took place outside the schools. The outstanding Hebraists of the twelfth and early thirteenth centuries did not hold university chairs: Nicholas Manjacoria was a Cistercian monk; Andrew of St Victor, though he studied and taught at the school of St Victor at Paris, published his commentaries as books, not lecture courses; Herbert of Bosham left Paris to make his career as Archbishop Becket's secretary and wrote his commentary on the Hebraica version of the Psalter in retirement after his master's murder; Ralph Niger and Alexander Nequam were canons, though with teaching experience. If we turn to the Grecians, we meet Robert Grosseteste. He had the best understanding ever shown by a medieval scholar of the value of Greek in biblical scholarship. He learned it. He studied the text of the LXX and of the Greek New Testament for certain books. He read Greek commentators. His work for linguistics overlapped from his teaching period at Oxford to his life as bishop of Lincoln. Friar Roger Bacon, a passionate admirer of Grosseteste and pleader for linguistic studies, never lectured on Scripture because he was never a master of theology. He wrote in isolation and at one stage in prison, though the pope took an interest in his plans. The best minds in the schools turned elsewhere. The great schoolmen were philosophers and theologians, who did not even acquire the skills available at the time. Only the industry and vision of lesser men ensured that biblical scholarship should get some recognition in the syllabus.

Hebrew studies at Paris drew their inspiration from Hugh of St Victor, as did so much else. The tradition passed into the schools through secular masters and thence to the friars. A few masters struggled with the Hebrew tongue and consulted Jews at first hand. Many more made their bow to the subject by quoting Andrew of St Victor. The Dominicans and Franciscans compiled lists of textual variants known as *correctoria*. These lists joined the *Gloss* and the *Historia scholastica* as standard classroom equipment, to judge from the number of quotations from them in lectures. The most exciting monuments to thirteenth-century Hebrew studies which survive are a number of interlinear verbal translations, complete or incomplete, written into Hebrew texts of the Old Testament, especially the Psalter. We know almost nothing of their authorship or provenance, except that one is said to have been written into a psalter of Robert Grosseteste. This *Superscriptio Lincolniensis*[1] was known to later scholars, but none of the new translations enjoyed the popularity of the *correctoria*. The success of the latter derived from the fact that they had been prepared for school purposes under the aegis of leading masters. More Greek patristic and Byzantine commentators became known in translation. Thomas's *Catena aurea* on the Gospels gave them wide currency.

Medieval scholars had excellent authority for studying the original texts, *veritas in radice*. Jerome had set an example. They knew, if only at second hand, that the Latin of the Vulgate, so far removed from the

[1] See p. 152.

rules of classical Latin, depended on an oriental tongue which had its own idiom. They realized too that when you have a correct text and can read it in the original language, you still need a knowledge of the milieu before you can understand it properly. Of course they did not think in terms of historical change and development as we do. Development at a religious level they could appreciate; it followed from the basic tenets of Christianity. But they imagined the patriarchs, kings and prophets of the Old Testament, like the heroes of classical antiquity, as wearing medieval costume and as following medieval fashions of warfare and social behaviour. The story gained for them in immediacy and vividness what it lost in accuracy. Nevertheless, they could observe the fact that different peoples had peculiar customs of their own. So must the children of Israel have had theirs. Each people had a store of traditions about its past. The modern Jews had theirs. Jerome had consulted Jews about their traditions as well as their language. The quest for information which today takes the form of archaeology was conducted in the twelfth and thirteenth centuries by tapping the brains of rabbis. An eager scholar conversing with a rabbi felt like an archaeologist digging on a promising site. He resembled those enthusiasts of an earlier generation than ours who did not distinguish between the various layers to be excavated, but would throw together pell-mell all the objects that they uncovered. What conflicted with Christian doctrine must be laid aside as false, though it much intrigued him. The rest he treasured, whether it came from the Talmud or rabbinic legend or Rashi or his successors. Hence a mixed assortment of Jewish lore filtered into the classroom. It came through the *Historia scholastica*, through various commentaries, especially Andrew's, and through fresh conversations; some of the friars carried on the inquiries.

The early-fourteenth-century revival of biblical studies included scholarship. A new and promising sign was its direction from the centre. The Council of Vienne in 1311/12 decreed that chairs of Greek and oriental languages should be set up and endowed in the principal schools and universities of Christendom. In England at least the ecclesiastical authorities took steps to enforce the decrees by allocating revenues to the proposed chairs. Nothing came of it either at Oxford or Paris; perhaps it was too hard to find competent teachers. The interest which inspired the decrees, however, bore fruit in encouragement to two keen Hebraists, the Oxford Dominican, Nicholas Trevet, and the French Franciscan, Nicholas of Lyra. Both were quoted by later fourteenth-century masters. Lyra, whose work was more comprehensive, covering the whole Bible, became a household name.[1] His *Postilla litteralis* supplanted earlier books and took its place as a classic, to be quoted by all teachers who wished to ground their pupils in 'the findings of modern scholarship'. Lyra was by no means the first to study 'Rabbi Salomon' (Rashi); but he did so more thoroughly and consecutively than had been done before. We also catch sight of attempts to arrive at the original meaning of the Song of Songs, that most difficult of books. Lyra's use of Rashi, cautious as it was, stimulated criticism and discussion.

The story of biblical scholarship breaks off here. Its development after Lyra's death in 1349 has not yet been traced. One deduction can be made from the fact that Erasmus shocked his contemporaries by reviving what was really a sound medieval tradition. The scholars of the period about 1100 to 1350 had tried to study the originals and to produce clean texts. The fifteenth century must have forgotten or disowned its ancestry: the dossier as a whole gives an impression of stunted growth. Biblical scholarship never achieved the standing of a separate discipline within the framework of sacred science. Students of theology got no preliminary training in language. It was left to the individual master or pupil to choose how much he would specialize: hence the role of the gifted freelance. The reason for failure must surely be that so technical a subject needs very strong stimulus to keep it healthy. Zeal for converting the infidel supplied one motive. It accounts largely for Roger Bacon's and Raymond Lull's pleas for the study of language and for the arrangements made at the Council of Vienne. Some friars engaged in mission work, but opportunities for it narrowed in the political conditions of the later middle ages. A deep belief in the Bible as a teaching book and source of doctrine led Grosseteste and others to urge a return to the original. But short cuts proved to be too tempting. Desire for knowledge to serve a distant end, let alone 'for its own sake', will move individuals; it will not bring changes in established academic practice. Reformers have generally forced their way in from the outside.

[1] See also pp. 261, 304.

CONCLUSIONS

'The citizen should be moulded to suit the form of government under which he lives.' The masters of theology like the educators in Aristotle's perfect state aimed at producing citizen rulers. Their better pupils left the schools well equipped for prelacy. They had the Bible and its glosses at their finger tips. They knew the answers. They were aware of biblical scholarship; ignorance of its existence would have shamed them. They had high standards of professional conduct but low expectations, having been brought up on satire. Whether saints or cynics, they could not be naïve. They had notebooks crammed with matter for sermons. And the system worked. Medieval doctors of theology count a tiny proportion of rebels among their number: Wyclif stands out as the great exception and he proves the rule. He read for his degree in theology at Oxford in the slackest period that we know of. We do not know what lectures he heard: his teachers, if they lectured at all, certainly did not publish. He grew up in a vacuum without the education which would have moulded him into shape, perhaps.

4. THE BIBLE IN LITURGICAL USE

In imitation of Jewish practices, the Bible has always served three fundamental purposes in Christian public worship: instruction, community prayer and lyric expression. Instruction was given by a single person reading to the congregation extracts or pericopes from the Old or the New Testament. The Psalter, because of its nature and use as a prayer book and reading primer, was excluded from instructional reading. Community prayers were chanted alternatively by either the congregation divided into two half-choirs or the congregation and one person or a choir. Here, in the main, only psalm texts were used. Soloists and choir gave lyric expression to instruction or prayer in the form of elaborate chants. Their repertoire was taken from the whole Bible, poetry being preferred to historical accounts.

From apostolic times Christian public worship has centred around the celebration of the Eucharist and the performance of prayers of praise. Thus the two principal types of liturgy developed, the Mass and the Office. The organization of the former grew naturally out of Church life in general, i.e. the life of clergy and faithful. The latter owes its development predominantly to various forms of asceticism which culminated in the monastic life. The threefold manner in which the Scriptures have been used and these two forms of worship suggest the scheme followed in the subsequent pages.

INSTRUCTION

For religion ignorance is a deadly poison. But during the first fourteen centuries of Christianity the ordinary faithful had only two ways of obtaining religious instruction, by looking and by listening. Visual aids were provided by paintings and pictures, sculptures and stained glass, by religious drama and similar media. Oral instruction, however, was by far the most important: with few exceptions, even the well-educated only understood what they read by listening to their own voice. Paul had already put his finger on this problem: 'Faith comes by hearing' (Rom. x. 17). Hence in liturgical services ample arrangements were made for and much time was given to this form of instruction. At first, all sorts of religious documents were read along with the Bible. In the Mass only the latter has survived. Since 'to read aloud' (*legere*) was identical with 'to sing' (*cantare*), ordinary speech was stylized into recitation tones. They carried the reader's voice and underlined the phraseology, imposing a hieratic character on his diction.

Liturgical Bible-reading is not another form of Bible-study or a catechetical instruction in church on past religious issues for their own sake. The Old Testament is read predominantly for its prophetic and typological value. Hence it illustrates the subsequent lesson from the New Testament, the mystery of the day, ecclesiastical discipline, the significance of the stational church—where the service took place—or the life of its patron saint. Nor are New Testament lessons read solely as historical accounts from which the audience might gain edification. The liturgical message is always new; it is God's word to this particular assembly, a proclamation in and for the present, the economy of salvation here and now. Hence the texts are 'accommodated'. The principles guiding this vary, and the relationship with the present is often restricted to the opening or closing words of the pericope; or even a few catchwords contain the leitmotif of the day.

Reading was naturally followed by comments and exhortations. The homily, therefore, is only another aspect and a logical conclusion of biblical instruction. Its importance grew when the natural objective of reading—understanding of the text by the audience—clashed with venerated traditions of the secret language.[1] The ensuing problem was solved differently according to the spirit of the age. At times understanding was favoured; thus liturgical reading became bilingual or vernacular. In the West particularly, more attention was paid to tradition. And once the congregation failed to understand the instruction, certain tones became more and more florid. Their melodies made the text still more incomprehensible, but they underlined the solemnity of the occasion.

At Mass

The older portion of the fore-Mass[2] originally began abruptly with reading. Justin's allusion to it[3] allows the interpretation that one person read continuously while the faithful were assembling. And Hippolytus[4] (*c.* 200) clearly states that readers succeeded each other until all were present. At times this reading was done in one church (*collecta*), whence the whole congregation, after a final prayer, went to another church (*statio*) for the celebration of the Eucharist proper. The Roman liturgy

MASS

Fore-Mass

preparation:

> *antiphon* Ps. *42* (*43*) *antiphon*   (psalm abolished by decree,
> *verse   response*   26 Sept. 1964)
> confession
> *verses   responses*
> prayers by celebrant in silence

prayer service:

> *introit:* ant.   psalm   doxology   ant.
> *Kyrie eleison*
> Gloria in excelsis
> *greeting*   invitation   prayer of the assembly
> (collecta)   *acclamation*

---

[1] For the use of Hebrew for Old Testament reading and the liturgical importance of the second column (Hebrew in Greek letters) in Origen's Hexapla see the comprehensive note by B. Kipper in *Ephemerides liturgicae*, LXXVII (Rome, 1963), 396. For the transition from Greek to Latin see Ch. Mohrmann, *Liturgical Latin: Its origins and character* (London, 1959).

[2] See the scheme of the Mass, in which items connected with the Bible are printed in italic.   [3] *Apol.* i, 67, 3.   [4] *Traditio apostolica*, can. 20.

The exposition and exegesis of Scripture

reading service:

   epistle   acclamation
   intermezzo chants: gradual   Alleluia or tract
   greeting   acclamation   gospel   acclamation
   creed
   homily

Offering

   greeting   invitation to prayer
   prayers of the faithful   *acclamations*   (reintroduced 1964)
   offering
   offertory   responsory
   prayers by celebrant in silence
   washing of hands: Ps. 25 (26)
   invitation to prayer
   prayer over offerings (secreta)   *acclamation*   (since 1964 said aloud)

Eucharistic prayer

dialogue   preface   *Tersanctus*
prayers
institution narrative
prayers
final doxology   acclamation
⎫
⎬ anaphora or canon
⎭
   (said aloud since 1964)

Eucharistic meal

prologue   *the Lord's prayer*   (since 1964 said or sung by
                           all)

prayer (embolism)   *acclamation*   (since 1964 said aloud or sung
                           by celebrant)

breaking of host: *Pax domini   acclamation*
Agnus dei
prayer for peace   *kiss of peace*
prayers of preparation in silence
communion   *communion ant.* and *psalm*
greeting   invitation   prayer after communion
  (postcommunio)   *acclamation*
greeting   dismissal   *acclamation*
last gospel   (abolished by decree of 1964)

preserves this absence of introduction on Good Friday; the independence of the fore-Mass continues in the pontifical Mass, where the ceremonies hinge around the throne of the bishop, not the altar.

From the fourth century, psalm-singing was introduced before the reading, and only then was there question of a kind of reading-service. The idea therefore that this goes back to the practice of the Synagogue cannot be upheld. The relationship is only a natural one, based upon the facts that the Christians inherited the Old Testament from the Jews and that they observed common practices of public reading (*kerygma*) and prayer (*latreia*). At the Synagogue, two passages were read at each meeting: one from the Law, the other from the Prophets. Reading from the Law was continuous; the text was taken up where the last reader had left off, and all books were read through within a fixed period. The pericope from the Prophets was chosen either at random or in accordance with the occasion. According to New Testament accounts it was followed by a homily, but the more usual arrangement was that this came after the lesson from the Law. Every assembly also had community prayers. For want of records, however, neither their place nor their manner is clear. If a priest were present, the meeting ended with a blessing, otherwise with a final prayer.

All elements of this organization, without any obvious relationship in detail, appear in the early accounts of Christian services: reading, prayers in the form of intermezzo chants, homily, and final prayer. Except for the latter, which disappeared from the Roman Mass before the sixth century, they are known as epistle, gradual (with *Alleluia* or tract—see below, p. 249), gospel and sermon.

Both the number and choice of readings have been subject to great variations. Syrian and Armenian liturgies possibly preserve the pattern of the Synagogue service: readings from the Law and the Prophets are followed by those from the New Testament. The latter were obviously preferred, since the Eucharist was plainly connected with the Lord's Resurrection, and the whole liturgical year is built around this mystery. The ancient western liturgies, such as the Gallican, Mozarabic and the still older Milanese rites, also have a lesson from the Old Testament and two from the New. But the common belief that the Roman Mass once had three lessons[1] is clearly contradicted by evidence to the con-

[1] An interesting project for the future is by J. Feder–M. Danchin, 'Choix de lectures pour la liturgie dominicale', in *Ephem. liturg.* LXXIX (1965), 249–316.

trary from the early fifth century. And from earlier times there is no evidence either for or against the idea. Still, some of the older liturgical week days, such as the Ember days and Wednesday and Friday in Holy Week, retain three lessons. The first is from the Old Testament, the second from the New Testament letters or Acts, the third from the Gospels. The permanent plan of the Roman fore-Mass, however, only knows two readings: on Sundays the first was from the Pauline epistles —hence the name epistle—and during Eastertide from other letters or Acts; on weekdays or ferias outside Eastertide the pre-Gospel reading is, as a rule, from the Old Testament.[1] For feasts, especially of the saints, no rule can be established.

As in the Synagogue, the early Christians read the Scriptures straight through. Eloquent proofs are the lengthy Bible commentaries of the Fathers, which are often simply their homilies upon the lessons just heard.[2] In the Roman liturgy vestiges of this continuous reading are visible in the epistles.[3] On certain Sundays after Whitsun and on the subsequent Wednesdays the epistles still form a series of pericopes in which Paul's letters are read in the order of the scriptural canon. Still, even here two methods of progressive or continuous reading are traceable. According to one system the Sunday lessons were continued on the following Wednesday; according to the other the Wednesday lessons themselves form a series independent of those read on Sunday.

Continuous reading was first interrupted for the greater feasts of our Lord, such as his revelation to the gentiles (Epiphany), his Resurrection from the dead (Easter), his return to the Father (Ascension) and the descent of the Holy Spirit (Pentecost or Whitsun), and for the feasts of the martyrs. On such solemnities passages were selected to illustrate the mystery of the day. Instances of such centonization, or selection, are particularly numerous in the Gallican rite. In fact, the

---

[1] R. Dubois, 'Hatte die römische Messe je eine dreigliedrige Leseordnung?', in *Heiliger Dienst*, XVIII (Salzburg, 1964), 129–37.

[2] An extensive list of their works is available in E. Dekkers–Æ. de Gaar, 'Clavis Patrum latinorum', in *Sacris Eruditi. Jaarboek voor godsdienstwetenschappen*, III (Steenbrugge, 1951), 2nd ed. 1961. For their actual liturgical use today see A. Hamman, 'Réflexions sur les lectures patristiques du bréviaire', in *Ephem. liturg.* LXXIX (1965), 340–7.

[3] E.g. on the Sundays from Septuagesima (I and II Cor.) where the famous *cri de cœur* in I Cor. xi. 19–33; xii. 1–9 is reserved for Sexagesima Sunday, when the station was at the basilica of St Paul, Rome.

oldest western system of selected passages goes back to fifth-century Gaul. In those early days, however, it cannot have been widespread. Egeria, the Spanish pilgrim to the Holy Land, was struck, again and again, by the fact that in Jerusalem the principal feasts of the year had lessons, psalms and antiphons chosen expressly for the occasion.

The early medieval Roman arrangement of the Gospels agrees fairly well with that of today. It is based upon the appointed Sunday and station services in Rome to which were added, gradually, the eucharistic celebrations on the fast days, Wednesday and Friday. This system of pericopes shows no trace of continuous reading. The Gospels were chosen freely, and the selection was inspired by the mystery of the day[1] or the season, by the life or passion of the stational saint[2] or by the place and function of his church.[3] In some cases the epistle affected the choice, for the Roman liturgy shows preference for a common theme in epistle and Gospel. Often this harmony, visible in many Lenten Masses, is slight indeed. Because of the different principles of reading— the epistle being continuous and the Gospel selective—the Roman Mass lectionaries present several instances in which a whole set of epistles and Gospels has been shifted by one Sunday. Thus the modern pericope system has lost much of its significance.

The liturgical setting of the lessons consists, first of all, in a title or announcement on the origin of the passage (*Lectio libri* or *epistolae...*; *Initium* or *Sequentia sancti evangelii secundum...*), words of address (*Fratres, Carissime,* etc.) or other introductory notes (*Haec dicit dominus, In diebus illis, In illo tempore*). Closing formulae are rare in the western Mass liturgy, although prophecies regularly end with *dicit dominus omnipotens*, and readings from Paul with the author's leading concept *in Christo Ihesu domino nostro*. All such titles, introductions and clauses are however of a later date; up to the present the most ancient readings, e.g. Good Friday and Easter vigil, omit them.

[1] On the feast of the Assumption of the Virgin (15 August) the pericope was, until recently, Luke x. 38–42, only because of the last sentence: 'Mary has chosen that good part, which shall not be taken away from her.'

[2] On Thursday in the third week of Lent the station in Rome was at Sts Cosmas and Damian's, both physicians. The Gospel (Luke iv. 38–44) recounts the healing of Peter's mother-in-law.

[3] On Thursday in the second week in Lent the station was at St Mary's in Trastevere in the Jewish quarter. The Gospel (Luke xvi. 19–31) tells the parable of the rich man and Lazarus. The ancient Church regarded them as symbolizing the Jews and the Christians.

At Mass, lessons are also introduced in much the same way as the principal prayers, by formulae which arouse the attention of the congregation. The Mozarabic rite knew a call for silence (*Silentium habete*) before the readings, to which the people answered *Amen* (So be it). In the Milanese rite the salutation *Dominus vobiscum* (The Lord be with you) (see below, p. 240) preceded both the epistle and the Gospel. In Rome it was restricted to the Gospel alone.

The hierarchy of lessons is expressed in various ways: in the tones of recitation, in the choice of readers and in the place where the reading was done. Although the lessons in the western fore-Mass have generally been kept free from melodic complications, the medieval Gospel tones were richer than those for the epistle, while the latter were slightly more melodious than those for the prophecies.[1]

Originally anyone sufficiently literate could be chosen as a reader; but the office of lector goes back, at least, to the second century and is the oldest of the minor orders. Boys were educated for this office, which was the basis of any further ordination. But innocence alone was no longer considered to be sufficient for the reading of the Gospel; it was given to the highest order before the priesthood, to the deacon. By the seventh and eighth centuries, stational reading of the epistle had become the task of the subdeacon. Even so, during the later middle ages any educated cleric or even server was allowed to read, also at private Mass. Hence the rubric in the Roman missal that during sung Mass the epistle should be sung by some lector vested in surplice rather than by the celebrant. The recent reform is inspired by more modern principles and has changed the practice considerably.

In order to make himself easily heard, the lector would turn towards the congregation and read from an elevated place. Instead of holding the book in his hands, he would put it on a desk, thus avoiding any muscular strain on the chest. Soon an *ambo* or pulpit was erected, either between the sanctuary and the nave or projecting into the side railings of the enclosure reserved for the choir (see the plan of the basilica). The *ambo* became the traditional place not only for reading but also for the performance of solo chants and the delivery of the homily. Amalar of Metz (*d.* 852 or 853) is the first to mention that the Gospel should be

[1] Since 1907 the traditional melodies are in the various editions of the *Graduale sacrosanctae Romanae Ecclesiae*, in the part entitled *Toni communes Missae*, also in the unofficial but widespread *Liber usualis* ed. by the Benedictines of Solesmes, Desclée.

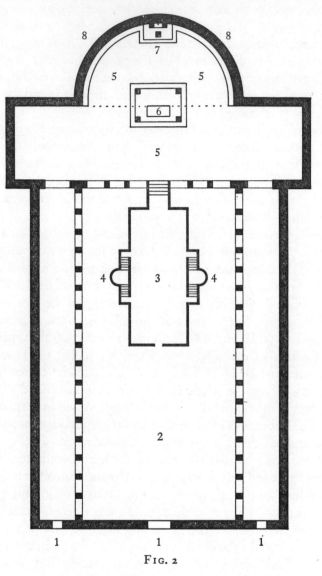

FIG. 2

PLAN OF A LATIN BASILICA

1 Entrances from courtyard.	5 Sanctuary.
2 Nave.	6 Altar under baldachin.
3 Place for Schola Cantorum.	7 Bishop's throne.
4 Ambo with steps on either side.	8 Apse.

chanted 'from an excellent place'. In the tenth-century Roman Order II the epistle was sung from a step of the *ambo* stairs but not the highest one. From this latter, the deacon, and he only, was to chant the Gospel.

From the later middle ages the Roman rite scarcely preserved any trace of these very logical requirements of public instruction. The subdeacon read with his back to the people; the deacon usually turned to the north side. This unfortunate tradition was due to mis-interpretations of rubrics during the centuries when the congregation no longer understood the liturgical language, and when the plan of the ancient basilica had undergone complicated and, for the congregation, unpractical architectural changes. Since September 1964 the lessons must be read or sung towards the people from an *ambo* or pulpit or from the sanctuary rail.

The epistle: The Roman ceremonial of the epistle is of great simpli-city. The reader says no prayer of purification beforehand, asks no blessing from the celebrant; he has no escort to the *ambo*; traditional melodies are plain and the people sit during the reading. This preserva-tion of simplicity, while the ritual of the Gospel was being developed increasingly, must have been intentional. From the eleventh century, however, the epistle was made more impressive on important feasts by the insertion of tropes, that is, short sentences of non-biblical origin. In the Sarum rite, among others, the epistle of the midnight Mass on Christmas (Isa. ix. 2, 6–7) was sung by two clerics alternating text and interpolated tropes.[1]

The Gospel: High esteem for the word of Christ is seen not only in the care and wealth expended on the writing, decorating and binding of the Gospel book, which began with the Celtic and Anglo-Saxon civilizations, but also in the fact that, with the sacramentary or the missal, it was allowed to rest on the altar. A Roman baptismal order of the sixth century even placed the reading of the Gospel on a level with the confession of faith in the Creed, and dismissed the catechumens before the Gospel at the scrutiny Masses during the period of prepara-tion. Gradually the carrying of the Gospel book to the *ambo* developed into a formal procession. Its origins go back to the Gallican liturgy at least. When towards the end of the seventh century the Roman Order I

---

[1] The latest ed. is by A. Jefferies Collins, 'Manuale ad usum percelebris Ecclesiae Sarisburiensis', in *Henry Bradshaw Society*, vol. xci (Chichester, 1960), Appendix 1 (from the Paris ed. of 1526).

was written, the deacon kissed the feet of the pope, who pronounced a blessing over him. Then, going up to the altar, he kissed the Gospel book, which he carried to the *ambo* not with his bare hands but through his chasuble. He was accompanied by two torch-bearers and two sub-deacons, one of whom had a thurible. Light and incense were accepted honours, since the days of Constantine the Great (*d.* 326) transferred from high civil officials to church dignitaries. To the procession were added, at times, a cross bearer and a cleric carrying a cushion upon which the book was placed during the reading. Further dramatic elements are the greetings and acclamations, the sign(s) of the cross, the listening erect, the putting aside of canes, sticks and swords, the removal of headgear by men and dignitaries. After the Gospel, the book was handed round by the subdeacon to the attendant clergy for veneration by a kiss.

In the Office

From the beginning of the ascetic life spiritual reading, particularly of the Scriptures, occupied much time. But when the liturgical Hours were first organized as community acts, they consisted solely of psalms and prayers. Only on the advice of the elders, the monks in Egypt added scriptural readings to their prayer service: one from the Old, the other from the New Testament; on the Sabbath and during Eastertide both were from the New Testament, the second was from the Gospels.

Among the monks of the West a prolonged reading during the night Office of matins is attested from as early as the fifth century. At Lerins they had long lessons at all Hours, except at vespers. The rule of St Benedict[1] knows the two types of Office reading which were generally accepted in the West: long lessons at matins, and short ones, called (little) chapters (*capitula*), at the other Hours.[2]

At first the secular Office too had no reading. In the West the first testimony comes from Illyria about 400, but elsewhere it was unknown up to the late sixth century. The Scriptures again formed the principal matter of instruction. But while all other works were gradually

[1] If the order of the Office in this rule is by St Benedict, it dates from before *c.* 547. The saint's authorship however is much discussed. Either this order, which is a separate unity within the rule, or the whole rule may date from *c.* 600; see O. Klesser, *Officium divinum. Inquisitio de originibus Officii divini Romani hodierni. cursus ecclesiastici et monastici syntheseos* (Heeswijk (Holland), 1966).

[2] See the scheme of the Office, in which items connected with the Bible are printed in italic.

The exposition and exegesis of Scripture

(secular of nine lessons)

Matins

Introduction:

opening versicles   responses   doxology
invitatorium to praise: *ant. Ps. 94 (95)*
hymn

first nocturn

prayer service:

ant.   psalm   ant.
ant.   psalm   ant.
ant.   psalm   ant.
versicle   response
the Lord's prayer   conclusion

reading service:

absolution   *acclamation*
blessing of lector   *acclamation*
scriptural lesson   acclamation   responsory
blessing of lector   *acclamation*
scriptural lesson   acclamation   responsory
blessing of lector   *acclamation*
scriptural lesson   acclamation   responsory

second nocturn

prayer service:

(as above)

reading service:

(as above; lessons from the Fathers or from the saint's legend)

third nocturn

prayer service:

(as above)

reading service:

(as above; 7th lesson preceded by opening sentence of *gospel pericope*;
lessons from homily of the Fathers)
Te deum or *9th responsory*

Lauds

opening versicle   response   doxology
ant.   psalm   ant.
ant.   psalm   ant.
ant.   psalm   ant.
ant.   canticle   ant.
ant.   psalm   ant.
(*little*) *chapter   acclamation*
hymn
versicle   response
great ant.   canticle Luke i. 68–79 (*Benedictus*)   *ant.*
greeting collect *acclamation   greeting*
conclusion

Prime

opening versicle etc.
hymn
ant.   3 psalms   ant.
(*little*) *chapter   acclamation*
short responsory
versicle   response
greeting collect *acclamation   greeting*
conclusion
chapter Office: reading of martyrology   *versicles   responses*   final collect
   blessing of lector etc.   *chapter* etc.   conclusion with blessing

Terce, sext, none

opening versicle etc.
hymn
ant.   3 psalms   ant.
(*little*) *chapter   acclamation*
short responsory
versicle   response
greeting collect *acclamation   greeting*
conclusion

Vespers

opening versicle etc.
ant.   psalm   ant.
ant.   psalm   ant.
ant.   psalm   ant.

ant. psalm ant.
ant. psalm ant.
(little) chapter acclamation
hymn
versicle response
great ant. canticle Luke i. 46–55 (*Magnificat*) *ant.*
greeting collect *acclamation greeting*
conclusion

Compline

blessing of lector
(little) chapter acclamation
versicle response
the Lord's prayer
confession
opening versicle etc.
ant. 3 psalms ant.
hymn
(little) chapter acclamation
short responsory
versicle response
ant. canticle Luke ii. 29–32 (*Nunc dimittis*) *ant.*
greeting collect *acclamation greeting*
conclusion with final blessing

excluded from the eucharistic liturgy, they were added more and more to the Office; hagiographical literature dates from the fifth and sixth centuries;[1] reading from patristic homilies and sermons seems to be of monastic origin and is attested by the rule of St Benedict. It has the same purpose as the oratorical explanations of the homily at Mass.

In Rome Bible-reading was introduced long before Gregory the Great (*d.* 604). In principle all books of the Bible were covered within a year, starting with the Heptateuch just before Lent, that is, on the Sunday nearest to the beginning of the civil year (March). But the Pauline letters were read on Sundays at the third nocturn of matins and in agreement with the epistles at Mass; so were the Gospel pericopes.

Because of the development of the liturgical year and a too frequent repetition of the *Apostolus*, a new order of Bible-reading was issued at

[1] B. de Gaiffier, 'La lecture des Actes des martyrs dans la prière liturgique en Occident', in *Analecta Bollandiana*, LXXII (1954), 134–66.

Rome, probably during the first half of the eighth century. The scheme, observed in the main up to the present, is as follows:

from Septuagesima to Passion Sunday the Heptateuch; with the reorganization of the station liturgy under Gregory II (*d.* 731) the Thursdays in Lent were given the stational gospels with their homilies;

during Passiontide the prophecies and lamentations of Jeremiah;

during Eastertide and the Whitsun octave the Acts, Catholic letters and the Apocalypse;

from the Sunday after Whitsun to the end of July Kings and Proverbs;

during August Solomon; during September Job, Tobias, Judith, Esther and Esdras; during October Maccabees; during November Ezekiel, Daniel and the Minor Prophets;

in Advent Isaiah;

from the feast of the Innocents (28 December) to Septuagesima the Pauline letters.

The differences between this scheme of continuous reading and that of the epistles is obvious. The Office lectionary is adapted to the seasons of the year; the Mass lectionary follows the ancient scriptural canons. Another difference is noteworthy. Mass pericopes were fixed and listed in a special catalogue (*comes* or *capitulare*); those of the Office never were. Apart from the fact that they had to be much longer, their length depended upon various factors, for example the interrupting occurrence of feasts with proper readings, the changeable length of summer and winter nights, and so on. At times a whole book had to be finished in a few nights. True, this Bible-reading was often continued in the refectory during meals, but the custom had arisen of including also Jerome's introductions to each book. Moreover, both patristic and hagiographical literature had steadily increased. Finally, towards the end of the middle ages, the reorganization of the choir books—resulting first in the choir breviary and then in the portable breviary—made curtailment of pericopes necessary. This reduction of the liturgical lessons and, consequently, of Bible-reading was largely an unavoidable result of late medieval liturgical book-production. But it became an established tradition, notwithstanding some valiant attempts by the early printers to introduce longer pericopes. Since no system of detailed selection was ever produced, the length and choice of passages were proportionate to the increasing number of manuscripts and prints. The lack of uniformity and organization in this point is still visible in the Roman breviary of today.

According to the rules of Caesarius of Arles (*d.* 542) and of 'the Master' (*c.* 570), one of the Gospel accounts of the Lord's Resurrection was read every Sunday at the third nocturn. Later the Gospel pericope of the Mass was adopted into the Office with a relevant homily. From the tenth century onwards, the latter began to supersede the former. Reduced to one or two opening sentences, ending with the formula *Et reliqua* (etcetera), the Gospel fragment is still a formal, but most unsatisfactory, introduction to a homily.

In the archaic Office there was no uniformity in the number of lessons, although three lessons in each nocturn were usual, in agreement with a threefold reading in the fore-Mass. Nor was there any proportion between the number of psalms, lessons and responsories. In the sixth century, suburban bishops of central Italy promised to say with their clergy nine psalms with an equal number of lessons and responsories on Sunday, three of each on weekdays in the summer and four of each in the winter. Two centuries later the Roman custom was nine psalms, lessons and responsories on feasts, three psalms, lessons and responsories during Eastertide, nine lessons and responsories (with eighteen psalms) on Sundays and three lessons on ferias (with twelve psalms). The Sunday lessons of the first nocturn were biblical, those of the second either biblical or from the Fathers. In the third nocturn they read, at first, the epistle and Gospel of the day with comments from the homilies; later on, with the placing of the Pauline letters after Christmas, the Gospel alone was kept with three portions from the homily. In ferial Office all lessons were biblical, except during Lent, when there was a gospel and homily. On feasts there was and still is a great variety. Biblical saints often have Bible pericopes in the first nocturn, a sermon and a Gospel with homily in the second and third. For other saints scriptural reading was often replaced by lessons from the legends or passions. Since the reform of Pius V (*d.* 1572) all feasts have scriptural lessons in the first nocturn.

Short lessons or chapters taken from the Bible existed in the early Office after the prayer services of terce, sext and none. In the Benedictine Office, which has them at all Hours, they had to be said from memory. Unlike the lessons at the night Office, they are not preceded by a blessing; nor are they said by a lector but by the person who officiates

that particular week (hebdomadarian) or feast day (the abbot, etc.).
St Benedict had already prescribed spiritual reading after supper, which
was immediately followed by compline, the night prayers. This reading
is the origin of the chapter at the opening of this Hour. Its incorporation into the Office did not do away with the preceding blessing.

COMMUNITY PRAYERS

Community prayers required some form of guidance from someone
apart from the congregation. Throughout the medieval period and up
to the present, two types of guidance can be distinguished. The first,
the least explicit, arose from the social and hierarchical nature of the
meeting, and comprises invitations and replies, acclamations, dialogues,
ejaculatory prayers of versicles and responses, and so on. The second is
more formal, often requires some musical knowledge in the leader, and
is commonly known as psalm-singing or psalmody.

Four principal methods of psalm-singing have been accepted in the
West: continuous, responsorial, antiphonal and alternating chant. The
first consists in the uninterrupted sequence of psalm verses sung by a
soloist or choir, while the congregation listens. The second is a heritage
from Jewish worship: one person (psalmist) sings the psalm verses,
while the choir or congregation answers (responds) with either the
same text or some refrain (*a capite*) or even part of a refrain (*a latere*).
The third method is much older than Christianity but was not practised
among the Jews, nor by the Christians before the fourth century: one
person, again, sings the psalm verses, but the refrain, or part of it, is
repeated alternately by a divided congregation or choir. The fourth
method has, in the course of time, grown into the most common
practice of performing the Office: there is no soloist, but the two
groups of the congregation alternate the consecutive verses.

Responsorial and antiphonal chant allowed for many variations in
the manner of alternating and in the choice of the refrain. The most
primitive form of responsorial chant, the repetition of every phrase or
verse, is adequate in a community where few master the text. Repeating
a motto from the first verse of the psalm is modelled upon the accepted
version of the Song of the Three Children (*Benedicite*) and of Ps. 135
(136) or upon Ps. 113 (114–15) where, according to Jewish tradition, an
Alleluia (praise God) was added after each verse or group of verses.[1]

[1] See G. Oury, 'Psalmum dicere cum Alleluia', in *Ephem. liturg.* LXXIX (1965), 97–108.

Refrains or respons(ori)es taken from other verses of the psalm or even from other sources were also customary. Augustine seems to mention alternate singing of verses—'People partly listen to the psalm, partly sing it'. If this was responsorial chant, it scarcely differed from true antiphony. For, indeed, the distinction between responsorial and antiphonal psalmody gradually disappeared and several intermediate forms were created. Already in the days of Benedict the performance of the *invitatorium* (below, p. 245) was called either antiphonal or responsorial.

The difference in the choice of the refrain gave rise to a complicated problem during the Carolingian era. The Romans used to repeat the entire responsory or antiphon as it had been given before the psalm. The Spaniards and Gauls 'halved' it by repeating the last portion only. When the Roman chant-books were adopted by the Gallican church, the curtailment of the Roman texts obviously created peculiar difficulties. The repetition of a truncated text after the verse did not necessarily make sense; both text and chant had to be adapted and amended for such dovetailing. In the Roman responsorial many items were revised in this manner by a commission of liturgists from the imperial court of Louis the Pious (*d.* 840); one member is known by name, abbot Helisachar. The result of his work is obvious in the present-day Roman books. Only in the introits and in some cases of Office responsories is the Roman method preserved.

Of the various Latin translations of the Psalter two only have been widely used for liturgical purposes. Perhaps the oldest of these goes under the name of the Roman Psalter. Until 1930 it was thought to be Jerome's first translation, but his authorship is now disputed (above, pp. 84, 111). His second translation, a somewhat hasty revision made with the aid of Origen's *Hexapla*, was introduced into Gaul by Gregory of Tours (*d.* 593) and adopted elsewhere as the Gallican Psalter, particularly through the propaganda of Alcuin (*d.* 804). The Roman Psalter was still commonly used in Rome during the thirteenth century; the canons of St Peter's in the Vatican have followed it up to the present. Remnants of it are found in the *invitatorium* at matins and throughout the Roman Mass chant books.

At Mass

The *Liber pontificalis* (before 530) records that Pope Celestine (422–32) 'ordered the singing of the 150 psalms of David before the sacrifice, which was not customary before, except for the letters of the apostle Paul and for the gospel'. Although the authority of this book cannot be wholly trusted, one may conclude with certainty that long before this statement was written antiphonal prayer filled in the time while the people were gathering and waiting for the reading service to begin. Before another century had passed, the singing was done by a choir of clerics[1] or, in the awe-inspiring papal liturgy, by the *schola cantorum*[2] during the entrance procession from the sacristy (St Thomas's near the main door of the Lateran basilica) to the altar. The many introit antiphons composed since then are not popular refrains but neumatic chants[3] requiring expert musical skill. Still, in the station liturgy they retained their antiphonal character. In churches with limited proportions and ceremonial the entrance procession was reduced or omitted and the psalm consequently shortened. Thus the antiphon was sung only twice, before and after the psalm, and the psalm itself curtailed to one verse followed by the short doxology (*Gloria. Sicut*). Outside Rome the antiphon continued to be repeated thrice on solemn feasts, the second time after the *Gloria*.

The introit is a variable chant, a prelude to the Mass, announcing the predominant mystery and theme of the day.[4] Many are not taken from the Psalter but from other books of the Bible; a few are by early Christian writers. In the modern Roman liturgy all verses are taken from the psalms; in the middle ages they were occasionally from other books.[5]

---

[1] *OR* xv, no. 13; ed. M. Andrieu, III, 97. For the date and origin see van Dijk, 'Recent developments in the study of the Old-Roman rite', in *Studia patristica. Studies presented to the fourth international conference on patristic studies . . . 1963*, VIII (Berlin, 1967), 316 f.

[2] *OR* I, nos. 44 ff.; ed. Andrieu, II, 81 ff.   [3] See below, p. 248.

[4] Accommodation, above, pp. 221, 226, is often striking: Saturday in the fourth week of Lent, the text is from Isa. lv. 1: *Sitientes, venite ad aquas . . .* (All you who thirst, come to the waters, says the Lord; and you without money come and drink with joy). The station church in Rome was St Nicholas's at the Prison, near a much used well. Sunday after Christmas, the text is from Wisdom xviii. 44 f.: *Dum medium silentium . . .* (While all things were in quiet silence and night was in the midst of her course, your almighty word, O Lord, came down from heaven from your royal throne), a text referring to the angel of death in Egypt, applied to the coming of the Word.

[5] St Peter's Chains (1 August): intr. *Nunc scio vere* ℣ *Et Petrus ad se reversus*; St Andrew (30 November): intr. *Dominus secus mare* ℣ *At illi relictis retibus*.

In the same way as the entrance of the clergy was adorned by the introit, so the processions of the people offering their gifts and receiving holy communion were enlivened with offertory and communion psalmody. If the technique of the former was originally perhaps anti-phonal, at an early stage the responsorial style replaced it. From the eleventh century the offertory procession was first gradually restricted to the greater feasts and then almost completely omitted. The verses are retained in manuscripts of the Milanese and Mozarabic rites; they disappeared from the Roman liturgy, except in the Mass of the dead, at which, to the present day, even the offering procession is observed in many places.

The offertory chant is, again, variable, often taken from biblical books other than the Psalter. But the texts seldom express the idea of offering and sacrifice.[1] At times they are accommodated to the mystery of the day to form a common theme with the other variable chants;[2] usually they have a general content of prayer or praise.[3] From a musical point of view, the offertories must be grouped with the elaborate, melismatic chant of the great responsories. Both refrain and psalm reflect the medieval lyricism of soloists and experienced chanters in the papal *schola cantorum*; they are frequently specimens of grandiose melodic construction and dramatic expression.

The communion is undoubtedly the oldest and simplest procession song at Mass. The oldest documents date from the fourth century, when the chant appears as responsorial. After each verse of Ps. 33 (34) the people answered with the refrain 'O taste and see that the Lord is sweet' (in the Mozarabic rite *Alleluia*), or after each verse of Ps. 144 (145) they repeated 'The eyes of all wait upon you; and you give them their food in due season'. As in the previous cases the choir took over the chant of the communicants and sang refrain and psalm antiphonally, in N. Africa already in the days of Augustine, in Rome not much

[1] Epiphany (*Reges Tharsis*), Dedication feast of a church (*Domine deus*), Mass of the dead (*Domine Ihesu*), the two offertories from Ps. 44 (45): 15–16: *Afferentur* (adapted to *Offerentur*) *regi virgines* ... (The virgins that follow her shall be brought (offered) to the king; her neighbours shall be brought (offered) to you with gladness and rejoicing; they shall enter into the palace (temple) of the king, the Lord). For manuscript evidence of responsory and verses of this offertory see R.-J. Hesbert, *Antiphonale Missarum sextuplex* (Brussels, 1935), *passim* (see index).

[2] As on first Sunday in Lent (*Scapulis suis*), all chants from Ps. 90 (91).

[3] Hence such cues as *Ad te levavi*, *Benedicam*, *Benedicite*, *Confitebor*, *Exaltabo te*, *Iubilate*, *Meditabor*, etc.

later, perhaps on the saint's authority. With the increase of the musical repertoire and the influence of the papal *schola*, the antiphon became variable and was chanted before and after the psalm. The history of the Roman communion runs parallel with that of the introit, but the psalm was dropped during the tenth century. Melodically the antiphon remained simpler than any of the other variable chants.

The text of the communion was not always chosen in relation to the day. On the weekdays in Lent, except for the formulae on Thursdays (Gregory II), Psalms 1–26 follow in the order of the Psalter up to Palm Sunday; similarly on the Sundays after Whitsun from Psalm 1 to 118. Whenever the antiphon is taken from the Psalter, the corresponding psalm followed; otherwise that of the introit was used. On feasts reference to the occasion is sought; in a few Masses there is an additional eucharistic theme in agreement with the action taking place.[1]

All prayer services in both Mass and Office are concluded with a solemn prayer (prayer of the assembly, prayer over the gifts, prayer after communion) by which the celebrant or officiant collects the preceding private and silent prayers and intentions of the congregation. Usually it is preceded by a greeting and implicit request for attention. The call *Dominus vobiscum* from Ruth ii. 41 is answered by the assembly with the Semitic expression, used also by Paul (Gal. xvi. 18, etc.), *Et cum spiritu tuo*. At pontifical high Mass, when the *Gloria in excelsis*, the hymn of peace, is sung, originally reserved to the bishop alone, the greeting is *Pax vobis*, words used by the risen Christ to greet his apostles (John xx. 19). Neither the exhortation to prayer (*Oremus*) nor the subsequent prayers themselves are biblical texts. However, their conclusion (*Per dominum*, Through our Lord Jesus Christ) and the Hebrew acclamation *Amen*, whereby the congregation confirms the prayer of their speaker, are common in the Pauline letters and the Gospels.

The preface to the *canon*, the *anaphora* or great eucharistic prayer, opens with a dialogue between celebrant and congregation which is of a most venerable tradition. Its precise origin is unknown, but connections with biblical and Jewish liturgical formulae are obvious. The New Testament also inspired much of the description of the heavenly liturgy at the

---

[1] E.g. first Sunday in Advent Ps. 84 (85): 13: *Dominus dabit benignitatem...* (The Lord shall give that which is good: and our land shall yield her fruit), referring to both the Virgin and the Eucharist.

end of the preface itself, while the conclusion of the *Tersanctus* is a Christian paraphrase of Old Testament texts (Isa. vi. 3; Ps. 117 (118): 25–6). Its oldest melody being a mere continuation of the preface recitative, this Latin *trisagion* was, at least up to the twelfth century, an outcry of praise where the congregation joined in with the celebrant.[1] With the gradual disappearance of congregational singing the *Sanctus* melodies increased in both number and complexity. A comparatively modern custom, due mostly to the development of polyphony, of singing the second part (*Benedictus*) after the consecration has been recently abolished.

In addition to these variable prayers, the Mass also has a number of invariable ones. In the Roman liturgy they are collected in the Order of the Mass and only a small portion of its prayers have a directly biblical origin; they are a few verses and responses from the psalms surrounding the confession at the very beginning of the fore-Mass, the *Kyrie eleison*, the *Sanctus* already mentioned, the institution narrative in the great eucharistic prayer, the Lord's prayer and the *Agnus dei*. Except for the eucharistic prayer, which is said by the celebrant, they are all community prayers.

The short Greek invocation *Kyrie eleison* (Lord, have mercy) is frequent in the psalms and a popular refrain in eastern liturgies. It was even known in the pagan world, while the Christians used it privately long before it was adopted into public worship. The oldest testimony to its liturgical use in the West comes from Rome. Pope Gelasius (492–6) suppressed the General or Bidding Prayers, still preserved in the Good Friday ceremonies, and introduced a series of fourteen invocations into the fore-Mass. The first seven of these have the *Kyrie* refrain, the last, *Praesta, domine, domine*, is the Latin equivalent of another Greek exclamation, *Paraschu kyrie*. By the sixth century the *Kyrie* was popular throughout Italy, whence it spread to Gaul. Gregory the Great simplified the Gelasian litany into a supplication in which clergy and faithful alternated first the *Kyrie*, then another traditional cry, *Christe eleison*. On ferial days this supplication was prolonged. In the stational liturgy it was omitted whenever the litany of the saints was sung during the procession from the *collecta* (see p. 222). The threefold grouping in the present-day Roman Mass dates from the eighth and

[1] Ed. in the Roman gradual, see above, p. 227 n. 1, and in the *Kyriale simplex. Editio typica* (Vatican City, 1965).

ninth centuries, when congregational singing was already a thing of the past.

Some of the plain, litany-like melodies of the old *Kyrie* are well known. But with the introduction of the papal chant, its performance was taken over by the *schola cantorum* (Roman Order I), and the musical form of the *Kyrie* was quickly elaborated. From the ninth to the twelfth century it also gave the greatest scope to the development of farcing or troping. Each invocation was amplified to a full line of prose or verse and the long-drawn, melismatic melody distributed in single notes over the text. The vast literature of these *Kyrie* tropes extends to the fifteenth century.[1] Still, the invocation itself remained alive among the people. The terms 'carol'[2] and 'lay' (Flemish *leis*) recall the days when *Kyrieleis(on)* was a popular refrain to macaronic and vernacular hymns.

The name *canon* (rule) for the great eucharistic prayer is typical of the Roman and Ambrosian rites. It indicates that these rites had only one basic text, while the other Latin and eastern rites varied the text according to circumstances. Except for the Nestorian *anaphora* (offering) of Addai and Mari, they all contain an institution narrative which, although based upon the New Testament accounts of Matt. xvi. 26–8, Mark xiv. 22–4, Luke xxii. 19–20 and I Cor. xi. 23–5, is nowhere directly taken from the original documents. In the Roman Mass it may well be built upon the Old-Latin version of Matthew with expression from I Corinthians;[3] but it remains peculiar that it has so little in common with Mark. Many literary and theological principles or motifs have contributed, in all liturgies, to a development of the various liturgical narratives. That of the Roman rite shows typical features of Latin rhythm (*cursus*) and of adaptation to the other prayers in the *canon*; but eastern elements are equally noticeable. The earliest western text goes back to Ambrose of Milan (*d.* 397), the next one, a most surprising version, comes from an Irish palimpsest sacramentary of 640–85, which may well depend upon a Coptic source.[4] The central

---

[1] Texts of 29 items used in England are edited, e.g., by W. G. Henderson, *Missale ad usum insignis Ecclesiae Eboracensis*, II, in Surtees Society, vol. IX (1874), 243–52.

[2] M. Sahlin, *Étude sur la carole médiévale* (Uppsala, 1940).

[3] E. C. Ratcliff, 'The institution narrative of the Roman Canon Missae', in *Studia patristica. Papers presented to the second international conference on patristic studies...1955* (Berlin, 1957), 64–82.

[4] Ed. A. Dold–L. Eizenhöfer, 'Das irische Palimpsestsakramentar im CLM 14429 der Staatsbibliothek München', in *Texte und Arbeiten* 53–4 (Beuron, 1964).

place of the institution narrative within the eucharistic prayers is obvious. Its function, however, as part of the whole *anaphora* and the communion has not always been clearly understood. Even the present-day ceremonies and their typographical presentation in the Mass books separate the institution account from its liturgical context, placing it in another, dogmatic context of a psychological nature.

Of the two versions of the Lord's prayer (Matt. v. 9–13; Luke ix. 2–5) only the longer one given in Matthew is used in western liturgies. Jerome believed that its recitation at Mass was instituted by Christ himself, while Gregory the Great asserted that the apostles consecrated (i.e. broke the bread) with this prayer. The same pontiff probably changed the place of the 'Our Father' to that which it now occupies, immediately after the *canon*, as an introduction to the whole communion rite. Although he rejected the accusation that, in doing so, he had imitated the Byzantine custom,[1] the fact remains that it had this place in both the Byzantine and other eastern rites. In Africa and in the Roman liturgy the Lord's prayer was sung by the celebrant only. The recent reform by which it is said by the entire congregation is inspired by the long-standing practice among the Greeks. The liturgical doxology *Quoniam tua est virtus et gloria in saecula*, already present in the *Didache*,[2] was a widely used conclusion in East and West. It is still known in the Anglican church: 'For thine is the kingdom, the power and the glory...' In all liturgies the Lord's prayer has always been preceded by a short prologue on its divine origin with an exhortation (*Praeceptis salutaribus moniti*... Mindful of our Saviour's bidding...). It is not of scriptural origin.

Inspired by Jewish Passover ritual and the Apocalypse (v. 6 ff.), the *Agnus dei* was brought into the Roman liturgy perhaps by Sergius I (687–701), a Syrian by descent, as an element from the West Syrian liturgies. An accompaniment not of the communion but of the breaking of the host, it was chanted alternately by clergy and people until the end of the ceremony. All invocations ended with *miserere nobis* (have mercy on us). When the ritual of the breaking was shortened, they were reduced to three, and from the tenth century the third refrain was increasingly altered to *dona nobis pacem* (give us peace). The influence of

[1] *Epist.* ix, no. 12, to John of Syracuse.
[2] *Didache* viii, no. 2.

the preceding salutation of the celebrant (*Pax domini*) and the kiss of peace, given a few moments later, is obvious. Like the *Kyrie*, the *Agnus dei* was a favourite text for troping.

In the Office

The early Christian veneration for the Psalter as a private and public prayer book is strikingly evident from a ceremony of unknown form, attested by documents from as far apart as Naples and Lindisfarne: the Psalter was officially presented to the catechumens on the third Sunday in Lent, a few weeks before they were similarly entrusted with the Creed. Western devotion is also vividly expressed, from the eighth century onwards, in the rich embellishment of Psalter manuscripts. It is most obvious from the prayer service of the Office, which is based not just upon the singing of psalms but upon the continual singing of the Psalter.

Until the eighth century the organization or *cursus* of these euchological services in western monasticism differed widely. Unity was obtained gradually through the acceptance of the rule of St Benedict, who, apart from his discreet personal contributions, combined Roman and local monastic traditions.[1] These ancient monastic Offices had one thing in common with the Milanese rite, namely that they divided the Psalter into two parts. In Milan they were meant to be sung in two weeks, in Rome in one. During this week the first part of the Psalter (1–108) was sung in connection with the morning Office, the second part (109–47) with the evening service:

	Sun.	Mon.	Tu.	Wed.	Th.	Fri.	Sat.
Nocturns:	1	26	38	52	68	80	96
	etc.	etc.	etc.	etc.	etc.	etc.	etc.
Vespers:	109	114	121	126	131	137	143
	etc.	etc.	etc.	etc.	etc.	etc.	etc.

In seven daily Hours all psalms and a certain number of canticles were chanted. Ferial matins and lauds differed from those on Sundays and feasts.

The *cursus* of the secular clergy too varied from place to place. Their original devotions of Sunday vigils and daily lauds and vespers (morning and evening prayers) were strongly influenced by the monastic

[1] D. Knowles, *Great Historical Enterprises* (London, 1963); see also above, p. 230 n. 1.

movement. If Pope Damasus (366–84) is the author of a complete Roman *cursus*, celebrated by the monks and partly by the clergy of the basilicas, it has not been traced. Gregory the Great perhaps corrected this archaic Office; maybe his arrangement was a compromise between the custom of the Roman monks and that of the clergy. But it is certain that at an early stage several changes took place: some psalms were taken out of the order of the Psalter because of some motif related to a particular time of the day; they found a place in one of the other Hours. In imitation of the Benedictine Office Gregory prefixed to matins Ps. 94 (95), the *invitatorium* which, previously, was said on Fridays. Its removal made it necessary to shift back all psalms said on the previous nights. He probably also reduced the number of psalms in the second and third nocturns on Sunday. Those left over (Ps. 21–5) were prefixed to the existing ones at prime. When, after all the vicissitudes, the Roman secular Office obtained its established form in the twelfth century, the liturgy of the papal court had the scheme of the weekly Psalter as shown on p. 246.

A slight curtailment of this scheme was introduced under Pius V (1568): for pastoral purposes the lengthy series of psalms at Sunday prime was shortened; the Psalms 21–2–3–4–5 were distributed over the weekdays (Fri.–Th.–Mon.–Tu.–Wed.). Only in 1911 was this Roman ferial Psalter thoroughly revised. The twelve psalms at matins were reduced to nine. This principle made $9 + 4 + 3 + 3 + 3 + 3 + 5 + 3 = 33$ places available daily for all Hours and weekly $7 \times 33 = 231$ places. In order to fill these with the 150 psalms Benedict's method was adopted, by which the longer psalms were divided into two or more parts. The ancient division was maintained: at vespers practically the same order (109–47) was preserved, while the first division (1–108) was distributed over all other Hours. But the psalms opening with the words *Dominus regnavit, Cantate, Lauda* or *Laudate* were reserved for lauds. The result of this reform is still seen in all modern Roman Office books.

At first the weekly Psalter was only interrupted by the principal feasts of our Lord (Christmas, Epiphany, Maundy Thursday, Good Friday, Ascension, etc.). On such days psalms, antiphons, lessons, etc., were deliberately chosen in conformity with the mystery. Feasts of saints were celebrated with a proper night Office (matins and lauds) chanted before that of the day. This twofold night Office is the origin of the grading of doubles, that is, solemnities with, originally, a double

Ferial Psalter of the thirteenth-century Roman liturgy*

	Sun.		Mon.	Tu.	Wed.	Th.	Fri.	Sat.
matins	1	15	26	38	52	68	80	97
	2	16	27	39	54	69	81	98
	3	17	28	40	55	70	82	99
	6	18	29	41	56	71	83	100
	7	19	30	43	57	72	84	101
	8	20	31	44	58	73	85	102
	9		32	45	59	74	86	103
	10		33	46	60	75	87	104
	11		34	47	61	76	88	105
	12		35	48	63	77	93	106
	13		36	49	65	78	95	107
	14		37	51	67	79	96	108
lauds	92		50	←	←	←	←	←
	99		5	42	64	89	142	91
	62+66		←	←	←	←	←	←
	Dan. iii²		Isa. xii	Isa. xxxviii	I Sam. ii	Exod. xv	Hab. iii	Deut. xxxii
	148–50		←	←	←	←	←	←
prime	21	53	53	←	←	←	←	←
	22	117	118^1	←	←	←	←	←
	23	118^1	118^2	←	←	←	←	←
	24	118^2						
	25							
terce	118^3		←	←	←	←	←	←
	118^4		←	←	←	←	←	←
	118^5		←	←	←	←	←	←
sext	118^6		←	←	←	←	←	←
	118^7		←	←	←	←	←	←
	118^8		←	←	←	←	←	←
none	118^9		←	←	←	←	←	←
	118^{10}		←	←	←	←	←	←
	118^{11}		←	←	←	←	←	←
vespers	109		114	121	126	131	137	143
	110		115	122	127	132	138	144
	111		116	123	128	134	139	145
	112		119	124	129	135	140	146
	113		120	125	130	136	141	147
compline	4		←	←	←	←	←	←
	30 [1–6]		←	←	←	←	←	←
	90		←	←	←	←	←	←
	133		←	←	←	←	←	←

* The numbering throughout is that of the Vulgate.

Fig. 3

Office. Such 'vigils' of the saints with three or nine psalms and lessons persisted throughout the middle ages for feasts of local and patron saints.

In the Roman and Benedictine Offices all psalms ended with the short doxology, except for the last three days of Holy Week and for the Office of the dead. Originally it served as a signal to end the silent prayer which followed the psalm. Elsewhere this silent prayer was, in its turn, followed by a collect, made up from the preceding psalm. Three series of such psalter collects are preserved, all of which go back to the fifth and sixth centuries.[1] They were widely used in the Gallican and Ambrosian rites but disappeared with the spreading of Roman customs.

Once antiphonal chant was established as a new form of community singing, the antiphon was repeated after each psalm verse. The practice is mentioned by Amalar of Metz early in the ninth century. By that time, however, the tendency to shorten the canonical Hours by reducing the numerous repetitions had made itself felt. Still, three centuries later the canons at St Peter's in the Vatican continued to sing the antiphon after two or three verses; this has remained customary at the *invitatorium*. In most churches, however, the refrain was restricted to the beginning and the end of the psalms, although on principal feasts the great antiphons to the *Benedictus* and the *Magnificat* continued to be repeated several times. Another connection between the grading of feasts and the repetition of the antiphon goes back to the same period. On ferias, ordinary Sundays and feasts of lower rank the refrain was only chanted after the psalm. Before the psalm the precentor hummed or pre-intoned its cue to indicate the melodic mode of the subsequent psalm. Written and printed in books without musical notation, the texts of these intonations persisted in public and private recitation for many centuries. They have only recently been abolished, though Humbert of Romans (*d.* 1277) even in his day had stressed the absurdity of this practice.

Of the four types of antiphons, those taken from the actual psalms are the most ancient. The matins of Christmas, Epiphany, Holy Week, Easter, Ascension and Whitsun, as well as the eighth-century Commons of the saints have, as a rule, this type of psalmodic antiphon. In Rome

---

[1] L. Brou (ed.), 'The Psalter Collects', in *Henry Bradshaw Society*, vol. LXXXIII (London, 1949); H. Ashworth, 'The psalter collects of pseudo-Jerome and Cassiodorus', in *Bulletin of the John Rylands Library*, XLV (1963), 287–304; F. Vandenbroucke, 'Sur la lecture chrétienne du psautier au Vᵉ siècle', in *Sacris Erudiri*, V (1953), 5–26.

the *Alleluia* was the sole antiphon at lauds on all Sundays during the year, except for Lent. Gospel antiphons, chosen from the pertinent Gospel pericope, often frame the New Testament canticles at lauds and vespers. Historical and independent antiphons, either based upon the legends or passions of the saints or free compositions, increased from the eighth century onwards. Although often inspired by biblical expressions, they do not belong to the present study.

In the archaic Office the singing of psalms was concluded by a short ejaculatory prayer, a versicle and response, taken from the psalm and often repeating one of the antiphons. In the Roman *cursus* these versicles and responses have kept their original place only in the nocturns of the night Office. At lauds, vespers and compline they were separated, first, from the psalms by the (little) chapter and, later on, from this chapter by the introduction of hymns; both elements are from the Benedictine Office. At the Little Hours they precede the final collect and follow the short responsories. The latter follow the chapters in the same way as the great responsories follow the lessons of the night Office. In their textual and melodic simplicity they still continue the Hispano-Gallican technique of responsorial chant.

LYRIC EXPRESSION

Both reading in public and conducting community prayers require preparation and expert knowledge. But far more arduous was the study needed before a medieval chanter could fulfil his liturgical duty of soloist. Prior to the invention of the musical stave by Guido of Arezzo, shortly before 1026, six to eight years were just sufficient to master the liturgical repertoire and to understand its notation. The psalm tones and Office antiphons remained, generally speaking, simple (syllabic chant). Even in the rhymed and rhythmical Offices of the Gothic period they retained this characteristic feature. Antiphons and psalm tones of the *Benedictus* and *Magnificat* were already more complicated (neumatic chant). So were the chants of introit and offertory, especially the latter, once they had lost their character of community chant. But the items demanding most knowledge and virtuosity were those meant primarily not as prayer or embellishment of ceremonies but as compositions to be enjoyed for their music (melismatic chant). In the western liturgies these are the intermezzo chants between the readings at both the fore-Mass and the night Office. Musical language here completes the instruction just given. Where reading prepared the mind, the lyric expression endeavours to move the heart.

These intermezzo chants constitute a most ancient musical heritage of Christian worship, but, again, their original purpose differed from that mentioned here. The early Christian era made scarcely any distinction between prayer and song. The chants linking the various readings were responsorial prayers, psalms and hymns, to which the assembly responded. However, since the text and the leadership was in the hands of soloists, this type of performance was, from early days, open to artistic influence. In the East it was poetry that changed both its nature and purpose; in the West it was music which, moreover, upset the responsorial structure. This is more evident in the Mass than in the Office.

At Mass

Epistle and Gospel are usually linked by two chants, the gradual and the *Alleluia* or, in its place, the tract. During Eastertide two *Alleluias* are sung. The fact that, as a rule, two chants follow one reading is, according to those who hold that originally the Roman fore-Mass had three lessons, a relic from the period when the gradual followed the first, the *Alleluia* the second reading. When, they say, the first reading disappeared, the *Alleluia* had become a preparation to the Gospel rather than an echo of the epistle. Thus both items remained. In actual fact, the gradual was originally a responsorial prayer of the assembly. It offered the occasion to extract the basic idea from the reading for meditation and thus provided the first response of the community to the Word of God. In Africa this responsorial psalm was directed by the lector who had just read the lesson; in Rome it was either the lector or the deacon. Gregory the Great replaced the deacons by special chanters (Synod of Rome, 595). The *Alleluia* however was at all times a chant performed by experts.

Once the responsorial psalm was entrusted to special chanters, embellishment of its music was only a matter of time. Already in the early papal liturgy the performance is entirely done by the *schola*. The psalm is shortened to two verses, the responsory proper (R℣) and one psalm verse (℣). The name gradual is derived from the *gradus* or step of the *ambo* on which the chanter stood. Today the refrain is no longer repeated: the choir sings the responsory, the soloist the verse, and both join in the last words.

The *Alleluia* is another responsory. The acclamation, already developed among the Jews into a long-drawn melody on the last syllable, is a refrain, still repeated by the choir before and after the verse. At first used in Rome for the Easter vigil, as a Resurrection cry, and for Eastertide, it was soon extended to all Sundays and major feasts, including the liturgy of the dead. Since the days of Gregory the Great the *Alleluia* has not been sung during Lent, nor in the liturgy of the dead. From 817 onwards the period of Lent was extended to that from Septuagesima Sunday to Easter. In that period it is replaced by the tract, which, however, is not a song of penance or sorrow but, probably, the oldest form of intermezzo chant, a solo-psalmody. The origin of the term tract is uncertain: it is either a translation of the Greek word *heirmos* (a melody constructed to fixed rules) or a derivation of the medieval Latin adverb *tractim*, meaning subsequently, without interruption. Apart from noteworthy exceptions, such as the tracts of the first Sunday in Lent, Palm Sunday and Good Friday, the psalm is reduced to three or four verses. From the later middle ages the performance was animated by dividing them among a soloist and choir or among two choirs. Like the gradual, the *Alleluia* (and tract) were chanted from the *ambo* steps but by another soloist.

All intermezzo chants are variable; graduals and tracts are almost always taken from the Psalter, the *Alleluia* versicles often from other books of the Bible. They still illustrate the preceding or subsequent lessons.[1] In the melismatic melody (*sequela, melisma, jubilus*) lies the origin of a complicated musical history, first of the *prosula* and then of the sequence and prose. The most ancient example of the former goes back to about 830.[2]

In the Office

There is no evidence that the great responsories of the night Office were, like those at Mass, chanted with the entire psalm. The earliest responsorials present their texts in almost the same manner as the modern

---

[1] A clear example is the last (5th) Sunday after Easter, the last Sunday before the Ascension: *Alleluia ℣ Surrexit Christus....Alleluia ℣ Exivi a patre...*

[2] J. Smits van Waesberghe, 'Over het ontstaan van sequens en prosula en beider oorspronkelijke uitvoeringswijze', in *Orgaan koninklijke nederlandsche toonkunstenaars/vereeniging* XII, feestafl. (September 1957), 50 ff. B. Stäblein, 'Zwei Textierungen des Alleluia Christus resurgens in St. Emmeram-Regensburg', in *Organicae voces. Festschrift Joseph Smits van Waesberghe angeboten anlässlich seines 60. Geburtstages 18. April 1961*, Instituut voor middeleeuwse muziekwetenschap (Amsterdam, 1963), 157–67.

books, namely responsory proper with one verse. A few exceptions to
this rule have always existed, like for instance the first responsory of the
liturgical year (*Aspiciens*). But the variety of verses found in Amalar's
antiphonal were only alternatives, sung whenever a responsory was
repeated during the week. The same antiphonal also bears witness both
to the Roman manner of repeating the whole responsory after the verse
and the Spanish and Gallican custom, whereby only the last phrase was
intercalated (above, p. 237). Only in a few cases is something of the
original Roman method preserved (*Aspiciens, Hodie coelorum, Angelus
domini, Libera me*).

The Office responsories can be divided in the same manner as the
antiphons. Of interest here are the psalmodic and biblical ones. The
former, compiled from one or more psalms, often include slight textual
changes, adaptations, omissions or additions. Three series stand out:
after the Epiphany the responsories follow, in a general way, the order
of the Psalter; during Passiontide most of them are made up to illustrate
the season; during the last two weeks of Eastertide they are of a general
content which has little connection with the reading matter of the
period. The biblical responsories are distributed in sets over the various
seasons of the liturgical year in the same way as the reading from the
Bible. Since the eleventh century these sets have become known as
responsorial *historiae*, histories, such as the [hi]story of Kings, of Job,
etc. Those for the period after Whitsun, in particular, were also quoted
by the cues of the first responsory of the set: the [hi]story *In principio,
Si bona*, or *Adonai*, etc., or by the name of the person to whom they
refer: the [hi]story of Adam, Abraham, Joshua, etc. Especially noteworthy are the historical responsories based upon the passion
narrative of Matthew. These are sung during the last three days
of Holy Week together with others which are the work of Roman
composers. They all represent a refined literary art of the early middle
ages.

As for their musical aspect, here, as in all items of Roman origin
mentioned previously, it should be borne in mind that since 1950 the
study of medieval Roman chant has gradually entered an unexpected
and new phase. We now know that a large proportion of the repertoire
that goes under the name of Gregorian chant can have had little to do
with Gregory the Great. Certainly those traditional chants which
require(d) expert musical knowledge cannot antedate the middle of the

seventh century. They formed an integral part of a majestic and spectacular papal liturgy which, strongly influenced by and often modelled upon practices of the imperial court of Byzantium, was devised as a dazzling symbol of papal sovereignty, a liturgy in which the people had no active part. The corresponding chant, though newly composed, was based upon an older and venerated repertoire of a different character. From the second half of the eighth century it rapidly superseded the Old-Roman and Gallican ones, except in the Eternal City itself. Here the ancient tradition, reduced to an urban rite, was tenaciously maintained in the basilicas and title churches, until its last traces were destroyed during the second half of the thirteenth century. Both the liturgical and musical problems arising from recent discoveries are complicated.[1] And renewed study of the subject will undoubtedly reveal unknown attitudes of the contemporary mind, even towards the liturgical use of the Bible.

5. THE STUDY OF THE BIBLE IN MEDIEVAL JUDAISM

The study of the Torah or Pentateuch is a biblical commandment. In Deut. vi the father is enjoined to teach his children all the commandments, statutes and ordinances; and teaching comprises both what the text says and what it means. Interpretation is known by the term *derash*. Its justification is derived from the verse in Deut. xiii: 'thou shalt inquire, and make search and ask diligently...' Rules of interpretation were developed to enable the rabbis to establish laws and regulations to meet the needs of the day. Minute investigation of the biblical text was called for, and far-fetched interpretation was sometimes needed to derive such laws from the Bible. But this method succeeded in preserving the Bible as the Word of the living God and as the perpetual foundation of Judaism. In this way, there arose gradually a 'fence round the Torah', considered necessary in response to the commandment to Israel to be 'a holy nation unto the Lord'. Holiness is understood in its basic meaning of separateness; unless Israel is

[1] S. J. P. van Dijk, 'The urban and papal rites in seventh- and eighth-century Rome', n *Sacris Erudiri*, XII (1961), 411–87; idem, in *Studia patristica*, 1963 (see p. 238 n. 1), 301–21; idem, 'Papal schola *versus* Charlemagne', in *Organicae voces*, 21–30; idem, 'Gregory the Great founder of the urban schola cantorum', in *Ephem. liturg.* LXXVII (1963), 335–56.

separate it cannot attain holiness. The fence developed into the oral Torah, eventually codified in the Talmud. The written Torah comprises not only the Pentateuch but all the Canon of Old Testament Scripture. Adherence to the whole Torah as *Halakhah*, the way to God, secured Jewish survival. Yet there was modification, adaptation, change and even abrogation in a continuous attempt to preserve the biblical heritage. Flexibility was essential, and it could only be maintained by ever fresh study and reinterpretation. The bulk of post-biblical Hebrew and Jewish literature is in fact interpretation of the Bible. Leo Baeck expressed this truism thus: 'It is a principle in Judaism that truth has to be discovered in, and through, the Bible. The book of "revelation" must again and again be revealed by the teacher. For every sentence and story in this book not only tells something, it also means something. It does not merely describe what has been and now ceased to be. It manifests something permanent that attains actuality again and again.'

The rabbis of the first centuries of the Common Era coined a terminology of interpretation which reflects the dynamic character of their diligent search for the truth of the Bible. This was not a theoretical ideal, or an intellectual exercise of the contemplative life; it was a wrestling with a text which was alive with meaning, a practical guide to individual and social conduct, a 'tree of life' for the Jewish people. 'Turn it and turn it, for all is in it' aptly describes the fundamental importance of the Torah and the constant, ceaseless activity of those qualified to interpret it. The fruit of this endeavour is to be found in the Midrash literature, apart from the Aramaic and Greek versions of the Old Testament. As the Torah contains preceptive matter, formulated in laws and statutes, and moral, edifying instruction and stories, these *Midrashim* are *halakhic* or *aggadic*, legal exposition and homily. Thus, we have two different approaches and methods side by side, the literal and the homiletical, figurative interpretation of the Bible. To guard against creative imagination running wild and undermining the obligatory character and significance of the preceptive side, the rabbis asserted a basic hermeneutic principle: 'No verse in Scripture can lose its literal (plain, simple) meaning.' This *peshat* or literal meaning must not be explained away by an allegorical or mystical interpretation; it always remains basic. But alongside it, *derash* or homiletical, figurative, meaning can be deduced from the text as a legitimate additional meaning.

In the period under discussion, this principle of biblical exegesis assumed great importance, and *peshat* became the dominant method of interpretation in the West from the eleventh century onwards.

This survey of medieval Jewish exegesis in the Christian West is necessarily brief. But even its general character cannot become clear unless we realize—against the background of this sketch of the purpose of exegesis—that it is but a part of a continual activity of long standing. Together with the observance of Jewish law, the fulfilment of the commandments as developed and interpreted in the *Halakhah*, continuous exposition of the basic teachings of the Hebrew bible in literary form guaranteed the meaningful survival of Judaism as a distinct religious way of life, an enclave in Christian and Muslim Europe. Living within the 'fence round the Torah' the Jews were sometimes tolerated but often persecuted as a separate group. This group, which did not profess either of the regnant religions, was determined to live a life of its own in accordance with its own religious and cultural heritage, intent to preserve and, if necessary, to defend it against attack and especially against any attempt at conversion. The 'fence' was not an impenetrable wall; it was more like a rampart. The Jews, while maintaining their separateness, were open to the spiritual currents and movements of the times. They drew into their own civilization what appealed to them among the ideas and institutions of the world around them, striving for a synthesis between the indigenous and the extraneous in religious thought—both in theology and in philosophy—and to some extent in social organization. This was effected by interpretation. For this reason it is important to see this activity clearly. Its task was twofold. Its principal object was to explain the tenets of biblical religious culture to each generation in order to give the life of the community and the individual member guidance and direction, and to strengthen their faith in the existence and absolute, simple unity of God, his revelation in history through the Torah, his promise of the kingdom of God on earth and the final redemption at the end of days through the Messiah, son of David. The second objective was the defence of these concepts against Muslims and Christians in so far as these two daughter-religions claimed to have superseded Judaism.

Our concern in this section is only with the Christian claim, or more specifically with the arguments the Jewish commentators on the Hebrew bible used against it. In particular, two issues were of vital importance from the days of the Church Fathers to the end of the medieval period: the divine–human nature of Jesus and his Messiahship and, connected with it, the validity of the Torah. In fact, the double purpose of Jewish exposition is basically one and the same, but it is so to speak a struggle on two fronts, an internal and an external one.

Internally, traditional normative Judaism had to be maintained: against the sectarian tendencies of the Karaites, who denied the oral Torah of rabbinic Judaism; against extreme rationalism; and against mysticism in so far as it developed into antinomianism. Externally, the Christian claim that Jesus was the Messiah promised in the Old Testament, and that he had replaced the Torah, had to be refuted. Since it was less relevant to convince the Christians than to confirm the Jewish belief that the Messiah was still to come and with him final redemption, and thus to fortify the Jews to withstand Christian attack and attempts at conversion, medieval Jewish exegesis was primarily concerned with the exposition of Judaism for the Jews. But Christian endeavours to convert the Jews, persecution, and general insecurity imposed on the Jewish leaders the task of emphasizing the simple unity of God, Messianism and imminent redemption. Hence we meet with a strong element of anti-Christian polemic, coupled with the stress on the literal as against the spiritual meaning of Scripture, in particular of its messianic passages in the Torah, in the prophets, especially in Isaiah, and in the Psalms. The twofold aspect of this exegesis is seen in its methods and also in its terminology. Both testify to the relevance and topicality of such exegesis.

Leaving aside the Jewish–Muslim controversy and Jewish commentaries written in Arabic, we confine ourselves to the Jewish–Christian issue and to the commentators writing in Hebrew. They give us a clear idea of the mental climate of the time; of close personal relations between Jews and Christians—closer, it appears, the more hostile the attitudes and measures of the Church against the Jews became. They also show us how great the messianic expectancy was among the Jews and what a vital part the eschatological teaching of the Hebrew prophets played in the daily lives of the hard-pressed Jews. All this goes to show how relevant the Bible was in those days and what a practical and active part its exposition played in the preservation of Judaism and in the survival of the Jews. But before we can tell the story of this exegesis we must briefly mention what made it possible for the Jews of Spain, southern and especially northern France and Germany to develop the literal interpretation of the Hebrew bible into a fine art and a powerful instrument, and to lay the foundations for the modern scientific study of the Bible.

As has been stated at the beginning, the literal interpretation is not the invention of the medieval commentators. Already the Church Fathers opposed to the *sensus Judaicus* (by which they mean the literal sense) the *sensus mysticus*. For the disciples of Origen the Jews were a *carnalis populus*, *amici litterae*. Jerome shared this view, although he made a valiant attempt, with the help of Jewish teachers, to get back to the *Hebraica veritas* in his Vulgate. Augustine also showed a more positive attitude to the literal meaning, as long as the spiritual or mystical sense was the one accepted by Christians. Dr Smalley has shown in her researches in the school of St Victor how the *peshat* found an entry into the exegetical work of Hugh and Andrew of St Victor, and how Jewish explanations are quoted by them, by the Chanter, by Langton and the Comestor; and Raphael Loewe has traced Herbert of Bosham's indebtedness to medieval Jewish exegesis, to mention only two of the more recent investigations. We shall come back to this question later in this section. Suffice it to say that even in the later middle ages, Jewish exegesis was always connected with the literal sense, and while it promoted a more accurate understanding of the Hebrew text it hampered Christian missionary activity and militated against the Christological interpretation, especially of the messianic prophecies. But it was on this ground of *peshat* that Jews and Christians met as Bible scholars in a common search for the truth of the Bible, irrespective of their theological presuppositions.

In the middle ages, the pioneering efforts in grammatical and lexicographical studies of Saadya Gaon (880–942) laid the foundation for the exegetical work of the Spanish Jews, who in turn enabled the French school in north and south to give an entirely new meaning and content to the method of *peshat*. Saadya established Hebrew philology as the prerequisite for the study of the literal sense of the Bible, a method he employed in his Arabic translation and in his Arabic commentaries on the Pentateuch, Isaiah, Proverbs and Job, which are extant in critical editions with French translation. He naturally brought the traditional rabbinic interpretation to bear on the text, to which he also applied the findings of reason. For he was steeped in Islamic culture and made full use of the secular knowledge of his time, the result of the renaissance of Greek science and Hellenistic philosophy. On the one hand, he stressed the paramount importance of the literal meaning. On the other, he allowed the inner, hidden meaning only if the literal sense ran counter to reason or established tradition, or was in opposition to another scriptural passage. In his case, the close attention to, and concentration on, the plain meaning of Scripture was forced upon him by the Karaites, who, as their name implies, went back to the Bible for guidance while rejecting the rabbinic interpretation of it as it crystallized in the *Halakhah*. These sectarians were a grave danger to rabbinite traditional Judaism, and Saadya, rising to its defence, employed the weapons of his opponents. Another danger threatened from the rationalist thinkers of Islam; hence Saadya clearly defined when and where a departure from the literal meaning was justified, or required. He contrasts the secular knowledge of the philosopher, consisting of three 'roots' (sense-perception, reason and logical deduction), with the knowledge of the religious thinker, who adds a fourth 'root', true trustworthy tradition deriving from the Torah and the Books of prophecy. He insists on the complementary unity of reason, of Torah as divine instruction, and of tradition based on prophecy, i.e. instruction through revelation. He thus laid the foundations of Jewish medieval religious philosophy, which, like every manifestation of the Jewish mind, is in a very special sense interpretation of the Bible. Rational inquiry and speculation are limited by the overriding demands of divinely revealed truth. We shall touch upon the philosophical interpretation of the Bible later in this section.

Saadya's aim in his exegesis, as we learn from his commentaries, is to show the theological and ethical significance of the Bible as a guide to God and to moral or social conduct. For him the Bible is a unity and so is every one of its books. Thus, his comments supply missing links as his translation does also by supplying suitable adverbs or conjunctions. Indeed, his translation shows the well-known characteristic of all translation: that it is interpretation, the translator's understanding of the original text. He says at the end of the introduction to his version of the Pentateuch that his translation is 'a simple, explanatory translation of the text of the Torah, written with the knowledge of reason and tradition'.

In his commentary on Proverbs he defines wisdom and analyses its various aspects. He is always lucid and to the point and deals with special topics like wisdom, justice, or knowledge in a little excursus, keeping the literal interpretation separate. It is to him that medieval Jewish religious philosophy owes the division of the commandments of the Bible into those of revelation and those of reason. Space does not permit much detail, but it must at least be mentioned that Saadya prefaces his comments with an introduction which sets out the contents of the book and points to its difficulties in order to facilitate its understanding. His approach is throughout rational, and he has recourse to metaphor, but not to allegory, typology or symbolism. In this he may have been reacting against Christian biblical exegesis.

With the decline of Babylonian Jewry the centre of cultural activity shifted to Muslim and Christian Spain, and biblical studies flourished there under the influence of Saadya and of Arab linguistic and philosophical studies. Hebrew grammar and lexicography were developed to a high degree, and a lasting and scientifically sound foundation was laid for the systematic study of the Hebrew language. The interpretation of the Hebrew Bible greatly benefited from this linguistic approach. The demarcation line between *peshat* and *derash* became more pronounced, and the literal meaning was worked out by close attention to Hebrew grammar and syntax. Besides, the text was examined in the light of past history, to which greater attention was now paid. Naturally, it was largely directed at the historical books of the Bible, until towards the end of the period Don Isaac Abravanel widened the scope of historical studies by including extra-biblical and non-Hebrew sources, as we shall see below.

The intensive study of the Hebrew language in the West begins with Menahem ben Saruk (*c.* 960) and his able critic Dunash ibn Labrat, and it culminates in Abraham ibn Ezra and the Kimhi family. Menahem wrote his *Dictionary* (*mahbereth*) of biblical Hebrew in Hebrew, which was also the language Dunash used in his objections. A century later Rashi, the most influential of the medieval Jewish exegetes, mainly relied on Menahem in his own linguistic observations and comments. It was important for the application of his findings to the interpretation of the Bible that Menahem, sometimes in opposition to Saadya, attempted a systematic presentation of the Hebrew roots, their formation and meaning, on the basis of reason and study, as he puts it in the introduction to his dictionary. He also tried to find the meaning of a root from the context. It seems that he recognized the well-known characteristic of Hebrew poetry, parallelism, at least as far as synonymous parallelism between the two verse halves is concerned. For him, as for Saadya, the unity of the Hebrew language is a fact, and he often explains a biblical word by a Mishnaic one. Needless to say both authors have recourse to the Targum, the Aramaic version of the Pentateuch.

Dunash, a disciple of Saadya, severely criticized Menahem in the light of a comprehensive and systematic investigation of Hebrew morphology, grammar, and syntax and a comparative study of Hebrew, Arabic and Aramaic, the Massorah and the traditional rabbinic rules of interpretation. Undoubtedly his critique of Menahem marks an advance, even though his empiricism sometimes led him astray. He was on the way to discovering the principle of triliteralism in Hebrew roots; he flatly rejected single-letter roots and tried to replace biliteral by triliteral roots. His terminology was more exact and he distinguished, more successfully than Menahem, the form and significance of Hebrew words.

Of their successors, divided into adherents and opponents, Hayyuj, a disciple of Menahem, outshone his master and Dunash; he was the first scientific Hebrew grammarian in the strictest as well as the widest senses of this term. He established the triliteral theory of Hebrew roots scientifically, applying them to the so-called weak verbs, and succeeded in establishing definite laws and rules for the vowel changes and the different grammatical forms. What followed his work is only a development and modification of his results. He tells us in the introduction to his important treatise on the weak verbs that he based his investigations exclusively on the text of the Hebrew Bible, drawing, as a rule, conclusions from what he found there to what he did not find in the Bible. In this way he illuminated many problems of morphology and verbal structure. His contribution to a better understanding of the Hebrew noun, based on extensive Massoretic studies, also deserves mention. Throughout he employed, in his works written in Arabic, the terminology of Arabic grammar. The man who completed Hayyuj's work was Ibn Janah, known by his Hebrew name, Rabbi Jonah. He, too, engaged in linguistic studies in order the better to understand the Hebrew bible. He looked upon himself as one who added to and completed the work of his master Hayyūj. Beyond this work he gathered his own advanced researches and original observations into his *magnum opus* in two parts: a grammar and dictionary. His *Book of roots* was for centuries largely forgotten because of David Kimhi's dictionary of the same title. But even Kimhi's father largely depended on R. Jonah. In our context, R. Jonah's contribution to biblical exegesis is significant. For he also paid systematic attention to matters of biblical style and diction, thus furthering a correct understanding, and critically evaluated the traditional rabbinic exegesis from the point of view of his linguistic attainment.

Moses ibn Gikatilla was the first to translate Hayyuj's principal studies into Hebrew, and Abraham ibn Ezra recorded many of Gikatilla's philological interpretations of biblical passages in his own grammatical and exegetical writings. Moses wrote in Arabic, as did Judah ibn Balaam. These two were the most important Bible commentators of Spain before Abraham ibn Ezra. Both applied to their exegesis the linguistic findings and aids of Hayyuj and R. Jonah. Moses ibn Gikatilla's writings are no longer extant and we have only extracts from his commentary on Isaiah and the Psalms quoted by Abraham ibn Ezra. These comments represent an attempt to give a historical explanation, coupled with an exposition based on grammatical analysis. He refers some psalms to the Exile and the prophecies in Deutero-Isaiah to the Second Commonwealth, to quote two examples. Similar comments on passages in the Minor Prophets are quoted by Abraham ibn Ezra. We possess a modern edition of Judah ibn Balaam's commentary on Isaiah; in this he seems to be dependent on Saadya. He also wrote a commentary on the Psalms. With regard to the miracles reported in the Bible Judah holds fast to the traditional, literal view, opposing Moses ibn Gikatilla's rationalistic interpretation.

Before dealing with the greatest Spanish exegete, Abraham ibn Ezra, we turn for chronological reasons to the school of biblical exegetes in northern France. It is significant that many representatives of this school were at the same time engaged in expounding the Talmud. Their knowledge of the traditional rabbinic exegesis was, therefore, unsurpassed and it was brought to bear on the literal interpretation. At times, the traditional homiletical interpretation (*derash*), as it is enshrined in the Midrash-collections, was by some accepted as *peshat*, and the borderline between the two methods became at times rather fluid. The linguistic foundation of their method of *peshat* was not as pronounced and systematically applied as among their Spanish co-religionists, and often the historical interpretation was in the foreground. This naturally varied with the individual exegetes. Yet with all of them, the attention to the plain, simple, literal meaning of Scripture was paramount. It resulted in highly competent commentaries of permanent value and significance. Their output was extensive and covers practically the whole of the Hebrew Canon. Its importance is by no means confined to the Jewish tradition. For they were in personal contact with the Christian exegetes of France and England and, together with the work of Abraham ibn Ezra and David Kimhi, their commentaries were of considerable help to the reformers and the biblical exegesis of the Reformation, in particular to its choicest fruit, the Authorized (King James) Version of the English Bible.

Another important aspect of their literal interpretation is that it was closely linked with the refutation of Christian exegesis, in particular the Christological exposition of the messianic prophecies in Isaiah and of the Psalms. On the Jewish side this centred round the concept of the absolute, simple unity and uniqueness of God, round the Christian claim of the divine–human nature of Jesus, who fulfilled for the Christian the messianic prophecies of the Old Testament, and round the eternally binding character of the Torah as the revelation of God, who made a covenant with the people of Israel.

By far the greatest and most enduring impact was made by Rashi (Rabbi Solomon ben Isaac of Troyes, 1040–96), who commented on almost the entire Hebrew Bible. Though he was more famous for his great commentary on the Talmud, his biblical commentaries, especially that on the Pentateuch, have always had a special appeal and fascination for countless generations of Jews. Christian exegetes from his day onwards, from the Victorines to the humanists and translators of the Authorized Version, carefully noted his direct, simple, often homely explanations, more often with approval than rejection, and he was aptly called by Reuchlin *ordinarius Scripturae interpres*. Nicholas of Lyra quoted him so often that Reuchlin remarked that not many pages would remain over if one took away references to 'Rabi Salomon' from Nicholas's *Postillae*. His exegesis figures largely in the Latin translation of Sebastian Münster, who so decisively influenced the Puritan scholars and translators. Rashi's comments can be detected in Tyndale, Coverdale and the Genevan and Bishops' Bibles, important forerunners of the King James Version, whose chief architect, John Reynolds, refers to him—as Reuchlin had—as 'the author of their ordinary gloss' in his commentaries on Haggai and Obadiah.

What is it that appealed so much to Rashi's contemporaries and subsequent generations? It was his combination of the method of *peshat* with the best in the rabbinic *derash*. Rashi was not uncritical of traditional exegesis and often opposed the literal meaning to it. But he was not rigid in the application of the *peshat*, aware as he was of its significance for a correct understanding of the Bible. He wrote for the people, learned and ordinary folk alike, and the occasional homily from tradition helped to establish the strictly literal, direct, plain meaning. He was not out to instruct merely to increase knowledge, but by instruction to strengthen the faith of his generation and to foster their hope of redemption and their belief in messianic fulfilment. We must remember that he was active in an atmosphere which produced the crusades, and he saw with his own eyes what that meant for the Jews. Many a comment on a passage in the Pentateuch, in Isaiah, Jeremiah, Ezekiel or the Psalms is concluded with the statement that his interpretation is according to the plain sense and serves as 'an answer to the Christians'. References to contemporary events and institutions are not wanting, for example, to the crusades, and to conversions and persecution in his comments on Isa. liii. 9 or Ps. 38: 18. They show that Rashi was not a recluse, an academic, but a man who lived with his people and mixed with Christians in his native Troyes and on his travels. Besides, they are a vivid testimony to the relevance of the Hebrew Bible for his time.

For what was more important than refuting Christian exegesis was providing the Jews with a Jewish interpretation. Thus the second psalm refers to David, not to Jesus, and Ps. 45 refers to Israel and not to the Church. Rashi shares with other Jewish exegetes of the period the interpretation of Edom as Rome; he identifies the *Kittim* with Christian Rome. Against the Christian interpretation of Zech. ix. 4 as referring to the second commonwealth, Rashi refers it to the days of the Messiah. In general, he tried to combat Christian interpretation even if he had to depart from traditional exposition. This is clear from his interpretation of Psalms 9 and 10 or 21 and of the 'servant songs' in

Isa. lii–liii, or of Zech. vi. 12. There can be little doubt that, except where he was forced to reject the rabbinic exposition on linguistic grounds, as in Psalm 9, it was the contemporary Jewish–Christian controversy which led Rashi to an interpretation in opposition to the rabbis. Yet the anti-Christian slant is only the negative side of his exegesis. The Christian interpretation—referring a prophecy or a psalm to Jesus or the Church—is countered by the positive assertion that it refers to a biblical historical person or event and, if plausible linguistically and historically, that it contains a promise of the future redemption of Israel. Thus, he says that Ps. 22: 27 points to 'the time of our redemption, the days of our Messiah'. Psalm 68 foretells Israel's final redemption. Verses 10–14 of Ps. 10 refer to Israel when the rule of Ishmael (Islam) and Edom (Rome) has come to an end and they have been driven from the land of Israel; then God will be king for ever. These examples must suffice to show the twofold character of anti-Christian polemic as we find it in Rashi and his successors, notably David Kimhi. They also indicate the strength of messianic expectation among the Jews and their eschatological preparedness. In this context it must not be forgotten that eschatology is also partly at the back of the crusading movement. Thus, the exegetical literature of the middle ages is, as has been claimed at the beginning of this section, among other things a source of knowledge of the state of mind of the period.

An unexpected by-product of Rashi's commentaries and of those of his school is the large number of French glosses which have preserved many a medieval French word for which there is no evidence in French contemporary literature. They have been collected and analysed by Blondheim, Darmesteter and Brandin, and number over 3,000 in Rashi alone. Rashi used these words to explain to his readers—another indication that he had not only scholars like himself in mind—difficult Hebrew phrases or words.

Primarily an exegete, Rashi did not leave separate grammatical treatises. Nor was he a systematic linguist, and we have seen that he relied on Menahem ben Saruk's *Mahbereth* in many cases. But he had a well-developed sense of the peculiarities of the Hebrew tongue, and his commentaries are full of grammatical observations, prompted by his close study of the context and similar passages elsewhere in the Bible and by his frequent use of the Targum of Onqelos on the Penta-teuch. Rashi often coined his own terminology; Hayyuj and R. Jonah

18-2

were unknown to him. Steeped in traditional lore as Rashi was, he studied and made use of the Massorah as well. His success can be measured by the unusually large number of manuscripts of his commentaries on the several books of the Bible, especially on the Pentateuch, and of the many super-commentaries, begun by his pupils and continued for many generations. Fortunately, enough of these manuscripts have escaped the vigilance of Christian censorship and we can recover Rashi's original text. Critical editions of his commentaries on Isaiah, the Minor Prophets and the Psalms, based on such uncensored manuscripts, were only published some twenty years ago. Incidentally, his commentary on the Pentateuch was the first Hebrew book to be printed, in 1475. This no doubt facilitated the acquaintance of the humanists and reformers with his exegesis, apart from the Latin tradition, briefly touched upon earlier on in this chapter.

Rashi inaugurated in northern France the movement towards the literal interpretation and the refutation of Christological exposition of many messianic passages within biblical commentaries. There were also public disputations, based on scriptural passages, and special pamphlets. These too were devoted to the Christian claims that the Messiah promised in the Old Testament had already come in the divine–human person of Jesus and that the Law had been superseded; they too provoked Jewish denials. This is not the place to go into detail about the disputations and pamphlets. They are mentioned to indicate at least the background to the Jewish–Christian controversy carried on in commentaries on the books of the Old Testament. To this literary struggle must be added, alongside the public disputations forced upon the Jews (in 1240 in Paris, 1263 in Barcelona, 1413 in Tortosa), the burning of the Talmud as a manifestation of the relentless campaign of the Church to convert the Jews. It is, therefore, the more remarkable that the growing hostility of the Church did not prevent friendly intercourse between Christian and Jewish scholars who met to discover the truth of the Bible, which was for both sides the Word of God. These meetings were a true dialogue between students of the Bible. For while the Jews gave their Christian partners the Jewish interpretation which they could not obtain unaided from the original texts, the Christians in turn acquainted the Jews with the Vulgate, the interpretation of the Church Fathers, and their own interpretation according to the fourfold method of biblical interpretation dating back to the Venerable Bede and

Rabanus Maurus (see above, pp. 186–7), to which we shall refer when discussing the mystical exegesis of the Kabbalists.

In this context it is not possible to discuss, even very briefly, the Jewish–Christian controversy outside the strictly exegetical literature, such as the tenth-century anonymous *Altercatio Aecclesie contra Synagogam* or *Gisleberti Crispini Disputatio Iudei et Christiani* of the last decade of the eleventh century. The first tract is directed as much if not more against judaizing heretics as against Jews, and is one of many such writings. Crispin's *Disputatio* had a considerable circle of readers until the middle of the twelfth century when the censor altered the text and transformed the Jew from an attacker into a passive, pale figure on the defensive. This reflects the changed situation caused by the crusades, which forced the Jews on to the defensive. Nor can we consider Moses Nachmanides' report of his role in the disputation at Barcelona with Paul, a Jewish convert to Christianity, as his opponent. The questions discussed were those which we meet again and again in the Jewish commentaries under discussion. This shows that these theological questions formed a live issue at a time when the western world, though divided between three religions, was at one in its fervent faith in God. It was thus by no means a purely academic question who was the *verus Israel*, the Church or the Synagogue; or whether the Messiah had already come in the person of Jesus, as the Christians claimed, or was still to come, as the Jews maintained. Both parties appealed to Scripture as sole authority, or to Scripture and Reason. In our context, the most sustained Jewish 'answer to the Christians' is to be found in David Kimhi's commentary on the Psalms and in Don Isaac Abravanel's three messianic treatises, two of which will occupy us a little later.

First, we must consider one or two of Rashi's successors in the field of exegesis. All without exception adhere to the *peshat* method of interpretation, and most of them combine it with a refutation of the Christological interpretation. In this respect they show a growing familiarity with the Vulgate, but it is difficult to decide whether they read the Vulgate themselves or obtained their knowledge from their Christian partners in conversation.

Joseph Bekhor Shor stands out among them; he combats Jerome, pointing out his mistakes and stressing the correct meaning arrived at by the application of the method of *peshat*, especially in Jerome's translation of the Psalms. His references to the history of Israel and to contemporary events show historical sense, an open mind and acute observation. He criticized the Christians' interpretation of almost all the passages which they claimed for their faith, more so than any other Jewish exegete before him. He was concerned about the anthropomorphisms in the Bible, just as was Saadya, who went far beyond the Targum in this matter. His attempt at whitewashing the patriarchs is ingenious, but very far-fetched, and his explanation of the miracles in the Old Testament is rationalistic. Many of his comments are based on the customs of his age and country. Like Rashi, he sometimes admits the *derash*, but more often prefers the sense required by Hebrew usage.

Brief mention must be made of Samuel ben Meir's commentary on the Pentateuch. He was a grandson of Rashi and on the basis of Rashi's commentary developed the literal interpretation to a fine art. His linguistic ability was exceptional without being systematically trained and scientifically developed; he relied on Menahem ben Sarūk, but not uncritically, thanks to a natural gift for languages and a profound knowledge of the whole Bible. Like his grandfather, who taught him and whom in all deference he often criticized, he wrote his commentary for a practical purpose: the instruction of the people to strengthen their loyalty to their inherited faith. With reverence for tradition he combined independent judgement, which he often followed against traditional exegesis. Thus, he disagreed with both Jewish and Christian exegesis of Gen. xlix. 10, since neither is consonant with the strictly literal meaning. *Shiloh* does not refer to Jesus as the promised Messiah; the Vulgate is wrong in translating *qui mittendus est*. So is the Jewish interpretation. The right explanation is that Shiloh is the name of a town, near Shechem, to which the king of Judah, namely Rehoboam, the son of Solomon, is to come. In two other places he opposes the translation of the Vulgate: in Exod. xx. 13 and Deut. xxxii. 39. These and a number of anti-Christian passages are not to be found in the printed editions of the Hebrew Pentateuch with rabbinic commentaries; they only occur in a critical edition of Samuel ben Meir's commentary on the Pentateuch, based on an uncensored manuscript.

Next, we pass to Abraham ibn Ezra (*d.* 1167), who in a long, unsettled life of travel mediated the achievements of the Spanish school of exegesis to the Jews of Italy and northern France. During his stay in England he composed two largely exegetical works, one on the Sabbath, the other on the reasons underlying the biblical commandments and their division. His weightiest commentary is on the Pentateuch as a whole; a second recension of the important introduction exists. A separate long commentary on Exodus, particularly rich in grammatical observations, and commentaries on Isaiah, the Minor Prophets, Psalms, Job, Esther, Ruth, Song of Songs, Ecclesiastes and Daniel illustrate his originality, wide range of knowledge, independent judgement and remarkable insight into the theological and ethical content of the Bible. On the foundations of the Spanish school, of Saadya's work in linguistics and exegesis, and of the sum total of secular knowledge of Muslim Spain, Abraham ibn Ezra composed commentaries which betray an exceptional mind and a colourful personality. He often shrouds his innermost thoughts in riddles and speaks of secrets hidden in commandments, stories and expressions. He is fond of allusions and hints, but is at pains to demonstrate with great learning and skill the literal meaning, especially of the preceptive part. His commentary on the Pentateuch ranks next to Rashi's in popularity; it has also produced many super-commentaries. But his commentary was in fact much more in need of explanation, through its terseness and its allusions. Daring in his independent approach, in his insistence on the *peshat* and rejection of the *derash*, and much in advance of his time in his literary criticism of the text of the Pentateuch and of Isaiah, he still stood four-square on the ground of traditional acceptance of the Pentateuch as Mosaic. But he held that some additions were made after Moses to the Pentateuch and that we have to distinguish a Second Isaiah from the first, although the latter opinion is more hinted at than openly expressed. But there applies to him what holds good for the religious philosophers as well: they accepted the revelation of the Torah on Sinai in the sight and hearing of the assembled children of Israel as an axiom of faith, because it was for the Jew a historical fact, not a myth. It would be wrong to make of Abraham ibn Ezra a Bible critic centuries before Higher Criticism. He was not only essentially a medieval man, but also a responsible spiritual leader of a community fighting for survival. Only in respect of one biblical book, the Song of Songs, did Abraham ibn Ezra adopt the allegorical method of interpretation, following Jewish tradition unquestioningly. He says in the introduction to his commentary that a secret meaning is contained and sealed up in this most excellent of all the songs of Solomon. But even in this commentary the allegorical method is only one other method next to the literal exposition, true to the general principle stated at the beginning of this chapter. For he says that he provides a threefold commentary: in the first place he explains every obscure word, next he sets out the contents according to its simple meaning, and in the third instance according to the method of *derash*.

His own method of interpretation is explicitly stated in the introduction to his commentary on the Pentateuch, and is set against four methods. The method practised by the *Geonim*, the spiritual leaders of Babylonian Jewry, contains unnecessary extraneous matter; yet he shows in his own commentaries a high regard for the greatest among them, Saadya Gaon. The method of the Karaites falls short of the true understanding of Scripture because it leaves out of consideration the accumulated tradition which, he holds, is of great help to the contemporary commentator. The method of Rashi and his school pays too much attention to the *derash* contained in Midrashic literature; it does not sufficiently follow the results of the scientific study of the Hebrew language and the dictates of reason. He allows the 'method of Midrash' only as a means of finding the inner connection of passages and chapters. Only by the strictest application of the laws of language and logic can we hope to penetrate to the plain, literal meaning of the text. For that reason, he completely rejects the allegorizing interpretation of the Christian sages, as he puts it, who say that the whole Torah consists of riddles and allegories, not only the whole of Genesis, but also all the laws and statutes and ordinances. To them, everything is a hint, an allusion. Thus, the twelve tribes typify the twelve apostles, and other words and passages are typologically interpreted to point to the Church as the heir of the Jews. We find the same attitude in David Kimhi, who, in his commentary on the Psalms, employs Christian terminology to refute Christian claims. Ibn Ezra denounces this method as vanity and hot air and insists that every commandment and every word is to be interpreted according to the scriptural wording. He admits that the Torah contains secrets, such as the tree of knowledge or paradise, and he appeals to the intellect implanted in us by God, to be a witness to the *peshat*. Once again, we see how closely linked are the literal meaning and the refutation of the Christian, spiritual, interpretation.

This is particularly striking in the case of David Kimhi (1160–1235), the son of Josef, a noted grammarian and exegete, and a brother of Moses who taught him. David began with grammatical studies and wrote his commentaries only afterwards. They were incorporated in the first printed Hebrew bibles, next to Rashi's. David Kimhi composed commentaries on all the prophets, on Chronicles and on Psalms. Of his commentary on the Pentateuch only that on Genesis has so far survived. The Kimhis completely share Ibn Ezra's attitude and method. David Kimhi is equally distinguished as a grammarian and lexicographer and as a Bible commentator. Of special interest is his commentary on the Psalms, which contains an introduction dealing with the phenomenon of prophecy (distinguishing it from inspiration by the Holy Spirit), and 'answers to the Christians'. He appended these to his comments on certain psalms claimed by the Christian interpreters to refer to Jesus. These 'answers' were collected into a separate treatise and frequently copied. Critical editions have been prepared of parts of Kimhi's commentaries over the last seventy years, based on manuscripts which had escaped censorship and which contain the refutation of Christological interpretation applied to parts of Psalms 2, 15, 19, 21, 45, 72, 87, and 110. A Latin translation by the Christian Hebraist Genebrardus was printed in 1566 at Paris.

It need not be stressed that these statements were by no means academic exercises; their topical relevance is also clear from Kimhi's introductory formulas, such as 'if somebody were to object, you must answer', or 'the Christians interpret this psalm as referring to Jesus' (or 'the Nazarene', 'that man'), or 'to their faith', 'but you must answer them [i.e. object]'. Kimhi insists, against the Christian claim that 'son' of Psalm 2 means Jesus, on the absolute, simple, undivided unity of God which makes it impossible for God, who is not body, to be divided as would be necessary on the Christian interpretation, since the Son is of the same kind as the Father. Moreover, the Son must be later than the Father, hence tri-unity is not possible. For if both were co-existent from all time one ought to call them twin brothers, not father and son. We can, he asserts, speak only metaphorically of God. He then deals with the Christian claim that the phrase *ask of me and I will give you nations as your inheritance* refers to Jesus. The logic of his rejoinder can hardly be denied, but in matters of faith this is not necessarily conclusive.

But since he, like all the Jewish exegetes who 'answered' Christian interpretation of this sort, was not aiming primarily to convince the Christians of the fallacy of their claim, but rather wished to provide an answer which would enable the Jews to withstand Christian proselytising activity and would fortify them in their inherited faith, his answers are not without interest. Says he:

if the son is God why should he ask his father? Has he no power over nations and the ends of the earth like him? They might point out that this happened after he had become flesh; God had referred to his humanity and promised, so to speak, inheritance to the son as man. But this is not so since he [Jesus] had no kingdom while in the flesh, nor any dominion over any nation. If they [the Christians] say that the psalm speaks of their faith...[object to them] that the majority, be they Jews or Muslims, have not accepted it.

This argument of the minority is also used by Ibn Ezra in his comment on Gen. xxvii. 40.

Another example is Kimhi's objection to the Christian interpretation of Psalm 19. The Christians maintain 'that the Torah has a limited time of validity, namely only until the time of Jesus' coming. Prior to his coming it was *corporealiter*, but when he came he commanded that it be understood *spiritualiter*. But their words are wind and vanity. For the commandments, which in their view are metaphorical and cannot be understood in their literal meaning, have been revealed by God with a clear exposition, not in a metaphor. Therefore, the other commandments must also be understood by man according to their literal meaning, not as an allegory.' He quotes Deut. xxx. 11–14 to prove that the commandments are actual and clear; if they were allegorical, men would be in doubt about them, and one would explain the hidden meaning one way and another another way.

Kimhi's arguments in the other psalms mentioned are similar in nature. He insists on the *peshat*, and on the basis of the unity and uniqueness of God denies the divine nature of Jesus; he asserts the continuing validity of the Torah and denies the messianic character of Jesus, since he has not fulfilled the prophecies concerning the Messiah at the end of days. The means which he employs are an appeal to grammar, e.g. in Psalm 87, and to history, and his demand for consistency when he denies that one can explain one passage of a psalm *corporealiter* and another *spiritualiter*. The few examples quoted show how he uses Christian terminology. Lack of space does not permit further examples in full, but I must at least refer to his denial that Psalm 110 refers to Jesus. He again resorts to grammatical objections which are incontrovertible and to prophetic passages (Malachi) which to his mind prove that the Torah will never be abrogated or changed, but will remain for ever as it was given to Moses on Sinai—adding that it was not given to Jesus. Elijah has not yet come again and will not come until the time of the Messiah (the Jews believe that Elijah will herald the coming of the Messiah and the final redemption). Kimhi insists that the *peshat* demands that this psalm be referred to David.

Assuredly, this polemic is only a small part of medieval Jewish exegesis. But it is an integral part of it, since its complement is the messianic interpretation which, as already stressed, occupies such a large space in the commentaries of Rashi and Kimhi and the others. They countered the Christian claim to the messiahship of Jesus with the positive assertion that the promises of the Messiah contained in the prophets, especially in Isa. ix and xi, and of the final redemption of Israel suffering in exile have still to be fulfilled. They see, therefore, references to their own time and to the redemption in many psalms as well, not only in the prophets. This is strikingly demonstrated by Kimhi in his commentary on the Psalter, for example on Psalms 10, 12, 29 and especially those contained in the fifth book, such as 108 and parts of 119–150. In addition, we meet with many a philosophical interpretation, often dependent on Maimonides' *Guide to the Perplexed*, for example in his definition of prophecy, in his teaching on the soul and the hereafter or in his exposition of the meaning of wisdom. In his ethics Kimhi leans on Ibn Gabirol and especially on Bahya ibn Pakuda, and a Neoplatonic strain is unmistakable. While such comments will have been appreciated by those of his readers who were acquainted with the religious philosophy of their day, Kimhi was not forgetful of the ordinary reader and tried to serve his needs as well. While strengthening his faith in redemption he gave him hope of messianic deliverance from exile if the Jews showed true repentance of their sins, were devout in loving service of God—he gives a moving definition of the 'servant of God'—by loyally fulfilling the commandments, which are not meant metaphorically and are still and will always remain obligatory. We see here again how the defence of Judaism against Christian claims and attempts at conversion was uppermost in his mind, as it was in that of many other exegetes whom we have met in this section.

The same features characterize the last great representative exegete at the end of our period, Don Isaac Abravanel (1437–1509). If anything, the Jewish position was by now much worse; the danger threatening from Dominican zeal was at its height, defection rife, and despair and despondency among those loyal to their religion and tradition growing deeper from day to day until 1492 brought the expulsion of the Jews from the Iberian peninsula. We must confine our attention to Abravanel's work as commentator; to this he brought many accomplishments which put him in a class apart from his predecessors, on whom he naturally leant. Philosophy and philosophical Bible exegesis are subordinated to a conservative reiteration of tradition and strict adherence to its sufficiency. He had learnt much from his Jewish predecessors, but also from Christian exegetes such as Jerome, Bede, Isidore of Seville, Albertus Magnus, Nicholas of Lyra and Paul of Burgos, a convert from Judaism. His method is scholastic in that he carefully reviews previous exegesis before giving his own explanation. He shows sound sense in his criticism, born of an unrivalled knowledge of affairs in the service of that king of Spain who decreed the expulsion of the Jews, and of other princes. His knowledge of past history, which he gained from Latin chronicles, is considerable and used judiciously, together with Jewish historical writings (*Josippon* or Pseudo-Josephus, Abraham ibn Da'ud's *Chronicle*). There is something of the humanist of the next age in him, something approaching the scientific spirit of the Renaissance. He anticipated what we call today the science of introduction to the Old Testament by his close attention to questions of date and authorship of the historical books of the Bible and of the hagiographa. His method of interpretation is naturally that of the *peshat*, and his strictures on his predecessors such as Rashi, Nachmanides and Abraham ibn Ezra were hardly justified, except in a purely formal sense and in so far as he sifted traditional material more critically, thanks to his greater resources. As a son of his age, he was more conservative in his attitude to rabbinic material, searching as his historical and literary criticism of it is. But Judaism had been forced back on itself, with terror, intimidation, discrimination and persecution growing in volume. Hence his insistence on the *peshat* within the confines of the text itself, and his reluctant recourse to a figurative interpretation where, and only where, a literal interpretation is contrary or inaccessible to human reason. For him the divinely revealed Torah is clear in its own terms; our understanding of it is aided by traditional exegesis used with discernment. His presentation—prefaced by a number of questions and an exposition of difficulties which are to be dealt with on the basis of previous Jewish and Christian exegesis—is orderly and systematic. His principal aim is the same as that of his Jewish predecessors, only its urgency is greatly heightened by the contemporary situation. Thus, he wanted 'to rouse his people Israel from the sleep of exile' by expounding to them the good tidings of the prophet Daniel. He demonstrated again and again with all the knowledge at his disposal that not one of the messianic prophecies had been fulfilled in Jesus during the second common-wealth. For him, that period was but an interlude and the first exile was still in being; soon, he was confident, to be terminated by the grace of God, who would send his promised Messiah to gather the exiles from the four corners of the earth and to redeem the land of Israel. In this vein he collected in a special treatise all the messianic passages in Scripture which might inspire hope in his generation, just as he held up Daniel as an example and preached repentance. As with his pre-decessors, the second purpose was the refutation of the Christian claim to the messiahship of Jesus, which the Dominicans maintained energetically in sermons which the Jews were forced to attend, and in treatises such as those of Geronimo de Santa Fé. Abravanel could claim to have provided a better answer than Nachmanides at Barcelona.

To illustrate his method of exegesis, his inquiry into the general character and meaning of Scripture under the four categories of Aristotelian philosophy may be sketched very briefly. Applying the three categories of purpose, matter and form to the Jewish and Chris-tian division of the Canon, he tries to show the superiority of the Jewish division into Law, Prophets and Writings over the four parts of the Christian division into legal, historical, prophetic and Wisdom literature. David must not, in his view, be counted among the prophets, for his Book of Psalms is only written under the influence of the Holy Spirit, as are the Writings. Therefore the Christian designation of *sapientes* is inadequate as it places these books on the same level as the writings of Aristotle and other philosophers.

That he should refer to contemporary events is only natural. Of poignant interest is a reference to the Marranos, or neo-Christians, many of whom secretly still practised their Judaism. Thus we read in his messianic treatises *The Salvation of His Anointed* and *The Wells of Salvation* (Commentary on Daniel):

...that in the midst of all the anguish and persecutions many of our nation leave the religious community and this is heresy, for through the wickedness of the nations hundreds of thousands of Jews have forcibly left the Lord... *until all kingdoms are changed to heresy* shows that this refers to all nations in general or to the wicked in particular, be it to Rome where our own eyes see in the kingdom of Spain that heretics increase and where they burn them because of their heresy *in thousands and myriads*...Also all the priests and bishops of Rome in this time run after profit, accept bribes and do not care for their religion...

These were clear signs that the Messiah would soon come and with him the end of the exile and the promised redemption. The prophecy of Daniel was about to be fulfilled. Rome, the fourth empire, was full of sin and corruption; it staggered to its destruction. Then the fifth empire, that of the king Messiah, would dawn upon mankind and bring redemption to the righteous of the Jews and of all nations.

Although the method of *peshat* had gained and maintained ascendancy over the figurative method, there were groups in medieval Jewry who raised their powerful voice in defence of a strictly rational interpretation of Scripture in order to bring out the inner, hidden (and to them real and true) meaning. For they would not admit that Reason could be in conflict with Revelation. Truth is one and indivisible, and revealed truth, contained in Scripture, contains nothing which runs counter to philosophical truth established by demonstrative proof. We have seen how Saadya dealt with this problem, balancing Reason with trustworthy tradition based on Revelation. Among his successors this balance was not always maintained, and often tilted towards a philosophical interpretation which set aside the plain meaning. This is not the place to argue about the possibility of complete agreement between the revealed truth, set forth in a comprehensive, prophetic law, and the Greek-Hellenistic philosophy and its man-made law. In our context, it is significant that the starting-point for the religious philosophers and exegetes alike was the Bible as revealed truth which had to be accepted as the basis of their speculation. Maimonides' *Guide* is largely philosophical interpretation of the Bible in an attempt to reconcile its doctrines with Aristotelian philosophy. For him the Bible contained

what philosophy taught. This necessitated at times a figurative interpretation and meant setting aside the literal meaning. But Maimonides
(1135–1206) was careful not to touch the basic tenets of his faith nor to
undermine the foundations of the Torah. This is evident from his
acceptance in its literal sense of the creation out of nothing, against
Aristotle's assumption of the eternity of matter. Since Aristotle did not
convince the metaphysician Maimonides, the traditionalist believer had
no difficulty in accepting the Word of God as it stood. But God being
incorporeal, anthropomorphisms had to be metaphorically explained
away. Angels were Aristotle's separate intelligences. On the other hand,
providence or reward and punishment were religious doctrines absolutely necessary for the life and faith of the people of Israel, the ordinary
believer as well as the elect few.

It is understandable that a storm broke over this allegorical interpretation of biblical doctrines and that contemporary Jewry was divided
into followers and opponents of Maimonides. The fact that the Church
relied on allegorical interpretation of the Old Testament complicated
the situation. In any case, the continued existence of Judaism demanded
the wholehearted fulfilment of the commandments, and any tampering
with the literal sense carried with it the danger of antinomianism. But
the addition of a philosophical interpretation to the literal one received
a tremendous stimulus through Maimonides' masterly exposition, and
we find in David Kimhi's commentaries frequent philosophical comments, including even Maimonides' interpretation of prophecy as a
natural phenomenon, the most controversial of all his teachings and
that which aroused most hostility among the traditionalists. Abravanel
did not defend Maimonides as Kimḥi had done, but occupied a middle
position. He respected the author of the *Guide* as his master so long as
he could square the philosophical explanation with the traditionally
accepted one based on the *peshat*. He accepted Reason as the handmaid
of Revelation, but he could not subscribe to the philosophers' opinion
that agreement between the two was possible and that it was rational
man's duty to achieve it. For him 'the way of the sages of Israel in their
wisdom received by tradition is as far removed from the ways of the
philosophers in their speculations and thoughts as East is from West'.
This is most marked in his concept of prophecy as the free gift of God
to any man he chooses, irrespective of his natural disposition and moral
and intellectual preparation and perfection. Maimonides differed from

Alfarabi, who furnished him with his psychological theory, only in his insistence that God could, if he so wished, withhold the gift of prophecy even from a man whose imagination and intellect were perfect. Yet in many a detail Abravanel followed Maimonides. The inescapable fact remains, as the poet-philosopher Judah Ha Levi (Hallewi, 1085–1141?) said, that the God of Abraham is not the God of Aristotle. A personal God of love, mercy and forgiveness, who in his goodness created the world for the good of man, and did so not of necessity but of his own free will, is the indispensable basis of Judaism, Christianity and Islam. Even the strictest of the Aristotelians among the Jews, Gersonides (Levi ben Gerson, 1288–1344), maintained this, though he accepted the eternity of matter. But he upheld voluntarism in God and creation in time and was a most acute exegete, combining *peshat* with a strictly Aristotelian philosophical interpretation.

The rational explanation of those biblical commandments which human reason could understand, as provided by Maimonides, did much to retain the loyalty of those whose contact with the regnant philosophy of the day had caused doubt and confusion in their minds. Before Maimonides, Saadya's division of the commandments—taken over from Muslim theology—into commandments of reason and commandments of revelation was widely accepted. The divinely revealed law contained both to perfection and both were equally obligatory for the faithful. Maimonides replaced this division by that into ceremonial laws, the reasons for which man cannot know, and judicial laws. In this as in others of his doctrines he influenced the scholastics, notably Alexander of Hales, Albert the Great and Thomas Aquinas, who often refers to 'R. Moyses'. Contact is not limited to such fundamental problems as the knowledge and perception of God, the creation out of nothing, divine attributes, angels and prophecy, but in the case of Thomas Aquinas extends even to Maimonides' detailed discussion of the biblical commandments in the third book of his *Guide*. A few illustrations may show this.

Thomas adds to Maimonides' two sources of the knowledge and perception of God, Revelation and Reason, a third, intuitive vision. It is the perception of God which for both leads man to his ultimate happiness in the hereafter. Both religious thinkers agree that the necessary foundation even for that knowledge which we can gain in this world already is faith. Thomas states the five reasons of 'R. Moyses' why this is so. Both accept Avicenna's doctrine that in God existence and essence are identical. Thomas goes some way with Maimonides in the latter's description of the divine attributes, but differs from him in his assumption that God's qualities are identical with his essence and then develops his own theory in conscious opposition to that of Maimonides, which he explicitly states.

A similar agreement in large measure can be seen in the question of the creation of the world. Thomas accepts Maimonides' arguments against its eternity, but seems to think that the creation out of nothing can be proved by demonstration, whereas Maimonides cannot find conclusive proof, and relies solely on faith which raises the philosophical possibility to religious certainty. Thomas uses Maimonides' exposition of the biblical creation story, but disagrees with the latter's view that the celestial bodies possess a soul. He also opposes his views on the angels and on prophecy, but agrees with his evaluation of the prophetic character of Moses as unique, that is, outside the natural disposition.

In dealing with the reasons for the biblical commandments Thomas Aquinas, like Alexander of Hales, sees in the ceremonial laws—going beyond Maimonides—a mystical significance in that they serve as a pointer to Christ. Thomas entirely agrees with Maimonides' explanation of the sacrifices and other specifically Jewish laws like circumcision or Sabbath observance. In the matter of judicial laws Thomas often accepts Maimonides' exposition, but he excludes the moral laws from them.

The philosophical exegesis was not only combated by those who adhered to the *peshat* and upheld the sufficiency of tradition, but also by the adherents of the *Kabbalah*, the Jewish mystics, from the twelfth century onwards. Like the rationalist thinkers, the mystics insist on the inner, hidden meaning of Scripture which they place above the literal sense and which they reach by a combination and manipulation of the letters making up a word in the text of the Bible and by computations based on the numerical value of the letters of the Hebrew alphabet. They recognized the literal meaning because they were, with few exceptions, anxious to remain loyal to Jewish tradition and to maintain normative Judaism intact and flexible. The century between 1150 and 1250 saw the mystical movement in Germany transplanted there from the East by the Kalonymos family. Eleazar of Worms made a notable contribution to biblical exegesis by his mystical explanations of the secrets hidden in the Torah, incorporating the teachings of Judah the Devout. The eschatological element was strong under the impact of the crusades, and the ideal of piety or devotion was expressed in the exegesis of the Bible as the 'tree of life' of Judaism. The German *Hasidim* ('pious', 'devout') had a tendency to asceticism and, according to I. F. Baer, were influenced in their social teaching and organization by a similar Christian movement, the Franciscan 'spirituals'. The mystical movement gathered momentum in Spain in the thirteenth century and the resultant literature centres in the Bible. The main influence was Nachmanides (Moses ben Nachman, 1195–1270), whose commentary on the Pentateuch contains mystical allusions and hints in addition to the primary exposition according to the *peshat*. His disciple Bahya ben Asher also wrote a commentary on the Pentateuch from 1291 onwards, which contains explanations employing four different methods of exegesis, *peshat*, *midrash*, *sekhel* and *kabbalah*. The first two are the well-established methods, the third is the philosophical exegesis which Bahya accepts as long as it does not run counter to the text and tradition. The fourth is the new method, which he stresses and which he develops on the basis of earlier mystical works. The four methods roughly correspond to those adopted by the basic mystical work of the middle ages, the *Zohar*, which exercised such a tremendous influence over the Jews for centuries and is at the centre of the kabbalistic vogue in the sixteenth century among Christians. They are, adapted to Jewish concepts and needs, the Christian methods of *historia* (*peshat*), *tropologia* (*derash*), *allegoria* (*remez*, 'allusion', 'hint') and *anagogia* (*sod*, 'mystery', 'hidden secret'). Bahya combines in his term *kabbalah* both *remez* and *sod*. The *Zohar* is now ascribed to Moses de Leon, who, according to G. Scholem, came from philosophic enlightenment to mysticism. The *Zohar* is the answer of the late thirteenth century to rationalism; it interprets the Torah mystically and, according to G. Scholem, attempts to preserve the substance of naïve popular faith. The Torah is a vast *corpus mysticum* wherein the Kabbalists 'discover layer upon layer of hidden meaning'. An investigation of its literary sources has underlined the basic unity of Jewish exegesis, which allows of several meanings alongside each other while stressing now the one and now the other. All the commentators discussed in this section occur in quotations in the *Zohar*: Rashi, Kimḥi, Ibn Ezra, Nachmanides, and there is evidence of a sound knowledge of the grammatical and lexicographical literature. The mystics pursued the same aim as the philosophers and the traditionalists, though their ways were different from each other, namely to draw near to God in knowledge and love. All four methods of biblical exegesis are pressed into the service of this task.

Medieval Jewish exegesis succeeded in keeping alive the spirit of the Bible; together with the fulfilment of the commandments, it preserved Judaism for the Jews; it also made an important contribution to Christianity by helping to establish that *Hebraica veritas* at which the Reformation aimed in its struggle for the authority of the Word of God.

CHAPTER VII

THE 'PEOPLE'S BIBLE': ARTISTS AND COMMENTATORS

In the eyes of the biblical writers, the course of history seemed to be not only the training-ground of the human spirit but also a sphere in which were displayed the workings of the power of God. History might thus provide abundant examples of the faithfulness, or the perversity, with which mankind responds to the unshakeable 'commandments and statutes and judgements of the Lord', yet it is more than the 'storehouse containing all the countless lessons of the past', which Cicero held it to be, since it bears the majestic impress of the divine. The richly significant run of events is therefore to be valued, both for its own sake, as a story with a moral, and as offering intimations and symbols of a deeper truth: in the language of Sir Thomas Browne, 'unspeakable mysteries are delivered in a vulgar and illustrative way' because 'while we are veiled in with mortality, truth must veil itself too, that it may the more fully converse with us'. The historical writings of the Old and New Testament serve to teach men the lessons which make them wise unto salvation, and also by their hints of 'something far more deeply interfused' propose limitless subjects for contemplation and reverence. Christian history teaches and suggests, and what applies to Christian history applies to Christian art as well.

The early painters and sculptors record biblical scenes in faithful and naïvely literal fashion; yet symbolism keeps breaking in, since the events acquire fuller dignity and importance as offering glimpses of supernatural truth. In other words, the picture is used to express something beyond that which is, or was at the time, immediately apparent, and to arouse in the spectator feelings and thoughts derived from the event which is actually portrayed. The earliest Christian art, that of the Roman catacombs, is symbolic through and through. In the graceful, if sometimes roughly executed, forms of the contemporary Pompeian style which they readily adopted, Christian artists decorated the catacombs with such badges as the anchor, suggesting 'hope' in accordance with the language of Heb. vi. 19, or a dove, type of the Divine Wisdom and of gentleness, as indicated by Matt. x. 16. Another emblem, found in the crypt of Lucina and elsewhere in the catacombs, is the fish, which serves at once to recall the feeding of the five thousand and the continuance of this miracle in the common life of the Church through the provision of the Eucharist by the Lord, who is referred to, in the second-century *Inscription of Abercius*, as 'the huge, pure Fish from the fountain which faith provides as food'. Such emblems suggest rather than define; and, though the eucharistic associations of the fish-symbol appear to be uppermost in the artist's mind, there may well be an allusion also to the sacrament of baptism whereby, as Tertullian puts it in a contemporary treatise, 'we little fishes, following the example of our Fish, Jesus Christ, are born in water'.

Anchor, dove and fish, however, act but as badges which remind the faithful of scriptural passages and their import. Elsewhere in the catacombs, scenes from the Gospel story or from Old Testament history are set forth realistically enough but with concise simplicity. Mark, writing his Gospel to show that Jesus is the Christ and to provide convenient stories for use by the preachers of salvation, leaves out many interesting points of biography and nowhere attempts a description of the Master's appearance. So in the paintings which bedeck the walls of the catacombs all unnecessary detail is omitted, and the artist concerns himself with the task of showing just so much of the incident which he depicts as declares it to be a mighty work of God. Noah stands in his ark without any of the attendant beasts or the members of his family who play their part in the narrative of Genesis, while, to take a New Testament example, the healing of the paralysed man (Mark ii. 1–12) may be depicted in so curt a fashion that the paralytic is to be seen clasping his bed on to his back but the Healer nowhere appears.

The choice of subjects, no doubt influenced by the fact that catacombs are places of burial, serves to stress God's victorious might, which will uphold the believer in the day of persecution and bring him safely through the valley of the shadow of death. Moses striking the rock with his rod so that 'the water came forth abundantly' is the scene from the Old Testament that is most frequently illustrated. Next in popularity comes Jonah, whose colourful story of deliverance no doubt gained added lustre from its use in the Gospel (Matt. xii. 40) to prophesy resurrection. Daniel in the lions' den and Noah with his ark also occur quite often, followed, in order of choice, by the sacrifice of Isaac and by the three young men in the fiery furnace (Daniel iii). Scenes of this kind, put forth in the crabbed and allusive style of painting which would yet be clear enough to the initiate who knew anything of the Scriptures, served as a kind of pictorial litany whereby God is reminded of the help which he has bestowed on the heroes of old in their distress and invited to continue that help in the no less troubled days of Marcus Aurelius or Decius.

A similar principle governs the choice of subjects drawn from the New Testament, of which the raising of Lazarus, occurring some fifty-three times in the Roman catacombs, was the favourite. Jesus, clad in an ample robe, is shown holding up a magician's wand as if to proclaim that to him alone has been entrusted all power in heaven and earth. He extends his hand towards a tomb, constructed in the form of a little shrine, in which the mummified form of Lazarus, tightly bound in his grave-clothes, stands upright. (Plate 4.) No attempt is made to include Mary or Martha or the band of spectators mentioned in the Johannine account. The opportunity to produce a vivid picture with attractive groupings of characters, and the portrayal of a wide range of emotions, is utterly disregarded, the aim being not so much to represent the occurrence exactly as to draw out its essential meaning for the early Church. Another picture frequently to be seen in the frescoes of the catacombs is that of the miraculous feeding, though the artist does not always make it clear whether he has in mind the feeding of the five thousand or the meal eaten by the sea of Tiberias (John xxi): some-times, indeed, he seems concerned only to show, in general terms, a solemn fellowship meal which prefigures the heavenly feasting to be enjoyed in the pastures of the blessed.

It is notable that, while several of the Lord's mighty works are freely, if compactly, shown forth on the walls of the catacombs, neither the Crucifixion nor the Resurrection is anywhere depicted. The reasons for this have been long debated. Some have held that the motive which restrained the artists was fear lest the deepest mysteries of the faith should be openly declared to pagan eyes, though this is not a very convincing argument when applied to an underground burial place. A more likely explanation is that the Church took over from its Jewish ancestry a horror of any attempt to represent the divine and a mood of reverence which instinctively felt that the incarnate Lord, in the most

solemn moments of his earthly life, must elude the normal methods of
artistic usage. Be that as it may, no earlier representation of Christ
crucified is to be found than that carved on the wooden door of the
church of S. Sabina at Rome, which was built about 430. (Plate 5.)
In the paintings of the catacombs, Christ is frequently shown forth as
Saviour, but, here again, a compressed and allusive style is preferred.
Instead of narrative pictures illustrating particular incidents of the
Gospel story, Christ appears no less than 114 times in the guise of a
shepherd boy bearing a sheep upon his shoulders. (Plate 6.) The precise form of the picture no doubt owes something to earlier representations of Hermes, for the Christian artists had few scruples about
adapting pagan art-forms to their own uses, but the inspiration is
scriptural. Ezekiel (xxxiv. 23) had proclaimed the divine message 'I will
set up one shepherd over them, and he shall feed them, even my servant
David; he shall feed them and he shall be my shepherd', or, in the words
of the second Isaiah (xl. 12), 'He shall feed his flock like a shepherd; he
shall gather the lambs with his arm'. Language of this sort found an
echo in the parable (Luke xv. 4) of the shepherd who searches for the
lost sheep and a fulfilment in the Johannine discourse concerning 'the
good shepherd who layeth down his life for the sheep'. Christ is therefore presented to the worshippers in the catacombs not simply in
realistic terms as a Galilean peasant who lived when Pontius Pilate was
procurator, but rather as a second David, powerful to deliver his sheep
from harm and uphold them even in death. Over against this representation of the Saviour often stands the *Orans*, or figure with hands raised
in supplication, and the message of the Bible is thus compressed into
the two figures which stand for mankind pleading and God answering
prayer.

The paintings, executed in about the year 240, in the oldest Christian
house-church still existing, at Doura Europus on the upper Euphrates,
reveal the same interests and the same treatment of biblical texts. On
the west wall Adam and Eve are to be seen, placed one on each side of
the fatal tree, with pilasters to indicate the walls of the earthly Paradise.
Above, and on a much larger scale, stands the Good Shepherd, with a
huge ram on his shoulders. The seventeen horned sheep which make up
the flock are shown, without any of that symmetry which Italian artists
preferred, in what has been called the 'narrative style of the east'. The
north wall exhibits three scenes, one of which may be the women at

Christ's tomb, though the interpretation is far from certain. The other two can be recognized easily enough. In the first place, the paralytic man of Capernaum appears, bearing away his bed upside down on his back (Mark ii). But now the occasion is depicted with greater fullness than is usual in the catacombs, for as well as its triumphant conclusion the beginning of the miracle is shown, where Christ, a beardless young man dressed in tunic and mantle, stretches out his hand in a gesture of compassionate power over the invalid. Nearby Peter's attempt to walk on the water (Matt. xiv) is illustrated. Peter's whole posture, as he reaches upwards to grasp Christ's hand, suggests that he is about to sink, while the brightly painted ship and the varied colours of the tunics worn by the apostles stand out sharply against the drab foreground of light brown water. On another wall of the Doura house-church are painted David and Goliath, now much damaged, and, nearby, the Samaritan woman (John iv) stooping in a free and graceful manner over the well. When compared with the catacomb paintings, those at Doura exhibit a similar interest in proclaiming God's power to intervene in time of need, but they tell their story in a somewhat less curt and impressionistic fashion and allow the introduction of figures subsidiary to the main action.

A similar development is seen in the stone coffins, or sarcophagi. The earliest Christian sarcophagi take over the themes of the Good Shepherd and the *Orans*, and to these is added the typical 'philosopher', half-naked, with unkempt hair and ecstatic gaze. The philosopher is often shown clasping a book, to indicate that the sincere Christian finds, through the Gospel, the true, indeed the only important, knowledge which enables him to pass safely through the shades and enter the gates of paradise. A little later, this simple scheme acquires a clearer biblical reference. The sarcophagus preserved in the church of S. Maria Antiqua at Rome, for instance, shows not only the basic symbols of Good Shepherd and *Orans* but also, as a reminder of effective prayer, Jonah cast up by the whale, over against the *Orans*, while a representation of Christ's baptism in Jordan, placed near the figure of the Good Shepherd, indicates the redeeming power of God and the means whereby, in the Church, man may avail himself of it. The Christian sarcophagi of the third century are nearly always so designed as to convey through their carvings a message of the dangers of life, typified by ferocious lions, together with the certainty of death and the need of a Saviour. But the mood of confidence which followed the accession of Constantine caused a certain widening of interest as well as an alteration of style in Christian art. The time-honoured figures—Jonah, Lazarus, the young men in the fiery furnace—who recalled mighty deliverances wrought by God, still find a place, at any rate for a time, on the carved sarcophagi, but they are jostled, in the crowded compositions which came to be the fashion, by a variety of biblical scenes. In selecting these, the sculptor seems to have been influenced by the thought that the events recorded in the Bible possess high value as declaring God's nature and proclaiming his glory. Sometimes the desire to include as many scenes as possible makes them not only less attractive but also difficult to interpret. By the middle of the fourth century, however, a combination of eastern rhythm and narrative power with western orderliness serves to produce sarcophagi on which the carving is of high artistic quality and the Bible stories are illustrated by a series of panels divided from each other by columns. The most famous example of this style is the stone coffin of Junius Bassus, dated 359, and found in St Peter's church at Rome. (Plate 7.) Here the sculptures are arranged in two lines, and the subjects run thus: (i) the sacrifice of Isaac, (ii) the arrest of Peter, (iii) Christ, shown as a beardless youth, sitting enthroned above the pagan sky-god with Peter and Paul standing on either hand, (iv) Christ being led before Pilate, (v) Pilate on his judgement-seat, with a servant preparing the water so that he might wash his hands before the multitude, (vi) Job seated disconsolate on his dung-hill, (vii) Adam and Eve, with the serpent coiled round the tree, (viii) Christ's triumphal entry into Jerusalem, (ix) Daniel in the lions' den (a modern restoration), (x) Paul led off to execution. Inset between the two rows of panels diminutive carvings of animals appear which in allegorical fashion suggest (i) the three men in the fiery furnace, (ii) a miracle attributed to Peter whereby, like Moses of old, he produced water by striking a rock, (iii) Christ's baptism, (iv) the multiplication of loaves and fishes, (v) Moses receiving the Law, and (vi) Lazarus.

The whole carving displays skill of a high order, each panel being marked by vivid realism, but the run of the scenes is not quite as might have been expected, and it has been suggested that the sculptor transposed the sacrifice of Isaac, which would better suit the Old Testament subjects in the lower row, and Paul being led to execution, which accords well with the New Testament scenes above. The three representations of Christ offer interesting contrasts in the manner of interpreting his nature. He sits on the donkey that bears him to Jerusalem and to his doom, as a graceful and attractive youth—a second David—with an expression on his face of thoughtful, half-smiling resolve. But when he appears before Pilate it is, in the late medieval fashion, as a 'man of sorrows and acquainted with grief'. Shown, however, as enthroned above the sky-god, he is, once more, portrayed as a youth with long, curly hair, though this time he is unsmiling, calm and dignified, as befits a heavenly judge, and clasps the roll of the Gospels in his left hand, while his right hand is raised in the act of blessing.

In the course of the fourth century, then, artists felt free to draw out now one aspect, now another, of Christ's person and work. The primitive symbolism of the Good Shepherd yields to the biblical Christ shown forth not only as deliverer but also in glory, and fashions of portraiture are set which continue throughout the years.

As the architecture of Christian churches developed, so the paintings which decorated the walls became more elaborate. But their primary purpose was to instruct. Nilus of Sinai laid down the rule, in about 430, that churches should never be decorated with such pictures as hunting-scenes, but that incidents drawn from the Old Testament and the New should appear on the walls of churches, so that those who were unable to read might contemplate the paintings, note the example of the saints and strive to copy in their own lives the virtues thus suggested; for it appears to be true that, as Horace said, 'less keenly are our spirits stirred by what passes through the ear than by what is set before our trustworthy eyes'. Just as the great majority of paintings in the cata-combs had illustrated events recorded in the Old Testament, so the artists commissioned to provide a series of pictures whether in manu-scripts or on the walls of churches showed the same preference at first for incidents in the history of the Old Israel. Eastern examples are hard to find, since the tendency in Asia was rather towards magnificence of decoration than any attempt to illustrate Bible stories, and those Byzantine chroniclers who attribute to Constantine the desire that his churches should display in sequence the incidents of Christ's life for the benefit of the unlettered are attributing to him ideas which were not current in imperial circles until a much later date. But in the West it was different. As early as about 500 the 'Vienna Genesis' appeared, displaying an attractive series of forty-eight miniatures arranged in orderly fashion to illustrate events from the Fall to the death of Jacob. (Plate 8.)

One example may be taken, the scene (Gen. xxxii. 6–8) where Jacob 'divided the people that was with him' and the animals into two companies so that, if Esau should attack one company, the other might have opportunity to escape. The text is written above, on a purplish ground; then, in the illustration, two angels are shown: their white garments are shaded with blue and they have long white wings touched with gold. The artist evidently made a mistake, and supposed the 'messengers' referred to in the story to be angels. Jacob stands before them, his hands raised in a gesture of anxious questioning.

In a second scene, below this, Jacob stands between the two groups into which his followers have been divided. At his right is a woman clothed in white and, next to her, another woman wrapped in a cloak of brilliant red. On his left are two more women clad in garments of bright and contrasting colours, while on both sides a varied selection of vigorously drawn animals is to be seen. The style, as in other more or less contemporary manuscripts, is that of unadorned narrative which presents a marked contrast to the crabbed symbolism often found in the catacombs. For, in general, the practice of extracting a small part of a well-known incident and using it to represent the whole yields to keener artistic and historic sensibilities which demand a fuller and more arresting picture. The sketch of Moses striking the rock in order to provide water for the Israelites is now amplified into a graceful scene which includes the figures of the men assuaging their thirst, while Daniel in the lions' den is shown, according to the story found in *Bel and the Dragon*, eating the dinner provided by the prophet Habakkuk, whom the angel had raised up by the hair of his head and deposited in Babylon.

The extension of one picture into two or more may be due to a desire to give the cause of some notable incident, as when the popular illustration of the three young men in the fiery furnace is accompanied by another showing their refusal to worship the golden image set up by Nebuchadnezzar. Biographical interests have also to be reckoned with. The Jews produced their Haggadah and the Christians their body of apocryphal legends in order to satisfy the curiosity of those who asked what happened next to famous persons who drift off into darkness from the biblical page; and this desire to know the rest of the story is ministered to by the artists no less than by the writers. Again, such accounts as those of Adam and Eve demand more than one picture if their various aspects are to be stressed and their theological implications drawn out. It is no longer felt sufficient to show the ancestors of the human race standing on either side of the tree: this scene has to be prefaced with one or more illustrations of the way in which God creates the world, and the oldest of such representations is perhaps the carved panel of a sarcophagus found in St Paul's church, Rome, in 1838. Here, in the first scene, three men appear, bearded, reverend and grave. One, seated on a throne, raises his hand in a solemn gesture. Before him stands another such figure, placing his hand on the head of a diminutive human being, who appears to be Eve, while Adam lies naked on the ground nearby. The third bearded figure stands quietly behind the throne, and it seems that, though some interpret them as angels, the three in fact represent the Trinity. It is however curious that in the next scene the figure, no doubt the Word of God active upon earth, who offers a handful of corn-stalks to Adam and a lamb to Eve is a beardless youth: the fashion of representing Christ as the second David prevails over consistency. This attempt to depict the Trinity in terms of three stately personages became frequent from the tenth century onwards. God had been described as saying 'Let us make man in our image' and these words were taken to imply one person talking to two other persons of identical appearance. Sometimes the artist went so far in his desire to show the unity in trinity that he draped a large mantle over all three figures. Others, however, declined to treat the subject with such naïve realism, and composed a picture in which the Father sits, in impressive majesty, on his throne, while the Son hangs on the Cross and the Holy Ghost, in the form of a dove, hovers nearby. This doctrine of the threefold nature of God could be portrayed in still more symbolic fashion; and as early as 400 Paulinus, bishop of Nola, described a wall-painting in the basilica of St Felix in which the Lamb of God appears, accompanied by the Dove, while from the clouds above stretches down the hand of God which typifies the creative power.

The early popularity of Old Testament subjects is exemplified by the splendid mosaics to be seen in the church of S. Maria Maggiore, at Rome. (Plate 9.) The nave is decorated with a series of panels, possibly part of the structure erected by Pope Liberius about 360, but more probably the work of Xystus III eighty years later. Twenty-seven panels remain out of an original forty-two, illustrating a variety of events from the meeting of Abraham with Melchizedek down to the execution by Joshua's orders of the five kings captured in the cave of Makeddah. Some of the incidents possess theological importance, and for that reason became favourites at any period, while others, as it would seem, owe their place to the appeal exercised on the artist by a colourful and vigorous story. When Abraham entertains the three angels by the oaks of Mamre, the scene is no doubt intended to suggest the Trinity to fifth-century Romans just as it did to Russians a thousand years later when Andrew Rublev painted the most famous of all icons. The appearance of Melchizedek is no less significant. In the Epistle to the Hebrews he had been taken as an Old Testament type of Christ, and the early Fathers were not slow to point out significant details in the narrative of Genesis whereby Abraham, the father of the Israelite nation, pays tithe to Melchizedek, the mysterious priest-king 'without father, without mother', who in his turn offers the gifts of bread and wine which could be held to anticipate the Eucharist. The sixth-century mosaics of S. Apollinare in Classe at Ravenna draw out the meaning. (Plate 10.) An altar is shown covered with an embroidered white cloth and having upon it circular loaves and a two-handled cup. At one side of the altar stands Abel offering a lamb while opposite him Abraham presents his son. Behind the altar Melchizedek is to be seen, wearing priestly garments and a royal diadem. He is portrayed on a larger scale than the other figures and, holding a loaf in his hands, he consecrates it in the manner of Christ. In other words, an Old Testament character, with all the associations attaching to him, is shown as a substitute for the person of whom he is regarded as the type. At S. Maria Maggiore, then, some of the scenes were no doubt chosen for their figurative value, but no pictures of New Testament events actually accompany them. The symbolism is still concealed, and it was left for later artists to draw this out into the open by setting Gospel fulfilment alongside the earlier event. It was felt that God, while directing the course of Israelite history, was also pointing onward to more important events, so that what appear to be quite trivial incidents in the biblical record may be charged with deep significance as prophecies, and in this way a close connection and sympathy exist between Old Testament and New (see above, pp. 157ff. and 195 for considerations of typology).

This view of Old Testament incidents as possessing both historical interest and importance in that they are prophecies or types of what is to come seems to have been that of Christ himself. 'As Moses lifted up the serpent in the wilderness, even so must the Son of Man be lifted up': thus, according to John's Gospel, did Christ foretell his crucifixion in terms of the occasion (Num. xxi) when Moses preserved the people of Israel from the attacks of fiery serpents by 'making a serpent of brass and setting it upon a standard'. By means of a similar argument it is explained that 'as Jonah was three days and three nights in the belly of the whale, so shall the Son of Man be three days and three nights in the heart of the earth'. Paul treated the Old Testament Scriptures in the same fashion. Abraham's two sons, 'one by the handmaid and one by the freewoman' (Gal. iv), are real persons whose adventures help to make up the history of the chosen people, but they have value also, for those who have eyes to see, as indicating the contrast between the earthly Jerusalem, standing for Judaism, and the spiritual Jerusalem in which every Christian has a share. Again, the experiences of the Israelites as they journeyed towards the promised land (I Cor. x) have, in the providential ordering of things by God, a lasting function to serve as lessons for the Church: 'they were written for our admonition, upon whom the ends of the ages are come.'

It was of even greater importance for Christian artists that, in the Epistle to the Hebrews, close parallels are drawn between the tabernacle and the sacrifices of the old covenant on the one hand and the sacrificial death of Christ on the other. For this clearly implies that the ordinances of the old covenant offer hints and intimations of the new. Here too there is no thought that the Hebrew sacrifices had been empty gestures as far as the men of earlier days were concerned. Rather the argument runs that the one God, who speaks in both Testaments, so ordained Israelite forms and directed Israelite history that these serve as valuable pointers preparing men for fulfilments in the Christian dispensation. A keen, Hebraic sense of the historical and the concrete kept most Christian writers from drifting over into vague allegorizing, but it is not surprising that their Neoplatonist rivals exclaimed in vexation against people like Origen who 'boast that the things said plainly by Moses are riddles, and treat them as divine oracles full of hidden mysteries'. The lines of scriptural interpretation which prevailed throughout the middle ages are laid down by Augustine (*Comm. in Exodum* 73) when he says *In veteri testamento novum latet, in novo vetus patet* (In the Old Testament the New lies hid; in the New Testament the Old becomes clear), a principle which Vincent of Beauvais amplifies in the words: 'The new law is contained in the old just as corn is contained in the ear: for everything which the New Testament puts forward for us to believe clearly and openly is to be found in the Old Testament by implication or in symbol.'

It is often quite impossible to understand a medieval artist's treatment of an incident drawn from the Bible story unless his love of symmetry is remembered, and his conviction that events described in the New Testament are the richer and more significant counterpart of those recorded in the Old. Whereas in our own day much store is set by originality and freshness in the choice of a subject, the painters or sculptors of the middle ages were well content to restrict themselves to quite a small number of favourite themes, which seemed to provide an unending stimulus to devout contemplation. The original text of the Bible, difficult to understand and not always easy of access, was not frequently consulted by such persons, who tended to rely on popular summaries. As early as about 520 Elpidius Rusticus, a deacon of Lyons who became court physician to the Ostrogoth kings, composed verses in which events of the Old Testament and the New are paired together; for instance Isaac bears the wood (*lignum*) of sacrifice as Christ bears the wood (*lignum*) of the Cross, or again just as Joseph was sold by his brethren so was Christ sold by Judas. A century later Isidore, bishop of Seville, composed handy books of reference which contained a wide variety of Old Testament texts and prophecies ranged over against incidents recorded in the life of Christ; indeed, on Isidore's view the whole of Scripture with its boundless store of history, allegory and moral instruction is rightly compared to a harp with strings of infinite resonance. And it was not only a matter of texts. In the Epistle to the Hebrews (xi) occurs a long line of patriarchs who displayed exemplary faith even though they 'received not the promise'. The Church Fathers, from the time of Clement of Rome onwards, used these and other such heroes of the Old Testament as instructive patterns of moral conduct. Isidore treats them in a different manner, which was to have considerable influence on the course of medieval art, for he takes them to be symbols of Christ and his work. The notices about each figure are concise but to the point; the first three run as follows: 'Adam displayed the characteristics of Christ; for just as he was made on the sixth day in the image of God, so in the sixth age of the world the Son of God put on the form of flesh, that is to say he received the form of a servant in order that he might create men again in the likeness of God.' 'Eve stands for the Church that was brought into existence through the mysterious stream which flowed from the side of Christ as he was dying.' 'Abel, pastor of the sheep, hinted at Christ, who is the true pastor, laying down his life for his sheep, and sure to come again as ruler of his faithful people.'

This discovery of significant correspondences between the Old Testament and the New was diligently pursued. It receives artistic expression in one of the medallions which the abbot Suger introduced, about the middle of the twelfth century, into his church of St Denis, near Paris. Christ is here shown standing between two female figures. With his right hand he crowns the Church, while with his left hand he tears away the veil with which the face of the Synagogue has been covered. A short inscription provides all that is needful by way of commentary: 'What Moses veils, the teaching of Christ unveils.' Another medallion, now destroyed, in this series used to present similar teaching in an equally popular but slightly different form. The prophets were shown pouring grain into a hand-mill, while Paul turned the wheel and collected the flour. Another text offered the explanation: 'You, Paul, by driving the mill-stone round, produce flour from chaff; you make clear the meaning of the details of the law of Moses.' In other words, the rough, crude material of which many Old Testament prophecies consist is purified and transformed, when Paul is there to play the part of interpreter, into the saving doctrines of the New Testament.

An indication of the widespread and influential nature of this kind of biblical criticism is furnished by the so-called *Biblia Pauperum*. (Plates 12–13 and see also pp. 332 ff.) The name, which is lacking in the earliest manuscripts, seems to mean that the book was a bible rendered in a compressed and popular manner that might supply poor preachers of no great intellectual attainment with material for their sermons and with pictures which could be shown to simple and un-lettered folk. Each *Biblia Pauperum* contained thirty-four scenes (forty or even forty-eight in some late examples), drawn from the New Testament, beginning with the Annunciation and ending with the descent of the Holy Ghost and a subject not derived from the biblical narrative, the coronation of the Virgin. Each of these pictures was set between representations of two Old Testament incidents which seemed to prefigure the happening recorded in the New, while above and below appeared four prophets with appropriate texts. The page was completed by some explanatory comment on the two Old Testament scenes. The triumphal entry into Jerusalem may be taken as an example. In the centre Christ is shown quietly riding on the donkey and raising his right hand to bless the crowd. Peter, distinguished by a large key which he holds, walks alongside, and the crowd is represented by some children, one of whom has climbed up into a palm tree while others pluck off its lower branches.

One of the Old Testament types is the scene when the women of 'all the cities of Israel' come out to meet David, after his victory over Goliath. David, a boyish figure, holds Goliath's head in his left hand and a large sword in his right. Three women stand opposite, one beating a tambourine with two sticks. The other Old Testament incident shown is the 'sons of the prophets' coming to greet Elisha in the conviction that 'the Spirit of Elijah doth rest on him' (II Kings ii. 15). At the top of the whole picture the crowned figure of David may be seen, together with his text 'Let the daughters of Zion rejoice in the King', a variant of Ps. 149:2. On the other side is Solomon, also crowned, and bearing his text, which may be drawn from Song of Songs iii. 11, 'Go forth, O ye daughters of Zion', but sometimes echoes the language of Zechariah.

Below the illustrations are two other prophecies. A man in a peaked hat, who must be Isaiah, proclaims (lxii. 11) 'Say ye to the daughter of Zion, Behold, thy King cometh', 'King' being substituted for the word 'salvation', found in the original text, by confusion with the prophecy of Zechariah, who appears opposite Isaiah, wearing a round hat and declaring (ix. 9) that the King would come 'riding upon a colt the foal of an ass'. The form of presentation is the same throughout. Thus, on the next page, Christ is shown raising his scourge in order to drive the money-changers from the Temple. On the left, Artaxerxes is shown granting the Jews, represented by Ezra, leave to rebuild the Temple (Ezra vii), while, opposite, three Jews stand before Judas Maccabaeus, who has arranged for the Temple, which the Gentiles had profaned, to be dedicated afresh (I Macc. iv).

The oldest manuscripts of the *Biblia Pauperum* date from the beginning of the fourteenth century, and the almost complete identity in the selection of scenes and in the commentary points to an original from which others were quickly copied. But, though the oldest examples of this book belong to South Germany or Austria, their typological scheme so closely suggests that which may be seen in the statuary of the elaborate façades of the cathedrals at Reims, Chartres and Laon as to make it seem certain that the first *Biblia Pauperum* was drawn up in northern France. The strictly biblical form of its typology receives no additions in the shape of those symbolic animals—lion, pelican, phoenix or unicorn—which achieved high popularity in the later middle ages, and the original text was probably composed, without illustrations, in the eleventh century.

Another influential commentary which helped to dictate the forms of medieval art was the *Glossa Ordinaria* (Plates 14–15) or 'Standard Commentary on the Bible', which may be compared with the standard commentary drawn up by twelfth- and thirteenth-century lawyers of Bologna to accompany the body of Roman law as this had been codified by Justinian (see above, pp.145ff.,190,205). The biblical *Glossa Ordinaria* has often been attributed to Walafrid Strabo, who became abbot of Reichenau in 838, but it is more correctly assigned to Anselm of Laon and his pupils working at Laon and Auxerre. Anselm and the members of his school, in producing their vast compilation, were indebted to such earlier commentators as Isidore of Seville and Rabanus Maurus, whose zeal for encyclopaedic study earned for him the title 'tutor of Germany'.

The *Glossa Ordinaria*, then, contains a hotch-potch of material drawn from the writings of the early Church Fathers and added to in the spirit of those who regard all Scripture as a 'mystery' and who seek, in the manner of Origen, to 'discover in every expression the hidden splendour of doctrines veiled in common and unattractive phraseology'. Early manuscripts of the *Glossa Ordinaria*, which was probably the source from which the author of the *Biblia Pauperum* collected his material, are so arranged that on each page a small portion of text is surrounded by a considerable amount of commentary. The notes vary in character. Some are critical and scholarly, but a large number reflect the spirit of a meditative and monastic piety. One example may be selected: the passage (Gen. vi. 14–16) where Noah is ordered to build the ark: 'Make thee an ark of planed timbers: rooms shalt thou make in the ark and shalt smear it within and without with pitch. And this is how thou shalt make it: the length of the ark three hundred cubits, the breadth of it fifty cubits, and the height of it thirty cubits. A window shalt thou make to the ark, and with a cubit shalt thou finish off its height; and the door of the ark shalt thou set in its side.' The commentary starts with a discussion of the meaning of the words which appear in the Vulgate as *ligna levigata,* or planed timbers, but are more accurately rendered as 'of gopher wood'. Then the author allows himself to speculate on the subject of the rooms which the ark contained, and he comes to the conclusion that there were five of these; a place for refuse, then a store-room, then, higher up, quarters for 'savage animals and serpents', for tame animals, and, finally, for men and birds. The commentary continues:

Noah built the ark of incorruptible timbers as Christ built the Church with men who were going to live for eternity, and the Church floats above the waters of tribulation just as the Ark floats on the waves. The ark is made up of squared timbers; so the Church, made up of saints whose life is firm and ready for all good works, resembles squared timbers that stand firm at every point. The timbers are fixed together with pitch inside and outside, so that this compact unity may symbolize charitable patience, the virtue which prevents the Church from being so disturbed by those within or without as to depart from brotherly concord. For pitch is the hottest and strongest form of glue and it symbolizes the fervour of charity and its strength for holding together a society which endures all things. Now the fact that the ark is six times as long as it is broad and ten times as long as it is deep presents an exact likeness with the human body in which Christ was made manifest. For the length of a body from the crown of the head to the sole of the foot is six times the breadth, that is to say from one side to the other, and it is ten times its height, that is the measurement from the back to the belly. Then, the broad expanse of fifty cubits symbolizes the manner in which the heart expands under the influence of that love which the Holy Ghost inspires, as the apostle said: 'the love of God hath been shed forth in our hearts'. For it was on the fiftieth day after the Resurrection that Christ sent forth the Holy Spirit which expanded the hearts of the faithful. Now a length of three hundred cubits amounts to six times fifty, and in the same way the whole extent of time falls into six ages, in which Christ was proclaimed without ceasing: in the fifth he is the subject of prophecy, while in the sixth he is openly proclaimed in the Gospel.

Of the words 'three hundred cubits' Isidore, quoted in the *Glossa Ordinaria,* remarks that the wood of the Cross can be indicated by that expression. 'For the symbol of this number is a T, which clearly indicates a cross, whereby we, made sharers in his Passion through baptism, obtain the full length of eternal life.' 'Now the height extends to thirty cubits, one tenth of the length, because Christ is our lofty height and he, reaching the age of thirty years, put forth the sacred teaching of the Gospel proclaiming that he came not to destroy the Law but to fulfil it. But since the essence of the Law is proclaimed in ten commandments, the length of the ark is completed in ten times thirty cubits.'

And so it goes on. The words 'with a cubit shalt thou finish off its height' are explained 'in such manner the Church, gathered together in one, is raised up on high and completed', while the door set in the side of the ark is made to serve as a reminder that 'no one enters the Church except through the sacrament of the remission of sins which flowed out from an opened side'.

This type of exegesis, symbolic and often fanciful, particularly where numbers are in question, and concerned to demonstrate the unity of God's revelation by linking the New Testament closely with the Old, is found illustrated in the artistic achievements of the middle ages. When Abbot Suger was writing his report about the buildings erected at St Denis, he referred to an altar cross as 'having the foot decorated with the four evangelists and the shaft most delicately enamelled to show the story of the Saviour together with testimonies of an allegorical type drawn from the Old Law'. Suger goes on to mention that the work on this cross was carried out by 'several goldsmiths of Lotharingia', and thus indicates that by the middle of the twelfth century the practice of using enamel-work to illustrate biblical scenes arranged on the principle of Old Testament type and New Testament fulfilment had become established on the borders of France and Germany. It is therefore not surprising to find that it was an artist from those parts, Nicolas of Verdun, who was called upon in 1181 by Abbot Wernher to construct for Klosterneuburg the magnificent altar-piece which, in spite of damage caused by a fire in 1322, exists today. (Plates 16–17.) This altar-piece consists of a central panel and two wings: it is decorated with enamelled plaques in three rows ranged one beneath the other. The first three scenes in each row combine to make up a related group, as do the second triplet, the third and so on. Half-figures of the prophets together with appropriate texts are added to each picture. The two groups at the end are concerned with the Last Judgement and stand apart from the main scheme, but the other fifteen groups are so arranged that a New Testament scene is placed between two incidents drawn from the Old Testament. Thus the Annunciation occurs between the prophecy of Isaac's birth and the prophecy of Samson's birth; the kiss of Judas is flanked by Cain slaying Abel and the death of Abner; the blessing of Jacob and Samson bearing away the gates of Gaza accompany the picture of the Resurrection. A further touch of theological refinement is added in that, of the two Old Testament types, the first is usually drawn from the period before the giving of the Law while the second belongs to the time when Israel was 'under the Law'.

But the most notable examples of Old Testament characters and events used to prefigure the Gospel record, 'like a preliminary model for a statue' as Origen put it, are provided by the carved porches and stained-glass windows of such French cathedrals as Chartres, Bourges or Le Mans. (Plate 19.) One of the great thirteenth-century windows at Bourges may be chosen as an example. This is the window put in at the expense of the local butchers, who felt it to be entirely natural that pictures illustrating the deepest mysteries of the faith should be accompanied by panels showing a pig being killed, a calf being led away and a butcher's stall laden with meat. Apart from these homely illustrations, the window contains two large medallions of glass, each containing a New Testament scene in a quatrefoil with four Old Testament subjects depicted around it. There are also two smaller, round medallions and two half-quatrefoils, one on each side. The lower large medallion contains, as its central quatrefoil, a representation of Christ bearing the Cross and being helped by Simon the Cyrenean. The Old Testament scenes which were thought to be hints and anticipations of the Crucifixion are as follows: (i) Abraham, holding a knife in his hand, strides vigorously ahead of Isaac, who carries the wood for the sacrifice arranged in the form of a cross. 'Just as Isaac carried the wood on which he was to be placed, so Christ carried the Cross on which he was to be nailed', observes the compiler of the *Glossa Ordinaria*. The only other object in the picture is a thornbush. (ii) As Abraham prepares to slay his son, an angel with his left hand clutches the raised knife while with his right he points to a ram standing demurely by the thicket. (iii) Two Hebrews are carefully marking the lintel and the side-posts of their house with the blood of the Passover lamb, slain that day for the first time (Exod. xii. 21). The comment is added *Scribe*

Thau, as though the Hebrews had been ordered to make the mark on their house in the form of a T, or cross. The writers of the New Testament, and the Church Fathers after them, found in both persons and events of the Exodus particularly close parallels with the life of Christ and the Church. Just as the first-born of the Jews were saved from destruction with the help of the lamb's blood, so the members of the New Israel are preserved, in spite of their failings and sins, through baptism, whereby they become sharers in the victorious power made available by the blood of the Lamb of God. (iv) A woman has gathered two pieces of wood, which she holds in the form of a cross. Behind her is the diminutive figure of her son. A bearded figure, with hand raised in solemn affirmation, is addressing her. This is Elijah, in his encounter with the widow of Zarephath (I Kings xvii). Elijah was held to stand as a symbol of Christ, particularly by virtue of his miraculous ascension into heaven, and the widow of Zarephath then becomes emblematic of the Gentile Church, which accepted the Gospel whereas the Jews rejected it. Significance is attached in the *Glossa Ordinaria* to the water which the widow draws for the prophet, and which indicates a willingness to submit to baptism in order to obtain the salvation which the wood—the wood of the Cross—will bring.

The central quatrefoil of the second medallion shows the Resurrection. Christ rises triumphant from the tomb attended by two angels, one holding a censer while the other clasps a candlestick, in postures of adoration. No guards are to be seen. Ranged round this picture are four scenes which foretell or symbolize it. (i) At the bottom on the left is shown a king, seated on a throne and holding a scroll. This is David, mentioned in the first verse of Matthew's Gospel as the ancestor of Christ, a connection emphasized in the early speeches of the Acts of the Apostles (ii and xiii). Nearby a pelican, 'in her piety', pecks at her breast to feed two young birds with her blood. The pelican (Plate 20) is one of the birds mentioned in *Physiologus*, 'The Naturalist', a treatise which seems to have been composed in a monastic community near Alexandria at a very early date but not to have become influential until translations were made into German and other European languages during the eleventh century. The purpose of such bestiaries, as they came to be called, was to draw out lessons which might be learned from the behaviour of the various living creatures. Of these the lion, the phoenix, the unicorn, the pelican and a mysterious bird known as the chaladrius all typified some aspect of the life of Christ. The pelican feeding her young with her life-blood naturally represented the sacrifice of Christ on the Cross, so that Dante can go so far as to describe Christ as 'our Pelican'. (ii) The picture on the right side at the bottom discloses two lions, one of which is licking the diminutive corpse of a lion cub. Here again the medieval bestiaries help with an explanation. The figure of a lion, a courageous beast, splendid but frightening, was used as a symbol either of good or evil, of Christ or the Devil. But the custom gradually prevailed of allowing the lion to typify the 'lion that is of the tribe of Judah, the root of David' mentioned in the Apocalypse. The window at Bourges, however, illustrates the belief, found as early as the works of Origen and popularized by *Physiologus*, that lion cubs are born dead and lie inert for three days. At the end of this time the old lion utters a tremendous roar, or according to some versions breathes into each cub's mouth, and thus the cubs are aroused. In the same way, it is pointed out, Christ lay dead in the sepulchre for three days until he was revived by the voice of the Father exclaiming 'Awake up, my glory'. The lions therefore suitably remind us of the Resurrection, as does the third picture in this medallion, which shows Jonah being cast up by the whale after three days inside it. The scene in the top left corner, Elisha bending over the son of the Shunammite woman to arouse him from the sleep of death (II Kings iv), fits in no less appropriately.

The circular panel at the top of the window depicts Jacob blessing the two sons of Joseph (Gen. xlviii). There is no attempt at realistic portrayal of a dying man, for Jacob sits in Christ-like majesty with his right hand on the head of the boy at his left, his left hand on the head of the boy at his right. His arms thus form a shape which, as the *Glossa Ordinaria* points out, significantly suggests a cross. 'He showed that this would be a stumbling-block to the Jews but the glory of Christians, and he indicated that the elder would change over from the right hand to the left through the mystery of the Cross and that the younger would move from left hand to right': in other words, the Crucifixion would mark the time when the New Israel of the Christian Church superseded the Old Israel of the Synagogue. This theme is continued in the central medallion, for here Christ is shown on the Cross, with a woman standing on either side of it. The figure on the right, clothed in a rich robe and wearing a crown, represents the Church. She looks straight at the Saviour and catches in a bowl the blood which flows from a wound high up in his side, and which suggests the sacraments of which the Church is guardian. The figure opposite has her head lowered in dejection; her crown is falling off, the staff of the flag which she holds in her hands is broken, her eyes are bound with a handkerchief in token that she, the Synagogue, is blind to the deepest truth. She is shown as fulfilling the prophecy of Jeremiah (Lam. v. 16): 'The crown is fallen from our head: Woe unto us for we have sinned. For this our heart is faint: For these things our eyes are dim.'

The two half-quatrefoils, at the sides of the Bourges window, both contain the figure of Moses. In one scene he is striking the 'rock in Horeb' with his wand and causing water to flow 'that the people may drink' (Exod. xvii), in the other he is pointing to the serpent of brass set upon a standard (Num. xxi) while certain Israelites show by their gestures that they appreciate its virtues as a specific against snakebite.

Moses, striking the rock in order to obtain water for the thirsty Israelites, provided one of the favourite themes for illustration by artists of the primitive Church, and when this incident was shown, painted on the walls of the catacombs or carved on sarcophagi, it symbolized baptism and the salvation to be derived from that sacrament. The story of a deliverance through water naturally suggested deliverance from sin by means of water, and Cyprian supplies as good a commentary as any of the Fathers on this theme (*ep.* 63). 'Whenever', he writes, 'water alone is the subject of a passage of Scripture, there is a reference to baptism...God, speaking through the mouth of the prophet, foretold that, in places which had hitherto been parched, rivers should flow and quench the thirst of the chosen people of God, that is to say those who have been made sons of God by baptism...What he says is: "If they are thirsty in the deserts, God will supply them with water: he will make it flow out of the rock for them: the rock will be cleft and the water will flow and my people will drink."' In the middle ages, however, the emphasis is different. Basil had said 'The rock represents Christ, and the water which flows from the rock represents the life-giving power of the Word'; so now the rock serves as a type of Christ in his suffering. 'The thirsty people', as the explanation runs in the *Glossa Ordinaria*, 'in their desire for water murmured against Moses, so God ordered him to show them a rock from which they might drink. In the same way, if anyone reads the books of Moses and murmurs against him and finds the letter of the Law unsatisfactory, Moses points out to him a rock, that is to say Christ, and leads him thereto, so that he may drink and appease his thirst. . . The striking of the rock indicates Christ, who, when on the Cross, was struck by the Jews, while the rock corresponds to the wood of the Cross which caused water to flow forth to meet the needs of the faithful.' The book of Wisdom lays it down that the brazen serpent was a 'token of salvation'; and Jesus, according to the narrative of John's Gospel (iii. 14), speaks in a somewhat similar way. The serpent is represented as foretelling not merely the death of the Son of Man but also the circumstances of his death; and this death, so far from being the fiasco which a casual and earth-bound glance might suppose it to be, proves to offer the supreme opportunity for the exercise of faith, 'that whosoever believeth may in him have eternal life'. Augustine notes (*de Civ. Dei* 9. 8) that the brazen serpent was 'both a present help for the snakebite and a type of the future destruction of death by death in the passion of Christ crucified', while the medieval view, in general, showed little advance on the explanation given in the second-century *Epistle of Barnabas*: '"Whenever one of you", said Moses, "is bitten, let him come to the serpent that is placed upon the tree and let him hope in faith that it, though dead, may be able to give life, and straightway he shall be saved." And they did so. In this also you have a forecast of the glory of Jesus.'

Moses appears, in the Bourges window, as a venerable, bearded figure with two horns projecting from his head. It may well be asked where the horns come from, since there is nothing to suggest them in the biblical narrative as it appears in the English versions. The answer is that they are a tribute to the authority of the Vulgate. For the horns of Moses owe their origin to a mistake which Jerome made in his translation. Exod. xxxiv. 29 records that 'Moses wist not that the skin of his face shone by reason of his speaking with God' on Mount Sinai. Jerome, however, misled by a confusion between the word *qaran* ('to shine') and *qeren* ('a horn'), wrote *Moses ignorabat quod facies sua cornuta esset*—'he knew not that horns had sprouted on his head'. In such high regard was the Vulgate held that this bizarre picture of Moses with horns sprouting from his head was accepted and standardized by medieval artists (see Plate 22).

As the fourteenth century yielded to the fifteenth, those responsible for the decoration of churches were inclined to indulge the popular interest in lives of the saints and in apocryphal stories. But the biblical themes continue to appear and to be treated, in the traditional manner, as illustrating the unity of God's revelation and the close concord that existed between Old and New Testaments. The *Glossa Ordinaria* maintained its influence, and another work which dictated the manner in which subjects drawn from the Bible should be treated in art was the *Speculum humanae salvationis*, which seems to have been composed by Ludolph of Saxony, a Dominican friar, about the year 1324. (Plates 24–5; see also p. 334.) The book is arranged in a methodical fashion. There are forty-two chapters, each containing a hundred lines of Latin verse. The first two offer an account of the history of the world from the Fall to the Flood: thereafter each chapter, in the seventy manuscripts or so which are complete with pictures, occupies two pages, each page having two columns of twenty-five lines with an illustration at the head of every column. The first of the four pictures in each set shows an incident taken from the Gospel story, the other three pictures being types, or anticipations. The *Speculum* differs from the *Biblia Pauperum* here in that, though the types are usually drawn from the record of the Old Testament, some derive from pagan history as related by such authors as Valerius Maximus. The whole experience of mankind thus serves, in some sort, to prefigure God's decisive work of salvation.

The Annunciation may be taken as an example of the way in which the Bible text is illustrated in the *Speculum*. In the picture of this event, Gabriel is shown kneeling, with hand upraised, in front of Mary. A jar containing flowers stands between them, and a house appears in the background. God the Father is seen looking down from a cloud in the sky, while the Holy Ghost descends in the form of a small bird. The first antitype is Moses and the burning bush. Moses kneels on one knee before a flaming bush out of which proceeds the figure of God. His right hand is raised, while with his left hand he clasps a scroll. Rabanus Maurus and other doctors had laid it down that the burning bush was an appropriate symbol of the Virgin, for, just as the bush blazed without being consumed, and allowed the form of God to be manifested in the midst of the flames, so Mary received the flame of the divine love within herself without being consumed. Next comes the story of Gideon's fleece (Judges vi). Gideon is represented as kneeling in prayer: above is the firmament of heaven with three large stars, while, in one part only of the foreground, rain pours down on some plants, the fleece not being visible. The lesson here is that the dew of the divine power descended upon Mary alone, the rest of the earth being left dry. The last picture on the page shows Rebekah standing in front of Eliezer, the servant of Abraham, who kneels to drink water from a flagon which she offers to him. Abraham had sent his messenger to find a maiden for his son and she, by providing water for him to drink, made it clear that she gave her consent. The whole action is prophetic of the time when God the Father should send Gabriel to find a pure virgin who should accept her destiny with the words 'Behold, the handmaid of the Lord; be it unto me according to thy word'.

The fashion in artistic style changed notably during the middle ages and the austere, majestic symbolism of the thirteenth century yielded to the greater realism of the fifteenth, with its interest in people for their own sake, and with its awareness of the emotions and the pathos of human life; but the belief that history provided hints and intimations of the fuller truth that should be revealed in Christ persisted, and most of the puzzles which sometimes appear in the great stained-glass windows of the Perpendicular period may be explained by reference to the *Glossa Ordinaria* or to the *Speculum humanae salvationis*. In the latter work are included four scenes concerned with the early life of the Virgin which served as a legendary supplement to Scripture. The scanty and abrupt references to the Virgin which are contained in the Gospels and the Acts of the Apostles were felt to be intolerably jejune by her medieval devotees, who were thus constrained to draw on such apocryphal works as the third-century *Book of James* in the attempt to obtain fuller details. The *Speculum humanae salvationis* offers illustrations of the Annunciation to Anne, the Nativity of the Virgin, her Presentation in the Temple and her Betrothal to Joseph. The Betrothal is thus described in Caxton's version of the widely influential 'Golden Legend': 'In the fourteenth year of Mary's age, the bishop commanded in common that the virgins that were instituted in the Temple, and had accomplished the time of age, should return to their houses and should after the law be married.' Mary protested 'that her father and mother had given her all to the service of our Lord', whereupon prayer was made and a voice proclaimed that 'all they that were of the house of David and were convenable to be married and had no wife should bring a rod to the altar, and his rod that flourished and, after the saying of Isaiah, the Holy Ghost sat in the form of a dove on it, he should be the man that should be desponsate and married to the Virgin Mary'. Joseph was elderly and somewhat shy and it was only 'by the command-ment of the bishop' that he 'brought forth his rod, and anon it flowered, and a dove descended from heaven thereupon' so that it was 'the advice of every man' that he should 'espouse the Virgin Mary and return unto his city of Bethlehem'. Old Testament prophecy is regularly taken to forecast not only the events of Christ's life but also the history of the Virgin. In this particular case, Isaiah's words (xi. 1) 'there shall come forth a shoot out of the stock of Jesse, and a branch out of his roots shall bear fruit, and the spirit of the Lord shall rest upon him' seem to have dictated the form of a simple narrative which artists followed when they showed Joseph holding a rod with a flower at the end and a dove perched in the middle. A commentary is supplied by the author of 'Miracles of Our Lady', written under the influence of St Bernard:

> Elle est la fleur, elle est la rose
> En cui habite, en cui repose
> Et jour et nuit Sainz Esperiz.

It was on the authority of such works as the *Speculum humanae salvationis* that incidents from the early life of the Virgin were included together with the scriptural scenes when a full cycle of Gospel pictures was set forth in the fifteenth-century glass of Malvern priory church or when, seventy years later, 'the story of the olde lawe and of new lawe' was illustrated on a vast scale in the windows of King's College chapel, Cambridge. Some of the well-loved apocryphal stories might gain so wide an acceptance that they were treated as Scripture, but artistic licence was checked and popular enthusiasm restrained by the scholarship and abiding influence of men like Nicholas of Lyra. Nicholas was born in Normandy, entered the Franciscan order and became a lecturer in the University of Paris about 1310.[1] He made a special study of the Hebrew language and of the Jewish commentators on the Old Testament, so that he was well aware of differing traditions in exegesis. Though prepared to allow that the student requires the assistance of symbolism and allegory in the task of biblical interpretation, Nicholas made it his prime concern to arrive at an exact understanding of the

---

[1] On Nicholas of Lyra see also p. 219 above.

literal sense of Scripture, and at the beginning of his *Postillae*, which were a recognized supplement to the *Glossa Ordinaria* and printed along with it in a number of early editions, he declares: 'The beginning of Genesis is involved in many extremely difficult matters, and their obscurity is proved by the variety and the number of interpretations offered by Jewish and Christian scholars. And, since confusion of this sort is harmful to understanding and memory alike, I propose to avoid this multitude of interpretations and in particular those which seem remote from the literal sense, since it is this sense which I propose to stress in accordance with the grace which the Lord has bestowed upon me.' Nicholas, in fact, recognized the dangers of unchastened speculation, and his sober scholarship was one of the factors which prevented biblical history from slipping, by way of allegory, into reckless fantasy. (Plate 23.)

A straightforward, even childlike, literalism is thus to be discerned in the work of medieval artists side by side with details which point to subtle speculations, so that a blend of simplicity and sophistication, of *naïveté* and philosophic shrewdness, marks the treatment of the august themes with which such men concerned themselves. Two examples may be selected. The clerestory windows on the south side of the nave at Malvern priory display a series of Old Testament episodes. The first picture illustrates the opening words of Genesis in a fashion different from the Trinitarianism of the sarcophagus at St Paul's, Rome. Within a framework of two piers supporting an elaborate canopy God is shown as a bearded figure clothed in blue tunic and white mantle, both garments being bordered with jewels. The halo behind God's head is decorated with rays and a four-armed cross. A cruciform halo is often used to distinguish Christ, and it may be that the figure here should be understood as God the Son carrying out the work of creating heaven and earth in accordance with the scriptural doctrine that 'all things were made' by the Word: on the other hand, in the Malvern glass a halo of this type is assigned to God when he is establishing the covenant with Abraham and in other Old Testament scenes. The Creator stands with right hand raised, while with his left he clasps a pair of compasses, the points of which rest on the ground. He is, in fact, shown forth as the omnipotent Master-craftsman described by Isaiah (xl. 12): 'Who hath measured the waters in the hollow of his hand, and meted out heaven with the span, and comprehended the dust in a measure?' This picture of God with compasses in his hand is found in such earlier manuscripts as the Anglo-Norman 'Queen Mary's Psalter', and it enters literature by way of Dante and Milton's *Paradise Lost* (vii. 221), when it is said of the Son

> Him all his Traine
> Follow'd in bright procession to behold
> Creation, and the wonders of his might.
> Then staid the fervid wheeles, and in his hand
> He took the golden Compasses, prepar'd
> In God's Eternal store, to circumscribe
> This Universe, and all created things.

In the Malvern window, the Creator is confronted by a golden disc from which rays of light force their way downwards through the surrounding circle of blue cloud, while other pictures in the same series illustrated the making of the heavenly bodies, plants, birds and animals. Elsewhere the various moments of Creation are often compressed into one scene: thus the *Glossa Ordinaria* printed at Lyons in 1528 (Plate 25) starts with a block-print in which God stands with hand upraised, as at Malvern, though lacking his compasses. Overhead six stars shine in the firmament, at his feet a plant springs up, while before him two fishes push their noses out of the sea, and the heads of a horse, an ox and a pig emerge from the elaborate initial I of the *In Principio*.

Another example of the medieval way of handling a motif is provided by a painting of the Resurrection which dates from about 1385 and forms one of a set of wooden panels, enriched by gesso work, now excellently repaired and displayed in Norwich cathedral (Plate 26). Christ is shown stepping forth from a stone coffin. His face, framed by a cross-halo, wears an expression of benevolent majesty; his body is covered by a mantle of purple lined with blue, from which his right arm projects, the hand upraised in blessing; his left hand clasps a processional cross decorated with the pennant of victory. Three armed soldiers, fast asleep, crouch round the coffin and Christ's right foot presses on the shoulder of one of them as he emerges triumphant.

Although the Resurrection was the principal element in the Gospel message as this was proclaimed in the apostolic age, the first generations of Christian artists were most reluctant to show forth either the Crucifixion or the Resurrection in a narrative picture. Nowhere is the

Resurrection clearly recorded in the paintings of the catacombs (p. 282), and the formula found on the carved sarcophagi is that suggested by a fourth-century sarcophagus preserved at the Lateran. Here, flanked by scenes of Christ's Passion, a plain cross is displayed and, above it, the labarum, or chi–rho monogram, enclosed within a wreath. Beneath each arm of the cross a sleeping soldier is to be seen; on one or two sarcophagi the place of the soldiers is taken by the women proceeding with spices to embalm Christ's body. This compact symbolism served as a reminder of the Resurrection, without recourse to a literalism which might attempt to portray mysteries too august for easy definition.

In the East, this hesitation was sometimes overcome. The Gospels of Rabula, a Mesopotamian manuscript illuminated in 586, offer a large picture of the Resurrection, as does a Byzantine ivory, now preserved at Munich (Plate 27), which is probably of still earlier date. On this ivory is shown a sumptuously decorated tomb with two soldiers, one awake and one asleep, nearby. In front sits an angel, his hand raised in a gesture of solemn explanation to the three women who stand in a row, listening attentively. Above, Christ is ascending a mountain-side on which two apostles crouch in an attitude of amazement as the hand of God reaches down from the clouds to welcome the Saviour on his victorious return to Heaven. But, even in the East, such frank and dramatic compositions are rare at first, and the Resurrection is usually indicated rather than fully portrayed, as for instance in the ninth-century mosaics of the church of the Holy Apostles at Constantinople, merely by an illustration of the three women at the tomb. This scene was almost invariably used to signify the Resurrection in the western Church down to the twelfth century. There is no need to imagine, as is sometimes done, that it was adopted under the influence of the liturgical drama which was enacted in English churches at Eastertide from the time of Dunstan and in France perhaps a century earlier. The Easter drama came to include certain incidents, such as the attempt by an unscrupulous spice-merchant to sell his wares to the three women at an exorbitant price, which were reproduced now and again in medieval art; but the principal scene, the women face to face with the mystery of the empty tomb, derives naturally from the reticence of the Gospel narrative itself.

Although the developed mystery plays might contain striking representations of the risen Lord, nothing of the kind seems to have been known as early as the twelfth century. Yet the Klosterneuburg altar-piece, and a Romanesque capital of about the same date, now preserved in the museum at Toulouse, mark a bold departure from the quieter symbolism. Christ is there shown stepping not indeed from any Palestinian rock-tomb but out of a stone coffin from which the lid has been victoriously flung back. This motif, copied and popularized by etchers such as Schongauer, became the dominant one in northern Europe and served as the model for the painter of the Norwich panel, though his artistic sensibility prevents him from crowding his composition with such details as the coffin-lid or the attendant angel. In Italy the change usually took a rather different form. The Florentine painter Taddeo Gaddi shows Christ, with his banner of victory, hovering in a radiance of light over the empty tomb, on which two angels are seated, while the women with the spices stand on one side and Christ appears to Mary Magdalene on the other. This theme of Christ exalted in glory above the tomb possesses such clarity and force that it superseded the earlier methods by which Italian artists strove to suggest the Resurrection, and it continued in popularity until the eighteenth century and even after that. Realistic details, however, intrude. For instance, the soldiers are commonly shown in earlier examples as asleep, this being the medieval way of interpreting the Gospel comment that they 'became as dead men', while later artists were inclined to depict the soldiers, more dramatically, as holding up their shields to ward off the blinding light and thus paying their tribute of fear in face of mystery. But, as recent years have shown, the pendulum swings to and fro, and a determined realism may in the end lead to a turning back in the direction of symbol as men seek to declare, in the language of their own age, that which in its deepest nature must ever elude expression.

CHAPTER VIII

BIBLE ILLUSTRATION IN MEDIEVAL MANUSCRIPTS

Biblical illustration in the middle ages is a vast subject whose study is still very much in its infancy. It is, therefore, impossible to give more than a brief sketch of the variety of forms which it takes. By now it is clear that illustrations of the books of the Bible were already in use by the fourth century of our era and that certain Jewish communities also had access to representations of biblical subjects. This is indicated by the paintings in the synagogue at Doura Europos which date from the middle of the third century and have scenes from the stories of Moses, Elijah, Esther and the vision of Ezekiel. The Moses series at Doura suggests that these may occasionally have been fairly complete cycles. It is difficult to be certain whether the Jewish communities of this period possessed bible picture-books. Naturally the scrolls of the Law bore no decoration, and early illustrated Jewish books have not survived. Christians seem to have been less reluctant to illustrate their bibles, though the earliest examples are by no means lavish in their provision of pictures.

In this chapter an attempt will be made to indicate something of the various methods of providing bible pictures in manuscripts between about 600 and about 1450. If the material were to be confined to the Bible as a composite work this would produce an extremely incomplete picture, since some of the fullest series of illustrations are to be found in volumes devoted to a single book or a group of books such as the book of Genesis, the Pentateuch or the four Gospels. The appearance of copies of the complete Bible in one or more volumes provided with a large number of illustrations is comparatively late and reaches its peak in manuscripts of the eleventh and twelfth centuries. Whether completely illustrated bibles existed in the early days of the Church is doubtful. It seems much more likely that the long series of pictures developed in the smaller units, and these, therefore, will be discussed as well as the bibles themselves.

There are two main types of illustrations found throughout the whole of the middle ages. The first is the 'direct' subject where the text is transformed as nearly as possible into a pictorial form. This is found in such books as Genesis or Kings where there is a strong narrative element, as well as in the Gospels. The second may be called 'typical'. Already in the Gospels the use of types and antitypes appears in such passages as John iii. 14, 'And as Moses lifted up the serpent in the wilderness, even so must the Son of Man be lifted up'. In this verse, the type of the Crucifixion is the raising of the brazen serpent in the wilderness by Moses in Num. xxi. 9. Such juxtapositions became extremely elaborate in works like the *Biblia Pauperum* and the *Speculum humanae salvationis*. The illustrations of the Psalter also provided many opportunities for 'typical' treatment, though the 'direct' method is also made use of.

As has already been mentioned, the illustrations of the large bibles of the early middle ages are sparse, particularly those of the Latin bible. The earliest that has survived is the *Codex Amiatinus*, now in the Laurentian Library in Florence (pp. 113 ff. above). It was written shortly before 716 in one of the two Northumbrian monasteries of Monkwearmouth or Jarrow at the order of Abbot Ceolfrith, who intended it as a present to the pope. The text, which is the most important witness of the Vulgate, is written in uncials of a particularly accomplished variety. It has three illustrations. Before the Old Testament is a picture of Ezra the Scribe revising the Scriptures and a large diagram of the Tabernacle with the vessels of its ritual. Before the New Testament is a full-page miniature of Christ in majesty with the four evangelists and their symbols. All three miniatures are derived from sixth-century originals probably coming from the library of Cassiodorus at Vivarium and brought to England in the second half of the seventh century by Benedict Biscop, abbot of Monkwearmouth and Jarrow. They are remarkable witnesses to the skill of English illuminators of that early period. It will be seen that the choice of illustrations is particularly appropriate. First is Ezra the reviser of Old Laws, secondly the representation of the Tabernacle, the seat of the Old Law, and thirdly the New Covenant expressed by the majesty and the evangelists.

There is evidence that there was a large bible at St Augustine's Canterbury at the end of the eighth century which was comparable in size and magnificence to the *Amiatinus*. This is British Museum Royal

MS 1 E. VI.[1] Today it is only a fragment containing the four Gospels. The illustrations are missing, but it is possible to reconstruct those for the Gospels of Matthew, Mark and Luke, since the verses describing them are found written on purple leaves at the beginning of each Gospel. Matthew appears to have had an elaborate miniature representing the Lamb of God and the four evangelists which must have resembled in design a page at the beginning of the New Testament in a ninth-century bible from Tours now at Bamberg.[2] Before Mark was a miniature of the baptism of Christ, and before Luke the appearance of the angel Gabriel to Zacharias in the Temple. It would appear that these were full-page miniatures. These larger pictures may be compared with miniatures found on a much smaller scale in the Carolingian Gospels of Saint Médard at Soissons in the Bibliothèque Nationale in Paris and the related gospel book in the Harleian manuscripts in the British Museum.[3]

From the Carolingian period a number of large bibles survive. Some have no illustrations, others a few. In no case, however, does there yet appear a bible with a vast series of illustrations, such as will be found in some of the later bibles of the eleventh and twelfth centuries. The most important group of Carolingian bibles are those which can be ascribed to the scriptorium of Tours (pp. 133 ff.). Although the influence of Alcuin, who had been abbot at Tours, may have been the inspiration, it must be remembered that the most famous of the Tours-illuminated bibles, the Bamberg Bible, the Grandval Bible in the British Museum, Add. MS 10546, and the Vivian Bible in the Bibliothèque Nationale in Paris (fonds lat. 1), all date from the middle of the ninth century and long after the death of Alcuin himself. The Bamberg Bible has only two illustrations: the first of the history of the Creation and the Fall in front of the Old Testament and the second before the New Testament of the Lamb of God with the four symbols of the evangelists. Both the Grandval and the Vivian Bibles have more pictures than the Bamberg Bible (see Plate 28). Those which are common to both the Grandval and the Vivian are thought to derive from the fifth-century original. They consist of the following four miniatures: the Creation and Fall of

---

[1] See P. M. McGurk, 'An Anglo-Saxon Bible fragment of the late eighth century', *Journal of the Warburg and Courtauld Institutes*, XXV (1962), 18–34.

[2] W. Koehler, *Die Karolingischen Miniaturen*, I, 'Die Schule von Tours', Taff. 1, 56b.

[3] W. Koehler, *Die Karolingischen Miniaturen*, II, 'Die Hofschule Karls des Grossen', Volume of plates.

Man before Genesis, and scenes of Moses receiving the Law on Mount Sinai and of Moses teaching the people before Exodus. In front of the Gospels is a Christ in majesty with the evangelists and prophets, and before the Apocalypse the Lamb and the Lion of the Tribe of Judah opening the Book, with, below, the revelation of the Almighty by the Four Living Creatures. Koehler has suggested that this choice of subject may reflect doctrinal controversies of the fifth century and that the originals used by the Carolingian illuminators came from an early bible.[1] The Vivian Bible adds four more miniatures: scenes from the life of Jerome, a David miniature before the Psalter, scenes from the story of the conversion of Paul before Acts, and fourthly a picture of the emperor Charles the Bald receiving the book from the abbot Vivian and the monks of St Martin's at Tours. It will be seen, therefore, that the illustrations of the Tours bibles are of special and rather restricted choice.

Of the great Carolingian bibles the most richly illustrated is that preserved in the monastery S. Paolo fuori le Mura in Rome. It was made, probably at Reims, between 870 and 875 for Charles the Bald. A number of its illustrations seem to be derived from the Vivian Bible from Tours, but there are many more both in the Old and New Testaments, particularly fine ones being those of the wanderings of the children of Israel in the wilderness. They may be derived from one of the lavishly illustrated copies of the Pentateuch which were current in the early Christian period. This can be confirmed to a certain extent by comparing a miniature of the Blessing of the Tribes and the Death of Moses in the St Paul's Bible with a miniature of the same scene in the eleventh-century manuscript of Ælfric's Heptateuch in the British Museum, whose very long series of pictures seems to go back to an early source.[2] (Plates 29, 30.)

During the tenth century large bibles are rare, and large illuminated bibles very rare. It is only in the eleventh century that they reappear in any quantity, and from that date until the end of the twelfth century they become more and more numerous. Although this must not be insisted upon, it seems very likely that their great popularity was due to the re-establishment of the reformed Benedictine monasticism which is such a feature of the religious life of the period. This was also a great

[1] W. Koehler, *op. cit.* I, 2, 'Die Schule von Tours', pp. 164–212.
[2] See Hanns Swarzenski, *Monuments of Romanesque Art* (1954), nos. 131, 132.

time for the refurbishing of monastic libraries and, with this, the expansion in production of what in modern parlance would be called 'large paper' copies of the Fathers of the Church as well as the Bible itself. The inspiration may originally have come through the Cluniacs, though this cannot be proved. By the twelfth century, at any rate, there must have been hardly a cathedral church or important abbey that did not possess a large bible of this kind.

Unlike the Carolingian bibles, which were restricted in their schemes of illustration, the great bibles of the Romanesque period were much more lavish in decoration, and some have very long series of pictures. These are usually of two kinds. First is the miniature, which can occupy a whole page or part of a page, and, as in the Carolingian books, several biblical scenes can be included in one miniature. Second and very important is the much extended use of the historiated initial, in which an illustration is placed within the bow or body of a large ornamented capital letter placed at the beginning of one of the biblical books. The historiated initial had of course existed at an earlier date, but the eleventh and twelfth centuries saw a vastly increased use of them. By no means all initials of this time were given pictures, but many were, and this naturally increased the quantity of biblical illustrations.

Among the earliest illustrated great bibles of this period is that pre-served in the Colegiata of San Isidoro in León in north-western Spain. From the colophon at the end we learn that it was completed by the presbyter Sanctius with the help of Florentius, a monk. The manuscript is written in two columns to a page and the illustrations are introduced into the columns of writing and are thus in close connection with the corresponding passages of the text. Such an arrangement is certainly not new and may be found in copies of early texts such as the fragment of the Ravennate Annals in Merseburg.[1] The distribution of the illustrations in the Bible of San Isidoro is very uneven. Whereas Genesis has only two pictures, Exodus is richly illustrated, as are also the books of Kings. Leviticus and Numbers have nothing, and the same is true for the four Gospels and the Apocalypse. This suggests that the ultimate sources of these illustrations were individual books of the Bible in single volumes and not a bible with a long series of miniatures of its own.

Among the most completely illustrated bibles are two Spanish bibles:

[1] See Kurt Weitzmann, *Illustrations in Roll and Codex* (Princeton, 1947), pp. 76, 91.

313

the Bible of Sant Pere de Roda in the Vatican Library and the other from the monastery of Santa Maria de Ripoll, sometimes called the Farfa Bible, in the Bibliothèque Nationale in Paris. Both are infinitely more richly provided with pictures than the San Isidoro book and include a long series of illustrations for the Gospels. Curiously enough the Apocalypse, of which a great number of illustrations were available in earlier and contemporary Spanish manuscripts, is rather poorly represented. This again suggests that the sources were richly illustrated individual books and not complete bibles.

It is impossible to enumerate the characteristics of the great twelfth-century bibles. Their variety is too great. On the whole, very long series of illustrations of the kind found in the Spanish bibles are rare, and in many cases there is only one illustration to a book, often, as we have seen, placed in the opening initial. Their choice is by no means uniform and must have been dictated by what was available to the artist. The Gospels and epistles usually have pictures of the evangelists and the writers of the epistles, but sometimes these are of a more elaborate nature. For instance in the great twelfth-century bible from the Premonstratensian abbey of Floreffe in Belgium, each Gospel is provided with a miniature in which a typological system of illustration is employed. (Plate 31.) Thus for Luke's Gospel there is a miniature divided into two compartments. In the upper compartment is Christ on the Cross; on one side is a bust of Paul, who holds a scroll inscribed with the text from Heb. ix. 12, 'but by his own blood he entered in once into the holy place', and on the other side David holding the verse from Ps. 110: 4, 'Thou art a priest for ever after the order of Melchizedek'. In the lower compartment is a scene showing the sacrifice of the calf by the High Priest. On one side stands David holding a scroll inscribed with Ps. 69: 31, 'This also shall please the Lord better than an ox or bullock that has horns and hoofs'. On the other side is Luke holding his symbol and a scroll with the words from Luke xv. 22, 23, 'But the father said to his servants: Bring hither the fatted calf and kill it'. It will be seen at once that what we have here is an elaborate typology in which the sacrifice on the Cross is equated with the Old Testament sacrifice of the fatted calf. In this too Luke's symbol, the calf, also plays a part.

In England a number of these giant bibles survive. One of the most magnificent is that from Bury St Edmunds, now in the library of Corpus

Christi College, Cambridge. This has miniatures preceding some of the books of the Old Testament. Although they are magnificent specimens of illumination, they are fairly simple in iconography and show such scenes as Moses and Aaron addressing the children of Israel. The book of Job is, however, rather more elaborate. (Plate 32.) It is a composite picture in which in the upper portion Job is seen with his sons and daughters; below he is shown with his wife. In the Lambeth Bible, which may have come from Canterbury, the illustrations are more elaborate than those in the Bury Bible. (Plate 33.) A comparatively new feature is the introduction of the Tree of Jesse to stand at the beginning of Isaiah. It is of course an illustration of one of the most famous prophecies of the coming of Christ: 'And there shall come forth a rod out of the stem of Jesse, and a Branch shall grow out of his roots.' Jesse lies on the ground, the Virgin stands in the tree, and above in a roundel is the bust of Christ surrounded by seven doves which are the seven gifts of the Holy Spirit. There are figures of prophets, virtues and the Church and Synagogue.[1] Prof. Dodwell has shown that some of the iconography of the other pictures in the Lambeth Bible may well have ultimate Byzantine origins, probably coming through Sicily.

In the thirteenth century the fashion for large bibles was superseded by a fashion for very small ones. This reduced format did not encourage elaborate illustration, which for the most part was confined to historiated initials placed at the beginning of each book. The initials at the beginning of the Old and New Testaments are sometimes more elaborate. They begin with the letters I (In principio creavit...), and L (Liber generationis), both having long ascenders, and within these are placed, in the Old Testament small scenes of the Days of Creation, and in the New Testament the Tree of Jesse. The other books sometimes have small scenes such as Ezekiel's vision of the Four Living Creatures for his book. For the most part the New Testament has little but figures of the evangelists and the authors of the epistles. The Apocalypse sometimes has John writing on Patmos surrounded by the seven churches.

The pattern just described lasted until the end of the middle ages. Giant bibles are still found as well as some small ones, though their place was often taken, particularly in France, by bible histories in the vernacular (pp. 448 ff.). These have illustrations placed at the beginning of

[1] For a fuller account of the illustration cf. C. R. Dodwell, *The Great Lambeth Bible* (London, 1959), Pl. 4.

each book, but they appear to have been derived for the most part from their Latin predecessors and display little iconographical invention.

It is clear, then, that the complete bibles did not provide the richest sources of biblical illustration for the medieval artists. Far more extensive sets of pictures were to be found in copies of a single book, such as Genesis, or groups of books, such as the Pentateuch. Certain of them, particularly those works containing much drama and action, could naturally provide more illustrative material than the others, which contain more abstract ideas. Genesis is more abundant in incident than some of the Minor Prophets, and the Gospels more fruitful for the miniaturist than the epistles. Yet this distinction is not an absolute one, since among the richest in invention were the illustrations to the Psalter, and the fantastic imagery of the vision of John provided a series of remarkable pictures.

As has been pointed out in connection with the Spanish bibles, it is likely that already by the late antique period there were a number of biblical books in circulation having large cycles of pictures. An early survival is the copy of the book of Genesis in Greek which was once one of the treasures of the Cottonian collection now in the British Museum. This manuscript, Otho B. VI, now almost a complete wreck through fire, was of the fifth century. It was provided with a large picture cycle, each miniature being placed within a rectangular frame.[1] Another early manuscript with an extensive Genesis cycle is the early-sixth-century Vienna Genesis, which has a Greek text written on purple vellum having at the foot of each page a series of unframed illustrations. The figures enacting the various incidents are arranged within what appears to be a continuous landscape so that the eye is carried on without difficulty from scene to scene. Whether these were originally conceived as an uninterrupted narrative or whether they were, as has been suggested, a series of single textual illustrations removed from their related text and combined together, cannot be proved.[2] What is important about them is that they represent a method of pictorial composition much favoured throughout most of the middle ages. A third method of composition was to place within the framework of a large composition a story told in several separate scenes which are unified by

[1] See Kurt Weitzmann, *Illustrations in Roll and Codex*, pp. 140, 141, 176, 177.
[2] *Ibid.* pp. 89–91.

some such device as a landscape or architectural framework. An early and important example of such a system is to be seen in the seventh-century Latin manuscript of the Pentateuch in the Bibliothèque Nationale in Paris, known as the Ashburnham Pentateuch.[1]

How or where these great narrative cycles were produced is unknown, but it is probable that they go back at least to the early days of the Peace of the Church. Some of the Old Testament ones may be even earlier and have had their origin within a Jewish milieu. This certainly seems true of the Ashburnham Pentateuch, where a few of the miniatures show an acquaintance with Aramaic paraphrases of the Bible.[2] It is, however, dangerous to assume that miniatures showing some apparently Jewish features postulate the copying of Jewish illustrated manuscripts in early times. These features may derive from Jewish literary, not pictorial, sources.

Some Old Testament picture-books dating from the later middle ages seem to reflect and even contain elements from books similar to those early ones which have just been discussed. Occasionally the texts which they illustrate have been considerably reduced, sometimes almost to what are no more than explanatory titles. One of the earliest is the paraphrase of the Pentateuch and the book of Joshua by Ælfric of Eynsham, formerly at St Augustine's Canterbury, and probably made there (see p. 375). It is now Cotton MS Claudius B. IV in the British Museum. There are numerous illustrations, some of which are unfinished. They were certainly not invented for Ælfric's text and are derived from something a good deal older. Their iconography points to pre-iconoclast cycles of bible illustrations with some details suggesting a relationship to the same tradition as that found in the Cotton Genesis.[3]

Several types of illustration are found in the Claudius manuscript. There are large full-page miniatures containing a single scene, or two or more scenes are combined into one in the manner of the Ashburnham Pentateuch. More frequently there are a number of small scenes, often

[1] Paris, Bibl. Nat. nouv. acq. lat. 2334, see O. von Gebhardt, *The miniatures of the Ashburnham Pentateuch* (London, 1883).
[2] See Joseph Gutmann, 'The illustrated Jewish manuscript in antiquity', in *Gesta*, v (Jan. 1966), 39–44.
[3] See O. Pächt in O. Pächt, C. R. Dodwell and F. Wormald, *The St Albans Psalter* (London, 1960), pp. 80, 81, also G. Henderson, 'The sources of the Genesis cycle at Saint-Savin-sur-Gartempe', *Journal of the Royal Archaeological Association*, Third Series, XXVI (1963), 11–26.

in frames of a rather irregular shape. At first sight it might seem that they indicate that the originals from which these miniatures were derived were in the form of column illustrations such as are found in the bible of 960 in San Isidoro at León. What is more probable is that they are portions of larger compositions containing a number of different scenes which were subdivided into smaller units.

Although behind these miniatures there may be a late antique original, this is no reason for assuming that there were early Christian manuscripts of the Old Testament in Canterbury in the eleventh century. The early tradition could run through many stages and still display its ancient origin, much in the same way as a manuscript of a text may preserve early readings in spite of its late date. Many details can be altered, but above all the style of the archetype can be completely lost. What suggests the nature of the source is an accumulation of iconographical individualities. When it is said that the pictures in Ælfric's Pentateuch belong to the tradition of the Cotton Genesis this statement is based upon iconographical details and not on artistic evidence.

Another important Old Testament cycle of pictures is to be found in the famous Cædmon manuscript of Old English poetry in the Bodleian Library at Oxford.[1] This was also probably made at Canterbury in the early eleventh century. It contains a series of drawings in ink illustrating portions of Genesis. The decoration is incomplete, though it is clear from the gaps left in the text that a much more extensive plan of illustration was envisaged. An interesting feature of this plan is the introduction of apocryphal elements. This may be seen not only in the drawings representing the story of the Rebellion and Fall of the Angels which illustrate a particular portion of the poem, but also in the curious representation of the translation of Enoch which may be derived from an ancient source such as the Book of the Secrets of Enoch. (Plate 34.)[2] How these apocryphal elements were transmitted is unknown, but they may well have been already in the early archetype in the same way as the early Jewish elements are present in the miniatures of the Ashburnham Pentateuch.

The thirteenth century saw the production of two magnificent series of bible pictures which are related to each other. First is the picture-book

[1] Bodl. MS Junius 11 reproduced in full by I. Gollancz, *The Cædmon Manuscript of Anglo-Saxon Poetry* (Oxford, 1927).

[2] See O. Pächt, *The Rise of Pictorial Narrative in Twelfth-century England* (Oxford, 1962), pp. 7, 8.

made in Paris probably for St Louis and now in the Pierpont Morgan Library in New York. This contains nearly three hundred scenes illustrating Old Testament stories, from the Creation to the beheading of Sheba the son of Bichri in II Sam. xxi.[1] No descriptive text as far as can be seen at present was provided, though at a rather later date a series of Latin titles was added by an Italian scribe. Artistically the Morgan picture-bible is one of the finest examples of French Gothic illustration. The sources of the scenes depicted cannot be shown to go back to very ancient originals, though one of them may have been the Greek Octateuchs of the middle Byzantine period, which certainly had influence in western Europe from the second half of the twelfth century. The second series is in an abbreviated version of the Old Testament in Old French written and illustrated in the crusading kingdom of Acre in the middle of the thirteenth century again probably for St Louis.[2] It has twenty miniatures each of which serves as the frontispiece to one of the twenty books. Some of these miniatures are derived from the Byzantine sources, but others, such as those preceding Esther, Tobit and Ruth, have no parallels in Byzantine art but belong to a western tradition. Thus it will be seen that the habits of the artists could be quite eclectic, taking one set of illustrations from one tradition and another set from an entirely different one. Even in their borrowings they make alterations. For instance, a story which was in the source depicted in three scenes may be reduced to one by combining certain figures from all three and omitting the remainder.[3] This habit was common to all medieval miniaturists and was one of the most significant ways in which an artist might show his originality.

Two other Old Testament picture-books should be mentioned. Both date from the fourteenth century. The earlier is English and the later Italian, though it seems clear that the artist of the former was influenced by fourteenth-century Italian painting.[4] British Museum, Egerton MS

[1] Reproduced by M. R. James and S. C. Cockerell, *A Book of Old Testament Illustrations of the Middle of the Thirteenth Century* (Cambridge (Roxburghe Club), 1927).

[2] H. Buchthal, *Miniature Painting in the Latin Kingdom of Jerusalem* (Oxford, 1957), pp. 54–8, Pls. 62–81. And see pp. 443 ff. of this book.

[3] For a valuable account of this method see K. Weitzmann, *Illustrations in Roll and Codex*, pp. 141, 142.

[4] Otto Pächt, 'A Giottesque Episode in English Mediaeval Art', *Journal of the Warburg and Courtauld Institutes*, VI (1943), 51–71. The whole manuscript has been reproduced by M. R. James, *Illustrations of the Book of Genesis* (Oxford (Roxburghe Club), 1921).

1894, known sometimes as the Egerton Genesis, contains one hundred and fifty scenes extending from the Creation to the story of Joseph in Gen. xliv. (Plate 35.) It is incomplete, and thus it is not known how far the series extended. The miniatures themselves are unfinished. A text in Anglo-French which has some connection with the *Historia Scholastica* of Peter Comestor (p. 206) was added after the pictures were already drawn. From the point of view of the history of biblical illustration the most important feature was the acquaintance by the artist with a very early cycle of Genesis illustrations belonging to the tradition of the Cotton Genesis. As has been seen, this tradition was known in England as well as in Italy, so the immediate source of his knowledge cannot be determined. The second picture-book is much more extensive. This is a late-fourteenth-century Paduan manuscript divided now between the British Museum and the Biblioteca dell'Accademia dei Concordi at Rovigo near Venice.[1] It contains the Pentateuch, Joshua and Ruth, and the pictures are arranged usually with four to a page. The cycle is, consequently, a very large one. In certain respects the Genesis pictures in the picture-book have some fairly close parallels with the Egerton Genesis pictures.[2] It is possible, therefore, that both made use of the same tradition for some of their illustrations and that it was an ancient one, though in both cases modified to suit the requirements of the fourteenth century.

What has been said will indicate that behind the numerous Old Testament pictures in the middle ages there may lie a good deal of early material, though it is hard to recognize. This does not mean that the artists merely copied earlier manuscripts. They altered them constantly, adding and subtracting as they wished. An undoubtedly important source for the Byzantine illuminators were the illustrated Octateuchs containing the Pentateuch, Joshua, Judges and Ruth. They do not appear until the middle Byzantine period, though they may well contain in them earlier iconographical matter. From the tenth century onward they become a vitally important influence which spread beyond the bounds of the Byzantine world. As has already been noticed in connection with the picture-bibles in the Pierpont Morgan Library and

---

[1] Add. MS 15277 and Rovigo MS 212; both parts have been reproduced by Gianfranco Folena and Gian Lorenzo Mellini, *Bibbia Istoriata Padovana della Fine del Trecento* (Venice, 1962).

[2] For a valuable list of picture-bibles, see O. Pächt, *op. cit.* p. 61 n. 1.

the Arsenal Bible in Paris, their illustrations were already known in western Europe by the twelfth century. This may not mean that a complete Greek Octateuch was available, but that some of the icono-graphical features of the Octateuchs were circulating through other manuscripts and copy-books.

With the possible exception of the Gospels, the most popular book of the Bible in the middle ages was unquestionably the Psalter. It enjoyed supreme popularity from the eighth century onwards and was only superseded by the Books of Hours in the Latin West during the fourteenth century. From the beginning of the eleventh to the middle of the fifteenth century it was consistently the book produced in the most luxurious copies for princes and the nobility, whether lay or ecclesiastic. This pre-eminence is hardly surprising in view of the fact that it formed the basis of the canonical Hours of the Church, being recited in full during the course of one week (p. 246). The Psalter was also the basis of much private devotion.

As a literary work the Psalter does not present very easy material for the illustrator, being a series of poems without any narrative running through them. Nevertheless a number of attempts were made to provide textual illustrations in both Latin and Greek manuscripts. They take a variety of forms. By far the most elaborate are those in the Latin Psalter known as the Utrecht Psalter which was made probably in the abbey of Hautvillers near Reims in the second quarter of the ninth century. Each psalm is preceded by a drawing composed of small scenes illustrating some of the verses of the psalm unified by placing them within a single landscape (see Plate 36). If we take the illustration to Psalm 15 (16), on the extreme left Christ is seen bending down and pulling the figures of a man and a woman from a pit, *v.* 10: 'thou shalt not leave my soul in hell.' This group has been borrowed by the artist from a picture of the harrowing of hell. Above on the right a figure holds out a cup, *v.* 5: 'the Lord himself is the portion of my heritage and of my cup' (*calicis*). In the middle is the scene of the women at the sepulchre, which certainly illustrates the second part of *v.* 10: 'neither shalt thou suffer thy holy One to see corruption.' On the right at the top is Christ with angels and below him a group of men who are presumably 'the saints that are in the earth' in *v.* 3. On the extreme right are three persons lying on beds who may represent *v.* 9, 'my soul also shall rest in hope'. From this it will be seen that the artist who composed these miniatures was beset by considerable difficulties. Some of the figures, such as the man with the cup from *v.* 5, are clearly direct illustrations of the text, but the figures of the harrowing of hell and the women at the sepulchre for *v.* 10 are borrowed from the New Testament picture cycles. This is natural in view of the fact that this verse is quoted in Peter's speech in Acts ii and has always been associated with the Resurrection story.

Besides such composite illustrations as those found in the Utrecht Psalter, where an attempt is made to illustrate the whole psalm, a number of psalters from the seventh century onwards make use of marginal illustrations; either these are placed near to the relevant text, or the text is in some way marked to bring text and picture together. Marginal illustrations of this kind are found in both Greek and Latin manuscripts, and in both appears the same ingenuity as that found in the Utrecht Psalter. There is also the same borrowing of scenes which really belong to some other set of pictures. For instance, in the Greek psalters with marginal pictures, Psalm 104, which recalls the Almighty's protection of the children of Israel in the wilderness, is provided with a number of scenes borrowed either from the Octateuch pictures or from an illustrated copy of Exodus.[1]

One of the most beautiful and original of the psalters with marginal illustrations was made at Bury St Edmunds in the second quarter of the eleventh century. It is now in the Vatican. (Plate 37.)[2] The artist who composed it was particularly ingenious. On the whole, psalters with marginal illustrations of the kind just mentioned are rare. Occasionally a rather similar device is found when textual subjects find their way into the illuminated initials at the beginning of each psalm. In the twelfth-century St Albans Psalter now in St Godehard's, Hildesheim, the small scenes in the initials illustrate a passage of the psalm which has been written out at the head of the psalm, so that it is quite clear to which verse the picture refers. The choice of verse is highly individual, being made to stress a lesson of particular significance for the religious for whom the book was made. (Plate 38.) For instance for Psalm 21 (22), verse 13, 'Many calves have surrounded me, fat bulls

[1] See K. Weitzmann, 'Die Illustration der Septuaginta', *Münchner Jahrbuch der bildenden Kunst*, Dritte Folge, Bd. III/IV (1952/3), pp. 108–10.

[2] MS Regin Lat. 12, see F. Wormald, *English Drawings of the Tenth and Eleventh Centuries* (London, 1952), Pls. 26–8.

have besieged me. They have opened their mouths against me, as a lion ravening and roaring', has been chosen because it may be interpreted by reference to the psalter commentaries as showing the soul escaping with God's help from the temptations of lust and pride.[1] These particular verses were not, therefore, chosen at random but, as it were, are visual glosses on the text. A late and somewhat jejune example may be found in the fourteenth-century English psalter made for a member of the Bohun family and now in the Nationalbibliothek in Vienna, where the subtleties displayed in the St Albans Psalter are completely absent.[2]

A far more general way of illustrating the psalters was to place a miniature or a more elaborate initial with a picture in it at certain specified points throughout the book. The simplest method was that used by some Byzantine illuminators, consisting of a large picture or group of minatures before Psalm 1 and another before Psalm 77. The Greek psalters were divided up into twenty kathismata, and Psalm 77 is the beginning of the eleventh kathisma and therefore of the second half of the whole book. Another division used often in the western Church was to split the Psalter into three, with pictures or historiated initials before Psalms 1, 51, and 101. This is sometimes called the Celtic division and it is certainly found in some Irish psalters. On the other hand it may be earlier than the seventh century. The abbreviated version of Cassiodorus' Commentary on the Psalms in the eighth-century copy in Durham cathedral MS B. II. 30 had originally three frontispieces, one to each part, and there is no reason to believe that this tripartite division had been invented in Northumbria where the manuscript was made.[3] A third and also very common division was to introduce miniatures or elaborate letters before the first psalm to be sung at Matins on each day of the week, and before the first psalm sung at Sunday Vespers. This gave rise to the eightfold or liturgical division with pictures or figured initials before Psalms 1, 26, 38, 52, 68, 80, 97 and 109. Occasionally in sumptuous copies both the threefold and the eightfold divisions are combined.

[1] See C. R. Dodwell in O. Pächt, C. R. Dodwell and F. Wormald, *The St Albans Psalter*, pp. 181–97, 214.

[2] Vienna, Nationalbibliothek, cod. 1826, described and reproduced by M. R. James, *The Bohun Manuscripts* (Oxford (Roxburghe Club), 1936), pp. 33–46, Pls. xxxix–lvi.

[3] R. A. B. Mynors, *Durham Cathedral Manuscripts* (Oxford, 1939), p. 21.

In the later middle ages, in the thirteenth and fourteenth centuries in particular, a fairly uniform system of illustration was evolved for the eightfold division; in this David, the supposed author of the Psalter, can be seen engaged in certain acts mentioned in the opening words of the psalm. Thus for Psalm 38 (39), 'I said I will take heed to my ways that I offend not in my tongue', the appropriate picture shows David pointing to his mouth, or again Psalm 52 (53), 'The foolish body hath said in his heart: There is no God', may have David addressing a fool or even a fool by himself.[1] (Plate 39.) In spite of the fact that these kinds of illustration seem to be the commonest there was certainly no hard-and-fast rule as to what must be put to illustrate a particular psalm, and David does not always take the leading part. In Psalm 68 (69), 'Save me O God: for the waters are come in, even unto my soul', Jonah belched forth by the whale is often found and any reference to David is omitted.

One of the most magnificent compositions found in psalters dating from the twelfth century onwards is the great Tree of Jesse which often stands before Psalm 1 in place of the picture of David and his musicians which was the earlier practice. This shows Jesse sleeping at the foot of a great ornamental tree which grows from his loins, and in its branches and convolutions are seen David with kings and prophets ending with Christ and sometimes the seven gifts of the Spirit. The idea of it lies in the prophecy of Isaiah 'And there shall come forth a rod out of the stem of Jesse, and a branch shall grow out of his roots...'. It does not appear before the twelfth century but after that date it was increasingly popular.[2] The whole shape can be easily manipulated into the form of the great B (for Beatus) with which every psalter text must begin. Consequently a number of magnificent books, such as the Gorleston Psalter in the British Museum, have a Jesse Tree within their first initial.

Besides the actual text of the psalms, most psalters were provided with a series of scriptural canticles, such as the Magnificat and the Nunc Dimittis, which came at the end of the book. These also were sometimes given pictures, particularly in Byzantine manuscripts. Their

---

[1] For the various methods in use in the thirteenth century see Günther Haseloff, *Die Psalterillustration im 13. Jahrhundert* (1938).

[2] Isa. xi. 1–3, see A. Watson, *The Early Iconography of the Tree of Jesse* (Oxford, 1934).

illustrations are usually borrowed from the appropriate scriptural pictures. For example the Canticle of Moses, from Exod. xv, is illustrated by a miniature of the crossing of the Red Sea with the destruction of Pharaoh's army, which can be related to the illustrations to the book of Exodus in the Octateuchs.

Many Latin psalters from the eleventh century onwards, besides using the eightfold system, have a series, sometimes very large, of miniatures placed at the beginning of the book. These may consist of pictures representing the important incidents in the life of our Lord, the subjects apparently being determined by their importance as illustrating the more important liturgical feasts and theophanies. The series relating to the Infancy begins with the Annunciation and ends with the temptation in the wilderness. This is then followed by a second group beginning with the entry into Jerusalem and ending with the descent of the Holy Spirit. They are in fact a kind of pictorial preface, and stress the teaching well known in the middle ages that in the psalms can be found reflections of the Incarnation, Passion and Ascension of Christ. These preparatory pictures are by no means uniform, and were added to and expanded at will by the introduction of other matter such as Old Testament pictures and scenes from the lives of saints and the Virgin. The earliest example of their use is in the psalter from Winchester, now Cotton MS Tiberius C. VI in the British Museum, made in the middle of the eleventh century. This shows scenes from the life of David and of Christ, the latter being mainly devoted to the Passion (entry into Jerusalem, Christ washing the feet of his disciples, the betrayal, Christ before Pilate, Christ crucified, the women at the sepulchre, the Harrowing of Hell, doubting Thomas, the Ascension, Pentecost). There is also Michael slaying the dragon.[1] Besides these, the artist placed pictures before Psalms 1, 51 and 101, thereby using the threefold system of psalter division. He also placed large decorated initials at the points required by the eightfold system, with a miniature of the Trinity before Psalm 109. Another magnificent set of prefatory pictures is found in the late-twelfth-century Ingeburg Psalter in the Musée Condé at Chantilly. They include not only Old and New Testament illustrations, but also the death and coronation of the Virgin and two miniatures with four scenes from the story of Theophilus, who did homage to the devil and

---

[1] Reproduced by F. Wormald, 'An English eleventh-century psalter with pictures', in *Walpole Society*, xxxviii (1960–2), 1–13, Pls. 1–30.

was rescued by the Blessed Virgin from damnation. It is, therefore, important to remember that the choice of what was put in and what was left out of these prefatory pictures was not prescribed by rigid rules, but was governed rather by the requirements of the individual for whom the copy was intended. In some manuscripts these prefatory illustrations are very considerable, the result being that we have really a bible picture-book incorporated into a Psalter.

Unquestionably the most sumptuous manuscripts of any part of the Scriptures produced in the middle ages were the copies of the four Gospels bound in one volume, frequently with splendid covers of ivory and metalwork. The Gospels were regarded with particular veneration by the faithful, and an eighth-century writer compares the entry of the gospel book at Mass to the entry of Christ himself (and see p. 230). Emperors and princes made presents of them to the monastic houses and churches under their protection. Their immense popularity lasted until the end of the twelfth century, when with the introduction of a missal in which all portions of the Mass were included their use became diminished and they fell out of fashion. They did not entirely disappear, and some splendid copies were produced in both the fourteenth and fifteenth centuries. The great period of their production was from the ninth to the middle of the twelfth century, and no great ecclesiastical establishment could be without one.

The contents of the gospel books are fairly uniform, and are made up of prefatory matter, lists of chapters and the Gospel texts themselves.[1] An important decorative feature is formed by the canon tables ascribed to Eusebius of Caesarea, which are frequently found at the beginning. These tables were designed to show which passages in each Gospel were in agreement with any of the other three. They are arranged in columns of figures under decorative arches, sometimes of great elaboration, and occasionally provided with scenes or the symbols of the evangelists. (Plate 40.) They are to be found in both Greek and Latin manuscripts.[2] Before each Gospel is a miniature of the appropriate evangelist, who is commonly shown seated, though he may be in some cases standing. Above his head is his symbol: Matthew an angel, Mark a lion, Luke a calf and John an eagle. The setting in which the evangelist

[1] For Latin gospel books dating from before 800, see P. McGurk, *Latin Gospel Books from A.D. 400 to A.D. 800* (Ghent, 1960).
[2] See Carl Nordenfalk, *Die Spätantiken Kanontafeln* (Göteborg, 1938), 2 vols.

is sitting is sometimes in the form of an elaborate architectural structure or may be some kind of landscape placed in a rectangular frame. He may be provided with a desk and writing paraphernalia. From their pose and general appearance it seems plausible to suggest that these figures are derived from representations of ancient philosophers and writers. Occasionally the function of the symbol seems to be that of inspiring the evangelist, as in the splendid Reims Gospels now at Épernay. Although not strictly speaking illustration, the large initial pages with which each Gospel begins should be mentioned, as they form an important element in the decoration of these books. They appear first in manuscripts from Great Britain and Ireland of the sixth and seventh centuries. The Lindisfarne Gospels in the British Museum, made in Northumbria at the end of the seventh century, have all the decorative elements just referred to. In some manuscripts the evangelist is not accompanied by his symbol and appears as a simple late author portrait, as is found in the early-ninth-century Coronation Gospels of Charlemagne now in the Schatzkammer in Vienna.[1]

Long cycles of illustrations to the Gospels were certainly known to both Greek and Latin Christians by the sixth century and probably earlier. The Greek Gospels of Rossano and the Sinope fragment now in the Bibliothèque Nationale in Paris, both dating from the sixth century, and both written on purple vellum, contain long series of pictures which indicate that the cycle used by the artists was a very complete one. The Sinope fragment includes illustrations, some of the miracles, and the Rossanensis some parables, and miracles, as well as scenes of the Passion.[2] In the Rossanensis the pictures are gathered together in a group at the beginning, forming a kind of preface of illustrations, while in the Sinope fragment they are placed in the lower margins of the page and interlock with the relevant text. On the whole, before the tenth century, gospel books with many illustrations are uncommon.

The earliest series of illustrations of the life of Christ in a Latin manuscript are those found in the gospel book from St Augustine's Canterbury, now MS 286 in the library of Corpus Christi College,

[1] Reproduced by W. Koehler, *Die Karolingischen Miniaturen*, III, Pls. 18, 20, 22, 24.
[2] For the Rossano Gospels, see A. Muñoz, *Il Codice purpureo di Rossano e il frammento Sinopense* (Rome, 1907). For the Sinope fragment see A. Grabar, *Les peintures de l'Évangéliaire de Sinope* (Paris, 1948).

Cambridge.[1] (Plate 41.) This manuscript was written probably in Italy towards the end of the sixth century and was by the early eighth century already in England. The illustrations seem to have been distributed over eight miniatures, two to each Gospel, and it may be calculated that in all as many as eighty-four scenes may have been represented. This number cannot of course be compared with the enormous series of illustrations found in some of the Greek gospel books of the eleventh century or in the later *Bible Moralisée*; nevertheless when complete the cycle must have been an impressive one. What remain today are twelve scenes from the Passion and twelve depicting incidents in Luke's Gospel. (Zacharias and the angel, Christ among the doctors, Christ teaching from the boat, Peter falls at Christ's feet, the raising of the son of the widow of Nain, the call of Levi, Christ and the lawyer, Christ hailed by a woman, Luke xi. 27, foxes have holes, the parable of the fig-tree, the miracle of the dropsical man, Christ and Zacchaeus.) Both groups stand before Luke's Gospel. The Passion pictures are placed in twelve small squares set in a rectangular frame forming a single miniature. The scenes from Luke stand between pairs of columns set on either side of a large figure of the evangelist. From what evidence we have it would seem that the large square miniatures showed pictures from the life of Christ, and those flanking the evangelist were devoted to scenes found in the relevant Gospel. Another gospel book now in Munich has been thought to contain remains of an early cycle. This manuscript seems to have been in the possession of one Hatto, who has been identified with an early-ninth-century abbot of the great abbey of Reichenau on Lake Constance. Two leaves with scenes from an Infancy cycle (adoration of the Magi and the massacre of the innocents) and pictures of events after the Resurrection have been inserted. They are considered to be Ottonian copies of sixth-century originals.[2]

Unlike the Carolingian gospel books, where illustration was for the most part restricted to the portraits of the evangelists, the gospel books of the Ottonian period have a large series of pictures which include illustrations of the parables and the miracles as well as cycles showing

[1] Reproduced by F. Wormald, *The Miniatures in the Gospels of St Augustine* (Cambridge, 1954).

[2] Munich, Bayr. Staatsbibliothek Clm. 23631, reproduced by A. Boinet, *La Miniature Carolingienne* (Paris, 1913), Pls. I, II. For the Ottonian dating see Catalogue of the Munich Exhibition, *Ars Sacra, Kunst des frühen Mittelalters* (June–October 1950), no. 58.

the Infancy and the Passion. The magnificent Gospels made at the abbey of Echternach as a gift by the emperor for the cathedral of Speyer in 1045–6, and now in the Escorial, introduce illustrations into the text as well as having canon tables and evangelist pictures.[1] Another splendid gospel book, also from Echternach and dating from about two years earlier than the Escorial book, is now in the Germanisches National-Museum in Nürnberg. Its pictures are arranged in groups of four miniatures at the beginning of each Gospel. They form a fairly continuous cycle beginning with the Annunciation and ending with Pentecost.[2] Rather earlier is the gospel lectionary made for Egbert, archbishop of Trier about 980, known as the *Codex Egberti* and now preserved in the Stadtbibliothek at Trier. The artist of this book absorbed most successfully the style of fourth-century painting, and one of his sources may well have been an early series of gospel illustrations. He made use, however, also of contemporary Byzantine illuminations, and in any case seems to have modified his models to meet his own requirements. This changing and modifying of models can also be seen in the two Echternach manuscripts, whose artists appear to have had knowledge of the *Codex Egberti*. The arrangement of the pictures in the gospel lectionaries follows the order of the Gospels as read at Mass. This may, therefore, be said to follow a liturgical rather than an absolutely strict Gospel order, though the cycles begin with the Annunciation and end with Pentecost.

Whereas in Germany, and occasionally in Italy, the illustrated gospel books and the lectionaries continued in fashion until the early twelfth century, such places as England and France retained the more limited Carolingian practice of canon tables, evangelist portraits and large initial pages. Their pictures of the life of Christ, at any rate from the twelfth century onwards, were to be found (as has already been mentioned) in the pictures preceding the psalters. Earlier they are found in sacramentaries and benedictionals. A particularly interesting series is found in four leaves of the second quarter of the twelfth century, two in the Pierpont Morgan Library in New York, and one each in the British Museum and the Victoria and Albert Museum. These have also some Old Testament pictures, but the majority of the scenes are devoted

[1] Reproduced by Albert Boeckler, *Das Goldene Evangelienbuch Heinrichs III* (Berlin, 1933).

[2] Reproduced by Peter Metz, *The Golden Gospels of Echternach* (London, 1957).

to the life of Christ and contain, like the Ottonian cycles, scenes of parables and miracles, including a Dives and Lazarus which should be compared with the same subject in the Escorial manuscript. The leaves were probably made at Canterbury and were available to the miniaturist who in the early thirteenth century decorated a copy of the Utrecht Psalter which is now in the Bibliothèque Nationale in Paris. If we compare the two manuscripts we can see how one miniaturist could use the work of the other. For instance the saying by Jesus in Luke ix. 58, 'Foxes have holes, and birds of the air have nests; but the Son of Man hath no where to lay his head', is illustrated in the British Museum leaf by two small scenes placed one above the other. In the Paris version it is arranged in two strictly separated rectangular scenes. The figures too have been changed, though the general plan has been retained. This miniature shows well the way in which artists modified their models.

Another important source of Christological subjects was the picture-books of the kind already mentioned in connection with the Egerton Genesis and the Rovigo picture-bible, in which the illustrations are more important than the text, which is very much abbreviated. Occasionally both Old and New Testaments are combined, as in the Velislav picture-bible made in Bohemia in about 1340 and containing nearly 750 illustrations usually in two registers,[1] comprising a series from the Old Testament, a cycle on the Antichrist, part of a Passion cycle and the Acts of the Apostles and an Apocalypse. There is also a cycle dedicated to the legend of St Wenceslas.[2] A comparable mixture of scriptural and apocryphal material is to be found in the rather earlier English picture-bible once at Holkham Hall and now in the British Museum.[3] This includes a short series of scenes from the Old Testament from the Creation to the drunkenness of Noah, followed by a much longer Christological cycle into which has been introduced a series of pictures of the apocryphal miracles of Christ's infancy. This set ends with the Ascension and is followed by a section containing the 'Last Things',

[1] See J. Květ, *Czechoslovakia, Romanesque and Gothic Illuminated Manuscripts* (New York (UNESCO), 1959), Pls. xxiv–xxvi.

[2] See exhibition catalogue, Paris, Musée des Arts Décoratifs, *L'Art Ancien en Tchécoslovaquie* (1957), no. 108, for a short bibliography.

[3] Brit. Mus., Add. MS 47680, reproduced by W. O. Hassall, *The Holkham Bible Picture Book* (London, 1954); see also M. R. James in *The Walpole Society*, XI (1922–3), 1–27.

among which are the fifteen signs immediately preceding the Last Judgement, which is also represented. Picture-books of this kind must in many cases have provided illuminators and preachers with extra material. Infancy miracles are found on tiles and the fifteen signs in painted glass and sculpture. In the Holkham Hall picture-bible the choice of scenes was certainly influenced by the *Historia Scholastica*. Like the Egerton Genesis and the Rovigo Bible, the explanatory text is in the vernacular, whereas in the Velislav Bible it is in Latin. In all these picture-bibles of the fourteenth century both costumes and architecture have been brought up to date. The Holkham Bible is particularly rich in accessories interesting to students of costumes and contemporary life.

Last in this examination of the decoration of individual books of the Bible is the Apocalypse.[1] After the Psalter and the Gospels this is the book most frequently found in fully illustrated copies. Its popularity has a long history, and examples come from the beginning of the ninth century to the end of the middle ages. Curiously enough, Greek illustrated copies appear late on the scene, but the evidence indicates that the Latin Church had them from the sixth century. The earliest evidence of a complete cycle comes from Bede's *Lives of the Abbots*. He tells how Benedict Biscop at the end of the seventh century brought back from Rome pictures of the Apocalypse to decorate his church of St Peter. What these were like is not recorded, but four manuscripts of the ninth century give some idea of the nature of these early cycles. There is a pair at Trier and Cambrai which were copied from the same model. From the style of the ninth-century copies, and they seem to be good ones, the archetype was probably a manuscript of the sixth century. Every moment of the book is illustrated in the seventy-four subjects. There are also two other ninth-century Apocalypses, one in the Bibliothèque Nationale, nouv. acq. lat. 1132, in Paris, the second in Valenciennes. These again show signs of being fairly accurate copies of earlier archetypes.[2] The Valenciennes manuscript may have been copied from the Anglo-Saxon intermediary model, so the Paris copy gives one a more accurate rendering of the late antique original.

[1] For the whole question of illuminated Apocalypses, see M. R. James, *The Apocalypse in Art* (London, 1931).

[2] Paris, Bibl. Nat., nouv. acq. lat. 1132, has been partly reproduced by H. Omont, *Bulletin de la Société française de Reproduction de Manuscrits à Peintures* (1922).

With the exception of the Spanish Apocalypses, which form a separate group, the centuries between the ninth and the thirteenth did not produce many illustrated copies of this book, though there is a cycle in the manuscript of the Liber Floridus of Lambert of Saint Bertin at Saint-Omer in Wolfenbüttel which is copied from a manuscript probably dating from the eighth century, and one in a manuscript of the Commentary of Haimo of Auxerre in the Bodleian Library at Oxford. The Spanish group represented by the manuscripts of the Commentary on the Apocalypse of Beatus of Liebana have illustrations which also suggest that they are derived from early sources, though their origin is unknown.[1]

By far the most productive period of illustrated Apocalypses is the thirteenth and fourteenth centuries, from which more than ninety examples exist. They are in most cases accompanied by a text and often short commentaries as well. They appear in England and France towards the middle of the second quarter of the thirteenth century. (Plate 42.) This large mass of material has been divided into two families, the first being distinguished by the introduction of pictures from the Life of John the Evangelist and by the appearance of scenes relating to the Antichrist which have been intruded into the episode of the Two Witnesses in chapter xi. The manuscripts of this first family are really a series of picture-books, whereas the second family has a more complete text and the copies are far more numerous; Antichrist is missing. Though often most splendidly written and illustrated, the actual text is sometimes carelessly transcribed and bad. The first family provided an important part of the archetype for the block-books of the Apocalypse.

The last class of illustrated bible to be discussed is that in which the pictures are accompanied by others which are used to explain or comment on them. They are in fact pictures glossed by other pictures. The two most important types are represented first by the *Biblia Pauperum* (p. 292) and the *Speculum humanae salvationis* (p. 302), secondly by what is known as the *Bible Moralisée* (p. 448). The first type is rather different from the second, in that its basic function is to show how incidents in the life of Christ are prefigured by many others in the Old

---

[1] The whole question of the Spanish Apocalypses has been very fully investigated by W. Neuss, *Die Apokalypse des Hl. Johannes in der Altspanischen und Altchristlichen Bibel-Illustration* (Münster in Westfalen, 1931), 2 vols.

Testament and ancient history. The second type is a much more extended affair in which each of the chosen incidents in the Bible is accompanied by a miniature illustrating its significance according to the principles of medieval exegesis. The result is occasionally extremely subtle, perhaps even somewhat far-fetched.

As has been mentioned, the foundation of the *Biblia Pauperum*, which seems to be a creation of the thirteenth century, is the fore-shadowing of the life of Christ by a number of Old Testament incidents and prophecies (see also pp. 155ff. and Plate 43). The life of Christ is seen as the fulfilment of all preceding human history. It was based upon a method of interpreting Scripture which is very old, being found in both the Old and New Testaments, and which also appears in early Christian and early medieval art, as has been indicated in an excellent sketch published recently by Fr Floridus Röhrig of Klosterneuburg. During the twelfth century interest in this method grew and finds full literary expression in such works as *Pictor in Carmine* from England and the *Rota in Medio Rotae* from Austria.[1] The pictures which form the *Biblia Pauperum* are conceived on a more or less uniform plan. In the middle is the New Testament scene or antitype, which is flanked on either side by Old Testament or other scenes providing the types. There are also heads of prophets associated by some quotation which was considered relevant.[2] Besides these there is usually a short text which explains the scene. Thus the two types of the Last Supper, which are the meeting of Abraham and Melchizedek and the rains of manna, are explained thus. For Abraham and Melchizedek the explanation is as follows: 'It is read in Genesis that when Abraham returned from the slaughter of his enemies and brought a great booty which he had taken off his enemies Melchisedech the priest of God offered him bread and wine. Melchisedech signifies Christ, who gave to his disciples the bread of the body and the wine of his blood to eat and drink in the Last Supper.' For the rain of manna the text says: 'It is read in Exodus that the Lord commanded Moses to say to the people that each man should collect of the manna from heaven as much as should suffice him for that day. That manna which God gave to the children of Israel signified the

[1] For *Pictor in Carmine* see M. R. James, 'Pictor in Carmine', *Archaeologia*, XCIV (1951), 144 ff. Floridus Röhrig, *Rota in Medio Rotae* (Klosterneuberg, 1965), pp. 7–12, where further bibliography will be found.
[2] G. Schmidt, *Die Armenbibeln des XIV. Jahrhunderts* (Graz–Köln, 1959).

holy bread, even that of his most sacred Body which he gave to his disciples at supper when he said: "Take eat all of this. This is my body, etc."'

Naturally there are a variety of textual families within the large number of manuscripts of the *Biblia Pauperum*, but on the whole the arrangement just described is valid for all of them. In choosing scenes to be used as the antitypes the author of the original work seems to have taken only the most salient points in the Gospel narrative to be illustrated. For instance, few miracles are used and naturally no parables. Thus the main source of the pictures are the great liturgical cycles. Those who have studied the manuscripts suggest that the original examples came in all probability from south-eastern Germany and were made in the middle of the thirteenth century. Certainly some of the beautiful early-fourteenth-century examples come from Austria.[1] As a type of illustrated book it remained popular and appears in the fifteenth century in the form of the block-book. A rather later and more elaborate picture-book, which is similar to the *Biblia Pauperum*, is the *Concordantia Caritatis*.[2] This also is based upon typological interpretation of the New Testament by the Old, but introduces scenes from natural history which are also shown as types of the scenes selected to illustrate the life of Christ.

Rather similar in aim is the *Speculum humanae salvationis* (see also p. 302 and plates 24–5), which appears in Germany in the early fourteenth century.[3] Its circulation was much wider than either the *Biblia Pauperum* or the *Concordantia Caritatis*, and copies from as far apart as England and Italy are known. The usual arrangement of the *Speculum* is to place each antitype with its type so that the antitype comes on the left and then three types. The whole is spread in four columns over a single opening. Besides the two Old Testament types is a third which may come from another source and is sometimes more allegorical in tone. Thus the Last Supper has the same two Old Testament scenes as are found in the *Biblia Pauperum*, but adds the paschal lamb as the third.

[1] See also Hildegard Zimmermann, 'Armenbibel', in *Reallexikon zur deutschen Kunstgeschichte*, ed. Otto Schmitt, I (1937), 1072–84, where the various types are set out.

[2] See Alfred A. Schmid, 'Concordantia caritatis', in Schmitt, *Reallexikon*, III, 833–53.

[3] T. Lutz and P. Perdrizet, *Speculum Humanae Salvationis* (Mulhouse, 1907), 2 vols.

Far more elaborate than any of the three works which have just been described is the *Bible Moralisée*. This was a work of the thirteenth century, almost certainly composed in Paris for St Louis, probably in a Dominican milieu. Its aim was to provide a completely illustrated bible history accompanied by a commentary, which was also illustrated in full. The method is to provide each biblical scene and its commentary with an illustration. Enormous ingenuity and care was lavished upon its production. The explanatory pictures are of great variety and by no means confined to typology, though this naturally plays a part. Even contemporary figures such as Dominican friars appear. In arrangement the relationship of the text to the commentary is fairly uniform. The page is divided into columns, a narrow one with the written text followed by a broad one with the illustrations. In the thirteenth-century copies these are often placed in roundels giving the appearance of stained-glass windows. First comes the biblical picture and immediately below it is the scene illustrating the commentary. On the whole, copies of the *Bible Moralisée* are naturally rare since their production must have been a most expensive and laborious business. By far the finest date from the thirteenth century, though a superb copy which was partly illuminated by the Limburg brothers dates from the early years of the fifteenth century. (Plate 44.)

It has been thought simpler to leave the question of how and where illustrated bibles or books of the Bible were made to the end. The first and most important point to stress is that from this aspect bibles were no different from any other illuminated manuscripts. Normally the text was written first, in the early middle ages on carefully prepared skin of some kind, in the fourteenth and fifteenth centuries occasionally on paper. Spaces were left by the scribes for the inclusion of the pictures. Such spaces may be seen in many books, for example the Cædmon manuscript at Oxford. Next the illuminator made a sketch, usually in light ink or plummet. After that the gold was added and certain broad areas of colour. This was then more carefully worked up until finally the completed miniature emerged. The last stage seems to have been to redraw the outline. Many bibles show these stages, the great Winchester Bible being a particularly good example. Occasionally the under-drawing is by a different artist from the one who did the painting; sometimes a long time may pass before the drawing is painted over. In the Winchester Bible, the painting seems to have been completed by at least two different artists working in two different styles.

As has already been seen, the sources from which the artists obtained their models were extremely various. In western Europe the miniaturists were much less bound by iconographical tradition and were constantly altering and adapting their models to suit their requirements. In the Byzantine empire and in those places where Byzantine art was most influential the iconographical tradition was more rigid, though the artists were capable of expressing ingenious variations on what seems at first sight to be a somewhat restricting tradition. The sources which provided the illustrations may be roughly divided into three categories: first illuminated manuscripts themselves or other monuments; secondly model books; and thirdly written descriptions of miniatures composed for the use of the artists. An example of direct copying of one bible from another is the second Bible of León dating from 1162, which is a copy of the first Bible of San Isidoro, which was made in 960. Much more frequent is the copying of individual miniatures such as those in the Carolingian bible from there. This copying of miniatures was attended by many changes, so that frequently only the faintest remnant of the iconographical tradition remains, and nothing of the original style. This makes iconographical study such a delicate business, since in one miniature several traditions may be combined.

One of the reasons for these combinations must be the existence of artist's model books.[1] It is obvious that many more must have once existed, but they are now among the great rarities of medieval art. Figures from a model book could be easily combined into scenes. Equally a model might be taken from a miniature in a book and modified by other figures introduced from a model book. One of the most interesting survivals is the sketch-book made in Saxony about 1230 and now in Wolfenbüttel, where the artist certainly had access to Byzantine models, some of which have been shown to come from a Greek gospel lectionary. (Plate 45.)

The third category is one which has hardly received any attention. It was sometimes the custom for those who were in charge of a programme of illumination to write, usually in the margin, a brief description of the miniature. These are often quite simple directions which are

[1] R. W. Scheller, *A Survey of Medieval Model Books* (Haarlem, 1963).

sometimes accompanied by a rudimentary sketch. In the Ashburnham Pentateuch there are some directions of this kind. They take the form of marking the places on the spaces left for the miniature with the name of the person who is enacting that particular portion of the scene. A much more elaborate version of such directions exists in the description of two psalters which may have come from the abbey of Saint Bertin at Saint-Omer. They date from the twelfth century and read almost like an extract from a modern catalogue.[1] The Last Supper is described thus: 'A table, three disciples on the right and three on the left. The Lord in the middle. John having his head on His Breast. Judas in front of the table, to whose mouth the Lord offers a bit of bread.' A short description like this could circulate quite easily and be equally useful as a marginal direction.

Two extremely difficult questions must be asked. Where were these illuminated bibles made and who made them? Neither question can be answered satisfactorily. The probability is that until about the middle of the twelfth century they were made either in monasteries or in other large ecclesiastical centres. By the end of the thirteenth century it would seem that shops run by laymen were already in existence, and there is evidence of lay illuminators at work in places like York, Oxford and Paris in the thirteenth century. The names of some are known, such as Master Honoré in Paris and not very much later Jean Pucelle. Even before the lay shops begin to appear it is clear that the illumination was not always the work of monks, even though it was executed in monasteries for monastic patrons. There was an artist called Nivardus who was brought from Lombardy to Fleury on the Loire in the early eleventh century, and the miniatures in the magnificent bible from Bury St Edmunds in Corpus Christi College, Cambridge, are the work of one Master Hugo, who was almost certainly a layman. Both Nivardus and Hugo were men of parts. Nivardus seems to have been a sculptor as well as a painter. Master Hugo cast the bronze doors once at Bury and carved statues in wood for the rood there. This does not mean that none of the works discussed in this chapter were the work of monks. Many artists were monks, but the evidence indicates that the lay artist had a most important part to play.

[1] F. Wormald, 'A Medieval Description of Two Illuminated Psalters', *Scriptorium*, VI (1952), 18–25.

CHAPTER IX

THE VERNACULAR SCRIPTURES

1. THE GOTHIC BIBLE

One of the fascinations of the study of the Gothic bible is that it is almost the only literary monument of a race which played so great a part in laying the foundations on which modern Europe eventually arose.

The historian Jordanes relates a popular tradition of about the middle of the sixth century according to which the Goths, leaving Scandza, i.e. the southern part of the Scandinavian peninsula, with a king at their head, arrived by sea at the Vistula delta. One of their branches, the Gepidae who established themselves there a little later, gave the name of *Gepidoios* to the islands situated at the river mouth. The Goths conquered and dispersed the inhabitants of the coast and also subdued the Vandals who were already established there; and according to Tacitus (*Germania* 43) and Ptolemy (*Geographia* 3. 5. 20), they remained on the lower Vistula until the middle of the second century A.D.

A new migration took the Goths by stages across the Pripet marshes towards the steppes of the Ukraine and as far as the Black Sea, where their presence is noted in 238. They are then found in Moesia and in Thrace, in contact, and often at war, with the Romans. Finally, certain Goths established themselves within the borders of the empire, north of the Danube and in Dacia (257), while others became mercenaries in the Roman army.

The Goths founded, on the two banks of the Dniester, a great empire stretching from the Don to the Danube. In the fourth century the natural frontier of the Dnieper separated two great tribes: in the east the Ostrogoths (*Austrogoti* or *Greutingi*), in the west the Visigoths (*Visi*, then *Visigoti* or *Tervingi*). These compounds were very early interpreted according to this geographical distribution, as though they meant 'Eastern Goths' and 'Western Goths'.

In 375 the Ostrogothic empire was attacked by the Huns, and its fall started a new migration. Some of the Ostrogoths fled to the Crimea, but the great majority was driven westwards. The Visigoths, under the leadership of Alaric, sacked Rome in 410 and founded in 412 the kingdom of Toulouse. More will be said later on the history of the Goths in the fifth century.

After the death of Attila (453) and the fall of his empire, the Ostrogoths established themselves in Pannonia. It was from there that Theodoric left in 488 for his campaign against Odoacer, which culminated in the conquest of Italy, where he reigned till his death in 526. It was Belisarius, the Byzantine general, who in 555 made an end of the Ostrogothic supremacy in Italy.

Not all the Goths, however, had left the Balkans. In Lower Moesia the *Goti minores* are noted as being peaceful herdsmen towards the end of the sixth century. There were still Goths living in the Crimea in the sixteenth century; but these are only a freakish survival: as a political factor the Goths counted for little after the sixth century, if we except the Gothic-Spanish kingdom in Spain which survived until its destruction by the Moors in 711.

ULFILAS

The most important source for the life of Ulfilas is Auxentius. The relevant passages may be found in F. Kauffmann, *Aus der Schule des Wulfila*, fol. 304–9, 349. The other main authorities are the *Ecclesiastical Histories* of Philostorgius (2. 5), Socrates (2. 41; 4. 33, 34), Sozomen (6. 37) and Theodoret (4. 33).

Ulfilas was descended from a Christian family of Cappadocia, originating in the town of Sadagolthina. According to Philostorgius, his grandparents were led into captivity in 264 by the Goths, during the invasion which ravaged Asia Minor in the reigns of Valerian and Gallienus. Among the captives there were also some priests who propagated the Christian faith among the Goths. In fact there seems no doubt that the Goths were acquainted with Christianity before Ulfilas, though missionary work in their territory had been mainly carried out among Roman captives. It is Ulfilas who has the right, in any event, to the title 'Apostle of the Goths'.

Ulfilas was probably born about 311, and if his mother was Cappadocian we can suppose that his father was a Goth. His name is very Gothic. The old historians wrote it Οὐλφίλας, Οὐρφίλας, Ulfila, Wulphilas, Vulfila. The Gothic form can only be Wulfila, a diminutive formed from *wulfa* ('wolf').

339

He must have had an excellent education, since he spoke and wrote Greek and Latin as well as Gothic. At the early age of thirty, on the occasion of a mission to Constantinople, he was singled out by Bishop Eusebius of Nicomedia and was raised to the episcopate. On his return to his native country he successfully ruled for seven years his little community of Christian Goths. His proselytizing, however, alarmed King Athanaric, persecutions broke out, and he decided to exile himself and his flock. He crossed the Danube and took refuge in Moesia, where the emperor Constantius had offered him shelter at the foot of Mount Haemus, not far from Nicopolis (348). This colony was still in existence two centuries later, and, under the name of Goths of Moesia or *Goti minores*, was engaged in breeding cattle.

For thirty-three years Ulfilas governed these Goths, both as bishop and as temporal leader. He is said to have taken part in numerous councils; it was at Constantinople, where he had gone to attend a synod, that he fell ill and died. The date of his death is usually given as 382.

Ulfilas was a definite, if moderate, Arian, and he spread the doctrines of Arius among his converts. At about the end of the fourth century Arianism disappeared from the East, but in the course of their migrations the Visigoths propagated it in the West, where it almost triumphed. Thanks to the zeal of the Visigoths, Arian Christianity also reached numerous Germanic tribes.

THE MANUSCRIPTS OF THE GOTHIC BIBLE

These manuscripts consist of:

1. The *Codex Argenteus* (CA), the Gospels written on purple parchment in silver and gold ink. Its exact origin is not known, but it belongs obviously to the same class as the *Codex Brixianus*, a Latin copy of the Gospels on purple parchment which comes from Brescia, a town which was an important centre of Gothic-Lombard influence. The *Codex Argenteus* contained 330 folios; 187 have survived. The order of the Gospels, Matthew, John, Luke, Mark, is that of the *Codex Brixianus* and of other Latin bibles prior to the Vulgate.

This manuscript is mentioned for the first time between 1550 and 1560 in the correspondence of German scholars. At that time the *Codex Argenteus* was at the monastery of Werden near Cologne. It is conjectured that it was brought there from Italy in about 795 by Liudger, a disciple of Alcuin, and founder of the monastery. At the beginning of the seventeenth century the MS was at Prague in the collection of the emperor Rudolph II. In 1648 the Swedes took the town and the *Codex Argenteus* formed part of the booty they carried away. After passing through several more hands, the MS was bought by Count de la Gardie, Chancellor of Sweden, who had a silver binding made for it and presented it in 1669 to the University of Uppsala, where it still is. The University Senate had a phototypographic reproduction made of it in 1927 (*Codex Argenteus Upsaliensis Iussu Senatus Universitatis phototypice editus*) as perfect as possible having regard to the present state of the MS and the use of ultra-violet rays.[1]

2. The *Codex Gissensis* (Giss.), at Giessen, discovered in Egypt near the ancient town of Antinoë. It consists of a double folio of parchment, and contains fragments (Luke xxiii–xxiv) of a Latin–Gothic bilingual of the Gospels.

All the other MSS are palimpsests originating from the monastery of Bobbio. They are:

3. The *Codex Carolinus* (Car.) at Wolfenbüttel (formerly at Wittenberg). It contains the Latin–Gothic text of Rom. xi–xv.

4. The *Codices Ambrosiani* (Ambr.), four in number (A, B, C, D) in the Ambrosian Library at Milan. A and B contain the Pauline epistles, C fragments of Matt. xxv–xxvii, D fragments of Neh. v–vii. It is probable that the Ambrosian Codices A and B and the *Codex Carolinus* derive from a not-far-distant common ancestor. Kauffmann's view that Codices A and B were copied from the same original is untenable. The fifty-three marginal glosses contained in Codex A are an inconclusive foundation on which to base a conclusive argument.[2]

5. The *Codex Taurinensis* (Taur.) at Turin, is, strictly speaking, part of *Codex Ambrosianus* A, and contains, on four very badly damaged folios, fragments of the Epistles to the Galatians and the Colossians.

THE TEXT OF THE GOTHIC GOSPELS

The *Codex Argenteus* represents a Byzantine text with a number of western readings. One of the main problems of the Gothic Gospels is to ascertain which of these western readings go back to the original translation. This is a difficult problem, since it often happens that a western

[1] See Otto von Friesen and Anders Grape, *Om Codex Argenteus, dess tid, hem och öden* (Uppsala, 1928).
[2] See G. W. S. Friedrichsen, *The Gothic Version of the Epistles*, pp. 62–128.

reading may derive from the Ulfilian Greek, or alternatively it may be the result of textual corruption caused by the influence of the Old Latin Version.

Streitberg has outlined the methods which he has followed in composing his suggested reconstruction of the Greek text from which Ulfilas translated the Gospels. On page xlv of the Introduction to *Die Gotische Bibel* he says:

In isolated instances it cannot always be determined with complete certainty whether the divergence of the Gothic text from the Byzantine is due only to the influence of the Old Latin, or whether the element foreign to the Byzantine text had already penetrated to the Greek original: probability mainly suggests the first assumption, particularly in the case where the text of the Old Latin is supported only by purely Alexandrian MSS...Wherever Greek MSS, whose readings can sometimes be found also in the Gothic text, give the Old Latin reading, this reading has been incorporated in the Greek Gospel text of the edition: this only indicates that in these cases the *possibility* of the influence of the Greek original exists.

This procedure is sound in principle: in particular cases it must be emphasized that extreme caution should be exercised in admitting western readings into the Greek underlying the Gothic Version.

The difficulty of determining the original Greek text of the Gothic Gospels is increased by the unhomogeneous character of the *Codex Argenteus*. This text bears a strong resemblance to that of Chrysostom and the Cappadocian Fathers. It is also similar to the text of the MSS E (eighth century), F (ninth century), G (ninth–tenth century), H (ninth–tenth century), S (tenth century), V (ninth century) and to a lesser degree to the text of K (ninth century), U (ninth–tenth century), Γ (tenth century), Λ (ninth century), Π (ninth century). At the same time the original Greek text, even allowing for displacement caused by textual contamination, cannot be completely identified with any existing Greek manuscript.

The most important point to be made in regard to the translation technique of the Gothic Gospels is that the translator has aimed at rendering every word in the Greek text by a corresponding word in the Gothic. Even particles like μέν and ἄν are represented in the Gothic, although such words, being peculiar to Greek, must almost necessarily, when reproduced in any other language, be unidiomatic or meaningless. The adherence to the word-order of the original is equally rigid.

It would be incorrect to criticize Ulfilas for the slavish literalness of his translation, since he was merely following a system of imitation which in his time was imposed by respect for the sacred text. Moreover it is precisely this literalness of rendering which facilitates the task of reconstructing the Greek underlying text and therefore adds so much to the value of the Gothic Version.

The second most marked feature of the style of the Gothic Gospels is the uniformity with which any word in the Greek is translated by the same Gothic word, wherever that word occurs, provided the sense permits. Thus λέγειν, 'say', 'speak', appears as *qiþan* 504 times out of 508, whilst λαλεῖν, 'speak', 'say', is rendered by *rodjan* in all but two of the eighty passages where it occurs. This uniformity of rendering often provides valuable evidence in deciding between the relative merits of two conflicting readings.

The translation technique of the Gospels has an important bearing on the interrelationship of the various Gospels. If a comparison is made of the translation technique of the four Gospels, the following points may be observed: (1) Of the renderings which are unique or peculiar to one Gospel, the largest number, both relatively and actually, occurs in Luke. (2) The total amount of variation in the application and use of the common vocabulary is relatively sixty per cent greater in Luke than in Matthew. (3) Matthew shows a more primitive technique and a greater simplicity of rendering than the other three Gospels. Thus in Matt. xi. 19 ἐδικαιώθη 'justified' is translated literally by *uswaurhta gadomida warþ* 'judged righteous', whereas in the parallel passage in Luke vii. 35 the same Greek word is rendered more freely *gasunjoda warþ* 'defended'. (4) Loan-words are more closely modelled on the Greek in Matthew than in the other Gospels. By way of illustration the translation of ἀντίδικος, 'opponent', may be cited. This is rendered in Matt. v. 25 by *andastaua* and in Luke xviii. 3 by *andastaþjis*. *Staua* 'judgement' exactly corresponds to the Greek δίκη, whereas *staþjis* derives from the word meaning 'place'. (5) In regard to 'dual renderings' (i.e. cases where a Greek word is rendered by two different words in Gothic) the more common rendering predominates in Matthew and John, while the alternative rendering is relatively much more frequent in the other two Gospels. Thus in the translation of θεραπεύειν the more common *hailjan* occurs three times in Matthew and six times in John, while the alternative rendering *lekinon* is found six times in Mark, but not once in Matthew or John. (6) Multiple renderings are found everywhere but in Matthew, showing strikingly the simplicity of diction in the first Gospel compared with the rest.

There thus emerges a greater uniformity of vocabulary, a simplicity of diction and a more primitive translation technique in Matthew, and to some extent in John, as against the other two Gospels. Two views have been advanced to account for this. It may be argued that since the first Gospel was in all probability the first to be turned into Gothic, we might here expect a meticulousness of method and a scrupulous subservience to the mechanical technique that were never again quite so rigidly observed. Alternatively the distinguishing characteristics of Luke and Mark may be attributed to the influence of the Old Latin Version and to subsequent revision. It is true that these factors cannot be held responsible in every case, and therefore some of the peculiar features of these Gospels may be as old as the Ulfilian text. Nevertheless, these differences cannot all go back to the original translation. Hence we should attach due importance to the influence of later hands in differentiating Luke and Mark from Matthew and John.

To what accident is it due that the text of Matthew and John, as preserved in the *Codex Argenteus*, seems to have escaped the changes that characterize the Argentean text of Luke and Mark? By the time that Theodoric had established his kingdom, the Visigoths had enjoyed a century of dominion in Toulouse. Not only, then, will these Visigoths have felt the need for a Gothic–Latin bilingual earlier, but their greater social and political stability must have favoured the critical revision of their Bible, influenced perhaps by the example of Jerome, at a time when the Ostrogoths still wandered over the Balkans. It is just such a revised and Latinized text that we have in the Argentean Luke and Mark, and it may, therefore, reasonably be suggested that these two Gospels go back to a Visigothic original, whilst Matthew and John were Ostrogothic texts.

The development of the Gothic text of the Bible can only be fully appreciated if it is seen against the political background of the period. During the fourth and fifth centuries the ever-growing intimacy between Goth and Roman is a factor which must be borne in mind.

Since the last decades of the fourth century the Goths had been recruited in increasing numbers into the Roman army. It was the

Goths who had won victories for Theodosius at the battles fought near Aquileia in 388 and 394. By the time of Valentinian III (425–55) the native Italians had become a very slight ingredient in the mass, and the Goths were now the backbone of the Roman army.

Even closer was the contact with Italians of the Gothic auxiliaries, who under the general command of Stilicho were billeted in the towns of northern Italy at the end of the fourth century. It was their active support that contributed to the Empress Justina's success in inducing Valentinian II (375–92) to issue an edict granting free right of assembly to the Arians.

The beginning of the fifth century saw a complete change in the relationship between the Goths and the Latin-speaking world: the foreign mercenaries now became masters of the soil. In 412 Athaulf led his Visigoths into Gaul, where the kingdom of Toulouse, which later came to embrace Spain, maintained itself until the Frankish Clovis in 507 drove the Visigoths over the Pyrenees. Contemporaneously with the Goths the Burgundians settled in the Rhone valley, where their smaller but more compact kingdom continued independent until 534. In 409 the Vandals invaded Spain, and thirty years later the capture of Carthage by Gaiseric marked the beginning of a powerful Vandal kingdom in Africa. Finally in 489 the Ostrogoths, who during this period had remained behind in the Balkans, were led by Theodoric into Verona and Milan. By the end of the century Theodoric was virtually master of Italy.

The attitude of the conquerors towards the native inhabitants was generally one of goodwill and admiration for Roman institutions. The civic and political union of Goth and Roman was symbolized by the marriage in 414 of Athaulf to Galla Placidia, the daughter of Theodosius. This trend culminated in Theodoric's conscious policy of unifying the two nations.

The relations between the two peoples in matters of religion are not easy to determine. But it appears probable that the Visigoths treated the Catholics (i.e. orthodox non-Arians) with justice and tolerance, with the exception of the persecution of Euric (466–85). At the Burgundian court Catholicism met with active sympathy. Finally, Theodoric's reign inaugurated an era of extreme religious tolerance.

Such political and religious conditions made the production of bilingual copies of the Bible desirable, and indeed necessary. We possess fragments of two such Gothic–Latin bilinguals, namely the *Codex Gissensis* and the *Codex Carolinus*.

Thus we see that for a hundred and twenty-five years before the *Codex Argenteus* came to be written, influences were tending towards the Latinization of the bible-texts of Burgundians, Visigoths and Ostrogoths. With these the Vandals should probably be included, although their religious policy contrasted sharply with the toleration shown by the three nations mentioned above.

The intermingling of Goth and Roman is reflected in the close connection between the Gothic and Latin bibles. The intimate relationship between the *Codex Argenteus* and the Old Latin Version may throw fresh light on some of the problems concerning Latin MSS.

If we consider the provenance of the chief witnesses of the Old Latin Version, it will be seen that they are chiefly the product of northern Italy and southern Gaul. But this was precisely the area where Gothic power was always strongest. It may therefore plausibly be conjectured that the preservation of these MSS in just this corner of Europe may have been due to their use by the Goths.

One of the questions posed by the Africana (the name given to the MSS of the Old Latin Version which originated from Africa) is why a MS like k (a fifth-century African MS) should be found on Italian soil at all, when there were two native products, the Itala (the Italian MSS of the Old Latin Version) and the Vulgate, apparently in general use.[1] The answer may be that the African text was imported into Italy by the Goths in the fifth century; that the African text may have penetrated to Europe via Spain when the Visigoths occupied parts of that country in the second decade of the fifth century; or, if we take a later date, the importation of the African text into Europe may have been the result of the Vandal invasion and settlement of Africa.

If then the African text was an importation incidental to the occupation of Italy and Gaul by the Goths, it is possible that the 'Europeanizing' of the Africana was the work of the Goths themselves. This theory will accord with the sporadic Africanisms in the Gothic text of the four Gospels and the much more frequent agreements with e in Luke.

The Goths may also be the key to the palaeographical difficulties presented by k and e (fifth-century African MSS). Burkitt has asked

[1] See Hans von Soden, *Das Lateinische Neue Testament in Afrika zur Zeit Cyprians*, p. 359.

'where and why an African text full of the strange clerical blunders which we find in the text of k came to be transcribed in the generation before the Saint (Columbanus) was born'.[1] By way of illustration the k reading of Matt. v. 29 may be cited:

> *abrode aps te exredist tibi ut sicreat*

for > *abripe abs te: expedit tibi ut pereat.*

One explanation of this palaeographical puzzle is that these MSS were the work of Gothic scribes who, having spent most of their lives in the seclusion of an eastern scriptorium, had never acquired more than a scraping acquaintance with the Latin language.

The original Greek manuscript or manuscripts, from which Ulfilas made his translation of the Gothic Gospels, belonged to the Byzantine group with a sprinkling of western readings. Consequent on their migration into western Europe, the Goths came into even closer contact with Roman culture, and the Latin Gospels, which belonged to the western family of MSS, began to influence the Gothic Gospels. Thus during the period which elapsed between the original translation by Ulfilas and the production of the *Codex Argenteus* in the first half of the sixth century, a number of western readings from the Latin Bible infiltrated into the predominantly Byzantine text of the Gothic Gospels. Hence it came about that the *Codex Argenteus*, our only extant MS of the Gothic Gospels apart from the Giessen fragment, contained many more western readings than were present in the translation of Ulfilas (we have no trace of the original translation, but the *Codex Argenteus* is a descendant of it).

One of the main problems in connection with the Gothic Gospels is to trace the alterations to and corruptions of the original text of Ulfilas. These were due to two main factors: the influence of the Old Latin Version, and assimilation of the Gothic text in parallel passages. Where parallel passages occur in different Gospels or in different parts of the same Gospel relating to the same biblical event or saying, the wording in one passage is often made to conform to the wording of the other, producing a fresh uniformity from the old diversity.

In the history of the development of the text of the Gothic Gospels four phases may be distinguished. In the first stage there is a partial accommodation of the four Gospels to the Latin text by the adoption

---

[1] F. C. Burkitt, *Old Latin and Itala*, p. 11.

of a number of Latin readings and renderings. This assimilation was not systematic but sporadic and haphazard, and reflects only the inevitable result of the Romanizing influences to which the Goths were from an early date exposed. This general Latinizing of the Gospels shows itself least in Matthew and John, which in the *Codex Argenteus* represent an older and purer text. The second phase represents a more thorough assimilation to the Latin text, affecting especially Luke and Mark, but manifesting itself most strongly in Luke. The third phase is marked by the production of the Brixian Bilingual (see below), in which the Gothic text seems to have been more definitely fixed, while the Latin portion has been made to conform to it. Finally in the interval between the Brixian Bilingual and the appearance of the *Codex Argenteus* a further period of textual activity may be observed. These phases in the evolution of the text of the Gothic Gospels will now be considered in greater detail, with the exception of the first, which need not detain us.

The renderings in the Gospel of Luke which seem to reflect the mutual influence upon one another of the Gothic and Old Latin Versions may be divided into two classes. The first category consists of passages which appear to have been affected by the Old Latin generally, while in the second category there is a similarity with two or three MSS of the Old Latin Version at the most. If a list is made of the twenty-one passages in this second category, it will be found that e (the fifth-century *Codex Palatinus*) occurs twenty times in this list, d (the sixth-century Latin half of *Codex Beʒae*) five times, and f (the sixth-century *Codex Brixianus*) four times. An ancestor of the Argentean Luke, then, would seem to have come into close contact with a MS akin to the *Codex Palatinus*. Having documentary proof of the existence of two bilinguals in the *Codex Carolinus* (Romans) and the Giessen fragment (Luke), we may adopt as a reasonable hypothesis the theory that a predecessor of the Gothic text of Luke as we have it once formed part of a bilingual of which some near relative of the *Codex Palatinus* formed the Latin half. This may be referred to as the Palatinian Bilingual.

The influence in the bilingual between the Gothic and the Latin text was reciprocal. In some cases the Gothic has clearly been affected by the Latin. Thus in Luke ii. 10[1] εὐαγγελίζομαι is translated in the Gothic by *spillo* and in e by *adnuntio*. *Spillon* is unique as a rendering for εὐαγγε-

[1] See also Luke i. 63, v. 26, xvi. 20.

λίζεσθαι in the *Codex Argenteus* and probably derives from *adnuntio*, which is characteristic of the African text.

The Gothic text, on the other hand, was not without influence on its Latin partner. For example in Luke vi. 48[1] for ἐβάθυνεν 'deepen' the *Codex Argenteus* reads *gadiupida* and e *exaltavit*. *Gadiupida* is just what we might expect in Gothic, while *exaltare* in e regularly translates ὑψοῦν the exact antithesis of βαθύνειν. This extraordinary rendering is best explained as an attempt to give a Latin equivalent for the Gothic *gadiupida*.

In other cases it is impossible to say which text has influenced the other.

There are a number of features common to the *Codex Brixianus* f (a sixth-century Old Latin MS) and the *Codex Argenteus*: they were approximately contemporaries, written in the same region, and in addition share a number of peculiar readings. To proceed a step further, there is bound in with the *Codex Brixianus* the preface to a Gothic–Latin bilingual. The fact that this preface, or *Praefatio*, to give it its Latin title, forms part of the same codex as f makes it natural, in the absence of evidence to the contrary, to identify the Latin half of this bilingual with an ancestor of f. In view of the close relationship between f and the *Codex Argenteus*, it is not unreasonable to suggest that a predecessor of the *Codex Argenteus* was its Gothic partner in this bilingual, which for convenience we may term the Brixian Bilingual. This argument is reinforced by a further consideration. The author or authors of the *Praefatio* indicate that they have provided the text of the bilingual with *wulþres* or *adnotationes*—a special type of marginal gloss (see below). Now there is no trace of these *wulþres* in f, but it is clear that they are associated with the text of the *Codex Argenteus*. These facts are explained if we assume that ancestors of *Codex Brixianus* and the *Codex Argenteus* together formed a bilingual. The words in the *Praefatio* relating to the *wulþres* can then be taken as referring to the Gothic and not the Latin half of the bilingual.

Neither the Palatinian nor the Brixian Bilingual has survived. A certain element of doubt cannot be eliminated from our contention for the existence of the Palatinian Bilingual or the composition of the Brixian Bilingual as outlined above, but there are good grounds for making these assumptions.

---

[1] See also Luke i. 9, ii. 8, iii. 23.

The accepted opinion before the researches of Burkitt was that the Latin influenced the Gothic half of the Brixian Bilingual. But Burkitt[1] adduced cogent arguments in support of the view that in fact the text of f, where it differs from the readings of the Old Latin, has been altered in accordance with the wording of the Gothic. Thus in Matt. ix. 8 the Gothic and f conflate the Alexandrian reading ἐφοβήθησαν 'they feared' with the Byzantine reading ἐθαύμασαν 'they marvelled' to read *ohtedun sildaleikjandans* 'marvelling they feared' and *admirantes timuerunt* respectively, while all the other MSS of the Old Latin Version support the Alexandrian reading. The fact that in a number of passages f is the only Latin MS to agree with the Gothic makes it reasonable to assume that f has borrowed from the Gothic and not vice versa. Moreover the hypothesis of Gothic influence will explain why f, more than all other known Latin texts, is full of Byzantine readings.

The purpose of the Brixian Bilingual was twofold. The first aim was to eliminate the deviations from the original text which had accumulated since the time of Ulfilas. In this we may in all probability detect the guiding hand of Theodoric, who, comparing the purity of his native Gospels with the corrupt state of the Gothic Gospel text which he found in the West, may well have decided to institute a revision to purge the text of these errors. It cannot be said that the authors of the bilingual completely succeeded in achieving their object. Some of the corruptions we meet with in the text of the *Codex Argenteus* may be attributed to the short post-Brixian period, but a number of passages even in the Brixian text would not have borne comparison with the readings of the Ulfilian Greek. Nevertheless the purity of the Gothic Gospel text as compared with that of the epistles may in part be attributed to the influence of the Brixian Bilingual.

The second aim of the bilingual was to revise the existing text of the Gothic Gospels on the basis of an idiomatic rather than a completely literal translation. The authors emphasize, if we may paraphrase their words, that, if anywhere there should seem a discrepancy (either between the Gothic or the Latin and the Greek, or between the Gothic and the Latin renderings) owing to the rules of language (*si pro disciplina linguae discrepationem ostendit*) or differences in the meanings of words (*declinationes sonus vocis*), the meaning is nevertheless the same (*ad unam intentionem concurrit*). In other words, the authors imply that

---

[1] See *Journal of Theological Studies*, I, 129–34.

they are endeavouring to render the actual meaning of any passage rather than its strictly literal and linguistic form.

The *wulþres*, according to the *Praefatio*, were designed to demonstrate that renderings which were not syntactically or linguistically consonant with the Greek or Latin, yet had an identity of sense.[1] For example in Matt. xxvii. 38 *gadomiþs warþ* 'was condemned' was the type of *wulþre* which might have stood in the margin of the Brixian Bilingual as a synonym for the Argentean reading *du stauai gatauhans* 'was brought to judgement', which rendered the Greek κατεκρίθη more literally. Some of these *wulþres* have disappeared, others have been incorporated into the text of the *Codex Argenteus* and yet others are probably among the marginal glosses of the extant Gothic text.

The *Praefatio* has traditionally been attributed to the two Gothic clerics named Sunnja and Friþila, whom Jerome addresses as Sunnia and Fretela; but this view will not really bear examination. Palaeographically the *Praefatio* is much more nearly contemporary with the sixth-century *Codex Brixianus* than it is possible to assume, if we ascribe the former to Sunnja and Friþila, who flourished at the beginning of the fifth century. Furthermore, the principles of the two documents are different. The Brixian Preface is concerned with renderings, as well as readings, whilst Sunnja and Friþila are only anxious about the readings of their text; the latter challenged the addition of any word not in the original Greek, whereas the writer of the *Praefatio* favours a liberality of rendering which is quite in accordance with the translation technique of Jerome. If, as is probable, the Brixian Bilingual may be assigned to the reign of Theodoric, allowing an interval between the Brixian Bilingual and the *Codex Argenteus*, we may give *c.* 500 as a tentative date for the execution of the bilingual. This date is supported by the palaeographical evidence.

In a few cases it can be shown with a strong degree of probability that the Gothic text has been altered since its partnership with the Latin in the Brixian Bilingual. Thus in Mark iv. 19 the Gothic *þizos libainais* 'of this life' for the Greek τοῦ αἰῶνος τούτου 'of this age' is the result of assimilation to Luke viii. 14. The fact that the *Codex Brixianus*

---

[1] For the precise meaning to be attached to the crucial word *etymologias*, which occurs in the third paragraph of the *Praefatio*, see G. W. S. Friedrichsen, *The Gothic Version of the Gospels*, pp. 204–11. For a somewhat different interpretation of the *wulþres* see Fr. Kauffmann, *Zeitschrift für deutsche Philologie*, XXXII, 304–16.

reads *saeculi huius*, while all the other Latin MSS omit *huius* 'this', points to the fact that the Gothic half of the Brixian Bilingual originally read *þis aiwis* 'of this age' and that the Latin was made to conform to this.

One factor in the corruption of the Gothic text was the absorption into the *Codex Argenteus* of marginal glosses. Some of these glosses found a place in the text side by side with the original reading. By way of illustration Luke ii. 2 may be cited. In this passage the gloss *wisandin kindina Swraisis* 'being governor of Syria' occurs side by side with *raginondin Saurim* 'governing the Syrians' for the Greek ἡγεμονεύοντος τῆς Συρίας. The textual activities of Gothic scribes continued even after the production of the *Codex Argenteus*. This is shown by the presence of fifteen glosses in the margin of the *Codex Argenteus*. In nine cases the gloss refers to a parallel passage or to the immediate context, the alternative usually being synonymous with the word in the text. Thus in Luke vi. 49 the *Codex Argenteus* renders the Greek ποταμός 'stream' by *flodus*, and the marginal gloss *awa* brings verse 49 into line with the preceding verse, where *aƕa* is the word used to translate ποταμός.

Other glosses are alternative renderings indicating a simple preference or intended for the improvement or the correction of the text. By way of illustration Luke ix. 34 may be cited. The words ἐφοβήθησαν δὲ ἐν τῷ ἐκείνους εἰσελθεῖν εἰς τὴν νεφέλην 'and they were afraid as they entered the cloud' are rendered in the *Codex Argenteus* by *faurhtidedun þan in þammei jainai qemun in þamma milhmin* (finite verb). The marginal *Jah at im in milhmam atgaggandam* (absolute participial construction) follows the Latin *et intrantibus illis in nubem*, the dative corresponding to the Latin ablative and the intrusive *jah* ('and', 'also', 'even') to the Latin *et*.

The influence of the Old Latin Version far outweighed that of other manuscripts but there is evidence to show that the Gothic text was also compared with Greek codices. Where the Greek text was good, and the Gothic properly conformed to it, the revision would naturally not leave any trace in the *Codex Argenteus*. Most of the instances, therefore, of this type of revision will be examples of blundering readings, that owe their existence to the fact that some graphic variant such as ει for η has been taken at its face value. Or else they result from the confusion of pairs of words of similar appearance, such as τρυφή–τροφή, καθῆκαν–κατέθηκαν.

It must always be borne in mind that errors in the *Codex Argenteus* may be due to post-Ulfilian revisions with Greek manuscripts rather than to Ulfilas or to his Greek original. The grosser errors probably occurred late in the history of the text, since obvious blunders, disturbing the sense, and contrasting sharply with the Latin readings, would be unlikely to survive for long.

As has been said, assimilation in parallel passages was one of the two main factors in the corruption of the Gothic Gospel text. The number of cases where the *Codex Argenteus* has been influenced by parallel passages bears witness to the degree to which revisional tendencies have been at work in the Gothic Gospels. It must be remembered that a parallelism may derive from the underlying Greek text, or from the Latin, or, thirdly, from another passage in the Gothic text itself. It is this latter type of parallelism with which we are here concerned.

In regard to these parallelisms within the Gothic text the source of influence may be sought for in the immediate context or else it may be more remote, either in another passage in the same Gospel or a parallel passage in another Gospel. An example of a contextual parallel has been dealt with in the consideration of Luke vi. 49 in relation to marginal glosses in the *Codex Argenteus* (see above).

Luke xix. 23 may be cited as an example of the second type of parallelism. In this passage ἐπὶ τράπεζαν, 'to the money table', is rendered by *du skattjam*, 'to the money changers', in conformity with the parallel passage in Matt. xxv. 27, τοῖς τραπεζείταις, 'to the money changers'.

In regard to the Greek text underlying the Gothic Gospels Odefey[1] has attempted to support a number of isolated readings in D (*Codex Beʒae*) by reference to the Gothic, basing his findings on the supposed excellence of the Gothic textual tradition. But the hypothesis of a pure Gothic text, as has been shown, is not supported by the facts. We should therefore rather follow the conservative policy of Streitberg and von Soden[2] in giving the authority of the Ulfilian Greek to no more than the possible minimum of western readings in the *Codex Argenteus*. In individual cases the decision as to whether or not a western reading should be included must depend on the internal evidence of the passage.

[1] P. Odefey, *Das Gotische Lukasevangelium*, p. 26.

[2] Hermann von Soden, *Die Schriften des Neuen Testaments in ihrer ältesten erreichbaren Gestalt*, p. 1469.

The extent to which the Gothic Gospels were Latinized reflects the thoroughness with which the Visigoths had become Romanized. By the end of the fifth century, perhaps, the connection between the *Graeca Veritas* and the Gothic text had lost much of its historical significance.

Odefey (*op. cit.* p. 140) has propounded the theory that the *Codex Argenteus*, as we have it now, was put together from various MSS, probably mere fragments. But a scribe entrusted with the production of a magnificent luxury edition of the Gospels would be more likely to work from one or two codices than to seek to patch up his text from any stray fragments that came to hand.

There is no definite proof, but good grounds for presuming, that the *Codex Argenteus* was copied from the Gothic half of the Brixian Bilingual, or else from a near-descendant of that bilingual. Having regard to the post-Brixian revisions mentioned above, the second is the more probable alternative.

The Brixian Bilingual was compiled at a time very little remote from the execution of the *Codex Argenteus*, perhaps not much earlier than the beginning of the sixth century. Whether the Gothic portion of the Brixian Bilingual was copied from one complete codex, or from separate copies of individual Gospels, we have no means of judging; but the evidence of the Argentean renderings shows that the Brixian Gospels ultimately derive from two quite different types of text—on the one hand the ancestor of Matthew and John, and, on the other, the predecessor of the Argentean Luke and Mark.

Matthew and John exhibit an older, more primitive text, and a more ingenuous workmanship; Luke and Mark show far more evidence of textual interference and a more advanced translation technique. Most striking is the greater amount of variation in vocabulary that distinguishes Luke and Mark from the other half of the *Codex Argenteus*, especially the very excessive preponderance in Luke, which Gospel is further distinguished by its close connection with the *Codex Palatinus*. In this respect it detaches itself from Mark, for the evidence of connection with the Palatinus is almost entirely wanting in the case of the other Gospels.

The differences between Matthew and John on the one hand and Luke and Mark on the other are best accounted for on the assumption that Matthew and John were Ostrogothic texts and thus for long preserved from western textual contamination, while Luke and Mark were in use among the Visigoths and owed their distinctive characteristics to the Romanizing influences to which they would be subject under these conditions. We cannot tell precisely by what means the four Gospels finally came to be united, but in view of the close relations between Theodoric and the Visigoths the presence of Visigothic bible texts in Italy need cause us no surprise. In spite of inevitable minor differences in pronunciation, and to some extent of vocabulary, Vandal, Visigoth and Ostrogoth spoke a language essentially the same, and hence there is nothing improbable in the hypothesis that Ostrogothic Gospels were united with Visigothic Bible texts in one codex.

We can only assign an approximate date to the *Codex Argenteus*. On palaeographical grounds we are safe in placing it in the sixth century. The reign of the great Theodoric is the most likely period for the appearance of a codex of such magnificence, and if we allow a short interval between the Brixian Bilingual (about 500) and the *Codex Argenteus, c.* 525 emerges as the most probable date for the completion of the work.

THE TEXT OF THE GOTHIC EPISTLES

As in the Gospels, the original Greek text in the epistles was of the Byzantine type, with a number of western readings. This text represents the mid-fourth-century stage in the development of the Byzantine text, and differs very little from the fully developed *Textus receptus* of the later period. The MSS with which the underlying Greek text has closest affinities are the ninth-century codices K L M P. With these, as in the Gospels, is associated the text of Chrysostom, which is within a generation of the traditional origins of the Gothic Version.

The Gothic text, as it stands, differs considerably from the text of the original translation. The comparison between the Greek text of Streitberg's edition and the Gothic text will provide an indication of the extent to which the original translation has been disturbed, usually by conformation to the Old Latin. The difference between the extant Ambrosian text of the epistles and Streitberg's ideal original stands in sharp contrast to the almost exact correspondence of the primitive Argentean text of Matthew with its Greek original.

Where the Greek MSS fall into two clearly defined groups, with Byzantine authorities on the one side and Alexandrian MSS on the other, the Byzantine reading may be assumed for the Ulfilian original with a very strong degree of probability. But where the Byzantine witnesses are divided, we are faced with the necessity of deciding which of the competing readings represents the original. In a number of passages the reading of K L and Chrysostom differs from that of P. The fact that P exhibits fewer Byzantine readings than K L is not in itself a reason for rejecting its attestation in favour of the two other codices in any specific reading, for it might be that just in this instance P preserves for us an earlier reading shared by the Ulfilian original, but which has disappeared from the more modernized text of K L. Nevertheless, the constant association of P with the older MSS and the Old Latin against K L and Chrysostom has to be borne in mind when weighing its claims against those of its more regularly Byzantine collaterals.

As in the Gospels, the majority of non-Byzantine readings in the epistles belong to the western group of MSS. After the elimination, however, of those readings which are the result of accommodation to the Old Latin Version, there remains a residue of readings which are sponsored by the Alexandrian MSS. These MSS, especially B (*Codex Vaticanus*), not infrequently present western readings, of which some go back to the third-century Chester Beatty papyri. It is therefore possible that some of these readings were present in the text from which the epistles were translated.

Four main influences have contributed to the corruption of the text of the Gothic epistles: the influence of the Old Latin Version, the Latin commentaries, exegetical renderings and assimilation in parallel passages. Each of these factors will be considered in turn.

The Old Latin Version

Bernhardt[1] thought it highly probable that Ulfilas consulted the Latin Version in his work of translating from the Greek. A number of passages may indeed be adduced where it may be said that the rendering was modelled after the Latin by the translator, or adopted from the Latin at a subsequent period in the history of the Gothic text. But such instances all suffer from the same inherent disability: it is impossible to prove that any one in fact belongs to the original version. There is therefore no definite proof that any individual Latinism reaches back to

[1] *Vulfila*, Einleitung, p. xxxviii.

the translator's pen, and therefore no positive evidence that the Latin Version was consulted, even occasionally, by the translator.

Turning now to renderings which have been assimilated to the Old Latin Version by the hands of later revisers, it will be found that the contamination of the original Gothic text by the Old Latin Version is far more extensive than was the case in the Gospels.

The MS which has played the principal part in the Latinization of the Ulfilian original is codex d (the Latin half of the Graeco-Latin bilingual *Codex Claromontanus*). There remain, however, a substantial number of readings sponsored by the other Old Latin texts and the contemporary Latin writers, among whom Ambrosiaster and Augustine are specially prominent.

Where the Gothic retains its original reading against d, the retention of the Byzantine reading, as far as can be seen, is not traceable to the influence of any specific Old Latin text or group of texts, like, for example, the Ambrosiaster. Chance and the mood of the scribe seem to have been the determining factors in the incidence of the Latin influence.

The Latin commentaries

The influence of eastern exegesis on the Gothic text was negligible. Of the Latin commentaries, Pelagius, Augustine and Jerome may be held responsible for an occasional rendering. But the Latin commentaries are completely overshadowed by the so-called Ambrosiaster, written at the end of the fourth century. For example, in Phil. ii. 28 the Gothic *hlasoʒa sijau* 'that I may be gladder', rendering the Greek ἵνα κἀγὼ ἀλυπότερος ὦ 'and that I may be less anxious', seems to be directly inspired by Ambrosiaster's comment...*et Apostoli animus laetaretur* 'and that the heart of the Apostle might rejoice'.

Exegetical renderings

The choice of rendering must to some extent be dependent upon the context, and even in a strictly literal, word-by-word translation the claims of contextual influence cannot be entirely ignored. The version of the epistles however goes further in this respect than the translation of the Gospels. We find renderings which reach out even beyond the implications of the literal context, and are modified so as to include some idea which may be supplied by the general explanation of the passage. The translator is encroaching upon the function which is properly the task of exegesis. Thus in I Cor. v. 7 τὸ πάσχα ἡμῶν ἐτύθη χριστός the word ἐτύθη has been translated *ufsniþans ist*: the literal 'sacrificed' gives way to the contextually interpretative 'killed'.

The influence of parallel passages

Renderings due to the influence of parallel and reminiscent passages are proportionally more numerous in the epistles than in the Gospels. This is not entirely due to the greater amount of contextual interference that characterizes the Ambrosian text, since many of these passages are concerned with remoter parallels and reminiscences. This is striking testimony to the keenness with which the Pauline epistles were studied by the Goths.

In regard to translation technique the epistles may be divided into two groups. The first consists of Romans and I and II Corinthians, and the second of the remaining epistles, in which the alternative rendering seems relatively more frequent than it is in the first three. It is *a priori* not unreasonable for any translator to vary his choice of renderings as the spirit moves him and were it not for the remarkable degree of uniformity with which the Gospels, especially Matthew and John, were rendered into Gothic, the phenomenon would not cause us surprise. But the question of the variations within the epistles is to some extent involved in the wider question of the differences in translation technique between the Gospels and the epistles. The epistles are far less stereotyped in style than the Gospels, dual and multiple renderings occurring relatively three times as often as in the Gospels. To some extent this is explained by the intrinsic difficulty of understanding Paul's language and the thought underlying it and the consequently greater difficulty of expressing this in the vernacular.

It has been suggested that, the epistles being presumably translated later than the Gospels, freedom and variation of rendering might increase with the experience and facility of the translator and that this would account for the greater amount of variation in the epistles. But the theory of an evolving translation-technique could only partially account for the very striking stylistic differences within the Gospels. (It is reasonable to assume that the Gospels were translated in the order traditional in Byzantium. It has been seen however that a definite process of textual revision may be traced both in the Gospels and the epistles, whether the source of inspiration was the Old Latin, the study of parallel passages, the context, or the commentaries. It is plausible therefore to conjecture that many of the variant renderings may be the result of a similar series of alterations, differing both in time and in place of origin. If such were the manner in which these variants were introduced subsequent to the original version, the limits of time and space within which these changes could have been effected are wide enough to justify this hypothesis, for the history of our codices goes back for over a century and a half, and the wanderings of the Goths are almost coextensive with the vast territories covered by the Roman empire.

If there is one fact in connection with the origins of the Gothic epistles that may be affirmed without hesitation, it is that they were rendered into Gothic from the Byzantine text represented by K L P and Chrysostom. The readings which agree with the text of the Old Latin alone are secondary and belong to the later history of the Gothic text. The hypothesis of an original of mixed type, recovered by re-translating the existing Gothic into Greek, of the kind postulated by A. Jülicher[1] and, more recently, by Lietzmann,[2] is unsupported by any existing evidence.

The Latinizing of the Gothic text may have been effected in Visigothic Gaul, or, from the time of Stilicho, in Italy, or in both regions simultaneously. However, the palaeographical evidence[3] suggests their Italian origin. The Latin texts that have affected the Gothic renderings, as well as the occasional contacts with Ambrose, Jerome, and Augustine—and especially with the text of Ambrosiaster, which has further influenced the Gothic text in its exegetical renderings—point in the same direction.

The Latinized renderings derive from the Old Latin Version in general and in particular from d (the predominant influence on the Gothic text), Augustine and Ambrosiaster. Of Ambrosiaster Dr Souter[4] writes: 'the text used by Ambrosiaster is a European text, perhaps specifically a Milanese text—as Berger would have it, though I cannot think the evidence adequate to establish certainty—of the epistles of St Paul, a sister text to that of Victorinus, and belonging to the same

[1] A. Jülicher, *Zeitschrift für deutsches Altertum und deutsche Literatur*, LII, 365 ff.

[2] H. Lietzmann, *ZfdA*, LVI, 249–78.

[3] O. von Friesen and A. Grape, *Codex Argenteus Upsaliensis, Introductio*, chapter II, *passim*.

[4] A. Souter, *The Earliest Latin Commentaries on the Epistles of St Paul*, p. 61.

class as d and g: in other words, that type which was readiest to hand in Italy when Jerome set out to make his revision.' And it is just such a text, as represented by Ambrosiaster, akin to but not coincident with d, characteristic of Northern Italy, of which Milan was the centre, that has left its impress on the Gothic text.

The adoption of readings and renderings from the Old Latin is not the only source of corruption of the original Ulfilian text; there is besides the influence of the Latin commentaries, the exegetical renderings of domestic origin, and the influence of parallel passages. The close attention to the Latin text implies the neglect of the original Greek, on which the Ulfilian tradition was founded, and points to a period when the Goths were being rapidly Romanized. This phase of textual activity is further illustrated by the influence of the Latin commentaries, notably Ambrosiaster. In the exegetical renderings the letter of the text tends to be subordinated to its contextual implications. Finally the accommodation of the original text to parallel passages goes beyond the comparatively modest degree of subjectivity of interpretation to be found in the Gospels.

It will be found that, with the exception of the influence of Ambrosiaster, both the Gospels and the epistles exhibit the same kinds of textual corruption, but the contamination of the original text has been far more extensive in the epistles. One indication of this fact is the presence of a far greater number of interpolated glosses in the Ambrosian Codices than in the *Codex Argenteus*. The greater purity of the Gospel text may be attributed in part to its history and in part to the expurgating influence of the Brixian Bilingual.

The evidence for the date of the Gothic epistles is conflicting. Palaeographically the Ambrosian MSS belong to the mid-sixth century. On the other hand the epistle text shows no sign of having been affected by the revisional movement associated with the Brixian Bilingual (*c*. 500), which we should have expected if the epistles were written after that date. These facts are best explained if we assume that the ancestor of the Gothic epistles was written in the fifth century, and that the actual Ambrosian MSS were copied during the sixth century and somehow escaped the revisional influences of the reign of Theodoric.

THE GOTHIC OLD TESTAMENT

It is clear that the fragments of the Gothic Old Testament have been translated from the Greek rather than from the Hebrew. Opinion has been divided in regard to the character of the Greek underlying text. Langner[1] and Streitberg[2] have claimed that the text was Lucianic. Kauffmann[3] on the other hand has detected rather a mixed text consisting of a Lucianic basis with an admixture of Hesychian and Origenic readings.

Most of the deviations from the Lucianic text in the Gothic Old Testament can be explained on the assumption that the original text has been altered by subsequent revisers to conform with parallel passages and with Greek manuscripts. Neh. vii presents special difficulties by reason of the number of apparent divergences from the Lucianic text. Many of these difficulties have been removed since the work of W. Braun on Codex D in 1910–11 introduced a number of fresh readings into the text of Neh. vii. For example, in Neh. vii. 21 Braun has the reading *Aʒeiris*, which agrees with the Lucianic Aʒηρ, as against the old reading *Ateiris*, which reflects the reading Aτηρ of B (*Codex Vaticanus*). Other deviations from the Lucianic text can be explained, if we remember that the list of names in Neh. vii would inevitably be compared with the parallel lists in Esdras A v (=I Esdras v) and Esdras B ii (=Ezra ii) and adjustments made accordingly. It is also legitimate to attribute some of these differences to scribal lapses in a passage containing so many names and numbers. It can therefore be said that the internal evidence presents no insuperable obstacles to the hypothesis of a Lucianic text underlying the Gothic Old Testament.

In view of the very small amount of material available to aid us in our investigation into the vexed question of the precise nature of the Gothic Old Testament text (the fragments of Neh. v–vii, the only part of the Gothic Old Testament to survive, occupy only sixty lines in Streitberg's edition), it is natural that we should inquire what light the findings of research on the New Testament can shed on the Old. If we assume that Ulfilas was the sole translator of the Gothic bible, we should expect to find the same type of text and textual outlook in the Old Testament as

[1] E. Langner, *Die Gotischen Nehemia-Fragmente.*
[2] W. Streitberg, *Die Gotische Bibel*, Einleitung, pp. xxxi–xxxv.
[3] Fr. Kauffmann, *Zeitschrift für deutsche Philologie*, XXIX, 312–37.

in the New. Having established a comparatively pure Byzantine text in the New Testament we should anticipate a relatively unmixed Byzantine text in the Old—in this case a Lucianic text, this being the Old Testament text current in Byzantium. But here a word must be said on the authorship and composition of the Gothic bible. We are told on the authority of Philostorgius that Ulfilas translated the whole of the Bible with the exception of the books of Kings. But we must not underestimate the difficulties involved in translating the whole Bible into a language which had hitherto not been a vehicle of literary expression. Apart from his work as translator Ulfilas had arduous pastoral, missionary and episcopal duties. It is therefore not unreasonable to suggest that he may have called in a colleague or two to help finish the translation. Alternatively the great task may have been completed after Ulfilas' death. The book of Nehemiah, being one of the less important books of the Old Testament and therefore probably one of the last to be translated, would be particularly likely to be the work of a second hand. If then in the Old Testament we have to reckon with more than one translator, the results of research on the Gothic New Testament cannot be applied to the Old.

The evidence however on the whole points to the fact that the translator or translators of the Gothic Old Testament used a substantially pure Lucianic text. But this thesis can be stated with less assurance than was the case in the New Testament. Indeed, the extremely fragmentary remains of the Gothic Old Testament are a precarious foundation on which to build a conclusive argument.

The Greek original of the Gothic Old Testament is most nearly allied to the MSS 19, 82, 93 and 108. Of patristic authors it is Chrysostom, as in the New Testament, whose text bears the closest affinities to the Gothic.

2. ENGLISH VERSIONS OF THE SCRIPTURES BEFORE WYCLIF

How a moderately educated man of the middle ages esteemed the Bible may be best understood by thinking of the attitude of a moderately educated man of the nineteenth century towards those select Greek and Roman authors known as the classics. To the Victorian these classics would be a body of writings incompletely surveyed in his own education: some texts would be known well, some passages by heart. What he knew would be taken as representative of the quality of the assumed whole. But the line separating the classics from other writings of antiquity he would consider fixed, yet often indistinct in relation to any particular author known only by repute. He would often have not been quite sure if in his own reading he had been dealing with myth, history, allegory, aspiration or propaganda. Furthermore, our Victorian may, surreptitiously, have used a crib such as Kelly's *Keys* to get out the meaning, but he would have understood almost from the beginning that this was a somewhat shameful way of proceeding. He had learnt that the classics stood for ever, inviolable, in their own language. They were essentially and necessarily untranslatable. Educated men read Latin and Greek. Only the uneducated and under-privileged would need the cribs. It was not very clear that such people should need to be acquainted with the classics at all.

The classics of medieval Englishmen were to be found in the Bible. It existed in a learned language, accessible only to an élite. As a physical collection of books it was truly *bibliotheca*—often at least two or three large volumes in folio—ponderous, rare and very expensive. The moderately educated man, usually a monk, a cleric by definition, seldom saw the Bible as a whole. Many clerics, probably most parish priests up to Wyclif's time, were unable to construe even the Latin of the Mass. Of the clergy who could read, most would still know the Bible in single books and extracts, primarily of course in the extracts of the service books. Medieval liturgies are bewildering mosaics cut and shaped for a purpose out of the Scriptures; and if this process gives a prodigious enrichment to meaning, it obscures almost completely the flow and scope of the original. But if our medieval cleric had at any time submitted to a course of intensive education—and such a training was comparatively rare—he would probably have known individually some of the Wisdom books, some of the Pauline epistles, perhaps the Song of Songs or the book of Revelation. Often he would come to the Scriptures through the commentaries. Gregory's *Moralia* provided an inexhaustible introduction to the book of Job and to much else. By the thirteenth century in a good centre of learning the range of commentary and homiletic material would be extensive (see chapter VI).

Nowadays no one is likely to deny that it is possible to acquire a very considerable knowledge of a text from reading the notes to it provided by a succession of editors, even though the total impression may be different from that obtained from reading the plain text itself. Many men during the middle ages knew the Bible very well indeed. But the whole prospect of the Bible presented to the medieval student was very different from that which confronts the modern general reader. For us, the leather binding (or the cloth boards) is a physical indication of the limits of the Canon. In the middle ages these limits were blurred for other reasons than the lack of this physical sign. Very frequently, especially in the earlier centuries, the treatment of Scripture shows uncertainty as to the authority of the Old Testament and New Testament apocryphal writings. Bede, Aldhelm, Ælfric all protest against the widespread popular use of some of these works. All three themselves used others. Works such as the latter books of Esdras, or the romantic Passions and Apocalypses of the apostles, had a deep fascination for the Anglo-Saxons.

The use made of these and other apocryphal writings in vernacular compositions requires separate study. Round the great nexus of interest in sacred story—around the Creation, the Fall, the Prophecies, the birth and Passion of Christ, the Harrowing of Hell, the life of the Virgin from the Conception to the Assumption, the fates of the apostles, and the four last things—were assembled vivid, earnest detail and sensational incident provided by the uncanonical writings. Often this accumulation gave an inescapable character and an inseparable shape to the original theme. The medieval hell, for example, has very little canonical authority. It was largely and horribly furnished from traditions established in the Apocalypses of Peter and Paul, and elaborated in the visions of men who had fed on such documents. From some practical points of view, the elaboration which insistent traditions could provide made an acquaintance with the bare canonical text of Scripture superfluous.

Our Victorian, reflecting on his inheritance and conscious that his classics stood in a shining aura of esteem, would still agree that they represented nothing more than a supreme human achievement. But for the early English, the Scriptures, however unclearly discerned, were not only the supreme documents of human achievement, they were divine oracles, texts numinous in themselves, whose full meaning was linked by divine arrangement with the language in which men received them. The very order of words was meaningful, as Jerome asserted. All words, not only biblical words, had an innate force and mystery for these people. The art of writing was of a divine origin—the gift of Mercury, the successor to Woden. The very volumes of Scripture possessed miraculous power. Roger of Hoveden records that the eyes of a murderess fell from her head as soon as she gazed on an open Psalter. How the great book of the Lindisfarne Gospels delivered itself out of the sea unharmed is a well-known story; and even now the visitor to the British Museum can catch a shadow of the awe and wonder which sight of this splendid book must have originally aroused.

The Anglo-Saxons knew of three sacred languages, Hebrew, Greek and Latin, but in practice Latin alone was accepted as the language of all high knowledge. Alcuin explained to Charlemagne that the whole temple of Christian wisdom was borne upon the seven pillars of the Latin liberal arts, as these had been taught in the schools of Rome. Culture and learning for the Anglo-Saxons meant Roman culture. In our phrase, 'the middle ages', we still incline to think of our early history as a stage in the general transformation of antique into modern culture. The Anglo-Saxons, naturally enough, did not regard their own times as an interim period. Unlike even some of their contemporaries in Mediterranean lands, they saw their own situation as a prolongation of the past. Scriptural history, Roman history, and their own all fall into the same scheme. For them, there was no clash between Cicero and Virgil and the Scriptures. They were never troubled by the barbarousness of the Bible as the young Augustine had been. For them, Cicero was plainly inferior to Solomon in wisdom, and Virgil a lesser prophet than Isaiah. Bede found it perfectly natural to apply the rules of classical rhetoric to an examination of Scripture. The art of letters, as the Anglo-Saxons understood it, found its ideal and absolute in the Latin bible. In our century, we have been urged to read the Bible as literature. In dealing with the early English, we must turn the phrase about: the Anglo-Saxons tended to read all literature as the Bible and judged all writing by the standards that they found implicit there. They saw little point in translating it into a sub-standard dialect, unless they had a very special and very limited object in view.

In any case, success in translating the Bible depends, it would seem, on the conjunction of two factors. No translation is possible before an acceptable interpretation of the original has been established. It is rash to render an ambiguous oracle. But an interpretation of Scripture implies the existence of a theology. The pressure that precise theological ideas exert on translation is, in English history, most clearly and quite simply seen in More's objections against Tyndale's use of 'senior' and 'congregation' for 'priest' and 'church'. The new words implied a new theology. But the pressure of theology on translation always exists. The corollary, of course, is that existing translations in turn continue to exert control over theology. The verbal character of any new translation is determined by a great number of assumptions, usually unexamined, about what is theologically as well as linguistically acceptable. Thus, there are many systems of communication which an educated person nowadays would count slightly horrifying as mediums for biblical translation. For many centuries, a medieval counterpart of a modern educated person would have counted English one of the highly unsatisfactory mediums. The vernacular appeared simply and totally inadequate. Its use, it would seem, could end only in a complete enfeeblement of meaning and a general abasement of values. Not until a vernacular is seen to possess relevance and resources, and, above all, has acquired sufficient cultural prestige, can we look for acceptable and successful translation. And the times at which a language possesses this cultural prestige may not coincide with the times at which theology permits its basic terminology a certain fluidity. It happens occasionally. The desirable conjunction occurred in late-sixteenth-century England. It had occurred in Jerome's time too. Jerome's triumph as translator was won in that creative war-embrace of his Christianity and his Ciceronianism.

But the full conjunction did not occur in England before the sixteenth century. It was still only partial in Wyclif's time. But the history of early vernacular treatment of the Bible in England must keep these regulating principles in view. Over the six hundred years separating Bede from Wyclif, both the theology of the Bible and the prestige of the vernacular submitted to change. If, in the eighth century, the Bible tended to be looked upon as oracle, by the fourteenth it was already being presented as a plain rule of life. By the middle of the eleventh century, on the other hand, the vernacular had slowly won and already begun to lose a literary standing and serviceableness which were not fully regained for another five centuries.

The medieval church in England never clearly envisaged even the possibility of what we should call translation of the Bible. Her teaching policy as regards the Scriptures conformed in general with the twin aims set out by Augustine in *De Doctrina Christiana*. First it was necessary for the preacher to understand the full meaning of the Scriptures: secondly, it was necessary for him to learn how to communicate this special knowledge. The very complexity of the first process, however, was thought to demonstrate the unsuitability of any attempt to achieve the second by mere translation. To translate the Latin Bible would have been to transform the whole frame of knowledge, human and divine.

In a profound sense, all early English writing, poetic as well as practical discourse, in Latin and in the vernacular, is written within the biblical ambience. The consequences are sometimes surprising. When Alfred drew up his code of laws, he began by enacting the Mosaic laws of Exod. xx–xxiii. The royal genealogies, which were still being copied out in the thirteenth century, traced the descent of the Old English kings back through the heroes of Germania, through Woden to Methuselah and Noah, back to Adam 'that is Christ'. The Frisian people, with whom the Anglo-Saxons retained close cultural ties, went even further; for the Frisians in their national chronicles rearranged the chronology of their history in order that it should conform with the sequence of events in the Old Testament. But with the Anglo-Saxons, too, the Bible is the fount of tradition. Anglo-Saxon history, as the Anglo-Saxons conceived of it, goes back behind the Fall of the Angels, and the beginning of their Christian literature in the vernacular is a Creation hymn.

Bede in the *Ecclesiastical History*, v, 24, tells how Cædmon, a layman, a cowherd at the monastery at Whitby, was visited one night by a heavenly messenger who commanded him to sing a song of the Creation. To his own astonishment, and to the astonishment of his fellows and superiors at the monastery in the morning, Cædmon found that he possessed thenceforth a remarkable poetic gift. Installed more fittingly in the monastery, he was told stories from the Bible and after meditating on them he was able to rework them into the highly complicated verbal and metrical forms of traditional vernacular verse. According to Bede's narrative, Cædmon sang, at different times, of the Creation of the world and all the history of Genesis, of the departure of Israel out of Egypt, and many other histories; of the Incarnation, Passion, Resurrection and Ascension of Christ, of the coming of the Holy Ghost and the preaching of the apostles; also of the terror of Judgement, the horror of hell and the delights of heaven.

The full significance of this story becomes apparent only when it is
attached to the body of Anglo-Saxon thought about the nature of
biblical inspiration. For Anglo-Saxon scholars as for Gregory the
Great, 'our own very special English Gregory', as Alcuin called him,
the named authors of Scripture were the penmen of the Holy Ghost.
Neither Gregory nor the Anglo-Saxons took the explanation metaphorically. The Bible was essentially prophetic, the divinely inspired
disclosure of secret wisdom. Prophetic modes of thought were acceptable to the Anglo-Saxons. In so far as they ever acquired a theology,
they displayed most interest in prophetic theology, a theology of
origins, destinies and ends.

There can be no doubt that Bede saw at work in Cædmon a power
similar in kind to that possessed by the original penmen of Scripture,
almost as if Cædmon had acquired by divine gift that liberation of
utterance which according to Augustine belongs to the prophet whose
interpretative translation of Scripture can in some measure replace the
original. The very transcendence of the Bible gave Cædmon and his
successors a certain freedom in handling scriptural material. 'What are
the sayings of truth', Gregory had asked, 'unless we turn them into
nourishment of the soul?' Cædmon, privileged by his gift, used it to
feed the faithful with food they could digest.

Apart from the original hymn on Creation, nothing survives which
can be convincingly ascribed to Cædmon, although in one of the great
manuscript collections of Anglo-Saxon poetry (MS Junius 11, ed.
G. P. Krapp, *The Anglo-Saxon Poetic Records*, 1) a series of pieces,
known individually as *Genesis, Exodus, Daniel* and *Christ and Satan*, so
well corresponds with parts of Bede's catalogue that the poems are still
often referred to as the Cædmonian poems. But these pieces illustrate
well enough the kind of thing Cædmon achieved and his successors
emulated. They are in many ways learned poems; verbally they are
highly wrought. It is difficult to believe that they were ever popular in
the sense of being easy to listen to: the diction is ornate, the narration
obscure, the allusion sometimes remote. Yet there can be no doubt that
such poems circulated through England, that they were imitated, and
copied out for centuries. A remarkable piece, the so-called *Genesis B*,
which has a curious history of its own, seems to have been composed
in the ninth century. *Judith* (edited by E. van K. Dobbie, *The Anglo-
Saxon Poetic Records*, IV) may well belong to the tenth. Despite the

general homogeneity of these pieces, they display different degrees of dependence on the Scriptures. *Daniel* and *Judith* are close paraphrases, but in others various material is gathered round the basic story and often a particular slant is given to the narrative. This is particularly noticeable in *Exodus*. The prime source is Exod. xii. 17–xiv. Almost every phrase of these three chapters is echoed in the poem. A wide acquaintance is shown with other books of the Bible also, and scraps of obscure learning suggest the influence of Irish catechesis. At the same time the poem is to be related to the liturgy of Easter Saturday with its emphasis on baptism. If this sort of treatment is to be called translation, it is translation which renders the Bible in the same spirit as it was read by a learned scholar. The poet is relying not only on the text, but on the whole Christian cosmopoesy which it sustains. At the end of *Exodus* the poet speaks about the leadership of Moses, how he provided enduring wisdom so that men may still find in the Scriptures every law truly enjoined upon them by the Lord for their journey through life. 'If the interpreter of life, bright in the breast, the guardian of the body, will unlock the great treasure with the keys of the spirit, the mystery will be resolved, the right course of action emerge' (*Exodus* 523–6). Always the kernel of spiritual truth must be carefully picked out of the words. This call to the wise man to discern what the mystery of words imports is sounded again and again in Anglo-Saxon verse. The elusive mists of special meanings and the splendid obscurities of types and antitypes closely enfold early poetic treatments of Scripture in the vernacular.

Cynewulf, probably a Midland poet of the early ninth century, a bookish, thoughtful writer, well-read in Christian Latin literature, was less concerned with biblical narration than with the expression and exercise of piety. His work indicates how the Cædmonian poetry of direct scriptural content was sophisticated into pious verse. The bulk of the surviving Old English poetry, the work of divers hands, treats secondary, non-scriptural themes in this way. A representative treatment may be observed in what many modern readers consider the most attractive piece of Old English verse—the *Dream of the Rood*. The dream setting here retains the basic prophetic convention of Old English religious verse, and this convention, as usual, releases the writer from a strict conformity with Scripture and at the same time sanctifies the variation. Within this setting in the poem, the narrative of the Passion depends less upon Scripture than upon the liturgical practices associated with the veneration of the Cross. The general didactic and aspirational character of the piece is made evident in the conclusion.

The use made of the Psalter at this time shows how unclearly liturgical prayer and private devotion were distinguished. The Psalms had, of course, their regular weekly place in the monastic offices. But many holy men recited the Psalter daily and knew it by heart and used it as a devotional manual. Godric, the recluse of Finchale, acquired a finger permanently curved through constantly holding his psalm-book. Outstanding men, capable of private vocal prayer—and they were few —would still fit their prayers to the familiar phrases. So fundamental was the Psalter to the devotional and educational system of the monasteries that it is not surprising to find that English aids to under-standing were provided. Some of these aids were no more than odd glosses to hard words. But nearly fifteen psalters, some of the Roman, some of the Gallican, text, survive with a continuous gloss in Old English. The best-known of these glossed psalters is the ninth-century *Vespasian Psalter* (BM Cotton MS Vespasian A. i), copied from a still earlier gloss. The tradition lived long. The twelfth-century *Canterbury* or *Eadwine Psalter* (Trinity College, Cambridge, MS R. 17. I) is a remarkable piece of work. Here the text is provided of the so-called 'Hebrew' version and of the Roman as well as the Gallican Latin versions, and an Anglo-Norman gloss is provided for the 'Hebrew' and an English gloss for the Roman version.[1]

There were freer treatments of the Psalms in Old and Middle English than the glosses. In the *Paris Psalter* (BN Paris, *fonds latin* MS 8824, see G. P. Krapp, *The Anglo-Saxon Poetic Records*, v) beside the Roman text of the Psalms stands an Anglo-Saxon translation—of Psalms 1–50 in continuous prose incorporating a fair amount of interpretative comment, and of Psalms 51–150 in rather crude verse. According to William of Malmesbury, King Alfred had been engaged in translating the Psalter, but had scarcely finished the first part of it at the time of his death. The prose version of Psalms 1–50 in the *Paris Psalter* may

---

[1] For the variety of the Latin texts of the Psalter available in Anglo-Saxon England, and an account of the glossed psalters, see *Introduction* (particularly Appendix I, pp. 47–52) to the *Salisbury Psalter*, edited from Salisbury Cath. MS 150 by Celia and Kenneth Sisam, Early English Text Society 242 (1958).

preserve this venerable translation. The verse translation of Psalms 51 onwards is of later date, but very closely related metrical versions of many of these Psalms occur in the Old English *Benedictine Office* (edited by James M. Ure (1957)), in MS Junius 121 of mid-twelfth-century date from Worcester, a monastery with strong vernacular interests. But in England generally up to the end of the medieval period, English versions of the Psalter continued in use and several fresh translations were made. Some pages of the *Eadwine Psalter* seem to depend directly on the *Paris Psalter*. In the fourteenth century, the *Surtees Psalter*, Richard Rolle's *English Psalter* and the *West Midland Prose Psalter* (edited by K. D. Bülbring, Early English Text Society, 97 (1891)) belong to the same general tradition of devotion.

Among the Anglo-Saxons, glossing was not restricted to the Psalms. There exist Old English glosses, some sporadic, some continuous, on Proverbs, on part of Ecclesiasticus, and of course on many non-scriptural texts; but most impressive and most interesting are the glosses on the Gospels. Over the Latin text of the Lindisfarne Gospels, a word-for-word gloss was written in later, probably shortly after the middle of the tenth century, under the supervision of a scribe Aldred. Another gloss of the Gospels, the Rushworth Gloss (MS Bodley *auct.* D. 2. 19), seems to have been worked by two men. It was initiated by a priest Farman, who perhaps also made final corrections to what had been carried to completion by a scribe Owun, who based his part of the work on the Lindisfarne gloss. Farman's rendering of Matthew and of part of John is something more than a gloss: it reads as literal, continuous prose, and thus stands as the earliest piece of direct scriptural translation into English which has survived.

Glossing was part of Anglo-Saxon pedagogy. The interrelations and interdependence of most of the monastic glosses suggests that the activity was traditional. It was a normal instrument of instruction when the younger members of a monastic school were introduced to the Scriptures through oral teaching in the vernacular. The Life of Alcuin gives an account of Alcuin's schooldays at York. There Egbert taught grammar and the other liberal arts as a preparation for the study of the Scriptures. 'Sitting on his bed from sunrise until the sixth hour of the day, and often until the ninth hour, Egbert would explain the mysteries of Holy Writ to his pupils as far as they were prepared to receive them.' Cuthbert's letter describing the death of Bede, who had been Egbert's teacher, discloses a similar scene of instruction. It is in this letter that Cuthbert tells how Bede in his last sickness turned two little books into English—the Gospel of John up to chapter vi, and a work of Isidore of Seville. On the strength of this story, Bede has often been credited with finishing off with his last breath the first translation into English of a book of the Bible. But Cuthbert's words will not easily bear such an interpretation. The work has not survived, but on the whole it seems unlikely that Bede provided a readable vernacular version of the Gospel. Cuthbert makes it quite plain that the little work was designed for teaching purposes in the monastic school. A similar appreciation of the use of the vernacular for instructional purposes, though in a wider field, is manifested in Bede's last letter to the same Egbert of York, where Bede reminds the new bishop of the essential pastoral duty of instructing his people. Let those who can read Latin, he urges, use Latin to increase their knowledge of the faith. This is the best method. But let those, priests and laymen, who know only the vernacular, use the vernacular for the purpose. For the unlettered, Bede recalls that he himself has translated the Creed and the Lord's Prayer into English.

Western Christendom owes much to the learning and teaching methods developed by Bede. The later Anglo-Saxons regarded their pedagogical traditions with a degree of pride and veneration which may have chilled somewhat the genial current of learning. In dealing with the Bible they became all too conscious of the great weight of dogmatic and ecclesiastical tradition, and grew more cautious in the interpretation and use of Scripture. This conservatism and caution were already marked in the work of Alcuin (735–804). Alcuin was charged by Charlemagne to establish a standard text of the Bible. His standardization of the Vulgate text was accompanied by a stabilization of interpretation. Alcuin worked with a sure belief that the full sense of Scripture was already deposited by the Fathers.

Alcuin's work initiated a scholastic approach towards the Bible which endured for centuries. From now on, Scripture was not considered to be directly accessible to an intelligent reader, nor would such a reader consider himself free to draw out of it or put into it his own associations of meaning. Each verse of the Bible became a cluster of meanings provided by tradition out of the Fathers. Any reading of the Bible implied acceptance of a huge network of orthodox associations. The Vulgate and its latinity became ever more inviolable. For us, many of the connections of meaning are difficult to make: most modern readers will be at a loss to see the relevance of many of the scriptural quotations in *Piers Plowman*, for example.

But during the time that the implications of the shift in biblical theology were still being worked out into monastic training, there occurred in the ninth century a remarkable extension of the usefulness of the vernacular in England. Writing in 894 and looking back over his troubled reign of a score of years, King Alfred recalled that when he came to the throne there were very few clergy anywhere in England who knew or could translate Latin. By the end of his reign the position had much improved. There was a body of learned clergy, and with their aid Alfred had put through a scheme of education in two phases. First, he with his helpers translated into English certain basic books of knowledge, and then the freeborn youth of England who could be maintained at schools were set to acquire at least the ability to read English. Those who were called to the priesthood were expected to stay on to learn Latin. Although in Alfred's scheme, which has the character of an extension on a national scale of Bede's methods in the cloister, the vernacular was plainly regarded as a preparatory course to Latin, the cultural standing and the literary standardization of English must have been enhanced when it was taught in the schools.

We have already noted the uncertain tradition that Alfred translated the Psalter for devotional use. None of the translations associated with his educational policy is scriptural, yet they have a distinctive character. Thus Gregory's *Pastoral Care* becomes in Alfred's translation a work emphasizing the Church's duty in instructing the people. The translations as a group imply an obligation on all free men of learning. An ideal of Christian wisdom is implicitly established and it is an ideal which is not exclusively the prerogative of the clergy.

The real achievement of Alfred's educational policy is usually measured by the quality of the monastic revival in England in the tenth century. But the legacy did not fall immediately to the monasteries. At the court of Athelstan, 'the most literate king that ever ruled', according to William of Malmesbury, many scholars put their learning into royal service; and a boy could acquire learning there, as Dunstan did for a time. Nor was learning confined to the royal court. Oda, who became archbishop of Canterbury in 942, had been educated in a thegn's household. During the first half of this century, learning was livelier among the secular clergy than in the monasteries. It is significant that the New Minster founded by Edward the Elder at Winchester was a house for clerks, not monks.

The monastic reform of the latter half of the tenth century was pushed through with single-minded force. We have indeed only the reformers' view of events and, for them, to live in an unreformed house of canons was to live like Lot in Sodom. As a result of this Benedictine revival the stamp of monasticism was impressed on late Old English culture. Whereas the effect of Alfred's policy must have been to enhance the status of the vernacular, the emphasis of the new reform served to develop Alfred's second and ultimate aim—the creation of a more learned priesthood. But the policy was promoted now in a strict monastic setting. A highly disciplined army of monks increased the intellectual driving force of the time, but their serious interests were bound to Latin. Their interest in the vernacular was mainly antiquarian, even faintly sentimental.

But to the end of the Anglo-Saxon period there was a high culture among some of the lay aristocracy. The most remarkable figure is the Earl Ethelweard, Ælfric's patron, who wrote a Latin chronicle. More important than the literary achievement was the advanced spirituality of well-born Englishmen and women. With people such as Byrhtnoth of Essex, Ethelwine of East Anglia, and, in the next century, Earl Leofric, Lady Godiva and Earl Waltheof, emerges a type of austere but gracious piety which remained long a characteristic of English religious life before and after the Reformation.

Ælfric, the greatest of Old English prose writers and the most important figure of the history of the Bible in the English vernacular before Wyclif, was brought up at Winchester, at the centre of the strictest Benedictinism. In 987 he was serving at Cerne as mass-priest, and presumably it was there that he composed for his own congregation, which would include laymen, those sermons which, about 994, at the request of Earl Ethelweard he gathered into the two series of the *Catholic Homilies* (edited by B. Thorpe (1844–6)). These were followed by the homilies known as the *Lives of the Saints* (edited by W. W. Skeat, Early English Text Society, 76, 82, 94, 114 (1881–1900)). Together these homilies provided sermons for the full monastic year, and include many passages of scriptural translation, in which Ælfric endeavoured, as he said, to give exact sense for the sense in the Vulgate.

Ælfric is however an excerpter and expositor rather than a translator. When he speaks of having turned Scripture into English, his practice is best thought of as adaptation. It is important to bear this in mind when we read Ælfric's own account of his handling of Scripture which he provided in his *Tract on the Old and New Testament* (edited by S. J. Crawford in the *Heptateuch*, etc., Early English Text Society, 160 (1922)). This tract, written about 1010 for a layman Sigeweard, is the most important treatment in English of the question of vernacular Scriptures before the Purvey tracts. But Ælfric, incidentally, also gives an account of his own labours. He has turned the Pentateuch into English, often dealt with the Creation story, translated Joshua for Ethelweard, treated Judges, Kings, Job, Esther, and the Maccabees. He notices that Judith is also available in English but does not claim it as his own. For his work on the New Testament he refers to his series of homilies. All this makes a very substantial list. But no book of the Bible received anything like full translation. Even in Genesis, the least abridged of all Ælfric's versions, lengthy lists of names are omitted, difficult poetical passages, descriptions and detailed instructions reduced. Ælfric's intention was to reproduce accurately the outlines of the biblical story, what he called the 'naked narrative'. This is the process, carried to extremes, which enabled him to reduce the four books of Kings to what makes less than fifteen pages of print and offer it as a single homily.

The need for some opening up of Scripture to the laity Ælfric admitted. 'At this time', he writes in one of the homilies, 'much more knowledge is necessary for laymen, because all the world is far spent in its manifold miseries.' Yet he was uneasy about appearing to follow a policy of deliberate translation. The *Tract* gives an appearance of method to his work on the Bible which was not apparent even to Ælfric himself as he produced the scriptural handlings which make up the list. The handlings emerged unsystematically, in response to particular requests or requirements. In the Preface to the *Catholic Homilies* he had declared that 'henceforth I will never translate Gospel or exposition of the Gospel'; and later in his preface to Genesis, addressed to Ethelweard, 'I dare not and I will not translate any book of the Bible after this book'.

The *Tract on the Old and New Testament* establishes his position precisely. Here he courteously accedes to Sigeweard's request for an account of Scripture, yet as firmly, if obliquely, denies the possibility of full satisfaction. He writes for Sigeweard, but, as a note at the head of the text observes, what he has to say is profitable to many. The Christian layman, he reminds Sigeweard, is saved by a life of good works. If the layman wants to know more about the Scriptures, he must first justify this ambition by such a life. God is concerned primarily with good works. The Bible is the record of God's own good works and these provide the spiritual meaning of the scriptural narrative. For instance, behind the Mosaic account of the Creation lies the operation of the Trinity and the actual Fall of man. It is not easy for the layman to see these meanings behind the words. In all the old history 'God in these things spoke by works and wonders and the works were put into words to keep men mindful of their true significance'. Nor can Sigeweard expect to receive the full content of the New Testament. Again, Christ loves deeds more than smooth words: words pass, works stand. Ælfric tells at some length an apocryphal story of John, of which the moral seems to be that too much forwardness on the part of an enthusiastic convert is not always a good thing. It is important for men to observe degree and status. Society is built on three pillars: labourers, warriors and men of prayer. If one order fails, society collapses. If Sigeweard's duty is to defend the right and administer justice, let him remember that God loves righteous judgements. Knowledge of the Word is not bound to profit. The Jews, to whom the Word was first preached, gave it no belief and perished miserably. 'When I was with you, you plied me with drink too liberally. Know, dear friend, that whosoever forces another man to drink more than he can take, he shall answer for it.' Should not Sigeweard have understood that Holy Scripture was strong wine indeed for a layman to take in excess and undiluted?

But Ælfric, who in this *Tract* would hold much back, had given the English much already. His influence was deep, if somewhat narrow. He was no national educator as Alcuin or Alfred had been. He wrote for groups of pious people, and by similar groups he continued to be read long after the Conquest. His style of thought as well as his style of writing undoubtedly contributed something to that tradition of vernacular religious writing which was to be eventually crowned by the Authorized (King James) Version. Ælfric himself worked in the channels provided and his matter is almost entirely derivative. His intention is didactic, his manner cautious, his flights and fires under strict control. His English prose is highly skilled, fluent, lucid, slightly orotund. He pays careful attention to rhythm and makes successful and unobtrusive use of rhetorical figures. His is a style which could be modified to suit almost any theme.

Ælfric's performance no less than his reluctance in handling Scripture shows the precarious and unstable position in which ecclesiastical policy would find itself, accustomed as it had become over centuries in the West to withholding Scripture from those ignorant of Latin. Now already in England at the end of the tenth century, the vernacular was reaching out to grasp at the sacred text. Kings and bishops and men of state cared for vernacular writings. Great books were made in English and ceremoniously donated. Yet this respect for the vernacular went forward in a world where ecclesiasticism was hardening and where intellectual leadership was being drawn more narrowly into firmer monastic moulds.

Ælfric was not the only purveyor of scriptural material at this time. It seems likely that another version of Genesis existed, though Ælfric's part in this so-called Anglo-Saxon *Heptateuch* is uncertain. Furthermore, it is probable that it was during his lifetime that there appeared from another hand the first translation of the entire Gospels which approximates to modern requirements in translation—the *West-Saxon Gospels*[1]—a full, accurate, readable, if literal, translation. Where, by whom, and why this version was made we do not know. That it appeared when it did is significant. That it is completely anonymous is perhaps also significant. It exists in several closely related manuscripts, none of which is the original. In one of the earliest copies (Cambridge University Library MS Ii. 2. 11), which was given to Exeter cathedral by Bishop Leofric (*d.* 1072), rubrics relate the Gospel text to the openings of the liturgical gospels throughout the Church's year. But it is unlikely that the Gospels were ever read in English at the Mass. One text of the *West-Saxon Gospels* (BM Royal MS 1 A. xiv) is of twelfth-century date: another (Bodleian Hatton MS 38), copied from the Royal MS, is somewhat later still. Modernizing glosses inserted in the Royal MS and the thoroughgoing linguistic revision of the Hatton text show that the Old English version of the Gospels was being seriously studied well into the thirteenth century.

[1] Edited by W. W. Skeat, *The Holy Gospels in Anglo-Saxon*, etc. (1871–87), and separately by J. W. Bright, *The Gospels in West Saxon* (1904–6).

Five hundred years of organized Christian life in England were not cancelled by the events of 1066. The continued use of the *West-Saxon Gospels* and the sustained popularity of Ælfric's works are outward signs of a continuity of spirit which survived the Norman Conquest. But the spirit came to inhabit new forms. The monasteries remained the instruments which determined intellectual development, but the Norman ecclesiastical system was very different from the Anglo-Saxon. It had short if strong roots, and no vernacular culture was attached to them. It was fiercely and proudly grounded in contemporary latinity. The native learning of England was unacceptable to the new order, not because it was the learning of a subject culture, but because it had the wrong tone. It appeared old-fashioned, unpractical, diffuse, unsuitably attached to old precedent and forgotten sentiment. At its worst it was hopelessly dreamy or fantastic.

By the end of the eleventh century nearly all the great monasteries of England had been brought under new management and conformed with Lanfranc's ideals—except for some monasteries in the secluded west of England. Particularly in the diocese of Worcester, where even in late Anglo-Saxon times the links between Church and society had never been strained so hard as in other parts where the monastic reformers were more militant, the vernacular continued to flourish awhile, even to develop. From this western area in the late twelfth century comes the remarkable group of homiletic and devotional texts commonly referred to as the Katherine Group texts. None of these texts provides direct handling of the Scriptures, but they all exhibit a profound knowledge of the Bible and a habit of trained scriptural exposition. And furthermore, they employ a style of English—sophisticated, subtle, instructedly rhetorical—which exploits Ælfric's achievement. But special local conditions keep the traditions vital in the west Midlands. Elsewhere these traditions ceased to be consciously preserved and the English language as a cultural medium was all but destroyed. And even in Worcester, by the end of the twelfth century, men knew that the old ways, the old learning, were passing. An unknown cleric laments: 'Saint Bede was born here in Britain among us and learnedly he translated books by means of which the English people were instructed... Abbot Ælfric ...was a scholar and translated [the Pentateuch]... These taught our people in English... Now is the learning lost and the people forlorn... Those who teach the people now are men of other tongues...'

By the mid-twelfth century a new literary vernacular is being developed in south and east England, an Anglo-Norman language for the new managers of English society. So far as its literature deals with scriptural material, the treatment is not original. Most of the men who wrote Anglo-Norman works, and many of the people for whom they were written, were lineal descendants of those who had cherished Anglo-Saxon literature. Guichard of Beaulieu in an Anglo-Norman verse sermon made direct borrowings from Ælfric. More commonly, of course, things go the other way round, and Anglo-Norman writings of the twelfth and thirteenth centuries provide the bases of English works in the thirteenth and fourteenth.

In the twelfth century appeared two influential Anglo-Norman versions of the Psalter. The Proverbs of Solomon were expounded for a Lincolnshire lady, Alice de Condé (*c.* 1140). A prose version of the books of Kings is probably of English origin. From the thirteenth century come other versions of the Psalter, a number of Passion narratives, and several comprehensive manuals which indicate the new importance attached to confession at this time. Of this character is the translation with commentary of Revelation made by William Gifford for the use of nuns. For a similar purpose is William of Waddington's *Manuel des Pechiez* (turned into English at the beginning of the fourteenth century by Robert Mannyng of Brunne), although the scriptural material here is limited. Robert of Greatham put together a translation of the Sunday gospels, *Les evangiles des domees*, for the use of a lady Aline, probably a member of the de Montforts, a family as famous for its piety as its politics. Other popular works were *Lumere as Lais*, an elaborated version of *Elucidarium* by Honorius (of Autun), and *Speculum Ecclesie* by Edmund Rich (1170?–1240), archbishop of Canterbury. Ostensibly most of the *Speculum* deals with meditation on Holy Writ, but it is not direct scriptural meditation that Edmund has in mind, but consideration of the familiar, carefully arranged topics falling within the framework of the seven deadly sins, the ten commandments, the seven virtues, etc. If a monk wants to know the Bible he is advised to listen to sermons.

Writings in Anglo-Norman were more sophisticated, as might be expected from the class of reader for which they were intended, than contemporary works in English. But all vernacular works concerned with Scripture were, in the main, mere attenuations of contemporary

Latin literature on the Bible. All serious work was done in Latin, and biblical scholarship during the twelfth and thirteenth centuries was drawing further and further away from the vernaculars. It was becoming specialized and technical to an unprecedented degree. By the end of the twelfth century it would be more than even a well-trained cleric could manage—even a cleric trained in youth in the disciplines of the new theology at Paris—to keep up with the development of advanced scholarship and the successive refinements of method. The elaboration of scholarship is illustrated by the vast apparatus produced—the succession of Sentences, and Summas, the books of Questions, the concordances, biblical dictionaries, collections of allegories, etymologies and ambiguities.[1] Little that Paris or Oxford taught could be easily transferred to the edification of the unlearned. Moreover the intense free speculation possible in a university made many who participated, and more who did not, decidedly unwilling to communicate with untrained minds. Heresy was the almost inevitable product of free speculation. The Bible was dangerous. To handle its text directly, as would be necessary in providing translation, would have been to court disaster. Already there was an effective, if often a self-imposed, system of censorship in operation. It was much safer, much better for the salvation of all concerned, to stick to the accredited expositions, to avoid direct handling of Scripture and to use instead, in the pulpit or in popular books, the theological schemes provided by Peter Lombard or the biblical history of Peter Comestor (pp. 205, 206). The dilemma in which Ælfric had found himself would now have been quite simply resolved. The prohibitions against vernacular translation formulated on the Continent were symptomatic of the general European development. Walter Map, the witty archdeacon of Oxford (from 1197), and a man who, within the closed republic of letters of his time, was decidedly anti-monastic in sympathy, tells in revealing fashion and to his own satisfaction how he discomfited a handful of Bible-reading Albigensians, who had the simplicity to believe what they read of Scripture and lived by the light of their understanding.

During the thirteenth century, then, the situation was unpropitious for vernacular translation. English languished, Anglo-Norman was necessarily the language of a colonial culture, and the esotericism of

[1] See J. de Ghellinck, *L'Essor de la Littérature latine au XIIe siècle*, 2nd ed. (1955), pp. 93–102, and chapter IV of this book, especially sections 2 and 3.

Latin learning and the fear of heresy preserved the documents of salvation from common use. All that could be provided for the unlearned had to be carefully filtered, made unequivocally clear, sterilized of infection and guaranteed to conform with formulations of the faith which were of course made only in Latin. What the laity could receive through words was no more than an extreme simplification of a highly systematized abstract of the Bible.

Towards the end of the twelfth century vernacular preaching revived. It would be unwise to generalize for the rest of the middle ages on the regularity with which the Mass gospel was preached to the Sunday congregation, or on the attentiveness with which it was received when it was preached. But these Sunday sermons must have given most unlettered men some indirect acquaintance with the word of Scripture. There were, of course, as we are often reminded nowadays, other ways—confessional practices, wall-paintings, minstrelsy and plays, for example—by which some knowledge of the central concepts of Christian belief could be implanted.

As a body the parish clergy leave almost no mark in the history of the English bible. Nor, rather surprisingly, do the Dominicans, the preaching friars. Much more successful in diffusing some vernacular knowledge of the Scriptures were the canons, particularly the Augustinians. The debt of the English to these orders cannot be properly assessed. Their work was obscure and often submerged in local conditions. But their contribution in re-forming the literary language and establishing new traditions must be counted of first-rate importance.

A touching example of Augustinian zeal, if not of Augustinian effectiveness, is provided by the canon Orm, writing in the north-east Midlands *c.* 1200. Orm intended to provide in English a full Gospel harmony with interpretations, by assembling the Mass gospels according to the chronology of Christ's life. The work as it exists is incomplete. Orm assured his brother Walter in the dedication that he had carefully checked everything but he still expected detractors to charge him with lack of judgement. To make sure he was not misunderstood he wrapped huge swathes of words round the smallest bundle of meaning and devised his own spelling system to ensure accurate delivery for reading aloud. To little purpose, we may well believe. The *Ormulum* (edited by R. M. White and R. Holt (1878)) was little read and had no imitators. It dropped straight into a philologist's limbo. The verbal flabbiness of the writing is a convincing demonstration of lack of confidence in English as a literary medium.

Orm's method of rearranging liturgical material into scriptural paraphrase must have been obvious enough. The same method appears basic to a great northern collection of the thirteenth century still largely unedited—the verse *Northern homily cycle*. There are however many manuscripts of this work exhibiting a great variety in form and content. Material is dropped or incorporated in each revision. A prologue in an early version indicates that the author—probably an Augustinian canon—intended to recount and explain the Mass gospels for the sake of unlettered parishioners. But again it is unlikely that the book was for reading aloud in church. It is more likely to have been a handbook for the preparation of sermons. At the end of each section of gospel paraphrase is added an illustrative tale. Some later manuscripts simply collect these tales and omit the scriptural material altogether. Other revisions add a variety of saints' legends. This development is elaborated in other manuscripts by a division of the *Cycle* into two parts—one consists of the regular Sunday gospels, corresponding with a *Temporale*, the other deals with saints' days throughout the year. Still further modification is exhibited elsewhere when to the *Temporale* is added an independent *Legendary*. Such accretions testify to notable developments in late medieval religious writing for the laity. As the demand for the Bible became more vocal with Lollardism in the fourteenth century, so the uneasiness among the orthodox in offering Scripture to the laity increased. Saints' legends and pious fictions were much less controversial.

Another vast, amorphous collection, similar in character to the *Northern homily cycle*, is the so-called *Southern legend collection*, which was first put together in the thirteenth century, but was still being used in the sixteenth. This work, originally a gathering together of saints' lives, was swelled with apocryphal material of the Infancy of Christ and the Harrowing of Hell, etc., and with some Old Testament material, so that one version (St John's College, Cambridge, MS B. 6, *c.* 1400) provides a fairly comprehensive coverage of the biblical story from Creation to the destruction of Jerusalem.

Such a comprehensive treatment had behind it the example of the *Historia scholastica* by Peter Comestor, who taught at Paris in the second half of the twelfth century. The *Historia* recounted the whole biblical history, drew upon a great number of non-biblical authors and inserted at appropriate places the histories of the Persians, the Greeks and the Romans. This learned work lost something of its high authority in the universities but remained popular throughout the medieval period. It was known to Chaucer and Gower and much drawn upon in preaching, in biblical versifications (for example, the fifteenth-century *Metrical Paraphrase of the Old Testament*, edited by H. Kalén (1923)) and in popular drama. An early extended use of it was made in *Genesis and Exodus* (edited R. Morris, Early English Text Society, 7 (1865)), written *c.* 1250 in south-east England. The author explains that he is composing a 'song' (in 2,500 lines) with 'words small' for recitation to laymen. The 'song' is a bald verse narrative remote from the biblical text. The story of Exodus in another 2,500 lines forms a sequel. Of much the same date and provenance is a shorter verse piece, *Jacob and Joseph* (edited by A. S. Napier (1916)), a minstrel composition, which shows the character often given to stories from Holy Writ in late medieval times. Doctrinal exposition has been replaced by emphasizing the human, romantic interest.

The most important English work to draw upon Peter Comestor is *Cursor Mundi* (edited by R. Morris, Early English Text Society, 57, 59, 62, 66, 68 and 99 (1874–92)), a northern composition of about 1300, which was still being copied and read at the end of the fifteenth century. It deals in over 25,000 lines with more or less the whole Old and New Testament story. Apart from the *Historia scholastica*, it draws on many apocryphal writings and many secondary sources. There are also some direct contacts with the Vulgate. The work, as its title indicates, is a running through of world history and shows the range and scope of scriptural knowledge possible in the vernacular during the fourteenth century. The range is indeed impressive, and the variations from Scripture no less astonishing to the modern reader. The story is framed in the usual scheme of the seven ages, but it is offered as a pious substitute for popular romance. This is the best and most delightful of all stories, the author avouches, just as the Virgin, in whose honour the poem is put together, is the best of all lovers. This is her romance, the full story of her doings and those of her kin. Mary's part in this grand scheme of Christian renovation gives a slack unity to the poem, a unity not easily comprehended, it must be admitted, as the couplets, often effective and well-pointed, pour on in their vigorous thousands.

The work of bringing religion to the laity in the thirteenth century by 'preaching peace and penitence for the remission of sins' is the special glory of the Franciscans. Despite the apostolic character of their lives, their preaching was not notably scriptural. Apart from works designed to aid personal devotion, numerous hymns and carols for instance, or versions and imitations of the pseudo-Bonaventuran *Meditations on the Passion*, the Franciscans contributed little to the history of vernacular Scripture, except by reaction, later. Francis himself, it will be remembered, deprecated the possession and private use of any books. In his sickness he declined the offer of being read to from the Bible. Christ poor and crucified was sufficient for his meditation. In the new movement of devotion, the crucifix, or some other representation to the senses of the humanity of Christ, is used with all the assurance with which the Bible has been used in other ages as the focus for meditation. Reading was regarded by some as a superfluity, even as a distraction. For contemplatives, the kernel of truth was embedded in the personal experience, but for men of ordinary clay the results of the new devotion were perhaps less satisfactory. Unless they are reinforced by moral instruction, special devotions, designed to produce an initial response leading to a personal experience, tend either towards an excessive sacramentalizing of the devotional life, or towards the senti-mentalizing and cheapening of the experience. By the fourteenth century, hearing without understanding Latin services was accorded a sacramental value. From this time too, saints' lives, as we have seen, provided reading more orthodox than Holy Scripture. Few churchmen took their suspicion that the Bible was a good only to the extent that it was not understood, as far as a Friar Claxton, a doctor of divinity, 'who said that Holy Scripture was a false heresy'.

During the fourteenth century the friars were the bitterest and most active opponents of an English Bible. There were ecclesiastical and political grounds for their opposition. But there were also reasons more directly concerned with biblical theology. The Franciscans, almost from their origins, had contributed much to the development of a new approach to the Bible which, rejecting spiritual interpretation, concentrated upon the extrication of the literal sense. The movement, initiated late in the twelfth century by such men as Andrew of St Victor and Stephen Langton, was revolutionary (pp. 206 ff.). The Bible lost its oracular character. It emerged instead as another literary text—

the supreme one, of course—requiring full editorial treatment. Roger Bacon is probably the most vociferous in proclaiming the new programme of studies. Literal interpretation did not mean looking for a plain sense. Interpretation, abandoning allegory and typology, relied instead on the whole wide store of human learning, on Aristotelian philosophy and natural science and on detailed philological and linguistic knowledge of the sacred languages. The whole Bible was exposed to scientific inspection. The unlearned had plainly no place in this work. It took fifteen years of hard study by the keenest mind to become a doctor of theology.

Franciscanism in many modes of spiritual activity worked towards ends which the friars themselves so bitterly opposed in the fourteenth and fifteenth centuries. Paradoxically, the desire for translation makes itself evident first among people of the kind which St Francis himself would have been best pleased to work with—humble contemplatives, often lay people, seeking to know Christ experientially. But we may remember, if mystical experience is primarily a seeing, what is to be seen must already have been given a shape by some symbol-system, and usually this system is bound to rest, at bottom, on words. To furnish the forms of his hoped-for experience the Christian contemplative was brought back in this way to Holy Scripture. We find in England, as we find still more remarkably in Germany and the Low Countries during the same centuries, that a desire for vernacular Scripture with a new object arises among lay contemplatives. Often these are women with no knowledge of Latin. They are often the people most skilled in the new devotional methods. They require the Bible not for moral guidance, nor for knowledge, nor for any good of Church or state, but in order to acquire the ground and forms of private mystical experience.

The mystic Richard Rolle (*c.* 1300–49) is the last significant figure before Wyclif. In Rolle were knotted many threads of the past. He knew some of the old devotional works in the vernacular and maintained thus a tenuous link with Ælfric. His English commentary on the Psalms shows also points of contact with the *Surtees Psalter* (*c.* 1300, edited for Surtees Society (1843–7))—a northern vernacular version in short couplets; and both Rolle's commentary and the *Surtees Psalter* seem to have a remote dependence upon the Old English Psalter glosses. But not only old native traditions were alive in Rolle. He was well grounded in European learning of the twelfth century. In his Latin works he uses a fantastic 'Hisperican' style which would have been admired by many of Bede's contemporaries, however baffling it may be to us. All through his work stretch those tentacular roots of language and expression which a literary culture must acquire before it can flower.

The bulk, if not the most interesting, of Rolle's works are expositions of Scripture, but, except for his second treatment of the Psalter, these scriptural works are in Latin. The *English Psalter* (edited by H. R. Bramley (1884)), based on Peter Lombard's commentary, was written in the vernacular for the use of the recluse Margaret Kirkby, but it acquired a popularity which it retained up to Reformation times as much among the orthodox as among the Lollards, who were to produce an interpolated version of it. Rolle's other English works are manuals of contemplation or pieces of devotion produced for the use of women. Although, when writing in English, Rolle is less systematic and less diffuse than in his Latin treatises, there is no marked simplification of the theory of contemplation. His own knowledge of the Scriptures was profound, and with pardonable idealism he expected a deep knowledge of Scripture among all people in religion. He thought of Scripture as a mystery. 'God wishes his Scriptures to be shut lest a passage of entry into the treasury of the Lord be exposed to enemies, who would glory in their own vanity and not in God, and would esteem the divine words too lightly.' It was not a mystery of words, but of meanings. For the secrets were directly open to the mystical lovers of Christ, who by virtue of their endowment and training seize directly upon the truth. These truths are most peculiarly relevant to the contemplative himself. Scripture is not envisaged as the message of joy and fear passed from lip to lip among an expectant people: it is the glass in which the solitary can darkly but surely discern in a series of portraits the lineaments of his own growth to perfection. Preaching and expounding Holy Writ is an activity inferior to self-knowledge. 'Here may we see that none should be so hardy to translate or expound Holy Writ but if he feeled the Holy Ghost in him, that is maker of Holy Writ, for soon shall he err that is nought led with him.' Rolle's attitude recalls Augustine's or for that matter Cædmon's, but this belief in divine illumination in relation to an understanding of the Bible had a very different import in fourteenth-century England from what it had had in Bede's Northumbria. Many vernacular writers in the fourteenth century repeat and develop Rolle's lines of thought. Such writers were accustoming the English language to deal with the most intimate concepts of religion.

The verbal achievement of an English translation of the Bible had as its essential prerequisite the enfranchisement of English. It is well to remember that Chaucer was celebrated among his contemporaries and successors for his achievement in high style above all else: for the splendour and dignity and range of his utterance. Chaucer did not translate the Bible, he was too wise and too cautious. He had the good sense to present the most orthodox doctrine in the most traditional form when he told the *Tale of Melibeus* and set the *Parson's Tale* last in the *Canterbury Tales*. But, following a line of fourteenth-century literary activity, he did translate non-scriptural Latin books into English. He had no direct connection with any of the biblical translation of the fourteenth century. He never aspired to more than a layman's knowledge. Yet his very achievement as a layman shows that the charmed circle of clerical learning is broken. His writings are the unmistakable sign of what Englishmen were coming to accept and expect in the vernacular. A writer like Chaucer is not bred in one generation. The English language had slowly acquired cultural standing and was seeking to become coterminous with contemporary life. But its range was still limited. There are still areas of contemporary life and thought which Chaucer cannot touch or touches only equivocally. As a result it is difficult sometimes to realize that Chaucer's world was also Wyclif's, or for that matter Langland's or Hilton's. But Chaucer's success over a wide but still restricted field is the palmary sign of the literary conditions which made the limited success of the Wycliffite translation of the Bible possible.

3. THE WYCLIFFITE VERSIONS

The culmination of the movement for the translation of the Bible into English in the middle ages is found in the activities of that group of men who surrounded John Wyclif at Oxford and at Lutterworth up to the time of his death in 1384, and who completed after his death the work which he had inspired and initiated.

From the end of the fourteenth century onwards the name of Wyclif has been associated with this work. Archbishop Arundel writes to Pope John XXIII in 1411:

This pestilent and wretched John Wyclif, of cursed memory, that son of the old serpent...endeavoured by every means to attack the very faith and sacred doctrine of Holy Church, devising—to fill up the measure of his malice—the expedient of a new translation of the Scriptures into the mother tongue.

The continuator of Henry Knighton's *Chronicle*, writing probably a little later, is more direct:

This Master John Wyclif translated from Latin into English—the Angle not the angel speech—the Gospel that Christ gave to the clergy and doctors of the Church...so that by his means it has become vulgar and more open to laymen and women who can read than it usually is to quite learned clergy of good intelligence. And so the pearl of the Gospel is scattered abroad and trodden underfoot by swine.

At about the same time John Hus in Prague, with information presumably derived from those disciples of Wyclif who had taken refuge with him, can write:

By the English it is said that Wyclif translated the whole Bible from Latin into English.

The evidence from friends and foes alike is unanimous for Wyclif's responsibility for the translation. If we now try to identify copies of it, we shall probably find that any moderate-sized collection of medieval English manuscripts will include at least one containing in a late-fourteenth- or early-fifteenth-century hand some part of the Bible translated into English. The British Museum Library possesses over forty such manuscripts, the Bodleian Library nearly as many, the John Rylands Library in Manchester fourteen. Single manuscripts are found in the libraries of many Oxford and Cambridge colleges, in the libraries of the older cathedrals such as Lincoln, Worcester and Hereford, and further afield in Dresden and Wolfenbüttel, in New York and San Marino, California. The physical appearance of these manuscripts, of which nearly two hundred are known, varies greatly. Some are large one- or two-volume works, containing the whole Bible carefully written, with elaborately decorated initials and fine bindings; such are B.M. Royal MS I C viii, which once belonged to Henry VI, B.M. Egerton MSS 617, 618, which probably belonged to Thomas of Woodstock, Duke of Gloucester, Bodley MS 277 and Bodl. Fairfax MS 2. Others are more workaday volumes, perhaps in quarto and containing only part of the Bible, often the New Testament, with simple decorations in red and blue. Still others are small volumes containing only a single book; Bodl. Douce MS 36 has only Tobit, Harley MS 984 only the Gospel of Matthew. Or they may be in a plain, even rough, hand with no decoration of any kind.

Of these many manuscripts, all but a small handful contain translations clearly related, though differing amongst themselves in some details. Since the time of Humphrey Wanley, the pioneer of English palaeography, they have been regarded as containing 'Wyclif's' translation of the Bible; the consensus of opinion on their origin has been challenged only once, in an ill-advised essay by the late Cardinal Gasquet, whose conclusions have since been proved untenable. Our main concern in this section will be with this great majority of the manuscripts, though the small handful that preserve different translations are of some importance and interest, since their very existence can be held to show that at the end of the fourteenth century several people or groups of people were devoting some of their time to translating parts of Scripture. Significantly, perhaps, it was the New Testament that was selected now for translation; if the Psalter was the most popular choice for translation in the early part of the century, it was not so in the later part of the century. Instead, we find versions of the Pauline epistles, some of the Catholic epistles, and of Acts. One of the versions of the Pauline epistles, preserved in a single manuscript, Corpus Christi College Cambridge MS Parker 32, contains the Latin text followed by an English rendering with a few short explanatory or interpretative glosses. Such a work is, like Rolle's *English Psalter*, probably designed as a help to the understanding of the Latin rather than as a substitute for it.

The same manuscript contains the Gospels of Mark and Luke, again in Latin with an English translation and a much longer commentary; what appears to be a parallel treatment of the Gospel of Matthew is found in other manuscripts, and in one of these, C.U.L. Ii. 2. 12, is introduced by a brief prologue in which it is stated that the translation was undertaken 'at the suggestyon of Goddys servant' and that 'gretly in this doyng I was comforted of other Goddys servauntys divers'— remarks that have been interpreted as meaning on the one hand that the translator was in sympathy with or even in association with the known

Wycliffite translators and on the other hand that the translations were in some way within the pale of the Church. The former view has perhaps more to support it. From the form of the language, it is considered that these Gospels derive from the north Midlands; from the same area apparently comes a translation of Acts which in the fifteenth century was more widely copied (it is in five manuscripts) and in modern times has been more extensively referred to. In two manuscripts this translation of Acts is combined with a version of the Pauline and Catholic epistles from an originally southern and probably therefore independent source, in another with the four Gospels in what we are to consider further, the Wycliffite version. An extensive prologue or tract is prefixed to two of the manuscripts, in which a 'lewed and unkunnynge' brother and sister—that is, apparently, orthodox religious—ask their brother superior to give them instruction for their souls' health. It is not made clear that it is specifically the translation of Scripture that is required of him, but the superior expresses some reluctance to do as they ask, adding 'ʒif y wolde answere to thyn axynges y moste in cas underfonge the deth'. This has been interpreted as a reference to the penalty for heresy laid down in 1401, and it is thought therefore that this translation dates from after that time. Several problems are raised by this tract, but perhaps for our present purpose it will suffice to point out that these other translations of biblical books, whatever their origin, are few in number and slight in importance when put beside the vast mass of closely related manuscripts containing what has been claimed as the Wycliffite versions, and to these we now return.

Few of them have any indication of the date of their copying. Even fewer have any indication of the date or authorship of the translation. This is perhaps not very surprising, since in the late fourteenth century even original works are not always credited to their author. Yet the authorship of Trevisa's translations is known on manuscript authority, as is that of Rolle's *Psalter*, and it might reasonably have been expected that the author of a widely copied translation would be well enough known to be mentioned by name in some manuscripts at least, particularly if he was as prominent a scholar as Wyclif. But translations of the Bible, and in particular those of the bare text without explanatory comment, were regarded with suspicion by the Church, and those produced by the heretic Wyclif were specifically condemned in 1407.

The opposition of the Church to translations was based on several grounds. The understanding of Scripture, with its fourfold interpretation, was felt to be possible for the priest only by virtue of the grace of his priesthood, and was therefore altogether too difficult for the layman who would be most likely to read a translation. In any case, the earthly hierarchy should be a model of the heavenly one, in that grace should be mediated from the higher ranks to the lower, from upper clergy to lower, and from lower clergy to laymen. Private Bible-reading by lay-people or by priests not intellectually equipped to follow the Vulgate themselves was liable to lead to heresy. Minor practical objections were also adduced: the preparation of an accurate translation would be a work of impossible subtlety; it would be impracticable to ensure the accuracy of copies of an English bible, copied anywhere and by anyone, though Latin bibles, produced in or near the university, could always be supervised. But despite such general objections, no universal and absolute prohibition of the translation of the Scriptures into the vernacular nor of the use of such translations by clergy or laity was ever issued by any council of the Church or any pope. There are, however, a number of surviving papal letters which could reasonably be taken to represent condemnation of translations. One of the most important, that of Innocent III in 1199 on the Waldensian translations, condemns the users of these, especially those who used them as a basis for usurping the office of preaching, for holding secret conventicles or for setting themselves up against priests of less learning. Nevertheless, Innocent had earlier carefully inquired about the author of the translation and his intention. The answers he received have not been preserved, but his very inquiry makes it plain that there was not at this time any known precedent for universally condemning all translations. Later he speaks as if he had condemned these particular translations, but his condemnation was not couched in such broad terms as to constitute a clear prohibition of all translations at all times, and the part of his condemnatory letter incorporated into the *Decretals* of Gregory IX was directed not against translations but against conventicles and lay preaching. On the other hand, those responsible for the day-to-day administration of the Church, particularly those responsible for the extirpation of heresy, diocesan bishops, papal commissioners and inquisitors, all seem to have worked on the principle that possession of vernacular Scriptures was in itself sufficient evidence to warrant the presumption of heresy. In theory, a licence to possess a vernacular translation could be given by the diocesan, but how widely such permission was given must be largely a matter of speculation. One English New Testament (John Rylands Library English MS 77) has a note which seems to indicate that it has been approved by two doctors of divinity for use by a layman or laywoman, but permission must often have been given verbally to members of the nobility and royal persons. That Anne of Bohemia, wife of Richard II, was given such permission we know from a reference in the funeral oration preached for her in 1394 by Archbishop Arundel. In praising her piety he said that he had read and approved for her use an English version of the four Gospels with glosses upon them—a work which, as we shall see, was almost certainly a product of the Wycliffites. But such individual licences to members of royal or noble houses are a very different matter from a general permission to the whole population, or even to particular classes of it.

In England, the question of the legality of biblical translations and their use did not come to the fore until the last quarter of the fourteenth century. Old English versions of biblical books seem to have aroused no antagonism, and to judge by the number of manuscripts extant, Rolle's *Psalter* must have had a fair popularity, and possibly therefore official countenance. But the aim of the Wycliffite translators was undoubtedly to set up a new and all-sufficient authority in opposition to the Church. By now the Church sanctioned much that was un-biblical and did not satisfy Wyclif's criterion for ecclesiastical institutions: that they should conform to the practice of Christ and his followers as recorded in the Scriptures. The Wycliffites therefore appealed to 'Goddis lawe' and 'Christis lawe'—their regular names for the Bible and New Testament. Moreover, they asserted that these laws were open to the direct understanding of all men on the points most essential to salvation. For such understanding it was necessary that all men should be able to study the Gospels in the tongue in which they might best understand their meaning.

The start of the work of translation cannot now be dated to 1382 quite so confidently as it used to be, but the evidence still points to a date about then. Wyclif's own attention seems to have been directed to the question of authority when in 1374 he went to Bruges as a royal commissioner to discuss with representatives of Gregory IX certain payments claimed by him. During the next ten years he was developing his theories of civil and ecclesiastical dominion. In the *De Veritate Sacrae Scripturae* (1378) he is already appealing to the Scriptures as his prime authority, but there is as yet no demand for a translation. By the year of Wyclif's death (1384), translations of the Gospels and epistles were being copied by a professional scribe, William Smith of Leicester; at any rate, at his trial in 1392 he confessed to having been copying them for eight years, though it is not stated if he began to do so on their first appearance. From about 1384 they were apparently copied continually. Thomas of Woodstock, Duke of Gloucester, executed in 1397, had an English bible in two volumes and an English New Testament; a priest in York bequeathed a book of the Gospels in his will in 1394; so did a Bristol burgess in 1404. But such books were confiscated if found in the possession of known or suspected heretics. Smith's copies were taken from him, and the Lollard William Thorpe had his Psalter confiscated in 1407.

During this whole period the opposition to Wyclif had been growing within the Church. Some points in his teaching were condemned by a bare majority in a commission specially appointed by the chancellor of Oxford in 1381, and more decisively in May 1382 by a special synod summoned by the new archbishop of Canterbury, William Courtenay, and meeting at the house of the Black Friars in London. Wyclif's influence was strong within the university, and it was only by exerting powerful pressure that Courtenay ensured the publication of these condemnations. He did not relax his pressure until the best-known of Wyclif's supporters within the university had recanted or been scattered; by the end of 1382 the university had been purged so thoroughly that it ceased to be a centre of heresy. Yet for many years individual Lollards were pursued and brought to trial; in 1397 the Church authorities pressed for the death penalty for heretics; in 1401 the statute *de heretico comburendo* introduced such a penalty, and in 1407, alarmed by rumours of a renewal of heresy in the university, Archbishop Arundel made a visitation, secured the condemnation of a number of points of Wyclif's teaching and brought forward a number of 'Constitutions' against Lollardy. One of these reads:

We resolve therefore and ordain that no one henceforth on his own authority translate any text of Holy Scripture into the English or any other language by way of a book, pamphlet or tract, and that no book, pamphlet or tract of this kind, whether already recently composed in the time of the said John Wyclif or since, or to be composed in the future, be read in part or in whole, publicly or privately, under pain of the greater excommunication, until the translation shall have been approved by the diocesan of the place, or if need be by a provincial council.

This constitution provided, for England at least, what had not till now existed, a clear prohibition on the making and use of vernacular translations; and the prohibition was sternly enforced. The number of prosecutions recorded for owning or reading English bibles is considerable; the details have been collected by Professor Margaret Deanesly. Thus the very possession of an English bible was a potential danger; if the bible contained any evidence of Wycliffite authorship or recent date the danger would be increased. Perhaps it is significant that one manuscript (Bodl. Fairfax MS 2) has at the end, 'The eer of the lord m.ccc & viij this book was endid', with a fourth c erased; a book copied in 1308 would be exempt from the prohibition, while one copied in 1408 would not. It is not therefore surprising that the surviving manuscripts give so little information about the translators and scribes responsible for their production; but the consequence is that the student of the Wycliffite Bible must rely for evidence of its development not upon the usual mixture of internal and external evidence, but almost solely upon the former, as provided by the manuscripts themselves.

Since the concern of the medieval scribe was with the matter of his text rather than its linguistic details, and there was as yet no standard literary dialect and no standardized spelling, these manuscripts will show considerable variations in grammatical forms and in spelling. Present participles may end in *-and, -ande, -end, -ind, -inde, -ing, -inge, -yng, -ynge*; 'their' may be *her, here, ther, their* or *thair*; 'them' may be *hem, ham, hom, them, tham, theim, thaim*. 'Eye' may be spelled as *eiȝe, eȝe, iȝe, yȝe, eighe, eigh, eghe, egh, ehe, ei, ee*, 'flesh' as *fleisch, fleish, flesch, flesh, flehs, flessh* and so on. They may also show slight differences of vocabulary; one will have *clepe* where another has *call*, or *clothed* where another has *clad*. Because scribes are human and fallible, there may be mistakes, omissions, alterations and repetitions. Such variation is to be expected, but close examination of the manuscripts reveals that they differ among themselves in more than these details; constructions, word-order, translation method are seen to be different. In these respects the manuscripts fall into two main groups, one considerably larger than the

other. Of the copies of the Psalms, for example, the smaller group consists of eight manuscripts, the larger of thirty; of the Gospel of
Matthew, whether in complete bibles, New Testaments, with the other
Gospels or on its own, there are some eighteen copies in the smaller
group and nearly 100 in the larger, with one or two that seem to be
mixed and a few others—perhaps five—insufficiently known to be
assigned to either group. This division of the material was made over
a century ago by the first scholars to work extensively on the Wycliffite
bible, the Reverend Josiah Forshall and Sir Frederic Madden, and
though in some details their work has had to be modified, the distinction remains valid.

Specimens of the translations found in the two groups of manuscripts
are printed here from a number of manuscripts, together with the Latin
from which they are translated. The smaller group is represented by the
left-hand column, the larger by the right-hand column.[1]

JOB i. 6–12

Quadam autem die cum venissent filij Dei vt assisterent coram Domino,
affuit inter eos etiam Satan. Cui dixit Dominus: Vnde venis? Qui respondens,
ait: Circuiui terram, & perambulaui eam. Dixitque Dominus ad eum:
Numquid considerasti seruum meum Iob, quod non sit ei similis in terra,
homo simplex, & rectus ac timens Deum, & recedens a malo? Cui respondens
Satan, ait: Numquid Iob frustra timet Deum? nonne tu vallasti eum, ac
domum eius, vniuersamque substantiam per circuitum, operibus manuum eius
benedixisti, & possessio eius creuit in terra? Sed extende paululum manum
tuam, & tange cuncta quæ possidet nisi in faciem benedixerit tibi. Dixit ergo
Dominus ad Satan: Ecce, vniuersa quæ habet, in manu tua sunt: tantum in
eum ne extendas manum tuam. Egressusque est Satan a facie Domini.

On a day forsothe, whan the sones of Forsothe in a dai, whanne the sones
God weren come that they shulde of God weren comun to be present
stonde niȝ biforn God, was niȝh bifor the Lord, also Sathan cam
among them and Sathan. To whom among hem. To whom the Lord

---

[1] In printing from the manuscripts, capitalization and punctuation have been modernized. The spelling of the manuscripts has been retained, except that *th* has been substituted
for the obsolete letter þ; ȝ, which in Modern English is sometimes represented by *gh* and
sometimes by *y*, has been retained. The frequent abbreviations have been expanded
without notice. Words printed in italics are underlined in the manuscript. The Latin is
taken from P. M. Hetzenauer, *Biblia Sacra Vulgatae Editionis* (Innsbruck, 1906), since
neither the Vatican Vulgate nor Wordsworth and White is available for all the books of
the Bible.

seide the Lord, 'Whenne comest thou?' The whiche answerende seith, 'I have enviround the erthe, and thurh gon it.' And the Lord seide to hym. 'Whethir hast thou not biholde my servaunt Job, that ther be not to hym lyk in erthe, a man simple and riȝt and dredende God, and goende awey fro evel?' To whom answerde Sathan, 'Whether in veyn Job dredeth God? Whether hast thou not strengthid hym and his hous and al his substaunce by envyroun? To the werkes of his hondes thou hast blissid, and his possessioun wex in the erthe; but strecche out thi hond a litil, and touche alle thinges that he weldeth, but in the face he blesse to thee.' Thanne the Lord seide to Sathan, 'Lo! alle thinges that he hath in thin hond ben; onli in hym ne strecche thou out thin hond.' And Sathan is gon oute fro the face of the Lord.

Christ Church, Oxford, MS 145

seide, 'Fro whennes comest thou?' Which answeride and seide, 'Y have cumpassid the erthe, and Y have walkid thorou it.' And the Lord seide to him, 'Wher thou hast biholde my servaunt Ioob, that noon in erthe is liyk hym? *He is* a symple man and riȝtful and dredinge God and goinge awei fro yvel.' To whom Satan answeride, 'Wher Ioob dredith God veynli? Wher thou hast not cumpassid him and his hows and al his catel bi cumpas? Thou hast blessid the werkis of hise hondis, and his possessioun encreeside in erthe; but holde forth thin hond a litil, and touche thou alle thingis whiche he hath in possessioun; if he cursith not thee in the face, *bileve not to me.*' Therfor the Lord seide to Sathan, 'Lo! alle thingis whiche he hath ben in thin hond; oneli strecche thou not forth thi hond in to him.' And Sathan ȝede out fro the face of the Lord.

B.M. Cott. MS Claudius E ii

ISAIAH ii. 1–3

Verbum, quod vidit Isaias, filius Amos, super Iuda & Ierusalem. Et erit in nouissimis diebus præparatus mons domus Domini in vertice montium, & eleuabitur super colles, & fluent ad eum omnes gentes. Et ibunt populi multi, & dicent: Venite & ascendamus ad montem Domini, & ad domum Dei Iacob, & docebit nos vias suas, & ambulabimus in semitis eius: quia de Sion exibit lex, & verbum Domini de Ierusalem.

The word that Ysay sawȝ, the sone of Amos, upon Iudam and Jerusalem. And ther schal ben in the last daies beforn maad redy the mount of the hous of the Lord in the cop of mounteynys, and it schal be rerid out upon hillis, and ther schuln flowe to it alle

The word which Ysaie, the sone of Amos, siȝ on Iuda and Ierusalem. And in the laste daies the hil of the hows of the Lord schal be maad redy in the cop of hillis, and schal be reisid above litle hillis, and alle hethene men schulen flowe to him, gentilis, and ther schul gon many peplis and seyn, 'Cummeth, stey we up to the mount of the Lord and to the hous of God of Jacob, and he schal techen us his weyes, and we schul gon in his stijes *or pathes.*' For fro Syon schal gon out the lawe, and the word of the Lord fro Jerusalem.

B.M. Additional MS 15580

and many puplis schulen go and schulen seie, 'Come ʒe! stie we to the hil of the Lord, and to the hous of God of Iacob, and he schal teche us hise weies, and we schulen go in the pathis of him.' Forwhi the lawe schal go out of Sion, and the word of the Lord fro Ierusalem.

Corpus Christi College, Oxford, MS 20

MARK X. 42–5

Iesus autem vocans eos, ait illis: Scitis quia hi, qui videntur principari gentibus, dominantur eis: & principes eorum potestatem habent ipsorum. Non ita est autem in vobis, sed quicumque voluerit fieri maior, erit vester minister: & quicumque voluerit in vobis primus esse, erit omnium seruus. Nam & Filius hominis non venit vt ministraretur ei, sed vt ministraret, & daret animam suam redemptionem pro multis.

Sothli Jesus clepinge hem, seith to hem, 'ʒe witen, that theie that semen *or ben seyn* to have princehed on folkis lordschipen *or ben lordis* of hem, and the princes of hem han power of hem. Forsothe it is not so in ʒou, but who evere schal wolle be maad more schal be ʒoure mynystre, and who evere schal wolle be the firste in ʒou schal be servaunt of alle. Forwhi and mannis sone cam not that it schulde be mynystrid to him, but that he schulde mynystre, and ʒyve his soule *or lyf* redempcioun *or a ʒenbiyng* for manye.'

Bodl. Douce MS 369 second part

But Jesus clepide hem, and seyde to hem, 'ʒe wyten, that thei that seemen to have princehood of folkis ben lordis of hem, and the princis of hem han power of hem. But it is not so among ʒou, but whoever wole be maad grettere schal be ʒoure mynystre, and whoevere wole be the first among ʒou schal be servaunt of alle. Forwhi mannus sone cam not, that it schulde be mynystrid to him, but that he schulde mynystre, and ʒeve his lijf aʒenbijng for manye.'

B.M. Harley MS 5017

LUKE i. 5–14

Fuit in diebus Herodis, regis Iudæ, sacerdos quidam nomine Zacharias de vice Abia, & vxor illius de filiabus Aaron, & nomen eius Elisabeth. Erant autem iusti ambo ante Deum, incedentes in omnibus mandatis, & iustificationibus Domini sine querela, & non erat illis filius eo quod esset Elisabeth sterilis, & ambo processissent in diebus suis.

Factum est autem, cum sacerdotio fungeretur in ordine vicis suæ ante Deum, secundum consuetudinem sacerdotij, sorte exijt vt incensum poneret, ingressus in templum Domini: & omnis multitudo populi erat orans foris hora incensi. Apparuit autem illi Angelus Domini, stans a dextris altaris incensi. Et Zacharias turbatus est videns, & timor irruit super eum. Ait autem ad illum Angelus: Ne timeas Zacharia, quoniam exaudita est deprecatio tua: & vxor tua Elisabeth pariet tibi filium, & vocabis nomen eius Ioannem: & erit gaudium tibi, & exultatio, & multi in natiuitate eius gaudebunt.

Ther was sum prest, Zacarie bi name, in the dayes of Heroude, king of Iudee, of the soort of Abya, and his wijf of the douʒtris of Aaron, and hir name Elizabet. Sotheli thei bothe weren iust bifore God, goynge in alle the maundementes and iustifiyngis of the Lord, withouten playnt. And a sone was not to hem, for that Elizabet was bareyn; and bothe hadden gon forth fer in her dayes. Sotheli it is don that Zacarie was sett in presthod in the ordre of his soort bifore God. Aftir the custom of presthod, bi soort he wente forth that he entride in to the temple of the Lord schulde putte encense. And al the multitude of the puple was withouten forth preyinge in the hour of encense. Sotheli an aungel of the Lord appeeride to him, stonding on the riʒthalf of the auter of encense. And Zacarie seeyng is disturblid, and drede fallide doun on him. Forsothe the aungel seith to him, 'Zacarie, drede thou not, for thi preyer is herd, and Elizabet thi wijf shal bere to the a sone, and his name shal be clepid Ioon. And he shal be ioye to thee and gladyng, and many shulen ioye in his nativyte.'

In the daies of Erode, king of Iude, ther was a prest, Zacharie bi name, of the sort of Abia, and his wif was of the douʒtris of Aaron, and hir name was Elizabeth. And bothe weren iust bifore God, goynge in alle the maundementis and iustifiyngis of the Lord, withouten playnt. And thei hadden no child, for Elizabeth was bareyne, and bothe weren of greet age in her daies. And it bifel that whanne Zacharie schulde do the office of presthood, in the ordre of his cours tofore God after the custum of the presthood, he wente forth bi lott and entride in to the temple to encensen; and al the multitude of the peple was withoute forth, and preiede in the our of ensensyng. And an aungel of the Lord apperide to him, and stood on the riʒthalf of the auter of ensence. And Zacharie seynge was affraied, and drede fel upon him. And the aungel seide to him, 'Sacarie, drede thou not, for thi preier is herde, and Elizabeth thi wif schal bere to thee a sone, and his name schal be clepid Jon. And ioie and gladynge schal be to thee, and many schulen have ioie in his nativete.'

ACTS xxviii. 17–20

Post tertium autem diem conuocauit primos Iudæorum. Cumque conuenissent, dicebat eis: Ego, viri fratres, nihil aduersus plebem faciens, aut morem paternum, vinctus ab Ierosolymis traditus sum in manus Romanorum, qui cum interrogationem de me habuissent, voluerunt me dimittere, eo quod nulla esset causa mortis in me. Contradicentibus autem Iudæis, coactus sum appellare Cæsarem, non quasi gentem meam habens aliquid accusare. Propter hanc igitur causam rogaui vos videre, & alloqui. Propter spem enim Israel catena hac circumdatus sum.

Forsothe after the thridde day he clepide togider the firste of Iewis. And when thei camen, he seide to hem, 'Men bretheren, I doynge no thinge aȝeins the puple or custome of fadris, I bounden at Ierusalem am bitaken in to the hondis of Romayns. Whiche when thei hadden axing of me, wolden dismytte me, for that no cause of deth was in me. But Iewis aȝeinseyinge, I am constreyned for to apeele Cesar, not as havynge eny thing for to acuse my folc. Therfore for this cause Y preiȝede for to see ȝou, and I spak to. Forsothe for the hope of Ysrael I am gird aboute with this cheyne.'

B.M. Egerton MS 618

And aftir the thridde dai, he clepide togidere the worthieste of the Iewis. And whanne thei camen, he seide to hem, 'Brithren, I dide no thing aȝens the puple either custom of fadris, and I was bounden at Ierusalem and was bitaken into the hondis of Romayns. And whanne thei hadden axid of me, wolden have deliverid me, for that no cause of deeth was in me. But for the Iewis aȝenseiden, I was constreynid to appelle to the emperour, not as havinge ony thing to accuse my puple. Therefore for this cause I preiede to see ȝou, and to speke to ȝou. For, for the hope of Israel, I am gird aboute with this chayne.'

B.M. Lansdowne MS 407

It will at once be obvious that the version printed on the left is the more literal. In it, the Latin order of words is often retained; Latin constructions such as the ablative absolute are imitated in the English; perfect passive tenses are translated by English present tenses; parts of the verb 'to be' are lacking because they are not found in the Latin; *autem* is translated always as 'forsothe' or 'sotheli'. In fact, this version can sometimes only be understood by reference to the Latin, whereas that on the right, though still reflecting to some extent the form of its original, is considerably more intelligible and idiomatic. That it was also more popular is suggested by the greater number of manuscripts. It is reasonable to assume that in any work of translation a literal version is more likely to be followed by an idiomatic one than an idiomatic one by a literal one, and this was certainly the order with some other medieval translations. Forshall and Madden therefore assumed that the left-hand version was the earlier, and such an assumption is confirmed by one or two other pieces of evidence.

The literal version contained in two Bodleian manuscripts ends abruptly in the middle of a verse—Baruch iii. 20. In one, Bodley MS 959, this break comes at the end of the second column of the page, just where the scribe would have to wait for his ink to dry before he turned over. In the other, Bodl. Douce MS 369, the break comes about a third of the way down the second column of the page. Immediately below the break, another hand contemporary with the original one has added 'Explicit translacionem Nicholay de herford' (Plate 48). A similar note has since been discovered[1] in Cambridge University Library MS Ee. 1. 10, inserted between verses 19 and 20 of Baruch iii, 'Here endith the translacioun of N, and now bigynneth the translacioun of J and of othere men'. Here we have two references, clearly independent, to a specific member of the Wycliffite circle, for Nicholas Hereford is known from documentary evidence to have been one of Wyclif's Oxford disciples, whose opinions were condemned with his master's in 1382. He appealed from the Synod of Black Friars to Urban VI, and went in person to Rome. Forshall and Madden, believing that Bodley MS 959 is the original holograph of his work, supposed that he left it unfinished because of his sudden departure. If this were so, it would give a definite date for part at least of the earlier version; but proof is lacking. When his views became known at Rome, Hereford was imprisoned by Urban VI, but was released in the summer of 1385 by the Roman mob during an insurrection; he returned to England and was active in the work of evangelization in the West country for some time. In 1387 Bishop Wakefield of Worcester issued a proclamation prohibiting five named Lollards from preaching. Hereford was named first in this proclamation, but he was in fact already in custody in Nottingham. Whether he was tortured, as his fellows professed to believe, or whether he found it better suited his temporal interests to conform, as Dr Workman has suggested, he recanted some time in or before 1390, and was soon taking part in the trials of his former fellows, in particular that of

[1] By the present writer, who apologizes for the error in transcription on its first publication.

Walter Brut in October 1393. The surviving records of this trial include an open letter to Hereford which contains a clear reference to his share in 'making clear the knowledge of Holy Scripture'. Various marks of royal and ecclesiastical favour were conferred upon Hereford before his retirement in 1417, apparently in extreme old age, to a Carthusian monastery. Hereford seems to have been a fierce controversialist, both for and against the Lollards; after his recantation he is said to have affirmed that he had 'greater favour and more delight to hold against them than ever he had to hold with them'. All that we definitely know of his share in the translation is that at least a part of the earlier version was ascribed to him, and that later reference could be made to his share in the work, yet these facts alone are of value, since they show that the work was done under the auspices of scholars of repute in the university. Moreover, the inclusion of his name in the two manuscripts mentioned is the clearest link connecting the mass of manuscript material with the work attributed to the Lollards by their friends and foes.

The other manuscript that breaks off abruptly at Baruch iii. 20 (Bodley MS 959) is of particular interest. It is written out by five different people, each of whom uses distinctive dialect forms, and it is freely corrected. Some of the corrections are made by the original scribe after his sentence is completed; others are by different hands, effected by frequent erasures, deletions and marginal additions. Forshall and Madden, with a perhaps unfortunate choice of words, called it the 'original version' of its part of the translation. Since it is written in five hands, it cannot be Hereford's autograph copy. Perhaps he dictated it to five different scribes; in that case we should expect to find greater dialectal consistency, since it is unlikely that a scribe would convert all that was being dictated into his own dialect as he wrote it down. Perhaps Hereford's responsibility for the translation was only one of general supervision. Recent work on the manuscript has shown a number of mistakes more characteristic of a copyist than of someone engaged in original work. However, our speculations on the significance of the corrections must remain speculations, since we have not the slightest knowledge how the work of translation was organized. But that Bodley MS 959 is a draft of an earlier stage in the translation than has survived elsewhere is clear. Either because he was using a poor Latin text or through ignorance, the man responsible for the first attempt often made gross errors; he translated *animo* by 'ʒeer', as if it were *anno* (Josh. ix. 2), *nisus est* by 'he is seen', as if it were *visus est* (Vulg. II Kings xxi. 16), *luctum* by 'cley', as if it were *lutum* (Job xxx. 31), *spuma* by 'thorn', as if it were *spina* (Wisdom v. 15). His first attempt too is sometimes more literal than his second. Thus the Latin ablative of comparison is translated by the bare pronoun, but later changed to 'than' with a pronoun, as in Deut. vii. 1 *robustiores te*, first 'the strenger' (i.e. thee strenger), then 'strenger than thou'. Parts of the verb 'to be', at first omitted since they are not found in the Latin, may later be supplied in the margin, as at II Chron. v. 13 and vii. 3, *quoniam bonus* 'for good', then 'for he is good'. The word-order too is occasionally closer to that of the Latin than in other manuscripts. The affiliation of the other manuscripts which contain the books to Baruch iii. 20 has not yet been worked out in detail, but a rapid survey of the manuscripts of the Psalms suggests that, with one exception, they form a close and compact group, and this in turn suggests that the text they contain is authoritative.

The exceptional manuscript, Cambridge University Library MS Ee. 1. 10, with the note about 'N' and 'J and othere men', contains an abridgement only of the Old Testament from Chronicles to Maccabees, including one or more verses from every chapter, the first verse being always given. What purpose such an abridgement could fulfil it is difficult to explain. The text has a number of divergences from that in the other manuscripts, all tending towards greater freedom of expression. The differences can perhaps be appreciated by comparing the parts of Job i. 6–12 included in it with those printed above:

Forsothe on a day, whanne the sones of God weren comen that thei schulden stonde nyȝ bifore God, and Sathan was nyȝ among. To whom seide the Lord, 'Whennes comest thou?' The which answering seith, 'Y have envirowned the erthe and thurh goon it.' And the Lord seid to him, 'Whether hast thou not biholden Job, my servaunt, that ther be not lijk to him in the erthe' *etc.* 'Thou hast blessid to the werkis of his hondis, and his possessioun wexide in the erthe; but strecche out a litel thin hond, and touche thou alle thingis that he weldeth *or hath*; but in the face he blesse to thee.' *etc.*

Several changes can be seen in these few verses: 'forsothe' as a translation of *autem* is brought forward as the first word in the sentence; the subject is made to precede its verb in a statement (and conversely, elsewhere, the verb precedes its subject in a question); the imperative is translated not by verb alone, but by verb and following pronoun.

Other changes are found elsewhere: nouns in the vocative case are brought forward to the initial position in the sentence; parts of the verb 'to be' are supplied; personal pronouns are supplied as antecedents to relatives ('He that goith in', not 'That goith in' for *qui ingreditur*); nouns are supplied in the translation of Latin absolute adjectives ('unpitouse men', not 'unpitous' for *impiorum*). Some of these changes may seem small, and they are not invariably made when they could be, but they are frequent enough to show that their introduction was deliberate, and their cumulative effect is quite noticeable. Since many of the changes are found also in the later version, we are justified in claiming that C.U.L. MS Ee. 1. 10 contains a—confessedly very in-complete—version of the Wycliffite bible intermediate between the two already distinguished. That it is the same manuscript that contains the note about 'N' is perhaps an embarrassment, since this version is not *ipsissimis verbis* the same as that preceding the other note about him; but perhaps scribes copying what was known to be dangerous material may be believed to have taken a certain satisfaction in emphasizing the connection between that material and one who was now a pillar of orthodoxy.

The existence of this revision of the earlier version, showing so clearly the types of change that the translators felt at first to be neces-sary, has not hitherto been generally known. When we turn to consider the parts of the Bible after Baruch iii. 20, and in particular the New Testament, it will be helpful to bear its improvements in mind. More than twice as many manuscripts of parts of the New Testament survive as of the Old, and some have mixed texts. B.M. Cotton MS Claudius E ii, for example, has a part of Luke's Gospel and the Epistle to Philemon in the earlier version, but the rest of the New Testament in the later one; Magdalene College, Cambridge, MS L. 5. 19 has John's Gospel in the later version, but the rest of the New Testament in the earlier. Such mixed texts indicate that the earlier version was not completely superseded on the production of the later one, but con-tinued to be copied. It is therefore possible for readings from the later version to have been introduced into manuscripts of the earlier version, contaminating the original text.

If the specimens of the earlier version printed above (pp. 395–9) are compared not with the later version but with each other, it will soon become apparent that even here there are marked differences in style.

The part before Baruch iii. 20 is very much more literal than that after it. The differences in style and translation method, to which there also correspond differences in vocabulary, were observed by Forshall and Madden and by them attributed to a change in translators. That Baruch iii. 20 completed Hereford's part of the translation they were informed by the note in Douce MS 369; what could be more natural than to assume that the differences after that point were introduced by the new translator? Exactly who he was no one has been able to determine conclusively. Forshall and Madden thought that the work was done 'not improbably by Wycliffe himself'—an opinion that has been frequently repeated without due qualification. But at this time, it has since been shown, Wyclif was in poor health and busily engaged in writing his most voluminous Latin treatises. There is in fact no convincing evidence for Wyclif's active participation in the work at all, and the failure of the manuscripts to provide any indication of his part that would support the clear statements of his friends and foes is the most puzzling feature of the Wycliffite bible.[1] Other names which have been suggested are those of John Trevisa and John Purvey. The former is known as a copious translator, and had close associations with known Wycliffites in Oxford, but it is impossible to connect him directly with biblical translation. The latter was Wyclif's secretary, and his name has been suggested on the general grounds that he would have been most likely to know the stage that the work had reached, and would probably have taken on the responsibility of completing it. Certainly the only contemporary evidence is the note from C.U.L. MS Ee. 1. 10, attributing the completion to 'J and othere men'. Such a note is too vague to identify any particular John—if J does stand for a Christian name and not for a surname—but specific enough to remind us that more than one man was associated with the work in the minds of contemporaries.

The extent of the stylistic differences between the two halves of the earlier version has however been unconsciously magnified by the fact that Forshall and Madden printed a somewhat revised form of the earlier version after Baruch iii. 20 which, though originally distinct from Douce MS 369, has at a later date been bound up with it. Their

[1] The view that Wyclif was an active participant is however consistently maintained by Dr Sven L. Fristedt in his writings (see Bibliography) and most recently in 'New Light on John Wycliffe and the First Full English Bible', *Stockholm Studies in Modern Philology*, (1966).

choice was determined by a belief that this and three other manuscripts, which constitute a reasonably close group, represented most
accurately the original text. But the manuscript that does this best has
now been shown to be Christ Church, Oxford, MS 145. This shows
most of the peculiarities that we have seen to be characteristic of an
early stage in translation. For example, the word-order is sometimes
close to that of the Latin; Matt. vi. 23 reads, as a translation of *ipsae
tenebrae quantae erunt*, 'tho derknesses hou grete shul thei be?', where
all the other manuscripts have 'how grete shulen thilke (*or* the ilke, tho
ilke, tho) derknessis be?'. The verb 'to be' is not supplied: in Matt. v,
in the Beatitudes, this is the only manuscript that has not 'ben', and in
Luke ii. 14, in the song of the angels, no part of the verb is supplied.
The prop-words 'man, woman, thing', used in translating Latin
absolute adjectives, are not always found; *haec* in Mark xiv. 9, referring
to Mary Magdalene, is translated simply 'this' in Christ Church MS 145,
but 'this woman' in all other manuscripts.

Perhaps most important of all, this manuscript is almost completely
without textual glosses. Apparently one of the most prolific sources of
change in the translation was a series of verbal glosses added in the text
and usually underlined in the manuscript. A difficult word in the Latin
was apparently first rendered by a literal translation, or was anglicized
into what must have been a quite unintelligible form. This was first
supplemented by, later sometimes used as a supplement to, and finally
completely displaced by, a more idiomatic translation. One of the
passages printed above (p. 397) has four of these glosses; it will be
instructive to see the various stages in the process as they survive in
different manuscripts.[1]

videntur:	ben seyn	*UVXY*
	semen or *ben seyn*	*AGKMNOPQSTW*
dominantur:	lordschipen	*MOPQTXY*
	lordschipen or *ben lordis*	*AGKNSW*
	ben lordis	*UV*
animam:	soule	*MOPQXY* (gloss added later in *Y*)
	soule *or lijf*	*AGKNSTW*
	lyf	*UV*

[1] For convenience, the sigla assigned to the various manuscripts in the printed edition
are used here, one or two manuscripts not collated for that edition being ignored. The
siglum of Christ Church MS 145 is *X*.

redemptionem: aȝenbiynge   *MPQXY* (gloss added later in *Y*)
    aȝeinbyinge *or redempcioun*   *T*
    redemcioun *or aȝenbiyng*   *AGKNSW*
    redempcioun   *OUV*

Though in these instances Christ Church MS 145 is only one of several manuscripts showing the literal translation standing on its own, in numerous other places this manuscript alone preserves it. So *praesides* (Matt. x. 18) is 'presidentis' in it, but 'presidentis *or meyris*', 'meyris *or presidentis*' in others, 'iustices' in some; the Good Samaritan's beast, *iumentum* (Luke x. 34), is 'iument' in Christ Church MS 145, 'iument *or hors*' in most of the manuscripts, 'hors' in three, and 'beest' in the later version. A recent writer has claimed that the literalism of the version in this one manuscript proves that the whole Bible was originally translated throughout on the same principles. Such a claim can hardly be admitted, however. Though the work of 'J' obviously underwent revision, the earliest form of it is more idiomatic than that of Hereford's portion.

In the preceding paragraph, it will have been noticed that where the gloss completely replaces the original literalism in two or three manuscripts, they are usually the same ones, *U* and *V*—B.M. Additional MS 11858 and New College, Oxford, MS 67. Other extensive changes are also found in the same manuscripts. Some Latin present participles are resolved into finite tenses, preceded or followed by 'and'; Latin perfect passive tenses are translated by preterites, not present tenses. So for the passage printed above (p. 399) from Acts xxviii, New College MS 67, has:

Forsothe aftir the thridde day, he clepide togidere the firste of the Iewis. And whanne thei camen, he seide to hem, 'Men britheren, I dide noo thing aȝens the puple either custom of fadris; and I was bounden at Ierusalem, and was bitaken into the hondis of Romayns. Whiche whanne thei hadden axid of me, wolden dismytte me, for that noo cause of deth was in me. But for Iewis aȝenseiden, I was constreyned forto appele to Cesar, not as havynge eny thing forto accuse my folc. I preiede therfore for this cause forto see ȝou and speke to ȝou. Forsothe for the hope of Israel I am gyrd aboute with this chayne.'

The resemblance to the later version is most marked, and Forshall and Madden themselves suggested that this manuscript might represent

'...a revision of the earlier text made by the second translator previously to the adoption of the principles by which he was finally guided in preparing his version'. This is likely enough; but they should have noticed that some of the improvements made in New College MS 67 are found also in the manuscript which they adopted as the basis of their printed edition and described as the earliest form of its part of the translation. Had they done so, they would probably have chosen a different manuscript to print, and so given to the general reader a more accurate impression of the nature of the two versions which they identified.

What emerges most clearly from this discussion is that the materials are probably still available for a more detailed examination of the development of the earlier version than has yet been made, and the various stages in the process of revision can perhaps still be definitely distinguished. We have seen that a very literal form of the translation can still be traced in one manuscript, and an extensively revised one in at least two. The greatest number of manuscripts lie between these limits, and even allowing for extensive correction from and contamination by the later version, seem to show two other stages in the revision. Certainly it would seem that scholars were continually altering and improving the text they had received. Such a process is only what we should expect, but it emphasizes the importance that these men attached to the work.

The text of the earlier version appears also in a series of works to which the title 'the Glossed Gospels' has been given. These survive, one or two to a manuscript, in seven manuscripts, with extracts in another two, and along with the text of the Gospels include a long commentary in English. It has long been recognized that the basis of the commentary is the *Catena Aurea* of Thomas Aquinas, and most scholars have dismissed these works as purely derivative and hence of little importance; but it now appears that they will be of more interest than has been thought. The longest form of the commentary is found in York Minster Library MS XVI D 2, which contains the Dominical Gospels only. In this, after the text of each Sunday's Gospel and long quotations from the Fathers, for which the *Catena Aurea* seems to have served as a convenient guide to the originals, there follows an introduction to a chosen topic: 'Therefore se what hooli scripture, hooli doctours and trewe lawis of the churche...seien of kyngis and domesmen'

(Luke vi. 36–43) or 'Se here what hooli doctours seyn of byndyng and assoilyng' (John iv. 46–53). Then come long quotations from Scripture, from other writers and from canon law, all of course in English and all fully provided with references. Though the Fathers predominate, such favourite authors of Wyclif as Grosseteste and 'Parisience' (Guillaume Pérault) are frequently quoted. Abuses that the Lollards denounced are stressed, though of course many such abuses were also condemned by orthodox moralists. The other manuscripts contain at least two forms of complete commentary for Matthew and two for Luke, one apparently derived from the other by selection and summary, and one each for Mark and John, and in them much of the material from the York manuscript is also found, that on 'binding and assoiling' for example at Matt. xvi, that on 'kings and doomsmen' at Mark xiii.

These *Glossed Gospels* show a careful scholar, working with an extensive library available; they may have provided for compilers of popular Lollard tracts in English a range of authorities not otherwise available. More important, they must have made the translator consider afresh the problems raised by translation. The literalism of the earlier version could hardly be sustained throughout the translation of comment sometimes twenty times as long as the text; and in such exegesis the words of Scripture are so often paraphrased, echoed or quoted that it is easy to see how a translator could be led on to a more idiomatic style, which he might then apply to biblical translation. Not that the form of the earlier version that he used was over-literal; whoever the author was, he had access to the revised form of the text found in New College MS 67, and like the scribe of that manuscript and of Additional MS 11858 included the first four verses of Luke, otherwise unknown to the Wycliffite translators. In his quotations from other parts of the Bible there are such frequent minor divergences from the text of both the recognized versions that it is clear the author cannot be using a manuscript of either; yet he is equally clearly not translating all afresh. Either he is revising the existing translation as he goes along, or he has previously gone through it, making such extensive revisions as to produce a text that is sometimes even more idiomatic than the recognized later version. The point is important, for the authorship of the *Glossed Gospels* has been credited to Purvey, who, as will be seen, is also regarded as responsible for the later version. The author adds a prologue and epilogue to some of the Gospels, in which he refers to himself as 'a synful caytiff', 'this coward synful caitif', 'this pore scribeler'. In the one extant work that is most probably his, Purvey used a similar pseudonym, and for this work borrowed the material from one of the prologues. Such evidence, in itself inconclusive, is reinforced by a reference in the epilogue to Luke to 'a pore caityf, lettid fro prechyng for a tyme for causes knowun of God'. Purvey was one of the five named Lollards who were inhibited from preaching in 1387 by Bishop Wakefield. He must then have been writing at some time after 1387; wherever he was, he had access to a good library and at least some contact with Oxford, since in the commentary on Mark he quoted from a sermon 'prechid late in Oxenforde'. The work must have been finished before 1394, because in that year Arundel said that he had approved for the use of Anne of Bohemia 'al the foure gospeleris on Engliche with the docturis upon hem'—an excellent description of the *Glossed Gospels* as they would appear to the casual reader. Several other works obviously from the Wycliffite translators are extant: versions of the Apocalypse with a commentary, a translation of Clement of Llanthony's Gospel harmony *Unum ex Quattuor*, translations of some Augustinian tracts. They show the same translation methods as, and in quotations from the Bible often identical wording with, the recognized Bible translations. The very volume of this translated material should constantly warn us of the danger of assuming that it can all be ascribed with certainty to the two or three men whose names we know.

Such a warning needs repetition as we pass to the much more numerous manuscripts of the later version. In some of these there is found also a long introduction to the Old Testament, known in modern times as the *General Prologue*. It begins with a statement about the canonical books of the Old Testament, goes on to assure 'symple men of wit' that they ought not to fear to study Holy Writ, and then passes to an extensive survey of the books of the Old Testament, summarizing their contents and pointing out the lessons to be drawn from them. Then it describes the fourfold interpretation of Scripture and concludes with a chapter justifying the translation, explaining some of the principles followed by the author, and exhorting the reader in the last few words to endure persecution. The writer stresses the care he has taken, with 'diverse felawis and helperis', to establish a true Latin text, and to consult 'manie gode felawis and kunnynge at the correcting of the translacioun'. He makes only a single reference to the earlier version as 'the English bible late translatid', but some of the principles he says that he has followed are just those we have seen being introduced into it: ablative absolutes and present participles in Latin may be resolved; word-order may be changed to give the normal English order; adverbs, conjunctions and prepositions need not always be rendered in the same way; words may be repeated if necessary.

There are enough references to contemporary events in the *General Prologue* to enable us to assign a date to the work, and to make a reasonable guess at the identity of the author. The date is given by a reference to a petition made known 'at the laste parlement'. This can be shown by external evidence to be that of January–February 1395; since the next parliament was held in January–February 1397, the *General Prologue* can clearly be dated to 1395–6. Included in it are a number of arguments which resemble a list of errors collected from John Purvey's works by one of his enemies, Richard Lavenham, and a list of errors that Purvey later repudiated. For this reason—which is perhaps not so conclusive as some of those who support the ascription claim—the *General Prologue* and the full version of the Bible to which it is prefixed have been ascribed to Purvey.

John Purvey is never officially referred to as a graduate, and a recent writer has suggested that it would be wise not to regard him as one of Wyclif's Oxford disciples. He was ordained in 1377 and for long was a prominent supporter of Wyclif, acting, it is thought, as his secretary and the popularizer and translator of many of his works. In 1387 he was prohibited from preaching; where he was living then is not clear, though if he was responsible for the *Glossed Gospels* he must have had access to a good library. Though the author of the *General Prologue* complains of not having necessary books to hand, this was some years later and his circumstances may well have changed.

In 1400 Purvey was in prison at Saltwood, Archbishop Arundel's castle, and in March 1401, just before the passing of the act *de Heretico Comburendo* and at the end of the week in which the first Lollard to suffer the death penalty, William Sawtry, had been burned, he recanted his errors. Thereafter he lived as a parish priest near to Saltwood Castle—under the archbishop's eye. In 1403 he resigned his living; from references to him made at a trial in 1407 it appears that he was then neither openly professing Lollardry nor wholeheartedly on the side of the authorities. After this he disappears from view, even the date of his death being unknown. No such clear manuscript evidence connects Purvey with the later version as connects Hereford with the earlier; a distich and a monogram in Trinity College, Dublin, MS A. 1. 10, which Forshall and Madden thought were in his own handwriting, are not now accepted as certainly by him. If Purvey did write and translate all that has been attributed to him by modern scholars, he must have been indeed an industrious scholar and a worthy intellectual leader of the Lollards, but there has perhaps been too great readiness to credit him with the authorship of anonymous works on a very general resemblance in subject-matter and style, and to give him sole credit for work done more probably by the co-operative efforts of a number of scholars.

The large numbers of manuscripts of the later version surviving and their wide geographical distribution have hitherto prevented any attempt to investigate closely the relationships between them. There is no *a priori* reason to assume that all the books of the Bible were revised the same number of times, or published in their final form together; but Forshall and Madden did call attention to the remarkable uniformity of the text in all the manuscripts they had handled. Certainly there is much greater agreement among the manuscripts of the later version than among those of the earlier. Though two manuscripts—Bodley MS 277 and Corpus Christi College Cambridge MS 147—have been described as showing signs of further desultory revision, there is to a much greater extent than is usual in medieval writings a text that can be regarded as authoritative. It presumably gained acceptance and discouraged further extensive revision simply because it provided an accurate and intelligible English text, the best that contemporary scholarship could provide. It exemplifies the belief of the author of the *General Prologue*

. . . that the best translating is out of Latyn into English, to translate aftir the sentence [meaning] and not oneli aftir the wordis, so that the sentence be as opin, either openere, in English as in Latyn, and go not fer fro the lettre; and if the lettre mai not be suid [followed] in the translating, let the sentence euere be hool and open.

An attempt to render the translation not only more idiomatic but also more comprehensible to the general reader is shown by the addition in some manuscripts of exegetical notes and comment, both in the margin and within the text itself. Those to the Acts and Pauline epistles were clearly designed originally to accompany a revised form of the earlier version, and so presumably date from about the same period as the *Glossed Gospels*; those to the Old Testament books were meant to accompany the later version. Their general agreement from copy to copy makes it clear that they are not the casual additions of occasional readers, and in three passages in the *General Prologue* the author says that he has glossed Job, the Psalms and the major prophets and hopes soon to finish the gloss to the minor prophets. Of those he mentions, the glosses to Job, the Psalms and some chapters of Isaiah survive, but most of the rest seem to have been lost. The sources of these glosses are usually given; all seem to be taken from 'Lire', 'the glos' and 'Austyn'.[1]

The glosses are of various kinds. Sometimes a single word or short phrase explains the literal meaning of a difficulty, in the way we have already seen above. Sometimes an equally short gloss draws attention to one of the spiritual meanings; so at Prov. i. 8 'thi fadir' is glossed 'that is, God', and 'thi modir', 'that is, holi chirche', these being the allegorical meanings. But frequently such explanations are too long to be expressed in a short phrase; again, the meaning of a Hebrew or Greek word may be briefly discussed, or a particular rendering justified. Thus the comment on Job xvii. 13 'helle is my hous' reads:

Helle etc.: that is, birying withynne the erthe, for Y abide no more erthely prosperite; in this place and othere of this book for helle is an Ebreu word that signefieth ofte 'a diche' ether 'biriyng'.

B.M. Cotton MS Claudius E ii

The glosses to Isa. ii. 1–3, printed above (pp. 396–7), are:

In the laste daies: that is, in the tyme of grace; *the hil etc.:* that is, hooli chirche, that passith ech congregacioun ordeyned to Goddis onour fro the bigynnyng of the world; *above litle hillis:* that is, princes of the world; *alle hethen men:* that is, summe of alle hethen men. Lire here. *Fro Ierusalem:* apostlis and othere dissiplis ʒeden out fro Ierusalem and Iudee, to preche the feith of Crist to hethen men. Lire here.   *Ibid.*

[1] Nicholas of Lyra, the fourteenth-century Franciscan commentator whose *Postillæ* was a common textbook at the end of the century; the *Glossa Ordinaria* (see chapter VII); and Augustine (usually without more detailed reference).

There are two obvious dangers from such glosses. The first is that controversial matter will be added, to support the cause of the Lollards or to criticize institutions of which they disapproved. In fact, this does not happen; the marginal notes are as free of partisanship as the text itself, and so contrast with Tyndale's provocative glosses later. The second is that the text will be contaminated by the gloss, a danger foreseen by the scribe of Lambeth Palace MS 1033 in his rubric to Isaiah:

Here endith the prologe on Isaye, and here bigynneth the text of Isaye. With a short glose on the derke wordis; and loke eche man, that he wryte the text hool bi itself, and the glose in the margyn, ether leve it al out.[1]

In the Psalms, such contamination is not infrequent. Psalm 30: 16 (A.V. 31: 15) has *sortes meae*, in the earlier version 'my lottis', translated by 'my tymes', as if it were *tempora mea*, because Lyra gives that as the correct Hebrew reading; Ps. 41: 8 (A.V. 42: 7) has *in voce cataractarum tuarum*, earlier 'in the vois of thi gooteris', translated 'in the vois of thi wyndows', as if it were *in voce fenestrarum tuarum*, because of Lyra's explanation of the word; Ps. 15: 5 (A.V. 16: 5) has *pars hereditatis meae et calicis mei*, earlier 'part of myn eritage and of my chalis', translated 'part of myn eritage and of my passioun', because of Lyra's association of this verse with Matt. xxvi. 42. Such substitution of comment for text is not envisaged in the *General Prologue*, where the author claims that he has recorded variants in the margin, particularly in the Psalter, where the Hebrew differs from the usual Latin readings, yet it is found regularly in all the manuscripts. Outside the Psalms, few spiritual notes have led to variation in the text, but an occasional literal note is taken up, as in Job i (see p. 395), where Lyra corrects the euphemism *benedixerit* to its obvious meaning, *maledixerit*, and is followed by the later version.

From the first tentative and over-literal versions, it is a long way to the fluent translation with spiritual interpretations added or incorporated. Attention to the exactness of the work as a word-for-word construe has given way to concentration on the production of a readable version bringing out the full meaning of the original. The work has required some scholarship; the range of authorities consulted is impressive, and the emphasis by the author of the *General Prologue* on

[1] In fact, there are no glosses in this manuscript to Isaiah, and the whole reference to them is crossed through in the rubric.

the care taken to compile a true Latin text, to consult acknowledged experts and to associate with himself a number of other scholars increases our respect for him. The connection with the university that Hereford's participation in the work implied had probably been continued.

The translation was widely used. Some of the late-fourteenth- and early-fifteenth-century copies of the Primer, a book for private devotion, have their Bible extracts taken from the later version. Bishop Reginald Pecock, writing in English his *Repressor of Over-Much Blaming of the Clergy*, a polemical work against the Lollards that involved its author in a charge of heresy, quoted regularly from the later version, though he was fully capable of translating for himself if he wished. Only a few years before Tyndale published his New Testament, and therefore a full century after its first production, a Scot named Murdoch Nisbet turned the later version into his native Scots. That the nobility possessed copies we have already seen; orthodox religious too are known to have owned copies. One was presented to the brethren at Syon in 1517; Bishop Bonner, Queen Mary's most active supporter, possessed a fine copy which has survived. It was, however, never printed by any of the early printers. Though they were good businessmen, following public taste closely, and must have known that English bibles would surely sell well, they were probably unwilling to commit themselves to so expensive an enterprise in the face of the clear prohibition of the Constitutions of Oxford.

The nobleman's fine copies were meant for, and doubtless remained unused upon, his library shelves; but smaller and cheaper copies were intended for common use among the lower classes. Reading them together in small groups, as the evidence at trials shows that they did, they were in danger of prosecution and even death, but read them they did, and the small and secret Bible-readings and meetings that they conducted proved a fertile breeding-ground for that Puritanism or nonconformity that has never since died out. The Bible which permeated the minds of later generations shows no direct descent from the Wycliffite versions; at most a few phrases from the later version, particularly of the Psalms, seem to have found their way into the Tudor translations, and Tyndale's return to the original languages meant that translations based on the intermediate Latin of the Vulgate would soon be out of date. But in their insistence upon the immediacy of 'Goddis lawe' for every man and their efforts to present it to him in an accurate and understandable form, the Wycliffite translators showed themselves to be true precursors of the English Protestant tradition.

4. VERNACULAR SCRIPTURES IN GERMANY AND THE LOW COUNTRIES BEFORE 1500

We may say that the baptism of the Frankish king Clovis and his vassals on Christmas Day 496 marks the effective beginning of Christianity among the Germans. Two centuries later, Pepin of Herstal, the head of the now well-organized and expanding Frankish State, was urging the new faith upon neighbouring German-speaking tribes. Within a generation of this, in 716, the Anglo-Saxon Boniface began his memorable forty years of missionary work. Christianity now spread rapidly; during the course of the eighth century many religious centres were founded, and the few already existing took on new importance. By the time of Charlemagne's accession only East Frisia and Saxony remained heathen, but the East Frisians officially became Christian in 785 and before the turn of the century most of the Saxons had likewise adopted the new religion following repeated defeats at the hands of Charlemagne's Franks. After 804 no more is heard of Saxon resistance and the formal christianization of the Germans was concluded.

The Frisians, however, occupied a rather exceptional position within the Frankish realm. Though subject in name to the emperor, they resisted feudal encroachments with some success and maintained their traditional institutions better than the other tribes. Doubtless Christianity among them was for many generations more nominal than real. All the same we hear of the blind minstrel Bernlef, who in the closing years of the eighth century added to his repertoire of heroic lays the singing of psalms. There seems no reason to doubt this report since the Psalter was more frequently translated into the medieval vernaculars of Germany and the Low Countries than any other book of the Bible. Moreover a fragment of the Psalms in Old Frisian has come down to us, a few blurred lines on two pages of manuscript being all that remains of an interverbal version. The text cannot be dated accurately, though it could be as old as the eleventh century. Altogether records of religious writing in Frisian before 1500 are very sparse, though certainly there was literary activity, as a considerable law literature exists in medieval Frisian. However, the Bible penetrated all spheres of culture, jurisprudence not excepted. It is not surprising therefore that most of the legal codes quote, as the highest form of law, the Ten Commandments. Here by way of a sample is a text of the first five, dating from the second half of the thirteenth century:

Thet erste bod: minna thinne god fore feder ende moder mith inlekere herta. Thet other bod: minna thinne eunkristena like thi selwm. Thet thredde bod: fira thene sunnandei end there helche degan. Thet fiarde bod: minna thine feder end thine moder, hu thu longe libbe. Thet fifte: thet thu thi nowet ne ower hor.[1]

Biblical reminiscences occasionally occur elsewhere in these documents. Thus the editor of *Thet Autentica Riocht* ('The Authentic Law'), a fifteenth-century code, speaks of seven sins hateful to God; his definition of these is seen to be an almost verbatim translation of Prov. vi. 16–19.

Apart from these scanty Frisian records, all the relevant literature is written in one or other of the High or Low German dialects proper, the latter extending of course into the Low Countries. During the period under review, dialect writing was the rule, though by the fifteenth century, and especially after the invention of printing, attempts were being made to find linguistic forms which could reach out beyond the traditional dialect boundaries. This tendency was already marked in the administrative language of the chanceries, so that at the end of the period there arises a movement feeling its way towards a standard for the High German region of the south and centre, paralleled by corresponding movements in the north. In the earlier period each scriptorium set up its own rough standard based on the dialect of the area. Since the rate of natural linguistic change was rather rapid, texts soon became old-fashioned and needed modernizing. This was regularly, if often imperfectly, carried out when older texts were being copied. In practice, then, all the vernacular texts vary both according to dialect and according to the date of composition or copying. But the literary dialects did not diverge very much from each other. They were always close to natural speech. The spoken dialects almost everywhere merged

[1] W. Stammler, *Abriß der altfriesischen Grammatik* (1928), p. 91.

imperceptibly into one another, thus forming a continuum throughout the whole area. In this Frisia, too, may be included, for although historically definable as a separate language, Frisian was not far removed from Low German, the underlying genius being the same. When, as often happened, a text which arose in one dialect found its way to a centre where another dialect was in use, it would be transcribed more or less mechanically into the new dialect. In this way there was a constant and easy interchange of vernacular materials throughout the wide area from the Alps to the North Sea and the Baltic.

The first indications of theological work in German date from the Carolingian Renaissance. From the period before this scarcely anything in German has survived—only a few glosses and a little poetry—doubtless, too, very little was written. But in the age of Charlemagne there was at least a modest change. Charlemagne himself is said to have taken an interest in his mother tongue and to have ordered Latin works to be translated into the vernacular. It is therefore customary to regard a contemporary manuscript containing a rendering of certain Latin works as a product of Charlemagne's solicitude for the German language. The manuscript in question was written at the beginning of the ninth century in the monastery of Mondsee, near Salzburg. It is a transcript in the local Bavarian dialect, sixteen pages of which contain fragments of Matthew. In spite of some mistranslations the German is often idiomatic, though the order of words tends to be influenced by the Latin original. The date of the translation cannot be precisely established, but it could be prior to 800. Other very early documents are three versions of the Lord's Prayer, also associated with Charlemagne's policy, or more exactly with the order in the *Admonitio Generalis* of 789 that congregations were to be taught to understand the Lord's Prayer, and the directive in the *Capitulare Missorum* of *c.* 802 which took up again the old instruction in the Statutes of Boniface *ut omnis populus christianus. . . dominicam orationem memoriter teneat.* The first of the three documents is a Paternoster and Creed from St Gall. It is written in the Alemannic dialect in a late-eighth-century hand. Only slightly later is a Paternoster from Freising in Bavaria. Two manuscripts survive; one is not later than 825, the other with somewhat modernized text is to be dated perhaps as much as a century later. The original was composed in the first decade or so of the ninth century. In this text each verse of the prayer is followed by a few lines of explanatory matter also in Bavarian German. The third Paternoster, similarly accompanied by an interpretation, occurs together with Creeds and other theological matter in a collection of short texts known as the Weissenburg Catechism. The documents are in Rhenish Franconian and belong to the second decade of the ninth century. To these brief records may be added a number of German glosses. Such glossing of Latin scriptural texts was a usual activity at this period and the practice continued throughout the early middle ages.

More impressive records appear during the reign of Charlemagne's successor, Louis the Pious. About 830 in Fulda, then the most significant monastic centre in the northern half of Germany, the Gospel story was put into East Franconian German. The translation was not made from the canonical text, but from Tatian's Diatessaron. It is preserved complete in a copy dating from the latter half of the ninth century. The Latin and German are written in parallel columns. As a translation it is inferior to the Mondsee Matthew; it adheres more closely to the Latin in respect of word-order and often renders the foreign idiom quite mechanically, the German following the original so slavishly in one section as to approach the quality of an interlinear version. As to the purpose of such a work at this early date we can do no more than speculate. Much later, in the thirteenth century, new vernacular Diatessaron manuscripts arose in association with religious revival on a mass basis. But this cannot have been the case in the ninth century. All the same, the work was obviously addressed to persons with little or no Latin, perhaps to wealthy lay patrons of the church. It is likely that it enjoyed a certain vogue in its day. At any rate there are in existence, in addition to the complete ninth-century copy, fragments of a tenth-century copy and a late transcript of a lost medieval copy; two other manuscripts are known to have existed.

The Diatessaron was the primary source of another vernacular work, the *Heliand* ('Saviour'), so called by its first modern editor. The *Heliand* is a versified gospel in the form of a book epic, dating approximately from the decade 830–40. With its 5,983 alliterating long lines it has been preserved almost complete; only a few lines can be missing from the end. There are two main manuscripts, from the ninth and tenth centuries respectively, and two small fragments from the ninth century are also extant. It is most likely that the work was inspired by the tradition of Old English religious epic. The author has Germanized his milieu to some extent: Christ is depicted as the liberal giver of rings to his loyal liegemen, the disciples. But in essentials the unnamed poet was an orthodox compiler, following his main source quite closely and supplementing it with matter drawn from glossaries, commentaries, apocrypha, legend. Exactly where the work was produced is unknown, but the dialect is Saxon. The following extract is intended to convey some idea of method and style.

> Thie banon wîtnodun
> unsculdige scole: ni biscriƀun giouuiht
> thea man umbi mênuuerk: uueldun mahtigna
> Krist selƀon aquellian.   Than habde ina craftag god
> gineridan uuid iro nide,   that inan nahtes thanan
> an Aegypteo land   erlos antlêddun,
> gumon mid Iosepe   an thana grôneon uuang,
> an erdono beztun,   thar ên aha fliutid,
> Nîlstrom mikil   nord te sêuua,
> flôdo fagorosta.[1]

> The murderers slaughtered
> a guiltless band.   Nor did they hate one whit,
> the men, from heinous crime: they wished the mighty
> Christ himself to slay.   Him powerful God had then
> saved from their hatred,   him by night thence
> to the land of the Egyptians   the men led away,
> the men with Joseph   to the green meadow,
> the best of lands,   there a stream flows,
> the great Nile river   north to the sea,
> of rivers fairest.

Here the poet has elaborated on the Gospel account of the murder of the innocents and the flight into Egypt. The 'men' accompanying the fugitive family are the *pueri* of Pseudo-Matthew xviii, the concept of the idyllic region of the Nile is presumably from the same source, while the geographical detail 'north to the sea' is found in Dicuil; other authorities, such as Isidore of Seville, have 'south'.

One of the ninth-century manuscripts which preserves a fragment of the *Heliand* also contains 337 lines of an epic known as the *Genesis*. It is regarded as an imitation of the *Heliand* and dates from about the same time. The existence of this Old Saxon work was postulated in 1875 by

[1] O. Behaghel, *Heliand und Genesis* (1903), pp. 27–8.

E. Sievers, who from linguistic criteria surmised that 617 lines of the Old English poem *Genesis* were an adaptation of a lost Old Saxon original. The fragment of this original was subsequently, in 1894, discovered in the Vatican Library. Of the fragment twenty-five lines are also extant in the Old English adaptation and six of them are quoted below to illustrate the close similarity between Old Saxon and Old English at this period, a similarity which naturally encouraged mutual literary influences.

> Uuela, that thu nu, Eua, habas, quað Adam,   uƀilo gimarakot
> unkaro selƀaro sîð!   Nu maht thu sean thia suarton hell
> ginon grâdaga,   nu thu sia grimman maht
> hinana gihôrean: nis heƀanrîki
> gelîhc sulîcaro lôgnun: thit uuas alloro lando scôniust,
> that uuit hier thuruh unkas hêrran thank   hebbian muostun.[1]

> Alas, that you have now, Eve, said Adam,   evilly determined
> the destiny of us both!   Now you are fated to see black hell
> yawning greedily,   now its roaring you can
> hither hear: heaven is not
> like such flame: this was of all lands the fairest
> which we through the grace of our Lord   were allowed to possess.

The Old English adaptation:

> Hwæt, þû Êve hæfst   yfele gemearcod
> uncer sylfra sîð!   Gesyhst þû nû þâ sweartan helle
> grǣdige and gîfre?   Nû þû hie grimman meaht
> heonane gehŷran: nis heofonrîce
> gelîc þâm lîge,   ac þis is landa betst,
> þæt wit þurh uncres hearran þanc   habban môston.[1]

A second poem, worthy to be compared with the *Heliand*, was produced a generation or so later. This was the *Liber Evangeliorum* composed by Otfrid, a monk of Weissenburg in Lower Alsace. He is known to have finished his work between 863 and 871. His dialect is Rhenish Franconian. The poem is exceptionally well preserved in three complete manuscripts and fragments of a fourth, all from the ninth century. Although often referred to as Otfrid's Gospel Harmony, the poem is not a harmony proper. The writer presents selections from the life of Christ and was guided in his choice, so it seems, by a lectionary.

[1] Behaghel, *op. cit.* pp. 224–5.

Like the author of the *Heliand*, Otfrid embellishes the Gospel story with matter drawn from the usual sources. Interpretations of the basic text are frequent, with special chapters devoted wholly to exegesis. The work is well constructed and has 7,416 rhyming couplets. Alliteration as a poetic form has disappeared; even alliterative phrases are very rare. Examples however occur in the following passage chosen to show Otfrid's narrative at its best; he is otherwise generally very pedestrian.

> Tho quam bóto fona góte,   éngil ir hímile,
>   bráht er therera uuórolti   diuri árunti.
> Floug er súnnun pad,   stérrono stráza,
>   uuega uuólkono   zi deru ítis frono,
> Zị édiles fróuun,   sélbun scā Máriun:
>   thie fórdoron bi bárne   uuarun chúningạ alle.
> Gíang er in thia pálinza,   fand sia drúrenta,
>   mit sálteru in hénti,   then sáng sị unz in énti.[1]

There came a messenger from God,   an angel from heaven,
  he brought this world   glad tidings.
He flew the path of the sun,   the streets of the stars,
  the courses of the clouds   to a holy virgin,
To a high-born maid,   S. Mary herself:
  her forbears every one   were kingly all of them.
He entered the palace.   He found her in pensive (?) mood,
  the Psalter in her hand;   she was singing it through to the end.

In content as in form the poem is entirely within the orbit of Latin Christian culture. It cannot be called a popular work with a wide appeal as could be claimed for the *Heliand*. Still less had it a missionary function, as that work had in newly converted Saxony. Rather it was a labour of piety addressed to a select circle already familiar with the Gospels and the elements of exegesis.

The main part of the work is prefaced by a poem in German entitled *Cur scriptor hunc librum theodisce dictaverit*. The substance of this statement, why he chose to compose the work in German, is as follows. Noting that the Greeks and Romans had fostered a rich literature in their respective languages, Otfrid asks why should not the Franks do the same? The Franks, he says, are in no wise inferior to the Greeks or Romans or to any other race. They, too, are conquerors exacting

[1] O. Erdmann and others, *Otfrids Evangelienbuch*3 (1957), pp. 20–1.

tribute from neighbouring peoples. They are a civilized nation, skilled in the working of metals. Why then should not the Franks sing Christ's praise in their own tongue? It has never been done before, he says, but now a beginning is to be made. Otfrid was doubtless thinking of metrical compositions, as he expressly refers to and praises Greek and Latin scansion. He cannot have meant prose translation of scriptural texts, as a humble beginning in that direction had already been made. Much less is there any suggestion of German as a liturgical language. All the same, it seems remarkable that Otfrid felt the need to justify his writing in German. It may be emphasized that in the prefatory poem he nowhere implies that he is to write in German because some of his readers or hearers may understand no other tongue. This fits well with what we have inferred from the contents of the work, which indicate that it was intended for persons already acquainted with the material to some extent. These would be mainly clerics. It is perhaps not irrelevant to recall that Otfrid was composing his German work at the time of the controversy about the use of Slavonic instead of Latin in the Moravian church. Both the Roman papacy and the German barony were interested in drawing Moravia into the western orbit and were opposing the official use of Slavonic. They realized that this would mean a neglect of Latin and strengthen connections with the East. As the underlying political conflict was being fought out partly in terms of Latin versus a vernacular, the time would hardly be auspicious for writing in German either.

Apart from Otfrid the vernacular records from the second half of the ninth, and throughout the tenth, century are most meagre. There is a Bavarian paraphrase of Psalm 138 into thirty-eight lines of Otfridian verse made in the early tenth century, and a fragmentary poem of thirty-one lines on Christ and the Samaritan woman in the same metre from about the same date. The language of the latter contains both Alemannic and Franconian elements, but such mixing of dialect forms, due to imperfect transcribing from one dialect into another, is not unusual in manuscripts at this period. An equally modest document consisting of two pages from the second half of the tenth century contains fragments of the Cantica in Rhenish Franconian. Since the Cantica were regarded for liturgical purposes as belonging to the Psalter, it is not unreasonable to see here a trace of an otherwise lost Rhenish Franconian psalter.

The north at this period is represented by an interlinear version of twenty-five psalms in Low Franconian. This considerable text is known only from a seventeenth-century copy, but linguistic criteria suggest the tenth or late ninth century as the date of composition. The text is a transcription of a Middle Franconian original. This northern version was not isolated. Occasional references in book catalogues show that German psalters were in use there in the ninth century; one is described as being accompanied by a vernacular commentary. These references are corroborated by the evidence of two mutilated pages from about 900 with fragments of a Saxon commentary to Psalms 4 and 5. Further confirmation came to light as recently as 1923 when a few scraps of an actual translation of the Psalter into Saxon were found in the binding of an incunabulum. The work, an adaptation of a High German interlinear original, was executed about 850. Perhaps contemporary with these Saxon fragments are four pages of an interlinear Alemannic psalter, also recovered from book bindings.

A new era begins with the activity of Notker (*c.* 950–1022), a master in the monastic school at St Gall. Notker made translations into German on a large scale. He translated several profane works and also two biblical books: the Psalter and Job. The Psalter, followed in the manuscript by a translation of the Cantica, Paternoster and Creeds, is preserved entire in a twelfth-century copy; a few contemporary fragments have also survived. His Job however is not extant, but the manner of treatment was doubtless the same as in the Psalter, in principle as follows: a verse of the Vulgate is given, then its translation into Alemannic German, after which come some sentences of commentary in German. Here and there Notker interposes Latin words in the German text, especially words of a technical nature; sometimes they do duty for a German word, sometimes they are followed by the German equivalent. The German naturally contains loan translations from Latin, and its syntax is also affected by the Latin, but otherwise the renderings are idiomatic in style and testify to no mean skill on the part of the translator.

Notker's work served a pedagogical purpose—*propter caritatem discipulorum* as one of his pupils put it—and his technique is a development of the interlinear gloss. He devised his own exact orthography, and his zeal for his native language earned him the nickname *Teutonicus*. His work lived on after him. It was subsequently recast, but the use of

Latin words in the German text was discontinued. The major portion of such a revision, in Bavarian German, has come down to us from the twelfth century. Even in the fourteenth century his psalter served as the basis for a further adaptation. Here we now see clearly a continuous tradition in biblical translation, a thread which runs from the monk of St Gall to Martin Luther, the acknowledged creator of the modern German bible. Yet even Notker, for all his innovating labour, did not stand at the beginning, nor can he have worked in total isolation. If earlier influences cannot be pointed out in detail, this must be due to losses in transmission. There are immense gaps in our knowledge for this reason alone; and perhaps in the early period oral tradition was important too. At all events rudiments of tradition were present through the copying of glosses. But apart from glosses, a tradition is occasionally demonstrable in the period before Notker. The influence of the Low Franconian psalms, for instance, can be discerned in a Westphalian psalter of the fourteenth century.

The high standard of translation set by Notker was reached by another author later in the eleventh century. This was Williram, abbot of Ebersberg, whose German work was a paraphrase of the Song of Songs in the East Franconian dialect. It dates from the 1060s. Each page of manuscript is divided into three columns. The centre column contains in large letters the Vulgate text, the left-hand one the paraphrase in Latin hexameters, the right-hand one the German prose version or rather a German–Latin version, for Williram wrote in a mixed language of the sort found in Notker, and intended for didactic purposes. We quote a specimen:

Der cúning Salomon máchota ímo sélbemo êinan dísk des hólzes uóne *Libano*...daz míttelôde des dískes, daz uuás sámfto unte mínlîcho gegrâdet dúrh dìe iúnkfrôuuon, daz sîe lîhto ze démo díske ûf getrétan móhten. Der *verus pacificus*, dérder mit sînemo tôde *dissoluit inimicitias inter deum et hominem*, der hât uóre gegáreuuet sînen hólden êinan dísk da ze hímele, daz íst díu uuúnna des êuuegen lîbes, *quam nec oculus uidit nec auris audiuit, nec in cor hominis ascendit*, díuder îetemêr zegêt, dánne díu *cedrus, quae in Libano est*, iruûlet...Díu uuîb sínt *fragilioris sexus* dánne dìe mán...Dén neuuírt daz gesídele ze démo uuúnnedíske nìet uerságet.[1]

King Solomon made himself a table out of wood from Lebanon...the middle of the table was attractively low so that the young women could reach it easily.

[1] P. Piper, *Die älteste deutsche Litteratur* (1884), pp. 452–3.

The true peace-maker, who by his death dissolved the enmity between God and man, has prepared a table in heaven for his elect, which is the bliss of eternal life, that no eye has seen, nor ear heard, nor has it entered into anyone's heart and which can no more decay than the cedar upon Lebanon...woman's sex is frailer than man's...but she will not be denied a seat at the table of joys.

The paraphrase was exceptionally popular, so it seems, as no less than nine complete manuscripts from the eleventh and twelfth centuries have survived; including fragments, altogether thirty-seven manuscripts are known. Nor did its influence soon wane. It prompted a twelfth-century imitation, purely in German, the so-called S. Trudpert Paraphrase. Where this version arose cannot however be determined; the main manuscript, from the thirteenth century, shows both Alemannic and Bavarian features. And at the very end of the middle ages Williram's work is again noted as the source of another Paraphrase preserved in the Maihingen manuscript of 1483.

While Williram's work was being read and copied, other books or episodes from Scripture were being put into German. But now the medium was poetry. Like Otfrid and the author of the *Heliand* before them, the writers of the period must have had a strong feeling that verse was the natural form for a vernacular composition. The Germany they knew was full of native oral poetry; heroic epic, though still unwritten, constituted the national literature with a universal appeal. Apart from a few translations and adaptations of religious material, the German language had never been used for the writing of prose; that was the domain of Latin. About a score of poems have come down to us from the eleventh and twelfth centuries. We refer briefly to the first of these, a free rendering of Genesis produced in Carinthia about 1070. The poem is preserved chiefly in a carefully written, partly illustrated parchment of the twelfth century. Its style is unpretentious, not to say primitive, and like these texts in general artistically inferior to the secular poetry which was presently to be written in German. Here are the lines based on Gen. xxix. 10–12 where Rachel and Jacob meet at the well:

> Also si zů ime chom,
> abe wielz er den stein
> und tranchte daz uihe
> daz si dare hête getriben.

Do er si gesach so scône,
do wart ime uil liebe.
si dwngen sich ze den brusten,
ich weiz er si uil minnechliche chuste.
er begunde weinun,
sprach er ware ire basun sun.[1]

When she came to him, he rolled away the stone and watered the cattle she had driven there. When he saw how beautiful she was, he fell in love. They fell into a mutual embrace. I know he kissed her very tenderly. And then he wept, he said he was her father's sister's son.

There are the two twelfth-century poems based on the book of Judith. Judith's praises were a popular theme in the middle ages, and it is not entirely surprising that one of these poems should be composed in popular ballad style. The events of the story are described in this work in a lively fashion, but the deep religious emotion of the original is lacking. Other poems deal, for instance, with the men in the fiery furnace, the Babylonian captivity, the birth of Jesus and his life and deeds. These works treat the biblical accounts somewhat freely and make use of non-biblical sources, especially theological commentaries, so that those who read or heard these poems would not be able to distinguish between what the Bible actually says and what others made of it.

Compared with such free metrical versions, the amount of prose translation is small and much less varied. Apart from Gospel fragments, all that is known in the vernacular from this period—and from the next half century too—are psalters, a few complete, most mere fragments of a page or two. The interlinear version is still in evidence, though not in all cases. A complete psalter from Windberg in Bavaria dating from the second half of the twelfth century strictly follows the interlinear principle, but later versions aim at more idiomatic German. The texts of the fragmentary twelfth-century manuscripts are copies, sometimes of work done in the previous century, but the paucity of the surviving material greatly hinders research into origins. Several of the psalters, however, give evidence of the Notker tradition.

The relative meagreness of the prose records for the years 1050 to 1250 seems to throw some light on the attitude of the medieval Church

[1] V. Dollmayr, *Die altdeutsche Genesis nach der Wiener Handschrift* (1932), p. 73.

to vernacular Scriptures. This period was one of increasing material prosperity; there was a new interest in religion; it was the age of the Church triumphant; but all this led apparently to no notable upsurge in the production of vernacular translations of Scripture. No doubt only a small part of the translations actually made have come down to us, but this factor must equally have affected the fate of the metrical versions and paraphrases. It is also relevant to recall that during the second half of the period secular literature in German flourished as never before. Its leading representatives were poets of European significance, whose extant work fills many volumes—and this is only a small part of the total literature surviving from the time.

It is, however, necessary to admit an exception. The documents on which this general conclusion is based are all presumed to be orthodox; the Church did not disapprove of them. But what of translations produced in defiance of ecclesiastical authority? The demand for Bible study by the laity was first raised by the Waldensian movement, and translations into Provençal were made, notably of the Psalter and the Gospels. Then Waldensian ideas were introduced into Flanders by travelling weavers and merchants, and vernacular translations followed there too. The first reference occurs in a statement by Lambert le Bègue in 1177 in defence of his French version of the Acts of the Apostles, when he declared that a precedent had been set by a Flemish translation of the Psalter. About the same time an episcopal ordinance instructed priests to denounce as heretics those who translated the Psalter.

The earliest mention of heretical translations in German occurs in an account of a synod for the suppression of heresy at Trier in 1231; the offending books were immediately confiscated. It is certain that such translations, from which the heretics drew their religious inspiration, were current in Germany in the thirteenth century, for the sect was both numerous and influential. The New Testament and at least parts of the Old existed in German, as can be inferred from an inquisitor's tract written about 1260: 'For I have heard and seen a certain unlettered countryman who used to recite Job word for word, and many others who knew the whole New Testament perfectly.'[1] It is not impossible that all the Bible had been put into German before the end of the thirteenth century. Two parchment pages from this period contain fragments of various books in a central German dialect which are

---

[1] Quoted from M. Deanesly, *The Lollard Bible* (1920), p. 62.

unconnected with later versions and which could be regarded as the remnants of a comprehensive translation. It is not impossible that these fragments and other later texts are the work of heretics, but in general it seems more likely that they arose in more conventional circles, for the thirteenth century also witnessed the development of another popular religious movement interested in vernacular Scriptures which, by and large, remained within the jurisdiction of the Church. This we may now consider.

From the last quarter of the twelfth century onward the southern Netherlands and also the area around Cologne were the scene of popular religious revival. Great numbers of lay people, men and women, banded themselves together into communities to live apart in apostolic simplicity. These were the Beghards and the Beguines, whose devotional requirements subsequently led to the translation of many books of Holy Writ. Gospels were needed, and this need was in part met, conveniently and economically, by a composite Life of Jesus, in fact Tatian's Diatessaron. A striking document in this connection is a Dutch version, best preserved in a Liège manuscript from about 1270, but composed some twenty years previously. It is the earliest surviving vernacular biblical text in the Low Countries apart from the Low Franconian psalms. Its quality as a translation cannot be exactly appreciated since the source is lost, but the diction is superb throughout, idiomatic, vivid and sensitive. Artistically on a higher plane than the standard Dutch version, the *Statenbijbel*, with its stiff Hebraisms and Grecisms, the Liège Diatessaron may well be considered the Dutch peer of Luther's celebrated German translation. Though the language is now archaic, the means of expression are substantially the same as in modern Dutch, as the following verses show; they are Matt. vi. 26–7 + Luke xii. 26 + Matt. vi. 28.

Siet ane de vogle die vliegen in der locht· sine sayen nit noch sine ogsten nit· noch sine ghedren nit in schuren· eñ nochtan uudt se vwe hemelsche vader· Eñ sidi nit werder vor gode dan si syn? wie es van v allen die hem seluen mach langer maken enen uoet dan ne nature hef gemakt? eñ och gi nin cont ghedon dat gode so cleine es te doene war omme side besorgt vā din dat hem toe behorrende es? Eñ waromme sorgdi omme cleder tuwen lichame? Siet ane die lilien die wassen in den velde· noch sine pinen noch sine spinnen.[1]

[1] D. Plooij and others, *The Liège Diatessaron* (1929–38), pp. 80–1.

A fine example of the translator's unusual literary skill is the assonance in the last sentence, partly gained (we suppose) at the price of a slight modification of the original sense. A modern Dutch bible has *zij arbeiden niet, en spinnen niet* corresponding to the Vulgate *non laborant, neque nent.* In any case it is believed that the stylistic merit of the work was partly achieved by a somewhat free handling of the source.

The Liège Diatessaron is not only remarkable for its artistic pre-eminence: it is considered significant for the textual criticism of the New Testament. Apart from the Liège Diatessaron all the vernacular Bible texts are obviously translations from the Vulgate. Occasionally, to be sure, an Old Latin reading has been detected in a vernacular text, but the Liège Diatessaron, even allowing for stylistic liberties, varies so much from the Vulgate that an investigation into the origin of its Latin source is called for.

The language in which Tatian[1] composed his Diatessaron is not known. It may have been Greek, and a few lines of a Greek version were recovered fairly recently (published 1935). It can equally well have been Syriac, but a version in this language has not survived. It is how-ever known from an Arabic translation and an Armenian version of a Syriac commentary on the work. The Diatessaron was not unknown in the West, the oldest Latin manuscript going back to the sixth century. The Latin versions, however, have all been modified more or less to agree with the Vulgate. On the other hand the Liège Diatessaron shows a large number of peculiar readings which are held to derive from the lost Old Latin original. These primitive readings are other-wise unknown in the Latin tradition: hence the unexpected value of a thirteenth-century vernacular manuscript for the early history of the Latin Diatessaron and thus for the critical study of the New Testament text itself.

Two examples will give some idea of the importance which has been attached to the Dutch text in this respect. Corresponding to the first half of Luke iii. 3, καὶ ἦλθεν εἰς πᾶσαν τὴν περίχωρον τοῦ Ἰορδάνου (Vulgate: *et venit in omnem regionem Jordanis*), the Dutch reads: *Doe ginc hi vter wustinnen eñ quam in die geburte daer de jordane loept.* Here *vter* is ambiguous, it can be a contraction of either *vt der* 'from the' or *vt te der* 'out to', so that the translation runs 'then he went from (*or* out to) the desert and came into the region where the Jordan flows'.

[1] See pp. 33–5.

Neither of the readings 'from *or* out of the desert' occurs in any of the Gospels, but the Armenian version of the Commentary on the Diatessaron has 'into the desert'.[1] A striking example is afforded by the rendering of the last words of Luke ii. 42. From κατὰ τὸ ἔθος τῆς ἑορτῆς (Vulgate: *secundum consuetudinem diei festi*) we would expect Dutch *na de costume van den feestedage*, but instead there occurs the strange pleonasm *na de costume van harre gewoenten* 'after the custom of their habits'. An explanation is at once forthcoming on the assumption that a Syriac text is the ultimate source. In Syriac the word for feast ܥܐܕܐ is derived from the same root as the word for custom ܥܝܕܐ. The Dutch must reflect a misreading or a misunderstanding of (unpointed) Syriac ܥܐܕܐ in the unknown Old Latin original, with the important corollary that the Latin translation was made direct from Syriac and not from a Greek version.[2]

Other texts arose in the Netherlands in the last decades of the thirteenth century. About 1280 a West Flemish Book of Revelation appeared. More influential was an often-copied Southern Dutch Psalter of the same date. By the turn of the century the Gospels and epistles existed in Southern Dutch and circulated widely in plenaries. These Dutch texts also found their way into those parts of Germany, such as the districts of the Rhine valley, where the religious influence of the Low Countries was felt; here the attitude of the Mystics was favourable to the distribution of works in German. As these areas were important for the production of vernacular Scriptures, these Dutch texts undoubtedly made some contribution to the German tradition. Meanwhile Germans themselves were translating independently. Dominicans in Cologne were responsible for a Diatessaron made about the same time as the Dutch one. Several psalters are extant, the Gospels were translated and incorporated into plenaries, the earliest of which date from the latter part of this century, but the amount of material surviving from before 1300 is not large. Although there are signs of a change, poetry is still the chief medium for vernacular composition. Here reference must be made to the outstanding poet, Jacob van Maerlant, a layman, who in 1271 published his *Rijmbijbel*. As his work is based primarily upon Peter Comestor's *Historia Scholastica* (p. 206), then at the height of its popularity, it is a free account of the Bible story with many additions. It is to be noted that the author came under

---

[1] Cf. D. Plooij and others, *op. cit.* p. 38.   [2] *Ibid.* pp. 35–6.

ecclesiastical censure for his poem, according to his pupil Jan de Weert, because he thereby made the Bible available in the Dutch tongue.

With this mention of one of the best of all rhymed versions, we must leave the various free adaptations and concentrate exclusively on translations proper. Not that the Bible story did not continue to be told in free adaptations, but the documents of the fourteenth and fifteenth centuries show that there was now considerable demand for precise translations of the Bible text. True, the concept 'Bible' remained rather wide; it still could and usually did include extraneous legendary and exegetical matter, but many of the translations distinguish clearly between actual passages of Holy Writ and the secondary accretions.

We first consider the most significant texts produced in the Low Countries. Between about 1359 and 1390 an anonymous translator rendered a large number of books of both Testaments into Southern Dutch. Prefaces refer to opposition to vernacular Scriptures, but the translator expresses his conviction that the sacred text should be made available in a language all can read. The biblical text in the translation is interspersed with marked 'paragraphs' and 'glosses' culled from the Comestor, hence the name *Historiebijbel* often given to this Dutch version. Without a doubt, the work arose in a milieu influenced by the New Devotion and Gerard Groote's teaching. Groote himself, indeed, turned translator at the end of his life, when he prepared psalms and other portions of the Bible for his famous Dutch *Book of Hours* issued in 1383. This work fulfilled a great need and its popularity continued into the next century when it was printed many times and translated into Low German. Shortly after Groote's death in 1384, a translation of the New Testament and Psalms was issued by Johan Schutken. Into this slipshod work exegetical paraphrases from the Fathers were introduced without indication of their provenance. But it was the most widely used of the medieval Dutch texts and was also translated into Low German.

Brief mention must here be made of a text which has figured prominently in discussions of the Dutch bible as the 'first' *Historiebijbel*. The work is extant in eight manuscripts from the second half of the fifteenth century, one of which bears the date 1358; but this, as is now known, is unreliable, for linguistic criteria prove that the translation cannot be earlier than 1400. The work was not as influential as the other, really older *Historiebijbel*, to which it is in any case inferior in that the many

431

additions, principally from the *Historia Scholastica*, are not distinguished from the actual biblical passages. Nevertheless it does give some indication of what the middle ages could understand by the term 'Bible'.

Notable among High German translations from the fourteenth century is a complete New Testament, the so-called Augsburg Bible of 1350. Another famous New Testament was written in Bohemia about 1400. This is the *Codex Teplensis*, the publication of which in 1881 led to a lengthy but unresolved controversy about possible Waldensian origins. The Old Testament is best represented by the Wenzel Bible—it contains no New Testament material—made between 1389 and 1400. Considerable fragments of an Old Testament of similar age are found in a Munich manuscript. Separate books from both Testaments are also found in German.

As might be expected, the Psalter continues to be the most translated book, and a very large number of manuscripts are known. The new interest in the Old Testament is confirmed by German versions of Genesis, Kings, Prophets. The Gospels were translated at least three times; Acts, epistles, Revelation are all extant from this period in High German. The north of the country, always the poorer and more isolated part, is nothing like so richly represented, but five psalters in Low German are certainly datable to this century. Many of these translations, by far the greater number of which date from the second half of the century, have considerable literary merit. Some of the versions appear to be quite independent of each other, though research has by no means said the last word on this topic. On the other hand, many interconnections have been noted. The German Gospels of Matthew of Beheim, dated 1343, well known from their use in East German plenaries, go back to a new translation made about 1300. The best-known psalter was that prepared by Henry of Mügeln between 1365 and 1370, to which he added an up-to-date commentary in the shape of Nicholas of Lyra's postill. The work was skilfully and conscientiously executed. Henry, a layman, was a Meistersinger and court poet, but he broke with the emperor, Charles IV, after the issue of the Imperial Edict of 1369 prohibiting German translations of religious books. A less sweeping papal rescript of 1375 was likewise directed against vernacular Scriptures in Germany, but these measures could never become fully effective. The habit of vernacular Bible study even among the orthodox was too widespread to be rooted out now. Henry's psalter became a most successful publication. The laity, too, were interested and the work occupied a place of honour in many a burgher's home; thirty-one manuscripts attest its popularity, which continued into the era of printing.

The main texts from the period 1300–1400 have been known at least since the close of the last century; latterly, smaller fragments have come to light and some have been published. But the most significant discovery of modern scholarship was not the finding of a new manuscript. It was the recognition that the first printed German bible, the Mentel Bible of 1466, in spite of modernizations, actually reflects the language and translation technique of about the beginning of the fourteenth century. An analysis of the vocabulary suggests that the work was made in Nuremberg. The manuscript from which Mentel printed his bible has perished, but a comparison with other texts from the period shows that he used a version which was then at least 150 years old; the 1466 bible is thus really the first complete German bible. Here follows an extract, Dan. v. 5–6, with the corresponding verses of the Vulgate and an East Central German translation made by Claus Cranc about 1350 and representative of the freer, more idiomatic diction of the mid-century.

VULGATE	MENTEL	CRANC
In eadem hora apparuerunt digiti, quasi manus hominis scribentis contra candelabrum in superficie parietis aulae regiae: et rex aspiciebat articulos manus scribentis. Tunc facies regis commutata est, et cogitationes eius conturbant eum: et compages renum eius solvebantur, et genua eius ad se invicem collidebantur.	Zů der selben stund erschinen vinger als einer hand des menschen schreibent gegen dem kertzstal: an dem antlútz der wand des kúnigklichen hoffs. Und der kúnig schaute die gelider der hand des schreibenden. Do wart verwandelt das antlútze des kúnigs· vnd sein gedancken die betrúbten in: vnd die fúgungen seiner lankken wurden enbunden: vnd sein kny wurden zůsamengeschlagen.	in der selbin stunde irschenen vingir als einis menschen hant schribende keygen deme luchtere an der want des kuniglichen salis. und der kunic sach di gelit der schribenden hant. do wart vorwandilt des kunigis antlicze und betrubeten sine gedanken, und di senwyn sinir lenden wurden slaf und sine kny klappirtin zusamene.[1]

[1] F. Tschirch, *1200 Jahre deutsche Sprache* (1955), p. 106.

It is reasonable to suppose that Mentel printed this inferior text because it was the only one available to him. In spite of the deficiencies of the text, a printed German bible was in great demand. Eleven new editions were called for before 1500, but the frequent and often drastic alterations made in the later editions show how unsatisfactory this archaic translation was felt to be. All the same it held the field until eclipsed by Luther's version. It has been a common error of criticism to regard the Mentel Bible as typical of the pre-Luther stage of biblical translation. Recent researches however have shown that the elements of Luther's style are already present in a large measure in the manuscript literature of the fourteenth and especially the fifteenth centuries. Since something like 800 manuscripts are known from this period, it may be taken as certain that a strong tradition was being established, the importance of which has been hitherto obscured by the Mentel prints.

In the north, bibles more representative of the current tradition were printed. In 1477 an Old Testament was brought out at Delft. It was mainly a modernization of the work done in the previous century, but without the passages from the Comestor. The Psalms were not included, but followed in 1480 in Schutken's translation. A year or so after the Delft Bible, two editions of a bible in different forms of Low German came out in Cologne. This work made use of a manuscript of the Delft class, and one of its editions circulated widely in the Netherlands. We are reminded in the case of both these bibles that opposition to vernacular bibles was still very strong in some quarters. The publishers of the Delft Bible felt it necessary to justify their work in a preface, while the printer of the Cologne Bible found it expedient to withhold his name and the address of his place of business. Outright prohibition of Bible reading was scarcely feasible now, but the right to censor translations could still be exercised—witness the Censor's Edict of 1486 issued by the archbishop of Mainz. The tone of this edict is markedly hostile to vernacular translations of religious works and doubtless discouraged, if it could not prevent, the appearance of German bibles. In 1494 a Low German bible was published at Lübeck, a huge work of over a million words, as it includes a good deal of Lyra's gloss. It has close affinities with the Cologne Bible and hence with the Low German tradition generally. But with this work we come to the end of the Low German tradition as far as Germany proper is concerned. The Netherlands alone retained their own language for literary purposes and here the tradition of biblical translation culminated in the *Staten-bijbel* of 1637. Northern Germany was irresistibly drawn into the High German orbit, and High German established itself first as a literary medium, later as a spoken language. Low German bibles continued to be published for over a century after the Lübeck Bible, but were mainly calques of Luther's High German; after 1621 they cease altogether.

We close this summary account of the medieval vernacular Scriptures in Germany and the Low Countries with a reference to biblical texts in Judeo-German. Linguistically these texts are in all essentials virtually identical with contemporary High German, but they are written in Hebrew script. It goes without saying that Jewish attitudes to Bible reading are not always the same as Christian attitudes, and one main difference directly affects the present topic. According to the Roman church, acquaintance with the Bible is not necessary to salvation, and generally speaking there was no official encouragement of private Bible reading among the laity in the middle ages. Judaism on the other hand enjoins the personal study of the Hebrew Bible upon all Jews. There was no question of a struggle for the open Bible in the Jewish communities. Jews, high and low, seem to have been united in an enthusiastic, nationalistic reverence for the sacred text, and a knowledge of Hebrew was very widespread among them. However, an understanding of Hebrew requires no little schooling, and vernacular aids to study are called for. The first records of such aids in Germany appear in the form of Judeo-German glosses to biblical texts, a fair number of which are found in manuscripts of the fourteenth and fifteenth centuries. The glosses are of two sorts, either marginal renderings of difficult words or phrases, sometimes of whole sentences, or else separate collections of glosses to selected passages of Scripture. In one case glosses to the Psalms are so extensive as to amount to a continuous translation. How long such glossing in German had been current before these relatively late records cannot be ascertained. A slightly older document than the above is, however, known; it is a glossed commentary on the prophetic books going back to the end of the thirteenth century.

Translations proper appear in the fifteenth century in various manuscripts. The earliest, from the first half of the century, contains a vernacular rendering of the Psalter, Proverbs and Job. Another psalter, the first dated manuscript of its kind, was written in 1490, but it is a copy of a slightly older original. Two other manuscripts contain a vernacular Pentateuch, one of them has also a translation of Esther and the Song of Songs. Whereas the glosses were an aid to the acquisition of the original, the translations were certainly meant for that section of the community whose Hebrew was most likely to be deficient—the women. There is evidence for this in the manuscripts themselves. In one text the reader is addressed as 'Dear Sister'. In another, an expanded version of the Psalms and Proverbs, dated 1532 but based on an earlier recension, the writer assures his readers that if they will read the book they will attain to the wisdom of Solomon's mother Bathsheba and will rear their children in the fear of the Lord as she did. It is also known that the scribe was writing for a patroness.

5. VERNACULAR SCRIPTURES IN FRANCE[1]

True translations of the whole Bible into the vernaculars were rare in the middle ages. Usually their place was taken by summaries of Old Testament history, collections of individual books of Scripture with glosses and comments, bible picture-books with running captions, and poetic paraphrases. The medieval clerk who provided these popular aids to study was not a learned divine or deep metaphysician, but an unpretentious scholar who made it his main task to expound ancient texts (whether sacred or profane mattered little) to the uninitiate, by glossing rare words and terms and explaining historical allusions. He was not averse to moralizing, and even allegorizing, upon the text. He saw that the destinies of God's chosen race were interwoven at every point with the story of Greece and Rome, with which he was well acquainted, and he approached both types of history in the same serious and workmanlike spirit. The first thing was to explore the realities underlying the text: place-names, customs, political institutions. As in a modern French schoolbook, the learner was presented with *selections* strung together by *summaries* and accompanied by explanatory *notes*. The final aim was the edification of the reader. The demand of reformers

---

[1] This article owes a great deal to the detailed remarks of Professor Julian Brown and M. Jean Porcher on the style of decoration of manuscripts in the British Museum and the Bibliothèque Nationale. I am also much indebted to Dr Otto Pächt and Mr J. J. G. Alexander for examining the little-known Christ Church New Testament, and to Mr C. J. Liebman, Jr, for help with the two Pierpont Morgan manuscripts.

and Renaissance humanists for the bare text put an end to this tradition: in the French tradition, the chief originality of Jacques Lefèvre d'Étaples, whose bible appeared in the 1520s, was his elimination of the obtrusive medieval glosses.[1]

The Old Testament story of the warfare of Israel and Judah made a powerful appeal in the age of the crusades, and the historical books were frequently translated and widely copied. The Gospel events were independently known from homilies, from painting and sculpture, and from the mystery plays. The sapiential and prophetic writings and the Pauline epistles received scant attention before 1280; their subsequent diffusion (in *BHC*, after 1317) is all the more remarkable. The book of Scripture most widely possessed and studied by the French-speaking laity was the Psalter.

The Passion narrative was among the oldest themes of oral poetry in Romance: an ancient version in octosyllabic verse (*c.* 1000) comes from Saint-Cyprien de Poitiers, an important daughter-house of Cluny, and is composed in a curiously artificial dialect:

> Pilaz que anz l'en vol laisar
> No·l consentunt fellun Judeu:
> Vida perdonent al ladrun,
> 'Aucid, aucid' crident 'Jesum'.
>
> Barrabant perdonent la vide,
> Jesum in alta cruz claufisdrent:
> '*Crucifige, crucifige*'
> Crident Pilat trestuit ensems.
>
> 'Cum aucidrai eu vostre rei?'
> Zo dis Pilaz, 'forsfaiz non es:
> Rumpre·l farai et flagellar,
> Poisses laisarai l'en annar.'
>
> Ensems crident tuit li fellun,
> entro en cel en van las voz:
> 'Si tu laises vivre Jesum
> Non es amics l'emperador.'[2]

---

[1] For the unbroken continuity between medieval translations and all sixteenth–seventeenth-century Catholic and Protestant versions prior to Lemaître de Sacy, see Berger, pp. 307–20. Berger cites parallel passages from *BXIII*, Jean de Rély's *editio princeps* of *BHC*, the translations of Lefèvre d'Étaples and Olivétan, and the Louvain Bible of 1550, to draw attention to the many verbal agreements between all the versions.

[2] Luke xxiii. 19–22, cf. John xix. 15, 12.

Femnes lui van detras seguen
Ploran lo van et gaimentan:
Jesus li pius redre gardet,
Ab les femnes pres a parler.

'Audez, fillies Jerusalem,
Per me non vos est obs plorer:
Mais per vos et per vostres filz
Plorez assaz qui obs vos es.'[1]

Cum el perveng a Golgota
Davan la porta de la ciptat,
Dunc lor gurpit soe chamise
Chi sens custure fo faitice.

Il no·l auserent deramar
Mais [chi] l'aura[t] sort an gitad:
Non fut partiz sos vestimentz,
Zo fu granz signa tot per ver.

En huna fet, huna vertet
Tuit soi fidel devent ester:
Lo sos regnaz non es devis,
En caritad toz es uniz.[2]

The drama of the original is strongly brought out in these succinct verses, as in the semi-dramatized readings of the Passion narratives in Holy Week. The final clash of Pilate and the Jews is underlined by phrases borrowed from John xix, and a further motif from the same chapter, the seamless coat of Christ, is made the subject of a brief allegory: the seamless coat is the unity of Christ's church. The Saint-Cyprien *Passion* is the forerunner of many octosyllabic narratives which in turn furnished the outline for the later medieval Passion plays—a characteristic expression of the biblical interests of the laity.[3]

Another channel of scriptural knowledge was the homily on the gospel, or *prône*, deriving from the Gallican liturgies and linked with the litanies for all conditions of men and the whole estate of Christ's church, in which the congregation were led by a deacon. Since the

[1] Luke xxiii. 27–8.   [2] John xix. 17, 23–4.

[3] The Passion plays are clearly distinct in origin and social background from the liturgical Easter plays, on the Resurrection and the appearances of Christ, which arose in a tenth-century monastic context, and are mainly in Latin. The source is the troping of the Easter introit; the complete corpus of these plays is published by Karl Young, *The drama of the medieval church*, vol. I (Oxford, 1933).

homily was originally reserved for the bishop, it was stylistically linked with the elaborate episcopal benedictions which occurred at the end of the eucharistic liturgy in the Gallican rites. The whole tradition is epitomized in the gospel homilies attributed to Maurice of Sully, bishop of Paris from 1160 to 1196; the antiphonal quality of liturgical chant is echoed in the cadences of his Old French prose:

Nostre Sire, qui savoit bien que li cuer des apostres estoient triste e torblé de sa Passion, si les conforta si com dist l'evangiles d'ui, e si lor dist, le juesdi absolu le soir devant sa Passion: 'Vos ploërrés,' dist Nostre Sire a ses aposteles, 'e li mondes avra joie; mais ne vos esmaiés pas, quar la vostre tristece sera müee en joie, e en tele joie que jamais ne le perdrés, ne nus ne le vos pora tolir.' Issi com il lor dist, ensi lor avint; quar il furent triste de sa Passion, qu'il soffri a l'endemain, e furent en grant deshait jusqu'al tierc jor qu'il le virent relevé de mort, e qu'il le jor de l'Asention le virent monter el ciel, e qu'il le jor de la Pentecoste lor envoia le Saint Esperit. Lors fu la tristece müee en joie; e quant meesmement en la fin de lor vies de la dolor de cest siecle les traist en sa glorie, lors fu veraiement lor tristece müee en joie, en tele joie que jamais ne perdront.

There are sets of pericopes (or gospel lessons) for the use of Cambrai and the use of Metz; and about 1333 Jean de Vignay translated both epistles and Gospels for the queen of France.[1]

The Psalter was widely known in the vernacular, first of all by means of a continuous interlinear gloss which in the twelfth century was assembled to form a highly literal version of the Vulgate text (Montebourg Psalter, Arundel Psalter). The middle ages possessed three redactions of the Latin psalter: the Vulgate text, which is an Old Latin version based on the Septuagint; the Roman revision of St Jerome; and his *Hebraica veritas*, which is a fresh translation based directly on the pre-Massoretic Hebrew text (pp. 84, 88). The revival of biblical studies by the Victorines led to renewed interest in the original Hebrew text and the rabbinic interpretation, especially in England; we possess a complete commentary on Jerome's *Hebraica* by Herbert of Bosham, the

---

[1] The Waldensian New Testament was the subject of intensive interest and bold speculation in the age of Raynouard and Fauriel, who stimulated a revival of Provençal studies; this translation was assumed to be very ancient and to derive from Catharist versions. E. Reuss showed that the fifteenth–sixteenth-century Waldensian manuscripts are based on a current Vulgate text (showing Hussite and even post-Erasmian influences), whereas the Catharist interlinear gloss, published by Clédat, was based on a distinctive Vulgate text in use in Languedoc.

biographer of Thomas Becket. The Eadwine Psalter, made at Christ Church, Canterbury, perhaps about 1160, contains the three Latin texts, the Vulgate being accompanied by the *glossa ordinaria*, the Roman revision by an Old English interlinear gloss, and the Hebraica by an Old French interlinear gloss.

As time went on, translators attempted more idiomatic renderings; the Metz Psalter (*c.* 1300) is very close to the Psalter of Raoul de Presles (*c.* 1380), which reappears in the early printed editions of *BHC*:

Icist dragun le quel tu formas a escarnir lui: tutes choses de tei atendent que tu dunges a els viande en tens. Dunant tei a icels, cuildrunt, aovrant tei la tue main, tutes choses serunt aempli de bunté; desturnant acertes tei ta face, serunt turbé; tu toldras l'espirit d'els e defirunt e en lur puldre repairerunt. Tu forsmetras tun espirit, e serunt cried, e renoveras la face de terre.

Montebourg Psalter (twelfth century)

Cilz dragons que tu as formét pour joer et moker de li, toutes [choses] s'attendent a ti a fin que tu lour donnes lour viande et a mangier quant temps serat. Quant tu lour donras il la recoilliront; et quant tu overras ta main, toutes choses seront remplies de ta bontét et de touz biens; et se destournes et repons ta face, il seront troublez; tu osteras lour esperis et il defauront tuit et en lour pourre retorneront. Envoie ton esperit et il seront creez et tu renoveleras la face de la terre.

Metz Psalter (*c.* 1300)

The former is a mere construe, retaining even the absolute construction (*aperiente te manum tuam*); the latter has a more idiomatic syntax, and uses a vocabulary which is already close to that of classical modern French (*s'attendre à*, [*se*] *moquer de*, *ôter*, *recueillir*, *détourner*, *troubler*, *défaillir*, *renouveler*).

There are many beautifully illuminated psalters, such as André Beauneveu's psalter made in 1380–5 for the Duc de Berry, and some homely, unpretentious copies. Harley 273 is a French miscellany (*c.* 1300) which once belonged to John Clerk, grocer and apothecary to Edward IV; it contains Grosseteste's *Rules for husbandry*, the *Chronicle of Turpin*, a calendar of the church of Ludlow, and the Psalter in French, and measures eight and a half by three and a half inches. Two early-thirteenth-century copies (fonds fr. 963 and 22892) contain Peter Lombard's *magna glossatura* in French; there were also several verse translations of the Psalms.

The most remarkable of all French commentaries on the Psalter was begun for Laurette, a daughter of Thierry d'Alsace, who after several marriages retired to a convent near Brussels in 1163, and her mother-in-law Sibylle, who died at Jerusalem in 1165. The work was eventually revised and completed at Paris and in England, and survives in three folio volumes, still at Durham, which were probably copied for Bishop Hugh du Puiset (*d.* 1195). The text of the first volume is preserved in a Beauvais cathedral manuscript now in the Pierpont Morgan Library, New York, which is decorated in a style akin to that of the Ingeborg Psalter (Paris, *c.* 1200). This first volume contains many personal allusions; the author is a disciple of the biblical school of Laon and he refers to persons living in the first quarter of the twelfth century: Gautier Hurel, count of Hesdin, the emperor Henry IV, William of Corbeil, archbishop of Canterbury, and also to 'Nicholas [Brakespear] who was afterwards Pope Hadrian'. On folio 129^v, after the words 'Bele Lorete', a later hand has added 'e vos bele Elyanor'—an allusion to Eleanor of Vermandois (1152–1213), a daughter-in-law of Laurette and the faithful friend of Queen Ingeborg. The second volume is known only from manuscripts of English provenance, and the third volume is found only at Durham, in a different format from the other two and copied in different hands. This great treasury of twelfth-century French prose, containing the essence of Augustine's commentary in his *Enarrationes*, still awaits an editor.

The north-east of France was a great centre of biblical and patristic translation. The movement came under suspicion from the authorities, and in 1199 Innocent III ordered a commission of inquiry. The books mentioned in the report (Gospels, epistles, Psalter, *Moralia in Job*) have a very traditional air, and no heterodox doctrine (indeed no theological emphasis of any kind) has ever been detected in Old French scriptural versions. However, Lambert the Stammerer (le Bègue, p. 427), one of the suspects, was imprisoned by Bishop Radulph of Liège in the fortress of Rivogne. There in chains he translated the Acts of the Apostles with a stylus bestowed on him in a vision by the apostle him-self. Eventually he was absolved at Rome, and returning built the church of St Christopher where he lies buried.

In France, the cause of biblical translation, like that of Aristotelianism a generation later, was rapidly won after initial ecclesiastical suspicion and even opposition. The way lay open for a complete vernacular translation; but this was not achieved until 1280, owing to the limited and sporadic interest shown by the laity in the literal text of Scripture. The Apocalypse had an immense appeal, and there were numerous translations; but these are often found in illuminated manuscripts where the text is only roughly adapted to a pre-existing cycle of miniature paintings. The subject is thus linked with the taste for pictorial narrative recently studied by Dr Pächt. What the laity mostly required was a bible picture-book with running headings which could be read out to the unlettered owner.

Poles apart from these works for the semi-literate is that great living masterpiece of French prose, the four books of Kings, which survives in a splendid late-twelfth-century manuscript in the Mazarine Library at Paris. This contains a good deal of erudite commentary, and may be compared with another contemporary example of medieval scholarship, the *Fet des Romains*—a massive life of Julius Caesar (*c.* 1213, at Paris), based on Caesar's own commentaries and on Sallust and Suetonius. Just as this biography begins with a sketch of Roman institutions, defining the duties of senators, consuls, dictators and tribunes, and later delves deeply into the geography of Caesar's Gaul, so the translator of Kings interweaves his version of i. 1–3 with sound information about Hebrew names, rites and customs:

En cel cuntemple fud une cité Sylo, de part Effraïm, que Deu out a sun oes saisie e sacree. La fud e out estéd li tabernacles e li sanctuaries Deu, des le tens Josue ki le pople Deu en terre de promissiun cunduist e guiad. La fud l'arche, la fud li propiciatories. C'est l'arche en qui fud repost e guardez li tresors precïus des tables u Deu meïmes escrist la lei, e partie de la manne ki del ciel vint e le pople quarante anz en lieu de vitaille corporel sustint, e la verge Aaron, u Deu sa vertud mustrad, kar en une nuit fuilli e fluri e fruit portad.

The reader thus gleans a good deal of information about the Jewish temple; a marginal note adds: *Paulus in epistola ad Ebreos quid in archa.* Hence he is better able to appreciate a later passage in which the ark is shown to be carried out to assist the Hebrews in battle against the Philistines:

E cume l'arche vint en l'ost, li poples Deu duna un merveillus cri que tute la terre rebundi. Li Philistien oïrent cest cri e distrent: 'Que deit cest cri k'il funt en l'ost?' Aperceurent sei que l'arche fud venue en l'ost. Poür urent merveilluse e distrent entre sei: 'Deus est venuz en l'ost.' E firent plaintes e plureïz e horrible guaimenteïz e redistrent: 'Nen ourent pas tel hait en l'ost ne hier ne avant hier. Ki nus guarderad encuntre ces halz deus? Ço sunt les deus ki flaelerent e tuerent ces de Egypte el desert. Mais ore vus haitez e seiez forz champïuns Philisthiim que vus ne servez as Hebreus si cume il unt servi a vus.' Puis cume vint a la bataille, la descunfiture turna sur Israel, e fuïrent tuit ki einz einz, chascuns a sun tabernacle. La ocisïun fud forment grande, kar il i chaïrent trente milie de gelde. E prise i fud l'arche, e morz i furent les fiz Hely, Ofni e Phinees.

The sacred awe and terror inspired by the ark of the covenant, indeed the whole atmosphere of warfare between theocratic tribes, is wonderfully conveyed; the erudition and the feeling for language challenge comparison with the work of the Elizabethan translators in England four hundred years later.

The book of Judges was separately translated for members of the Order of the Temple. Judges, Kings and Maccabees were later incorporated in a vast compilation, now BN *fonds français* 6447, made in Flanders *c.* 1275. It contains local annals, a poem by Huon de Cambrai, and a life of St Martha dedicated to Margaret, daughter of Baldwin (*d.* 1280), who was the first western emperor of Constantinople.

An earlier and more important compilation is found in the Acre Bible in the Arsenal Library, now placed in its proper context by Dr Buchtal (and see pp. 319, 321). It contains:

(*a*) Genesis, Exodus, Numbers, Joshua and Judges, illuminated in a Byzantine style;

the four books of Kings (the twelfth-century version);

Judith, Esther, Job and Tobit, illuminated in a thirteenth-century Parisian style.

(*b*) Selections from the sapiential books, with a painting of Solomon as a Byzantine emperor enlightened by the divine Wisdom;

Maccabees, a historical link with the New Testament (from Peter Comestor's *Historia Scholastica*), and the book of Ruth, illuminated in the Parisian style.

It is very probable that this book was made for St Louis during his residence in the Holy Land (1250–4). There are several other copies of this collection. One, now lost, belonged to the Gonzaga family at Mantua; another, still extant (nouv. acq. 1404), omits Esther, Job, Ruth and the sapiential books; there is even a Provençal version.

This Bible of St Louis represents the highwater mark of early medieval translation from the Old Testament, a movement which is closely linked with the military orders and the crusade. The version of the book of Job is the oldest in any western vernacular language, and one of the finest:

Un home fu en un terre que l'en apeloit Us, et si avoit nom Job. Cest home si estoit simples et droiturier, et doutoit Deu, et li desplaisoit touz maus. Il avoit VII fiz et treis filles. Et ot en sa possession VII mile berbiz et CCC chamiaus et v cens jous de bues et v cens ahnesses, et grant maisnee de genz. Cest home esteit granment henorés et sovrain entre trestouz les orientaus. Et les fiz de ce proudome faisoient mangiers et festes chascun jor et chascun en son jor, et enveoient, et faisoient apeler lor treis serors, que manjassent e beüssent avuec eaus. Et quant aucuns jors passerent, le pere si les visiteit, et les beneisseit, et se leveit mout matin, et faiseit sacrefice por chascun de ses fiz, et disoit ensi: 'Par aventure mes fiz ferunt aucun pechié, que Nostre Sires ne se corrouce encontre eaus.' Ensi faisoit le proudome chascun jor. Un jor fu que Sathan vint devant Nostre Seignor. Et Nostre Sires li dist: 'D'ou viens tu, Sathan?' Et cil li respondi: 'Je ai serchee la terre et par alee tote.' Et Nostre Sires li dist: 'Et n'as tu donc pris garde de mon serf Job, que en toute la terre n'est nus qui le resemble, home simple et droiturier et qui doute Deu, et se retrait de toz maus?' Et Sathan li respondi: 'Et il ne le fait mie en vain, car tu as bien garnie sa maison, et lui, et tout ce que il a tout environ, et beneis toutes les oevres de ses mains, et toz ses biens li creissent de jor en jor. Mais fai une chose. Laisse moi covenir avuec lui, et verrons com il se provera vers toi.' Et Nostre Sires li dist: 'Or va que totes ces choses que il a soient en ta main, mais garde que n'atochier a sa persone.' Et Sathan s'en ala...

En cele hore se leva Job, et descira ses vestimenz, et deschevela sa teste, et cheï en terre, et aora et dist: 'Nus issi dou ventre de ma mere, et nu i retornerai. Deu m'a doné et Deu m'a tolu, et ensi com il plaist a Deu, ensi est fait. Le nom de Deu soit benoit.' En totes ces choses ne pecha Job, ne ne parla nulle fole parole envers Deu.

Apres de ces VII jors, Job parla, et maudist au jor qu'il fu né, et dist: 'Perisse le jor ouquel je sui né, et la nuit en laquel je sui conceü. Et Deu ne la requiere desus, et ne soit mention de lui. Et soit oscuré par teniebres, et l'ombre de la mort la cuevre, et nuble et oscurté et amert[um]e la cuevre. Icele nuit que je sui conceü soit pleine de tenebros estorbeillons, et ne soit contee es jors de l'an, et ne soit trovee es meis...Deus, por coi ne fui je mors dedenz la nature de ma mere, ou quant je nasqui, que je ne morui tantost? Deus, por coi fu norriz? Deus, por coi alaitai les mameles de ma mere? Car se je fusse morz, je me reposeroie avuec les rois et avuec les conseilliers de la terre, o vos, princes qui poseez l'or. Ou por coi ne fui je come avorton, ou come ceaus qui nasquirent et ne virent lumiere? Car en la mort cessent li mauvais dou travail, et en la mort se reposent ceaus qui sunt las, et ceaus qui furent vencu senz molesté pieça, oïrent la voiz de l'enemi. Li petit et li grant sunt la, et le serf est franc de son seignor. Deus, au cheitif por coi li donas clarté? Et ces qui sunt en amertume, por coi ne sunt morz, qui atendent la mort, et ele ne vient, et qui desirent le monument, come ceaus qui chavent a trover le tresor?...'

Et touz ses frere vindrent a lui, et toutes ses serors, et tuit cil qui premiere-ment l'avoient coneü, et mangerent avuec lui pain en sa maison, et moverent lor testes desur lui, et le conforterent dou mal que Deus li avoit doné. Et chascun li dona une berbiz et un an[el d']or. Et Nostre Sires beneï les derreenes choses de Job plus que il ne fist au comencement. Et trova que il avoit XIIII mile berbiz, et II mile chamiaus, et mil jous de bues, et mil ahnesses. Et ot VII fiz et treis filles. Et l'une ot nom Diem et l'autre Cassiane, et la tierce Cornutibia. En toute la terre ne furent trovées ausi beles femmes com furent les filles de Job. Et le pere lor dona heritages entre lor freres. Job vesqui puis cest flaelement cent et XL anz, et vit ses fiz et les fiz de ses fiz jusques a la quarte generacion. Et morut veillart et plein de jors.

A different selection of scriptural books appears in the sadly mutilated De Thou Bible (*c.* 1280), now *fonds français* 899, which contains the *BXIII* text: the whole of the Octateuch (without glosses), Kings, Tobit, Judith, Esther and Job; then the Psalter and the Gospels, with the unintelligent glosses peculiar to *BXIII*; and finally the Acts and the Catholic epistles (here James and I Peter only) in the inferior transla-tion of *BXIII*. A fifteenth-century copy (to the end of the Gospels) is in the Widener collection in Philadelphia. Yet another selection is in *fonds français* 24728: the historical books as in the De Thou Bible; then Daniel and minor related works, Jonah, Esdras and Maccabees; finally the Apocalypse, Ecclesiastes, James and I Peter, and Proverbs.

The complete 'Bible du xiiie siècle' (*BXIII*) is made up thus:

Volume I: The Octateuch (Genesis, Joshua, Judges and Ruth have glosses derived from the *glossa ordinaria*);
  Kings;
  Chronicles to Esther;
  Job, with a few glosses;
  Psalter, in a traditional version, ill transcribed, with unintelligent glosses
    peculiar to *BXIII*.

Volume II: Sapiential books;
  Maccabees;

Prophets;

Gospels, with unintelligent glosses as for Psalter;

Pauline epistles;

Acts and Catholic epistles in an inferior translation;

Apocalypse: a garbled transcription of an older version.

Apart from the glosses, and the condensation, omission or mis-translation of individual passages, *BXIII* resembles any modern translation from the Vulgate. But it is a compilation, not a work of literature; a publishing venture carried out by anonymous editors financed by a group of stationers in Paris or Picardy. The Psalter and the Apocalypse represent an archaic stratum; the Acts and the Catholic epistles the work of an inferior hand. The remainder is clear, succinct and transparent, but without the rugged strength and the poetic fire of the old translation of the books of Kings. The glossing is very uneven, and in some cases trivial or absurd.

It is possible (although the contrary view was defended by Berger)[1] that *BXIII* arose out of partial translations made in the second or third quarter of the century. Important stages in its growth may be discerned in the isolated copies of the Gospels, and the New Testament as a whole. The Gospels appear in the De Thou abridged Bible, and also in a Champenois miscellany side by side with the *Queste del saint Graal*, the *Tresor* of Brunetto Latini, some lyrics of Thibaut de Champagne, and the *Devisions des Foires de Champagne* (the copy of the *Tresor* is dated 1284). Two early copies of the New Testament are preserved in English

[1] Of the various abridged bibles and selections from the Old Testament described above, only two were known to Berger in 1884, the Acre Bible and the De Thou Bible, and both of these he seriously misdated. Unaware of the near eastern origins of the former, he was baffled by the costumes depicted in the Byzantine miniatures, and attributed them, for want of a better explanation, to direct imitation of lost Carolingian prototypes; he placed this manuscript around the year 1200, and regarded the De Thou Bible as contemporary with the Latin bible of the Paris Dominicans, *fonds latin* 16719–22, *c.* 1250. He dated *BXIII* soon after the Parisian revision of the Vulgate in 1226, and assumed that the De Thou Bible was a subsequent abridgement of it. The whole of this chronology is unacceptable since the researches of Vitzthum and his successors on Parisian and non-Parisian manuscript decoration; whereas the Acre Bible is dated *c.* 1250–4, the whole of the remaining corpus of material under discussion is not earlier than *c.* 1280. The movement leading to the constitution of *BXIII* belongs to the latter half of the century; the existence of the Acre Bible suggests that some of the abridged bibles may be earlier than the complete ones. *BXIII* in the extant manuscripts overlaps with the age of Guyart des Moulins, whose work was carried out in 1291–5, and the creation of the complete Bible leads directly to the composite *BHC* (before 1317).

libraries. The Christ Church manuscript is a remarkable volume, transcribed and illuminated for a wealthy patron in a non-Parisian atelier, about 1280. The miniatures are everywhere numerous, and in the Fourth Gospel and the Pauline epistles there is a plethora of decorative illustration, with an elaborate design occupying a large part of the margin to mark the head of each chapter. Paul, bearing a symbolic sword, is shown addressing his hearers in innumerable roundels, generally incorporated in a vertical strip of colour often running the entire length of the page, the prevalent tints being a hard, chilly blue and gold (or ochre). The general effect is reminiscent of the Gospels of the Sainte-Chapelle—or indeed of the stained glass of the Sainte-Chapelle itself. The New Testament is also found in an unpretentious manuscript copied a few decades later in England, now Royal 20 B v in the British Museum. The non-Parisian background of all these early New Testament manuscripts (apart from the De Thou selection) is evident.

There is also one early copy[1] of the Old Testament alone, divided into two volumes: Genesis to Chronicles, and Esdras to Maccabees, without glosses on the Octateuch. This is the Sanford Bible, which (though seriously mutilated) agrees in its style of decoration with English manuscripts of the final decades of the thirteenth century;[2] there is evidence that the book has remained in England until the present day. It seems possible that the unglossed version of the Octateuch and the translation of the Gospels had separate origins and were first

[1] Another copy may have existed, for a fifteenth-century note on the flyleaf of Cambridge University Library MS Ee 3 52 states '...[Thomas Croftys] comunitati canonicarum de Flyxton contulit simul et donavit Vetus Testamentum in duobus voluminibus gallici ydyomatis...', and another note adds 'Primum volumen Veteris Testamenti ex dono Thome Croftys armigeri. Q. R. M.'. But this volume extends as far as the book of Job, and so resembles a first volume of *BXIII*, rather than the first half of an Old Testament. The notes show however that an Old Testament in two volumes was a recognized type of book in fifteenth-century England.

[2] 'The remains of the illumination seem to me to show that the MS was made in England in the last quarter of the 13th c. The evidence for the date of the decoration seems all to come from the second volume, which has little figures in the margins, but the two volumes seem to be contemporary. The birds in the margins and certain more or less naturalistic leaves in the initials recall Royal 3 D. VI (*c.* 1283) and Add. 24686 (dated 1284); and the early "cabbage leaf" foliage in vol. II, fol. 1, seems to me indisputably English and probably rather late in the century, since "cabbage leaf" comes in with the Peterborough and Arundel Psalters which are generally thought to belong about A.D. 1300' (letter of Professor Julian Brown, 9 January 1959). Similar datings are suggested by Professor Brown and M. Porcher (and indeed already by Vitzthum) for practically the whole corpus of manuscripts associated with the *BXIII* text.

assembled in the De Thou–Widener compilation; the remainder of the Bible was assembled some time between 1280 and 1300.

At the present time about half a dozen copies of the complete *BXIII* are known to exist or can be surmised to have existed (complete copies in two volumes dating from about 1300 are now in the British Museum, in the Pierpont Morgan Library, and at Chantilly, and odd copies of volume one have come to light elsewhere; a fifteenth-century copy for the baron de Villars has long been known, *fonds français* 6–7). The second volume had a much wider circulation, since it was appended to *BH* some time before 1317, and the composite work *BHC* survives in some seventy copies. French-speaking families on both sides of the Channel had a great and growing familiarity with Scripture in their mother tongue during the century before Wyclif. A different and very literal translation in Anglo-Norman dialect was possessed by John de Welles (*d.* 1361); this family bible crossed the Channel and passed into the collection of the kings of France, where it is now *fonds français* 1.

The climax of the new translation movement started by the late-thirteenth-century stationers was reached with Guyart des Moulins's expanded translation of Comestor's *Historia Scholastica*, known as the *Bible Historiale* (*BH*), which attached to itself a vast train of scriptural books in translation and grew into a medieval biblical encyclopaedia (*BHC*). Guyart was a canon of St Peter's church at Aire (near Saint-Omer) and was dean from 1297 until some time after 1312. He set to work in June 1291 and finished in February 1295; the fair copying of the work must have taken some years, for the author refers in his preface to his election as dean on the feast of S. Rémi, 1297.

His history covers the same ground as the books of the Acre Bible: the Old Testament histories, the Gospels and Acts. He follows Comestor to the end of Kings, there inserts a selection of Proverbs and the beginning and end of Job, goes on with Tobit, the age of prophets and the stories of the captivity, and provides a historical link with the New Testament. The first book of Maccabees, however, is a direct translation from the Vulgate with explanations drawn from the *Historia*. This new method is greatly extended in the New Testament history: gospel passages are given in the order of Comestor's gospel harmony, and accompanied or followed by commentary from his book. The gospel text is written first in a large hand (*de grosse lettre*), and the commentary is added in a smaller hand (*de delïe lettre*): shorter comments are inserted as glosses, longer expositions are reserved for the end of the scriptural text, but both are in the smaller hand. In Acts, as in Maccabees, we have a direct version of Scripture interspersed with commentary from the *Historia*.

Encouraged by Guyart's example, copyists from the earliest years of the fourteenth century embodied large but variable portions of *BXIII* into their copies of *BH* until very nearly the whole Bible, apart from the Octateuch and Kings, had become a part of *BHC*. These copies were generally in two massive folio volumes, splendidly illuminated, and the composite work replaced all earlier biblical compilations and translations in the public favour.

The text when properly copied has the layout of a scholastic manual, or a modern annotated edition. There are very few apocryphal additions (the legend of the True Cross, the penance of Adam and the life of Pilate). I Maccabees and Acts are the earliest known examples of the translation of complete books of Scripture with a distinct and separate commentary. Unfortunately they were rarely copied. In fact, few manuscripts retain the original form of Guyart's work. *Fonds français* 155 contains all but the apocryphal pieces (an Apocalypse has been bound up with it as a supplement). The 'pearl of the Guyart manuscripts' is the copy made by Thomas du Val of Clairefontaine (near Chartres) in 1411: this is our only source for the Apocrypha, but the copyist added a version of Job and the Psalter. There is also the three-volume copy made at Bruges for Edward IV; the first two volumes were made to the king's order, but the third volume, dated 1470, contains the king's name over an erasure and had been kept in stock. Other manuscripts which keep very close to the primitive form of *BH* are the Crèvecœur and Calais Bibles (although they substitute the poorer version of Acts from *BXIII*). The De Croy Bible adds not only Job and the Psalter but the sapiential books, and ends with the Apocalypse and the prophetic books, after the gospel harmony.

All these are random and even disorderly borrowings from *BXIII*. But already in 1317 a Parisian scribe had signed a copy of *BHC* in its classical form: 'J. de Papeleu in vico scriptorum.' This follows a simpler plan: it pursues Guyart's work as far as the stories of the captivity and adds a historical link with the New Testament; it then concludes volume one with the Psalter. The second volume is simply identical with the second volume of *BXIII* and contains the sapiential and prophetic books and the New Testament. There was some overlapping. Some of the finest parts of Guyart's work (especially Maccabees and Acts) were sacrificed to make way for a direct translation of the latter half of the Bible, while on the other hand the historical part of Scripture, as far as Job, is replaced by Guyart. This is the 'petite bible historiale'; the 'bible moyenne' adds the full text of Job; the 'grande bible historiale' adds to this Chronicles, Esdras and Nehemiah. About seventy copies of this massive two-volume work were examined by Samuel Berger.

All these different types of bible had some currency on both sides of the Channel, and we should not underestimate their influence on the minds of that powerful and wealthy section of the laity who had them in their possession. The royal house of France encouraged the copying, illuminating and re-translation of the Bible; but the Bible of Jean de Sy (before 1355), a work of real originality, remains unfinished in the eighteenth chapter of Jeremiah (the fragment survives in a single manuscript), and his successor Raoul de Presles (*c.* 1380) did no more than revise the text of *BXIII* down to the Gospel of Matthew. Raoul's patron Charles V and the king's brother, the duc de Berry, were enthusiastic collectors whose library catalogues have been preserved. At the discovery of printing it was *BHC*, strongly represented in the royal collections, which drew the attention of an editor, Jean de Rély, confessor of Charles VIII. His *editio princeps*, with a modernized psalter text from Raoul de Presles, ran into a dozen further editions between 1487 and 1545.

The pioneer of modern biblical criticism, Richard Simon, spoke slightingly of these medieval compilations, ignoring the very considerable amount of scriptural material contained in them; and for a long time serious study of them was frustrated by their inaccessibility. Jealously guarded in royal palaces and provincial châteaux, they illustrate every phase of later medieval book illumination; some were mutilated for the sake of their miniatures. Like family ikons, they were revered not studied during the Ancien Régime. The history of individual bibles is often astonishing. The Bible of Jean II contains a note on the flyleaf in a fifteenth-century hand:

Cest livre fust pris ové le roy de Fraunce a la bataille de Peyters, et le bon counte de Saresbirs, William Montagu, la achata par cent mars et le dona a sa compaigne Elizabeth la bone countesse, qe Dieux assoile, et est continus dedcins le Bible enter ové tixt et glose, le mestre de Histoires et incident, tout en memes le volym. Laquele lyvre la dite countesse assigna a ces executours de le vendre pur .xl. livers.

This book is now in the Royal collection in the British Museum. The Bouillon Bible can be traced from the day in June 1410 when the duc de Berry gave it to his chamberlain, Jean Harpedenne, through half a dozen hands until, in 1785, it was passed on by Godefroy de Bouillon (the last reigning duke of that family) to his adopted son Philippe d'Auvergne, afterwards an admiral in the British navy. It passed through the Ashburnham and Yates Thompson collections, and is now in the Walters Art Gallery, Baltimore. Some important witnesses to the development of *BXIII* (including the three oldest complete copies, now in London, New York and Chantilly) remained in private hands and only came into the open between 1900 and 1930. The difficulties of Reuss and Berger in convincing the learned public of the mere existence of *BXIII* ('une assertion non justifiée de S. Berger', according to Paul Meyer) are due to this inaccessibility of the principal pieces of evidence. There is some excuse for still more recent historians who, like Margaret Deanesly, have assumed that the translation movement of the 1380s, in France and England, was a quite new departure.

The conclusion to be drawn is a simple one. In the north of France, and in French-speaking circles in England, the translation of Scripture was neither licensed nor prohibited by diocesan authority (but see pp. 391 ff. for opposition to English versions, and p. 434 for opposition in Germany). It was a stationers' venture and encountered no official opposition or criticism. The restriction of complete bibles to the wealthy, or even to court circles, was perhaps economically inevitable. The Latin bible, assured of a wide sale, could be mass-produced. The vernacular bible appealed from the outset to a limited public, and an undecorated copy might have been an unsaleable commodity. Scriptural knowledge was never censored, merely rationed by the purse. But the New Testament was relatively easy to copy and handle, and at least one unpretentious copy, with simple red and blue initials, has survived from fourteenth-century England.

How far were these massive manuscripts read and appreciated? It is perhaps an indication to find François Villon, who had access to the great libraries of the princes of the royal house, quoting from Job:

Mes jours s'en sont allez errant
Comme, dit Job, d'une touaille
Font les filets, quant tisserant
En son poing tient ardente paille...

It is still more revealing to find that an unknown contemporary had bound up the book of Tobit with the works of Alain Chartier (*fonds français* 25435). But the main line of approach to the Bible was historical and erudite; the deeper meaning of Holy Writ was embodied in the mystery plays; and the full appreciation of its literary value had to await the Renaissance.

6. VERNACULAR SCRIPTURES IN ITALY

Given the relatively late emergence of a vernacular literature in Italy, it is not surprising that the Bible began to be translated into Italian later than into French, Provençal and German. It is however generally agreed that Italian versions of substantial parts of the Bible existed from about the mid-thirteenth century, if not earlier, though none of the manuscripts is older than the fourteenth century. Among the first books to be translated were the Gospels and the Psalter. These earliest Italian versions have not yet been thoroughly studied in detail, so that a summary account of them, such as will be attempted here, must be in part rather tentative. To the fourteenth century belong our earliest manuscripts of more or less complete Italian bibles, almost certainly composed, for the most part, of versions made in the previous century. The social and religious background of these manuscripts is fairly clear. Finally, in the second half of the fifteenth century the first printed Italian bibles, representing the remarkable achievements—however limited in some respects—of the medieval translators, bring our period to a close. With the following century a new era opens. The medieval material may be treated under five heads: principal manuscripts and incunabula; general description of the versions; the translators; the sources of the versions; the use and influence of the versions.

PRINCIPAL MANUSCRIPTS AND INCUNABULA
Principal Manuscripts

(i) Originally more or less complete bibles. Siena, Bibl. comunale, I. V. 5 (fourteenth century): Genesis; Exod. i–xxviii; I–IV Kings;

Judges (the story of Samson); Tobit i–xii; I Macc. i–xiv. Siena, Bibl. comunale, F. III. 4 (fourteenth century): the whole Old Testament.[1] Rome, Bibl. Angelica, 1552–3 (fourteenth century): the whole Old Testament. Florence, Bibl. Riccardiana 1252 (fourteenth century): Ecclesiastes to Apocalypse. Paris, B.N. Ital. 1 and 2 (fifteenth century): the whole Bible except Daniel, in part, and Romans. Paris, B.N. Ital. 3 and 4 (second half of fifteenth century): all the Bible from I Esdras. (These two Parisian manuscripts formed part of the library of the Aragonese kings at Naples; they were appropriated by Charles VIII of France in 1495.) Florence, Laurenziana, Ashburnham 1102 (fifteenth century): Genesis to Psalms. (ii) Old Testament, separate books. Florence, Bibl. Naz., conv. soppr. B, 3, 173: Proverbs. *Ibid.* Cl. XL, 47: Proverbs; Ecclesiastes. Florence, Bibl. Naz., Pal. 2 (fourteenth century): Psalms and Song of Songs. Venice, Marciana I, 57 (fourteenth century): Psalms and Song of Songs. (iii) New Testament Siena, Bibl. com. I. V. 9 (fourteenth century): Harmony of Gospels; epistles; Apocalypse. Rome, Vatican, Pal. lat. 56 (fourteenth century): Harmony of Gospels. Florence, Riccardiana 1250 (fourteenth–fifteenth century): the whole New Testament. Venice, Marciana 4975 (fourteenth century): Harmony of Gospels. *Ibid.* I. it. 2 (fourteenth century): the whole New Testament.

Incunabula

Two complete bibles were printed at Venice in 1471. The first, printed by Wendelin of Speier and dated 1 August, was compiled by a Camaldolese monk, Niccolò Malermi (*c.* 1420–81). In his preface Malermi claimed to have translated all the Bible, but his work is not strictly a translation, but a revision of earlier versions to bring them closer to the Vulgate and incidentally to make their language less Tuscan and more Venetian. His work proved very popular and was often reprinted. The last edition came out at Venice in 1773. The other bible was printed by N. Jenson and is dated 1 October. It was compiled anonymously, and with no attempt at revision, from existing versions, the books of the Old Testament, except most of the Psalter, being taken from manuscripts (chiefly Siena F. III. 4) while for most of the New Testament the compiler drew upon the Bible of Malermi. This Jenson Bible was almost forgotten until the nineteenth century, when the increasing

---

[1] To this text corresponds, in general, the Cambridge manuscript of an Italian Old Testament, dating from the end of the fourteenth century: U.L. Add. MSS 6685.

interest—partly patriotic, partly literary—in the language of the Trecento caused it to be regarded, not without exaggeration, as a treasure of the purest Tuscan. It was edited by Carlo Negroni, in ten volumes, with an interesting and enthusiastic but now very dated introduction (*La Bibbia Volgare*, Bologna, 'Collezione di opere dei primi tre secoli della lingua', 1882–7). Of this bible there were many nineteenth-century editions of selections and fragments (see Negroni's Introduction, pp. xxx ff.).

THE VERSIONS

The manuscripts listed above contain only versions made by and for Christians. What of the Jews in medieval Italy? Did they too have their versions of the Scriptures? The question has been disputed, and fifty years ago a negative or, at least, a sceptical answer was strongly recommended by the authority of M. Steinschneider. This great Jewish scholar was not convinced that there existed any Jewish Italian version of the Bible, or of substantial parts of it, in the middle ages; there were only translations of liturgical prayers, incorporating certain Old Testament texts, and some glossaries of Hebrew terms.[1] But in recent years the contrary view has gained ground: U. Cassuto, its chief representative, maintains that manuscripts of the late fifteenth and sixteenth centuries contain an Italian version—written in Hebrew characters—of the complete Jewish Bible, substantial parts of which transmit a version or versions made at least as early as the thirteenth century. These, Cassuto says, were in central Italian dialect, a 'marchigiano-umbro-romanesco', which formed a sort of medieval '*koiné* giudeo-italiano' which in time was to become more or less 'Tuscanized'. And there seems to be evidence that the Roman rabbis in the thirteenth century authorized a version of biblical texts for liturgical uses.[2]

Leaving the question of Jewish versions, we shall confine our attention now to those made for Christians. Among Italian Christians in the middle ages the parts of the Bible for which translations were in most demand seem to have been the Gospels and the Psalter, Proverbs, with

---

[1] See *Monatschrift für Geschichte und Wissenschaft des Judentums*, XLII (1898), 117, 317–19; *Jewish Quarterly Review*, XVI (1904), 734–64.

[2] *Encyclopaedia Judaica*, 4, pp. 610–11; *Miscellanea di studi ebraici in memoria di H. P. Chajes* (Florence, 1930), pp. 19–38.

the other 'sapiential' writings, and the Apocalypse. Genesis, Job and Tobit were also fairly popular (this term being of course relative). On the whole the New Testament was read in translation more than the Old Testament.

Of the Pentateuch only one version, probably, has survived in the manuscripts (apart from an interesting 'essai individuel' (S. Berger)[1]— the version of Genesis made or revised by the Florentine Romigi de' Ricci, and now in the Biblioteca Riccardiana, 1655). Of the Psalter, contained in at least fourteen manuscripts, A. Vaccari distinguishes three Tuscan versions (Berger had distinguished only one) and one in Venetian dialect.[2] Next to the Psalter, Proverbs seems to have been the book of the Old Testament most in demand in separate copies; there were at least four versions of it. Of the books of Kings and Judith, S. Berger distinguished two versions: an earlier one, freely paraphrased, and a later, more literal version. There were perhaps three versions of Job, which differ in the same way.

Of the books of the New Testament, the Gospels were easily the most popular, especially in the form of harmonies derived, in the first place, from Latin versions of Tatian's Diatessaron. Berger counted twenty-five manuscripts of the Gospels in translation, including harmonies and the Gospels for Sundays and feast-days; and Vaccari has since drawn attention to many more manuscripts of Gospel harmonies, either separate or combined with other parts of the Bible.[3] Most of these harmonies are in Tuscan dialect and derive from a single version of the Latin translation contained in the *Codex Fuldensis* (cf. Migne, *PL*, 68, cols. 255–8). This Tuscan version seems to have been made early in the thirteenth century; a representative manuscript (which includes other parts of the New Testament) is the Sienese, I. V. 9. Of particular interest for the history of the Latin Bible is a Gospel harmony in Venetian dialect contained in a fourteenth-century manuscript, Marciana 4975. It is a freely glossed translation of a Latin version of the Diatessaron which Vaccari considers independent of, and probably earlier than, that contained in the *Codex Fuldensis*.[4] Of the Pauline epistles, two or possibly three versions have been

[1] See *Romania*, XXIII (1894), 366.

[2] *Enciclopedia Italiana*, VI, 900.

[3] 'Propaggini del Diatessaron in Occidente', *Biblica*, XII (1931), 326–54.

[4] The texts of both the Tuscan and the Venetian harmonies are printed in *Studi e Testi*, *81* (Città del Vaticano, 1938).

distinguished, distributed among some fifteen manuscripts—one of which, the Riccardiana 1252, has a chapter-division that differs from the Vulgate.[1] The Tuscan version of Acts is prefaced, in some manuscripts, by a short prologue by Domenico Cavalca (*c.* 1270–1342) in which this Dominican friar (see below) outlines his method of adapting the original to the limits, as he thought them, of the vernacular.[2] Of the Catholic epistles Berger distinguished two versions, in nine manuscripts, which differ in the same way as the earlier and later versions of books of the Old Testament. The Apocalypse is found in at least ten manuscripts, in one of which the version seems to derive from a Catalan text, itself derived from a French version.

Concerning the Italian Bible as a whole the following features may be noted. (*a*) So far as we know, the versions were never made from the original tongues, but always from Latin. (*b*) The language of most of the versions is Tuscan. There are however a few in Venetian dialect, and these include, besides the Gospel harmony mentioned above, two manuscripts of the Psalter; but the earlier of these (fourteenth century) is thought to be a Tuscan version copied at Venice. This general predominance of Tuscan is of course in line with the development followed by secular literature in Italy, which tended to be linguistically more or less Tuscan from the later decades of the thirteenth century. Therefore, as time went on the use of Tuscan forms of speech would not always and necessarily indicate a geographically Tuscan provenance. An anonymous translator, writing at the end of the fourteenth or early in the fifteenth century, expresses the opinion concerning the superiority of the Tuscan dialect which had become normal in Italy since the great Tuscan writers of the Trecento, Dante, Boccaccio and Petrarch: 'volgarizzando seguiteremo uno comune parlare toscano, però che è il più intero et il più aperto communemente di tutta Ytalia, e il più piacevole e il più intendevole de ogni lingua.'[3] (*c*) The versions are often interspersed with glosses in order to elucidate the sense or bring

[1] Berger (*Romania*, XXIII, 399) regarded this division as a compromise between the older, pre-thirteenth-century arrangements and the system introduced at Paris *c.* 1220. This point is relevant to the question of the origin of the Tuscan New Testament; see below.

[2] The gist of Cavalca's statement is that the depth and multiplicity of meaning in the original has compelled him sometimes to alter the order of words and insert glosses; cf. *Romania*, XXIII, 390–3.

[3] *Romania*, XXIII, 408–9.

out points of doctrine. Thus at Gen. iii. 1, the Vulgate *Qui dixit ad mulierem* is glossed: 'conoscendola di più fragile natura che l'uomo' (Siena, F. III. 4, the best of our Old Testament manuscripts); so, in a version of Tobit, at xii. 7, *sacramentum regis abscondere*, etc., the king's name, Raguel, is inserted to mark the contrast with Deus in the same verse, while two verses later we read 'libera da morte *eternale*'.[1] In general the older versions are rendered more freely than the later, though Cavalca's version of Acts is a notable exception. (*d*) Most of the manuscripts include supplementary material in the form of prologues translated from Jerome, and sometimes pieces of medieval commentary or a sermon of Bernard. In the Sienese manuscripts—reproduced in the Jenson Bible—Proverbs has exceptionally a commentary in Italian. A careful study of such additions might throw light on the social and religious setting of the versions.

THE TRANSLATORS

Writing in 1894 S. Berger concluded that the whole Bible had probably been translated into Italian, in north Italy, by the mid-thirteenth century or a little later; and though it has not yet been proved that the entire Vulgate was in Italian so early, Berger's conclusion may be regarded as fairly certain. But it is not clear how many distinct versions this Italian Vulgate represented. Nor can we identify any of the thirteenth-century translators. With regard to the New Testament at least, Berger's judgement that the version presupposed by our oldest manuscripts 'paraît être sorti tout entier d'une même plume' would now seem to call for re-examination in view of A. Vaccari's researches into the earliest examples of Gospel harmonies in Italian.[2] But no one has yet identified the authors either of these latter versions or of the New Testament texts examined by Berger.

What then of the fourteenth-century translators—if, in the strict sense of the term, there were any? But here too we are still mostly in the dark. Carlo Negroni, introducing his edition of the Jenson Bible, ascribed the bulk of the versions it contains to the Dominican Cavalca, a writer well known to students of early Italian prose. But the identification

[1] This interesting anonymous version of Tobit can now be read in G. De Luca's anthology of fourteenth-century religious prose, *Prosatori minori del Trecento*, vol. 1 (Milan–Naples, Ricciardi, 1954), pp. 363–79.

[2] *Biblica*, XII (1931), 326–54.

was sentimental and is certainly false. Cavalca certainly worked on a version of Acts; he says so himself in a prologue to that book contained in several manuscripts; but it has been shown that he did no more than freely gloss an earlier version (represented by Riccardiana 1252).[1] There is no reason to suppose that the basic version was his work. The fact is that in respect of most of the Bible we cannot name any Italian translator before the sixteenth century. Generally speaking the medieval versions are anonymous.

We are left then with various indications, in the manuscripts, which show or suggest one or other part of the medieval Italian scene—a group or region within which the vernacular bible, or some part of it, circulated. The region is usually Tuscany, and, more precisely, Florence. The Florentine predominance is remarkable. In no other city do we find the vernacular bible, as Berger puts it, 'si intimement mêlée à la culture des lettres et la vie de famille'. The majority of our manuscripts are preserved in Florentine libraries, and it is remarkable that many of these were copied by members of that wealthy mercantile class which was in effect the city's aristocracy. We have already mentioned the de' Ricci manuscript of the Old Testament, Riccardiana 1655, as containing the version of Genesis made or at least revised by a layman, Romigi de' Ricci, about 1400. Another Florentine layman, a Torna-quinci, translated a letter of Jerome included in a manuscript of the vernacular New Testament (Bibl. Naz. Pal. 5). But the most active copiers and propagators of the vernacular bible were naturally the friars, and especially, it would seem, the Dominicans. It was a Domini-can, a Master Zanobi, who prefaced the epistle of James with a version of one of Jerome's letters, 'per l'utilitade di chi non sae gramaticha' (i.e. Latin). Two other Florentine manuscripts come from the Domini-can library of S. Maria Novella; and one of the Parisian manuscripts was copied, presumably at Naples, between 1466 and 1472, by a member of that Order, Niccolò de Neridino.[2] In other cases the provenance seems Franciscan: the Riccardiana 1354 contains, with the Gospels, legends about St Francis; and another, from the same collection, some sayings of Jacopone da Todi. Another Florentine manuscript includes, with a version of Acts, some letters of the Vallombrosa monk Giovanni dalle Celle (c. 1396). It may not be unconnected with the interest

[1] *Romania*, XXIII, 394.
[2] See Quetif-Echard, *Scriptores Ordinis Praedicatorum*, I, 837.

shown by the friars in our versions that many of the manuscripts include translated passages from Jerome and St Bernard, since these authors were favourites with the friars.[1]

THE SOURCES

The first really critical inquiry into the question as to which texts of the Bible—Latin or vernacular—were used by the first Italian translators was made by S. Berger in the course of a series of articles on the Romance versions of Scripture, published in *Romania*, XVIII (1889), XIX (1890) and XXIII (1894). Berger's general conclusion was that the Italian translators depended in large measure on previous French and Provençal versions, and that, so far as Latin originals were concerned, they made use of a text or family of texts current in southern France and north Italy before the mid-thirteenth century and representing, in part at least, non-Vulgate versions. The dependence on a French original seemed especially clear in the case of the Psalter, and dependence on a Provençal original in respect of the New Testament as a whole. These conclusions have been accepted in the main by S. Minocchi,[2] E. Reuss,[3] U. Cassuto[4] and G. Ricciotti.[5] A dissident voice is that of A. Vaccari, who questions the dependence of the Tuscan New Testament on a Provençal version, and, implicitly, on any Romance version.[6] Nevertheless it seems reasonable, as a working hypothesis, to accept the more usual view, that the formation of the Italian Bible was influenced by transalpine versions. There are strong arguments in favour of this, while the contrary opinion of Vaccari was stated in too cursory a manner to effect the dislodgement of the majority opinion.

The more usual view then, as conveniently summarized by E. Reuss,[7] comprises three points. (*a*) The Italian thirteenth-century Bible was a translation, in part of the Latin Vulgate, in part of French and Provençal versions. (*b*) So far as a Latin original was concerned, the Italian Old Testament reflects a number of rare readings found in Latin

[1] The importance of the friars as propagators of the Italian Bible is particularly stressed by S. Minocchi in Vigouroux's *Dictionnaire de la Bible*, III, cols. 1012–38.
[2] Art. cit.
[3] *Realencyklopädie für protestantische Theologie und Kirche*, III, 140–2.
[4] *Encyclopaedia Judaica*, 4, pp. 610–11.
[5] *Enciclopedia Cattolica*, II, cols. 1556–8.
[6] *Enciclopedia italiana*, VI, 900–1.   [7] Art. cit. pp. 140–1.

texts current in southern France in the twelfth and thirteenth centuries; from which it appears that that version was made independently of the 'standard' mid-thirteenth-century Vulgate of Paris. (*c*) It is probable—not proved—that the first Italian versions were the work of Waldensian heretics or near-heretics, whether missionaries from France or, as would be more likely, Italians affected by their preaching.

The evidence favouring the first two of the above points will appear more clearly from a consideration of the book-order and chapter-divisions in Italian bible manuscripts, and of certain variant readings found in these. The more notable points are as follows.

(i) The Sienese manuscripts of the Pentateuch (I. V. 5 and F. III. 4) have an archaic chapter-division found only in Latin manuscripts prior to the thirteenth century. In Siena F. III. 4 Job has twenty-two chapters instead of the forty-two which it has had since the thirteenth century; and in one of the Parisian manuscripts it is placed after the Psalter. In the numbering of the Psalms traces of a French original are found in two of the oldest and best Italian manuscripts, Florence Bibl. Naz. Pal. 2 and Siena F. III. 4, which have 175 and 180 psalms respectively. These figures (due to dividing Ps. 119) are almost unknown in Latin manuscripts but approximate to French versions prior to the mid-thirteenth century. Turning to the New Testament, the Parisian manuscripts and the important Florentine Riccardiana 1252 show a book-order that is extremely rare in Latin manuscripts—Gospels, Catholic epistles, Paul, Acts, Apocalypse—and rare even in manuscripts of Romance versions (the Zürich manuscript of the Vaudois (Waldensian) New Testament has it; and this may be based on an early Provençal version). Again, the Riccardiana 1252 and other Florentine manuscripts give, for the Gospels, a chapter-division different from the Vulgate and almost certainly derived from a period not later than the mid-thirteenth century.

These features of the Italian New Testament admittedly only go to show an independence of the Vulgate in the form which this has taken since the thirteenth century. They do not prove a dependence on other Romance versions. This dependence is argued from a consideration of variant readings.

(ii) Our authorities have not adduced much evidence of such variants in the Old Testament, apart from the Psalter, the French origin of which is conceded even by Vaccari. Berger and his followers have rather concentrated on the New Testament, pointing out traces of a derivation from Provençal versions especially, and particularly in respect of the Tuscan Gospels. The following examples may suffice:

Matt. xxi. 9: *Hosanna filio David* (Vulgate).
   Riccard. 1251:[1] 'Facci salvi figliuolo di David.'
   Provençal MS, Paris B.N. fr. 6261 (fifteenth century): 'Salva nos, filh de David.'
   Vaudois MS, Carpentras Bibl. Mun. 22 (fourteenth century): 'fay nos salf.'

John i. 1: *In principio erat Verbum* (Vulgate).
   Riccard. 1252: 'Nel cominciamento era il figliuolo di Dio.'
   Provençal MS, Paris B.N. fr. 2425: 'Lo filh era al comensament.'
   Provençal MS, Paris B.N. fr. 6261: 'En lo comensamen era lo filh de Dieu.'
   Vaudois MS, Carpentras Bibl. Mun. 22: 'Lo filh era al comencament.'

John xi. 16, xxi. 2: *Thomas...Didymus* (Vulgate).
   Riccard. 1252: 'Tomaso...incredulo.'
   Provençal MS, Lyons Palais des Arts 36: '...no crescentz.'
   Vaudois MS, Carpentras Bibl. Mun. 22: '...dubitos.'

At Acts xvii. 27 the Riccard. 1252 has 'et diede a tucti ke ciercassono Idio', representing a rare Latin reading, *dedit hominibus quaerere Deum*, which is found in one Catalan and one Languedoc manuscript. At II Cor. viii. 18 the Riccardiana 1250 and the Parisian manuscripts insert 'il nostro frate Luca', which is not in the Vulgate but is found in the Provençal version and in some Latin texts from Languedoc. At Apoc. i. 13, the Vulgate *similem filio hominis* becomes, in most of the Italian manuscripts, 'simigliante al figliuolo della vergine', as in the Provençal, Vaudois and some French versions,[2] while at xix. 13 *verbum Dei* appears as 'son of God' in some Italian and Provençal manuscripts, corresponding to their rendering of John i. 1.

Not all the above examples are of equal weight, but taken together they suffice to recommend the thesis of a transalpine derivation of the earliest Italian New Testament—the view, as Berger expressed it, that the translator was 'accoûtumé au language religieux du midi de la France,

---

[1] This manuscript gives the most common Tuscan version of the Gospels. The Jenson Bible has 'Salvaci, figliuolo di David' (*Bibbia volgare*, IX, 118).

[2] *Romania*, XVIII, 400. This argument for a Provençal derivation is expressly rejected by Vaccari: '...l'interpretazione "figlio della vergine" per "filius hominis" si trova dappertutto', *Encicl. italiana*, VI, 901.

il a sous les yeux la même Bible latine qui était usitée dans ce pays et sa mémoire est pleine des versions provençales'.[1] But from this need one conclude that the Italian New Testament was the work of heretics? The view usually taken is that the inference is probably justified; firm grounds however for a final judgement are still lacking. Meanwhile this at least may be said: whatever the origins and uses of the Provençal New Testament may have been, its text is not doctrinally tendentious, and the same is true of the Italian Bible as a whole; as the manuscripts preserve it, it is doctrinally quite orthodox. This, to be sure, is not incompatible with its having been the work of Waldensians, for their 'heresy', in the early thirteenth century, was still a matter of ecclesiastical discipline rather than of doctrine. It is then not impossible that the Italian Bible, and particularly the New Testament, was put together under heretical influences originating north of the Alps. What is certain however is that it did not remain the patrimony of heretics. In the fourteenth century we find it associated with and used by the Dominicans and the Franciscans, the leaders of that counter-attack upon heretical tendencies which filled the thirteenth century. It is clear then that if the thirteenth-century Italian versions had originated among heretics, they were adopted in the course of time by the friars—and often freely glossed for purposes of doctrinal instruction. The friars had many and close contacts with the laity, especially in the cities, and their ideal of an apostolate of preaching and teaching adapted to the needs of the latter—who were now becoming more and more articulate and critical—naturally led the friars to make use of, and quickly to become the most conspicuous promoters of, vernacular versions of the Scriptures. Hence, as we have had occasion to note already, it was in the houses of the friars, Dominican and Franciscan, that we find, in the later middle ages, the chief centres for the diffusion—such as it was—of the Italian Bible. It is significant that a version of the Acts of the Apostles contained in the Vaudois manuscripts of the fourteenth–fifteenth centuries is the one made or revised a few decades earlier by the Dominican Cavalca. Heretics themselves, in this case, were now receiving back from Catholic hands material which the Church may, in the first place, have adopted from heretical sources.[2]

[1] *Romania*, XXIII, 405–6.   [2] *Romania*, XXIII, 392–3.

USE AND INFLUENCE OF THE VERSIONS

The religious literature of medieval Italy was neglected from the sixteenth to the nineteenth century, except by an occasional student of the Tuscan of the Trecento and a few pious readers. The old vernacular Bible was almost entirely forgotten with the rest. The nineteenth century brought a change. Italian literary historians and critics began to take an increasing interest in the 'spiritual' writers—in Catherine of Siena and Jacopone da Todi and Passavanti, to name the most conspicuous. To a large extent this was and remains an interest in the language of such authors rather than in their 'message', though in recent years the content too of their writings has been increasingly studied.[1] Yet, for all this, the Italian Bible still attracts curiously little attention from historians. It has been the subject, within the past thirty years, of some valuable studies in detail; but there is still no all-round historical assessment of its place in the literature and life of medieval Italy. The following remarks, then, should be taken as a summary of investigations which are still, for the most part, incomplete.

We can be sure that the vernacular Scriptures were not used in the liturgical worship of the Church. The extant versions, however, of passages from the New Testament which form part of the Missal show that translation did serve to some extent—no doubt a very limited one —as a medium between the laity and the official Catholic liturgy. There is evidence too that among the friars Bible versions were sometimes used for community reading; a fourteenth-century manuscript from the convent of the Dominicans at Ferrara has passages marked for this purpose. As for private reading of the versions, what has been said already will suggest that this must have been not uncommon, here and there, among the literate laity. The texts, we have seen, were usually much glossed for the sake of doctrine or edification; but we need not suppose that the readers' interest always stopped at these points; the surviving Gospel harmonies, with their text divided into paragraphs and the names of the evangelists inserted at the appropriate places, attest at least a degree of critical interest in the Gospels as a consistent historical narrative. At the other extreme a meditative elaboration of certain texts, notably the Penitential Psalms and the Song of Songs,

[1] See G. Getto, 'La Letteratura religiosa', in *Questioni e correnti di storia letteraria* (Milan, Mazorati, 1949), pp. 857–900.

resulted sometimes in virtually new compositions—for example, an interesting 'variation' on the Song of Songs recently edited by G. De Luca, who ascribes it, tentatively, to a Dominican, Simone da Cascina (*c.* 1420).[1] Yet another approach is represented by the extant specimens of versification of some part of the Bible: examples are the remarkably early *Splanamento de li Proverbi di Salamone* by the Cremonese Gerardo Pateg (first half of the thirteenth century) and the Venetian Jacopo Gradonico's verse version of the Tuscan translation of the Diatessaron (late fourteenth century).

A careful examination of the secular Italian writers of our period might reveal traces in their works of the vernacular Scriptures; but any direct influence on a large scale is most improbable. The case of Dante is especially interesting in this connection, not only because he twice alludes to translation of the Bible, but also and more because one of his works, the prose *Convivio* (1304–8), contains fifty-two quotations from the Bible in Italian—roughly two for every three chapters.[2] In his two references to translating the Bible Dante does not, in fact, mention Italian versions. In one case (*De vulg. eloq.* I. x. 2) he is giving his opinion that French holds the first place among the Romance vernaculars as the medium for prose, and the French Bible is mentioned as an example. In the other case (*Convivio,* I. vii. 14–17) it is the Latin Psalter that Dante mentions, to support his view that poetry could not be translated without the loss of all its beauty. The poet, it would seem, was not predisposed to find poetic beauty in the Italian Psalter. But in fact he does not mention it. As for the citations in the *Convivio,* there are thirty-five from the Old Testament and seventeen from the New Testament. The proportions are interesting. The three books which Dante ascribed to Solomon—Proverbs, the Song of Songs, Ecclesiastes —account for eighteen of the quotations; Psalms, Wisdom and Ecclesiasticus for thirteen; while Genesis, Isaiah and I Kings (Vulgate) are each cited once. Of the New Testament, the Gospels are quoted nine times, Paul six times, James twice. Apart from the predominance of the Old Testament, this choice, with its stress on the 'sapiential'

[1] *Prosatori minori del Trecento:* I, *Scrittori di religione* (Milan–Naples, Ricciardi, 1954), pp. 341–58. On Simone da Cascina (not to be confused with the better known Simone Fidati da Cascia) see A. Levasti, *Mistici del Duecento e del Trecento* (Milan, Rizzoli, 1935), pp. 1016–17.

[2] Some of them are considered, but not precisely as translations, in E. Moore's *Studies in Dante,* I, 47 ff.

writings, agrees with the normal medieval taste. That it also exactly suited Dante's aim in writing the *Convivio*, and that this aim was the instruction of the laity in philosophy, especially in ethics, are facts which indicate, one may suggest, the rather 'philosophical' bias of that taste; on the whole reflective material was preferred to mere narrative—at least so far as the Old Testament was concerned. As for the source of Dante's vernacular quotations, it is probable that he translated the texts for himself, as he needed them, from the Vulgate. His versions are quite different from those preserved in the Jenson Bible, so far as this reproduces the fourteenth-century manuscripts.[1] And in most cases Dante's version is decidedly closer to the Vulgate.

In conclusion, it may be said that the evidence adduced supports the view that the vernacular Bible was a fairly important factor in the religious life of pre-Reformation Italy, at least in Tuscany and in parts of the north. The various indications combine to give us, in Berger's words, 'une image assez nette et très vivante, d'une société catholique, dans laquelle la Bible italienne a sa place au soleil'. It is, finally, noteworthy that, so far as our evidence goes, the Church in Italy in those centuries showed no hostility in principle to the translation of the Bible, and placed no serious obstacle in the way of rendering it accessible to the people in their own language.[2]

7. VERNACULAR SCRIPTURES IN SPAIN

On opening the first volume of the Complutensian Bible (1514–17) we find the Latin Vulgate printed in the centre of the page with the Septuagint on the left and the Hebrew text on the right, and the Targum of Onqelos and its Latin translation in the lower margin. The orderly composition chosen by the editors of the first polyglot bible produced by any European press thus placed the Hieronymian text in the centre *velut inter Synagogam et Orientalem Ecclesiam*, to symbolize its unquestioned authority and unique position. In medieval Spain, as everywhere before the Reformation, the Vulgate was the natural source of quotations, the fountain-head from which sprang all paraphrases, condensations, rhymed versions, moralizations and translations for the

[1] Cf. L. Negri, 'Dante e il testo della *Vulgata*', *Giornale storico della letteratura italiana*, LXXXV, 441 ff.

[2] See the judgement of the Protestant scholar E. Reuss, art. cit. p. 141.

instruction of Christian people. The high scientific effort of the enterprise reminds us also of other more distinctive phases of Spanish
culture, and makes us think of the care with which old readings of the
Latin Bible had been preserved, and texts established, by the schools of
sacred palaeography at Seville and Toledo. We remember also the
revival of biblical scholarship in the *aljamas* of fourteenth-century
Castile.

The history of the vernacular Bible is inextricably bound to the
texts from which it springs, texts sacred and inviolable in their religious
character, yet worked over by long philological toil and never entirely
fixed, interspersed with prefatory and extra-biblical material, and
presented to the reader with Christian glosses or rabbinical commentaries. Hence we find great variety in the translations, none of which
bears an exact resemblance to any of the others. Although the number
of manuscripts preserved is less than that in other languages, the
diversity of the texts followed by medieval translators in the Iberian
peninsula makes the task of analysing and grouping the vernacular
bibles no less complicated and intriguing.

Without counting the biblical translations embedded in the *General
Estoria* and other medieval works such as those of Pero López de
Ayala, we know of fourteen Spanish biblical manuscripts; a small
number compared with the 189 codices Samuel Berger examined for
his history of the Bible in the *langue d'oïl* alone. Only three of these
have survived in their entirety, and none is complete to the last detail:
the Bible of Alba and two of the manuscripts belonging to the royal
collection of the Escorial under the seal of Philip II: I-j-3 and I-j-4 (to
be referred to, together with the other Escorial bibles, in the abbreviated
form of E plus the last number). All the rest are fragmentary. Some of
them, however, contain complementary parts of the Old Testament
(E 8 and E 6, E 7 and E 5), and certain similarities of language justify us
in grouping them together. Only one (E 6) goes back to the thirteenth
century; the others were written or transcribed in the latter part of the
fourteenth or the first half of the fifteenth century (E 8 in Aragonese
dialect). Some relationships have been ascertained: Evora CXXI 1–2
(ff. 348 to end), dated 1429, and the second part of E 5 are copies of
the same translation with frequent variants. E 3 and the Ajuda (Lisbon)
MS 52-VIII-I (Gen.–Jud.) are closely related. E 5 Jud. is almost
identical with E 19. The Academy of History manuscript belongs to the

family of the Alba Bible as regards the Major Prophets, while Minor Prophets, including Prologue, bespeak common origin with Biblioteca Nacional of Madrid MS 10288, the book of Daniel, and Prologue, with E 4. The latter is in turn related to Evora, Academy, Nac. 10288 and the Sephardic printed texts. In the same manuscript, the same passage, or even an entire book, such as Lamentations in Nac. 10288, is transcribed twice, from different sources. On account of the composite character of some of these manuscripts they must be collated in their entirety before a definite classification of mutual relationships can be attempted.

The situation is scarcely less complex in the case of the Catalan versions, though for different reasons. We know of a translation of the whole Bible into Valencian, made by Bonifatius Ferrer (*d.* 1417), presumably in the last year of his life, and printed in 1478. This edition, which would be most valuable to us, was destroyed so thoroughly that only the last leaf has been found and is preserved in a manuscript chronicle of the Carthusian Order, now at the Hispanic Society in New York. A psalter, probably of Barcelona, 1480, belonging to the Mazarine Library, claims to be a revised reprint of Ferrer's version. It is hard to say which of the other partial manuscript texts, Psalms and Gospels, are related to the Valencian Bible, and whether Ferrer himself leaned on some earlier version. There is yet another family of Catalan bibles: one complete in three volumes, known as the Peiresc manuscript of the Bibliothèque Nationale in Paris (MS esp. 2–4), and two others of one volume each, to be found in London (most of the Old Testament, Egerton 1526) and in Paris (Gen. ii. 21–Psalms, MS esp. 5). The writing places them in the fifteenth century; the latter two, moreover, are dated in the colophon: 1465 and 1461 respectively.

Are they copies of earlier versions? What relation, if any, do they bear to a bible which Alphonso II of Catalonia and Aragon had translated from the French in 1287? Samuel Berger points to certain similarities between the Peiresc manuscript and the Marmoutier New Testament (B.N.P. esp. 486; fourteenth century), and in turn between the Marmoutier manuscript and earlier French and Provençal versions. The glosses of the latter part of the Peiresc Old Testament are also reminiscent of those which we read in the second volume appended to Guyart des Moulins's great *Bible historiale*, containing a direct translation which was circulated widely in fourteenth-century France (p. 448).

The close interrelation between Catalonia and its northern neighbour is further proved by the translation from the Provençal of a brief compendium of Holy Scripture, interspersed with moral considerations and complete with Gospel and apocryphal texts: the *Genesi de scriptura* preserved in two slightly different manuscripts (one of them available in an edition of 1873). Moreover, a complete Catalan bible in rhymed couplets is also in consonance with French style, which used rhymed bibles as a popular means for the propagation of Scripture. Another genre, likewise prominent in France, found its way into the Peninsula: the *Bible moralisée*. The kings of Castile and Aragon coveted these bibles, so beautifully illustrated in France. The only vernacular example known today, however, and this in Spanish rather than Catalan, is the 'Osuna Bible', now at the Biblioteca Nacional in Madrid (10232). Though it contains no illustrations, its connection with the older groups in the family of French *Bibles moralisées illustrées* lies, as S. Berger has shown, in the detailed instructions given for the illumination of the Psalter, which the Spanish copyist or translator mistook for part of the text.

Even apparently irrelevant clues are important. A systematic study should be made of the Spanish bibles in the broad framework of Christian and scholastic culture, as within the narrower bounds of the Church and Synagogue in the Hispanic peninsula. Apart from the still insufficiently studied connection of the Catalan versions with French and Provençal texts, the vernacular bible in Spain is an offshoot either of the Latin or of the Massoretic text. By the time our bibles were translated the Vulgate was firmly established in Spain. E 8–E 6 follows the order which was fixed later by the Clementine edition. In E 2 the books of the New Testament are set in the sequence which we know from the ancient Visigothic manuscripts, with Acts after the Catholic epistles. The Prayer of Manasses and III Esdras are inserted also. The extra-biblical materials which accompany this manuscript belong to the tradition of the *Codex Toletanus* and the Bible of Theodulf. On the other hand, the translations of the Psalms in both E 8 and E 4 are more closely allied to the *Psalterium juxta Hebraeos* than to the Gallican Psalter.

However, what makes the history of the vernacular Bible so different in Spain is the fact that many translations are based not on the Latin but on the Hebrew, with a varying number of reminiscences of the Vulgate.

One such translation is the Psalter just mentioned, which contains Psalms 1–70 with a brief moral glossary. Other translations were made by Jews, and some of them for Jews. The division of the Hebrew Canon into Law and former and latter Prophets is followed by E 3, E 19, E 7, the Alba Bible, and the manuscript of the Academy of History. In the Hagiographa there is some divergence; E 3 coincides with the order most frequently found in the bibles copied in Spain during the middle ages.

Chapter-division as we have it today was unknown to the Jews. If we find such divisions (e.g. in E 7), they were probably introduced by a Christian hand. E 19 is distributed in 196 consecutive sections. E 3 is marked in the Pentateuch according to the synagogal reading or *parashioth*. In both these manuscripts certain poetic sections such as Exod. xv. 1–21 and Num. xxi. 18 are written in a peculiar fashion, filling the extremes of the first and third line and the middle of the second and fourth. In the vernacular this arrangement does not underscore a rhythmical pattern, but only illustrates the copyists' ambition to imitate the Hebrew text by following the Massoretic prescriptions wherever possible.

Although it is not clear to what extent, if any, the vernacular translations were used in the Synagogues, the liturgical notation of E 3 is very significant. However, some of the translations from the Hebrew as they stand today must have been copied by Christians; for such unmistakably Jewish bibles as E 3 and the Academy manuscript contain the books of the Maccabees. In the latter the version based on the Hebrew is placed alongside the Latin text. Deuterocanonical books are also contained in E 4 and Nac. 10288.

Vernacular translations are bound by textual traits to the Church or the Synagogue; but they should bridge the gap between the narrow circles of learning and ecclesiastical practice, and the broader world of the uninitiated. To what extent did the vernacular Bible in Spain fulfil the essential function of bringing the sacred page within the reach of those who did not know Hebrew or Latin? We shall try to answer this question by investigating the testimony of three types of sources: historical documentation manifested chiefly in patronage and prohibitions; the texts in their adaptations outside the Bible and in their intrinsic make-up; and the vernacular languages. It would be very important to determine the extent to which Spanish and Catalan followed the model of Hebrew constructions, biblical terminology, figures of speech and proverbs. Historical and textual evidence is fragmentary and uneven; the sedimentation of language is widespread and conclusive, although it is more difficult to assess.

The E 8–E 6 bible fits perfectly into the cultural milieu of mid-thirteenth-century Castile. Several generations of translators had made Toledo one of the cultural centres of the West, a conveyor of Greek philosophy and Arabic science. At first, Arabic translations of Greek works and original Arabic writing were interpreted orally by Jews and then written in Latin by Christians. When Castilian came into its own as a written language, translation into the vernacular became an end in itself. Spain was ready to have its bible, and it is at this moment that we place our translation of E 8–E 6 containing almost the whole text of Holy Scripture. In E 8, the heading of the Psalter attributes its translation to Hermannus Alemannus, whom we know as the translator into Latin of Arabic (Averroan) commentaries on Aristotle's Nicomachean Ethics and Rhetorics. Whether the attribution be trustworthy or not, it is significant that we find a biblical version associated with a scholar whose activity is attested in Toledo for the years 1240 and 1256. It is also noteworthy that we find the interpreter of this first Castilian psalter at work on the Hebrew text, even if he depended to some extent upon the *Psalterium juxta Hebraeos* and the Gallican psalms.

Alphonso the Wise, king of Castile, was credited by historians with being the first Spanish monarch to have the Bible translated into the vernacular. We should understand 'Bible' in the broad sense of the *Bible historiale*. The king regarded Holy Writ as a record of history written for the instruction of mankind. 'If we consider', he wrote in the Prologue of the *Crónica de España*, 'the benefit that flows from the Sacred Scriptures, we see that it lies in the instruction they give us regarding the creation of the world, the coming of the patriarchs, the going out from Egypt, God's giving the Law to Moses, the reigns of the kings of the holy land of Jerusalem, their exile, the promised coming of our Lord Jesus Christ, and his passion, resurrection and ascension.'

The preparation of the *Primera Crónica General* (1270), in which the story of Moses was told in one brief chapter as the background of the settlement of Spain by Tubal, son of Japhet, inspired the king to undertake another project, the *General Estoria*, a universal history of the world. In it the Bible was to be combined with profane sources, following the chronology of Eusebius' *Chronicle* and the pattern of Peter Comestor's *Historia Scholastica*. The result was a monumental work twelve times as extensive as its model, and much larger than the *Bible historiale* composed ten or twelve years later by Guyart des Moulins. It is in fact the largest of its kind produced in the middle ages.

The following is the distribution of biblical matter among the five volumes of equal size adopted by the editors: part I, Pentateuch; part II, Joshua–Kings; part III (as reconstructed from two manuscripts), Psalms, Song of Songs, Proverbs, Wisdom, Ecclesiastes, Joel and Isaiah (MS Escorial Y-j-8), Hosea, Amos, Jonah, Tobit, Job, Ezekiel and Chronicles with IV Kings intercalated at various points (MS Evora CXXIV 1–2); part IV (as represented by Vatican MS 539), Daniel, Obadiah, Zephaniah, Jeremiah, Lamentations, Baruch, Habakkuk, Judith, Ezra, Nehemiah, Haggai, Zechariah, Esther and Ecclesiasticus. For the fifth part we have to turn to E 2, which contains the same books as Vat. 539, plus Maccabees, and a literal translation of the New Testament from Matt. xviii to Jude. The literal rendering of the New Testament was probably tacked on to the *General Estoria* after the execution of the original plan had ceased.

The desire to read bible history uninterrupted by events alien to it caused some of the transcribers (of Escorial X-j-2, Y-j-8, Evora cxxv 2–3, and B.N. Madrid, U 38) to omit portions of the non-biblical content. Yet other copyists (Esc. Y-1-6 and X-i-1) went back to literal translations of the Scriptures. This would have constituted a change in the original plan, which was to paraphrase the Bible, using literal renderings only when the content warranted it. Thus, in part I of the *General Estoria* the canticles and benedictions of Moses in Deut. xxxii. 1–43 and xxxiii. 2–29 are rendered almost word for word, and the poetical and Wisdom books in the *General Estoria* are closer to the original than the narrative portions. A comparison of these passages of Deuteronomy with their equivalents in E 8 has shown that the compilers of the former probably used as a reference an earlier vernacular translation such as the text reproduced in E 8. Nevertheless, their main text is that of the Vulgate, which, in the passages freely paraphrased, they adapt to a more rhetorical style, avoiding parataxis and constant repetition, and often changing direct into indirect speech.

As regards contents, the authors of the *General Estoria* do their best to explain the structure of sacred history by showing the unity of its parts. From the commentaries of the Fathers and from medieval Latin exegetes they learned the canons of the spiritual interpretation of Scripture. They explain, for example, that 'the ark of Noah is the Church of the faithful, and the cubit's length is Christ, in whom the whole Church was completed' (28a35), although allegorical exposition, on the whole, remains relatively infrequent. The interpreters are more preoccupied with the moral lessons of Holy Writ, which they expound with scholastic precision (Cain's punishment, for instance, dealt out according to the seven capital sins, 9b31); they are even more pre-occupied with the where, when, how and why, amplifying the text with descriptions of places and things, calculations of chronology, sugges-tions of motives and judgements of biblical characters and their actions. The meaning and symbolism of Hebrew names is expounded, and the invention of arts and crafts pointed out with evident satisfaction.

For this the compilers of the *General Estoria* followed the example of Christian and non-Christian sources, especially Josephus, from whose *Antiquities of the Jews* probably come much of the Jewish legendary lore and some talmudic interpretations which penetrated into the Spanish text. Moreover, the collaborators of Alphonso the Wise had direct access to rabbinical and Arabic sources. These they handled with an astonishing degree of curiosity and with an open mind, as we see from the introduction to the account of the birth of Abraham according to the Arabic version: 'The Arabs have their Bible translated from Hebrew...they also have had their interpreters, and they bring forth their proofs on the sayings of Moses, and so do we and our interpreters, and even if they are mistaken in their beliefs because they do not have the faith of Jesus Christ, nevertheless they have said many good, certain and right words in this matter of the Bible...And in those things which they have said well, we think that it is not against reason to compare, where necessary, our sayings with theirs, since this is what our own saints have done and still do' (85b39).

Drawing data and interpretations from the most heterogeneous sources, the authors of the *General Estoria* wove an encyclopaedia of universal knowledge around the core of a paraphrased bible. The bulky volumes of King Alphonso's monumental work deterred printers from transmitting it to the readers of the printed page, but in previous centuries the work was copied many times, and even translated in part into Portuguese and Catalan, so that, if we add the manuscripts of the

General Estoria to those mentioned above, we more than double our count.

If we follow manuscript tradition we go from the second part of the thirteenth to the latter part of the fourteenth and first half of the fifteenth century, another period of fervent activity inspired not so much by the broad vision of universal history as by a zealous and somewhat indiscriminate erudition. In 1406 a great literary patron came to the throne of Castile in the person of John II, who is said to have been fond of having Scripture read and its secrets declared to him. It is with the names of the higher nobility that new translations or copies of previous versions are associated. In 1422, Luis de Guzmán, Grand Master of the Military Order of Calatrava, ordered a Jewish subject of his to produce a fresh translation of the Old Testament, the older ones being outmoded. In the same year a Franciscan friar began to translate the *Postillae* of Nicholas of Lyra, at the request of Alfonso de Guzmán (MS KK-3-8 of the National Library in Madrid). This work, as well as the *Bible moralisée* with a translation of the preface of Jerome, known as the 'Bible of Osuna', found its way into the private library of the Marquis of Santillana, who ordered or collected many biblical and patristic works along with translations of Josephus, Plutarch, Livy, and other historians and poets of antiquity. Later, the devotion of Isabel the Catholic and the zeal of the bibliophile Philip II were responsible for the preservation of most of the biblical manuscripts, while the 'Alba Bible', translated by order of Luis de Guzmán, stayed in the possession of his descendants, who were allowed to keep and read it by a decree of the Inquisition (1624). This aristocratic connection explains the escutcheons found on some of the ancient codices, and the miracle of their survival, as well as the more esoteric character of fifteenth-century texts, intended not so much for a reading public as for a select few who desired to nourish the spirit by having the Bible read to them when other occupations allowed.

An added insight is obtained into the history of the vernacular Bible if we consider the positive information supplied by royal and ecclesiastical prohibitions. We are not concerned so much with the decree of James I of Aragon in 1233 at the Council of Tarragona, since it reiterates a similar decision of the Council of Toulouse in 1229 against the Albigensians. The order to hand over to ecclesiastical authority all bibles *in romancio* is no direct proof that the bibles in question were written in any of the Hispanic vernaculars, nor have we proof that the decree was carried out. We are primarily interested in the documents and proceedings of the Inquisition. Soon after it was re-established in Castile (1478) and in Valencia (1484), Catalan and Spanish bibles and prayer books became its concern. The disappearance of the Valencian Bible of 1478 is the best proof that it was dangerous to own any such book.

At first the vernacular psalters and the liturgical Gospels and epistles escaped censure, and we see the latter revised as late as 1513 and re-printed several times by royal mandate. These biblical selections, mainly from the New Testament, are the only continuous texts which bridge the turn of the century and carry the tradition of the *Biblia romanceada* into the age of the Reformation and Counter-Reformation. Later, with the impending spread of Illuminism and Protestantism, versions of the New Testament came under the surveillance of the Inquisition.

At the end of the fifteenth century, however, the attention of the Inquisitors was directed mainly against the use of Scripture by the Jews and particularly by relapsed neo-Christians or crypto-Jews. Here, for the first time, we are prompted to use the term 'use of Scripture', because we find the Bible read not only as sacred history or a source of erudition, but as *the Book*. The Inquisition feared that the Jews were turning their former co-religionists back to the Old Law through the use of vernacular bibles. In the trials of the period, prayer is likewise mentioned as a point of accusation: prayer in Hebrew and prayer in the vernacular. The first Hebrew printer in Spain, Juan de Lucena, was mentioned in a trial for having printed a Jewish *siddur* of prayers in the vernacular. Although in earlier days translations of the biblical texts and shortened prayer books were probably intended for the benefit of women and the instruction of children, we may suppose that as persecutions grew and the study of Hebrew declined, a greater need was felt for vernacular versions.

This role of the Spanish Bible in the religious life of the Jews sets the translations made by Jews apart from those by Christians. Jewish bibles had characteristics all their own, not only because they were taken from the Massoretic text (the psalter of E 8 also is at least in part a translation from the Hebrew), but because they belonged to a tradition in which the vernacular played a different role. Unfortunately the

Jewish translations (late fourteenth and fifteenth century) are either fragmentary or bear traces of Christian intervention. In order to place them in the right perspective within the Judaeo-Spanish tradition, it might be well to invert the chronological order, and start from the vernacular Bible as the Jews printed it, as soon as they saw themselves relatively free to publish and circulate the book for their own use.

In 1547 there appeared in Constantinople from the press of Eliezer Soncino a polyglot Pentateuch in Hebrew characters containing a Spanish version. In 1553 the twenty-four Books of the Law were printed in full at Ferrara under the auspices of Ercole d'Este, but this time in Latin (black-letter) type.[1] The two texts, though separated in time and space, show striking similarities in language and manner of translation. The resemblance could be explained through textual tradition, for the manuscripts of the vernacular Bible, like the beautiful types that had been used in the early presses in Spain, could have followed the Jewish diaspora. Constantinople and Ferrara, via Venice, were not too far removed from each other in the sixteenth century. Soncino had himself come from Italy, where he had been an assistant of his father Gershom, the learned and pious printer who spent much energy in lending help to refugees from Spain.

The translators of the Ferrara Bible tell us that they had all the versions, both ancient and modern, at their disposal. In fact certain points of contact have been found between the Ferrara Bible and manuscript readings, especially in E 3–Ajuda. Yet even if the Jewish refugees had no Spanish versions tucked away among their possessions, we can safely say that they would have been able to reproduce much the same translations as we have in the two texts mentioned above. Through long years of memorizing and recitation, a certain biblical terminology and phraseology had become second nature to them, and they passed it on to the Portuguese Jews, even when the latter came to outweigh their Spanish co-religionists in number, as happened in the synagogue of Ferrara.

Since 1553 the Spanish Bible for the use of Sephardic Jews has been printed many times, along with their books of prayer. The scriptural texts of these editions go back substantially to the Ferrara Bible. What relation do they bear to earlier versions? A late-fifteenth-century

---

[1] *Cambridge History of the Bible: The West, from the Reformation to the Present Day*, p. 125.

fragment of a prayer book found in Cairo shows a great similarity with the printed texts in the *Shemone Ezreh*, while the psalms (114, 6–117) are somewhat further removed from the Ferrara Bible. We can therefore assume a tradition of long standing, probably oral, which explains the practical identity of the prayers and the similarity of the biblical texts.

Since so much textual evidence has been lost, both manuscript and printed, we have to make the most of the testimony of the Constantinople Pentateuch and the Ferrara Bible for what they are: not a medieval bible set in print, but two sixteenth-century interlinear translations, produced to a great extent by setting the traditional expressions and terminology between the lines of the Hebrew text. The Ferrara translators tell us plainly that they had not tried to imitate the niceties of contemporary speech. 'The phrase' reproduces the venerable and sententious language that was so natural to the Jews of old. In this sense, the Ferrara Bible can be said to be the main link between the vernacular Bible in Spain before 1500 and the religious literature of Sephardic Jews outside Spain, perpetuating a biblical tradition much more conservative and stable even than that of the English version.

Let us take the Ferrara Bible as the centre of a comparison. The two printed editions are slavish in their translations to the point of unintelligibility, reminding us of Aquila in antiquity. In the medieval Spanish versions faithfulness to the text is moderated by the desire to make the text understandable to the reader and to simplify somewhat the technical nature of certain portions of the sacred text. Much less frequent are some of the extreme Hebraisms of the Ferrara Bible, such as the postposition of the adjectives or the omission of the copula. The present participle imitating a similar form in Hebrew has not yet been shortened to the oxytonic form so characteristic of Judaeo-Spanish bibles and rituals. Yet, with the syntactical and even morphological traits of MSS E 3, E 19, E 4, Acad., Evora–E 5, and, to a somewhat lesser extent, of the Alba Bible, one could compose a goodly treatise of Hebrew grammar, illustrated with Spanish examples. Without the interposition of the latinity of Jerome, clauses follow one another in paratactical order. They are continually punctuated by the interjection *ahe* (*hinneh*, i.e. lo!, behold!), undeterred by repetitions, and derive different words from the same root, with extraordinary licence in word formation.

In Spanish guise the Semitic syntax sounds strange to the western ear, with its peculiar ways of introducing interrogative sentences, of paraphrasing relative pronouns in oblique cases and of expressing the superlative by means of the genitive. The exotic character of these renderings is further enhanced by the use, in most of the translations from the Hebrew, of the word *Adonay* for God, and by the transliteration of the tetragrammaton (*Yod He Vabf*). The preservation of the same number, whether it be singular (*tiniebra* vs. the Hieronymian *tenebrae–tinieblas*) or plural (*piadades*, 'mercies', *faces*, 'countenances', *vidas*, 'lives'), is another feature which makes the Jewish origin of these bibles immediately apparent. In some cases literalness may be due to the sheer routine of translation, and many an error is caused by the interpretation of a root in disregard of context. Fundamentally, however, faithfulness to the letter is a principle of translation inspired by respect for the sacred text. This respect is also responsible for many of the valid interpretations which have been confirmed by modern biblical scholarship. To the medieval mind, Jewish translations must have seemed to undermine the harmony between the Old Testament and the New, to sever the sayings of the prophets from Christ, and to withdraw the Bible from the speculations of Christian theology. That this might have been a concomitant intention of the Jews is not unlikely, and the Ferrara translators show it plainly (e.g. Isa. ix. 6).

By collating some key passages from the Ferrara Bible and the Constantinople Pentateuch one may group the earlier Spanish translations from the Hebrew and characterize them as unanimous in diminishing the messianic suggestions emphasized by Jerome (e.g. in using the abstract *justicia* or *justedad* instead of 'the just' in Isa. xii. 3, xlv. 8, etc.). They did away with the basis for Mariological interpretations (cf. Gen. iii. 15), and cut the ground from under the feet of those Christian theologians who saw in the Old Testament allusions to the Trinity (cf. Gen. ii. 18) or to the Holy Ghost and his gifts (cf. Isa. xi. 2). At times the ambiguity of the Hebrew text causes a divergence in the translations. One passage, however, must have been a touchstone by which Christians might detect the Jewish hand in a vernacular Bible: 'virgin' in Isa. vii. 14 is translated in the Ferrara Bible in three different ways; by *virgen* in some copies, and by the transliteration *alma* and by *moça* in others of the same edition. In the Alba Bible *alma* was finally allowed to remain (the manuscript shows evidence of the deletion of other words). E 3, E 5 and E 4 all have 'la virgen'. Other passages, however, no less divergent from Christian tradition, are taken literally from the Massoretic text, although some rabbinical interpolations have also been noticed: e.g. of the Targum of Onqelos in E 19 (Gen. xlix. 9, 12) and in E 4 (Gen. xlix. 25 and *passim*).

Literalness, as we have seen, manifests itself in form and content. A third criterion by which medieval translations can be distinguished by comparison with the Ferrara Bible is that of vocabulary. In the two sixteenth-century Judaeo-Spanish editions we find a striking mixture of Old Spanish words, which go back to the origin of the language, with recent borrowings from the Latin. A third, even more remarkable, category is that of vernacular terms, also found in Jewish documents of other Romance countries, which have acquired a technical or religious meaning in the translations of sacred Hebrew texts (e.g. *alsacion* for 'sacrifice', *templacion* for 'libation').

This, in brief, is the picture presented by the vocabulary of the Ferrara Bible and of the Constantinople Pentateuch which preceded it. Only a few of its terms (e.g. *meldar, oinar*) can be traced back to a Jewish *Sondersprache*, i.e. a parlance peculiar to the Jews, and even these words are absorbed into a bookish and artificial language which the translators shaped at will, in an effort to adhere as closely as possible to the Hebrew text. Whether ultimately some of the vocabulary of the Ferrara Bible goes back to a lost Latin translation of the Old Testament made by Jews in the early centuries of our era is not for us to decide. Their archaic and exotic character sets the Judaeo-Spanish bibles and prayer books apart from all others and gives them a tone reminiscent of the sacred language.

May the same be said also of earlier versions? None of our medieval manuscripts is so far from the normal prose of its century as the Ferrara Bible is from sixteenth-century Spanish. Still, familiarity with biblical Judaeo-Spanish or *Ladino* will make immediately apparent some unmistakable terms both in the bibles and in the prayer books. In the *Shemone Ezreh* of the latter part of the fifteenth century we read 'palacios de tu casa' for 'temple', 'enadimiento' for 'traditional offering', 'sangustias' for 'sufferings'. All these terms and others equally singular are found with more or less frequency in E 3–Ajuda, E 19, E 7, Evora–E 5, Nac. 10288, as well as in the Academy and Alba Bibles.

A comparison, however, of even solemn and often-recited passages like the Song of Moses in Exod. xv. 1–21 shows that distinctively Judaeo-Spanish terms were not used for the same verse by all the Jewish translators. We would have to collate a considerable portion of the biblical text in order to devise a scale of verbal concurrence. A short cut to valid conclusions would be the selection of a representative semantic cluster of synonyms, such as that of the concept of 'the wicked' which is so vividly represented throughout the Bible and especially in the Psalms. The E 8 Psalter, which is a translation from the Hebrew, but not in Judaeo-Spanish terminology, can be drawn upon for verbal comparison. To designate the 'sinner against God' and the 'enemy of the just' we find two expressions there which coincide with those of Jerome: *enemigos* (iii. 2, v. 9, vi. 8, vii. 6, ix. 14, used also where Jerome has *adversantes*, iii. 8, vii. 5, and *opprimentes*, vii. 7), and *obreros de maldat* ('workers of evil', v. 6 and vi. 8 for *qui operantur iniquitatem*); the third translation, *asaynnadores* (v. 9) or *ensannadores* (ix. 14, 'those who exert their hatred'), draws upon a typically Spanish word. In the Ferrara Bible, on the other hand, we have *enemigos* (iii. 8, v. 9) vying with *angustiadores* (iii. 2, vi. 8, vii. 5, 7) and *odiantes* (vi. 14), while the 'workers of iniquity' are *los obrantes tortura* (v. 6, vi. 9). If we add that, in v. 11, transgression is called *rebello*, we have the three roots *angust-*, *rebele-* and *tort-* or *tuert-*, i.e. the same roots which we find in medieval translations of the Bible made by Jews, in such expressions as *angustia*, *angustiador*, *angustiante*, *rebellar*, *rebellador* and *rebellante*, *tuerto*, *torticero*. These words are alien to the religious terminology of the Christian Bible and show that the versions of the Jews belong to a totally different tradition, whether they be of Latin or vernacular derivation. The same may be said of the names and attributes of God (particularly of *abastado* for *Saday*, instead of *Omnipotente*), of the expressions used to signify God's countenance, mercy and anger, and of the words for sin and salvation, hope and despair, and for all the other great themes of the Holy Scriptures. The medieval Spanish bibles contributed in varying degrees to the formation of a unique phraseology, which we find consecrated in the Ferrara edition of the Old Testament and in the devotional literature surrounding it.

There is still another way to classify medieval Jewish translations in relation to one another and to their milieu. Rabbi Mosse Arragel of Guadalajara, the translator of the Alba Bible (1422–33), gives us a clue to this when he says that 'the Christian nation had become very learned...and through intercourse with scholars...the knights and squires and the citizens *had* abandoned pure Castilian and mixed with it much Latin, so that Latin *had been* converted into Castilian'. Since many Latin words were commonly used in his time, he had decided to leave 'many Latin parts in the text and in the gloss without translating them'. However, in order to obviate any misunderstanding, especially by Jews, he would also give a vernacular interpretation of both Latin and Hebrew terms, 'so that the Jew would not be startled by the Latin nor the Christian by the Hebrew words'.

This promise was not entirely fulfilled. The Alba Bible contains a sufficient number of double translations to comprise a very interesting glossary of biblical terms. Other terms are explained in the introduction. The rest of the text is a mosaic of heterogeneous expressions, combining a good number of Judaeo-Spanish words, which Arragel employs without explanation, because they had become second nature to him, with a series of Latin or only slightly Hispanized words.

In the letters included there we read the request made by Luis de Guzmán to have a new translation of the Bible (with Jewish glosses); and the point-by-point reply of his cautious vassal asking to be excused from a task which he, a Jew, could not accomplish to the satisfaction of his Christian lord. The casuistical and self-abasing arguments of the rabbi provoked the anger of the Master of Calatrava, and it was settled that the Jew was to translate and gloss the Bible, for a fee; a Franciscan and a Dominican friar would supervise his work, Fr. Arias de Ensinas supplying the Christian glosses, and illuminators for the pictures that Arragel would describe.

In the whole middle ages we find no bible like that of Alba. In it rabbinic lore is combined with Catholic exegesis in the most heterogeneous fashion, and contradictory interpretations are given in succession: sound literal interpretations side by side with expositions of the symbolism of proper names; some enlightened historical explanations mixed with messianic glosses as naïve as those of the *Bible moralisée*. Even in the miniatures, which were supposed to be supplied by Christians according to Christian models, the Jewish and Christian traditions converge: 'This is a woman sitting in the midst of the amphora', the rabbi wrote as a direction for an illustration of Zech. v. 7 (cf. the Vulgate: 'et ecce mulier sedens in medio amphorae'); but the illuminator, more familiar with an *ephah* than with Jerome's *amphora*, made her sit in a square wooden box, which may well have been his interpretation of a corn-measure (*ephah*).

In medieval Spain it is impossible to draw a clear line of demarcation between the Church and the Synagogue. The Bible divided them and drew them together; it was the core of controversy as well as a source of mutual instruction wherein Christians could learn much from Jews. Beneath the differences of religious affiliation there was a common ground on which the adherents of the various faiths could meet. To Arragel Church, Synagogue and *almasgid* meant essentially the same thing.

How much of all this effort towards religious syncretism was prompted by the impelling necessity for Jews to find a modus vivendi with Christians as an alternative to feigned conversion it is hard to say. It is evident, however, from the preliminaries and glosses that philosophical interpretation is closest to Arragel's own way of expounding the books of the Law: Jacob's ladder symbolizes 'science and good habits'; Job is a model of 'political virtues'; the Song of Songs is the 'story of the soul'. Arragel is so taken up with philosophical issues, so full of Aristotelian and Stoic commonplaces, and so much concerned with the problem of free will, that the scholastic terminology in which those ideas are expressed not only permeates his commentary but overflows into his actual translation, as is evidenced by such words as *fillicidat*, *genus*, and *nichil*. His attitude and interests are very similar to those of other writers of his century. Theirs was not a humanism inspired by respect for pure classical forms, but rather an unrestrained enthusiasm for the wisdom of the past, and a desire to force the Spanish language into the moulds of a spurious Latinity.

In the translation of the Bible Arragel made a constant effort to harmonize the Hebrew and the Christian texts. For instance in the passage containing the famous interpretation of Aquila and Jerome of the 'horns of Moses' (Exod. xxxiv. 29), caused by confusing *qeren* and *qaran* ('horn' and 'ray', p. 301), E 3, E 4 and Ferr. take the metaphorical meaning, 'the skin of his face shone'. Arragel, mindful of both the Massoretic text and the Vulgate, tries to do justice to both. The English of his version runs: 'Coming down from the mountain Moses did not know that the skin of his face shone like rays that are bent backwards like horns'; and the illuminator surrounded the head of Moses with lines (rays) directed outwards and curled at the ends.

Such feats of ingenuity were not always forced on Arragel by the watchful eye of the friars. The vocabulary he uses provides internal evidence for his spontaneous and constant effort to Latinize Holy Writ. Adherence to Jerome's diction was only part of the process of minimizing the differences between Christians and Jews; part was due to the polishing of the texts to suit the taste of the times, as in the case of the Bible of Alba.

Arragel lifted entire phrases from the Vulgate, even those of such a marked ecclesiastical tone as Song of Songs iv. 7: 'toda eres tu fermosa, la mi amiga, e macula en ti no es', which to the ear of the Christian middle ages suggested the Immaculate Conception. None of the other Jewish translators went quite so far. Therefore the proportion between Latinisms of Hieronymian or other origin, on the one hand, and vernacular and Judaeo-Spanish terms on the other, should be used as a criterion in classifying the rendering made by the Jews.

In the first chapter of Isaiah, for example, we see Arragel writing 'el verbo del Señor', where the Academy MS has 'la palabra del Señor', 'lauadvos e mundificadvos', where the Academy MS has 'lavadvos, alimpiadvos'; inversely, we find in the latter codex expressions like *kalendas* whose Hebrew equivalent Arragel translates 'cabo de luna', and *cogitaciones* for which Arragel has *obras*. On the other hand, we also recognize in both many of the expressions common to Judaeo-Spanish translations, and which are represented more fully in E 3 and E 5. The terms which characterize the former in their effort at Latinization of the Hebrew Bible do not appear in E 3 and E 5, a fact which enhances the conservative character of the two latter bibles, and groups them together verbally and ideologically. The contrast, however, is not always as clear-cut as it would appear from this chapter of Isaiah. In E 4 this contrast underscores the composite character of the manuscript, since in the chapter just mentioned, as in most of the major prophets, E 4 is a copy of E 5, while in other books it shows a greater affinity to the diction of the Alba Bible.

Latinization is an important clue to the chronology of our biblical versions; it also reveals much about the milieu in which bible translations were made, the spirit which informed the interpreters, and the relations established between the sacred page and the reader. The admission of Latinisms and the creation of pseudo-Latinisms can also be taken as a touchstone for comparing translations made by Jews with those by Christians. In E 4, for instance, a word like *notificar*, for *dezir*, can be found both in the parts translated from the Hebrew and in those translated from the Latin, a peculiarity paralleled in the translation of the Sunday Gospels by Gonzalo García de Santa María (1484), where Christ is for ever *certifying*, instead of *saying*: 'Amen, amen, dico tibi' being rendered 'certifico, certificote'.

Jewish interpreters stood directly between the Hebrew and the Spanish, whereas Christian translators into the vernacular stood at the end of a long chain of texts from the Hebrew to the Vulgate through the Septuagint and the Old Latin. They could lean on Jerome and avail themselves of a ready-made terminology. Thus, among many other instances, *shekel* appears in E 8 as *siclo* while E 4 has *peso*; a Nazirite is a *nazareno* in E 8 while E 4 has *apartado*. Most biblical Hebraisms, such as Belzebub, Satanás, penetrated into Spanish through Christian usage. Words of Greek origin likewise came into Spanish through their adoption by Jerome from the Septuagint (e.g. *holocausto*, *profeta*), to say nothing of words derived from Latin expressions which Christian authors had adopted to express a new meaning, such as *bendecir*, *oblación*, *redención*, and many others.

Not all terms consecrated by the authority of Jerome, however, were incorporated into the vernacular Bible from its inception. *Scenophegia* for 'the feast of Tabernacles' is a typical transliteration appearing in the oldest translation from the Latin (E 6), while in E 8 we find 'la fiesta de las tiendas'. In many other instances the translators of the thirteenth century show a clear desire to interpret the Latin text and to express the content in terms of contemporary life and speech. Paul is not only an *apostol* but also a *mandadero* (I Cor. xv. 9, ix. 2, E 6), and *evangelium* is translated also as *mensajería*. A familiarity of tone and a vagueness of meaning are introduced by the use of popular terms: 'the *mysteries* of the Kingdom' become 'la *fazienda* del regno', 'the business of God', just as German mystics spoke of 'die Wirtschaft Gottes'.

E 8, E 6, E 2 and the *General Estoria* show us what the Spanish Bible might have been if a truly vernacular tradition had established itself. Like the early French translators, Spanish interpreters of the thirteenth century created a biblical vocabulary by taking some words from everyday speech, adopting others from Jerome, and adjusting still others to the sound-system and rhythm of the Spanish language (e.g. *afijamiento* for *filiatio, confessamiento* for confession, *sinoa* for synagogue). If these first translations had had a wider diffusion and authority they might have influenced the vernacular more permanently. As it is, those expressions which are used both in the Bible and in Christian doctrine and devotion are almost the only ones preserved today in their old form: *ayuno, diezmo, mandamiento* (one of the many words in *-miento* so typical of the old bibles). It is also noteworthy that of the verbs in *-iguar* only *santiguar* is still in use, but with the more specific and concrete meaning of 'make the sign of the Cross'. The same word in its more general connotation, together with words of similar formation, has returned to its Latin form, just as *aorar, batear* and *preigar* have been replaced by *adorar, bautizar* and *predicar*.

When the tendency to re-Latinize won the day, a whole set of new terms was taken over from the Vulgate: e.g. *abominar* for *aborrecer, consumir* for *destroir, contricion* for *quebranto*, to which the influence of post-medieval times added other neologisms such as *ázimo* for *cenceño, iniquidat* for *maldat, oprobio* for *denuesto*, along with such adjectives predicated of God as *altísimo, eterno, omnipotente* while *Dios nuestro Señor* and *todopoderoso* ('all-powerful') preserved the flavour of the old vernacular tradition.

With verbal innovation based on a foreign language, the self-explanatory or transparent character of the original words was lost and a new esoteric terminology was formed with a specialized function distinct from everyday language. We can deduce from the translation of the Sunday Gospels, referred to above, that the translator reserved the old term *denuesto* for insult with reference to man, but considered *blasfemia* proper to be used with reference to God. The Hebrew *racha* was reinstated at Matt. v. 22 instead of the *desmeollado* ('deprived of marrow', 'brainless') of E 6. Such Grecisms as *architriclino* and *gazofilacio* were introduced in Spanish and Catalan translations and were thenceforth a matter for homiletic elucidation.

Later, many of these learned terms were incorporated into the official lexicon of the Academy (1726), and to this day the Spanish dictionary abounds in second-hand scriptural references. The ascetical and mystical writers of the sixteenth and seventeenth centuries, from whose works the quotations of the lexicon originate, were the main intermediaries between Scripture and the general public after the Bible itself had become a closed book because of the remoteness of the language and the ban on its use in the vernacular. In the last decades of the fifteenth century, however, the process of Latinization had gone half-way, and had affected some parts of the Bible more than others. Several editions of the Gospels and of the Psalms, published before the close of the century, show a popular demand for at least some parts of Scripture, while the Valencian Bible of 1478, a de luxe edition of some 400–50 folios, falls into the tradition of fifteenth-century bibliophilia.

Vocabulary, which is itself an avenue of interpretation, is intimately connected with the short periphrastic glosses that we find in our texts. They may be attributed to the fact that the vernacular tongues by their very nature are more analytical than Latin. Moreover, the Christian translators had to make the Hebrew phraseology intelligible to the Western mind and bring the intricate terminology of Paul closer to the reader. Thus the interpreter of the Sobradiel Gospels lengthens Matt. v. 4 to read, *Posseyran la terra, ço es, la terra dels vivents* ('They shall possess the land, i.e. the land of the living'). Pseudo-erudition, especially in later translations, plays havoc with the text: *Echo* becomes 'the goddess Echo' in E 4, Wisd. xvii. 14, and *neomenia* is misspelled and misinterpreted by the same translator as a geographical term at Ps. 81: 4.

Apart from these glosses which grow out of the context, we have lengthy commentaries appended in the margins (complete in the Alba Bible; fragmentary in the Academy MS and in Nac. 10288), or short glosses interspersed within the text itself. Such is the case with the Christian translation E 8–E 6, whose few glosses bear some resemblance in places to the *Glossa ordinaria*. To a special category belongs the Spanish counterpart to the *Bible moralisée*, with its Latin and vernacular explanations alongside the biblical core. In 1490 a book of 'Evangelios moralizados', from Advent to Passion Sunday, was published in Saragossa under the name of José López and dedicated to the duchess of Arévalo. A few years before, the Aragonese jurist Gonzalo García de Santa María had translated, along with the Gospels and epistles for Sundays and propers of the Mass, the *Postilla* of William of Paris. Whereas the latter had made his compilation for the use of the lower clergy, the translator intended his work for the laity for private devotional reading. Another type of presentation of the New Testament which enjoyed great popularity was the *Vita Christi* of Ludolph of

Saxony, translated into Castilian by Fr. Ambrosio Montesino and published in 1502–3, with the passages from Scripture printed in 'broader letters' and accompanied by glosses according to the four senses of Scripture.

Other channels through which parts of the Bible reached those who did not know Latin include translations and compilations of Gregory's *Moralia in Job*, and the homilies of Origen, Chrysostom and other Fathers or, in the case of Hebrew, the translation of Maimonides' *Guide to the Perplexed* (p. 271) by Pedro de Toledo (1432), preserved in MS 10289 of the Biblioteca Nacional, Madrid. The life and teachings of Jerome were incorporated (as transmitted by Vincent of Beauvais) into the *Historia de los quatro dotores*. Jerome enjoyed great authority in Spain for his theories on translation and on the metrical system of the poetic sections of the Bible. However, in popular devotion and in literature he was cherished especially for the legendary elements of his biography and for his teaching on virginity and the duties of women.

Parts of the Bible, especially the penitential psalms, were singled out for special commentary in Spanish and Catalan. Moreover, since the Books of Hours, so rich in biblical content, were the main source of the interior life for the laity, it would be interesting to know to what extent the vernacular was used in them. Recently a leaf was found in a Latin codex of the library of the cathedral chapter at Tarazona, carefully written in Gothic letters (fourteenth century). It contains translations of two liturgical prayers and of Psalm 129. Offices in the vernacular, we may add, were also sought after by the Inquisition in the sixteenth century, and this may be one of the causes of their scarcity today and of the fact that the printed copies preserved in Spanish originated in Paris, Antwerp and Lyons. *Las Horas de Nuestra Señora con muchos otros oficios y oraciones* (Paris, 1499, B.N. Paris, Velins 1501) is a jewel of early typographical skill in which manuscript calligraphy and illumination are passed on to the art of printing. In it the translation of the psalms flows with ease, as if it had been rounded and smoothed by many generations of prayerful readers.

Preaching was another channel for the diffusion of bible texts in the vernacular. Unfortunately no sermons in Spanish are preserved that can compare in antiquity and extent with the French homilies of Maurice of Sully. Catalan fares better in this respect. In fact, the history of Catalan prose opens with a short fragment of a collection of sermons, strongly influenced by Provençal. This important document, in which the Gospels for several Sundays are explained (mainly according to the moral meaning), is known as the *Homelies d'Organya* and belongs to the end of the twelfth century. Two other series of homiletic materials of the fifteenth century have been found in Marseilles and Barcelona respectively. The latter manuscript (Biblioteca de Catalunya 479) is particularly interesting because it contains fragmentary notes in Catalan, in which the scriptural theme is set forth in threefold rhymed phrases. The use of this mnemonic device reminds us of the Catalan rhymed bible mentioned on p. 468, and of the devotional literature in rhymed couplets which was popular in the fifteenth century. The Marseilles manuscript (Public Library 1095) contains an extensive collection of homilies of the beginning of the fifteenth century or earlier, in which scriptural material is interwoven with apocryphal narratives. In Spanish the sermons intercalated in Ambrosio Montesino's *Epistolas y Evangelios* (1512) give us an idea of what vernacular homilies were like. Moreover, we have a translation of the *Speculum laicorum* that might have been used by preachers. The many biblical quotations appended to each of its chapters in idiomatic translation constitute a scriptural concordance in the vernacular under the headings of the Christian virtues.

Very revealing for the history of the exposition of the Bible in medieval preaching are the many sermons delivered by Vincent Ferrer. An ardent advocate of the study of the Bible, he preached in plain language, and only in Valencian. His sermons all follow more or less the same pattern: a brief quotation from Scripture, suggested by the Mass of the day; a doctrinal interpretation of the same with divisions of the subject-matter into three or four parts. Emphasis is successively laid on doctrine, the mysteries of the life of Christ, and the practical lessons for daily living.

Adaptations in the vernacular of biblical matter or of short biblical texts were also found in catechetical works, such as the *Biblia parva* which tradition attributes to Peter Paschasius (thirteenth century). In this, quotations from the Old Testament are woven into a rather disorganized assemblage of heterogeneous matter expounded in Valencian. To the first half of that century belongs a short treatise for confessors, which is one of the first specimens of Spanish prose, *Los diez mandamientos*. The Commandments are quoted in close adherence to the

Vulgate, but the vocabulary which the anonymous Navarrese cleric used is that of the vulgar tongue and reminds us of the thirteenth-century bible translations. If we compare this early text of the Commandments with a later catechism in verse, the *Doctrina de discrición* of Pedro de Veragüe, or with other documents of the same nature, we can see the process of gradual Latinization which has been mentioned above. In medieval Spanish literature also we are struck by the fact that the same biblical quotations appear in many different forms (e.g. Matt. xxii. 37–9, where *mens* was rendered as *voluntad* or *pensamiento*, or omitted, and *proximus* as *christiano, veʒino* and *cercano*, until *próximo* prevailed). The authority of the Vulgate and the spontaneous tendency to incorporate religious concepts into the language are two forces that pull vocabulary and phraseology in opposite directions.

The Bible is one of the favourite sources for the didactic treatises of the fourteenth and fifteenth century. It is quoted profusely in the *Castigos y documentos del rey D. Sancho*, where it is beautifully blended into the rest of the text. The Book of Tobit, a favourite source of instruction for Christian matrimony, inspires a long composition by Fernán de Guzman entitled *La doctrina que dieron a Sarra*. The exhortations given to Sarah by her parents as she goes off with her husband (x. 13) are translated and amplified at length. To modern taste the sixty-nine stanzas of this poem, heavy with polysyllabic words and dry doctrinal disquisitions, may not seem a very desirable wedding gift, but the noble ladies to whom the poem was dedicated would have been pleased with the erudite and authoritative counsel of their learned adviser. We may mention in passing that the Bible was exploited also for one of the favourite common-places of this type of literature, i.e. the warfare waged against or on behalf of the feminine sex. We shall cite only two examples: The *Libre de les dones* of Jaume Roig (*c.* 1456), in which Solomon is brought forward to heap upon women the responsibility for all the disasters of the world since the Flood, and the *Libro de las claras e virtuosas mujeres* of D. Alvaro de Luna, where the account of Creation and the authority of Paul (I Cor. vii. 4) are adduced to prove that man and woman are created equal as regards their eternal destiny. A gallery of biblical women is introduced to exemplify the virtues.

While allusion to characters of the Bible and citation of biblical passages and especially biblical proverbs were typical of didactic poets like the Marquis of Santillana or Juan de Mana and constitute a favourite ornament in the *Cancioneros*, a wider public was reached through religious drama. The scarcity or total lack of Latin liturgical drama in Castile was compensated for by the flowering of vernacular plays, as we can surmise from a 147-verse fragment of an *Auto de los Reyes Magos* of the twelfth century, found in the cathedral archives at Toledo. Other specimens (few and far between as compared with the unique flowering of the religious and biblical theatre of the Golden Age) go back to the fifteenth century: the *Representación del Nacimiento de Nuestro Señor* and the *Lamentaciones fechas para Semana Santa*, both by Gómez Manrique, and an anonymous *Auto de la huida de Egipto*, discovered in 1944. These pieces of simple dialogue illustrate the two cycles of plays for Christmas and Easter to which Alphonso the Wise had alluded in his *Partidas* (ed. Paris 1846, I, 115). They also show the important part played by popular traditions originating in the apocryphal books. Some elements, such as the Sibylline prophecy preserved in the description of the Toledan 'Sibila de la noche de Navidad', would lead us away from the Bible altogether. On the other hand, biblical texts may have been used. In the Valencian *Mystery of Elche*, ultimately of medieval origin, in the scene of the burial of the Virgin, the Apostles and the Jews are represented as singing together alternate verses from the psalm 'In exitu Israel'.

Spanish medieval literature as a whole belongs to our history of the Bible in the vulgar tongue, as regards both narration of scriptural or apocryphal stories (as in the *Libro de los Tres Reys d'Orient* of the first half of the thirteenth century), and the way in which biblical matter is interpreted (as in Gonzalo de Berceo's *Sacrificio de la misa*, where a parallel is drawn between the sacrificial rites of the old dispensation and the sacrifice of the Mass). In many cases we cannot speak of a direct contact with the Bible because other Latin sources stand in between, nor can we be sure whether the Latin text was used exclusively or together with a vernacular rendering. In any case, the translations of the Scriptures into the vulgar tongue can always serve as a term of comparison. Besides the Vulgate, Jews and converts writing in the vernacular had access to the Hebrew text or had it in their memory. The scholar Solomon Ha Levi, for example, who after his conversion bore the name of Pablo de Santa María, wrote in verse a universal history, *Las siete edades trovadas* (1418), in which he translates Gen. iii. 15 as

'la tu cabeza ell quebrantará' ('*he* shall crush your head'; Vulgate: *illa*).
It is significant of Spain's unique position that such a biblical story as
that of Joseph could be told not only from the Vulgate, as everywhere
else in Christendom, but also according to the Koran, and through a
combination of the Bible text and *yashar*. The latter adaptation, which
is in verse, *Coplas de Yoçef*, may have been recited for the feast of
Purim. It is preserved in rabbinical script and offers such unmistakable
traces of Judaeo-Spanish as the verb *oinar*, characteristic of the bibles
of the fifteenth century.

Writing in the vernacular, the Jews were instrumental in enriching
doctrinal literature with the wisdom of their race, particularly with
biblical maxims. They could do so without depending on the Vulgate,
and this freedom made their expression more effective. On the other
hand, the presence of the Jews and the *conversos* in Spain made the
Christians more attentive to the letter when quoting Scripture and
more aware of the differences between the various textual traditions.

It would be misleading, however, to emphasize the differences at the
expense of the similarities that bind Spain, and especially Catalonia, to
the rest of Europe. The spiritual interpretation of Scripture was used
and abused here just as much as anywhere else. The examples of this
are legion. One is afforded by the *Vita Christi* of a Valencian noble-
woman and abbess, Isabel de Villena. The canonical Gospels account
for only part of the narrative, yet this nun quotes continually from the
Old and New Testaments with the ease gained from long acquaintance
with Scripture and from reading and chanting the Office. In this work
biblical texts are generally quoted out of context and placed in a unified
framework of a different kind, in which the limitations of time and space
are abandoned and the Old Testament is interwoven with the New,
much as the Liturgy weaves the two together. Allegory embellishes it
with endless processions of personified virtues and with the enumera-
tion of articles of clothing and adornment which are interpreted
symbolically; thus the eight diamonds in the necklace of Mary are a
symbol of the Beatitudes. While we read Isabel de Villena's book we
marvel at her ability to piece together such a many-storied castle; but
in the end we wonder whether so great and complicated a construction
was not ready to fall under its own weight.

The waning middle ages lingered on in Spain longer than in other
parts of Europe. This is not the moment to talk of the spiritual move-

ments of the sixteenth century, and of the part Bible-reading and Gospel-preaching played in them. We shall only point out that although sixteenth-century translations have been an object of controversy and of historical research they have never been studied with internal criteria in mind as a part of a continuous tradition. When Francisco de Enzinas[1] offered his translation of the New Testament to Charles V in Brussels in 1543 he complained that while Spaniards prided themselves on being first in everything, in the matter of the Bible in the vernacular they were not even last. In reality the use of the vernacular Scriptures was not so foreign to medieval Spain as Enzinas and other dissatisfied reformers may have thought. It could be shown that their own translation owed much to the earlier tradition in the vulgar tongue. While the study of Luther's bible has led to the investigation of medieval German translations the same cannot be said of those in Spanish. For the most part, Spanish and Catalan bibles lie hidden in manuscripts scattered in many different libraries, awaiting those who will study and publish them.

[1] *C. Hist. Bible: The West, from the Reformation to the Present Day*, p. 125.

CHAPTER X

ERASMUS IN RELATION TO THE MEDIEVAL BIBLICAL TRADITION

Were we to take the title set for our study in any narrow sense, a single sentence would cover it completely: there is no relationship at all between Erasmus and the medieval biblical tradition. Read, for example, Miss Beryl Smalley's excellent book on *The study of the Bible in the middle ages*, after collating everything that Erasmus wrote on the Bible: we have the impression that Erasmus simply knew nothing whatever about all that Miss Smalley has taken for her subject-matter. Hugh of Saint-Cher and Nicholas of Lyra get only a cursory mention in the *Apology* to his New Testament. Though the name is not mentioned, he is probably referring to the *Glossa*—and that with some acerbity—in one page of the *Ratio* in which he denounces wrong quotations of the Fathers. And that is about all. So far as biblical studies are concerned, Erasmus's knowledge of the middle ages is pretty well limited to the dialectical use made by the later schoolmen of truncated texts, wrenched from their contexts. He acknowledges—rather distantly—Thomas Aquinas's exegetical principles; but so far as traditional exegesis is concerned he applies himself closely only to the Fathers, to Jerome especially, and then more and more to the Greek Fathers. His interest very soon fixed on textual criticism of the Bible, in particular of the New Testament, as it had been re-established (rather than simply revived) by Lorenzo Valla, under the influence of Jerome and the Origen of the Hexapla. Then, on this basis, he set himself to give new life to meditation on the divine word, and the preaching of it. This meditation and preaching owed their chief inspiration to the *Devotio moderna* and to Colet, and were strengthened by the example given by the Fathers: but of the whole medieval tradition they took practically no account at all.

This fact is the more natural in that—as Miss Smalley, following Samuel Berger, but in more detail, has made clear—medieval efforts towards a scientific exegesis were more or less limited to the Old

Testament. In effect, western exegetes of the middle ages could easily find some rabbi willing to initiate them into Hebrew and rabbinic exegesis. Real knowledge of Greek was much less accessible to them; and it might well have seemed to them (even though it was an illusion) that they had the ancient exegetical tradition of the first Christian centuries adequately summed up for them in such commentators as Ambrose and Augustine. Erasmus, on the other hand, was never a great Hebrew scholar, nor—even for his own day—a real specialist in the Old Testament. Rather he represents that first flowering of New Testament exegesis, based on criticism and philology, through which the Renaissance—while restoring the link with the patristic tradition, and especially with the Alexandrian—was to prepare the way for modern exegesis. So Erasmus's biblical work cannot be defined in terms of the influence on him of whatever authentic critical tradition there might be in medieval exegesis, nor even of his own conscious reaction against it. It was a kind of fresh endeavour, in a field virtually unexplored by his predecessors; even in the field alongside the one that was to be his own he was almost completely ignorant of what they had achieved, or projected.

In this study we shall attempt to set out in detail, step by step, Erasmus' awakening to biblical problems, and the circumstances and possible influences that were to orient him in his path. At the same time we shall see how his approach to these problems was gradually modified, and became clearer. After that we shall be in a position to review the enormous amount of work he devoted to the Bible, and appreciate it historically, taking account of our present knowledge of his more or less immediate predecessors; yet we must not forget that he shared that knowledge only in a very small degree, or in none.

I

Huizinga has very clearly demonstrated the paradox in Erasmus's earliest letters: the young monk of Steyn monastery, formed in the most austere and most puritanical traditions of the last great spiritual school of the middle ages, making his first appearance as an enthusiastic and slightly intoxicated disciple of Italian humanism. Renaudet rightly stressed, when he called his last book on him *Erasmus and Italy*, both this opening note and the most continuous *motif* of Erasmus' life. Yet from that moment Erasmus was a reader—and already a passionate one—of Jerome, and was shortly to become his editor. What is more—and what was to follow will show it more and more clearly—no matter how exasperated he may have been with religious in general and with his own congregation in particular, he had been ineradicably impressed by the *Devotio moderna* in which he was formed at Steyn. Nor is impressed a strong enough word: 'inspired', rather.

What was the *Devotio moderna*? After it had been propagated by Gerard de Groote amongst the canons of Windesheim and the Brethren of the Common Life, it had affected other congregations, amongst them the canons of Sion, to whom was attached the monastery of Steyn where Erasmus was taken in after his initial studies with the Brothers of Deventer. It was the fruit of the first reaction against decadent scholasticism; the depth and inwardness of the religious life were sought in meditation on the gospel: and this form of edification had already taken a moral and psychological character. Erasmus was not merely to keep all these characteristics to the very end: he was to develop them in a more and more personal fashion, and explicitly to make them the real object of those of his researches that, at first sight, seem most purely critical.

Then again we must not forget that this spirituality was a spirituality of teachers. By that very fact it was to clear the way for Erasmus's discovery of Italian humanism, even though, in the first flush of the discovery, he might seem to lose sight of the wholly interior and spiritual ideal of his first teachers. In effect, though we must wait a long while yet before formulating humanism into a humane ideal separate from the study of *litterae humaniores*, it is nevertheless Erasmus's humanity, with all its sensibility and its receptiveness to real life—far richer in his nature than at a superficial examination one might suppose—that was at once to feed avidly on the Italy and the ancient world that he was discovering anew. Far from eradicating the *Devotio moderna*, this fullness of humanity and this realism were simply to leaven it with a new substance, while in philological method he discovered the instrument both of his own personal response and of the renewal of a spirituality that had appeared to be exhausted. Erasmus was to find the key to the reconciling of these diverse elements, and their future full development, in what was probably the most crucial book he ever read: Valla's *Adnotationes* on the New Testament.

Erasmus discovered this book—apparently by chance—as late as

1504, at Louvain, at the Premonstratensian monastery. True, as a passionate disciple he had made a summary of Valla's *Elegantiae* when he was still just eighteen, and perhaps he also knew the *De voluptate* at about that time. But in 1504 the Italian master was still for him merely the most lucid exponent of literary humanism—contemptuous, no doubt, in a way that was bold and disturbing, of all that could be called worn-out or dead in medieval religiosity, offering instead a humanity eager for self-expression and full of self-confidence. Then suddenly Valla became for Erasmus the man who had put into his hand the instrument that would make possible a renewal of religious thought itself: the instrument was that resurgence of philological studies which might have seemed far more likely to favour a revival of wholly pagan ideas and feelings.

It is hard to estimate here just how far Erasmus, discovering this new aspect of Valla, was faithful to Valla's own deepest thought, or how far he submitted Valla to one of those modifying processes that entirely transform the very thing that one has taken most to one's heart. However unexpected the comparison may appear, there is here something analogous to what probably happened to Aquinas, in respect of the method he inherited from Abelard. To have made of Abelard's dialectical criticism—so vigorously opposed by William of Saint-Thierry and St Bernard—the chief prop of a radically renewed theology which still remained faithful to its own tradition is unquestionably no more astonishing an intellectual feat than Erasmus' own; the turning of Valla's philological criticism into the point of departure for a renewal of biblical studies firmly spiritual and evangelical in its orientation. And yet, just as Abelard's intention was much less profane than it might appear at first sight, so it seems too that Valla himself was not the mere hypocrite he has for too long been judged to be—his declarations of 'reforming' intentions may well have been belied by his sensualism more than by his criticism.

However that may be, Erasmus's reading of the *Adnotationes* was unquestionably dominated by his old familiarity with Jerome, and provides the connecting link between the spiritual accent of the *Devotio moderna* and humanism's regard for scholarship. In this way Erasmus was to arrive at a clear programme of biblical studies. He had already sketched it out in 1497, at Paris; and his first stay at Oxford a little later, together with his first contacts with Colet, had helped him to fill the lines in firmly, though not without some reservations in his mind; and these he was now about ready to define.

Certainly the Dean of St Paul's helped more than anyone else to restore and fortify Erasmus's faith, strengthening it by his own familiar example of what humanism could bring to a spiritual search freed from the narrow bounds of a decadent religious tradition. At the same time his rather improvised method had inspired very characteristic reservations in Erasmus: these are clearly to be seen in their very interesting friendly controversy about the Agony of Jesus at Gethsemane. It becomes quite clear here that Erasmus was to be one of those who can get no edification from exegesis where they suspect some misinterpretation. Then again, Erasmus had already moved over from studying Jerome to the direct study of Origen—doubtless after his stay at Saint-Bertin Collégiale at Saint-Omer in the company of his friend Jean Vitrier, warden of the Franciscans. Nevertheless, the discovery of the *Adnotationes* was to provide him with the instrument which he was looking for at this same period, in his first rather tentative commentary on the Epistle to the Romans. After he had had Valla's text printed, his second stay in England—marked particularly by his friendship with Sir Thomas More—led him to confirm most strongly the grand design that was to absorb him from then on; and in this he was profoundly helped by More's understanding, balanced as it was between real humanity and most Christian piety.

In the spring of 1506, by way of prelude to the critical editions that were to follow, he published a new Latin version of the epistles and Gospels, based on a manuscript doubtless discovered at St Paul's. The poem composed a short while afterwards on the road to Italy (where he was to take a doctorate in theology at Turin, without difficulty) witnesses to the fact that his project was now in definitive form. The letter of 28 October 1507 to Aldus Manutius shows what an important place a critical edition of the Greek New Testament had now taken in his plans.

The stay with Aldus himself in 1508 at Venice gave him leisure to deepen his knowledge of the Greek Fathers, particularly Gregory Nazianzen. The dedication of the *Adages* to Lord Mountjoy shows us Erasmus already in possession of that balanced view of exegesis that was to be completely his in the *Ratio verae theologiae*. Philological study of the text prepares the way for a meditation drawing together all that he found most sure in the spiritual exegesis of the Fathers, notably of Origen's school.

Renaudet has stressed the importance of the period 1521–9, as the decisive years in the life of Erasmus. And so they were, in so far as in those years his attitude to the Protestant Reformation and the positions that he was to take up were defined. But the years we have just summarized are perhaps still more important, for his solely personal orientation as a Christian humanist and as a thinker. It was then that the programme and the ideal were defined: those of Reforming humanism. And in order to defend both programme and ideal, Erasmus was to be led, between 1521 and 1529, to reject equally the Protestant Reformation and a purely conservative Catholic attitude of reaction. In this light what may have seemed to be tergiversation from a wholly exterior point of view shows itself more profoundly to be faithfulness to a design elaborated slowly, but already formed by 1508–9 at the latest. And this design was: to reform the Church from within by a renewal of biblical theology, based on philological study of the New Testament text, and supported by a knowledge of patristics, itself renewed by the same methods. The final object of it all was to nourish that chiefly moral and spiritual reform already quite clearly conceived in the *Enchiridion militis Christiani*, published at Antwerp in February 1504.

What we must stress, in fact, is how far Erasmus—under the influence of Colet and even more so of Thomas More—how far he was always to be from shutting himself up in a purely academic study of the Bible. For him, rigorously scientific biblical study must sustain an effort to renew the interior life, and the interior life must itself be at once the agent and the beneficiary of a renewal of the whole of Christian society. Not simply Erasmus's spiritual writings, but even the moral and political *Adages* and the *Institutio principis christiani* must be taken into account in the background when we study Erasmus's biblical work. We should otherwise lose sight of a dimension essential to the intellectual and moral search in which that biblical work had its setting.

II

After the period we have now reached, Erasmus's fundamental work was to progress methodically. From the point of view here adopted we may distinguish four different lines of work, parallel with each other, and complementary. First, the establishing and critical elucidation of the biblical texts; alongside it, the editions of the great patristic commentators; then, the exegetical works properly so called, in which these two fundamental researches yield their fruit; and finally, the methodological works, which in their first state constitute a sort of preface to the various other studies, but which—in return—were nourished and enlarged by them as they went along.

Let us try, first of all, to follow the first three lines of this vast whole: later we shall find in the fourth how they bear on each other. And that will bring us directly to our assessment of the constructive work of Erasmus, in relation to his medieval predecessors.

As regards his critical editions of biblical texts, clearly Erasmus's master-work is his edition of the Greek text of the New Testament with an introduction, new Latin translation, and notes. Envisaged, as we have said, at least as early as October 1507, and first suggested to Aldus Manutius, the edition was in great part prepared during a stay in England (notably at Cambridge, where Erasmus gave a course in the summer of 1511 on Jerome) but was finally given to Hieronymus Froben, at Basle, to print. It came out at the end of February 1516, under the title *Novum Instrumentum*. This title contributed at least as much as the actual or supposed boldness of some of the textual readings, of the notes, and of the Latin translation, to scandalize the die-hards.

In 1519 Froben produced a second edition in which, along with other things, Erasmus gave up the violently criticized title. He decided, on the other hand, to translate the *logos* of John by *sermo*: and this was a new cause for scandal, even though it represented a return to the oldest Latin translations. In 1522 the third edition, still more prudent, went so far—in the face of attacks, especially by Jerome Aleander—as to restore the *comma Johanneum*. Erasmus decided, at this same time, to take out his introduction, which he had notably developed over the preparation of the editions, and to publish it as a separate little work, the *Ratio verae theologiae*. (He had already published it under this same title in 1519, in its original state.) The fourth edition, of 1527, was to push the concessions to his opponents so far as to reproduce the Vulgate text alongside his own proposed new Latin version. The fifth edition, of 1535, the last in Erasmus's own lifetime, adds little fresh.

It is an exaggeration to maintain, as some still do, that Erasmus only used the Greek manuscripts that he had found in the library of the Basle Dominicans for his edition. He himself protested against accusa-

tions of this sort, in his dedicatory letter to Leo X. And it seems un-
deniable that he used notes, at any rate, which he had made on the
manuscripts that he had seen in England. The customary comparisons
with the polyglot edition of Alcalá, undertaken earlier, are scarcely
convincing evidence, since that edition was published much later.

Erasmus's Greek text was to remain the principal source for the great
editio regia of the printer Robert Estienne (1550), and hence of the
textus receptus that he was to establish. It corresponds to the manuscript
tradition which in fact prevailed in the Greek Church; and not until
the end of the nineteenth century were editions proposed that differed
other than on points of detail.

Alongside this basic work come the patristic editions undertaken by
Erasmus. They all, in his mind, had the main aim of making available
again the knowledge of an exegesis of the Bible at once truly traditional
in the Church and close enough to the cultural background of the New
Testament for its theological interpretation to remain laden with
literary and historical data of objective value.

The Cambridge course (of 1511) on Jerome was to be the immediate
preparation for several years of research, in which Erasmus was to
establish the text of that Father. The edition appeared—again with
Froben—two months after the *Novum Instrumentum*. Originally dedicated, like that work, to Leo X, it was in fact offered, when it came out,
in homage to Warham, archbishop of Canterbury.

1520, 1521 and 1525 marked stages in the edition of Cyprian. In 1522
the *De Civitate Dei* appeared, furnished with an ample commentary by
his friend Juan Luis Vives. In the same year 1522 Erasmus dedicated his
edition of Arnobius the Younger's Commentary on the Psalms to the
new pope, Adrian VI. The dedicatory letter set out a new programme
of biblical studies, as he conceived of them.

In 1523 it was Hilary's turn. And in this same year Erasmus outlined
his plan of complete editions of Origen and of Chrysostom. As the
printers hesitated before the amplitude of these designs, he gave up
1524–6 to re-editing Jerome. In 1525, 1526, 1527, and 1529 there
appeared nevertheless from Froben's press the separate works of
Chrysostom. In 1526 appeared the edition of Irenaeus. The following
year appeared Origen's Fragments on Matthew; then Ambrose.

1528–9 marked the great edition of Augustine, which had been
long promised. (It was dedicated to Fonseca, archbishop of Toledo.)

In 1530 he published the complete works of Basil (dedicated to Sadolet): he had previously edited Basil's Commentary on Isaiah in 1511 (and dedicated it to Fisher, bishop of Rochester). In 1535 he returned to Basle, which he had left in 1529 for Freiburg-im-Breisgau, and there devoted the last year of his life to preparing the long-awaited edition of Origen. Although for most of these labours he had a whole team of scholars working under his guidance, there is still something quite stupendous in the sheer extent of this work of bringing ancient exegesis and the ancient biblical theology up to date.

But we must turn to Erasmus's own commentaries, and more especially to his methodological works, to appreciate to the full the influence that his researches into the Fathers—combined with the application of the principles inherited from Valla to the biblical text and its literal interpretation—were to have on his own vision of the Bible.

At the time of his stay in Saint-Omer, in 1502, while still under the immediate influence of his first meeting with Colet, Erasmus had written four books of commentaries on Paul's Epistle to the Romans. This was to be the germ of a paraphrase of all the epistles, which took its final form in the Basle editions of 1523 and 1524. Yet in 1522 he published his paraphrase of Matthew, dedicated to Charles V; in 1523 his paraphrases first of John and then of Luke; and in the spring of 1524 his paraphrase of Mark.

Add to this some commentaries on Psalms (2, 3 and 4) which appeared in 1524–5; the commentary on Psalm 85 that came out in 1528; and the *Precatio dominica digesta in VII partes*, a Commentary on the Our Father, which, written in 1523, prefaces his treatise of the following year on Prayer (*Modus Orandi Deum*).

All these works set out to make clear, generally as succinctly as possible, the exact meaning of the Bible texts; and even within the treatises called *Paraphrases* there is a perpetual exchange between strict explanatory paraphrase and commentary of the most sober kind.

But if we would understand the idea which Erasmus gradually formed in his own mind of the new biblical culture whose foundations were to be laid by his work, and the instruments which his work sought to provide, then we must turn first of all to his great methodological treatise, in its finished form: the *Ratio seu methodus compendio perveniendi ad veram theologiam*. We may do so in the light of various other prefaces and apologies and dedicatory letters accompanying his edition of the New Testament or his *Paraphrases*. And a study of this treatise will put us in a position to assess Erasmus's biblical work.

III

The *Ratio* was gradually formed from a development of the Preface to the *Novum Instrumentum*, into which eventually the essential elements of Erasmus's thought on biblical studies crystallized. At the same time the *Ratio* sets out a whole programme of theological thought, and an ideal of spirituality. If there is a Reformism proper to Erasmus— previously sketched in the *Enchiridion*, later defined in the polemic against Luther in the *Hyperaspites*, and vulgarized in the *Ecclesiastes*— then assuredly we must look to the *Ratio* for its fundamental exposition.

The opening pages of the *Ratio* contain an implied polemic against the contentious theology of the last of the schoolmen. It has been emphasized how much this opposition owes to the influence of the *Devotio moderna*, but not sufficiently pointed out how close it is, above all, to those theological objections with which the Cappadocian Fathers—whose religious inquiries remained so reverent before the mysteries of Christianity— met the different forms of Arianism. Still more precisely we seem to feel in this work—like a kind of filigree— the constant presence of Gregory Nazianzen (notably his theological sermons) whom Erasmus had read in 1508 at Venice.

True theology is no mere matter of intellectual technique, but requires of him who would make progress in it a striving to become better, and a directly religious frame of mind. In fact theology is to be considered as a work of prophecy. It demands the inspiration of the Holy Spirit. Its end must be to make saints, not dialecticians. This in no way prevents Erasmus from at once insisting also on the intellectual resources that seem to him necessary in a theologian. The first of these, according to him, is a knowledge of the three languages: Hebrew, Greek and Latin. The first two are no less necessary than the third, because the existing translations are all inadequate; because there can be no perfect translations; and because the best translations cannot be used with certainty by those who are not capable of criticizing them with real competence.

The next section passes from there to the need for what we would call general culture: knowledge of nature, of rhetoric, and the poets.

There we find again the concept of theology as a simple elucidation of Scripture, and the concept of profane culture as a simple preparatory study to it, in much the same terms as we find in the last exponents of the medieval intellectual ideal, prior to the thirteenth century. But it is not a case of Erasmus's dependence on Anselm of Laon or William of Saint-Thierry, but of their common dependence on the Fathers. This is shown by what follows; Erasmus specifically contrasts the school-men with the Fathers, and reproaches the schoolmen with 'using' the sacred writers, and making them answer questions they never put to themselves, instead of learning from them. In contrast with these methods Erasmus then gives an all-important series of rules for the interpretation of Scripture: never take a quotation out of its context, nor out of the general way of thought of its author, nor yet out of the thought of the Scriptures as a whole. In this connection Erasmus under-lines the importance for the novice in theology of a perfectly objective summary of the content of the epistles and Gospels. Then come the questions of the place, the moment, the occasion, the intention, and the tone of the work being studied.

Thence he goes on to how the Doctors may be used to get deeper into the meaning of the texts. He is at pains to define and graduate their authority, giving first place to the Greeks and above all to Origen, and amongst the Latin Fathers setting Jerome, with his anxiety to be objective, above Augustine, whose expositions too easily sink into edification at all costs. But above all he stresses how one must never confuse the exegetical opinions of the Doctors with dogma; nor at any time become so attached to one of the Doctors that one is afraid ever to disagree with him, even for good reasons. Further on, Erasmus is to insist on the necessity of not taking for gospel any and every text ascribed to one of the Fathers, but to exercise in this respect a prelimi-nary rigorous criticism.

But study of the Fathers will lead us to what is the basic idea in all their commentaries (in particular those of Origen, so highly prized by Erasmus): that knowledge of Christ is the centre, the heart as it were, of all the Scriptures. In connection with this idea he brings in, and transforms, the famous argument of Justin and Clement of Alexandria: they observed that all the partial truths discovered by the philosophers were to be found in the Gospel, but there completed and unified into a coherent whole. Erasmus goes further; he says that all that is best, not just in the thought but in the lives, too, of the philosophers, is found again in the Gospel in unique fullness; and in the life and personality of Christ still more than in his teaching.

From this view, centred in Christ, comes the relative importance we should ascribe to the different books of the Bible, according as they bring us more or less directly to knowledge of him. Hence the idea, again taken from the Fathers, and particularly from Athanasius and Basil, that the later multiplicity of dogmatic formulae—made necessary because of heresy—must not blur the living unity of the divine person, who is the supreme object of faith, which feeds on the Scriptures. On the contrary, the multiplicity of aspects under which Christ appears to us in the Bible only renders this unity the more concrete to us. Then follows an excursus on the apparent contradictions of Scripture, which resolve themselves the moment we take account of all the historical circumstances against which each text must be read, when the continuity of the whole is found again. Erasmus develops at length from this general principle its application to what is told us both as to Christ's divinity and his humanity. He follows very closely here the fourth theological sermon of Gregory of Nazianzen, but softening its dialectical rigour.

Thus he comes to show how Christ drew the world to him: and after him the apostles, in imitation of him; not by violence, nor by any power of this world, but by the sympathy and purity of a loftier humanity that drew souls to the divine. Then finally follows a picture of that Christian spirit which *Vera theologia* must spread—flowering into charity founded on faith, as distinct from a wholly exterior religion that leaves the interior life unchanged. Not that we must reject the traditional rites and ceremonies of the Church, he takes care to add; only we must understand them properly, and use them in the light of that final end which they also themselves serve. All this part ends with what we might call the ideal psychology of the preacher, drawn from Christ and the apostles, according to the New Testament. The treatise closes with a series of counsels to exegetes, to help them to overcome the particular difficulties that a real and integral understanding of Scripture involves.

The most developed of these counsels in itself constitutes a whole dissertation on the literal meaning and the spiritual allegorical meaning. In it Erasmus reveals so profoundly penetrating a knowledge of the Fathers that it anticipates the best of the most modern works, such as those of Père de Lubac on Origen. His views are far removed from the abstract views systematized by Thomas Aquinas, on the literal meaning and the various figurative meanings. Following the exegesis that the biblical authors give of one another, he shows how not only are there cases in which the figurative sense is the only literal one, but further, how the development of Scripture presupposes the possibility of layers of different meanings for a single text, within the whole compass of revelation. Concrete examples, admirably chosen from different Fathers, show how carefully in this respect we must distinguish an artificial interpretation of a text, imposed on it from without, from the interpretation which the text itself suggests when we put it back in its place in the Bible as a whole.

Erasmus likewise examines the idiomatic expressions (particularly the Hebraisms) proper to the language of the Bible, and which are particularly confusing when we meet them in the New Testament texts: hyperboles, and other expressions to be taken in a wide sense. He does not forget that irony must be taken into consideration, not excluding certain sayings of Jesus. Lastly he insists on the danger of taking words in a sense they may well have in classical Greek, but which is not the sense in which they are used in the New Testament. He makes this clear by taking the best possible example: the Pauline meaning of the opposition between the flesh and the spirit.

He underlines again the absolute need for exegetes to quote Scripture always at first hand, paying attention at the same time to context. This gives him a good opportunity to set out a list of scriptural expressions misconstrued even by such writers as Ambrose, Bede or Augustine.

His conclusion reverts at greater length to an idea sketched out earlier: the usefulness of a concordance—not of words only, but also of ideas—which would trace right through the Bible the way its great themes are developed. In this connection he rehearses the rules that allow a commentator to compare texts fruitfully one with another.

If we would condense into a formula what Erasmus set out to do in the field of scriptural studies, we may say that he expressed the ideal of all Christian humanism as Giuseppe Toffanin defined it, and that he achieved this just as far as it was possible: the revival of traditional patristic culture, made new again, so that Scripture too should be rediscovered, and be at the heart of a reform of the Church entirely from within. The great originality of the period—and in this respect Erasmus is its greatest representative—was the use and perfecting of critical philology in order to fulfil the task. The method was taken over from Valla and developed so as to serve a truly historical understanding of the ancient texts, biblical or other.

Erasmus's medieval kinship is seen particularly in the psychological and moral bent of his interpretation of Scripture, reacting against a theology in which speculation had gone over into pure abstraction. In this he was faithful to the *Devotio moderna*; and indeed he even intensified its main lines.

But he is at least as much an innovator in his sense of history and in his attachment to the human content of biblical theology as in his conception of critical philology and his use of it as the basis of all biblical research.

But he is far closer to the ancient patristic writers, and to the Greek Fathers especially, than to the medieval writers, in the living sense which he recovered of the Church's tradition, and of Scripture seen, as it were, inside that tradition. This is what distinguishes him from the rationalist individualism of latter-day scholasticism, where recourse to the argument of tradition is made only in the form of texts that have been detached from their context and are simply offered as the point of departure for a wholly dialectical discussion of Scripture, itself likewise atomized.

So we may say that Erasmus offers one of the finest examples of a 'return to the sources' without taint of archaism: where what is newest ministers to a fresh and better understanding of what is oldest.

BIBLIOGRAPHY

PLATES

INDEX

BIBLIOGRAPHY

CHAPTER I

The Old Testament: manuscripts, text and Versions

The most important work on textual studies has been published in article form, and, with a few notable exceptions, cannot be included in the present list.

General works

Bruce, F. F., *The books and the parchments* (3rd ed. 1962).

Cross, F. M., *The ancient library of Qumran* (1958).

Eissfeldt, O., *Einleitung in das Alte Testament* (1st ed. 1934). English translation of 3rd ed., P. R. Ackroyd, *The Old Testament, an introduction* (1965).

Flack, E. E., Metzger, B. M. and others, *The text, canon and principal versions of the Bible* (1956).

Herklots, H. G. G., *How the Bible came to us* (Penguin, 1959).

Kahle, P. E., *The Cairo Geniza* (1st ed. 1947, 2nd ed. 1959).

Noth, M., *Die Welt des Alten Testaments* (4th ed. 1962). English translation, *The Old Testament world* (1966).

Price, I. M. (revised), *The ancestry of our English Bible* (3rd ed. 1956).

Robinson, H. W. (revised), *The Bible in its ancient and English versions* (2nd ed. 1954).

Rypins, S., *The book of thirty centuries* (1951).

Vandervorst, J., *Introduction aux textes hébreu et grec de l' Ancien Testament* (1935).

The Massoretic Text

Texts

Kittel, R. (with P. Kahle), *Biblia Hebraica* (3rd ed. 1937, and subsequent).

Snaith, N. H., *Sepher Torah, Nebi'im u-Kethubim* (1958).

Books

Edelman, R. (ed.), *Corpus Codicum Hebraicorum Medii Aevi*, Part II. Vol. I, A. Sperber, *The Pre-Masoretic Bible...Codex Reuchlinianus* (1956); vols. II and III, A. Sperber, *Codices Palatani*. 1. *Parma Pentateuch*, 2. *The Parma Bible*, 1. *Pentateuch–II Samuel*; vol. III, II. *Jeremiah–Chronicles* (1959). (The two volumes of the Parma Bible consist of facsimile plates of the whole Old Testament.)

Goldschmidt, L. (with P. Kahle), *The earliest editions of the Hebrew Bible, with a treatise of the oldest manuscripts of the Bible* (1950).

Goshen-Gottstein, M. H., *The Hebrew University Bible project. The Book of Isaiah. Sample edition with introduction* (1965).

Bibliography

Kahle, P. E., *Der Hebräische Text seit Franz Delitzsch* (1962).

Lehmann, O., *The Damascus Pentateuch and its manuscript. Tradition according to ben Naphtali* (1962).

Roth, C., *The Aberdeen Codex of the Hebrew Bible* (1958).

Sperber, A., *A grammar of Masoretic Hebrew, a general introduction to the pre-Masoretic Bible* (1959).

Weil, G. E., *Elia Levita — humaniste et massorète* (1963).
Initiation à la massorah. L'introduction au sépher zikhronôt d'Elia Levita (1964).

Würthwein, E., *Der Text des Alten Testaments. Eine Einführung in die Biblia Hebraica* (2nd ed. 1963). English translation of 1st ed. 1957.

Articles

Orlinsky, H. M., 'The Masoretic text. A critical evaluation'. Prolegomenon to the re-issue (1966) of C. D. Ginsburg, *Introduction to the Massoretico-critical edition of the Hebrew Bible* (1897).

Textus. The Annual of the Hebrew University Bible Project. (Editors: C. Rabin, later S. Talmon (1960–).)

The Septuagint

Texts

Brooke, A. E. and McLean, N., *The Old Testament in Greek*, vols. I–IV (the Cambridge Septuagint, 1906–40).

Septuaginta. Vetus Testamentum Graece auctoritate Societatis Litterarum Gottingensis editum (the Göttingen Septuagint, 1931–).

Rahlfs, A., *Septuaginta. Vetus Testamentum Graece* (1935 and subsequent editions).

Swete, H. B., *The Old Testament in Greek according to the Septuagint* (1st ed. 1887–94, subsequent editions until 1909).

Books

Barthélemy, J. D., *Les devanciers d'Aquila* (1963).

Field, F., *Origenes Hexaplorum quae supersunt*...(1875, reprint 1965).

Gerleman, G., *Studies in the Septuagint*, vol. I, *The Book of Job* (1946); vol. II, *II Chronicles* (1946); vol. III, *Proverbs* (1956).

Gooding, D. W., *Recensions of the Septuagint Pentateuch* (1955).

Kenyon, F. G. (revised), *Our Bible and the ancient manuscripts* (5th ed. 1958).

Leider, J. and Turner, M., *An index to Aquila* (1966).

Margolis, M. L., *The Book of Joshua in Greek* (1931–8).

Orlinsky, H. M., *The Septuagint. The oldest translation of the Bible* (1949).

Ottley, R. R., *A handbook to the Septuagint* (1920).

Rahlfs, A., *Septuaginta Studien*, vols. I–III (1st ed. 1904–11, 2nd ed. 1965).

Seeligmann, I. L., *The Septuagint Version of Isaiah* (1948).

Swete, H. B., *Introduction to the Old Testament in Greek* (2nd ed. 1914).

Wutz, F. X., *Systematische Wege von der Septuaginta zum hebräischen Urtext* (1937).

Bibliography

Articles

Gehman, H. S., 'Greek Versions of O.T.' in *Dictionary of the Bible* (ed. F. C. Grant and H. H. Rowley, 2nd ed. of *Hastings Dictionary of the Bible*) (1963). Numerous articles in various journals.

Wevers, J. W., 'Septuaginta Forschungen', *Theologische Rundschau* (1954), with full bibliography.

Samaritan Pentateuch

Castro, F. P., *Séfer Abisha'. Edición del fragmento antiguo del rollo sagrado del Pentateuco Hebreo Samaritno de Nablus.* 1959.

von Gall, A., *Der hebräische Pentateuch der Samaritaner.* 1914–18. Reprint 1965.

Targums

Texts

Berliner, A., *Targum Onkelos*, 1884.

Sperber, A., *The Bible in Aramaic*, vols. I–III (1959–62).

Stenning, J. F., *The Targum of Isaiah* (1st ed. 1949, reprint 1953).

Peshitta

Text

Vetus Testamentum Syriace, ed. S. Lee (1823).

Peshitta Institute, *The Old Testament in Syriac according to the Peshitta Version.* Sample edition (1966).

Books

Baumstark, A., *Geschichte der syrischen Literatur* (1922).

Moss, C., *Catalogue of Syriac printed books and related literature in the British Museum* (1962).

Peshitta Institute, *List of Old Testament Peshitta manuscripts* (*Preliminary issue*) (1961).

Vööbus, A., *Peschitta und Targumim des Pentateuchs* (1958).

Old Latin and Vulgate

Texts

Biblia Sacra iuxta Latinam Vulgatam Versionem ad codicum fidem, cura et studio Monachorum Abbatiae Pont. S. Hieronymi in Urbe O.S.B. (Benedictine Vulgate) (1926–).

Biblia Sacra Vulgatae Editionis Sixti V Pont. Max. iussu recognita et Clementis VIII auctoritate edita (Clementina) (1959).

Sabatier, P., *Bibliorum Sacrorum latinae versiones antiquae*, and B. Fischer, *Vetus Latina, Die Reste der altlateinischen Bibel nach Petrus Sabatier neu gesammelt u. herausg. v. d. Erzabtei Beuron* (1739–49, 1751, and 1949–54).

Sainte-Marie, H. de, *Sancti Hieronymi Psalterium iuxta Hebraeos.* Édition Critique (1954).

Bibliography

Books

Bea, A., *Die neue lateinische Psalmenübersetzung* (1949).
Schäfer, J., *Die altlateinische Bibel* (1957).
Stummer, F., *Einführung in die lateinische Bibel* (1928).

CHAPTER III

Early Christian Book-Production

The subjects studied in this chapter fall within the scope of what has in recent years come to be known as the science of codicology, i.e. the study of the material aspect of manuscripts as distinct from palaeography, which is concerned with the history and development of scripts. Indeed, 'The codicology of the early Christian book' might have been a more accurate, if somewhat pedantic, title.

Most of the best-known handbooks on palaeography and manuscripts, such as Sir Edward Maunde Thompson, *Introduction to Greek and Latin palaeography* (1912), or R. Devréesse, *Introduction à l'étude des manuscrits grecs* (1954), include sections on writing materials and the physical make-up of manuscripts, but generally speaking are not sufficiently up-to-date to take account of the striking additions to knowledge made in recent years. In English, the only comprehensive work dealing with the subjects of this chapter is Sir F. G. Kenyon, *Books and Readers in Ancient Greece and Rome* (2nd ed. 1951), which covers both classical and early Christian literature. Clear, accurate and eminently readable, it is nevertheless beginning to wear something of an old-fashioned look. An equally valuable survey, in German, is Wilhelm Schubart, *Das Buch bei den Griechen und Römern* (2nd ed. 1921); though containing much acute observation of permanent value, this is even more in need of modern revision, since the so-called '3rd edition' of the book, published in 1962, is merely a reproduction of the 2nd edition, shorn of its invaluable footnotes and references.

Probably the best all-round account at present available is to be found in that work of composite authorship, the *Geschichte der Textüberlieferung der antiken und mittelalterlichen Literatur* (Zürich, 1961). The two initial sections of volume I, *Antikes und mittelalterliches Buch- und Schriftwesen*, by H. Hunger, and *Überlieferungsgeschichte der Bibel*, by O. Stegmüller, cover between them all the topics discussed in this chapter. The information is accurate, authoritative, and up-to-date, with references and bibliographies. A later section, *Überlieferungsgeschichte der lateinischen Literatur*, by K. Büchner, contains a valuable discussion on the transference of literature from roll to codex. A masterly summary of the present state of knowledge is provided by E. G. Turner in the opening chapter (Chapter I: 'Writing Materials and Books') of his *Greek Papyri: an Introduction*, (Oxford, 1968).

As regards writing materials, J. Černý's inaugural lecture, *Paper and books in ancient Egypt* (1952), contains much useful information about papyrus and its use, which though related to the Pharaonic period is in many respects relevant to later ages. For the Graeco-Roman period N. Lewis, *L'industrie du papyrus dans l'Égypte gréco-romaine* (1934), remains indispensable. It is unfortunate that there are no similar works dealing with parchment, and indeed few of the writers who have attempted to deal with this subject have possessed the necessary scientific and technological qualifications. The first section of R. J. Forbes, *Studies in ancient technology*, vol. v (2nd ed. 1966), is concerned with leather in antiquity, and this includes a brief discussion of parchment (pp. 63–6), with valuable bibliography. Lastly, no comprehensive codicological study has yet been made of the Dead Sea scrolls, and none can be effectively undertaken until conservation and study of the material have reached a much more advanced stage.

For the codex, as stated in the text, the monograph of C. H. Roberts, 'The Codex', *Proceedings of the British Academy*, xl (1954), 169–204, is of fundamental importance. The arguments drawn by Roberts from the writings of Roman jurists have been carried further by F. Wieacker, *Textstufen klassischer Juristen, Abhandlungen der Akademie der Wissenschaften in Göttingen*, Phil.-hist. Kl., 3. Folge, Nr. 45 (1960), especially in his section 4, 'Rolle und Codex, Papyrus und Pergament', which deals comprehensively with the transition from papyrus roll to parchment codex, and its effects on literature; but this work must be used with caution, since it contains a number of careless misstatements. For the Yale papyrus mentioned on p. 71 see now the authoritative article by C. H. Roberts, 'P. Yale 1 and the early Christian Book' in *Essays in honor of C. Bradford Wells*, New Haven, 1966, pp. 25–8.

Lastly, for details of the bindings of the Nag Hammadi Gnostic codices (p. 74) see Jean Doresse, 'Les Reliures des Manuscrits coptes découverts à Khenobaskion', *Revue d'Égyptologie*, xiii (1961), pp. 27–49.

CHAPTER IV

Jerome

HUCA: Hebrew Union College Annual (Cincinnati, Ohio); *RSR: Recherches de science religieuse* (Paris); *TU: Texte und Untersuchungen zur Geschichte der Altchristlichen Literatur* (Leipzig); *VT: Vetus Testamentum* (Leyden).
The latest edition of Jerome's works is that of Vallarsi, whose 2nd edition is reprinted in Migne, *Patrologia Latina* [abbreviated as *PL.*] 22–30 (1845–6), to which references are here made. Migne's reprint is less accurate and has different numeration. For the epistles [*ep.* references] see the critical edition by I. Hilberg in *Corpus Scriptorum Ecclesiasticorum Latinorum* (1910–18) [*C.S.E.L.*]. This still lacks the indices. For an appreciation see A. Vaccari, *Biblica*, 1 (1920), 386–90.

For the Commentary on Jeremiah [*Comm. in Jer.*], see S. Reiter in *C.S.E.L.* (1913). *Commentarioli in Psalmos; Tractatus sive Homiliae in Psalmos, in Marci Evangelium aliaque varia argumenta; Tractatus sive Homiliae in Psalmos quattuordecim*, ed. G. Morin, O.S.B., Maredsoli (1895–1903) = *Anecdota Maredsolana*, iii, i, ii, iii. *De Viris Illustribus*, ed. E. C. Richardson in *TU*, xiv, i (1896); *De Situ et Nominibus Locorum Hebraicorum*, ed. E. Klostermann in the Berlin edition of Eusebius, iii. i. A Benedictine commission at Rome is revising the Vulgate in order, as far as possible, to restore the text to the form in which it left the hands of Jerome. The

New Testament revision, begun by J. Wordsworth and H. J. White (Oxford, 1889), is now complete. The Psalter from the Hebrew, ed. H. de Sainte-Marie, O.S.B. (Rome, 1954). *Select Letters of St Jerome* with an English translation by F. A. Wright (Loeb Classical Library, 1933).

Grützmacher, G., *Hieronymus: eine biographische Studie* (3 vols. Berlin, 1901–8). Cavallera, F., *Saint Jérôme, sa vie et son œuvre*, I, i, ii (Louvain–Paris, 1922). This work was never completed. Antin, O.S.B., P., *Essai sur Saint Jérôme* (Paris, 1951). Vaccari, S. J., A. P., *S. Girolamo* (Roma, 1921). Schade, L., *Die Inspirationslehre des hl. Hieronymus* (Freiburg i. B. 1910) (Biblische Studien, 15, 4–5). *Miscellanea Geronimiana* (Roma, 1920). *A monument to St Jerome*, ed. F. X. Murphy (C. SS. R., New York, 1952). On the name 'Vulgate', see A. Allgeier, *Biblica*, XXIX (1948), 353–90, and E. F. Sutcliffe, *ibid.* 345–52. Characteristics of Jerome's translation: A. Condamin, *RSR*, II (1911), 425–40; III (1912), 105–38; R. Loewe, *HUCA*, XXII (1949), 265–306; *VT*, II (1952), 261–72. On his pronunciation of Hebrew, see Sutcliffe, *Biblica*, XXIX (1948), 112–25, and on his Hebrew manuscripts, see *ibid.* 195–204. On the supposed washing of camels' feet, see A. Vaccari, *Biblica*, VII (1926), 439–43; VIII (1927), 94 f. On the discovery of the hexaplaric revision of the Song of Songs, see A. Vaccari, *Biblica*, XXXVI (1955), 258–60.

Reiter's edition of the Commentary on Jeremiah was reprinted in *Corpus Christianorum*, Series Latina, vol. 74 (Turnholti, 1960). Morin's edition of the *Tractatus sive Homiliae in Psalmos, in Marci Evangelium, aliaque varia Argumenta*, with additions and corrections, was reprinted in CChr vol. 78 (1958). CChr vol. 72 contains an extensive and recent bibliography of Jerome, and reprints with a few additional notes P. De Lagarde's editions of the *Hebraicae Quaestiones in Libro Geneseos*, and the *Liber Interpretationis Hebraicorum Nominum*, and also Morin's edition of the *Commentarioli in Psalmos*. It also includes a new critical edition by M. Adriaen of the *Commentariorum in Esaiam, Libri I–XI*. Vol. 73A (1963) contains Libri XI–XVIII, and reprints Morin's edition of the *In Esaia parvula Adbreviatio*. A new critical edition by F. Glorie of the *Commentariorum in Hieze-chielem, Libri XIV*, appeared in CChr vol. 75.

CHAPTER V

The medieval history of the Latin Vulgate

Note. The main *sigla* used to symbolize the manuscripts, and the families by which they are affiliated, are explained in the text, footnotes, and diagram (pp. 103–5); full lists are included in *Bibla Sacra* and *Novum Testamentum* (listed below). See also the bibliography to chapter IX, section 5 (below, p. 525). Of more recent works, those marked with an asterisk (*) contain further bibliographies.

Ayuso Marazuela, T., *(1) *La Vetus Latina Hispana*. I. Prolegómenos. Consejo Superior de Investigaciones Científicas (Madrid, 1953).

(2) *Origen del Códice Ottoboniano Latino del Eptateuco*. Miscellanea Biblica B. Ubach (=*Scripta et Documenta* 1), ed. R. M. Díaz (Montserrat, 1953), pp. 115 f.

Bibliography

(3) *La Biblia visigótica de la Cava dei Tirreni.* Consejo Superior de Investigaciones Científicas (Madrid, 1956).

(4) *La Biblia visigótica de San Isidoro de León; contribución al estudio de la Vulgata en España* (1965).

E.B., Articles published in *Estudios Bíblicos* (Madrid, 1941).

Berger, S., (1) 'Des essais qui ont été faits à Paris au treizième siècle pour corriger le texte de la Vulgate', *Revue de Théologie et de Philosophie*, XVI (Lausanne, 1883), 41 f.

(2) *De l'histoire de la Vulgate en France.* Leçon d'Ouverture (Paris, 1887).

(3) *Histoire de la Vulgate pendant les premiers siècles du moyen âge* (Paris, 1893).

(4) *Quam Notitiam Linguae Hebraicae habuerunt Christiani medii aevi temporibus in Gallia* (Nancy, 1893).

Biblia Sacra = *Biblia Sacra iuxta Latinam Vulgatam Versionem...cura... monachorum Sancti Benedicti..edita* (Rome, 1926–) (still in progress).

Bonnardière, A. M. la, *Biblia Augustiniana, A.T.*, II. *Livres Historiques* (Paris, Études Augustiniennes, 1960).

Boretius, A., see *M.G.H.*

Brewer, J. S., *Fr. Rogeri Bacon opera quaedam hactenus inedita*, I (London, Rolls Series, XV, 1859).

Bruyne, D. de, (1) 'Étude sur les origines de la Vulgate en Espagne', *Revue Bénédictine*, XXXI (Maredsous, 1914–19), 373 f.

(2) 'Saint Augustin, réviseur de la Bible', *Miscellanea Agostiniana*, éd. A. Casamassa, 2, Studi Agostiniani (Rome, 1931), pp. 521 f.

Burkitt, F. C., *The Old Latin and the Itala. Texts and Studies*, ed. J. Armitage Robinson, IV, 3 (Cambridge, 1896).

Chapman, J., *Notes on the early history of the Vulgate Gospels* (Oxford, 1908).

C.L.A., *Codices Latini Antiquiores*, assembled and annotated by E. A. Lowe (Oxford, 1934–).

Clark, C. Upson, *Collectanea Hispanica. Transactions* of the Connecticut Academy of Arts and Sciences, 24 (Paris, 1920).

Cordoliani, A., 'Le texte de la Bible en Irlande du Vᵉ au IXᵉ siècle', *Revue Biblique*, LVII (Paris, 1950), 5 f.

Corssen, P., 'Die Bibeln des Cassiodorius [*sic*] und der Codex Amiatinus', *Jahrbücher für Protestantische Theologie*, IX (Leipzig, 1883), 619 f.

C.S.E.L., *Corpus Scriptorum Ecclesiasticorum Latinorum* (Vienna).

Denifle, H., 'Die Handschriften der Bibel-Correctorien des 13. Jahrhunderts', *Archiv für Literatur- und Kirchengeschichte des Mittelalters*, IV (Freiburg im Breisgau, 1888), 263 f., 471 f.

Duckett, E. S., *Alcuin, friend of Charlemagne. His world and his work* (New York, 1951).

Duemmler, E., see *M.G.H.*

Durrow, Book of. Evangeliorum Quattuor Codex Durmachensis. Facsimile edition, 2 vols. Introduction, etc., by A. A. Luce, G. Simms, P. Meyer, L. Bieler. Olten, Switzerland, 1962. (N.B. A convenient summary in the review of *The Times Literary Supplement*, 22 Feb. 1963, p. 143.)

Fischer, B., (1) *Die Alcuin-Bibel. Aus der Geschichte der Lateinischen Bibel,* I (Freiburg im Breisgau, 1957).

(2) 'Codex Amiatinus und Cassiodor', *Biblische Zeitschrift,* N.F. VI (Paderborn, 1962), 57 f.

(3) 'Algunas observaciones sobre el "codex Gothicus" de la R. C. de S. Isidoro en León y sobre la tradición española de la Vulgata', *Archivos Leonenses,* XV (León, 1961/2), 29–30 (*Volumen conmemorativo...de la Biblia visigótica de... San Isidoro*).

*(4) 'Bibelausgaben des frühen Mittelalters', *Settimane di Studio del centro Italiano sull'Alto Medioevo,* 10 (Spoleto, 1963), pp. 519f.

(4a) 'Arbeitsbericht' (an abridged version of (4)), *Vetus Latina,* XII (Beuron, 1963).

Fontaine, J., *Isidore de Séville et la culture classique dans l'Espagne wisigothique* (Paris, 1959).

Frede, H. J., (1) *Pelagius, Der irische Paulustext Sedulius Scottus. Aus der Geschichte der lateinischen Bibel* (Freiburg im Breisgau, 1961).

(2) *Vetus Latina,* vol. XXIV, fasc. 1, *Epistula ad Ephesios* (Freiburg im Breisgau, 1962).

[Fritzsche, O. F. and] Nestle, E., 'Bibelübersetzungen, lateinische', in *Realencyclopädie für protestantische Theologie und Kirche,* ed. A. Hauck (3rd edition, Leipzig, 1897), vol. III, pp. 24 f.

Ganshof, F. L., 'La Révision de la Bible par Alcuin', *Bibliothèque d'Humanisme et Renaissance,* IX (Geneva, 1947), 7 f.

Gaskoin, C. J. B., *Alcuin: his life and work* (London, 1904).

Glunz, H. H., (1) *Britannien und Bibeltext. Der Vulgatatext der Evangelien in seinem Verhältnis zur Irisch-Angelsächsischen Kultur des Frühmittelalters. Kölner Anglistische Arbeiten,* XII (Leipzig, 1930).

(2) *History of the Vulgate in England from Alcuin to Roger Bacon* (Cambridge, 1933).

Goelzer, H., *Étude lexicographique et grammaticale de la latinité de Saint Jérôme* (Paris, 1884).

Hody, H., *De Bibliorum Textibus Originalibus, Versionibus Graecis, & Latina Vulgata* (Oxford, 1705).

Jones, L. W., *An introduction to divine and human readings by Cassiodorus Senator,* translated with an Introduction and Notes (New York, 1946).

Kells, Book of. *Evangeliorum quattuor codex cenannensis...Totius codicis similitudinem...exprimendam...prolegomenis auxerunt...Ernestus Henricus Alton ...Petrus Meyer.* 3 vols. (Berne, 1950–1).

Kenney, J. F., *The sources for the early history of Ireland. An introduction and guide.* I, *Ecclesiastical.* Columbia University Press Records of Civilisation (New York, 1929).

Kenyon, F., *Our Bible and the ancient manuscripts* (5th edition revised by A. W. Adams, London, 1948).

Kleinclausz, A., 'Alcuin', *Annales de l'Université de Lyon,* 3rd Series, XV (Paris, 1948).

Bibliography

Lindisfarne Gospels. Evangeliorum Quattuor Codex Lindisfarnensis Musei Britannici Codex Cottonianus Nero D. IV, Permissione Musei Britannici Totius Codicis Similitudo Expressa. Prolegomenis auxerunt T. D. Kendrick, T. J. Brown, L. S. Bruce-Mitford, A. S. C. Ross, E. G. Roosen-Runge, A. Werner. Vol. II (Olten and Lausanne, 1961).

Lowe, E. A., see *C.L.A.*

Loewe, R. J., (1) 'Herbert of Bosham's Commentary on Jerome's Hebrew Psalter', *Biblica*, xxxiv (Rome, 1953), 44 f., 159 f., 275 f.

*(2) 'The medieval Christian Hebraists of England. Herbert of Bosham and earlier scholars', *Transactions* of the Jewish Historical Society of England, xvii (London, 1953), 225 f.

*(3) 'The medieval Christian Hebraists of England. The *Superscriptio Lincolniensis*', *Hebrew Union College Annual*, xxviii (Cincinnati, 1957), 205 f.

(4) 'Latin Superscriptio MSS on Portions of the Hebrew Bible other than the Psalter', *Journal of Jewish Studies*, ix (London, 1958), 63 f.

Mangenot, E., *'Correctoires de la Bible', in *Dictionnaire de la Bible* (Paris, 1899), vol. II, cols. 1022 f.

Marazuela, see Ayuso Marazuela, T.

Martin, J. P. P., (1) *Saint Étienne Harding et les premiers recenseurs de la Vulgate Latine, Theodulfe et Alcuin* (reprinted from *Revue des Sciences Ecclésiastiques*, Arras) (Amiens, 1887).

(2) 'La Vulgate latine au treizième siècle d'après Roger Bacon', *Le Muséon*, vii (Louvain, 1888), 100 f.

(3) 'Le Texte parisien de la Vulgate latine', *Le Muséon*, viii (Louvain, 1889), 444 f., and ix (1890), 55 f.

Menéndez Pidal, R. (ed.), *Historia de España*, iii (Madrid, 1940), 395.

M.G.H., *Monumenta Germaniae Historica*.

Poetae Latini Aevi Carolini, i, ed. E. Duemmler (Berlin, 1881).

Capitularia Regum Francorum, *Leges*, ii, i, ed. A. Boretius (Hanover, 1883).

Epistolae iv, *Karolini Aevi ii*, ed. E. Duemmler (Berlin, 1895).

Mohrmann, C., *(1) *Latin vulgaire, Latin des Chrétiens, Latin médiéval* (Paris, 1955). (The third chapter reprinted from *Revue des Études latines*, xxix, Paris, 1951 ('52), 330 f.)

(2) 'Le latin médiéval', *Cahiers de Civilisation Médiévale*, xi (Poitiers, 1958), 265 f.

*(3) *Études sur le Latin des Chrétiens* (Rome, 1958). [Lists Miss Mohrmann's writings up to 1957.]

Mynors, R. A. B., *Cassiodori Senatoris Institutiones* (Oxford, 1937).

Nestle, E., see [O. F. Fritzsche and] E. Nestle.

Novum Testamentum, Novum Testamentum...Latine secundum editionem Sancti Hieronymi, ed. J. Wordsworth, H. J. White, H. F. D. Sparks, etc. (Oxford, 1898–1954).

P.G.L., *P.L.*, *Patrologiae Cursus Completus*, Series Graeca, Series Latina, ed. J.-P. Migne (Paris).

Power, E., (1) 'The lost ninth-century Bible of Carcassone', *Biblica*, v (Rome, 1924), 197 f.

Bibliography

(2) 'Corrections from the Hebrew in the Theodulfian MSS of the Vulgate', *ibid.* pp. 233 f.

Quentin, H., *Mémoire sur l'établissement du texte de la Vulgate.* Ière partie. *Octateuque. Collectanea Biblica Latina,* 6 (Rome–Paris, 1922).

Rand, E. K., 'A preliminary study of Alcuin's Bible', *Harvard Theological Review,* XXIV (Cambridge, Mass., 1931), 324 ff.

Roberts, B. J., **The Old Testament Text and Versions. The Hebrew Text in Transmission and the History of the Ancient Versions* (Cardiff, 1951).

Robinson, H. Wheeler, see Sparks, H. F. D.

Rönsch, H., *Itala und Vulgata. Das Sprachidiom der Urchristlichen Itala und der Katholischen Vulgata unter Berücksichtigung der Römischen Volkssprache* (2nd edition, Marburg, 1875).

Sainte Marie, H. de, *Sancti Hieronymi Psalterium iuxta Hebraeos. Collectanea Biblica Latina,* 11 (Rome, 1954).

Smalley, B., (1) 'Hebrew scholarship among Christians in thirteenth-century England, as illustrated by some Hebrew–Latin psalters', *Lectiones in Vetere Testamento et in Rebus Judaicis,* VI (London, 1939).

(2) *The study of the Bible in the middle ages* (2nd edition, Oxford, 1952).

Sparks, H. F. D., ***The Latin Bible', chapter 4 of *The Bible in its ancient and English Versions,* ed. H. Wheeler Robinson (Oxford, 1954, reprint).

Stephens, G. R., **The knowledge of Greek in England in the middle ages* (Philadelphia, 1933).

Stummer, F., **Einführung in die lateinische Bibel* (Paderborn, 1928; see pp. 125–58).

Sutcliffe, E. F., (1) 'The name "Vulgate"', *Biblia,* XXIX (1948).

(2) 'The Council of Trent on the Authentia of the Vulgate', *Journal of Theological Studies,* XLIX (1948).

Thiele, W., *Wortschatzuntersuchungen zu den Lateinischen Texten der Johannesbriefe. Aus der Geschichte der Lateinischen Bibel,* 2 (Freiburg im Breisgau – Beuron, 1958).

Turner, C. H., *The oldest MS of the Vulgate Gospels, St Gall MS 1395* (Oxford, 1931).

Vogels, H. J., *Handbuch der Textkritik des Neuen Testaments* (2nd edition, Bonn, 1955).

[Wattenbach, W.], Levison, W., and Löwe, H., *Deutschlands Geschichtsquellen im Mittelalter. Vorzeit und Karolinger* (Weimar, 1953).

Weber, R., *Le psautier romain et les autres anciens psautiers latins. Collectanea Biblica Latina,* 10 (Rome, 1953).

White, H. J., **Article 'Vulgate' in J. Hastings's *Dictionary of the Bible* (Edinburgh, 1902), vol. IV, pp. 873 f.

Wilmart, A., 'Nicolas Manjacoria, Cistercien à Trois-Fontaines', *Revue Bénédictine,* XXXIII (Maredsous, 1921), 136 f.

Wordsworth, J. and White, H. J., see *Novum Testamentum.*

Yglesias, S. M., 'El decreto tridentino sobre la Vulgata y su interpretación por los teólogos del siglo xvi', *Estudios Bíblicos,* V (Madrid, 1946), 137 f.

Bibliography

2. From Gregory the Great to St Bernard

Ayuso Marazuela, T., *La Vetus latina Hispana*, I. *Prolegómenos* (Madrid, 1953).

La Bibbia nell'Alto Medioevo (Spoleto, 1963).

Bischoff, B., 'Wendepunkte in der Geschichte der lateinischen Exegese im Frühmittelalter', *Sacris Erudiri*, VI (1954), 189–281.

Dudden, F. H., *Gregory the Great: his place in history and thought* (London, 1905), II, 298–309.

Fischer, B., 'Bibeltext und Bibelreform unter Karl dem Grossen', *Karl der Grosse. Lebenswerk und Nachleben* (Düsseldorf, 1965), II, 156–216.

Hermann, H., *The Bible in art: miniatures, paintings, drawings and sculpture inspired by the Old Testament* (London, 1956).

Leclercq, J., 'Écrits monastiques sur la Bible aux XIe–XIIIe siècles', *Medieval Studies*, XV (1953), 95–106.

The love of learning and the desire for God. A study of monastic culture (Fordham University Press, 1961), ch. V: 'Sacred Learning', pp. 87–109 (and: a Mentor Omega Book, New York, 1962, pp. 76–93).

'Bible and Gregorian reform', *Concilium*, XVII (1966), 57–68.

'Écriture sainte: S. Bernard et le 12e siècle monastique', *Dictionnaire de Spiritualité*, IV (Paris, 1960), cols. 187–94.

'La Bible dans les homélies de S. Bernard sur "Missus est"', *Studi medievali*, V (1964), 613–48.

Lubac, H. de, *Exégèse médiévale. Les quatre sens de l'Écriture* (4 vols. Paris, 1959–64).

McGurk, P., 'The Irish Pocket Gospel Book', *Sacris Erudiri*, VIII (1956), 249–70.

Ohly, F., *Hoheliedstudien. Grundzüge zur Auslegung einer Geschichte der Hoheliedauslegung des Abendlandes bis um 1200* (Wiesbaden, 1958).

Rost, H., *Die Bibel im Mittelalter* (Augsburg, 1939).

Smalley, B., *The study of the Bible in the middle ages* (Oxford, 1952).

Spicq, C., *Esquisse d'une histoire de l'exégèse latine au moyen âge* (Paris, 1944).

Stegmüller, F., *Repertorium biblicum medii aevi* (7 vols. Madrid, 1950–61).

Vagaggini, C. and Penco, G., *Bibbia e spiritualità* (Rome, 1966).

Vrégille, B. de, 'Écriture sainte: du 6e au 12e siècle', *Dictionnaire de Spiritualité*, V (Paris, 1960), cols. 170–87.

3. The Bible in the medieval schools

La Bibbia nell'Alto Medioevo (Settimane di Studio del Centro Italiano di Studi sull'Alto Medioevo, X, Spoleto, 1963).

Lubac, H. de, *Exégèse médiévale. Les quatre sens de l'Écriture* (Paris, 1959–64).

McNally, R. E., *The Bible in the early middle ages*, Woodstock Papers no. 4 (The Newman Press, Westminster, Maryland, 1959).

Smalley, B., *The study of the Bible in the middle ages* (2nd ed. Oxford, 1952).
English friars and antiquity in the early fourteenth century (Oxford, 1960).
Spicq, P. C., *Esquisse d'une histoire de l'exégèse latine au moyen âge* (Paris, 1944).
Stegmüller, F., *Repertorium Biblicum Medii Aevi* (Madrid, 1949–61), seven volumes, in progress.

4. The Bible in liturgical use

Andrieu, M., 'Les Ordines Romani du haut moyen-âge', vols. II–V, *Spicilegium sacrum lovaniense*, fasc. 23, 24, 28, 29 (Louvain, 1948–61).
Daniélou, J., 'The Bible and the liturgy', *Liturgical Studies*, III, University of Notre-Dame Press, 1956 (London, 1961).
Dijk, S. J. P. van, 'Sources of the modern Roman liturgy. The ordinals by Haymo of Faversham and related documents (1243–1307)', *Studia et documenta franciscana*, vols. I, II (2 vols. Leiden, 1963).
Diringer, D., *The illuminated book. Its history and production* (London [1958]).
Frere, W. H., *Studies in early Roman liturgy.* II. *The Roman gospel-lectionary.* III. *The Roman epistle-lectionary*, in *Alcuin club collections*, nos. XXX, XXXII (Oxford, 1934–5).
Gamber, K., 'Codices liturgici latini antiquiores', *Spicilegium friburgense. Subsidia* I (Freiburg (Sw.), 1963), pp. 192–9 (nos. 1001–50), 204–33 (nos. 1101–1290).
'Die kampanische Lektionsordnung', *Sacris Erudiri*, XIII (1962), 326–52.
'Oratio ad collectam. Ein beitrag zür römischen Stationsliturgie' in *Ephem. liturg.* LXXXII (1968), 45–7.
Hänggi, A.–Pahl, I., Prex eucharistica. Textus e variis liturgiis antiquioribus selecti, *Spicilegium friburgense*, XII (Freiburg (Sw.), 1968), 62 f., 81, 92 f., 112 f., 120 f., etc. (institution narratives).
Hennig, J., 'The first chapter of Genesis in the liturgy', *Catholic Biblical Quarterly*, X (1948), 360–75.
Hesbert, R.-J., Antiphonale missarum sextuplex...d'après le graduel de Monza et les antiphonaires de Rhenau, du Mont-Blandin, de Compiègne, de Corbie et de Senlis (Brussels, 1935).
  Corpus antiphonalium officii. I. Manuscripti 'cursus romanus'. II. Manuscripti 'cursus monasticus'. III. Invitatoria et antiphonae. Editio critica, *Rerum ecclesiasticarum documenta. Series maior. Fontes VII. VIII. IX* (Rome, 1963, 1965, 1968) (to be continued).
Hughes, A. (ed.), 'Early medieval music up to 1300', *New Oxford history of music* (Oxford, 1954).
Jungmann, J. A., *Missarum solemnia. Eine genetische Erklärung der römischen Messe* (3rd rev. ed. Vienna, 1952); 2 vols. with, under the same title: *Nachträge zur 3. Auflage* (Freiburg, 1958). English transl. by F. A. Brunner, *The Mass of the Roman rite. Its origins and development (Missarum solemnia)* (2 vols. New York, 1951, 1954).
  Der Gottesdienst der Kirche; auf dem Hintergrund seiner Geschichte kurz erläutert (2nd rev. ed. Tyrolia, 1957). English transl. by C. Howell, *Public worship* (London, 1957).

Bibliography

Kunze, G., *Die gottesdienstliche Schriftlesung*. I. *Stand und Aufgaben der Perikopen-forschung* (Göttingen, 1947); only 1 vol. published.

Le Roux, R., Aux origines de l'office festif. Les antiennes et les psaumes de matines et de laudes pour noël et le Ier janvier selon les cursus romain et monastique, *Études grégoriennes*, IV (1961), 65–170.

Etude de l'office dominical et férial. Les répons 'de psalmis' pour les matines de épiphanie à la septuagésime selon les cursus romain et monastique, *Études grégoriennes*, III (1963), 39–148.

Parsch, P., *Das Jahr des Heiles* (13th ed. Klosterneuburg, 1947). English transl. by W. C. Heidt, *The church's year of grace* (5 vols. Collegeville, 1957–8). *Messerklärung*. English transl. *The liturgy of the Mass* (Collegeville, 1960).

Quacquarelli, A., 'Retorica e liturgia antenicena', *Ricerche patristiche*, I (Desclée, 1960).

Reese, G., *Music in the middle ages. With an introduction on the music of ancient times* (New York [1940]), 57–193.

Righetti, M., *Manuale di storia liturgica* (2nd ed. 4 vols. Milan, 1950–9).

Willis, G. G., 'St Augustine's lectionary', *Alcuin club collections*, no. XLIV (London, 1962) (contains much information of later date).

5. The study of the Bible in medieval Judaism

Bacher, W., 'Die Bibelexegese vom Anfang des 10. bis zum Ende des 15. Jahr-hunderts', in Winter u. Wünsche, *Die Jüdische Litteratur...*, Band 2 (Trier, 1894).

Driver, S. R. and Neubauer, Ad., *The fifty-third chapter of Isaiah according to the Jewish interpreters*. Texts and translations (Oxford, 1876).

Heinemann, I., 'Die wissenschaftliche Allegoristik des jüdischen Mittelalters', *Hebrew Union College Annual*, XXIII (1950–1).

Loewe, H. and Trend, J. B. (eds.), *Isaac Abravanel* (Cambridge, 1937).

Loewe, R. J., 'Herbert of Bosham's Commentary on Jerome's Hebrew Psalter', *Biblica*, XXXIV (1953).

Poznanski, A., *Schiloh* (Leipzig, 1904).

Poznanski, S., *Eliezer of Beaugency's commentaries on Ezekiel and the minor prophets* (Warsaw, 1910–13) (German introduction espec.).

Rosenthal, Erwin I. J., 'Rashi and the English Bible', *Bulletin of the John Rylands Library*, XXIX, i (1940).

'Don Isaac Abravanel: financier, statesman and scholar', *ibid.* XXI, ii (1937).

'Sebastian Münster's knowledge and use of Jewish exegesis', *Essays presented to Dr J. H. Hertz*, ed. I. Epstein, E. Levine and C. Roth (London, 1943).

'Edward Lively: Cambridge Hebraist', *Essays and studies presented to Stanley A. Cook*, ed. D. Winton Thomas (London, 1950).

'Anti-Christian polemics in medieval Bible commentaries', *Journal of Jewish Studies*, XI (1960).

'Medieval Jewish exegesis: its character and significance', *Journal of Semitic Studies*, IX, 2 (1964).

Scholem, G., *Major trends in Jewish mysticism*[3] (London, 1955).

Bibliography

Smalley, B., 'Andrew of St Victor, abbot of Wigmore: a twelfth-century Hebraist', *Recherches Théologiques Anciennes et Médiévales*, x.
'The School of Andrew of St Victor', *ibid.* XI.
*The study of the Bible in the middle ages*² (Oxford, 1952).

CHAPTER VII

The 'People's Bible'

The classic works that deal with the representation of biblical history in art forms are:
Künstle, K., *Ikonographie der christlichen Kunst* (Freiburg, 1928).
Mâle, E., *L'art religieux en France*.
  1. *L'art du XII* siècle* (5th ed. Paris, 1947).
  2. *L'art du XIII* siècle* (8th ed. Paris, 1948). English translation by Dora Nussey (1913).
  3. *L'art de la fin du moyen âge* (4th ed. Paris, 1931).

Also of much general value:
Gardner, A., *English medieval sculpture* (Cambridge, 1951).
James, M. R., *The Apocalypse in art* (London, 1931).
Kondakov, N. P. (trans. E. H. Minns), *The Russian icon* (Oxford, 1927).
Rushforth, G. McN., *Medieval Christian imagery* (Oxford, 1936).
Smalley, Beryl, *The study of the Bible in the middle ages* (Oxford, 1952).
Talbot Rice, D., *Art of the Byzantine era* (London, 1963).
Tristram, E. W., *English medieval wallpainting* (Oxford, 1950).
Volbach, F. W. and Hirmer, M., *Early Christian art* (London, 1961).

Works of reference:
Aurenhammer, H., *Lexikon der christlichen Ikonographie* (Vienna, 1963–).
Dictionnaire d'archéologie chrétienne et de liturgie, ed. F. Cabrol and H. Leclercq (Paris, 1907–53).
Réau, R., *Iconographie de l'art chrétien* (Paris, 1955).

The Catacombs
Cabrol–Leclercq (as above), art. 'Catacombes'.
Elliger, W., *Zur Entstehung und frühen Entwicklung der altchristlichen Bildkunst* (Leipzig, 1934).
Grant, M., *The early Christians* (London, 1960).
Wilpert, G., *Die Malereien der Katakomben Roms* (Freiburg, 1903). This majestic work remains the standard storehouse of information on the paintings.

Doura-Europus
Hopkins, C. and Baur, P. V. C., 'The Christian Church', *Excavations at Dura Europus: Reports of the Yale Expedition*, 5 (1934).
Rostovtzeff, M., *Dura Europus and its Art* (London, 1938).

Bibliography

Sarcophagi

Gerke, F., *Die christlichen Sarkophage der vorkonstantinischen Zeit* (Berlin, 1940).
Wilpert, G., *I sarcofagi cristiani antichi* (3 vols. Rome, 1929–36).

The Churches of Rome

Corpus Basilicarum Christianarum Romae (in English), R. Krautheimer and others (Rome, 1962–).
Wilpert, G., *Die römischen Mosaiken und Malereien der kirklichen Bauten* (Freiburg, 1917).

Mosaics

Bartl, F. X. and Boehringer, J., *Ravenna: S. Vitale* and *Ravenna: S. Apollinare in Classe* (Baden-Baden, 1959).
Borini, G., *Mosaici di Ravenna* (Milan, 1956).
Cechelli, C., *S. Maria Maggiore* (Rome, 1956).

Stained glass

Aubert, M., Grodecki, L. and others, *Le vitrail français* (Paris, 1958).
Le Couteur, J. D., *English medieval painted glass* (London, 1926).

Special studies include:

Delaporte, Y. and Houvet, E., *Les vitraux de la cathédrale de Chartres* (Chartres, 1926).
Grodecki, L., 'A stained glass Atelier of the thirteenth century', *Journal of the Warburg and Courtauld Institutes* (1948).
Rackham, B., *The ancient glass of Canterbury Cathedral* (London, 1949).
Venier, J., *La cathédrale de Bourges et ses vitraux* (Paris, 1943).
Woodforde, C., *Stained glass in Somerset* (London, 1946).
 The Norwich school of glass-painting (Oxford, 1950).

Manuscripts

See bibliography and notes of chapter VIII.

Works on the Vienna Genesis include:

Gerstinger, H. (Vienna, 1955).
Hartel, W. von and Wickhoff, F. (Vienna, 1895).
Wellesz, E. (London, 1960).

Bestiaries

Druce, G. C., 'The medieval bestiaries and their influence on ecclesiastical decorative art', *Journal of the British Architectural Association* (1919 and 1920).
James, M. R., *The bestiary* (Roxburghe Club, 1928).
Millar, E. G., *A thirteenth century bestiary in the library of Alnwick Castle* (Roxburghe Club, 1958).

Bibliography

Illustrated commentaries

Speculum humanae salvationis:

James, M. R. (Oxford, 1926).

Lutz, J. and Perdrizet, P. (Mulhouse, 1907).

Biblia Pauperum:

Cornell, J. H. (Stockholm, 1925).

Heitz, P. (Strassburg, 1903).

Laborde, A. de, *La Bible moralisée* (Paris, 1911–27).

Schmidt, G., *Die Armenbibeln des XIV. Jahrhunderts* (Vienna, 1959).

Schramm, A., *Bilderschmuck der Frühdrucke* (Leipzig, 1920–39).

Strachan, J., *Early Bible illustrations* (Cambridge, 1957).

CHAPTER VIII

Bible illustration in medieval manuscripts

It is suggested that the footnotes be also used as instruments
of a bibliographical nature.

Beissel, S., *Geschichte der Evangelienbücher in der ersten Hälfte des Mittelalters*
(Freiburg im Breisgau, 1906).

Cornell, H., *Biblia Pauperum* (Stockholm, 1925).

Delisle, L., 'Livres d'images destinés à l'instruction religieuse et aux exercices de
piété des laïques', *L'Histoire Littéraire de la France*, XXXI (1890), 213–85.

De Wald, E. T., *The illustrations of the Utrecht Psalter* (Princeton, 1933).

Goldschmidt, A., *Der Albanipsalter in Hildesheim* (Berlin, 1895), pp. 1–25, contains
an important sketch of medieval Psalter illustration.

James, M. R., *The Apocalypse in art* (Schweich Lectures of the British Academy,
1927) (London, 1931).

'Illustration of the Old Testament; being an introduction to S. C. Cockerell
and M. R. James, *A book of Old Testament illustrations of the middle of the
thirteenth century*' (Roxburghe Club, Cambridge, 1927).

Laborde, A. de, *Étude sur la Bible Moralisée illustrée* (Paris, 1911–27).

Leroquais, V., *Les Psautiers manuscrits latins des bibliothèques publiques de
France* (Mâcon, 1940–1), I, pp. lxxxxvi–cxxxv.

Neuss, W., *Die Katalanische Bibel-illustration um die Wende des ersten Jahrtausends
und die altspanische Buchmalerei* (Bonn 1922).

Neuss, W., 'Bibel-illustration', an article in the *Reallexikon zur deutschen Kunstgeschichte*, ed. Otto Schmitt, II, cols. 478–517.

Rost, H., *Die Bibel im Mittelalter* (Augsburg, 1939), contains useful lists of
illustrations found in the *Biblia Pauperum*, pp. 220–1, the *Speculum humanae
salvationis*, pp. 235–6 and the *Concordantia Caritatis*, pp. 240–6.

Bibliography

CHAPTER IX

The Vernacular Scriptures

1. *The Gothic Bible*

(For a fuller bibliography the reader should consult 'Bibliographia Gotica' in *Medieval Studies*, XII, XV and XIX. A further supplement was due to appear in the volume for 1967.)

Balg, G. H., *A comparative glossary of the Gothic language* (Mayville, 1887).

Bardy, G., 'Ulphila', *Dictionnaire de Théologie Catholique*, XV (1950), cols. 2048–57.

Bennett, William H., *The Gothic commentary on the Gospel of John*. Modern Language Association of America (New York, 1960; Oxford, 1962).

Bernhardt, E., *Vulfila* (Halle, 1875).

Bradley, Henry, *The Goths* (London, 1898).

Burkitt, F. C., 'The Vulgate Gospels and the Codex Brixianus', *Journal of Theological Studies*, I (1900), 129–34.

Dietrich, E., *Die Bruchstücke der Skeireins* (Strassburg, 1903).

Feist, Sigmund, *Vergleichendes Wörterbuch der gotischen Sprache* (Leiden, 1939).

Friedrichsen, G. W. S., *The Gothic Version of the epistles* (Oxford, 1939).

The Gothic Version of the Gospels (Oxford, 1926).

'The Gothic Skeireins in the Greek original', *New Testament Studies*, VIII, no. 1 (1961).

Friesen, Otto von and Grape, A., *Om Codex Argenteus* (Uppsala, 1928).

Gabelentz, H. C. von der, and Loebe, J., *Ulfilas* (Leipzig, 1846).

Gwatkin, H. M., *Studies in Arianism* (London, 1900).

Henning, H., *Der Wulfila der Bibliotheca Augusta zu Wolfenbüttel (Codex Carolinus), herausgegeben und eingeleitet* (Hamburg, 1913).

Hodgkin, Thomas, *Italy and her invaders* (Oxford, 1880).

Kauffmann, F., *Aus der Schule des Wulfila. Auxentii Dorostorensis epistula* (Strassburg, 1899). (Texte und Untersuchungen zur altgermanischen Religionsgeschichte, 1.)

Kauffmann, F., 'Beiträge zur Quellenkritik der gotischen Bibelübersetzung', *Zeitschrift für deutsche Philologie*, XXIX (1897)–XLIII (1911).

Klein, Karl Kurt, 'Der Auxentiusbrief als Quelle der Wulfilabiographie', *Zeitschrift für deutsches Altertum und deutsche Literatur*, LXXXIV (1952), 99–152.

Lagrange, M. J., *Introduction à l'étude du Nouveau Testament*. 2ème partie, pp. 325–42, 523–5 (Paris, 1935).

Lietzmann, H., 'Die Vorlage der gotischen Bibel', *ZfdA*, LVI (1919), 249–78.

Linke, W., *Das gotische Markusevangelium* (Berlin, 1920).

Mossé, Fernand, *Manuel de la langue gotique* (Paris, 1956).

Odefey, Paul, *Das gotische Lukasevangelium* (Kiel, 1908).

Schmidt, K. D., *Die Bekehrung der Ostgermanen zum Christentum* (Göttingen, 1939).

Scott, Ch. A. A., *Ulfilas, apostle of the Goths* (Cambridge, 1885).

525

Streitberg, W., *Die gotische Bibel* (Heidelberg, 1950).
Vries, Jan de, *Wulfilae Codices Ambrosiani rescripti* (Florence, 1936).
Wrede, F., *Stamm-Heynes Ulfilas* (Paderborn, 1920).
Wright, Jos., *A primer of the Gothic language* (Oxford, 1954).

Editions of the Gothic bible

The following are the most important editions of the Gothic bible:

Bernhardt, E., *Vulfila oder die gotische Bibel mit dem entsprechenden griechischen Text und mit kritischem und erklärendem Kommentar nebst dem Kalender, der Skeireins und den gotischen Urkunden* (Halle, 1875). The first endeavour to establish the Greek original.

Gabelentz, H. C. von der and Loebe, J., *Ulfilas. Veteris et novi testamenti versionis gothicae fragmenta quae supersunt* (Leipzig, 1843–6). The text is out of date, but vol. II contains a complete glossary.

Streitberg, W., *Die gotische Bibel.* I. *Der gotische Text und seine griechische Vorlage mit Einleitung, Lesarten und Quellennachweisen sowie den kleinern Denkmälern als Anhang* (3rd ed. Heidelberg, 1950). II. *Gotisch-griechisch-deutsches Wörterbuch* (2nd ed. Heidelberg, 1928). The first serious attempt to reconstruct the Greek text used by Ulfilas.

Wrede, F., *Stamm-Heynes Ulfilas oder die uns erhaltenen Denkmäler der gotischen Sprache. Text, Grammatik, Wörterbuch* (14th ed. Paderborn, 1920).

For a fuller bibliography readers may consult F. Mossé, 'Bibliographia Gotica', pp. 255–63 in *Medieval Studies*, vol. XII.

2. *English versions of the Scriptures before Wyclif*

Editions of texts cited are given in the footnotes.

Crawford, S. J., *The Old English Version of the Heptateuch, Ælfric's treatise on the Old and New Testament and his Preface to Genesis*, Early English Text Society 160 (1922).

Krapp, G. P. and Dobbie, E. van K., *The Anglo-Saxon poetic records* (New York, 1931–53).

Skeat, W. W., *The Holy Gospels in Anglo-Saxon, Northumbrian and Old Mercian Versions* (Oxford, 1871–87).

For bibliographical information on other scriptural material in Old English, see N. R. Ker, *Catalogue of manuscripts containing Anglo-Saxon* (Oxford, 1957).

Cook, A. S., *Biblical quotations in Old English prose writers* (London, 1898). Introduction, pp. xiii–lxxx.

Deanesly, Margaret, *The Lollard Bible* (revd ed., Cambridge, 1965).

Glunz, H. H., *The Vulgate in England from Alcuin to Roger Bacon* (Cambridge, 1933).

Smalley, Beryl, *The Study of the Bible in the Middle Ages* (2nd ed. Oxford, 1952).

For bibliography of scriptural material in Middle English, see J. E. Wells, *A Manual of the Writings in Middle English 1050–1400*, and *Supplements* (New

Haven, 1916–); in Anglo-Norman, see J. Vising, *Anglo-Norman Language and Literature* (London, 1923): M. Dominica Legge, *Anglo-Norman Literature and its Background* (Oxford, 1963).

3. *The Wycliffite versions*

Texts. The only printed text of the whole Wycliffite bible in both the recognized versions is *The Holy Bible, containing the Old and New Testaments, with the Apocryphal books, in the earliest English version made from the Latin Vulgate by John Wycliffe and his followers*, edited by the Reverend Josiah Forshall and Sir Frederic Madden (4 vols. Oxford, 1850). Earlier editions of the New Testament alone, from different manuscripts, are: of the earlier version, *The New Testament in English, translated by John Wycliffe, circa MCCCLXXX*, edited by Lea Wilson (London, 1848); of the later version, *The New Testament. . .translated out of the Latin Vulgat by John Wiclif. . .about 1378. . .*, edited by John Lewis (London, 1731); *The New Testament translated from the Latin in the year 1380 by John Wiclif, to which are prefixed. . .an historical account of the Saxon and English versions of the Scriptures. . .*, edited by the Reverend Henry Hervey Baber (London, 1810); and *The English Hexapla, exhibiting the six important English translations of the New Testament Scriptures, Wiclif, Tyndale, etc.*, published by Bagster and Sons (London, n.d. (1841)). Since 1850, two parts of the later version have been separately reprinted from Forshall and Madden's edition: *The New Testament in English, according to the version by John Wycliffe. . .and revised by John Purvey* (with an introduction by the Reverend Walter W. Skeat) (Oxford, 1879) and *The Books of Job, Psalms, Proverbs, Ecclesiastes and the Song of Solomon, according to the Wycliffite version made by Nicholas de Hereford. . .and revised by John Purvey* (with an introduction by the Reverend Walter W. Skeat) (Oxford, 1881). See also *The New Testament in Scots, being Purvey's revision of Wycliffe's version turned into Scots by Murdoch Nisbet, c. 1520*, edited by Thomas Graves Law, Scottish Text Society (3 vols. Edinburgh, 1901–5). The earliest form of the earlier version is currently being edited, one volume being devoted to each scribe, by Conrad Lindberg: *MS Bodley 959. Genesis–Baruch 3. 20 in the Earlier Version of the Wycliffite Bible* (Stockholm Studies in English, vols. VI, VIII, X, XIII).

The other late-fourteenth-century translations are published as: *A fourteenth-century English biblical version*, edited by Anna C. Paues (Cambridge: printed privately in 1902, with a valuable introduction on medieval English biblical versions: reprinted without this introduction in 1904 and 1909), and *The Pauline epistles contained in MS Parker 32, Corpus Christi College Cambridge*, edited by Margaret J. Powell (London: Early English Text Society, Extra Series 116: 1916).

Studies. The introductions to Lewis's and Baber's editions are quite out of date. That to Forshall and Madden's edition is still important; it explains many features of their edition and gives the only available list of manuscripts (now in need of revision). It is the source of virtually every popular account of the Wycliffite versions in the last hundred years. To supplement and correct it there are two books, Margaret Deanesly, *The Lollard Bible and other medieval biblical Versions* (Cambridge, 1920), and Sven L. Fristedt, *The Wycliffe Bible: Part I: the principal problems connected with Forshall and Madden's edition* (Stockholm Studies in English, IV, 1953); a published lecture, Margaret Deanesly, *The Significance of the Lollard Bible* (London, 1951); and a few recent articles: E. W. Talbert, 'A note on the Wyclyfite Bible translations', *Studies in English* (Univ. of Texas Publ. 4026) (1940), pp. 29–38; H. Hargreaves, 'The Latin text of Purvey's Psalter', *Medium Ævum*, XXIV (1955), 73–90; S. L. Fristedt, 'The authorship of the Lollard Bible', *Studier i Modern Språkvetenskap*, XIX (1956), 28–41; H. Hargreaves, 'An intermediate Version of the Wycliffite Old Testament', *Studia Neophilologica*, XXVIII (1956), 130–47; and 'The marginal glosses to the Wycliffite New Testament', *Studia Neophilologica*, XXXIII (1961), 285–300.

Other works. The background to the Wycliffite translations and the personalities of Wyclif himself and his most important followers and opponents are most fully recorded in H. B. Workman, *John Wyclif: a study of the English medieval church* (2 vols. Oxford, 1926). A shorter and more stimulating account, with a different viewpoint, is that of K. B. McFarlane, *John Wycliffe and the beginnings of English non-conformity* (Teach Yourself History Series: London, 1952). Most of Wyclif's own philosophical and theological treatises in Latin are available in the volumes of the Wyclif Society from 1882 to 1913. English works by him and his followers— it is often impossible to be certain of the authorship of any work—are in *Select English Works of John Wyclif*, edited by Thomas Arnold (3 vols. Oxford, 1869), and *The English works of Wyclif hitherto unprinted*, edited by F. D. Matthew (Early English Text Society, Original Series 74: London, 1880), with an excellent selection in *Wyclif: Select English Writings*, edited by H. E. Winn (Oxford, 1929).

4. *Vernacular Scriptures in Germany and the Low Countries*

Bruin, C. C. de, *De Statenbijbel en zijn Voorgangers* (Leiden, 1937).

Buma, W. J., 'Geestelijke Literatuur in Oud-Friesland', *Trijeresom* (Grins (Groningen), 1950).

Knight Bostock, J., *A handbook on Old High German literature* (Oxford, 1955).

Rost, H., *Die Bibel im Mittelalter* (Augsburg, 1939).

Stammler, W. and Langosch, K., *Die deutsche Literatur des Mittelalters: Verfasserlexikon* (Berlin, 1933–55).

Waxman, M., *History of Jewish literature*, vol. II (New York, 1943).

5. *Vernacular Scriptures in France*

ABBREVIATIONS: *BXIII* = Berger's 'Bible du XIIIᵉ siècle' (redated *c.* 1280–1300, see p. 446 n. 1 and p. 447 n. 2; *BH* = *Bible historiale*, the original work of Guyart des Moulins (1291–5); *BHC* = 'Bible historiale complétée', a compilation in existence by 1317, in which *BH* is followed by the second volume of *BXIII*.

Select list of manuscripts

The following list is selective, and the reader who wishes for a completer account can consult Berger, pp. 321–435, a description of about 190 manuscripts. He will however find here several manuscripts unknown to Berger in 1884: these are marked with an asterisk.

Bibliothèque Nationale, Paris

Fonds latin 8846: a partial copy of the Eadwine Psalter, as far as Ps. 99 (98), without the Old English interlinear gloss; *c.* 1200.

Fonds français 1: an Anglo-Norman translation of the whole Bible as far as Hebrews xiii. 17, the family bible of John de Welles (*d.* 1361); partial copies of this text are in British Museum, Royal 1 C iii and fr. 9562.

6–7: *BXIII*, a copy made for baron de Villars (*d.* 1440).

152: the Calais Bible ('Calais. Nota' written twice in margin of I Macc. v. 51), *BH* with extracts from *BXIII*; after 1347 (siege of Calais).

155: *BH* complete but for the apocryphal pieces; first half of fourteenth century.

398: *BXIII* (or *BHC*), volume II, after 1280; belonged to Humbert Roy of Bourg-en-Bresse in the fifteenth century.

899: the De Thou abridged Bible, text of *BXIII*, after 1280.

5707: the Louvre Bible, bearing the names of Charles V, the duc de Berry, Henry III, Louis XIII and Louis XIV, *BXIII* (or *BHC*), volume II, dated 1363.

*6447: a compilation made for Flemish patrons, *c.* 1275, cf. *Notices et Extraits des mss. de la Bibl. Nat.* XXXV, 2 (1896), 1–78.

12581: a Champenois miscellany, *c.* 1280–90, containing the gospels, text of *BXIII*.

13091: a psalter made for the duc de Berry, according to the use of Bourges, illuminated by André Beauneveu, *c.* 1380–5.

15397: the translation of Jean de Sy (or Cis), dated 1355.

*24728: an abridged bible, related to the De Thou-Widener collection, text of *BXIII*, late thirteenth century.

*nouvelles acquisitions françaises 1404: a copy of the Acre Bible, latter half of the thirteenth century; cf. *Romania*, XVII (1888), 126–9, 132–5.

Bibliothèque de l'Arsénal, Paris

5056: *BXIII*, volume I, a copy almost identical with Harley 616; *c.* 1300.

5059: the Papeleu Bible, the oldest known copy of *BHC*, signed and dated 1317.

5211: the Acre Bible, a collection of mainly historical books from the Old Testament, probably made and illuminated for St Louis in the Holy Land, *c.* 1250–4.

Bibliothèque Mazarine, Paris

35 (684): *BXIII* (or *BHC*), volume II, *c.* 1300.

54 (70): the late-twelfth-century manuscript of the four books of Kings, followed by a slightly later copy of Maccabees.

312 (552): a most reliable copy of *BH*; according to Berger, pp. 164–77, it retains the original spelling of the author, and preserves a pre-1297 version of the work, without the prefaces; text of Acts borrowed from *BXIII*; latter half of fourteenth century, owned by the Crèvecœur family in the fifteenth.

382 (798): the Metz Psalter, fourteenth century.

Musée Condé, Chantilly
  *3: a derivative of the Acre Bible, fourteenth century.
  *4–5: *BXIII*, a complete copy in two volumes, early fourteenth century.
Bibliothèque Publique de Rouen, A 211: *BXIII* (or *BHC*), volume II, late thirteenth
  century.
Bibliothèque de la ville de Strasbourg, C iv 10: *BXIII*, volume I, thirteenth–fourteenth century; seen by Reuss, but destroyed by fire in 1870.
British Museum, London
  Royal I A xx: *BXIII* (or *BHC*), volume II, copied in prison at Paris by Robert
  de la Marche, 1312.
  18 D ix,x, 15 D i: *BH*, a copy in three volumes produced for Edward IV, the first
  two volumes copied in 1479; the third volume, taken from stock, is dated 1470.
  19 C ii: a copy of the Gospels, fourteenth century.
  19 C v: a copy of volume II of the Durham Psalter Commentary, c. 1200.
  19 D ii: *BHC*, the Bible of Jean II, lost on the field of Poitiers, 1356.
  19 D iii: *BH*, copied by Thomas du Val of Clairefontaine, near Chartres, 1411.
  20 B v: an undecorated copy of the New Testament from *BXIII*, England, early
  fourteenth century.
  Harley 273: an Anglo-Norman miscellany, once owned by John Clerk, grocer to
  Edward IV; contains the Psalter; c. 1300.
  616: the first volume of the Simonds d'Ewes Bible, *BXIII*, c. 1300; cf. Additional
  MSS 41751.
  Lansdowne 1175: the Bible of Raoul de Presles, with the translator's preface,
  copied by Henri de Trévou, late fourteenth century, with signature of duc de
  Berry.
  Arundel 230: Psalter with French interlinear gloss, c. 1200.
  *Additional 40619–20: the Sanford Bible, an Old Testament in the text of *BXIII*
  copied and illuminated in England, late thirteenth century.
  *41751: the second volume of the Simonds d'Ewes Bible, *BXIII*, c. 1300; cf.
  Harley 616 above.
Cambridge University Library, Ee 3. 52: volume I of an Old Testament (or more
  probably of a complete bible; the text goes down to the end of Job), text of
  BXIII; England, late fourteenth century; bequeathed by Sir Thomas Croftys
  to the canonesses of Flixton in 1442.
Trinity College, Cambridge, R 17. 1: the Eadwine Psalter, Canterbury, c. 1160.
Bodleian Library, Oxford, Douce MS 320: the Montebourg Psalter, end of twelfth
  century.
Christ Church, Oxford, 178: a splendidly illuminated New Testament, text of
  BXIII, after 1280.
Durham Cathedral Library, A ii 11–13: the Durham Psalter Commentary, perhaps
  before 1195; odd volumes in the Royal Collection and the Pierpont Morgan
  Library.
Bibliothèque Royale, Brussels 91 (II 987), previously Phillipps 379: *BH*, with Acts
  from *BXIII*, fourteenth century.
  97 (10993): Gospels in text of *BXIII*, fourteenth century.

Bibliography

Iena University Library, N. B. 97–8: *BH*, with a selection of books from *BXIII*; late fifteenth century, belonged to Charles de Croy (*d.* 1527), the godfather of the emperor Charles V.

Vatican Library, Regina 26: *BXIII* (or *BHC*), volume II, *c.* 1300.

Pierpont Morgan Library, New York, M 338: a copy of volume I of the Durham Psalter Commentary, early thirteenth century, similar in decoration to the Ingeborg Psalter; formerly in the collection of Lecaron de Troussures, from Beauvais Cathedral Library, Berger, p. 384.

*M 494: *BXIII*, a complete copy, two volumes bound as one; after 1280.

Walters Art Gallery, Baltimore, 501; the Bouillon Bible, previously Ashburnham Appendix 7, Berger, pp. 416–17 and Yates Thomson LXXVI; *BHC*, *c.* 1400.

**Library of Jos. Widener*, Lynnewood Hall, Elkins Park, Philadelphia, 2: a collection of scriptural books similar to the De Thou Bible, f. fr. 899; *c.* 1460.

Editions of texts

For early printed editions see E. Reuss (below), *Revue de théologie...* XIV (1857).

Marquis d'Albon, *Le Livre des Juges. Les cinq textes de la version française faite au xiie siècle pour les chevaliers du Temple* (Lyons, 1913).

D'Arco Silvio Avalle, *Cultura e lingua francese delle origini nella 'Passion' di Clermont-Ferrand* (Milan–Naples, 1962). [For this important MS now at Clermont-Ferrand, a copy of the Glossary of Ansileubus with two Romance poems added in blank spaces, see T. D. Hemming, *Medium Aevum*, XXXV (1966), 43–8 (origins at Saint-Cyprien de Poitiers) and G. de Poerck, *Scriptorium*, XVIII (1964), 11–33.]

Bonnardot, F., *Le Psautier de Metz* (Paris, 1885).

Bossuat, R. and Raynaud de Lage, G., *Les Évangiles des Domées* [use of Cambrai] (Paris, 1955).

Clédat, L., *Le Nouveau Testament traduit au XIIIe siècle en langue provençale, suivi d'un rituel cathare* (Paris, 1887).

Curtius, E. R., *Li Quatre Livre des Reis* (Dresden and Halle, 1911).

Delisle, L. and Meyer, P., *L'Apocalypse en français au XIIIe siècle*, 2 vols., Société des Anciens Textes Français (Paris, 1900–1) [prose version of f. fr. 403, in facsimile with transcription].

Hassall, W. O., *The Holkham bible picture book* (London, 1954) [in facsimile with introduction and commentary].

James, M. R., *The Trinity College Apocalypse*, Roxburghe Club, London, 1909 [facsimile of a prose version, Trinity College, Cambridge, R. 16. 2].

The Canterbury Psalter (London, 1935) [complete facsimile of the Eadwine Psalter]. Cf. T. S. R. Boase, *English art 1100–1216* (Oxford, 1953), pp. 158–60, 289–90.

Liebman, Ch. J., 'Le commentaire français du psautier et le MS. Morgan 338. Pour l'attribution à Simon de Tournai', *Romania*, LXXVI (1955), 433–76 [lengthy extracts from the Pierpont Morgan MS, containing contemporary allusions]; 'Remarks on the manuscript tradition of the French Psalter Commentary', *Scriptorium*, XIII (1959), 61–9 and Pl. 11–13.

Michel, F., *Libri Psalmorum versio antiqua gallica* (Oxford, 1860) [the Montebourg Psalter]; *Le livre des Psaumes*, Documents inédits (Paris, 1876) [the French text of the Eadwine Psalter].

Ratcliff, N. E., *The Acts of the Apostles*, Anglo-Norman Text Society (Oxford, Blackwell) [to appear in 1969; the Anglo-Norman text from f. fr. 1 and 9562].

Rhys, Olwen, *An Anglo-Norman rhymed Apocalypse with Commentary*, with a historical introduction by Sir John Fox, Anglo-Norman Text Society (Oxford, Blackwell, 1946) [poetic version, from the Giffard MS].

Robson, C. A., *Maurice of Sully and the medieval vernacular homily* (Oxford, Blackwell, 1952).

Theben, H., *Die altfr. Achtsilbnerredaktion der Passion* (Greifswald, 1909) and E. Pfuhl, *Die weitere Fassung der altfr. Dichtung...über Christi Höllenfahrt und Auferstehung* (Greifswald, 1909); another French text is in F. A. Foster, *The Northern Passion*, Early English Text Society (O.S.), CXLVII, 102 ff.

Secondary sources

Berger, S., *La Bible française au moyen âge* (Paris, 1884) (cf. P. Meyer in *Romania*, XVII, 1888, 121–44; on the Provençal, Catalan and Vaudois versions, see Berger and Meyer in *Romania*, XVIII, 1889, 353–438; XIX, 1890, 505–61).

Bonnard, J., *Les Traductions de la Bible en vers français au moyen âge* (Paris, 1884).

Buchtal, H., *Miniature painting in the Latin Kingdom of Jerusalem* (Oxford, 1957) [facsimile of pages from the Acre Bible, Pl. 62–81].

Lelong, J., *Bibliotheca Sacra*, I (Paris, 1723), pp. 313–24 [the most learned work before Reuss and Berger].

Mangenot, E., '(Versions) Françaises de la Bible', *Dictionnaire de la Bible*, ed. Vigouroux, II (1895), cols. 2346–73.

Pächt, O., *The rise of pictorial narrative in twelfth-century England* (Oxford, 1962).

Reuss, E., 'Fragments littéraires et critiques relatifs à l'histoire de la Bible française', *Revue de théologie et de philosophie chrétienne*, II (1851), 1–21, 321–43; IV (1852), 1–26; V (1852), 321–439; VI (1853), 65–96; XIV (1857), 1–48, 73–104, 129–60. (revised S. Berger), 'Romanische Bibelübersetzungen', *Realencyclopädie für protestantische Theologie und Kirche*, 3ᵉ Aufl. III (1897), 125–45.

Graf Vitzthum, G., *Die Pariser Miniaturmalerei von der Zeit des hl. Ludwigs bis zu Philipp von Valois und ihr Verhältnis zur Malerei in Nordwesteuropa* (Leipzig, 1907) [a fundamental work on book illumination; revises Berger's datings of the *BXIII* MSS].

See also R. Bossuat, *Manuel bibliographique de la littérature française au moyen âge* (Melun, 1951), nos. 3007–87, *Suppl. 1949–1953* (1955), nos. 6589–97, *Second Suppl. 1954–60* (1961), nos. 7742–7, especially for the verse adaptations of the Bible not dealt with in this article. For a general survey of biblical themes on the medieval French stage, see Grace Frank, *The Medieval French Drama* (Oxford, 1954), pp. 18–92, 125–35, 161–96.

Bibliography

6. Vernacular Scriptures in Italy

Berger, S., 'La Bible italienne au moyen-âge', *Romania*, XXIII (1894), 358–431.

La Bibbia volgare, ed. C. Negroni (10 vols. Bologna, 1882–7).

Cassuto, U., 'La tradizione giudeo-italiano per la traduzione della Bibbia', *Atti del primo Congresso nazionale delle tradizioni popolari* (Florence, 1930).

De Luca, G., *Letteratura di pietà a Venezia dal, 300 al '600* (ed. V. Branca, Florence, 1963), pp. 1–26.

Groppi, F., *Dante traduttore* (2nd ed. Rome, 1962), pp. 17–47, 147–56.

Minocchi, S., 'Versions italiennes de la Bible', *Dictionnaire de la Bible* (Vigouroux), III, cols. 1012 ff.

Steinschneider, M., 'Jüdische Literatur des Mittelalters', *Jewish Quarterly Review*, XVI (1904), 373–95, 734–64.

Vaccari, A., S.J., 'Propaggini del Diatessaron in Occidente', *Biblica*, XII (1931), 326–54.

Vaccari, A., S.J., Todesco, V., and Vattasso, M., *Il Diatessaron in volgare italiano*, 'Studi e Testi', no. 81, Città del Vaticano (1938).

Vaccari, A., S.J., *Scritti di erudizione e di filologia* (Rome, 1958), II, 378–90.

7. Vernacular Scriptures in Spain

The following bibliographical essays were published by the same author to accompany the chapter:

'Apuntes bibliográficos para la iniciación al estudio de las Biblias medievales en castellano', *Sefarad*, XX (1960), 66–109.

'Apuntes bibliográficos para la iniciación al estudio de las Biblias medievales en catalán', *Analecta Sacra Tarraconensia*, XXXI (1960), 271–90.

'Biblia romanceada y Diccionario histórico', *Studia philologica. Homenaje ofrecido a Dámaso Alonso* (Madrid, 1961), pp. 141–52.

Additional studies, published to date, include:

Castilian

General

Gormly, F., *The use of the Bible in representative works of medieval Spanish literature 1250–1300* (Washington, 1962); see also the rev. by D. Catalán in *Hispanic Review*, XXXIII (1965), 310–18.

Morreale, Margherita, 'Aspectos no *filo-lógicos* de las versiones bíblicas medievales en castellano (Esc. I-j-4 y Ac. 87)', *Annali del Corso di Lingue e Letterature Straniere presso l'Università di Bari*, V (1963), 161–87.

Language

Morreale, Margherita, 'Latín eclesiástico en los libros sapienciales y romanceamientos bíblicos...MSS Esc. I-j-6 y I-j-4', *Boletín de la R. Academia Española*, XLII (1962), 47–89.

'Arcaísmos y aragonesismos en el Salterio del MS bíblico escurialense I-j-8', *Archivo de Filología Aragonesa*, XII–XIII (1961–2), 7–21.

'Algunas adiciones... sacadas de las antiguas biblias judeo-españolas' (Esc. I-j y I-j-5)', *Revista Portuguesa de Filologia*, XII (1962–3), 383–93.

'El glosario del Rabí Mosé Arragel de Alba', *Bulletin of Hispanic Studies*, XXXVIII (1961), 145–52.

Review of R. Levy, *Contribution à la lexicographie française selon d'anciens textes d'origine juive* (Syracuse University Press, 1960), in *Revista de Filología Española*, XLV (1962), 345–50.

See also M. Bannitt, 'Une langue fantôme: le judéo-français', *Revue de Linguistique Romane*, XXVII (1963), 245–94.

Individual manuscripts

Translated by Christians:

Almerik, *La faⱬienda de ultramar. Biblia romanceada et itinéraire biblique du XIIe siècle*, ed. M. Lazar (Salamanca, 1965). This amazing document, already mentioned by Gallardo, was published several years after the completion of this chapter. It is a guide to the Holy Land, compiled at the request of Archbishop Raymond of Toledo (*d.* 1152) by one who calls himself archdeacon of Antioch. It contains large portions of Genesis, Exodus, Numbers, Deuteronomy, Joshua, Judges, and of the two books of Samuel and Kings, as well as some verses from Tobit, II Chronicles, and from the Prophets, literally translated from Hebrew, plus some verses from I and II Maccabees from Latin. The manuscript, probably transcribed early in the thirteenth century, bears no title.

General Estoria: cf. M. Morreale, review of the recent edition of part II in *Revista de Filología Española*, XLIV (1961), 455–7, and 'Fraseología bíblica...' in *Linguistic and Literary Studies in Hon. of H. A. Hatⱬfeld* (Washington, 1964), pp. 269–79.

E 6 (Esc. I-j-6); Montgomery, Th., *El Evangelio de San Mateo* (Madrid, 1962), review by M. Morreale in *Nueva Revista de Filología Hispánica*, XVII (1963); de Poerck, G., and Mourin, L., *Introduction à la morphologie comparée des langues romanes basée sur des traductions anciennes des Actes des Apôtres* (Bruges, 1961).

Margherita Morreale, 'De la comparación bíblica en un romanceamiento castellano del Siglo XIII (MS *ESC I-I-6*)' in *Litterae hispanae et lusitanae* (München, 1968), pp. 241–98.

MS 10138 of the Biblioteca Nacional, Madrid: translation of Job, allegedly from Hebrew, attributed to P. Lópezde Ayala, and edited by F. Branciforti, *El libro de Job* (Messina, 1962), lxiv, 175 pp. See also by the same editor another work abounding in biblical quotations: P. López de Ayala, *Las Flores de los 'Morales de Job'* (Florence, 1963), li, 336 pp.; review by M. Morreael in *Hispanic Review*, XXXIV (1966), 361–5.

Translated by Jews:

Morreale, Margherita, 'Las antiguas biblias hebreo-españolas comparadas con el pasaje del cántico de Moisés', *Sefarad*, XXIII (1963), 3–21.

'El Códice de los Profetas en latín y castellano que se conserva en la Biblioteca de la Academia de la Historia (87)', *Boletín de la Real Academia de la Historia*, CI. (1962), 133–49 [the call number now: 1].

'La Biblia de Alba', *Arbor*, XIV (1960), 47–54.

'La Biblia de Ferrara y el Pentateuco de Constantinopla', *Tesoro de los judíos sefardíes*, V (1962), lxxxv–xci.

Révah, I. S., in *Annuaire* (1962/3) [École Pratique des Hautes Études], pp. 144–7.

Jewish Iconography (in a vernacular Bible)

Nordström, C.-O., *The Duke of Alba's Castilian Bible. A Study of the rabbinical features and of the miniatures* (Uppsala: Acta Universitatis Upsaliensis, 1967).

Liturgical prayer

Christian:

Marín, T., 'Fragmento de un Libro de Horas romanceado', *Hispania Sacra*, IX (1956), 175–9.

Morreale, Margherita, 'El canon de la Misa en lengua vernacular y la biblia romanceada del s. XIII', *Hispania Sacra*, XV (1962), 1–17.

Jewish:

Baroja, C., *Los judíos en la España moderna y contemporánea* (Madrid, 1962), I, 422–4; III, 350–2.

Corré, A. D., 'The Spanish Haftara for the Ninth of Ab', *Jewish Quarterly Review*, XLVIII (1957), 13–34. On this see also R. D. Abraham, 'An Amsterdam Version of the Judeo-Spanish Haftara Paraphrase', *Romance Philology*, XIV (1961), 237–44.

Molho, M., *Literatura sefardita de Oriente* (Madrid: C.S.I.C. 1960), pp. 199–224.

Morreale, Margherita 'Libros de oración y traducciones bíblicas de los judíos españoles', *Boletín de la Real Academia de Buenas Letras de Barcelona*, XXIX (1961–2), 239–50.

'El Sidur ladinado de 1552', *Romance Philology*, XVII (1963), 332–8.

Révah, I. S., in *Annuaire 1963/1964* [École Pratique des Hautes Études], pp. 193–8.

Sirat, C., and Révah, I. S., 'Un maḥzor espagnol du XIIIᵉ siècle avec des prescriptions rituelles en Castillan', *Revue des Études Juives*, 3ᵉ sér. III (1961), 353–62.

Catalan

Bohigas, P., 'Los fragments catalans des Evengelis, restes de la traducció de la Biblia de Bonifaci Ferrer', in *Saggi e ricerche in memoria di Ettore Li Gotti* (Palermo, 1961), I, 171–85.

Ventura, J., *Els heretges catalans* (Barcelona, 1963), pp. 110–13.

CHAPTER X

Erasmus in relation to the medieval biblical tradition

The Correspondence of Erasmus is available in the excellent edition of P. S. and H. M. Allen, *Opus epistolarum Des. Erasmi Roterodami denuo recognitum et auctum* (Oxford, 1906–47, 11 vol). For the rest of Erasmus's works, the best complete edition is that of Le Clerc, in 11 folio volumes (Leyden, 1703–6).

NOTES ON THE PLATES

1 Paris, BN, nouv. acq. lat. 710. Exultet roll from Fondi; work closely allied to Montecassino; early twelfth century. Nearly all of the original drawing has been retraced. See A. M. Latil, *Le miniature nei rotoli dell'Exultet. Documenti per la storia della miniatura in Italia* (Montecassino, 1889), fig. 14; M. Avery, *The Exultet rolls of South Italy*, II (Princeton, London, The Hague, 1936), pl. 80.

2 Brussels, BR, lat. 9092, fol. 9ʳ. Treatise on the Lord's prayer, translated from Latin into French by Jean Mielot (*d.* 1472) at Lille in 1457. If this manuscript comes from Mielot's atelier there, its illumination is his most impressive work. See L. M. J. Delaisse, *La miniature flamande. Le mécénat de Philippe le Bon,* flemish transl. *De vlaamse miniatuur. Het mecenaat van Filips de Goede* (Brussels, 1959), p. 93.

3 Fol. 87 *a* from David Kimhi's Hebrew Commentary on the Book of Psalms, showing Ps. 110 subjected to Christian censorship.

4 The raising of Lazarus. Wall painting in the catacomb of SS Peter and Marcellinus, Rome. The paintings in the Roman catacombs represent the earliest form of Christian art and were of an essentially symbolic nature.

5 The earliest surviving representation of Christ crucified. Wooden panel in the door of the church of S. Sabina, Rome, built *c.* 430.

6 Christ as the Good Shepherd. Marble statue of the fourth century now in the Lateran Museum, Rome. The form of the statue is clearly adapted from pagan representations of Hermes.

7 Christ, shown as a beardless youth, enthroned above the pagan god of the sky with Peter and Paul on either hand. A carved panel on the sarcophagus of Junius Bassus, dated 359 and found in S. Peter's church, Rome. Now in the Vatican, Rome.

8 Öst-Nationalbibliothek. Cod: Theol: 31. Rebecca at the well (Genesis xxiv). From the 'Vienna Genesis', a series of forty-eight miniatures illustrating events from the Fall to the death of Jacob, *c.* A.D. 500.

9 Abraham entertaining the three angels by the oaks of Mamre (Genesis xviii). A mosaic panel from the nave of the church of S. Maria Maggiore, Rome, probably late fourth century. The scene is no doubt intended to suggest the Trinity.

10 Abel, Melchizedek and Abraham. A sixth-century mosaic from the church of S. Apollinare in Classe, Ravenna. Melchizedek is portrayed, wearing priestly garments and a royal diadem, as an Old Testament type of Christ.

11 The Stuma Paten, silver gilt, now in Istanbul Museum. The subject is the Communion of the Apostles, shown with the vigorous realism which characterizes Syrian art of the sixth century.

Notes on the Plates

12 St Florian, Austria, MS III 207. The Triumphal Entry into Jerusalem. *Biblia Pauperum, c.* 1310.

13 Öst-Nationalbibliothek, Vienna MS 1198. Christ drives the money changers from the Temple. *Biblia Pauperum.*

14 Worcester Cathedral MS 76. Page from the *Glossa Ordinaria*, probably by Anselm of Laon, showing the passage on the building of the Ark.

15 The vision of Ezekiel. From a version of the *Glossa Ordinaria* printed by Anton Koberger at Nürnberg in 1481.

16-17 Scenes in enamel work from the altar-piece at Klosterneuburg, constructed in 1181 by Nicholas of Verdun. The altar-piece consists of a central panel with two wings, the whole decorated with enamel plaques in three rows ranged one beneath the other. The scenes are grouped in threes with a New Testament incident between two Old Testament incidents.

18 Bodleian, Oxford, Auct. M. 3. 13. A Netherlands manuscript of the fifteenth century. Pentecost, with, as anti-types, Moses receiving the Law and Elijah's sacrifice on Mount Carmel. Reproduced by permission of the Curators to the Bodleian Library.

19 Bourges Cathedral. 'La nouvelle alliance' window. Jacob blesses the sons of Joseph. He sits in Christ-like majesty with his arms forming the shape of the cross. This is the top panel of an immense thirteenth-century window put in at the expense of the local butchers.

20 Norwich Cathedral choirstall. Wood carving of the 'pelican in her piety'. Representations of the pelican pecking at her breast to feed young birds with her blood, typifying the sacrifice of Christ on the Cross, became common after the appearance of Bestiaries in the eleventh century.

21 Worcester Cathedral. Misericord seats in the choir showing two Bestiary creatures: (*a*) the lion, crowned to represent the Lion of Judah (Revelation v. 5), and (*b*) the cockatrice (Isaiah xi. 8) being teased by weasels.

22 The Horned Moses. The 'horns' of Moses are due to a confusion made by Jerome between the words qaran (to shine) and qeren (a horn). Plate (*a*) shows a woodcut representing the beginning of Deuteronomy from a Bible printed by Anton Sorg (Augsburg 1477). Plate (*b*) a woodcut representing Moses, Christ and the Apostles from Günther Zainer's 'Belial' (Augsburg 1478).

23 The *Glossa Ordinaria* with further exegesis by Nicholas of Lyra. Printed at Lyons, 1528. The Third Epistle of John.

24-5 The *Speculum Humanae Salvationis*, composed *c.* 1324 by a Dominican friar, is another example of the illustration of biblical texts. In plate 24 the Annunciation (left) and its first anti-type, Moses and the burning bush (right). This was regarded as an appropriate anti-type, for as the bush burned without being consumed and allowed God to manifest himself, so the Virgin received the flame of divine love without being consumed. As Gabriel kneels with hand upraised before Mary, Moses kneels with hand upraised before God. (Bibliothèque Nationale, Paris, MS Lat: 9584.) Plate 25 shows the Coronation of the Virgin. Bodleian, Oxford, MS Douce 204. Reproduced by permission of the Curators to the Bodleian Library.

537

26   The Resurrection. A painted wooden panel dating from about 1385 and now in Norwich Cathedral. Christ steps out of a stone coffin, his right hand raised in blessing, his left hand holding a processional cross. Three sleeping soldiers lie round the coffin.

27   The Resurrection depicted on a Byzantine ivory of the fourth century. Christ leaves an elaborate tomb and ascends a mountain side—where two apostles crouch in wonder—into heaven. Two soldiers, one awake, stand by the tomb and in the fore-ground an angel addresses three attentive women. The ivory is now at Munich.

28   British Museum, Add. MS 10456, f. 5ᵛᵒ. Miniature from the Bible made at Tours, mid-ninth century, showing the following scenes: (1) Creation of Adam and the creation of Eve; (2) Eve presented to Adam; the Almighty indicates the forbidden tree to Adam and Eve; (3) the Temptation of Eve; Adam and Eve eat of the fruit; Adam and Eve dis-covered by the Almighty; (4) the angel expels Adam and Eve from Eden; Adam and Eve in exile from the garden. Reproduced by permission of the Trustees of the British Museum.

29   Rome, Abbey of San Paolo fuori le Mura. Bible of San Callisto, f. 49ᵛ, written and decorated at Rheims for the Emperor Charles the Bald, *c.* A.D. 870. The scene shows the death of Moses and the Numbering of the Tribes.

30   British Museum, Cotton MS, Claudius B. IV, f. 139ᵛᵒ. Aelfric's paraphrase of the Heptateuch in Old English, made probably at Canterbury, second quarter of the eleventh century. Miniature depicting the same subject as plate 29. Reproduced by per-mission of the Trustees of the British Museum.

31   British Museum, Add. MS 17738, f. 187. Bible made for the abbey of Floreffe in the diocese of Liège, *c.* 1155. The miniature which precedes St Luke's Gospel shows the Crucifixion and below the slaughter of the sacrifical calf; the latter being in the nature of a type and anti-type. Reproduced by permission of the Trustees of the British Museum.

32   Cambridge, Corpus Christi College MS 2, f. 344ᵛᵒ. Bible made for the abbey of Bury St Edmunds, Suffolk. Second quarter of the twelfth century. The miniature shows: above, Job in prayer with his seven sons and three daughters below him. Below, Job seated on a dung hill admonished by his wife. Reproduced by permission of the Master and Fellows of Corpus Christi College, Cambridge.

33   London, Lambeth Palace MS 3, f. 198. Bible, probably made at Canterbury *c.* 1150. The miniature shows the Tree of Jesse. At the foot lies Jesse from whose loins springs a tree. The Virgin stands in the centre. Above her is a roundel with the bust of Christ surrounded by the Seven Gifts of the Spirit in the form of seven doves. In the two lower roundels are prophets; in the middle pair, on the left 'Mercy and Truth are met together', on the right 'Righteousness and Peace have kissed each other'. In the upper pair of roundels are: on the left the crowned figure of the Church with two apostles; on the right the veil is being taken from the eyes of the Synagogue by two men, probably apostles. Reproduced by permission of the Archbishop of Canterbury and the Trustees of the Lambeth Palace Library.

34   Oxford, Bodleian Library MS Junius xi, p. 61. The Cædmon Manuscript of Anglo-Saxon Poetry, written and illuminated in England, probably at Canterbury,

eleventh century. The miniature shows the translation of Enoch. Reproduced by permission of the Curators to the Bodleian Library.

35 British Museum, Egerton MS 1894, f. 5vo. Bible picture-book made in England in the third quarter of the fourteenth century. The miniature shows the building of the Tower of Babel. The tall man on the right is Nimrod. Reproduced by permission of the Trustees of the British Museum.

36 Utrecht, University Library: the Utrecht Psalter, made at Hautvillers, near Rheims, second quarter of the ninth century. The upper miniature is the illustration to Ps. 14 (15): 'Who shall dwell in thy tabernacle, etc.', the text of which is written in Latin immediately below. At the foot of the page is the illustration to Ps. 15 (16); the text being on the next page, see also above p. 321.

37 Vatican, Cod. Regin. lat. 12, f. 73vo. Psalter, in Latin, made for the abbey of Bury St Edmunds, second quarter of the eleventh century. The drawing surrounding the text of part of Ps. 67 (68) shows the Ascension of Christ illustrating verse 19 (18): 'Thou art gone up on high, thou hast led captivity captive and received gifts from men.'

38 Hildesheim, Godehardskirche, The Albani-Psalter, p. 109. Psalter made at St Albans Abbey, *c.* 1120–6. In the initial, with which Ps. 21 (22), 'Deus, Deus meus, respice in me...', begins, there is the illustration of verse 13 (12): 'Many oxen are come about me: fat bulls of Basan close me in on every side.'

39 Oxford, Bodleian Library MS Rawlinson G. 185, f. 43vo. Psalter made in England in the third quarter of the fourteenth century for Stephanus de Derby, prior of Holy Trinity, Dublin. In the initial D at the beginning of Ps. 52 (53): 'Dixit insipiens in corde suo...', is an illustration of the opening words: 'The fool has said in his heart: There is no God.' This shows a fool seated in front of a Dominican friar to whom he says: 'Non est deus.' The friar replies 'Tu mentiris aperte'. Above is the head of the Almighty on whose scroll is written: 'ecce dicit insipiens.' Reproduced by permission of the Curators to the Bodleian Library.

40 British Museum, Harley MS 2788, f. 19. Gospel Book written probably at Aachen early in the ninth century at the order of the Emperer Charles the Great. The page shows one of the Canon Tables, the numbers in the columns indicating the passages in which the Gospels of Matthew, Luke and John are in agreement. Reproduced by permission of the Trustees of the British Museum.

41 Cambridge, Corpus Christi College MS 286, f. 129vo. Gospel Book written probably in Italy late in the sixth century and formerly preserved in the abbey of St Augustine's, Canterbury. It may be one of the books given by St Gregory the Great to St Augustine of Canterbury. The miniature shows St Luke seated with his symbol above him. At the sides are small scenes from the life of Christ. Reproduced by permission of the Master and Fellows of Corpus Christi College, Cambridge.

42 Oxford, Bodleian Library MS Douce 180, p. 46. Apocalypse made in England, *c.* 1270. The miniature shows the Dragon persecuting the Woman who is provided with wings, Revelation xii. 13–16. Reproduced by permission of the Curators to the Bodleian Library.

43   Vienna, Nationalbibliothek, cod. 1189, f. 15ʳᵒ. *Biblia Pauperum*, Austria, c. 1310. Above is the Cleansing of the Temple, with the types: on the left Darius commanding Esdras to rebuild the Temple; on the right Judas Maccabeus ordering the Cleansing of the Temple (I Maccabees iv. 36–60). Below the Last Supper with the types: Abraham and Melchizedek on the left; on the right the shower of manna.

44   British Museum, Harley MS 152, f. 52. *Bible Moralisée*, written in France, probably in Paris, c. 1250. The page is divided into eight scenes; four illustrating the life of Christ. These alternate with four which are in the nature of a visual commentary on them. The New Testament scenes illustrate the Betrayal of Christ and the incident of St Peter and the servant of the High Priest. Reproduced by permission of the Trustees of the British Museum.

45   Wolfenbüttel, Herzog-August-Bibliothek, Cod. 61. 2. Aug. 8°, f. 92ᵛᵒ. Page from a sketch-book from Saxony, c. 1230–40. The main figure of Christ is copied from a Byzantine miniature of the Anastasis, the Harrowing of Hell, and shows Christ seizing the hand of Eve, thus rescuing her from Hades.

46   A page from the *Codex Argenteus*, a Latin copy of the Gospels on purple parchment probably dating from the sixth century, now in the University of Uppsala, Sweden. This is one of the main manuscripts of the Gothic Bible and represents a basically Byzantine text with some western readings.

47–8   Two notes about the authorship of the earlier version of the Wycliffite Bible, (a) from Bodleian Douce MS 369 Part I, f. 250ʳ, and (b) from Cambridge University Library MS Ee. 1. 10 f. 61ᵛ. Both are at the same point in the translation—Baruch iii. 20— but are clearly independent. Reproduced by permission of the Curators to the Bodleian Library and the Syndics of the University Library, Cambridge.

1   Easter vigil: Deacon on ambo singing from a roll

2 The Lord's Prayer at Mass in the presence of Philip the Good

הללויה

3   Hebrew commentary on the Book of Psalms, subjected to Christian censorship

4   The raising of Lazarus. Wall painting in the catacomb of SS Peter and Marcellinus, Rome

5 Christ crucified. Wooden panel of the fifth century

6   Christ as the Good Shepherd

7   Christ enthroned above the pagan god of the sky. A panel on the sarcophagus of Junius Bassus

8 The *Vienna Genesis*: Rebecca at the well

9   Abraham entertaining the three angels. Mosaic from the church of S. Maria Maggiore, Rome

10   Abel, Melchizedek and Abraham. Mosaic from the church of S. Apollinare
in Classe, Ravenna

11   The Stuma Paten, sixth century: The Communion of the Apostles

12 The Triumphal Entry into Jerusalem: from the St Florian *Biblia Pauperum*

13   Christ drives the money changers from the Temple: from the Vienna *Biblia Pauperum*

inquit hominem quem crea
ui á facie terre ab homine
usq; ad animantia. á reptili
usq; ad uolucres celi. Peni
tet eni me fecisse eos. Noe u

Noe uir iustus a.p.ti.
Si nullus sine petco.
qm pfectus? pfecti
dur aliq. ñ sic sunt
pficiendi. qñ eqbunt
anglis dit scps̃t. ẽẽ.
impegnatione. vn
addit ingñatioib;
suis. i. sic p suo m
di gra potar. ẽẽ. pfec
tus. ñ sic in alia uirra
in qñ nec uolet. nec
peccare poterit. cu
do ambulauit uesti
gia ei. s. sequens;
sc̃; ñ estimate iusticie. h̃ iuxta
generationem suam.
.i. sedm iusticiam. pfectam p̃seum uite ñ h̃eiite.
nerationib; suis. cum deo
s sequens uestigia eius.
ambulauit. & genuit tres
snom ut noiar. callidus. latitudo.
filios. Sem. Cham. & Japheth.
homo qm quie eunera
Corrupta. ẽ. aute tra coram
creara. quo peccante omnia dur corrupta esse.

muenit

gram co

ram deo.

degenera

tiones noe

Noe uir iust

atq; pfect
comprehensor.
fuit in ge

deo. & repleta. ẽ. iniquitate
cumq; uidisset deus tram
ẽẽ. corruptam. omnis quip
s̃i. omnis homo. uirra. actiones.
pe caro corruperat uiam
quo peccante. omnis caro dicit corrupisse uia. qa
sua. sup tram: dr̃ ad noe.
p eum omnis caro creara.
s omnium mortaliu pter eos qui in archa erant sal
Finis carnis uniuerse. uenti
uandi. quasi seminarium sede originis.
s placito in iudicio habita
coram me. Repleta. ẽ terra
totes tre. p senna.
iniquitate á facie eoꝝ &
ego disperdam eos cum
s tradunt doctores. terre uigorem & fecun
ditatem. longe. ẽẽ. inferiorem p diluuiu
& ido hominib; esum carnium concessu
tu antea tm tre frutib; uicturarent.
s ut non sit suo more fructuosa.
s ecciam.
terra. Fac tibi archam de
s scis. alii qdrans. qa uirra scdm firma & stabil.
s.i. poluit. ne qd nociuum inhereret.
s in hebreo bituminatis.
lignis leuigatis. Fac archã
de. l. l.i. ꝯ. Hortib; s. & insolubilib; & bñ
coartatis. que alia tslatio dicit qua
d rata. ut nec iuuentorum nec inun
datione archa solueretur.

14   The *Glossa Ordinaria*: thirteenth-century manuscript at Worcester

15   Ezekiel's vision: from a printed *Glossa Ordinaria*

16　The Klosterneuburg altar-piece: Samson and the lion

17   The Klosterneuburg altar-piece: The harrowing of hell

18   Pentecost: a Netherlands manuscript of the fifteenth century

19 Bourges Cathedral: Jacob blesses the sons of Joseph

20   Norwich Cathedral choirstall: 'The pelican in her piety'

(*a*) The lion crowned to represent the Lion of Judah

(*b*) The cockatrice being teased by weasels

21   Worcester Cathedral misericords

(*a*) The beginning of Deuteronomy from a fifteenth-century bible

(*b*) Moses, Christ and the Apostles

22   (*a*) and (*b*)   The Horned Moses

E ¶Scd̃ a iohãnis vbi dr̃ in poſti. Senior:& hoc rõne ætatis, puetæ
ADDITIO.I. Beatus iohãnes (& ſtatus ſeu officiũ &c.
cãte humilitatis ſuit, q̃ in libris ſuis nõ no
minat ſe apſm̃:nec de ſe dicit aliqd̃ nomen dignitatẽ deſignans:
ſed noiat ſe in euangelio diſcipulũ quẽ diligebat Ieſus:non expri
mens nomen ſuũ propriũ ex humilitate. Siſr in prima ſua cano
nica nõ exprimit nomẽ ſuũ, nec offm̃, nec aliquid hm̃õi:q̃ue oma
nia ad magnã p̃tinẽt hũilitatẽ. Vñ ex hoc vr̃, q̃ cũ hic dr̃ Senior,
referẽdũ eſt ſolũ ad ætatẽ q̃ nõ iportat aliquã dignitatẽ nec ſtatũ
altiorem

GLO. ORDI.

¶Incipit epſa tertia eiuſdẽ.
Enior ga.ch.&c.
Gaius ſide chriſti
ſuſcæpta, bon9 in
actibus p̃dicato
res & auditores:
bi dei facul
tatibus miniſtrabat: ſicut in
epiſtola declaratur. Commẽ
dat autem hoſpitalitatem: &
ne ab ea deſiſtat exemplo, &
inſtinctu diotrepis inuitat.
Diotrepes em̃ aſſerebat inuti
lem eē hoſpitalitatem. Vide
tur gaius fuiſſe corinthi:vñ
1.Co.1.d. paulus:Gras ago deo meo, q̃
neminem vr̃m baptizaui niſi
criſpũ & gaiũ.Et alibi:Salu
Ro.16.d. tat vos gaius hoſpes meus &
totius eccleſiæ. b ¶Deo
mnibus orationib9 c.ſicut nũc
abundat tibi,& bona volũ
tas largiendi indigentibus:&
facultas operum, ita ſemp vir
tutibus plenam dñõ adiuuan
F te vitã ducere poſſis. c ¶Ga
iuſus ſumvalde. Indecēs eēt:
ſi deficiente ſide mõ dolerem
de quo hactenus gaudebã:&
iõ non tm̃ .ppter ſalutẽ tuam,
ſed ēt propter meã auctorita
tẽ ſiſiſte hoſpitalitati. d ¶Ma
iorẽ ho. lõ gauiſus ſũ:q̃ a ho
rũ fratrũ venientiũ nõ habeo
maiorẽ gratiã.i.qñ fratres ve
niũt ad me,in nullo facto vel
y̆bo eos, magis gaudeo:q̃ de
hoc q̃ annũciant filios meos
quos p̃dicãdo vel baptizãdo
genui:y̆irate recte fidei, & bo
nẽ opatioĩs obſuare. e ¶Cha
riſſime ſi.lõ nõ debes deficie
re ab hoſpitalitate, & elemo
ſynis:q̃cqd em̃ oparis in fres
fidelr̃.i.ſicut fidelis.i.ſicut de
cet fidelẽ facis nõ.p vana glia
ſed fide tua operibus oſtẽdis.
f ¶Pro no.cm̃ eius &c.Qui
vere ſunt honorãdi.nõ em̃ p

Incipit argu.in tertiã epſam eiuſdẽ.
Aium pietatis cauſa extol
lit:atq̃ vt in ipa pietate ma
neat exhorta:idiotrepẽ im
pietatis & ſupbiæ q̃ obiur
gat:demetrio aũt bonũ teſtimoniũ p
hibet cum fratribus vniuerſis.

Explicit argumentum.

Incipit epſa beati Ioha.apſi tertia.
¶ego.
¶Enior Gaio cha
riſſimo quem dili
¶nõ tpaliũ bonorum
gra,ſed,ppter æterna.
diligo inueritate.
Chariſſime de oi
a ¶hoc a dñbo crebris p
cibus exopto:vt bene
quod agis,bene perſiſcias.

bbus vſouñ ſacõ proſperè te ingredi
a ¶corpore & aio.b¶.pficit in elemoſynarum
operibus.¶vt ſicut aia valeas & corpe.c¶Iter
& valère : ſicut proſpere agit animã f
na mentis intentio. ¶ate.
c ¶tua.Gauiſus ſum valde venientibusg
¶peregrinis. a¶vera̅ charitati,q̃ nõ ceſſat ab
fratribus & teſtimoniũ p̃hibetib9ve/
opere.¶tam ſtudioſe reddunt teſtimoniũ
q̃ ſtudioſus tu es ad bene operandum.
ritati tuæ:ſicut tu iueritate ambulas.
d ¶Maiorẽ horum non habeo gratiã q̃
¶ſm̃ fidem. ¶vera fide.
vt filios meos audiã in veritate am/
e bulantes. Chariſſime fideliter facism
a ¶a quibus nihil expectas r̃pale.¶quos nõ no
qcqd oparis in fres:&hoci pēgrinos p
ſcis. a¶operibus miſericordiæ,
qui teſtimoniũ reddiderũt chãritati
a¶& ita exemplo tuo alij incitetur ad hoſpita
litatem. b¶dum apud te ſunt.
tuæ i cõſpectu eccliæ:quos bn̄ſaciẽs ſ

altiorẽ:ſed ſolum quãdam maturitatẽ q̃ cõiter in ſenib9 debet in
uenir̃.iuxta illud:In antiquis eſt ſapientia &c.& ſic nõ cõmẽdat Ioh.12.b
ſe ex rectoria ſeu p̃latia:ſed ſolũ ex ætig̃rate diẽr̃ ſm̃ quã ſuis ſmõ
nibus deber̃et acq̃eſcere,&ſic intelligẽdũ eſt in ſequẽri canonica.
¶In eadẽ epſa vbi dr̃ in poſtil.Non tanq̃ mandatum nouum.
ADDITIO.II. Qualiter intelligatur q̃ mandatũ de di
lectione dei & proximi non eſt nouum.
& qualiter debet intelligi eſſe nouum,habetur ſupra in additiõe
prima.ij.cap.vide ibi.

NIC. DE LY.

Eiuſdẽ expoſitio in tertiã epiſtolã Iohannis.
Enior gaio.Hæc epſa ſicut & p̃cedens Diuiſio.
diuidit in tres partes.ſ. ſalutationẽ:pro
ſecutionẽ:& cõcluſionẽ.ſcd̃a ibi chari
ſſime.tertia ibi:Multa.In prima p̃te de
ſcribit prio pſona ſalutans ex ætate &
officio.cum dicitur: a ¶Senior.in ſenib9 dictum eſt
in epiſtola p̃cedenti.Scd̃o perſona ſalutata ex no
mine & familiaritate cum dicitur: b ¶Gaio cha
riſſimo.Ille erat corinthius ille de quo dicit paulus
j.Corinẽ.j.b.Gratias ago deo meo,q̃ neminemve
ſtrum baptizaui niſi criſpũ & gaiũ.& de quo di
cit Rcm̃.xvj.d.Salutat vos gaius hoſpes meus:reci
piebat enim & ſuſtentabat p̃dicatores verbi diui
ni:propter qd̃ erat apoſtolo chariſſimus.Tertio p̃
tatur affectus ſalutantis ad ſalutatum,cum dicitur
c ¶Quem ego dſ̃.in ve.nonverbo ſolum aut lin
gua: d ¶Chariſſime.Hic incipit p̃ſecutio huius
epiſtolæ.in qua beatus iohannes primo monet ga
ium de perſeuerantia in bono.ſcd̃o de declinatiõe
a malo,ibi:Scripſiſſem.Circa primũ vt gaius eſſe
cacius recipiat ſuã monitionem:primo gr̃as agit de
ſuis bonis operibus p̃teritis,deprecans pro futu
ris,di.Chariſ.de omni.ſ.bonis operib9 q̃ facis.
¶Orationẽ ſn̄ pro te ſn̄ & vr̃ i.de bono in meli9
ſemper p̃ficere. ¶¶Sicut pro.agit a.t.q̃.d.iſta nõ
ſunt opera ficta:ſicut ſunt hypocritarũ opera,q̃ nõ
procedunt ex conſcia & intentione recta.iõ ſubdit:
g ¶Gaiuſus ſumval.ve.fra.i.p̃dicatoribus & pe
regrinis fidelibus. h ¶Et te phi.ve.tuæ.i.in fide &
operibus miſericordie. i ¶Maiorẽ horũ nõ ha
gra.i.nihil mihi eſt gratioſius audire. k ¶Quãt
ſi.me.au.non carnales:q̃a virgo in æuum perman
ſit:ſed ſp̃uales. l ¶Inveritate am.p̃ſeuiã fidei &
morum.ideo conſequenter in bono confirmat eũ,
di. m ¶Chariſſime fi.fa.erga deum & proximũ.
n ¶Quicquid.boni. o ¶Operaris in fra.per ba
ptiſmum regeneratos nobiſcu. p ¶Et hoc in pe.
ſupple maxime eſt acceptum deo.Dicuntur aũt hic
peregrini fideles de ſuis ciuitatibus .ppter fidẽ chri
ſti ab incredulis electi. q ¶Qui teſtimoniũ red
di.charita.tuæ.quam eis exhibuiſti. r ¶In con
ſpectu eccleſiæ.& ppr̃ hoc multi motiſunt ad ſiſe
faciendum exemplo tui. s ¶Quos beneſacies de
ducens &.deo.iungatur ſic litera:Quos ſcilicet pe
regrinos cum ad te venerint.Deduces,id eſt ſuis ele
moſynis p̃ouidens,vt inde tranſeant ad alia loca.
Beneſacies digne deo.i.ad honore domini.& ſub
dinurratio: t ¶Pronomine enim.i.pro ſideuñ9

191.di.c
legimus

G Ioh.12.b

H

23 The *Glossa Ordinaria* of Nicholas of Lyra

24   The *Speculum Humanae Salvationis*: The Annunciation *and* Moses' vision
of the burning bush

Xps rex celorū aſſūpſit maria ī celum·

In precedenti cū audi de beate virgis gueracōe
Conſequenter audiamo de iph felici aſſūpcione
Quantuz tempus maria ſupervixit poſt y aſſēaōz
de hoc non habemus certam determinacioes
Quidam dicit duodecim annos quidam vero plus

25   The *Speculum Humanae Salvationis*: Coronation of the Virgin

26   The Resurrection. Painted panel of the late fourteenth century

27   The Resurrection. Ivory panel of the fourth century

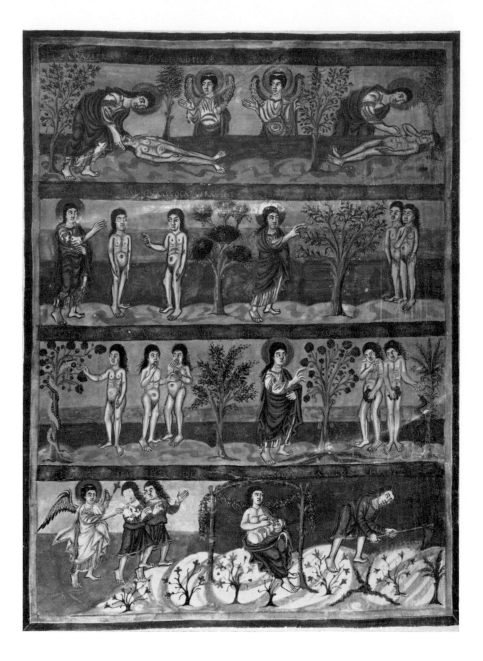

28   Adam and Eve. Miniature from the mid-ninth-century Tours Bible

29   The death of Moses. Bible of San Callisto, *c.* 870

30 The death of Moses. Paraphrase of the Heptateuch in
Old English, eleventh century

31   The Crucifixion, *and* the slaughtering of the sacrificial calf.
The Floreffe Bible, *c.* 1155

IRE RAT
TER ABS
NOMINE·

ıoв. Et erat uir ille simplex & rectus ac
timens dm̃. & recedens a malo. Natiq;
sunt ei septe̅ filii. & tres filie. Et fuit
possessio eius septem milia ouiu̅. & tria
milia camelo̅ꝝ· quingenta quoq; iu
ga boum. & quingente asine. ac fa
milia multa nimis. Eratq; uir ille
magnus inter om̅s orientale. Et ibā̅ꝝ
filii eius & faciebant conuiuiu̅ p domo.

unusq̃sq; in die suo. Et mittentes uo
cabant tres sorores suas. ut ede
rent & biberent cu̅ eis. Cu̅q; in o̅rbe̅
transissent dies conuiuii· mittebat ade
ıob & sc̅ificabat illos. consurgensq; di
luculo· offerebat holocausta p̃ sing̅lo̅s·
Dicebat eni̅. Ne forte peccauerint filii
mei. & benedixerint deo in cordibus
suis. Sic faciebat iob cunctis diebus·

347 v

32   Job in prayer (above) and seated on a dung hill (below).
The Bury St Edmunds Bible of the mid-twelfth century

33   A Tree of Jesse, *c.* 1150

34   The translation of Enoch: Cædmon manuscript, eleventh century

35 The Tower of Babel. Bible picture-book, English, fourteenth century

XIIII
Dnequishabita
bitintaberna
culotuo · Actquis
requiescitinmonte
scotuo ·
Quiincriditursine
macula · EToperatur
IUSTITIAM
Quiloquituruerita
TEMINCORDISUO ·
QUINONECITDOLU
INLINGUASUA

PSALMUS
Nichcitproximosuo
malum Etobprobriu
Nonaccepitaduer
susproximossuos
Adnihilumdeductus
EstinconspectuEIUS
malignus · TimEntes
Autemdnmglorificat
Quiiuratproximo
suoEtnondEcepit
Quipecuniamsua
Nondeditadusura ·

DAUID
ETMUNERASUPER
INNOCENTES
NONACCEPIT
QUIFACITHAEC · NON
MOUEBITURINAE
TERNUM

D

36   Illustrated psalter, ninth century. Psalms 14 (15) and 15 (16)

Oum discernit caelestis reges sup eam.
niue dealba buntur infelmon
mons dei mons pinguis.
Mons coagulatus mons pinguis. utquid
suspicamini montes coagolatos.
Mons inquo bene placitum est deo. habi
tare ineo. & enim dns habitabit infinem.
Currus dei decem milib; multiplex milia
laeantium dns meis insyna insancto.
Ascendisti inaltum cepisti captuitate.
accepisti dona inhominibus.
Etenim non credentes inhabitare
dominum deum.
Benedictus dns die cotidie. prspum faciat
nob ds salutarium nostrorum.
Ds nr ds saluos faciendi.
& dni domini exitus mostis.
Ve rumptamen deus confringa capita
inimicorum suorum uerticem capilli
per ambulantium indelictissuis.
Dixit dns exbasan conuestam.
conuestam inp fundum maris.
Vtintin guatur pes tuus insanguine

37   Psalter with marginal illustrations, mid-eleventh century.
Illustration to Psalm 67 (68), verse 19 (18)

circúidede

SI
rei
qu
de
m
d
m

n

&nocte &non adinsipientiam
Tu autem insco habitas: laus ist
In te sperauerunt patres nos
sperauerunt &liberasti eos.

38 Historiated initial from the St Albans Psalter, *c.* 1120

39   Historiated initial in a Psalter, mid-fourteenth century

40   Canon Table from a Gospel book, ninth century

41   Evangelist picture, late sixth century

oftmam uidit draco cr   Vitens diabolus se marimam multitudinem ese

42   Illustrated Apocalypse made in England, *c.* 1270

43 The cleansing of the Temple *and* the Last Supper. *Biblia Pauperum*, Austrian, *c.* 1310.

The cleansing of the Temple is enlarged in Plate 13

44　The *Bible Moralisée*, French, *c.* 1250

45   Christ rescuing Eve from Hades. The Wolfenbüttel sketch-book, German, c. 1230

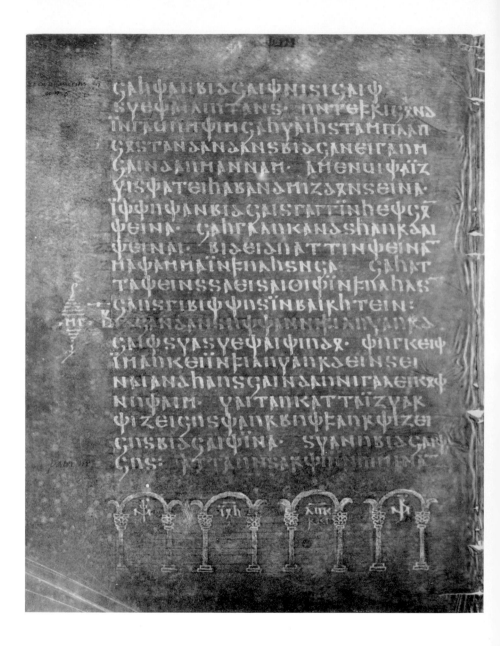

46 A page from the sixth-century *Codex Argenteus*

biddng of lyȝt ȝ of lytil flo
dr. whe bē lȝt of ȝē ȝ pe
es / who fonde his place.
ȝ who entre into hise tre
soures. whe ben pe pnas
of gentilis. ȝ p pat lord
schipe of bestis p ben up
on erpe. p pat i pe bnddis
of heuen plien. p pat tre
sore silu ȝ gold i whiche me
tristen ȝ p is noō eende of
pe pchasing of hē: p pat
forge silu ȝ ben bisie. ne
p is fynding of pe wer
his of hē: pei bē outlawe
de. ȝ p wentē dou to helle;
ȝ ope men i pe place of hē
risen ȝ cēssȝ ere endip pe
tūslacion of h̄. ȝ now bi
gȳnep pe tūslacion of .j.
ȝ of ope men

Iopeh p knewē not
pe wei of disciplne.
ne p vndurstoden pe papis

multitude schal be sued i to ye leste folc of lond· for ye y schal scatte for y not y mee schal not here ye puple· ye puple is for loue wt an hard nol z schal be sued to his lite· ye loud of his caitifte· z yei schul write for y au ye lord god of he· and y schal zyue to ye au lite z yei schul vndur stoude· z eres y yei schul here· z yei schulu pile me i ye loud of y caitifte· z unfeisful yei schul be of my name· z yei schul tru awei yeself· For y hau de rig· z for y childhed· for yei schul remembre ye wele of y fadris yat synueden i me· z y schal azee clepe he r to ye loud yat y swor to ye fadris of he abrahā· isaac z jacob· z yei schul lord schipen of it· z y schal multeplie ye· z yei schul not be lassid· z y schal sette to yem au oy testamet euedureude· y y be to yo i to a lord· z yei schul be to me i to a puple· z y schal no more moue my puple ye cou of irl· For ye loud yat yzat to ye

A nd now lord god of irl· ye soule i anguysshes z ye spir it tormentid· cryep to yee· here lord z haue mercy for god y art merciful· z haue mercy of vs for wee hau synued bifor yee yat sittist i to euer mor· z wee schul not pisse i to ye spirituel durig· lord god al myzti god of irl· he re now ye orisou of ye deade mē of irl z of ye cou of he for yei hau synued bi for yee· z yei hedeu not ye vois of ye lord y god· z ioyued be to vs euels· wile y not han mide of ye wickenesse of oure fadris· but haue mide of yi houd z of yi name i yis tyme· for y art lord oure god· z wee schul pile yee lord· for yi yt y hast zoue yi drede i youre hertes y wee iuward li clepe yi name z pile yee· oure caitifte· for wee schul be sued tio ye wickenesse of oure fadris yat synueden i yee· z to wee i oure caitifte ben to day y vs y hast sca tterd to irpf· z iw curlig· z i to syne· aft alle ye wickednesses of oure fadris yat wenteu awei tio yee lord oure god· here y irl· ye maundemes of lit· wt eres per ceyue y y wite sidence· what is irl· y i ye loud of ye enemys y art· you hast eldid i au alien loud y art defoulid wt dwale me· y art set wt me goende dou i to helle· y hast forsake ye welle of wisdū· for if i ye weies of god y haddest gō· y schuldist han dwellid for loye i pes vp on erpe· ler·ue wher be sidence wher be vtue· wher be vndstoudig y y wi re toyidr· wher be loug abidig of lit z of liflore· wher be hizt of ezen z pes·

who foud his place· who entide i to his tresores· wher be ye prices of jentilis z yat lordshipen of beestis yat ben vpon erpe· yat i ye briddes of heuene pleien· yat siluir tresoren z gold i whiche tristou me· z pis noon eude of ye purchasiug of he· yat siluir forgeten z ben besily wo y is studig of ye worchio of he· yei be out turned z to helle yei wente dou· z opir me i ye place of he risen· ye iuzre

Explec translacoum· Incipit Nicholay de herford·

INDEXES

GENERAL INDEX

Abelard 140, 143, 190, 205, 495
Abisha ben Pinhas 24
Abisha Scroll (found at Nablus) 24
Abraham 158, 160, 164, 289, 333
Abraham ibn Da-ud's *Chronicle* 272
Abraham ibn Ezra 258, 260, 261, 266–70, 272, 278
Abravanel, Don Isaac 258, 265, 274, 275–6; method of interpretation 272; method of exegesis 273; reason *v.* revelation 274
Academy Bible 478
Acre Bible 443, 446, 448
'Ada' Group 134
Adalhard 138
Admonitio Generalis 417
Adnotationes (*and see* Valla) 494, 496
Adrian VI, Pope 499
Aelfric of Eynsham 317, 364, 374, 377–80; *Catholic Homilies* 375; *Tract on the Old and New Testament* 375–6; link with Rolle 385
Africana MSS 346
Agnus dei 241, 243, 244
Alaric 87, 399
Alba Bible 466, 467, 469, 473, 476–9, 482; contains double translations 480; commentaries in margins 485
Alberic 143
Albertus Magnus 272
Albigensians (*and see* Heresy) 473
Alcuin 113–14, 131 n., 133–41, 187, 194, 237, 311, 365, 368, 371–2, 376; his Bible 110, 125, 139–40, 151; his text 113, 114, 120, 128–9, 137, 146–7
Aldhelm 364
Aldus Manutius 496, 498
Aleander, Jerome 498
Alexander the Great 58, 62
Alexander of Hales 276–7
Alexandria 29, 48, 57, 62, 177
Alexandrian text 29, 31, 32, 356

Alfonso II (of Catalonia and Aragon) 467
Alfonso the Wise (of Castile) 470, 489
Alfrabi 276
Alfred, king 139, 367, 373–4; translation of the Psalter 370, 373
Allegory 3 (*and see* Exegesis, Sense(s), Typology), 159–72
Alleluia 249–50
Altercatio Aecclesie contra Synagogam 265
Amalar of Metz 227, 247, 250
Ambo 227, 229, 230, 249, 250
Ambrose 53, 106, 142, 177, 185, 242, 359, 493, 499, 504
Ambrosian codices: interpolated glosses 360; text 355, 358
Ambrosian rite 242, 247
Ambrosiaster 53, 188, 357, 359, 360 (*and see* Ambrose)
Ammonius of Alexandria 191
Amphilochius of Iconium 53, 83
Anaphora 240, 242, 243
Andrew of St Victor *see* Victor, St
Andrieu, M. 104, 238
Andronicus of Rhodes 60 (*and see* Aristotle)
Anglo-Norman language 379, 380–1, 448
Anglo-Saxon: Bible 364, 365, 367, 372; Church 129; missionaries 130, 133; poetic records (MS Junius) 368–9; glosses 371; literature 379
Anne of Bohemia 392, 409
Anselm of Laon 190, 294 (*and see* Gloss); school of 132; and Erasmus 502
Antinomianism 275
Antioch 29, 30, 35, 37, 38, 82
Antiphon 238, 240, 247, 248
Aphraates 33, 35, 52
Apocalypse 32; decoration of 331; illustrated 332; commentary of Haimo of Auxerre 332; French translation 442, 449; Catalan text in Italy 456

Apollinarius, bishop of Laodicea 82, 86
Aqiba, Rabbi 1, 2, 3, 5
Aquila 17, 18, 22, 95, 476, 481; his Greek
    version 85
Aquinas, Thomas 202, 215–16, 276–7, 492,
    495, 504
Arabic science, translation and writing 470
Aramaic 22, 63
Argentean renderings (of Brixian Bilin-
    gual) 354–5
Aristarchean signs 18
Aristeas, Letter of 14, 15, 16, 95
Aristotle 200, 207, 211, 220, 273, 275; his
    MSS found at Scepsis 60; his God
    276; *Constitution of Athens* 56;
    Nichomachean Ethics and *Rhetoric* 470
Arius 340; Arianism 107, 176, 501; Arians
    345
Ark, and description of 295, 296
Ark of the Covenant 443
Armagh, Book of 132
Arnobius the Younger 499
Arragel, Rabbi Mosse 479, 480, 481, 482
Art, Christian 285, 290
Artaxerxes 293
Arundel, archbishop 387, 392, 409, 410;
    'Constitutions against Lollardy' 393–
    4
Ashburnham collection 451
Ashburnham Pentateuch 113, 317, 318,
    337
Asher, ben 6, 9–13 (*and see* Naphtali, ben)
Ashworth, H. 247
Athanaric, king 340
Athanasius 43, 52, 81, 177
Athaulf 345
Athelstan 373
Augsburg Bible 432
Augustine of Canterbury 136
Augustine of Hippo 365; principle con-
    cerning passages relating to Christ
    164; rendering of Latin commen-
    taries (Gothic epistles) 357, 359; as
    commentator 112, 169, 194, 237, 493;
    and chant of communicants 237, 239;
    De Doctrina Christiana 38, 179, 367;
    De Civitate Dei 8, 9, 301, 499;
    exegeses 183, 209; as teacher to
    St Gregory 186; lines of scriptural

interpretation 290; and Jerome 53,
    87, 89, 102, 110; works cited by
    Lanfranc 188; positive attitude to
    literal meaning 256; treatment of
    miracle stories 180–3; texts of
    Pelagius circulated under his name
    190; and Rolle 386; dominance in
    scholasticism 195; scriptural ex-
    pressions misconstrued 504; dis-
    approval of certain translations 96;
    advises caution with rules of Tyconius
    179
Augustinian Order 381
Auriole, Peter 207
Austin friars 200, 209
'Authorized Version' *see* Versions
Auto de la huida de Egipto 489
Auto de los Reyes Magos 489
Autpert, Ambrose 186
Auxentius 339
Auxerre, School of 132
Avicenna 277
Avitus, St, of Vienna 113
Avromān 63
Ayuso, T. 31, 103, 120–5, 127–9

Babylon 99
Babylonian liturgical drama 106; Talmud
    22
Bacon, Roger 106, 148, 149, 151, 217, 219;
    criticizes 'Paris' text 147, 148; *Homo
    sapientissimus* 150; views on Bible
    385
Baeck, Leo 253
Baer, I. F. 278
Baer-Delitzsch 12
Bahya ben Asher 278
Bahya ibn Pakuda 271
Bainet, A. 328
Baldwin, Frankish emperor of Constan-
    tinople 443
Baranina 92
Bar Cochba revolt 2
Bardy, G. 38, 115
Barnabas 49, 159, 168; Epistle of, 168
Barnouw 34
Barthélemy, Father D. 17
Basil, St, Commentary on Isaiah, edited
    by Erasmus 500

Basil of Caesarea 52
Basilica, plan of 228
Basilides 93
Becket, Thomas 440
Bede 107, 117, 118, 130, 137, 140, 142, 151, 186, 264, 272, 364, 366, 368, 371, 373, 378, 386, 504; *Lives of the Abbots* 331; *Ecclesiastical History* 367; *Letter to Egbert* 372
Beghards 428
Behaghel, O. 419, 420
Belisarius 115, 339
Benedict Biscop 107, 110, 310, 331
Benedict of Nursia 186, 230, 233, 236, 237, 244
Benedictine Office 235, 247, 248, 371
Benedictine Order 112, 191, 227, 312, 374
Benedictus, The 247, 248
Berengar of Tours 141, 204
Berger, Samuel 103, 107, 111, 113, 114, 120, 125, 127, 128, 129, 131, 135, 138, 139, 141, 143, 144, 145, 147, 148, 149, 150, 151, 152, 153, 359, 437, 446, 450, 451, 455, 456, 457, 458, 459, 460, 461, 465, 466, 467, 468, 492
Berliner, A. 22
Bernard of Clairvaux 183, 184, 191, 192, 193, 213, 457, 459, 495
Beuton 25
Bible 197–308; as basis of elementary education 196; commentaries by the Fathers 225; glossed more than any other text 196; helped to form vernacular languages 196; principal source for preachers 194; as source of private mystical experience 385; standardization under enactment of Dominican Chapter-General 149
Bible du treizième siècle 445–6
Bible Historiale 448, 449, 467, 470, 471
Bible Historiale Complétée 449
Bible Moralisée 328, 332, 335, 468, 473, 480, 485
Bible-reading, new order of introduced 233–4, 434
Bibles: Alba 466, 467, 469, 473, 476–9, 480, 482, 485; Arsenal 321; Bamberg 139, 311; Bishops' 262; Bouillon 451; Bury St Edmunds' 315; Cala-

horra 122; Calais 449; Carolingian 312, 313, 336; Cologne 434; Complutensian Polyglot 12, 465, 499; Coverdale 262; Crèvecoeur 449; De Croy 449; De Thou 445, 446, 447: Widener compilation 448; *Exemplar Parisiense* 146; Farfa 314; Ferrara 475, 479; Genevan 262; Grandval 138, 311; Holkham 330, 331; Jean II 450; Jean de Sy 450; Léon 336; Louvain 437; Lübeck 434, 435; Mentel 433, 434; Oña 125; pandects 106, 107: Alcuin's 137; Ripoll 129, 314; Roda 122, 123, 129; Rovigo 330, 331; St Germain 107; St Louis 443, 444, 445; St Paul 312; San Isidoro 313, 336; Sanford 447; *San Pere de Roda* (Vatican Library) 314; Sens 149; Siena 452, 453; Tours 122, 312; Tyndale 262; Valencian 467, 474; Vallicelli 138; Veleslav 330, 331; Vivian 311, 312; Wemzel 432; Winchester 335, 336
Bible picture books 436
Bibles, giant, of Romanesque period 79
Bibles, very small 146, 315; of thirteenth century 79
Biblia Pauperum 292, 293, 294, 302, 310, 332, 333, 334
Biblia romanceada 474
Biblical books
    Genesis 383
    Exodus 383
    Joshua 23
    Judges 23
    Isaiah 23
    James 303
    John 180
    Revelation 430
Blake, R. P. 31, 41
Blesilla 85, 87, 92
Blondheim, D. S. 105, 263
Bobbio (*and see* Codex) 132, 341
Boccaccio 456
Boeckler, Albert 329
Boniface, St, Anglo-Saxon missionary 115, 133, 415
Bonner, Bishop 414
Books of Hours 321, 431, 486

Brandin 263
Breviarium psalterii 189
Brewer, J.S. 106, 147, 148, 150, 151
Brixian Bilingual 348, 349, 350, 351, 352, 354, 355, 360
Brown, T. J. 118, 130, 436, 447
Bruno, St 188
Bruno of Asti 190
Bruno of Würzburg 188
Brut, Walter 401
Buchtal, H. 319, 443
Burkitt, F. C. 35, 36, 108, 110, 346, 347, 350
Byzantine art and iconographic tradition 336; customs and rites 243; illuminations 320, 329; MSS 324; sources for miniatures 319
Byzantine text 29, 30, 31, 32, 33, 36, 362

Cædmon 367, 368, 386; MS 318; poems 368
Caesarea 29
Caesarean text 30, 31, 32, 37
Caesarius, St 235
Cairo Genizah (*and see* Genizah fragments) 22, 23, 24
Cambridge Text 20, 21
Cancioneros 489
Canon, the 42, 44, 48, 49, 51, 53, 128, 179, 180, 240, 242, 243, 273, 364; Alexandrian 48, 49; African 51; Syrian 49; Western and European 49, 50; of Cyprian 53; formation of in Old and New Testaments 163; Muratorian 43, 49, 50
Canons Regular 190
Canterbury 136, 310, 317, 318; Early Christian MSS of the Old Testament, 318
Cantica, The 423; fragments in Rhenish-Franconian 422
Capitulare Missorum 417
Cappadocian Fathers 342, 501
Cappuyns 115, 116, 142
Carmelite Order 200
Carolingian period 125, 417; Bibles 312, 313, 336 (and *see also* Alcuin, Theodulf)

Carthage, Council of 53
Carthage, Synod of 53
Carthusian Order 209
Cassiodorus 76, 106, 115, 116, 117, 118, 119, 125, 135, 137, 186, 189, 310; commentary on the Psalms 323; *Institutions* 118
Cassuto, U. 454, 459
Castigos y documentos del rey D. Sancho 488
Castilian 470
Catalan: bibles 468, 474; homiletic materials 487; sermons 486–7; strongly influenced by Provençal 486–7; versions 467, 468, 484
Catena aurea 217, 407
Catena Group 21
Catharist versions 439 (*and see* Heresy)
Catherine, St, of Siena 463
Catholic Epistles 52, 53
Cavalca, Domenico 456, 458, 462; prologue to Tuscan version of Acts 456; version of Acts 457
Celestine, Pope 238
Celsus 174
Celtic text 132
Centonization 225
Ceolfrid, Abbot 107, 110, 117, 130, 136, 310
Champenois Miscellany 446
Chant books 237
Chantilly *BXIII* 448, 451
Chants, Roman and Gallican 252
Charlemagne 111, 131, 133, 134, 135, 136, 138, 365, 372, 415, 417; his Encyclical 134; his Bible (*and see* Bibles) 151
Charles V 450, 491, 500
Charles VIII 450
Charles VIII of France 453
Charles the Bald 131, 138, 312; his Bible 151
Chartier, Alain 452
Chaucer 383, 387
    Canterbury Tales 387
Chayim (Jacob ben) 12
Chester Beatty papyri 16, 18, 31, 32, 39, 40, 49, 68, 356; codex 32, 73
Christ 155, 156, 157, 158, 164, 178
Chronicle of Turpin 440

General Index

Chrysostom 52, 126, 177, 194, 342, 356, 362; and Erasmus 499; homilies 486; text 355, 359

Church, primitive 162, 165; Great 45, 46

Ciasca 34

Cicero 211, 280, 365; *De Republica* palimpsest 76

Cistercian Order 144, 191; psalter text 144

Clairemont Gospels 132

Clement of Alexandria 31, 43, 48, 49, 171, 172; and Erasmus 502

Clement of Leanthony 409

Clement of Rome 44, 50, 164, 166, 167, 170, 291

Clementine text 123, 132; edition 468

Clerk, John (Harley 273 MS) 440

Clermont list 43

Clovis 345, 415

Cluny 313, 437

Codex
 Christian preference for codex form 70
 origins and description of form 65
 Papyrus codex of Genesis (P. Yale 1) 71
 Aberdeen Codex of the Hebrew Bible 11
 Alexandrinus 20, 21; written in metallic ink 61
 Ambrosianus 26, 341
 Amiatinus 106, 113, 115, 116, 117, 118, 130, 132, 310
 Aniciensis 128
 Argenteus 340, 341, 342, 344, 346, 347, 348, 349, 350, 351, 353, 354, 355, 360
 Babylonian Codex of the Prophets 10
 Bezae 30, 32, 353
 Bobbiensis 28, 30, 38
 Brixianus 340, 348, 349, 351; and Praefatio 349, 351
 Cairo codex of the Prophets 10
 Carolinus 341, 346, 348
 Cavensis 113, 114, 121, 122, 123
 Claromontanus 52, 357
 Colbertinus 113
 Egberti 329
 Erfurt 11, 12
 Fuldensis 34, 113, 115, 133, 455
 Gissensis 341, 346
 Gothicus 122 (Isidore Bible *q.v.*)

Codex grandior littera clariore conscriptus 116, 117, 118 (*and see* Cassiodrous)

Great codices 19

Leningrad 10

Lindisfarniensis 327 (*and see* Lindisfarne; Gospels)

Marchalianus 19

Neofiri I 22, 23, 24

Ottobonianus 120

Palatinus 30, 348, 354; of Virgil 76

Paris 146

Regius 30

Reuchlin 11

Rossanensis 327

Sinaiticus 20, 21, 29, 30, 43, 49, 52, 75, 76, 77, 78, 79; written in metallic ink 61

Tarazona cathedral chapter library, in Latin 486

Taurinensis 341

Teplensis 432

Toledo 113

(Toletanus 468)

Ussher 131

Vallicelli 138

Vaticanus 19, 20, 21, 30, 75, 356

Vercellensis 30; old Latin version of New Testament 76

Veronensis 30

Colegiata of San Isidoro (Bible) 313, 314, 318

Colet 492, 497, 500

Collectio psalterii (attributed to Bede *q.v.*) 189

Comestor, Peter 190, 206, 256, 320, 382, 383, 430, 431, 434, 443, 448, 471

Comma Johanneum 498

Commentaries: eleventh and twelfth centuries 205; fourteenth century 203, 213; by Bonaventure, Thomas Aquinas and Albert 207; terminology and definitions 202–4

Commentators 187, 198, 199, 203

Concordances 207, 210, 504

Concordantia caritatis 334

Constantine the Great 230, 285; Letter to Eusebius 75, 78

Constantinople, Council of 83

Constantius, Emperor 340

Conversos (Spain) 490
Coplas de Yoçef 490
Coptic Manichean codices 73
Coptic text 31
Cordoliani 130, 131, 132, 133
'*Corrections*' 149, 150, 151, 152, 217
Counter-Reformation 206, 474
Courtenay, William, archbishop of Canterbury 393
Crispin, Gilbert 190
Croftys, Thomas 447
Crónica de España 470
Ctesias 63
Cureton 35
Curetonian Syriac MSS 30, 35
Curia 153, 199
Cursor Mundi 383
Cursus 242, 244
    of Pope Damasus 245
    Roman 248
Cuthbert, archbishop of York 371; letter, on death of Bede 371, 372
Cynewulf 369
Cyprian 29, 30, 32, 38, 39, 111, 172, 499
    Testimonia 157
Cyril of Alexandria 30

Da Cascina, Simone 464
Damasus, Pope 25, 83, 85, 245
Damian, Peter 141; the 'principle of agreement' 188
Danchin, M. 224
Dante 306, 456; *Convivio* 464, 465
D'Auvergne, Philippe 451
Dead Sea scrolls 2, 10, 13, 17, 18, 64, 65
    (*and see* Qumran *and* Murabba'at)
    and relations to Scriptures 158
Deanesly, Margaret 394, 427, 451
De Berceo, Gonzalo 489
De Berry Duc 440, 450, 451
De Bouillon, Godefroy 451
De Bruyne, Dom 45, 47, 84, 103, 106, 115, 116, 120, 121, 122, 123, 124, 128
Decius 282
De Condé, Alice 379
De Enzinas, Francisco 490
De Gaar, Ae. 225
De Groote, Gérard 431; propagates *Devotio Moderna* 494

De Guzmán, Alfonso 473
De Guzmán, Fernan 488
De Guzmán, Luis 473, 480
Dekkers, E. 123, 225
De Lagarde 20, 21, 23
Delisle, L. 127, 143
De Lubac, Père H. 504
De Luca, G. 457, 464
De Lucena, Juan 474
De Luna, D. Alvaro (*Libro de las Claras e Virtuosas Mujeres*) 488
De Mana, Juan 489
Demetrius, Bishop 39
Demosthenes (*De falsa iegatione*) 67
Denifle 123, 143, 144, 145, 146, 147, 148, 149, 150, 151
De Presles, Raoul 450
Derash 253, 260, 266, 262, 267, 268
    interpretation 252
De Rely, Jean 437, 450
De Rossi, J. B. 12
De Santa Fé, Geronimo 273
De Santa Maria, Pablo (*Las siete edades trovadas*) 489
Des Moulins, Guyart 446, 449, 450, 467, 471; translation of *Historia Scholastica* 448
De Sully, Maurice 439, 486
De Verague, Pedro 488
De Vignay, Jean 439
De Villena, Isabel 490
Devisions des Foires de Champagne 446
Devotio Moderna 431, 492, 494, 495, 501, 505
De Weert, Jan 431
De Welles, John 448
Dialects: forms and dialects 422
    High German 416
    Literary 416
    Low German 416
    Rhenish-Franconian 420
    Spoken 416, 417
Diatessaron 30, 33, 34, 35, 39, 41, 49, 52
    Armenian version of commentary on 430
    Dominican 430
    Liège 428, 429
    Tatian's 418, 428
    Tuscan translation 464
Didache 49, 51, 52, 167

Didymus 86, 87, 96
Diocletian, Edict of 75
Diodore of Tarsus 178
Dionysius of Alexandria 51
Diqduqe Ha-te'amim 6
Disputatio–Gisleberti Crispini Disputatio Iudei et Christiani 265
Dodwell, C. R. 315, 317, 323
Dominical Gospels 407
Dominican Order 148, 149, 151, 152, 200, 202, 217, 273, 335, 381, 462, 463
  copiers and propagators of vernacular Italian bibles 458
  Diatessaron 430
  Library of S. Maria Novella 458
  Library at Basle 498
  Synod of 400
Doura Europos 34, 63, 284, 309 (*and see* Painting)
Dream of the Rood, The 396
Dunash ibn Labrat 258, 259
Dunstan, St, archbishop of Canterbury 141, 307
Durand 149
Durham: 3-folio vols. of French commentary on Psalter 441
Durrow, Book of 132
Dutch Bible 428, 429 (*and see Rijmbijbel, Statenbijbel*)
  Texts, contribution to German Tradition 430
Du Val, Thomas, of Clairefontaine 449

Ecclesiasticus 93
Editio vulgata 106
Edward IV 440
Egbert of York 371, 372
Egeria 226
Egerton Genesis 320, 330, 331
Eleanor of Vermandois 441
Eleazar of Worms 277, 278
Elpidius Rusticus 291
Elucidarium 379
Emblems in Christian art 281
Enarrationes (St Augustine) 441
England 129, 130, 132, 152, 218
  medieval Church in 366
English Psalter, The, H. R. Bramley 386; Rolle 385, 389

English versions, pre-Wyclif 362; opposition to 451
Ephraem Syrus 34, 35, 52
Epiphanius 173
Epiphanius, bishop of Salamis in Cyprus 83, 86
Epistle, Roman ceremonial of the 229
Erasmus 206, 219, 492–505
  Adages 496, 497
  Apology to N.T. 492
  Enchiridion militis Christiani 497, 501
  Hyperaspites 501
  Institutio principis christiani 497
  Novum Instrumentum 498, 499, 501
  Ratio 501–3
  and humanism 494, 497; edits Jerome 494, 499; great edition of Augustine 499; undertakes edition of Origen 500; publishes complete works of Basil 500; commentaries 500; dissertation on literal and spiritual allegorical meanings 503; counsels to exegetes 503; contrasts schoolmen with Fathers 502; examination of idiomatic expressions 504; lists scriptural expressions misconstrued by Ambrose, Bede and Augustine 504; discovers Valla's *Adnotationes* 494, 495
Ercole d'Este 475
Erdmann, O. 421
Erigena (John the Scot) 131, 142
Essenes 4
Estienne, Robert (Stephanus) 149, 499
Ethelweard, Earl 374
Eucharist 289
Eumenes II 62
Eusebian canons, canon tables 326
Eusebius, bishop of Caesarea 18, 31, 35, 39, 43, 47, 51, 75, 78, 86, 87, 100
  his Chronicle 471; translated by Jerome 83
Eusebius of Nicomedia 340
Eustochium 92, 93
Evagrius 82
'Evangelios Moralizados' 485
Exegesis (*see also* Allegory, Sense, Senses, Typology) 192, 195, 197, 201, 210, 333, 493

Exegesis (*cont.*)
 Aquinas' definition of literal and spiritual sense 216
 of Augustine 182, 183, 209, 493
 four methods of Bahya ben Asher 278, 279
 Christian exegetes 158, 166; four methods 278, 279
 Christological interpretation of Bible 164
 four-fold method of interpretation 264
 Gregory the Great's methods 183–5, 195
 literal and spiritual allegorical meaning 503
 literal interpretation of Hebrew Bible 256
 Jewish 143, 145, 152, 160, 163, 271; and literal sense 256; medieval 254, 255, 279
 linking Old and New Testaments 296
 literal meaning 277
 Origen's 173, 195; and allegory 196; meaning and inner truth in Scripture 174–5
 rules of interpretation 252
 scientific 197
 of Scripture 155–279; and homiletics 212; spiritual interpretation in Spain 490
 Spanish school 266, 267
 study of 202
 typological 157, 162, 164
Exegetes and *General Estoria* (*q.v.*) 472
Exegetical methods and example of Epistle to the Hebrews 161
Exegetical renderings 357, 358

'False Decretals' 141
Farman (priest) 371 (*and see* Gloss, Rushworth)
Fathers 14, 118, 132, 135, 140, 142, 145, 162, 184, 187, 192, 194, 198, 207, 231, 264, 291, 372, 408, 431, 492, 497, 502, 503
 commentaries of, as basis for *General Estoria* (*q.v.*) 472
 homilies 486
Ferrer, Bonifatius 467
Ferrer, Vincent (Sermons) 487

Fet des Romains 442
Finian, St 131
Fischer 103, 106, 107, 110, 112, 113, 114, 115, 116, 117, 118, 119, 120, 121, 122, 123, 124, 125, 126, 127, 129, 132, 134, 135, 136, 137, 138, 139
Floreffe, Abbey of, and twelfth-century Bible 314
Florentinus 82
Flores Psalmorum 189
Floridus Röhrig, Fr 332–3
Fonseca, archbishop of Toledo 499
Fore-Mass 222, 223, 235, 241
Forshall, Rev. Josiah 395, 400, 401, 404, 406, 411
Fournier, P. 131
France (*see* French)
Francis, St 384, 458
Franciscan Order 151, 152, 200, 217, 278, 384, 385, 458, 462
Franco Scholasticus 141
Frankish Empire 125, 421, 422
Frede 106, 110, 132
Freising (Paternoster) 417
French: Bible, work encouraged by royal house 450–1; biblical and patristic work 441; commentaries on Psalter 440–1; exegetes 260–1; prône, role of 438; vernacular scriptures 315, 436–52; versions 132
Friars 201; as biblicists 207; opponents of English Bible in fourteenth century 384; promoters of vernacular versions 462–3
Fridugis 136
Friederichsen, G. W. S. 341, 351
Friesen, Otto von 341, 359
Frisia 415
Frisian: language 417; religious writings in 416; attitude to the Bible 367
Froben, Hieronymus 498, 499
Fulbert (Chartres) 204

Gaer, Ae. 123
Gaiffier, B. de 233
Gaiseric 345
Gallienus 339
Galuth-psychology 16
Ganshof, F. 133, 135, 136

Gatian, St, Gospels 133
Gelasian Decree 53; litany 241
Gelasius, Pope 241
Genebrardus 269
General Estoria 470, 472, 473, 483
General Prologue 409, 410, 411, 412, 413
Genesi de Scriptura 468
Genesis B 368
Genesis and Exodus 383
Genesis, The 419, 420
Genizah fragments 8, 9, 10, 12, 17, 23 (*and see* Kahle, Paul)
Geonim, The 268
Gepidae 338
Gerard of Huy 150
Gerbert (Pope Sylvester II) 204
Germany 113, 130, 132; *Hasidim* 278; mystics 483; vernacular scriptures 415, 432; opposition to versions in German 451
Gershom 475
Gerson, John 208
Gersonides (Levi ben Gerson) 276
Ghellinck, J. de 133, 380
Giessen fragment 347, 348
Gifford, William 379
Gilbert de la Porrée, 190; *Media Glosatura* 205
Ginsburg, C. D. 6, 12, 13
Giovanni dalle Celle 458
Gloss, The 132, 145, 146, 147, 151, 190, 205, 206, 207, 217, 294, 295, 297, 298, 299, 300, 302, 303, 305, 306, 412, 440, 485, 492
  to whole Bible, by Anselm and Ralph of Laon 205, 206
Gloss, Rushworth 371
Glossa ordinaria (*see* Gloss, The)
Glossaries 210
  of Hebrew terms (Italian versions) 454
Glossary of biblical terms in Alba Bible 480
Glossators 205, 214
Glossed Gospels 407, 408, 409, 410, 412
  attributed to Purvey (*q.v.*) 408
Glosses 122, 187, 203, 204, 214, 220, 371, 413, 424, 436
  in *Bible Historiale* 449
  in Erse 133
  Old English 371, 385

French 263
  to *General Prologue* 412
German 418
  interlinear 142; Alemannic psalter 423; Catharist 439; Notker's 423
  Italian versions 462
  Judeo-German 435
  marginal, in extant Gothic text 351, 352
  in Peiresc Old Testament 467
  periphrastic, in Spanish Bibles 485
  of Walafrid Strabo and Anselm of Laon 205
  verbal, in MS 145 (Christ Church, Oxford) 405
  visual 323
Gloucester, duke of 393
Glunz, H. 103, 107, 127, 130, 131, 132, 133, 135, 136, 137, 138, 139, 140, 141, 142, 145, 146, 147, 148
Gnosticism 50, 159, 168, 174, 176
Godric of Finchale 370
Goldbacher, A. 108
'Golden Legend' (Caxton's version) 303
Gonzalo García de Santa María 483, 485
Gospel books: in St Augustine's, Canterbury 327; Carolingian 328; Coronation, of Charlemagne 327; early medieval Roman arrangement of 226, 229; Echternach 329; Greek, Rossano 327; Harmonies 455; in Latin, revision and emendation by Jerome 83, 84; Lindisfarne 327; Lectionary, made for Egbert 329; Greek 336; Munich 328
  of Rheims 327
  translated into E. Franconian German, in Fulda 418
Gospels 30, 32, 36, 41, 45, 46, 47, 48, 49
Gothic Bible 338, 340, 344, 346, 361–2
  epistles 355, 356, 359
  gospels 343, 347, 348, 353, 354
  New Testament 362
  Old Testament 361, 362
  scribes' deficiency in Latin 347
Goths 338, 339
  migrations 338
  of Moesia 340
  'Romanization' of 348
Gower 383

Gradonico, Jacopo 464
Graeca Veritas and Gothic text 354
Grape, Anders 341, 359
Greek Bible 150
  New Testament papyri 39
  Philosophy 154
  Psalters 323
  Text (versions) 18
Gregorian Chant 251
Gregory, C. R. 68, 70
Gregory IX 392; *Decretals* 391
Gregory the Great 107, 121, 140, 151, 155,
    183, 186, 187, 193, 195, 213, 233, 241,
    243, 245, 250, 251, 368
  commentaries 184
  Moralia in Job 109, 486
  Pastoral Care 373
  reform of study of the Bible 198
Gregory of Nyssa 52, 177
  Theoria or spiritual sense 177
Gregory of Tours 111, 237
Groote, Gerard (*see* De Groote)
Grosseteste, Robert, bishop of Lincoln
    152, 207, 217, 219, 408
  Rules for Husbandry 440 (*and see*
    Psalter, Harley)
Guichard of Beaulieu 379
Guido of Arezzo 248
Gutmann, Joseph 317
Guyart des Moulins, *see* Des Moulins,
  Guyart

Habakkuk, Commentary on 159
Hadrian VI, Pope 441
Haggadah (of Jews) 287
Halakhah 254, 257
Hale, William of 142
Hamman, A. 225
Harding, Stephen 143, 144, 145, 148
Harkel, Thomas, bishop of 37
Harmouli, and MSS 40
Harnack, A. 43, 45, 47, 50
Hartmut 140
Hastings (*Dictionary of the Bible*) 68
Hatch 21
Hayyuj 259, 260, 263
Hebraica veritas 92, 188, 279
Hebraisms (and Erasmus) 504
Hebrew Bible 15, 153 (*and see* Jews);

Greek translation of 153; Jewish
  commentators of the, 254, 255;
  standardization of text of 73; texts
  14, 15, 18; language, study declines
  after Inquisition 474; Truth (*Hebraica
  veritas*) 92; University Bible 12
Hefele, C. J. 152
Helian, The 418, 419, 420, 421, 425
Helisachar, Abbot 237
Henry of Cossey 153
Henry of Langenstein 208
Henry of Mugeln's Psalter 432, 433
Heptateuch (Anglo-Saxon) 312, 377
Heracleon 39, 166; the Valentinian 173,
  174
Herbert of Bosham 145, 216, 256; commentary on Jerome's *Hebraica* 439;
  psalter text 145
Hereford, Nicolas 400, 401, 406, 411, 414;
  member of Wycliffite circle 400;
  translator of Wycliffite Bible 401
Heresy 380, 390, 391, 393; Trier synod
  for suppression of 427; possession of
  vernacular scriptures presumption of
  392; prosecution for reading or
  owning Bibles 394; *de heretico com-
  burendo* 410
Heretics 178, 462; works and translations
  of 427, 428
Herino of Hirschau 141
Hermannus Alemannus 470
Hermeneutics 16
Hermes 283
Hervé of Bourg Dieu 194
Hesbert, R.-J. 239
Hesdin, John 213
Hesychian Recension 19, 20
Hetzenauer, P. M. 395
Hexaemeron 205; by Henry of Ghent 212
Hexapla (Origen's) 18, 19, 20, 492
Hexaplaric Recension 20
Hexaplaric Septuagint 25
Hieronymic tradition 131; text 132
Hilarion (Life of, by Jerome) 87
Hilary of Poitiers 50, 53, 102, 177, 499;
  commentary on the Psalms and
  treatise *De Synodis* 82; interpretation
  of the Psalms 177
Hillgarth, J. N. 125, 131

Hippolytus 43, 49, 50, 51, 171, 222
Historia Scholastica (*and see* Comestor, Peter) 217, 218, 320, 331, 382, 383, 430, 432, 443, 448, 449
Historiebijbel 431–2
Holcot, Robert of Oxford 208
Homilies 212, 213, 221, 224, 487; II Clement 168; on Psalms, by Jerome 94; in France 438, 439
Homoousion 176
Honorius of Autun 190, 379
Hubert, St, Bible of 127
Hugh du Puiset, bishop 441
Hugh of St Cher 149, 150, 206, 492
Hugh of St Victor (*see* Victor, St)
Humanism: and Erasmus 497 (Christian: as defined by Guiseppe Toffanin 504); and science 495; and writers of Arragel's time 481
Humbert of Romans 247
Huon de Cambrai 443
Hurel, Gautier, count of Hesdin 441
Hus 208, 388

Ibn Ezra (*see* Abraham ibn Ezra); Gabirol 271; Janah (*see* Jonah, Rabbi) 259, 263
Icons 289
Ignatius 44, 45, 167
Illumination 79, 309, 310, 335, 337, 474
Ingeborg, queen 441
Innocent III, Pope 391, 441
Inquisition 473, 474, 486
Inscription of Abercius 281
Intermezzo chants 248, 249, 250
Interpretation (*and see* Exegesis, Senses): 215; of the Bible by early Church 155, 162; weakness of medieval methods in Scripture 184; of Old Testament prophecy 214; traditional rabbinic rules of 259
Introit 238, 240, 248
Invitatorium 237, 245, 247
Iona 131
Ireland 125, 129, 130, 131, 132, 133, 187
Irenaeus 30, 43, 47, 50, 170, 171, 499
Irish Psalters 323
Isabel the Catholic 473
Isidore, bishop of Seville 121–9, 145, 195,

272, 294, 295, 372, 419; *Etymologies* 124, 186; *Introductions* 186; *Sententiae* 187
Isidore of Pelusium 178
Israel, divine literature 183; prophets of 157
Itala MSS of Old Latin versions 25, 38, 346
Italian: Bible 452, 453, 457, 460, 462, 465; incunabula 453; text 122; versions 452–64; Florentine predominance of translations 458; glosses 456; sources of 459; translations 457 (*and see* Berger); Tuscan and Venetian dialect 456
Psalter 464 (*and see* Dante)
Italy 110, 112, 113, 125, 454

Jacob and Joseph 383
Jacopone da Todi 458, 463
James I of Aragon 473
James, M. R. 319, 323, 330, 331, 333
Jamnia (Jabne-El) Synod 4; Academy of 5
Jarrow 110, 117, 132, 136, 310
Jenson, N. and Bible 453, 454, 457, 461, 465
Jerome 19, 25, 27, 36, 37, 43, 53, 102, 105, 106, 107, 110, 111, 113, 116, 119, 120, 121, 124, 130, 135, 137, 139, 150, 174, 177, 185, 186, 188, 194, 217, 218, 234, 243, 256, 265, 272, 344, 351, 357, 359, 364, 457, 459, 476, 477, 479, 481, 483, 492, 494, 495, 496, 502; birth and baptism 80–1; settles at Bethlehem 85; Bible 131; at Chalcis 82; work on Chronicles 91; commentary on Psalm 88 (89) 94; engaged by Pope Damasus as secretary 83, 84; death 80, 110; *De Viris Illustribus* 80, 87; dream at Antioch 80; commentary on Ecclesiastes 94; Preface to Ephesians 93; exegesis 146; Exhortations to his correspondents 101; commentary on Epistle to the Galatians 92; revision of the Hebrew Canon 88; commentary on Jeremiah 91, 93, 94; preface to Job 96; work on Job 91; version from the Book of Kings 92; his letters translated by Tornaquinci and Master Zanobi

Jerome (*cont.*)
(Italy) 458; preface to Malachi 90, 91; first commentary on Obadiah 90; ordained by Bishop Paulinus 82; translation of Psalms from Hebrew 95; translations of Psalms 266 (*and see* Shor); translates fourteen homilies of Origen 83; translates Origen's commentaries into Latin 194; collates all the books of the Old Testament 86–9; final translation of the Old Testament 121; revision of the Psalms 88 (*and see* Psalter, Gallican); version from the Book of Samuel 92; and the 'senses' of Scripture 90; authority in Spain 486; studies 81, 82; style 88; teaching 486; triumph as a translator 366; attitude to the Version 95

Jerusalem (contrast between earthly and spiritual) 290

Jesse 324

Jews 152, 154, 214, 218, 224, 254, 255, 275, 279 (*and see* Hebrew); and Hebrew Bible 435; in Italy 454; in Spain 490; Bibles in Spain 474, 475, 478, 479, 483; Bibles in Germany 435, 436; interpretation 264, rhetoric 159; translations in Middle Ages 477

Johannine epistles 112; Prologue 48

John II of Castile 473

John XXIII (Pope) 387

John of Bristol 152

John of Damascus 33

John of Fécamp 189

John the Scot (*see* Erigena)

Jonah 102, 106, 281; and the whale 211, 290

Jonah, Rabbi 259, 263

Jordanes 338

Josephus 4, 14, 16, 20, 472, 473

Josippon (or pseudo-Josephus) 272

Jovinian (Jerome's controversial work against) 87

Judah Ha Levi (Hallewi) 276

Judah Ibn Balaam 260

Judas Maccabeus 293

Justin Martyr 46, 47, 169, 170, 222, 502; Christological typology of 168; *Dialogue with Trypho* 17, 168, 173;

exegesis 169; interpretation of the Old Testament 169

Justina, Empress 345

Justinian 294

Kabbalah 277

Kabbalists 265, 278

Kahle, Paul 2, 7, 12, 13, 14, 16, 17, 18, 19, 22, 24, 140; Schweich lectures 8 (published as The Cairo Geniza 1947 with 2nd edition 1959)

Kalonymos family 277

Karaites 255, 257, 268

Katherine Group texts 378

Kaufmann, F. 339, 351, 361

Kenney 130, 131, 143

Kennicott 12

Kenyon, Sir F. 56, 68, 113, 128, 133

Kimhi, David 260, 261, 263; Book of Roots dictionary 260; commentaries 265, 268–71; family 258

Kittel 11, 13; *Biblia Hebraica* 13

Klosterneuburg altar-piece 296–7, 307, 333

Knighton, Henry, *Chronicle* 388

Koehler, W. 311, 312, 327

Koran 490

Koriun 41

Kosowski 23

Kyrie eleison 241, 242, 244

Lactantius 162

Ladino (Judaeo-Spanish) 478

Lambert le Bègue 427, 441 (*and see* Heretics)

Lambeth Bible 315

Lanfranc of Bec 141, 142, 188, 204, 378

Langland 387

Langton, Stephen 147, 148, 256, 384; lectures on Bible and its glosses 206, 207

Langue D'Oil (Berger's 189 codices) 466

Laon, School of 132 (*and see* Anselm and Ralph of Laon, Glossa); theological instruction in 190

Lateran library 115

Latin: accepted by Anglo-Saxons as language of high knowledge 365

Latin Bible 153; text old Latin 112, 113; attempts at improvement 153–4;

Latin Bible (*cont.*)
could be mass produced 451; of
Paris Dominicans 446; text (Vulgate)
25, 32, 34, 36, 38, 45; Commentaries
357; Diatessaron 429; Influence on
Gothic epistles 360; Psalter 321
(Utrecht Psalter), 464 (*and see*
Dante); Rite 242
Latinisms in Spanish Bibles 482–5
Laurence of Durham 190
Laurentian Library, Florence 310 (Codex
Amiatinus)
Lavenham, Richard 410
Lazar of Pharpi 41
Lazarus 175, 383
Leander, St 123
Lectio divina 193, 194, 200
Lectionaries 33, 37; Jewish 104; used as
guide by Otfrid (*q.v.*) 420; in Roman
mass 226
Lector, office of 227, 234
Lectures 209, 210, 211, 212, 213
Lefèvre d'Étaples, Jacques 437
Legionensis Group 125
Lemaître de Sacy 437
Leo the Great 98
Leo X 499
Leofric, bishop 377–8
Leontius 33
Lerins 230
Leroquais, V. 143
Letteris (edition of Hebrew Old Testa-
ment) 13
Levasti, A. 464
Levison, W. 126, 134
Liber Evangeliorum, of Otfrid of Weissen-
burg 420
Liber Floridus, of Lambert of St Bertin
332
Liber Hebraicorum Quaestionum in Genesim
(Jerome) 100
Liber de Nominibus Hebraicis (Jerome)
100
Liber pontificalis 238
*Liber de Situ et Nominibus Locorum
Hebraicorum* (Jerome) 100
Liberius, Pope 288
Libro de los Tres Reys d'Orient 489
Lietzmann, H. 38, 47

Limberg Brothers 335
Lindisfarne 130, 131; Gospels 113, 117,
118, 130, 132, 365, 371
Liturgical message and bible-reading 221,
222; setting of lessons 226, 230
Liturgy 189, 194, 195, 198, 220–52 (*and see*
Mass, Office, Chants); Armenian 224;
Communion 239, 240; Community
prayers 236, 237; Community sing-
ing 247; Creed(s) 229, 423; Gallican
224, 225, 229, 248, 438, 439;
Gregorian chant 251; Milanese 224;
Mozarabic 224; Papal 252; two
principal types, mass and office 220;
Roman 225, 226, 241, 243; Syrian 224
Liudger, disciple of Alcuin 340
Loewe, Raphael 143, 145, 149, 152, 153,
256
Lollardy 382, 386, 393, 400–1, 408–14;
Lollard Tracts 408
Lombard, Peter 146, 190, 205, 380, 386,
446; four books of *Sentences* 198
Lord's Prayer, The (Commentary by
Erasmus) 500
Lothair Gospels 138
Louis, St 318, 319, 335, 443
Louis the Pious 237, 418
Low Countries, vernacular scriptures in
415, 416, 431 (*and see Historie-
bijbel*); religious revivals in 428
Low Franconian psalms 424
Low German 417, 424 (*and see* dialects);
Bible 434, 435
Lowe, E. A. 103, 118
Lowe, H. 126, 134
Lucan Prologue 47; Resurrection narra-
tives 155
Lucian's Recension 18, 19, 20
Lucinus 121
Ludolph of Saxony 302; *Vita Christi*
485
Lukyn Williams, A. 124
Lull, Raymond 152, 219
Luther: 434, 491; creator of modern
German Bible 424; translation of
Bible 428
Lyonnet, S. 41
Lyra, Nicholas of, *see* Nicholas of Lyra
Lyric expression 248

Mabillon, J. 141, 144
McGurk, P. M. 311, 326
Madden, Sir Frederick 395, 400, 401, 404, 406, 411
Madrio, Academy of History (MS2) 114
Magna Glosatura (*see* Gloss *and Glossa ordinaria*) 145, 146, 205, 440
Magnificat 247, 248, 324
Maimonides 10, 274, 275, 276, 277; *Guide to the Perplexed* 271, 274, 486; *Reason and Revelation* 275; translation by Pedro de Toledo (*q.v.*) 486
Mainz, archbishop of (Censor's Edict) 434
Malachi, allusion to pure sacrifice 167
Malchus, life of, by Jerome 87
Malermi, Niccolò 453
Mangenot, E. 148, 149
Manitius, M. 126
Manjacoria, Nicholas 144, 145, 148, 150, 216; *Libellus de corruptione et correptione Psalmorum* 144; *Suffrageneus Bibliothecae* 144
Mannyng, Robert, of Brunne 379
Manrique, Gomez 489
Manuel des Pechiez (William of Waddington) 379
Manuscripts: B.M. Or. 4445, 10; B.M. Or. 2626–8, 11, 13; B.M. Or. 2375 (Yemenite),13; Cassino, 114; Corpus Christi College MS 147, 411; Cotton Genesis, 317, 318, 320; Cottonian Collection, 316, 317, 325, 412; Egerton, 319, 320, 330, 331; Escorial, 466; Harleian, 311; Harley, 273, 440; Doridethi, 30; Liège, 428; Maihingen, 425; Mondsee, 417, 418; Northumbrian, 115; Otho B.M. VI, 316; Peiresc, 467; Pierpont Morgan, 436; Riccardiana 1252, 456, 458; 1354, 1655, 458; Salisbury, 142; *Shem Tob* (Sassoon Library), 13; Sienese (of Pentateuch), 460; Ussher, 132; Valenciennes, 331
Map, Walter 380
Marcion 38, 44, 45, 46, 47, 93, 170, 171; Apostolicon 45, 46; rejection of Old Testament 164
Marcus Aurelius 282
Mark (Marcan Prologue) 47

Marmadji 34
Marmoutier, N. T. 467
Marranos (or Neo-Christians) 273
Marsili, A. (Ed.) 137
Martène 149
Martial: poems 66, 67; codex 68, 70
Martin, J. P. P. 141, 143, 144, 145, 146, 147, 148
Masada texts 2
Mass 220, 222, 223, 227, 235, 238, 239, 240, 241, 249
Massekheth Sopherim 6
Massorah 1–13, 259
Massoretic annotations (*Tiqqune Sopherim; Itture: Qre: Kethib*) 7; prescriptions followed by Spanish copyists 469; studies 1–13; texts 1–15, 22, 23, 122, 481; and Spanish translations 478
Masters' teaching procedures 215
Matthew, testimonies 160
Matthew of Beheim 432
Maurdramnus (abbot of Corbie) 134, 138
Mazarine Library, Paris, MS, twelfth century in French prose 442; Barcelona psalter 467
Médard, St, of Soissons 311
Meditations on the Passion 384
Meir, Samuel ben, Commentary on the Pentateuch 266
Melchizedek 161, 289, 333
Melismatic chant 248; melody 250
Melito of Sardis 169
Mellini, Gian Lorenzo 320
Menahem ben Sarūk 258, 259, 263, 266; his dictionary (Mahbereth) 258
Menéndez Pidal 123, 124
Metrical Paraphrase of the Old Testament 383
Metz, Peter 329
Midrash, collections 260; literature 253, 268
Milan palimpsest 19
Milanese rite 227, 239, 244; text, used by Ambrosiaster 359
Milo Crispinus 141
Mimesis 162
Miniatures 310, 325, 328, 447; in Alba Bible 480; in illustrations of Psalters 325

Miniaturists, and iconographical traditions 336
'Miracles of Our Lady' 304
Mishna 5, 7, 8, 23
Missionaries 109, 110
Modus Orandi Deum (Erasmus) 500
Mohrmann, C. H. 38, 104, 105, 222
Monkwearmouth 110, 132, 136, 310
Montanism 46
Montesico, Fr Ambrosio 486, 487
Moralia of Gregory 363
More, Sir Thomas 366, 496, 497
Mosaics 288, 289, 307
Moses 104, 156, 271, 281, 290, 301
Moses de Leon 278
Moses ibn Gikatilla 260
Moses Nachmanides 265, 272, 273, 278; commentary on Pentateuch 278
Moses of Chorene 41
Mountjoy, Lord 496
Mozarabitic rite 227, 239
Münster, Sebastian 261
Murabba'at cave 2, 17, 58 (*and see* Dead Sea Scrolls *and* Qumran)
Muratori, L. A. 49, 50, 51
Mynors, R. A. B. 106, 116, 118, 119, 120, 135, 323
Mystery plays 452
Mystery of Elche (Valencian) 489

Nachmanides, Moses (*see* Moses Nachmanides)
Naphtali, ben 9
Naples Calendar 117
Nazianzen, Bishop Gregory of Constantinople 52, 83, 86, 496, 501, 503
Neckham, Alexander 149
Negroni, Carlo 457 (editor of Jenson Bible, Italy *q.v.*); 454 (and introduction to La Bibbia Volgare, Bologna) 454
Nehardea 5
Nequam, Alexander 216
Nestle, E. 141, 142
New Covenant 195
Niccolò de Neridino 458
Nicholas of Lyra 207, 219, 261, 272, 412, 432, 473, 492; gloss 434; *Postilla Litteralis* 207, 219, 305; studies of

Hebrew language, and Jewish commentators on Old Testament 304, 305; studies of Rashi 219
Nicodemus 92
Nicolas of Verdun 296
Niger, Ralph 216
Nilus of Sinai 286
Nineveh 179
Nisbet, Murdoch 414 (Scots version)
Noah 281, 295
Nordenfalk, Carl 326
North Africa, preference for Old Latin Bible text in 112
Northern homily cycle 382
Northumbria 130, 131, 133, 136, 386; text forms 132, 136
Notker ('Teutonicus') 423; his Psalter 424; high standard of translation 424; tradition in twelfth-century psalters 426
Novation 37
Nunc Dimittis 324

Ochla we-Ochla 6
Octateuch 114, 321, 325
Oda, archbishop of Canterbury 373
Odefey, P. 353, 354
Odo, bishop of Cambrai 143
Odo of Battle 190
Odo of Cluny 188, 190
Odoacer 339
Offertory chant 239, 248
Office, The 230, 231, 232, 233, 235, 236, 240, 244; archaic 235; night 245, 250
Old Frisian, fragment of Psalms in 415
Old Latin versions 37, 38, 45, 105, 183
Old Syriac version 35, 36, 38
Olivétan, P. 437
Onesimus, slave of Philemon, later bishop of Ephesus 44
Onqelos 22, 23, 140
Opiza MS 41
Orans, The 283, 284
Origen 18, 29, 30, 31, 43, 49, 83, 85, 86, 89, 90, 91, 96, 100, 165, 173, 174, 175, 177, 186, 191, 192, 194, 195, 222, 256, 290, 294, 299, 492, 496; and Erasmus 499, 502; Hexapla 86, 88, 95; homilies 486; school of 497

Orlinsky, H. M. 5, 6, 11, 13

Ormulum, The 381

Ostrogoths 338, 339, 344, 355; Gospels, united with Visigothic Bible 355; texts 344, 346, 354

Osuna Bible 468, 473

Otfrid 420, 421, 425; 'Gospel Harmony' 420; justifies writing in German 422 (*and see Liber Evangeliorum*)

Othlo of St Emmeran 188

Ottobonianus 98

Ottonian copies 328; cycles 330 (*and see* Munich Gospel)

Pachomius 40, 87

Pächt, O. 317, 318, 319, 320, 323, 436, 442

Paduan MS (part in B.M., part in Rovigo) 320

Painting: in catacombs 281, 282; at Douar Europus 283, 284; and Christian Churches 286, 288; in Norwich Cathedral 306, 308

Palatinian Bilingual (codex Palatinus) 348–9

Palestinian Syriac 37

Pammachus 96

Pamphilus 86

Papal curia 153, 199

Papyrus: 54–77 *passim*; Codex 71–6; Oxyrhyncus 59; Rylands 14, 18; Fouad 14

Parables, examples 161

Parallelism, characteristic of Hebrew poetry 259; in Gothic texts 353

Paraphrases (of Erasmus) 500, 501

Parashioth 469

Parchment 54, 61, 62, 63, 64, 67, 73; relative price of 76; codex: supremacy of 74, 75; technical factors 77

Paris 142, 208; Bible 123, 140, 144, 151; Doctors 147; 'little' Bibles 120; MS 127

Parisiense (Guillaume Pérault) 408

Paschasius, Peter (Biblia Parva) 487

Passion, narrative and plays 438

Passover ritual 243

Patrick, St 131

Patristic quotations 150

Patristic tradition 194, 195

Paul, St 14, 27, 28, 29, 36, 38, 40, 43, 47, 51, 156, 158; treatment of Old Testament scriptures 290; epistles 31, 35, 37, 38, 40, 44, 45, 46, 49, 50, 53, 115, 117, 118, 121, 145, 157, 205; canon 43, 44; codex 40

Paulinus of Antioch 83, 86

Paulinus, bishop of Nola 288

Pecock, Bishop Reginald 414

Pedro de Toledo 486

Pelagius 53, 110, 190, 357; Jerome's controversial work against 87

Pentateuch 22, 23, 24, 97, 140, 252, 261, 312, 316; Ashburnham 113, 317, 318, 337; Aelfric's 318; Paduan 320; represented by five loaves of the miracle 181; Italian version 455; Spanish version 469; polyglot in Hebrew characters in Spanish version 475; Constantinople 476–8

Pepin of Herstal 415

Perdrizet, P. 334

Peregrinus, St 121–5, 128; prefaces (prologues) 121

Pericopes 220, 225, 226; for mass 234; for use of Cambrai and Metz 439; Gospel 248

Pero López de Ayala 466

Peshat (*and see derash*) 260, 261, 262, 265, 267, 268, 270, 271, 272, 274, 275, 277, 278; dominant method of interpretation in the West from eleventh century 254; in exegetical work of Hugh and Andrew of St Victor 256; and *derash*, demarcation between 258

Peshitta, Syriac (*see* Syriac Peshitta)

Peter of Pisa 135

Peter of Poitiers (genealogical tables) 206

Peter the Chanter 206, 256

Petrarch 456

Philemon 50, 51

Philip II 473

Philo 14, 16, 20, 100, 160, 162, 169, 174

Philostorgius 339, 362

Philoxenian Syriac 52

Philoxenus (bishop) 37

Photius 33

Physiologus 298, 299

Pictor in Carmine 333

Piers Plowman 373
Pius V, Pope 111, 235, 245
Plenaries 430; East German 432
Pliny (*Natural History*) 55; and letters of
the Gracchi 59; and parchment 62
Plooij, D. 34, 428, 430
Plummer, C. 117, 130
Polena, Gianfranco 320
Polycarp 37, 44, 45
Pontifical Mass 224
Porcher, J. 436, 447
Postilla (William of Paris) 485
Postillae (Nicholas of Lyra) 473
Praefatio (attrib. to Sunnja and Fripila)
351 (*and see* codex)
Precatio dominica digesta in VII partes
(Erasmus) 500
Premonstratensians 191
Primer, The 414
Primera Cronica General 470
Priscillian, *Canons* of 121
Provençal versions 443, 460–2
Prudentius 126
Prudentius of Troyes, bishop 189
Psalms 26, 189, 255, 370 (*and see* Psalter);
penitential 463; Roman text 370;
Saxon commentary on Psalms 4 and 5
423; singing, four principal methods
236
Psalter 6, 25, 94, 111, 117, 122, 131, 133,
142, 205, 206, 220, 238, 239, 240, 244,
245, 250, 251, 310, 312, 316, 321, 324,
331, 370, 389, 413, 415, 449, 468;
St Albans 322, 323; Anglo-Norman
versions 379; Arundel 439, 447; Bury
St Edmunds 322; Canterbury (or
Eadwine) 370, 371; Cassino 111;
Castilian, first 470; Corbie 114;
Southern Dutch 430; Eadwine 440;
English fourteenth century 323; R.
Rolle 371, 392; Gallican 88, 100,
111, 128, 137, 153, 237, 370, 468;
German 423; Gorleston 324; Harley
440; illuminated by André Beauneveu
440; Ingeburg 325, 441; Italian
versions 454, 455; Iuxta Hebraeos
127, 153, 216, 370, 468, 470; Iuxta
Hebraicam Veritatem 111; and
French-speaking laity 437; widely
known in vernacular in France 439;
Flemish translations 427; glossed
370; Jerome's 128, 137; Latin 84,
111, 112, 237, 325, 370, 439; learned
by heart 196; MSS embellishments of
244; Metz 440; *West Midlands prose
psalter* 371; Montebourg 439, 440;
Mozarabic 108; Notker's translation
423; St Omer (from Abbey of
St Bertin) 337; *Paris* 370, 371;
Peterborough 447; Psalterin, translation into Saxon 423; psalters,
twelfth century 426; Quadruple
143; Queen Mary's 306; of Raoul de
Presles 440; readings 129; Rhenish-
Franconian 422; Roman 85, 111,
112, 237; Roman ferial 245 (*and
see* fig. 3, page 246); Roman version
370; *Surtees* 371; translations of
432; Tuscan versions 454, 455;
Utrecht 330; Verona 111, *Vespasian*
370 (BM); weekly 245; Westphalian
424; Winchester 325; Windberg
426
Ptolemies 59
Ptolemy 338
Pum Bedita 5, 8
Purim, Feast 490
Puritan scholars and translators 261, 262
Purvey, John 408–11; and Wyclif 404;
Tracts 375

Qaraites 7, 8
Quaestiones Hebraicae in Genesim 98
Quentin 103, 114, 117, 118, 124, 127, 128,
129, 134, 138, 141
Queste del saint Graal 446
Quetif-Echard 458
Quintilian 81
Qumran 2, 24; cave four 14 (papyrus
fragments); cave 1, 4, 5, 6 14
(papyrus fragments); commentaries
on Habakkuk and Nahum 158; leather
scroll of Samuel (*4QSam*^{a}) 60;
scrolls 3; *1QIsb* 3, 4; *1QIsa* 3, 4;
Psalms 4; sect 3

Rabanus Maurus 195, 265, 294, 302;
commentaries 187

Rabbinic exegesis 493; rules for sewing scrolls 65; rules for writing on different kinds of parchment 64
Rabbula of Edessa 35, 36
Rabula (bishop of), Gospels of 307
Radulph, bishop of Liège 441
Rahlf (*Septuaginta*) 20
Rand 139
Rashdall, H. 152
Rashi 218, 262, 266, 268, 269, 271, 272, 278; commentaries and interpretations 261, 262, 264; exegesis 263; identifies the *Kittim* with Christian Rome 262; inaugurated movement towards literal interpretation in Northern France 264
Ratherius of Verona 204
Ratio seu methodus compendio parveniendi ad veram theologiam (Erasmus) 500, 501
Ratio verae theologicae (Erasmus) 492, 496, 498
Ravenna papyrus 60
Ravennate Annals, fragment (Merseburg) 313
Recensions: Samaritan 14; Lucianic 14; of Hesychius 95; of Lucian 95; of University of Paris 99; in early history 19
Reformation 206, 261, 279, 386, 465, 474
Reichenau Abbey 328
Remigius of Auxerre 142
Renaissance 105, 151, 152, 452, 493; humanists 437
Renaudet 493; (and Erasmus) 497
Reportationes 201, 202
Responsorial Psalm 249
Responsories 251
Resurrection 306; depicted in Byzantine ivory 307; in mosaics at Constantinople 307; Reuchlin 261, 262
Reuss, E. 439, 451, 459, 465
Reynolds, John 262
Riccardiana, Biblioteca 455
Ricciotti, G. 459
Rich, Edmund, archbishop of Canterbury 379
Richard of Fourneaux 190
Rijmbijbel (Van Maerlant's) 430, 431
Rituale Armenorum 41

Robert of Greatham 379
Roberts, C. H. 68, 69, 70, 71, 72, 76
Roger of Hoveden 365
Roig, Jaime 488
Rolle, Richard 371, 385, 387; treatment of the Psalter 386, 390; writings 386
Roman: breviary 235, chant, study of medieval 251; fore-Mass 225; Mass 224, 241, 242; Office 247; Order I and II 229, 242; Psalter, *see* Psalter; Secular Office 245; rite 229, 242
Romance: poetry 437, versions 460; vernaculars 464 (*and see* Dante)
Romanesque period Bibles 313
Romigi de'Ricci 455, 458
Rota in Medio Rotae 333
Roth, Cecil 11, 118, 152
Rudolph II 341
Rufinus 53, 82, 102, 195; Apologia 102; Jerome's controversial work against 87
Rupert of Deutz 191
Ruricius, bishop of Limoges 76
Rylands, John 14

Saadya Gaon 8, 24, 256, 257, 259, 260, 266, 267, 268, 274; commentaries 258; division of the commandments 276; stresses importance of literal meaning 257; translations 257
Sadolet 500 (*and see* Erasmus)
Saint Cyprien de Poitiers (Romance poem) (*and see* Passion plays) 437, 438
Saint Gall 106, 117, 125, 129, 131, 133, 138, 141, 417, 423; MS 70, 115; Winithar of 114, 141
Sanctius 313
Sanctus 241
San Isidoro Colegiata 318
Santillana, Marquis of 473, 489
Sarcophagi, Christian 284, 285; St Paul's Church, Rome 288; Lateran 307
Sarum rite 229
Sawtry, William 410
Scholarship, biblical 216; in twelfth and thirteenth centuries 380; revival in fourteenth century 218
Schongauer, M. 308
Schoolmen 210

Schools of scripture 204
Scintillae 187
Scribes, Graeco-Roman 56, 65
Scriptorium, Scriptoria 138, 139, 147, 311, 416
Scripture (*and see* Exegesis) as library of oracles 163; Church's interpretation of 158; in religious life 183; interpretation of 157, 159; new meaning in light of Easter 156; and Philo 160; two methods of reading 193
Sedulius Scotus 143
Sense (*see also* Allegory, Exegesis, Typology), figurative (Erasmus) 504: Christological interpretation 214; and interpretation of texts 504; literal and spiritual 89, 90; spiritual, Gregory's explanation 184; spiritual, in commentary on the vision of Isaiah by Jerome 83; 'sublime and sacred way of understanding' 89; tropological 90
Senses: distinction between 215; Gregory's three 196; Historical and spiritual (Isidore) 178; literal, and distinction between inner meaning 214; literal or historical, in Scriptures 135, 214; Prodigal son, example of 89, of Scripture, glosses in Montesino's translation of *Vita Christi* (*q.v.*) 486; four senses of Scripture 196, 214
Sentences (Peter Lombard) 145, 146, 148
Sentences, Collections of, by students 198, 200
Sephardic Jews, Spanish Bible for 475, 476
Septuagint 3, 13, 14, 15, 16, 17, 18, 19, 20, 21, 22, 25, 26, 28, 88, 89, 94, 95, 99, 105, 122, 162, 166, 174, 176
Sergius I, Pope 243
Servant Songs 156, 262
Severian of Gabala 178
Shemone Ezreh 476, 478
Shepherd, the (Hermas) 43, 49, 51, 52
Shor, Joseph Bekhor 265; explanation of Old Testament miracles 266
Sibylline oracles 162; prophecy 489
Sigebert of Gembloux 141, 143
Sigeweard 375, 376
Simon, Richard 450
Sinai Covenant 155

Sinope fragment 327
Sixtus V, Pope 25
Smalley, Beryl 118, 131, 140, 141, 142, 143, 144, 145, 147, 148, 151, 153, 256, 492
Smith, William, of Leicester 393
Smits van Waesberghe, J. 251
Sobradiel Gospels 485
Soncino, Eliezer 475
Sondersprache (Jewish) 478
Song of Songs (biblical): paraphrased by Williram (*q.v.*) 424; studies of by Nicholas of Lyra 219; variation on 464
Souter, A. 37, 38, 359
Sozomen 43
Spain 120, 121, 129, 473, 481
Spanish: Apocalypses 332; Bibles 313, 314, 316 (*and see* Bibles); codices 114, 123, 125; Church 120; connections of 'Italian MSS' 114 (*and see* Quentin); and Catalan Bibles, many still lie hidden 491; Latin Bible 120; MSS 112, 121; pandect bibles 127; text 124, 125; texts take Jerome as their base 112; text types 113; treatise for confessors *Los Diez Mandamientos* 487, 488 (compare with *Doctrina de Discrición* by Pedro de Veragüe *q.v.*); vernacular scriptures 465, 466, 468, 469, 470; versions, influenced by Jerome 483; Vulgate 122; history of 120
Speculum de Scriptura Sacra 128
Speculum Ecclesie (Edmund Rich) 379
Speculum humanae salvationis 302, 303, 304, 310, 332, 334
Speculum laicorum 487
Splanamento de li Proberbi de Salamone (Gerardo Pateg) 464
Stained glass: windows of French cathedrals 297; Bourges cathedral 297–301; windows of La Sainte Chapelle 447; windows of Malvern Priory 304, 305, 306; windows of King's College Chapel, Cambridge 304
Statenbijbel 428, 435
Statutes of Boniface 417
Stegmuller, F. 114, 203
Stegmuller, O. 17
Stephen's Apologia (Acts vii) 159

Stilicho 345, 359
Strabo, Walafrid 111, 294
Streeter, B. H. 29, 30, 31, 32, 38, 46
Streitberg, W. 353, 355, 361; *Die Gotische Bibel* 342
Stubbs, W. 141
Studies, biblical, *see* Scholarship
Suger, Abbot 292, 296
Sunday Gospels (Spain) (*and see* Gonzalo García de Santa María) 483, 484
Sunnja (*and* Fretela) 351
Superscriptio Lincolniensis 152, 153, 217
Sura Academy 5, 8
Surtees Psalter 385; society 385
Symbols and Symbolism 280, 284, 286, 289
Symmachus 17, 18, 95, 99
Synagogue service 224, 225
Synod of Laodicea 52, 53
Synod of Sens 146
Syriac Peshitta, the 14, 25, 34, 35, 36, 52; as ultimate source of Dutch texts 430
Syriac writings 33; text 29, 30

Taddeo Gaddi 308
Talmud 8, 218, 253, 260, 261; Babylonian (Shebu'oth 26a) 2; (Kethuboth 106a) 5; burning of 264
Targums 8, 11, 14, 22, 23, 24, 26, 99, 266; Aramaic 13, 15; Aramaic version of the Pentateuch 259; pseudo-Jonathan 24; of Onqelos 263, 478
Tarragona, Council of 473
Tatian 30, 33, 34, 35, 39, 47, 115; Diatessaron 428, 429, 455 (and see *Diatessaron*)
Teaching in pre-scholastic period 204; methods of the masters 209, 210, 211
Tertullian 32, 38, 43, 51, 111, 172, 179, 281; exegesis 172
Tetrapla 19
Textus, Annual of the Hebrew University 8, 10, 13
Theodore of Mopsuestia 52, 177
Theodoret 52, 178, 339
Theodoret of Cyrrus 35
Theodoric 115, 339, 344, 345, 351, 360; influence of Brixian Bilingual (*q.v.*) 350; close relations with Visigoths 355

Theodosius 345
Theodotion 17, 18, 23, 88, 95, 99
Theodulf 113, 114, 123, 125, 126, 127, 128, 129, 134, 141, 143, 145; Bible 129, 133, 468; edition 128; influence 144; recension 121, 122
Theophilus' *Ad Autolycum* 170; of Antioch 170
Theotger, Abbot 141
Thet Autentica Riocht 416
Thibaut de Campagne 446
Thierry d'Alsace 441
Thompson, E. M. 143, 146
Thompson, Sir H. 39
Thorpe, William 393
'Three Chapters' controversy 124
Toffanin, Guiseppe 504
Toledo 470
Torah 6, 15, 16, 64, 252, 253, 254, 255, 257, 261, 267, 268, 271, 272, 275, 278; *corporealiter* and *spiritualiter* 270; Greek rendering of the 14
Totting, Henry 208
Toulouse, Kingdom of 344, 345; Council of 473; Museum 308
Tours 136, 137, 139
Translation (*and see* Vernacular Scriptures): of Acts, North Midlands version 390; of the Bible 365, 366; condemnation of 380, 391, 393, 434, 436; into English 387, into Provençal, of Psalter and Gospels 427; techniques, of Gothic Gospels 342, 343, 358; techniques in Matthew 344; traditions in biblical translations 424; Tudor 414; in sixteenth century 491
Trent, Council of 25, 106
Tresor (of Brunetto Latini) 446
Trevet, Nicholas 218
Trevisa, John 404; translations 390
Trinity, The, depictions of 288
Trisagion 241
Trudpert, S. Paraphrase 425
Trypho the Jew 169
Tyconius 164, 178, 179
Tyndale 262, 366, 414; his 'provocative glosses' 413
Typology 157, 158, 160, 161, 215, 335; 'direct' and 'typical' in Bible

Typology (*cont.*)
    illustrations 310; historical 163, 177; and Jerome 91; in Judaism 159; Melchizedek and Christ 161, 289, 333, 'type' and 'anti-type' 170

Ugaritic 99
Ulfilas 339, 340, 342, 343, 350, 353; sole translator of Gothic Bible 361, 362; translation of Gothic Gospels 347; use of Old Latin version in translating from the Greek 356; texts 344, 356, 360
Unitas Scripturarum 195
Universities: Bologna 200; Cambridge 199; Chairs in language teaching at Paris, Bologna, Salamanca and Oxford 152; course in theology 200, 201; Oxford 199, 200, 218; Constitutions 414; Friars 207; Paris 99, 145, 146, 200, 218; thirteenth-century theology course of eight years 201; schools 147, 199; rise of 209
Unum ex Quattuor 409
Urban VI 400
Uzziel, Jonathan ben 23

Vaccari, A. 34, 84, 111, 455, 457, 459, 460, 461
Valencian language 487
Valentinian II 345
Valentinian III 345
Valentinus 39, 42
Valerian 339
Valerius Maximus 302
Valicelli Library 118, 128
Valla, Lorenzo 492, 505; *Adnotationes* on the New Testament 494, 496; *De Voluptate* 495; *Elegantiae* 495
Vandals 338, 345, 355; Bible texts 346
Vandenbroucke, F. 247
Van der Meer, F. 106
Van Maerlant, Jacob 430 (*and see Rijmbijbel*)
Variants 28, 127, 128; Greek texts in pre-Christian era 16; Hebrew 15; in revisions of Alcuin and Theodulf 114
Vattasso 34
Vaudois MSS 462
Vegetius 211

Vera theologia 503 (Erasmus)
Vernacular scriptures 415–91 (*and see* Translation); and attitude of medieval Church 426, 427; not used for liturgical worship in the Church in Italy 463; Papal rescript against in Germany 432
Version 12, 13, 14, 16, 17, 19, 28, 35, 99
Versions: Arabic 14, 28
    Aramaic 37
    Armenian 28, 31, 41; old Armenian 41
    Bohairic 40
    Christian 22, 37 (origins)
    Coptic 28, 39, 52
    Cyprian 29 (text)
    Ethiopic 28
    Georgian 28, 31, 41; old Georgian 41
    Gothic 342, 343, 355
    Greek 16
    Harklean 37
    Jewish 22 (origins)
    King James' Authorized 39, 139, 261, 262, 376
    Latin 24, 32, 34; old Latin 28, 37, 38, 39, 99, 342, 344, 346, 348, 350, 352, 356, 357, 359; of Renaissance 108
    Palestinian Syriac 37
    Philoxenian 37
    Polycarp 37
    Renaissance 153 (of Pagninus, Arias Montanus and Munster)
    Sahidic 30, 39, 52
    Scots 414
    Syrian 28, 33; old Syriac 28, 35, 36, 37, 38
    Syriac 26
Verus Israel 265
Victor, Pope 37, 49, 50
Victor, bishop of Capua 34, 115
Victor, St, School of 256; Andrew of 216, 217, 218, 256, 384; Hugh of 148, 190, 206, 217, 256
Victorines 190, 261, 439
Victorinus 81; text of 359
Vienna Genesis, miniatures 286, 287
Vienne, Council of 218, 219
Vigilantius (Jerome's controversial work against) 87
Vincent of Beauvais 291
Visigothic MSS 468

Visigoths 338, 339, 340, 344, 345, 354, 355; Bible texts of the 346
Vita Christi (Ludolph of Saxony) 486
Vita Christi (Isabel de Villena) 490
Vitrier, Jean 496
Vitzthum 446, 447
Vivarium 76, 118; library 115, 310; monastery 115
Vives, Juan Luis 499
Vivian 138
Vocalization 7, 8; so-called Babylonian 7; Babylonian 8, 9; primitive Palestinian supralineal 7; Palestinian 9; Massoretic 98; Tiberian system 7, 8, 9
Vööbus, A. 35, 36, 37, 41, 42
Vulgate 13, 25, 53, 105, 106, 107, 115, 116, 119, 120, 121, 122, 124, 129, 130, 131, 139, 140, 142, 144, 146, 154, 183, 187, 195, 203, 256, 265, 266, 295, 301, 310, 340, 346, 383, 391, 429, 430, 433, 448, 465, 481, 483, 489, 490; and Alba Bible 480; Alcuin's revision of the 130; Alcuin's standardization of text 372; Aelfric's translation 374; authority of 488; *Biblia Sacra Iuxta Latinam Vulgatam* 25; Christians acquaint Jews with 264; Clementine edition 152; Clementine revision 25; continental and Irish influence 132; text and Erasmus 498; Isidore's recension 125; containing Jerome's translations 99, 100; Latin 102, 150, 199, 217, 218, 414; set text in Universities 197; old Latin version in use in the West in Jerome's time 99; Paul's text 110; Parisian revision 446; history to Renaissance 103 (diagram pages 104–5); scholarship in nineteenth and twentieth centuries 112; becomes firmly established in Spain 468; source of all quotations, etc., in medieval times 465; Sixtine revision 25

Wakefield, bishop of Worcester 400, 409
Waldensian heretics 460, 462; Italian Bible 462; movement 427; New Testament 439; translations 391
Wanley, Humphrey 389

Warham, archbishop of Canterbury 499
Wattenback, W. 126, 134, 137
Weissenburg Catechism 418
Weitzmann, Kurt 313, 316, 322
Wen-Amon 59
Wendelin of Speier 453
Werden monastery 340
Wernher, Abbot 296
Western texts 29, 31, 32
Wikgren, A. 40, 42
William of Corbeil, archbishop of Canterbury 441
William Le Breton (*Correction*) 149
William of Mara 149, 150
William of Malmesbury 370, 373
William of St Thierry 192, 495, 502
William of Waddington (*Manuel des Pechiez*) 379
Williram, Abbot of Ebersberg 424, 425
Wilmart 144
Winithar of St Gall 135, 141; verses of 138
Wisdom literature 207; lectures on 204 (by Robert Holcot)
Wordsworth, J. 149
Workman, Dr 400
Wormald, F. 317, 322, 323, 325, 328, 335
Wultres (*and see Praefatio*) 351
Wyclif, John 208, 220, 362, 363, 366, 374, 385, 387, 388, 390, 392, 404, 408, 448; in Bruges in 1374 392; death 393; Bible: Nicholas Hereford's part in translation of 401; specimens of translations 395–9; specimens of translations and variants 401–15; start of translation *c.* 1382 392; C.U.L. MS Ee.1.10 (incomplete version) 404
Wycliffite versions 387, 388, 389, 390, 392, 394, 395, 414; MSS 388; translators, other works 409; translators, true precursors of English Protestant tradition 415; *De veritata sacrae scripturae* 393

Xystus II 288

Zachary of Besançon 191
Zakkai, Johanan Ben 4
Zealots 4
Zohar, The 278

INDEX TO BIBLE REFERENCES

OLD TESTAMENT

Genesis, 20, 25, 268
  ii. 18: 477
  ii. 24: 182
  iii. 1: 457
  iii. 15: 99, 477, 489
  iv. 1: 100
  vi. 14–16: 294
  xv. 9: 97
  xxi. 21: 23
  xxiii. 16: 97
  xxiv. 32: 97
  xxvii. 40: 270
  xxix. 10–12: 425
  xxxi. 47: 96
  xxxii. 6–8: 287
  xliv: 320
  xlviii: 299
  xlix. 9, 12: 478
  xlix. 10: 266
  xlix. 25: 478
Exodus
  ii. 5: 114
  xii. 21: 297
  xii. 17–xiv: 369
  xv: 325
  xv. 1–21: 469, 479
  xvii: 300
  xx. 13: 266
  xx–xxiii: 367
  xxxiv. 29: 301, 481
Leviticus, 14
  x. 16: 6
  xi. 42: 6
  xiii. 13: 6
Numbers, 14
  xxi: 290, 300
  xxi. 18: 469
  xxix. 9: 310
  xxxiii. 21: 92
Deuteronomy, 14, 40
  vii. 1: 402
  xviii. 21: 96
  xxv. 4: 161
  xxx. 11–14: 270

  xxxii. 1–43: 471
  xxxii. 39: 266
  xxxiii. 2–29: 471
Joshua ix. 2: 402
Judges
  ii. 6: 114
  vi: 302
  xviii. 30: 7
Ruth ii. 41: 240
I Samuel
  v. 6: 145
  v. 9: 145
  xiii. 19–20: 183
II Samuel
  vii. 7: 97
  vii. 13–16: 97
  xxi: 319
I Kings xvii: 298
II Kings
  ii. 15: 293
  iv: 299
  xxi. 16: 402
I Chronicles xvii. 6: 97
II Chronicles
  v. 13: 402
  vii. 3: 402
Ezra vii: 293
Nehemiah
  v–vii: 361
  vii. 21: 361
Esther, 24
Job, 25
  i: 413
  i. 6–12: 395, 402
  xvii. 13: 412
  xxx. 31: 402
Psalms, 24, 25, 402
  1, 26, 28, 51, 52, 68, 80, 97, 101, 109: 323
  1–50: 370
  1, 51, 101, 109: 325
  2, 15, 19, 21, 45, 72, 87, 110: 269
  2, 9: 97
  9: 263
  9, 10, 21: 262

Psalms (*cont.*)
9, 14: 293
10: 263
10, 12, 29: 271
15. 5: 413
16, 10: 177
19: 270
22 (23), 1: 98
30, 16: 413
38, 52, 68, 1: 324
22, 27: 263
44 (45), 15–16: 239
41. 8: 413
45: 262
45, 3: 153
51–150: 370
68: 263
69, 31: 314
71 (72), 12: 98
72: 178
72, 10 ff.: 160
78: 159
78, 38: 6
80, 14: 7
81, 4: 485
82, 8: 182
87: 270
94 (95): 231
102: 169
108, 119, 150: 271
110: 271
110, 4: 314
117 (118), 25–6: 241
129: 486
138: 422
Proverbs
i. 8: 412
vi. 16–19: 416
viii. 22: 176
xiv. 21: 123
xvi. 11: 150
xxii. 20: 89
Song of Songs, 25, 159, 171, 178, 267, 463
iii. 11: 293
iv. 5: 171
iv. 7: 482
Isaiah
ii. 1–3: 396, 412

v. 10–14: 158
vi. 3: 241
vii. 14: 160, 173, 477
ix: 271
ix. 2, 6–7: 229
ix. 6: 477
ix. 9: 293
xi: 271
xi. 1: 304
xi. 1–3: 324
xi. 2: 477
xii. 3: 477
xiv. 12: 179
xl. 1: 7
xl. 12: 283, 305
xlv. 8: 477
lii–liii: 263
liii: 167
liii. 4–6; 10–11: 178
liii. 7 (61 ff.): 170
liv. 1: 168
liv. 11: 158
lv. 1: 238
lx. 17: 164
lxi. 10: 178
lxii. 11: 293
Jeremiah xxxi. 15: 160
Lamentations v. 16: 300
Ezekiel
ii. 2: 184
xxxiv. 23: 283
Daniel, 17
i. 14: 171
v. 5–6: 433
Hosea
xi. 1: 160
xi. 8: 99
Amos iv. 13: 176
Jonah, 40
iii. 3: 178
Micah v. 1–3: 160
Nahum iii. 3: 178
Habakkuk ii. 4: 158
Zechariah
v. 7: 480
vi. 12: 263
ix. 4: 262

Index to Bible References

APOCRYPHA
(see also Subject Index)

Tobit (Tobias), 20
  xii. 7: 457
  x. 13: 488
Wisdom of Solomon, 49
  v. 15: 402

xvii. 14: 485
xviii. 44 f.: 238
Baruch, 93
  iii. 20: 400, 401, 402, 403, 404

NEW TESTAMENT

Matthew, 36, 42, 46, 180
  v. 4: 485
  v. 9–13: 243
  v. 22: 484
  v. 25: 343
  v. 29: 347
  vi. 23: 405
  vi. 26–7: 428
  vi. 28: 428
  ix. 8: 350
  x. 16: 281
  x. 18: 406
  xi. 19: 343
  xii. 40: 281
  xiv: 284
  xvi: 408
  xvi. 26–8: 242
  xviii: 471
  xviii. 10: 145
  xix. 21: 40
  xxi. 9: 461
  xxii. 37–9: 488
  xxiv. 15–16: 179
  xxv. 26: 353
  xxvi. 42: 413
  xxvi. 64: 178
  xxvii. 48: 351
Mark, 31, 36, 47, 48, 71, 180, 281
  i. 1–v. 30: 30
  ii. 1–12: 281
  iv. 19: 351
  v. 31: 30
  vi. 32: 137
  ix. 15: 35, 39
  x. 42–5: 397
  xi. 26: 131

xiii: 408
xiv. 9: 405
xvi. 9–20: 28
Luke, 45, 46, 47, 48, 180
  i. 5–14: 397
  i. 46–55: 233
  i. 63: 348
  i. 68–79: 232
  ii. 11: 107
  ii. 2: 352
  ii. 10: 348
  ii. 14: 405
  ii. 42: 430
  iii. 3: 429
  iv. 38–44: 226
  v. 25: 142
  v. 26: 348
  vi. 36–43: 408
  vi. 49: 352, 353
  vii. 35: 343
  viii. 14: 351
  ix. 2–5: 243
  ix. 34: 352
  ix. 58: 330
  x. 34: 406
  x. 38–42: 226
  xii. 26: 428
  xii. 35: 140
  xv. 4: 283
  xv. 7: 107
  xv. 22, 23: 314
  xvi. 19–31: 226
  xvi. 20: 348
  xviii. 3: 343
  xix. 23: 353
  xix. 37: 137

Luke (*cont.*)
   xxi. 38: 28
   xxii. 19–20: 242
   xxiii. 19–22: 437
   xxiii. 27–8: 438
   xxiv: 182
   xxiv. 26–7, 44–7: 156
John, 42, 46, 47, 48, 49, 50, 53, 180
   i. 1: 461
   i. 1–2: 179
   i. 47: 131
   ii. 12–xx. 20: 39
   iii. 13: 310
   iv: 173, 284
   iv. 36: 173
   iv. 46–53: 408
   vii. 8: 137
   vii. 53–viii. 11: 28
   xi. 16: 461
   xix: 438
   xix. 15, 12: 437
   xix. 17, 23–4: 438
   xx. 19: 240
   xxi: 282
   xxi. 2: 461
Acts, 28, 32, 35, 37, 38, 40, 44, 48, 49, 50,
   52, 53
   ii: 298
   xiii: 298
   xvii. 27: 461
   xxviii: 406
   xxviii. 17–20: 399
Romans, 43, 47, 49
   i. 1–4: 178
   x. 17: 221
I Corinthians, 43, 47
   iv. 2: 483
   v. 7: 358
   vii. 4: 488
   vii. 10, 12, 25, 40: 45
   ix. 9: 89
   x: 290
   x. 1–11: 160
   x. 8–10: 89
   xi. 23–5: 242
   xi. 19–33: 225
   xii. 1–9: 225
   xv. 9: 483

iv. 2: 483
II Corinthians
   iii. 6: 89
   iii. 14: 50
   viii. 18: 461
Galatians, 47
   iv: 290
   iv. 24: 177, 178
   xvi. 18: 240
Ephesians, 43, 44, 47
   vi. 16: 180
Philippians, 52
   ii: 167
   ii. 28: 357
Colossians
   i. 7: 27
   iv. 16: 43, 47
I Thessalonians iv. 14: 45
II Thessalonians
   ii. 4: 178
   ii. 13: 45
II Timothy
   iii. 16: 174
   iv. 13: 66
Hebrews, 43, 47, 48, 49, 50, 51, 52, 53
   vi. 19: 281
   ix. 12: 314
   xi. 167, 291
James, Epistle of 32, 49, 53
   i. 1: 51
   ii. 23: 50
I Peter, 32, 49, 50
   iii. 18–22: 162
II Peter, 28, 36, 50
   iii. 15–16: 45
I John, 32, 49, 50, 51
II John, 36, 49, 50, 51
III John, 36, 49, 50, 51
Jude, 28, 36, 49, 51, 53
Revelation, 16, 36, 37, 38, 42, 47, 50, 51,
   52, 53
   ii. 17: 42
   iii. 12: 42
   v. 3–8: 42
   xiv. 1: 42
Apocalypse
   i. 13: 461
   xix. 13: 461